The Puzzle Palace

The Puzzle Palace

*A Report on America's
Most Secret Agency*

James Bamford

HOUGHTON MIFFLIN COMPANY BOSTON

Library of Congress Cataloging in Publication Data
Bamford, James.
The puzzle palace.
Includes bibliographical references and index.
1. United States. National Security Agency. I. Title.
UB251.U5B35   327.1'2'06073   82–3056
ISBN 0–395–31286–8   AACR2

Printed in the United States of America

S 10 9 8 7 6 5 4

FOR NANCY
who endured my puzzle
and sacrificed her palace

Any sound that Winston made, above the level of a very low whisper, would be picked up by it . . . There was of course no way of knowing whether you were being watched at any given moment . . . You had to live — did live, from habit that became instinct — in the assumption that every sound you made was overheard and, except in darkness, every movement scrutinized.

— George Orwell, *1984*

Secrecy is the first essential in affairs of the State.

— Armand Jean du Plessis, Cardinal de Richelieu, chief minister to King Louis XIII

The King has note of all that they intend,
By interception which they dream not of.

— William Shakespeare, *The Life of Henry V,* Act II, Scene 2

CONTENTS

ACKNOWLEDGMENTS

I AM DEEPLY GRATEFUL to the many people who gave unselfishly of their time, knowledge, and ideas in order to help me with this book. General Marshall S. Carter, Frank Raven, Dr. Solomon Kullback, Frank Rowlett, Edna Yardley, Raymond Tate, Wesley Reynolds, Richard Floyd, Dr. William O. Baker, Clark Clifford, General Preston Corderman, and others who will remain unnamed but not unthanked, all patiently endured my endless questions and offered me their kind hospitality and a piece of the puzzle.

Others helped me arrange the pieces in their proper place. David Kahn was the source of a wealth of helpful advice and kindly took the time to review a final draft of the manuscript. John E. Taylor of the National Archives constantly found time in his busy schedule to help me locate the most obscure government documents. Linda Melvern of London's *Sunday Times* provided me with continued support and assistance. Mark Lynch of the American Civil Liberties Union brought his considerable legal talents to my aid in a tug of war with the government over several documents. Tony Crawford and John Jacob of the George C. Marshall Research Library frequently went out of their way to assist me. And Claire Lorenz of the Margaret Clapp Library at Wellesley College, where I did much of my research, was never without a kind word and friendly smile as she pointed me to the right stack of Senate hearings or House reports. My appreciation also to Charles Sullivan, Gerald Everett, and the rest of NSA's D4 staff, who suffered through my torrent of Freedom of Information Act requests with professionalism and good humor.

Finally, I want to thank my editor, Robie Macauley, for the personal attention he has consistently shown to me and this project; Senior Vice President Richard McAdoo for his continued encouragement and patience over the years; my copy editor, Frances L. Apt, for her eagle eye in decrypting my manuscript; and all the other fine people at Houghton Mifflin who contributed to *The Puzzle Palace*.

The Puzzle Palace

1

BIRTH

AT 12:01 on the morning of November 4, 1952, a new federal agency was born. Unlike other such bureaucratic births, however, this one arrived in silence. No news coverage, no congressional debate, no press announcement, not even the whisper of a rumor. Nor could any mention of the new organization be found in the *Government Organization Manual* or the *Federal Register* or the *Congressional Record*. Equally invisible were the new agency's director, its numerous buildings, and its ten thousand employees.

Eleven days earlier, on October 24, President Harry S Truman scratched his signature on the bottom of a seven-page presidential memorandum addressed to Secretary of State Dean G. Acheson and Secretary of Defense Robert A. Lovett. Classified top secret and stamped with a code word that was itself classified, the order directed the establishment of an agency to be known as the National Security Agency. It was the birth certificate for America's newest and most secret agency, so secret in fact that only a handful in the government would be permitted to know of its existence. Even the date set for its birth was most likely designed for maximum secrecy: should any hint of its creation leak out, it would surely be swallowed up in the other news of the day — the presidential election of 1952.

•

Thirty years later Mr. Truman's memorandum is still one of Washington's most closely guarded secrets. Those seven pages remain "the foundation upon which all past and current communications intelligence activities of the United States government are based," according to a senior official of the National Security Council. And in its defense against a 1976 lawsuit seeking access to the memorandum, the NSA argued successfully against the release of even one word: "This Memorandum remains the principal charter of the National Security Agency and is the basis of a number of other classified documents governing the conduct of communications intelligence activities and operations, functions [and] activities of the National Security Agency." Even a congressional committee was forced to issue a subpoena in order to obtain a copy of the directive that implemented the memorandum.

Three decades after its birth the agency itself remains nearly as secretive and mysterious as when it emerged from the presidential womb. Its name is no longer classified information, but virtually all other details concerning the agency continue to be.

Newsman Daniel Schorr, in his book *Clearing the Air*, referred to the NSA as "one of the deepest secrets"; former CIA official Victor Marchetti has called it "the most secretive member of the intelligence community"; and Harrison E. Salisbury, the Pulitzer Prize–winning former editor and correspondent for the *New York Times*, has written that "not one American in 10,000 has even heard its name." Even Moscow's *Literary Gazette* once noted: "It has been observed that even the mouths of those in the 'intelligence community' . . . and literally of everyone, shut automatically at the slightest mention of NSA's secret operations, and their faces acquire a vacant look."

As a result of this overwhelming passion for secrecy, few persons outside the inner circle of America's intelligence community have recognized the gradual shift in power and importance from the Central Intelligence Agency to the NSA. Thus, it was to a surprised Congress that the Senate Intelligence Committee reported: "By the budget yardstick, the most influential individual [in the intelligence community] is the Director of NSA (DIRNSA), who, including his dual role as Chief of the Central Security Service, manages the largest single program contained in the national intelligence budget."

Victor Marchetti and John D. Marks, in *The CIA and the Cult of Intelligence*, reported that former CIA director Richard Helms was so frustrated by his lack of real authority within the intelligence community that he concluded, "It was unrealistic for any DCI [director of Central Intelligence] to think that he could have a significant influence on U.S. intelligence-resource decisions or the shaping of the intelligence community." According to Marchetti and Marks, Helms once observed to his staff that "while he, as DCI, was theoretically responsible for 100 percent of the nation's intelligence activities, he in fact controlled less than 15 percent of the community's assets — and most of the other 85 percent belonged to the Secretary of Defense and the Joint Chiefs of Staff."

Even with that bleak assessment, however, Richard Helms overestimated his true influence. According to the Senate Intelligence Committee, "as Director of the CIA, the DCI controls less than 10 percent of the combined national and tactical intelligence efforts." The committee went on to say "The remainder spent directly by the Department of Defense on intelligence activities in FY 1976 was outside of his fiscal authority." Then, pouring salt on the wound, the committee added, "The DCI's influence over how these funds are allocated was limited, in effect, to that of an interested critic."

So where, then, is the real power base in the U.S. intelligence community? Again, according to the Senate Intelligence Committee, in terms of both budget and size "the most influential individual is the Director of NSA."

Soon after his appointment by President Carter, CIA director Stansfield Turner realized how emasculated the position of DCI had become. He created a storm of controversy, shortly after his arrival at Langley, by suggesting the establishment of what amounted to an "intelligence czar," with absolute power over the sprawling intelligence community. The suggestion sparked a bitter battle with Secretary of Defense Harold Brown, who opposed any takeover of what he considered primarily defense-oriented agencies.

The dispute was resolved on January 24, 1978, with the issuance of Executive Order No. 12036, which reorganized the intelligence community and established greater restrictions on collection techniques. The order rejected Turner's concept and left overall control of the NSA and the other defense intelligence organizations with the Secretary of Defense, although it did give the DCI greater control over both assignments and the budget for the entire community.

Yet despite Turner's increased position in the intelligence community, the role of the CIA as a major intelligence collector continued its downward trend as a result of the continuing growth of technical intelligence and a corresponding decline of that gathered by human effort. James R. Schlesinger, the tough, organization-minded manager President Nixon picked in 1973 to replace Helms, arrived at CIA headquarters with a pipe in one hand and an ax in the other. During his brief five-month tenure Schlesinger chopped more than two thousand employees from the payroll. On taking office in March 1977, Admiral Turner picked up Schlesinger's bloodied ax and slashed away another 820 employees, thus nearly causing what one former agency official called "the CIA's first mutiny." Actually, Turner had been kind; he had inherited a Ford administration recommendation to cut from twelve hundred to fourteen hundred people. By 1978 the CIA's Operations Division had been reduced from a peak of eight thousand during the Vietnam War to less than four thousand.

Although the NSA had also suffered cutbacks, particularly once
the Vietnam War ended, by 1978 it still controlled 68,203 people —
more than all of the employees of the rest of the intelligence community put together.

Despite its size and power, however, no law has ever been enacted
prohibiting the NSA from engaging in any activity. There are only
laws to prohibit the release of any information about the Agency.
"No statute establishes the NSA," Senate Intelligence Committee
chairman Frank Church reported, "or defines the permissible scope
of its responsibilities." The CIA, on the other hand, was established
by Congress under a public law, the National Security Act of 1947,
setting out that agency's legal mandate as well as the restrictions
on its activities.

In addition to being free of legal restrictions, the NSA has technological capabilities for eavesdropping beyond imagination. Such capabilities once led former Senate Intelligence Committee member Walter F. Mondale to point to the NSA as "possibly the most single
important source of intelligence for this nation."

Yet the very same capabilities that provide the United States with
its greatest intelligence resource also provide the nation with one
of its greatest potential dangers. Noted Senator Church: "That capability at any time could be turned around on the American people
and no American would have any privacy left, such is the capability
to monitor everything: telephone conversations, telegrams, it doesn't
matter. There would be no place to hide." America had secretly constructed the eavesdropping equivalent of the H-bomb. Now the question was where to use it.

It was a difficult and dangerous road, a road that had its unlikely
beginning in the small southern Indiana town of Worthington during
the pastel, sunlit days before America's first war to end all wars.

2

PRELUDE

HERBERT OSBORNE YARDLEY was a dreamer. Terrestrially, the borders of his world were the small southwestern Indiana towns with such descriptive names as Coal City, Clay City, and Freedom. He was born on April 13, 1889, in Worthington, where the Eel River flows gently into the mightier White. He was the son of a railway telegrapher, and the rumbling thunder of an approaching train was more than simply a reminder of where his father worked; it was the sound in his dreams that led to distant cities and exotic lands with intriguing names.

He was the archetypical high school success — the boy with a talent for doing everything right. He was popular and outgoing; he was intelligent; he was an amusing talker. It was almost inevitable that he would become the president of his high school class, editor of the school paper, and captain of the football team. It was not quite so predictable that he would become one of the most addicted poker players in town.

In 1912 at the age of twenty-three, Yardley decided to get on that train which would take him into the bigger world of Washington, D.C. — a trip that eventually would bear him into history as the world's most famous cryptologist, the father of the first codebreaking organization in the United States, and one of the founders of the codebreaking bureaus of Canada and the Republic of China.

All that was some distance in the future, however. Yardley landed at Union Station in the quiet, prewar days when the United States was on the verge of becoming a world power — with all the complicated interests in communications that such power brings with it. On November 16, the young man from Worthington got a job as a $900-a-year code clerk and telegrapher in the State Department. His dreams had begun to come true, and, for him, the stuttering telegraph key on his desk was the sound of history being made.

It was, at least, the raw material of history — all of these department messages that flowed across his desk — but before that it was still the confidential information on which we based our foreign policy. Yardley worried. He knew that other countries employed "decipherers" to solve the puzzle of coded foreign messages, so why not the United States? "As I asked myself this question," he later wrote, "I knew that I had the answer . . . to a purpose in life. I would devote my life to cryptography."

When he went to the Library of Congress and was able to find no more than a few titles on the subject, most of those in foreign languages, he began to educate himself in the dark art. He practiced trying to decipher State Department messages; at the same time, he began to obtain copies of the coded diplomatic messages of some of the foreign embassies in Washington. Where and how he managed to filch these secret texts will probably always remain a mystery. In his later accounts, he simply alluded to "friendly connections previously established," presumably a co-conspirator in the telegraph company.

One quiet night in May 1916, the wire between the cable office in New York and the White House began to come alive. Ordinarily the State Department code clerks would pay little attention, since such transmission was direct to the White House and in an unfamiliar code; it simply passed through the equipment used in the Code Room. Yardley copied the coded message as the five hundred words began flashing across the wire. The cable was to President Wilson from his aide and personal representative, Colonel House, who had just come from speaking with the German Emperor. If ever there was a challenging code on which to test his ability, surely this must be it: a personal message to the President from his top aide.

To Yardley's amazement, he was able to solve it in less than two hours. Whatever respect he had for the American codes instantly vanished. He knew that messages from Colonel House traveled over cables that passed through England and that the Code Bureau in the Royal Navy intercepted all the messages. "Colonel House must be the Allies' best informant," Yardley concluded.

Throughout the next year the young Hoosier worked secretly on a treatise describing the sad shape of American cryptography and its vulnerability to analysis. As the shadows of the approaching war darkened the horizon, Yardley presented to his superior, David Salmon, his analysis, titled "Solution of American Diplomatic Codes." When he read it, Salmon was speechless. His first thought was that the British maintained a large bureau for solving diplomatic correspondence, and he asked Yardley whether he believed that the English code experts could solve the American code. Yardley answered with what would become a maxim in cryptology: "I always assume that what is in the power of one man to do is in the power of another."

A month later Salmon confidently handed the code clerk a number of messages encoded in an entirely new system. When Yardley placed the deciphered messages on his desk several weeks later, Salmon's optimism disappeared; he was resigned to the belief that nothing was indecipherable.

By now America had entered the war to end all wars. Yardley saw his future not in the State Department, where advancement was snail-paced at best, but with the War Department, which he felt "would soon rule America." On June 29, 1917, he pinned on the gold bars of a second lieutenant and took charge of Section Eight of Military Intelligence, MI-8, responsible for all code and cipher work in the division.

As the war progressed, Yardley added a variety of subsections to MI-8. Because of the likelihood that Germany was reading a great deal of the most confidential American traffic, he first added the Code Compilation Subsection, which began devising new code systems. Next, he established the Communications Subsection to provide rapid and secure communications with about forty military attachés and intelligence officers in foreign countries. Then the Shorthand Subsection, which could attack the most obscure foreign shorthand systems. To head up the Secret Ink Subsection, Yardley had the help of Harvard professor Theodore W. Richards, America's first Nobel laureate in chemistry. Finally, Yardley established the Code and Cipher Solution Subsection, which eventually deciphered a total of 10,735 messages sent by foreign governments.

At the time the Armistice was signed, on November 11, 1918, Yardley was in Paris, trying to develop greater cooperation with the secret French Chambre Noire. He was then directed by Washington to take charge of a code bureau attached to the American Commission to the Peace Conference. From two rooms in the Hôtel Crillon, the small band of cryptologists encrypted messages for the delegation and solved those of the other Allied nations. Much of the intercepted traffic related to the intrigues of secret agents and espionage operations that abounded during the conference, each nation doing its best to read each other's cards.

With the conclusion of the conference, Yardley sailed back to the United States and to an uncertain future. For some time he had been concerned about what lay ahead, now that America had entered a time of peace. "The situation is so uncertain," Yardley confided to a friend in December of 1918, "that I have already written . . . about getting some sort of job with the American Code Company." His days of peering into the secret codes of foreign nations, he feared, were over forever.

But by the time Yardley arrived in the United States, on April 18, 1919, there had already been a number of discussions on the possibility of retaining a capability to eavesdrop on foreign communications. General Marlborough Churchill, director of Military Intelligence, had recommended to the Army chief of staff that MI-8 "be retained in toto"; and in Washington, Captain John Manly, who had been in charge of MI-8 in Yardley's absence, had recommended "a large permanent organization" but added that he was anxious to get back to his professorship at the University of Chicago and suggested that Yardley be retained as chief of MI-8.

To his delight, Yardley was given the assignment to prepare a memorandum arguing for retention of MI-8 and its conversion to a peacetime organization. The proposal, submitted by General Churchill to the Army chief of staff on May 16, called for a bureau consisting of ten code and cipher experts, each employed at $3000 per year, fifteen code and cipher experts at $2000, and twenty-five clerks at $1200. The chief himself would receive the handsome salary of $6000 a year. The total budget, including rent, heat, electricity, and reference books, was set at $100,000, $40,000 of which was to be paid by the State Department and $60,000 by the War Department. The War Department was to submit its expenditure in a "confidential memorandum," which was not subject to review by the Comptroller General — and this probably represents the first American example of a secret intelligence budget.

The proposal also specified that the organization be composed of civilians, and cited the British policy of "searching the British Empire for the best code and cipher brains of the Empire." The type of mind needed in cryptologic work, it argued, is seldom found in the Army.

The day after the memorandum was submitted it was approved by Frank L. Polk, the Acting Secretary of State; and on May 20, 1919, as the ink from the signature of Chief of Staff General Peyton C. March began drying, America's Black Chamber was born.

For reasons of security, as well as the fact that the State Department's portion of the budget could not by law be spent within the District of Columbia, Yardley set up shop in New York City. After first considering a building at 17 East 36 Street, he finally settled on a stately four-story brownstone at 3 East 38 Street, owned by an old friend.

Secrecy was always the paramount concern; each new employee, as soon as possible, was given a memorandum that dictated a number of security precautions and outlined the Black Chamber's cover story: "Where you work and what you do are not matters for discussion, but rather than appear mysterious you may say that you are employed by the War Department in its translation department." In addition to a cover story, the Chamber also had a cover address, Post Office Box 354, Grand Central Station, New York, which was to be used for all correspondence.

To hide even further the true nature of the work (as well as to earn a few extra dollars) Yardley formed a commercial code business called Code Compilation Company, and operated it from the first floor of the brownstone. If anyone ventured in through the front door, he would find an apparently legitimate company. The firm did produce a commerical code, the Universal Trade Code, which it was able to sell profitably.

Yardley's tiny enterprise took off like a rocket. At midnight on Friday, December 12, 1919, that rocket reached its apogee. Five months earlier Yardley had promised General Churchill that he would solve the Japanese code within a year or resign. Now, out of a sound sleep, the solution had come to him. "My heart stood still, and I dared not move," Yardley would later write. "Was I awake? Was I losing my mind? A solution? At last — and after all these months!" An hour later, after successfully testing his theory, he locked the key to the solution of the Japanese code in his safe, told his wife to get dressed, and went out to celebrate. That decipherment was to be by far the most important achievement of the Black Chamber and Yardley's greatest personal triumph, though he did have some help from his brilliant assistant Frederick Livesey.

The timing could not have been better. During the summer of 1920 the major powers began to move toward a conference on the limitation of naval armaments, a sort of post–World War I SALT talk. The goal was a Five-Power Treaty between the United States, Britain, France, Italy, and Japan to set limits on the tonnage of capital ships. The treaty would stipulate certain ratios in terms of tonnage for each nation according to its current naval strength and require that these ratios be maintained.

The conference opened on November 14, 1921, in Washington's Pan American Building. Three days earlier, the American delegate, Secretary of State Charles Evans Hughes, had revealed the United

States position on the question of ratios: parity with England and a 10-to-6 ratio with Japan. Each point in the ratio meant 100,000 tons of capital ships, or the equivalent of about three battleships. Secretary Hughes was therefore seeking an agreement of a million tons for the United States versus 600,000 tons for Japan, the most aggressive nation attending the Washington Conference.

For Yardley, the armament conference was a chance to prove to the policy-makers in Washington the tremendous value of his Black Chamber. The first indication of a conference came in intercepted telegram No. 813, from Japan's ambassador in London to Tokyo, on July 5, 1921. From then on the Chamber began following closely each development as the messages were in turn deciphered and translated. Daily courier service was established between New York and Washington. It was learned early that Japan had set its bottom line with the United States at a ratio of 10 to 7. When the Japanese delegate, Admiral Tomosaburo Kato, went public with this position, it appeared that the conference had reached a stalemate. The deciphered messages, however, began telling a different story. Then, on November 28, the Black Chamber deciphered what Yardley considered "the most important and far-reaching telegram that ever passed through the Black Chamber's doors." It was from Japan's Foreign Office to the delegation in Washington and showed the first signs of a softening of Japan's 10-to-7 position:

> It is necessary to avoid any clash with Great Britain and America, particularly America, in regard to the armament limitation question. You will to the utmost maintain a middle attitude and redouble your efforts to carry out our policy. In case of inevitable necessity you will work to establish your second proposal of 10 to 6.5. If, in spite of your utmost efforts, it becomes necessary in view of the situation and in the interests of general policy to fall back on your proposal No. 3, you will endeavor to limit the power of concentration and maneuver of the Pacific by a guarantee to reduce or at least to maintain the status quo of Pacific defenses and to make an adequate reservation which will make clear that this is our intention in agreeing to a 10-to-6 ratio.
>
> No. 4 is to be avoided as far as possible.

An avid poker fan, Yardley now likened America's position to that of a stud poker player who knows his opponent's hole card: "All it need do was to mark time." Finally, on December 10, Japan threw in its hand and agreed to the 10-to-6 ratio.

By the time the conference drew to a close, on February 6, 1922, Yardley's health had taken a sharp turn downward. Overcome by exhaustion, on the verge of a nervous breakdown, and weakened by a mild case of tuberculosis, he remained in bed for a month. In March his doctor told him to pack his bags and go to sunny Arizona for a long rest. Three months without seeing a single coded message or rushing toward a deadline apparently did the trick, and in June he returned to the anonymity of the Black Chamber, fully recovered.

But things had changed. Gone was the eager anticipation in the halls and offices of the War and State Departments, anxiously awaiting the news that the latest decipherment would bring. The all-important conference was over, and America was enjoying a long-awaited peace. All this meant that the Chamber's once-endless stream of intercepted messages was rapidly drying up.

This had always been a serious problem for the Black Chamber; without messages there could be no solutions. During the war, obtaining cable traffic presented no problem because of mandatory cable censorship. This ended on the Far East circuits on December 21, 1918. The United States had wanted to end all remaining censorship later that month but the British and the French wanted the practice to continue; it was finally dropped by the United States in early 1919. Whether it was also ended by the British and French is unknown.

With the end of the war came another problem: the Radio Communication Act of 1912 was again in effect. This act provided that the government would guarantee the secrecy of communications:

No person or persons engaged in or having knowledge of the operation of any station or stations shall divulge or publish the contents of any messages transmitted or received by such station, except to the person or persons to whom the same may be directed, or their authorized agent, or to another station employed to forward such message to its destination, unless legally required to do so by the court of competent jurisdiction or other competent authority.

The law had been enacted after the proclamation of the International Radio-Telegraph Convention of July 8, 1912. Three days earlier, the United States had joined a great many other nations in London in affixing their signatures to the document. This was a very significant step for the United States, since it represented the first international convention of its type to which the country had adhered. To the Black Chamber, however, it represented a large obstacle that had to be overcome — illegally, if necessary.

By the time Yardley returned to the United States in April 1919, the State Department was already busy trying to establish a secret

liaison with the Western Union Telegraph Company. It was hoped
that Western Union would cooperate with the Black Chamber in providing copies of needed messages. For six months the State Department got nowhere; the Radio Communication Act provided harsh
penalties for any employee of a telegraph company who divulged
the contents of a message. Then Yardley suggested to General Churchill that he personally visit Western Union's president, Newcomb
Carlton. The meeting was arranged in September, and Churchill,
accompanied by Yardley, raised with President Carlton the delicate
matter of his secretly supplying the Chamber, in total violation of
the law, copies of all necessary telegrams. After the men "had put
all our cards on the table," Yardley would later write, "President
Carlton seemed anxious to do everything he could for us."

Under the agreed-on arrangements, a messenger called at Western
Union's Washington office each morning and took the telegrams to
the office of the Military Intelligence Division in Washington. They
were returned to Western Union before the close of the same day.

In the spring of 1920 the Black Chamber began approaching the
other major telegraph company, Postal Telegraph, with the same request. Officials of this company, however, were much more disturbed
by the possibility of criminal prosecution than were their counterparts
at Western Union. For this reason, negotiations with the Black Chamber were carried on through an intermediary, a New York lawyer
named L. F. H. Betts. All letters were carefully written so that no
outsider would be able to understand what was really being said,
and to camouflage the negotiations even further, Betts in one case
communicated with General Churchill through the general's wife.

In the end an agreement was reached, and that left only the smaller
All-American Cable Company, which handled communications between North and South America. Yardley, later that same year, began
negotiations with it through W. E. Roosevelt and Robert W. Goelet,
who himself had been a commissioned officer in Military Intelligence
during the war.

Regardless of whether All-American cooperated, by the end of 1920
the Black Chamber had the secret and illegal cooperation of almost
the entire American cable industry. American cryptology had lost
its virginity.

By early 1921, however, Yardley's delicately woven cooperation
with Western Union threatened to come unraveled. On the afternoon
of March 5, four miles off the warm sands of Miami Beach, American
sub chaser No. 154 aimed its forward gun at the Western Union
cable ship *Robert C. Clowry* and with an ear-piercing boom sent a

shell across her bow. Captain H. M. Smith of the *Clowry* was duly impressed. As he began to heave to and precede the sub chaser in to shore, a bitter dispute between Western Union and the federal government had dramatically reached its climax.

For months the giant cable company had been trying to lay a cable from Florida to connect with the British cables serving Brazil. But the link would have strengthened a British monopoly over communications between the United States and the South American country, a monopoly the State Department feared would be extremely detrimental to American commercial interests. At the time, the British had almost complete control of the world's cable systems, the principal channel through which all international business was negotiated. No matter where a cable originated or was destined — Asia, Africa, Europe, South America, or even the United States — the odds were that at some point it would have to pass through the British cable system. The State Department's consternation was increased when it learned that the British were secretly eavesdropping on all cable messages, commercial as well as governmental, a practice that originated long before the First World War and continues to the present.

American cables had been laid by another U.S. cable company into Santos and Rio de Janeiro, thereby making possible direct communication between the United States and Brazil. The problem, however, was that Western Union controlled the routing of messages originating in the United States and thereby could drive the other company out of business simply by routing all messages to and from Brazil over the Miami-British cable link. It was the assignment of Ensign William H. Klapproth, commanding officer of the sub chaser, to prevent that link from being formed. After the warning shot, the cable, four miles short of its goal, sank to the bottom as the *Clowry* headed into Miami.

The controversy was still raging when, on April 2, Yardley approached his Western Union contact, J. C. Willever, the vice president, and requested that he supply some messages that had been filed by an agent of a country in which the Black Chamber was greatly interested. But the request, bucked up the ladder to President Newcomb Carlton, could not have been more ill timed; still bitter over the action by the State Department and the Navy, Carlton refused any additional favors to the Black Chamber. Yardley, not to be outdone, went to Brigadier General D. E. Nolan, who had replaced Churchill as head of Military Intelligence and whom Yardley had known when Nolan was wartime chief of Military Intelligence in France. He suggested that Nolan have a conference with Carlton and possibly work out a modus operandi that would be satisfactory to both sides. Whether such an agreement was made may never be known; either the subject was too sensitive to be committed to paper or the documents were destroyed.

How long the cooperation of the companies lasted is also unknown. It does seem certain, however, that by the middle to late 1920s the volume of cable traffic to the Chamber had dropped quite sharply. One factor that may have had some influence was the enactment of the Radio Act of 1927, which greatly broadened the Radio Communication Act enacted in 1912. Whereas the 1912 act made it a crime only for the employees of the cable and telegraph companies to divulge the contents of the messages to unauthorized persons, the 1927 act closed the loophole by making liable to criminal penalties also those who received such unauthorized communications. One exception allowed for the acquisition of messages "on demand of lawful authority," but Yardley and his ultrasecret Black Chamber could hardly avail themselves of this channel.

As a result of the reduction in cables supplied by the cable companies, attention turned to the establishment of intercept stations to eavesdrop on communications sent by radio. During the war, this had been the responsibility of the Signal Corps. Its primary usefulness was at the front lines, where radio intelligence units would monitor German battle communications. In the United States, the Signal Corps maintained "mobile tractor" units stationed along the southern border to intercept some of the Mexican traffic, but radio was still considered too new and unreliable for long-distance communications between fixed stations.

As the war ended, so did the intercept material, a fact that came as a total surprise to Yardley and Military Intelligence. Just as they had taken for granted that the cable companies would continue to supply copies of all messages passing through their offices, they assumed that the Signal Corps would continue its wartime intercept activities, which would be at the call of the Black Chamber. Now that the cable companies were beginning to back off and supply less and less material, Yardley began looking again to the possible establishment of intercept stations.

In 1925 Military Intelligence began to consider setting up a listening post in China to monitor Japanese radio traffic. The Signal Corps also was enthusiastic over the idea and recommended that four expert telegraphers be sent on a special mission to China, where they would study the Japanese language and learn to read the Japanese radio code. It was hoped that this training would make them expert intercept operators and that they could, once they returned, be assigned to Military Intelligence and the Signal Corps as instructors.

Though the idea sounded good, it soon ran into a storm of bureaucratic static, and in 1932 the State Department formally scratched the plan.

At one other point Yardley had considered the establishment of an intercept station. In 1922 one of RCA's competitors confidentially informed him that "there existed in the office of this competitor an automatic wireless-receiving set which was used to monitor the traffic of the Radio Corporation of America for commercial purposes." The intercepts were made on a tape that could be read visually. With a similar receiving set, Yardley believed, he would be able to do his own intercepting. Tests were begun to see whether such a set, established either at Governor's Island, New York, or in Yardley's office, would be able to eavesdrop on the commercial telegraph station in San Francisco that, it was believed, broadcast the Japanese diplomatic messages. The tests proved a failure, however, and the project was abandoned.

During the mid to late 1920s this lack of both cables and intercepted radio communication proved to be a major problem for the Black Chamber, a problem that would never be totally overcome. Yardley's once-soaring rocket was beginning to fall back to earth, its fuel of messages rapidly being exhausted.

Traffic between the Black Chamber and the State and War Departments was passed in the form of "bulletins," which always began with the ambiguous phrase: "We learn from a source believed reliable that . . ." followed by the deciphered but paraphrased intercept.

By the fall of 1924 the bulletins were becoming scarcer as the traffic dropped off to zero. The Japanese desk cryptanalytic staff was now reduced to processing material dating back to the war and the peace conference — material acquired when the Black Chamber first established its secret liaison with the cable companies.

During all of 1926 the Black Chamber received only eleven Japanese messages, and these were radio intercepts. Since they were in several different systems it was hardly enough for the Chamber staff even to begin working out a solution. Nineteen twenty-seven proved substantially better, with 428 Japanese messages received, of which 150 were deciphered.

The lack of intercepts, combined with a governmentwide austerity drive, hit the Black Chamber like a sledgehammer. In May of 1923, Yardley was forced to cut back so drastically that he had to fire more than half his staff. Nine people, including such valuable assets as

Frederick Livesey, were dismissed, thus reducing America's entire corps of codebreakers to seven. In a letter written that month, Yardley indicated just how severe the budget cutbacks had become:

> In 1919 our organization called for an expenditure of $100,000. This was reduced to something like $70,000, and then to $50,000; next year we are reducing it to $35,000 and if the plans outlined above are followed we shall, for the following year, reduce it to $25,000. This means that in the year 1924–1925 we will be spending only ¼ of the money that was planned for this bureau when it was established in 1919, or a reduction of 75% in a period of five years.

In an effort to save on rent, and also because of a recent break-in, the Black Chamber was moved from the comfortable town house at 141 East 37 Street, where it had moved in June 1920, to several back rooms in a large office building at 52 Vanderbilt Avenue, where it again was hidden behind the cover of Yardley's Code Compilation Company.

In March of 1929, Herbert Clark Hoover told an inauguration crowd, "I have no fears for the future of our country; it is bright with hope," and then proceeded to the White House as the nation's thirty-first President. As his new Secretary of State, Hoover appointed the conservative Henry L. Stimson.

To Yardley, any change in Washington was viewed as a potential threat to his Black Chamber, and he advised his liaison at the State Department not to reveal the existence of the organization to the new Secretary for a few months, in the hope that any idealism Stimson may have had before taking office would become tempered by reality.

Then in May, after Yardley had deciphered a new group of Japanese messages, he decided the time had come to share the dark secret with the man who was paying the bills, and a few selected translations were laid on the Secretary's desk.

Stimson's reaction was immediate and violent. Branding the Black Chamber highly illegal, he at once directed that all its State Department funds be cut off. Since the Chamber was now getting almost its entire support from the State Department, that meant instant doom.

Yardley apparently took the news hard. The Black Chamber had successfully solved more than ten thousand messages, most of them diplomatic, including sixteen hundred during the armament conference alone. In addition, since 1917 Yardley and his staff, laboring in thankless anonymity, had managed to solve coded messages from Argentina, Brazil, China, Costa Rica, Cuba, Germany, Japan, Liberia,

Mexico, Nicaragua, Panama, Peru, the Soviet Union, El Salvador, Santo Domingo (the Dominican Republic), Spain, France, England, and had even studied the papal codes of the Vatican. Yet, after all this, it now fell on Yardley to inform what was left of his staff that, according to the new Secretary of State, "gentlemen do not read each other's mail."

That day was to be their last. So outraged was Stimson that he wanted the entire staff dismissed at once. It took a considerable amount of pressure by the assistant chief of staff for Military Intelligence to convince him that the immediate effect of throwing six people out on the street would be to invite possible "indiscretions which could be embarrassing to the Government and produce serious consequences as regards . . . national defense." Stimson apparently saw the logic in the argument, especially when it was also noted that the codebreakers had neither civil service status nor retirement benefits. It was therefore agreed that the actual work of the organization would end immediately, but that the personnel would be retained on the payroll during a period in which a reorganization would take place. In the summer of 1929 the six were given an advance of three months' pay, which was to tide them over until they were able to locate new jobs. Then, at midnight on October 31, 1929, the doors to the Black Chamber officially closed, as quietly as they had opened.

If Herbert Yardley had nightmares that evening, it had nothing to do with Halloween. Seven days earlier the bottom had fallen out of the stock market. Black Thursday. The Great Depression had begun. Now, for the first time in sixteen years, Yardley was without a paycheck, without a job, and with skills so arcane as to be almost useless.

Back in Worthington, and with no end to the Depression in sight, Yardley began toying with the idea of writing a book describing his exploits as chief of the Black Chamber. The idea at once attracted and repelled him — after all, it was he who had written to a friend, only half a dozen years before, "Ever since the war I have consistently fought against disclosing anything about codes and ciphers. My reason is obvious: It warns other governments of our skill and makes our work more difficult." Even earlier, he had written that if it should become known by the Japanese that the Americans could read their messages, "they may make such a violent change in their new codes that we could never read them."

But Yardley was convinced that the situation was now different. The book, he would argue later, could not injure the government, "because it proved to foreign nations that we would no longer stoop to this sort of espionage." His deepest and sincerest motivation, how-

ever, came from the feeling that the State Department had made a
terrible blunder based on a naïve and unrealistic view of the world.
He felt that by letting the American people know that their government had removed one of the most important tools in international
diplomacy, a tool designed to save lives in time of war and to fortify
America's diplomatic positions in time of peace, enough of a furor
would be created to force the government to rethink its position.
In addition, he believed that the present state of the American code
was so bad that almost any nation could read it anyway, and the
publicity might bring about the needed revisions.

The reasons for publication, Yardley decided, greatly outweighed
those against, and he set out to find an agent who might be able to
help him sell the idea. He selected George T. Bye & Company of
New York, a well-known literary agency with offices at 535 Fifth Avenue. Bye immediately saw the potential in such a book but recommended magazine publication as the first step. *The Saturday Evening
Post* liked the idea and agreed to serialize the text in three issues.
Finally, Yardley received the news that the Bobbs-Merrill Company
of Indianapolis had approved of his outline and agreed to publish
his book.

Military Intelligence had known of Yardley's publication plans almost from the beginning. In May 1930, Colonel Stanley H. Ford,
the assistant chief of staff for Intelligence at the War Department,
was told by "a prominent publisher" that he had been approached
by Yardley, who proposed to write a full account of his activities
while employed by the MID. Yardley had taken the publisher into
his confidence and told him fully of his activities under the War Department both before and after the Armistice. The publisher, after
conferring with Ford, agreed that going ahead with the publication
"would not be for the best interests of the United States" and therefore declined to accept Yardley's proposal.

After the publisher left, Ford contacted Lieutenant Colonel O. S.
Albright, who was one of the officers involved in closing down the
Black Chamber, and asked him to contact Yardley. When they met,
Albright pointed out to Yardley that if he made public his activities
after the Armistice, "it was possible that international unpleasantness
might arise." Yardley vaguely promised that he "would be careful,"
but he would not agree to submit any articles to the War Department
for screening.

On March 28, 1931, the panic began. In that week's issue, *The
Saturday Evening Post* announced Yardley's forthcoming series of articles. Emergency meetings were called in Washington to decide on

a course of action. Prosecution was considered but rejected, because
it was felt that such a trial would be compromising as well as embarrassing to the government. Suppression of the book was also considered, but, there being no precedent or legal basis, this too was rejected.

The *Post* articles, "Secret Ink," "Codes," and "Ciphers," which
appeared between April 4 and May 9, were a smash hit and whetted
the public's appetite for the publication, on June 1, of what was to
become one of the most controversial books in American publishing
history, *The American Black Chamber*.

The book was an immediate success. It was written in a thrilling,
melodramatic style, and it related the Chamber's most intimate secrets. The critics were as favorable as official Washington was horrified. One critic called it "the most sensational contribution to the
secret history of the war, as well as the immediate post-war period,
which has yet been written by an American." The State Department,
on the other hand, not only denied that it had been reading the
Japanese messages during the Washington Conference, but even
stated that Secretary of State Stimson had never heard of the Black
Chamber. A few days later, Stimson changed his denials to an embarrassed "no comment." General Douglas MacArthur, the Army chief
of staff, stated that he knew nothing about the Black Chamber; high
officials in the Military Intelligence Division did the same.

That fall, Yardley toured the country, lecturing to audiences about
America's past successes in cryptology and its bleak future without
them. He was, however, ambitious to produce another book. *The American Black Chamber* had been a popular exposé — it sold about eighteen
thousand copies in America — but Yardley wanted to be accepted
as a serious historian, as well. His new subject was to be the Japanese
role in the arms limitation conference of 1921–1922; as a basis for
the text, Yardley had a personal cache of the intercepted Japanese
messages that had been decoded in the Black Chamber. Such a book
would, he thought, provide its readers with a unique glimpse into
diplomacy, as they followed the secret communications of an adversary
during an international conference.

Because making a book out of the mass of Japanese telegrams was
a job for which, evidently, he had little patience, Yardley hired a
young free-lance journalist, Marie Stuart Klooz, who was recommended to him by his agent. The thirty-year-old graduate of Sweet
Briar had worked several years as a newspaper reporter and earned
a well-deserved reputation for speed. In two months, she produced
a 970-page manuscript. She and Yardley discarded such possible titles

as *Diplomatic Eavesdropping* and *Embassy Keyholes,* and settled on one guaranteed to glaze all eyes except the most academic: *Japanese Diplomatic Secrets: 1921–22.*

By late summer of 1932, rumors of the new Yardley book were beginning to circulate in Washington, and Yardley got wind of them. Afraid that this time the government would take some action, he decided to have his young ghost writer put her name on the manuscript as sole author.

Could a young lady who had been a Sweet Briar junior during the armament conference have decoded a whole volume of Japanese diplomatic traffic and written a scholarly book about it? Evidently America's finest cryptologist could invent no more baffling deception than that.

The finished manuscript was placed in seven brown manila envelopes and quietly delivered to the Bobbs-Merrill Company. But Yardley by now was too hot to handle, and D. L. Chambers, president of the publishing house, turned down the manuscript. Worried that the Justice Department was going to ban further publication of *The American Black Chamber,* and trying to curry some favor with the department, Chambers secretly notified Nugent Dodds, the assistant attorney general, about Yardley's new book, noting that it made heavy use of the intercepted Japanese messages.

Dodds immediately notified Stanley K. Hornbeck in the State Department's Division of Far Eastern Affairs. In a memo dated September 12, 1932, Hornbeck warned, "I cannot too strongly urge that, in view of the state of excitement which apparently prevails in Japanese public opinion now, characterized by fear of or enmity toward the United States, every possible effort should be made to prevent the appearance of this book."

The day after Hornbeck's memo, Dodds, who himself considered any sequel to *The American Black Chamber* both scandalous and a serious threat to national security, requested that Bobbs-Merrill wire him Yardley's current address. A few hours later, a Western Union telegram informed him that Yardley was now at home in Worthington, Indiana. He notified the Secretary of War, who issued an immediate order through his Adjutant General, directing that one officer, together with two witnesses, proceed at once to Yardley's home. There they were to demand the return of the Japanese messages and any other secret or sensitive materials he may have taken from the Black Chamber. So that there would be no written record of the action, the officer was ordered to instruct Yardley orally. "This demand must be made in the presence of two witnesses, preferably military," the

order stated, "for the reason that no copy of this communication
or demand will be furnished Mr. Yardley." The original copy of the
order was to be returned to the War Department.

Three days later, on the evening of September 16, Infantry Colonel
Oliver P. Robinson, a professor of military science at Indiana University, accompanied by Captains Frank E. Barber and Ernest C. Adkins,
called on Yardley at his home. When Yardley answered the door,
Colonel Robinson began to read the prepared order:

"The Secretary of War is informed and believes that you have in your
possession and under your control diverse original documents that came
into your possession during the time that you were an employee of the
United States Government in connection with the Military Intelligence
activities of the War Department, including those certain documents,
reproductions of which are set forth in a book written by you entitled
The American Black Chamber between pages numbered 48 and 49, and
168 and 169.

"The Secretary of War has also been advised that you have within
your possession and under your control diverse other original documents
belonging to the United States made and obtained by you while you
were connected with the United States Government in the capacity above
mentioned.

"It is, therefore, demanded of you that you deliver to the Adjutant
General, United States Army, War Department, Washington, D.C., which
officer is designated to receive such delivery, all such documents or copies
of documents hereinabove described by reason of the relation of such
documents and copies of documents to the National Defense, and that
you refrain from making or causing to be made any copies thereof of
any kind or nature whatsoever."

Yardley, obviously surprised by his evening visitors, first tried to
assure the trio that he was out of the exposé business by telling them
he had turned down an offer by *Cosmopolitan* magazine to write a
series of articles on espionage. He added, "I am not interested in
non-fiction." Then he declared, "I have no documents that could
injure the strength of the U.S. Government." As his surprise began
turning into anger, Yardley told the colonel, "I cannot understand
why the U.S. Government should attempt to embarrass me," and
demanded to speak to the Adjutant General about the matter.

Dodds had never really believed that Yardley would give up the
material voluntarily. Legally, there was very little he could do, since
Yardley's actions seemed to fall between the cracks of the espionage
statutes. Still, he was not about to have Yardley slip another *Amercian*

Black Chamber under his nose, and he was determined to get his hands on the new manuscript.

At 9:45 A.M. on the morning of the 16th, Dodds felt he might get his chance. At that time he was visited by Colonel Alfred T. Smith, the War Department's assistant chief of staff for Intelligence, who informed him that the manuscript was at present in the hands of Yardley's new literary agent, Viola Irene Cooper, at 9 East 59 Street in New York City, and that she "will endeavor (or has endeavored) to place it with the MacMillan [sic] Company."

Dodds immediately telephoned the United States Attorney's office in New York City and spoke with the first assistant, a dashing, thirty-year-old attorney with jet black hair and an Errol Flynn mustache. Dodds told the assistant, Thomas Edmund Dewey, to get in touch with the Macmillan Company "relative to the inadvisability of publishing this book."

Dewey telephoned George Platt Brett, Jr., heir to the Macmillan publishing empire and president of the company. Brett, whose father still held control as chairman of the board, had himself worn khaki during the war as an officer in Military Intelligence. He agreed totally with Dewey and vowed to cooperate in any way he could to prevent the publication of Yardley's new book. At the time he spoke with Dewey, Brett had not yet read Yardley's *The American Black Chamber,* so a short while later he picked up a copy for himself. Outraged at the revelations, he wrote to Dewey: "I can readily see why the government should object to the publication of that book. Not only is it in very bad taste, but it seems to me that it reveals information which never should be revealed to the public."

Brett's cooperation with the government, however, went much deeper. He not only took great care to avoid publishing anything that might violate the espionage laws; he went so far as to refuse books that might simply "embarrass" the government. Around the same time as his phone conversation with Dewey, Macmillan had received the manuscript for *The Dark Invader,* by Captain F. von Rintelen, a German spy who had operated in the United States. Brett voluntarily offered the manuscript to Dewey and asked to have someone review it for any possible violations of the espionage laws and for "anything which the government would rather not have us include in the book." He added, "We are naturally anxious to co-operate in every possible way."

A few days later, Dewey sent the manuscript off to Nugent Dodds, asking that the Justice Department comply with the publisher's request to return the book as soon as possible. "I assume the Department will endeavor to cooperate with him," Dewey wrote, "particularly in view of his courtesy in submitting the book for the Government's inspection, and his attitude that he not only desires to avoid any possible violation of the espionage laws, but also his general attitude that anything offensive to the Government, whether illegal or not, would be distasteful to him."

Dodds, in turn, sent the document off to an embarrassed War Department, which had never requested nor, indeed, wanted the manuscript. With censorship dead for more than twelve years, it had no legal authority to review any private publications. After a brief review, in which it was determined that the book might embarrass a few living persons but posed no security threat, the War Department returned the manuscript to Dodds with a warning that it was not in the literary review business. The assistant attorney general then shipped it back to Dewey without even attaching a letter. Dewey, perplexed, wrote back to Dodds and, noting that no letter was enclosed, asked, "Can you advise me at this time whether *The Dark Invader* offends the War Department?"

Dodds replied with the suggestion that Dewey get in touch with Brett by phone, apparently to avoid any written record, and inform him that the War Department "appreciates his courtesy in permitting it to examine the manuscript but regrets that it is unable to express any opinion concerning the propriety or the legality of publishing the same." He added that the propriety of publishing the manuscript "is one which must be considered by the publishers."

Four months later, on February 16, 1933, Brett called Dewey to inform him that George Bye (Yardley had returned to his former agent) was about to submit the manuscript of *Japanese Diplomatic Secrets.* Dewey immediately contacted Frank Parrish, who was the acting head of the Justice Department's Criminal Division, and said that if either the Justice Department or the War Department desired to read the manuscript secretly, he would be able to accommodate it, as long as the reading was done quickly. "The important thing is that Macmillan cannot properly keep the book more than about ten days," Dewey wrote.

Parrish got on the phone to Colonel Alfred T. Smith, the assistant chief of staff at the War Department, and also called a Mr. Castle at the State Department. Both were eager to see the manuscript, and Parrish so informed Dewey. By now it was Friday, February 17, and time was becoming a major factor. Dewey notified Parrish that Macmillan was due to get the manuscript from their reader the next day and would immediately forward it to Washington. "There is a pressing time element in this situation in as much as the author has wired them that he will be in New York on *Tuesday*, February 21, to discuss the manuscript," Dewey cautioned Parrish. He also told him that Macmillan had agreed to wire Yardley that the manuscript would not be back from their reader by the 21st, "but they will not be able to delay the author's trip to New York more than one or two days."

By the time Macmillan had received the manuscript on Saturday, it was too late. Dewey could not get the document down to Washington, have it reviewed by both the State and War Departments, and have it back to Macmillan by the time Yardley arrived on Tuesday. The only alternative now was to seize the manuscript, but this presented serious problems. No manuscript had ever (or has since) been actually seized by the government for posing a danger to the national security, and the legal justification for it was, to say the least, tenuous.

Dewey notified George Z. Medalie, the U.S. Attorney, that if a seizure was to be made, it had to be on Monday, before Yardley turned up. The approval was given. On Monday, February 20, 1933, Dewey sent a U.S. marshal to the Macmillan office to advise Brett that he was wanted at the Federal Building and that he was to bring with him the manuscript of *Japanese Diplomatic Secrets*. At the same time, Dewey sent another marshal to fetch George Bye, Yardley's agent, with instructions to have Bye accompany him to the Federal Building.

Brett arrived first, the seven manila envelopes containing the manuscript tucked tightly under his arm as he entered the Old Post Office Building. Bye had not been in his office when the marshal first arrived, but he appeared a short time later at the United States Attorney's office. He instantly gathered what had happened when he saw Brett sitting there with the manuscript in his lap. A few minutes later, Brett disappeared into the grand jury room. When he reappeared, he no longer had the manuscript; at the recommendation of Dewey, it had been impounded by the grand jury. *Japanese Diplomatic Secrets* thus became the first and only manuscript in American literary history to be seized and impounded for national security reasons by the United States government. Forty-six years later, in 1979, the manuscript was still in government custody, still packed in its seven manila envelopes, with portions still classified as secret.*

Bye was called in to testify once Brett left, and he was asked to produce Yardley the next day. Bye agreed and told the grand jury, quite to its surprise, that Yardley had been lecturing in the vicinity

* On March 2, 1979, as a result of a request by the author, the entire manuscript was finally declassified.

for some time. No charges were filed against Bye. He was told he was free to go but was advised to keep the whole matter secret.

Dewey considered the seizure so secret that he personally telephoned all the news media and requested that they not publish any information concerning the incident. They all agreed to cooperate. The *New York Times* had prepared an article on the seizure but agreed not to print it. It was inserted accidentally into one edition but was quickly removed from all others.

When Yardley arrived in Dewey's office the next day, he was informed that his manuscript had been seized pursuant to Title 50, Section 32, of the United States Code, the espionage statute. Dewey gave him the choice of continuing his efforts to get the manuscript published and thereby face probable prosecution or agreeing not to pursue the issue and thereby have all further action stopped. Reluctantly, Yardley agreed.

The battle had been won, but just barely. The State Department knew it was only a matter of time before Yardley would be back in front of his typewriter and that only by swift, tough legislation could his penchant for revelation be quashed.

Work began at once on the drafting of a comprehensive bill that would make it a crime punishable by up to ten years in prison to write or publish information concerning government codes. But the bill that was finally introduced, on March 27, 1933, by Hatton W. Sumners, a Texas Democrat and chairman of the powerful House Judiciary Committee, went much further. Entitled "For the Protection of Government Records," H.R. 4220 also made it a crime for any government employee to "sell, furnish to another, publish, or offer for sale" *any* government document, regardless of whether it was classified or dealt with any subject relating to codes, just so long as the release of information could be shown to be "prejudicial to the safety or interest of the United States." This amounted to little more than a ruse, since Section 3 of the bill added that "proof of the commission of any of the acts described herein shall be *prima facie* evidence of a purpose prejudicial to the safety or interest of the United States."

The bill was the closest America had ever come to anything like Britain's Official Secrets Act, whereby unauthorized reporting of even the number of cups of tea consumed by the Prime Minister could be technically prohibited.

On April 3, H.R. 4220 was quietly passed by the House without opposition, after being favorably reported out by the Judiciary Committee. The quiet soon turned to outrage, however, when the press learned of the bill. Complaining that the legislation smacked of censorship, was an abrogation of the freedom of the press, and was contrary to the First Amendment, the news media demanded a repudiation. Accordingly, when the bill was sent to the Senate, a subcommittee removed most of the objectionable portions, and it was passed by that body on Monday, May 8.

Absent during the vote by the Senate was the influential Hiram W. Johnson, a California Republican and former governor, as well as vice presidential candidate. On his return, the senator urged reconsideration of the bill, and on May 10, 1933, it was hotly debated for several hours, with Democrats generally in favor, Republicans opposed. One of the most vocal opponents to the new law was Indiana senator Arthur R. Robinson, who at one point exploded: "We cannot get the truth from the State Department up until this minute! Nobody knows why they want this bill passed — not even the Senator from Texas. We did our best to get them to tell us. We asked them how they got hold of the manuscript of Yardley. 'Did you steal it? Where did you get it?' Not a word. 'Do I have to tell that?' they whimpered."

In the end, despite Senator Robinson's charge that the bill was nothing more than a gag law, much like the old alien and sedition laws, H.R. 4220 became Public Law 37. The final version, signed by President Franklin D. Roosevelt on June 10, 1933, was as follows:

AN ACT for the Preservation of Government Records.

Be it enacted by the Senate and House of Representatives of the United States of America in Congress assembled. That whoever, by virtue of his employment by the United States, shall obtain from another or shall have custody of or access to, any official diplomatic code or any matter prepared in such code, and shall willfully, without authorization or competent authority, publish or furnish to another any such code or matter, or any matter which was obtained while in the process of transmission between any foreign government and its diplomatic mission in the United States, shall be fined not more than $10,000 or imprisoned not more than ten years, or both.

Today, changed only slightly, the law remains in the criminal statutes as Section 952 of Title 18 of the United States Code.

•

The closing of the Black Chamber in 1929, following Secretary of State Stimson's moralistic bombast, was more illusion than reality. His cutting off of funds for Yardley's maverick organization resulted not in an end to cryptanalysis, but merely in its transfer to another

department. Gentlemen would continue to read each other's mail —
only now they would be wearing Army green and the crossed flags
of the Signal Corps.

Months before the ill-destined intercepts ever reached Secretary
Stimson's desk, plans were under way to transfer responsibility for
cryptanalysis from Military Intelligence to the Signal Corps. The factors that went into this decision, made formal by Army regulation
on May 10, 1929, were numerous, but the most important was the
Army's desire for greater centralization and better preparation in the
event of a future war.

The need for centralization was obvious. In the past, while the
Signal Corps had responsibility for code compilation, the responsibility for the printing, storage, and issuance of the codes and ciphers
went to the Adjutant General. Responsibility for cryptanalysis and
detection of secret inks, however, had devolved on Yardley and his
Black Chamber, hundreds of miles to the north. The reorganization
was intended to consolidate this inefficient set-up under one authority — the chief signal officer, Major General George S. Gibbs.

On July 19, 1929, a hot Friday in Washington, General Gibbs called
a meeting in his office attended by three senior Signal Corps officers
and the civilian in charge of the department's tiny Code and Cipher
Section, William F. Friedman. They were there to discuss the establishment of a new organization, one that would bring together responsibility for codebreaking as well as codemaking, intercept as well as solution and translation, production as well as detection of secret ink.
The men agreed that the organization should be composed of four
divisions: Code and Cipher Compilation, Code and Cipher Solution,
Intercept and Goniometry (direction finding), and Secret Ink. They
then agreed that the name for the new organization would be the
Signal Intelligence Service and its chief, William F. Friedman. Just
how fortunate this final decision was would not be recognized until
a decade had passed.

The son of a Jew from Bucharest, he was born Wolfe Frederick
Friedman on September 24, 1891. At the time, his family was living
in the southern Russian city of Kishinev, now the capital of the Soviet
Republic of Moldavia near the Rumanian border, where his father,
Frederick, was employed as an interpreter and translator in the Rus-
sian Postal Service.

As a wave of anti-Semitism began to swell throughout the country,
Frederick began looking west and in 1892 set sail for New York.
After settling in Pittsburgh, where he got a job selling sewing machines
door to door for Singer, he sent for his wife, Rosa, and their two

children. On September 26, 1896, two days after his fifth birthday, Wolfe officially became William as his father took the citizenship oath in a Pittsburgh courthouse.

In high school, the youth found his main interest in electrical engineering but eventually became involved in a "back to the soil" movement and turned his attention to agriculture.

Graduating with honors, he enrolled at the Michigan Agricultural College in East Lansing in 1910 and soon discovered that his interest lay in the more specialized field of genetics. After learning about Cornell's grant of free tuition for students enrolled in the genetics field, he transferred there.

Friedman received his bachelor of science degree in February 1914 and eventually signed on as a geneticist at Riverbank Laboratories, a philanthropic research organization located on a five-hundred-acre estate in Geneva, Illinois, outside Chicago. Run by "Colonel" George Fabyan, an heir to a cotton fortune who chose to spend it dabbling in science, the wooded estate housed laboratories for acoustics, chemistry, genetics, and even one for cryptology, where a handful of scholars hoped to prove that the actual author of Shakespeare's works was Francis Bacon.

In short order, Friedman found himself head of both the Department of Genetics and the Department of Ciphers, and in June 1916 his Cipher Department began receiving work from a rather unexpected source: the United States government.

Fabyan had managed to let the word get out to a few selected officials in Washington that Riverbank had the ability and facilities for solving cipher messages. It was a purely voluntary gesture; he added that of course there would be no charge. At the time, Washington had absolutely no capability for dealing with messages written in code or cipher, and the various government departments slowly began to take Fabyan up on his offer.

As Friedman and his band of cryptologists began solving messages coming in from the Departments of State, Justice, and others, they became America's first de facto cryptologic organization. It was still a year before Yardley would form MI-8, the nation's first official cipher bureau.

Many of the messages that trickled into Riverbank were from Mexico, with whom American relations were less than amiable. According to Friedman, the messages were obtained "by various and entirely surreptitious means from telegraphs and cable offices in Washington and elsewhere in the U.S." They were attacked, solved, and returned, usually within a matter of days.

As the first few months of 1917 brought ominous warnings of an approaching war, Fabyan decided to offer the services of his Cipher Department to the War Department, which wasted no time in accepting. Lieutenant Joseph O. Mauborgne, one of the few outside Riverbank with any knowledge of ciphers, was dispatched to assess the laboratory's capabilities and came away impressed. On April 11 he wired the War Department that officers should be sent to Riverbank for training and that any intercepted messages should be forwarded there immediately for decipherment.

There was good reason for the urgency in his words. Only five days before, America had declared war on Germany.

Two months later, Yardley formed MI-8 in Washington, and from then on, most of the intercepted material was sent to his organization for solution, but Riverbank continued to serve as a training ground for officers before they were shipped to France. Under Friedman's tutelage, a group of four officers spent six weeks in October and November receiving a cram course in cryptanalysis. The course was so successful that the number of officers attending the second class, from January to February 1918, increased fifteenfold, to sixty. The last group, trained in March and April, was back to seven or eight.

Ironically, the War Department later discovered that the officers had been sent to Riverbank to learn crypto*graphy,* the making of codes, not crypt*analysis,* the breaking of codes. But until 1921, when Friedman coined the word *cryptanalysis,* the term *cryptography* had been used to mean both. The word that is now used to cover all aspects of code work is *cryptology,* also invented by Friedman.

In June 1918 Friedman was commissioned and sent to France, where he worked on the solution of German code systems during the final months of the war. He returned to the United States the following April and, after an unsuccessful search in New York for a position as a geneticist, he reluctantly went back to Riverbank. His stay this time was a brief eighteen months, however; on January 2, 1921, he became head of the Signal Corps's Code and Cipher Section, where his first chore was to revise the War Department Staff Code. Throughout the 1920s, Friedman and his sole assistant, a cauliflower-eared former prize fighter who was now a clerk typist, constituted the War Department's entire cryptographic department.

At seventeen minutes past the hour of ten o'clock on the morning of April 24, 1930, the Signal Intelligence Service was born. It was at that moment that the chief signal officer officially received the order from the Secretary of War setting out the duties and responsibilities of the new organization. As first head of the SIS, Friedman found that his new responsibilities included the "preparation and revision of Army codes and ciphers and, in time of war, interception of enemy radio and wire traffic, the goniometric location of enemy radio stations, the solution of intercepted enemy code and cipher messages, and laboratory arrangements for the employment and detection of secret inks."

To accomplish his mission, Friedman was authorized to hire four junior cryptanalysts at $2000 a year and one assistant cryptographic clerk at $1620. His choice to fill these positions would be one of Friedman's most important decisions and would affect the course of cryptology for years to come.

To fill the four junior cryptanalyst slots, Friedman sought people with a thorough background in mathematics and knowledge of at least one of four languages — French, Spanish, German, and, most important, Japanese.

The Civil Service Commission sent over to Friedman eight candidates, and from these he chose only three. The first was Frank B. Rowlett, twenty-two, a tall, broad-shouldered Virginian from Rose Hill who had graduated with honors in science from Emory and Henry College in Emory, Virginia, the previous June. Rowlett brought the total manpower of the infant SIS up to three when he joined Friedman and his secretary on April 1.

Nine days later Abraham Sinkov, a short, bespectacled high school teacher from New York, was picked to fill the French spot, the German one having been filled by Rowlett. Sinkov, also twenty-two, had graduated from City College in New York in 1927 and had recently earned his master's degree at Columbia.

The Spanish-language vacancy was filled on April 21 by Solomon Kullback, a Brooklynite who had celebrated his twenty-third birthday several weeks earlier. Like Sinkov, Kullback received his bachelor of science degree from City College in 1927 as well as his master's degree from Columbia in June of 1929. Within four years, both Kullback and Sinkov would also have their doctorates in mathematics from George Washington University.

With the selection of Kullback, Friedman could turn his full attention to the most difficult task of all — finding a native-born American fully qualified to translate Japanese. Just as he was searching, the chief signal officer received a call from Joe Shaffer, a Virginia representative who had heard of the Army's need for a Japanese linguist. He asked that his nephew, John B. Hurt, be given an interview.

More out of courtesy than expectation, Friedman arranged for the interview and an examination by Major David M. Crawford, G-2's Japanese expert. The results were better than Friedman could have ever hoped for. In all his experience, Crawford told Friedman, he had never met a non-Japanese as proficient in the Japanese language. Hurt was quickly hired, and several weeks later Friedman selected Harry Lawrence Clark as an assistant cryptographic clerk.

With the hiring of Clark, the manpower of the Signal Intelligence Service came to a grand total of seven, a number that would remain almost constant for the first seven years. From 1930 until 1937 the total annual budget of the SIS never exceeded $17,400.

Friedman's first task, once he had trained his new assistants, was to set up an adequate training program to provide a sufficient reserve of officers knowledgeable in all aspects of cryptology in case of future hostilities. The result was the Signal Intelligence School. And on September 8, 1931, its first (and only) student arrived for classes. This was Mark Rhoads, a first lieutenant in the Signal Corps who had been carefully selected for the assignment.

Lieutenant Rhoads proved to be a good student, but even after a year there was much more for him to learn, so it was agreed to extend the course, making it a two-year program. As Rhoads entered his second year, a new student, First Lieutenant W. Preston Corderman, a redheaded Signal Corps officer, took his seat as the new first-year student.

Once the school began functioning smoothly, Friedman turned his attention to the blacker side of the organization: interception and solution. Here, however, he found the problems considerably more difficult than those encountered in setting up the school. In addition to there being a law (the Communications Act of 1934) with severe penalties for the interception of communications, there was also the problem of former Secretary of State Stimson's stern ban against such activities. How could one adequately train personnel in the fine arts of interception and analysis, Friedman questioned, if one was not first permitted to engage in interception and analysis? It was cryptology's classic paradox, a choice between the law and the profession.

As usual, the latter won, and in the summer of 1931 construction began on an experimental intercept station in the Washington, D.C., area. The site chosen was Battery Cove, Virginia, where the War Department maintained the remotely controlled receivers for its Message Center in the Munitions Building. Once established, the station began churning out intercept traffic for Friedman and his latter-day Black Chamber. In addition, intercepts began arriving from small radio intelligence detachments set up in Texas, the Panama Canal, and the Philippines.

During this period, Joseph Mauborgne, the veteran codebreaker who was now a colonel in charge of the western United States for the Signal Corps, managed to acquire some automatic recording equipment and established his own intercept station in the basement of his California home. The tapes were sent to Friedman, who welcomed the helpful, if questionable, intercepts, apparently with one eye closed.

In 1933 Friedman's protégé, Mark Rhoads, set up the Provisional Radio Intelligence Detachment at Fort Monmouth, New Jersey. This unit spent most of its time engaged in research in the field of communications intelligence, although it did conduct some actual interception.

As a result of growing world tensions and apprehension over American involvement in another war, the SIS in November 1937 requested authorization to establish another intercept station at Battery Cove. The station, with receiving equipment to be located in the War Department Message Center, was needed to monitor the radio channel carrying the bulk of diplomatic traffic between Washington's Embassy Row and the commercial relay stations in New York. Also requested were two additional radio operators, who would be assigned to Washington to monitor communications during the twelve to fifteen hours of the day when the most "interesting" traffic was being handled.

The Signal Corps turned down the request primarily because by now the SIS was already receiving from other sources more intercept material than it could handle. In addition, there was a good likelihood that a new intercept station would be built at Fort Monmouth that would have the capability to monitor the same circuit. The station was, in fact, built the following year.

By 1938, in addition to the new station at Fort Monmouth, the Signal Intelligence Service had intercept bases in California, Texas, Panama, the Philippines, and Hawaii. Friedman would be sent the intercepted traffic once a week by registered secret mail.

Because of its strategic location, the station in Panama was considered one of the most important, and on January 26, 1938, the listening post was directed to begin scanning the ether twenty-four hours a day and to give first priority to diplomatic traffic between Rome and Tokyo. A secondary emphasis was to be placed on traffic between Berlin and Tokyo. In addition, "Abe" Sinkov, now in charge of the station, was ordered to monitor Japanese diplomatic traffic to and from Central and South America.

As the intercept activity increased, Friedman grew more worried about the illegality of the operations and the effect their disclosure might have. In order to protect the personnel with a record of official authorization, the assistant chief of staff for G-2 (Army Intelligence) sent a memorandum on March 26, 1938, to the chief of staff, recommending authority "to maintain and operate in time of peace under strictest provisions to insure secrecy, such radio intercept and cryptanalytic services" as were "necessary for training purposes." Four days later, Secretary of War Harry H. Woodring penned his approval, and Friedman and the SIS were off the hook. The Communications Act of 1934, however, was still in effect.

Now operating under color of authority, the SIS was put in overdrive. By the time German troops marched into Poland, on September 1, 1939, the SIS had increased its staff from seven to nineteen. When Japan struck Pearl Harbor, on December 7, 1941, the staff had grown to 331; by the time the war was over, the number had increased to over 10,000.

The increase in personnel had enabled the SIS to concentrate more heavily on the threat from the East. Friedman, who had been replaced several years before as head of the SIS so that he could give his full attention to the technical side of cryptology, began putting greater effort into the solution of the advanced Japanese systems.

Equally important, by 1939 the rivalry that had long marked relations between the Army and the Navy in the field of cryptology was at long last coming to an end. This "friendly competition," which had continued for close to two decades, not only resulted in duplication of effort, but, more seriously, gave rise to instances where one branch might unknowingly have the key to the other one's puzzle.

Like the Army, the Navy had long been involved in cryptology. Its beginnings can be traced back almost to the first wireless transmission from a Navy ship in 1899. During World War I, the Code and Signal Section of the Naval Communications Service handled cryptology, and in July 1922 it was assigned the organizational title OP-20-G, which, deciphered, meant that it was G Section (Communications Security) of the 20th Division (Office of Naval Communications) of the Office of Chief of Naval Operations (OP).

Two years later, in January 1924, a thirty-one-year-old Navy lieutenant, Laurance F. Safford, was ordered to establish a radio intelligence organization in the section. The Annapolis graduate established himself in Room 2646 of the Navy Department's ramshackle building on Constitution Avenue and began the time-consuming task of building the Navy's first intercept organization. It was a small unit in a large headquarters, but it did not lack dedication. "We were just a few then in Room 2646," one former officer recalled; "young people who gave ourselves to cryptography with the same ascetic devotion with which young men enter a monastery."

That young officer, Lieutenant Ellis Zacharias, after his seven-month apprenticeship under Lieutenant Safford in 1926, left his monastic surroundings for the intrigue of Shanghai, where he became chief of an intercept post located on the fourth floor of the American consulate. Here he was well placed to learn as much as possible from Japanese naval messages.

By the late 1930s the Navy's cryptologic organization had grown to seven hundred officers and enlisted personnel, with eavesdropping posts in Washington state, Maine, Maryland, Hawaii, and the Philippines. There were smaller stations at Guam, California, Long Island, and Florida.

Intercepts received from the various listening posts revealed that Japan was using at least nine different cipher systems and that the most important appeared to be a machine system known as Angooki Taipu A, or Cipher Machine Type A, reserved for high-level diplomatic traffic. The system, put into use before 1932, was attacked by the SIS in 1935 and broken the following year, thus enabling the codebreakers to read practically every message to and from the Japanese Foreign Office.

A short time after the breakthrough, Friedman became concerned about the fact that in both internal correspondence and official reports the machine was referred to as the "A" machine, the same name by which it was known to the Japanese. He decided to give the various systems code names based on the colors of the spectrum. The color selected for Angooki Taipu A was Red.

In late 1938 and early 1939 the Japanese Foreign Office completed distribution of a new diplomatic cipher machine designed to replace their "A" machine. Known to the Japanese as Angooki Taipu B and to the SIS as Purple, the machine was far more complex than its Red predecessor; and on March 20, 1939, when the first Purple message was flashed between Warsaw and Tokyo, the pipeline began to quickly run dry.

The new system was as deep and mysterious as its chromatic code name implied. As a result, its solution was given the highest priority. At the time, the Signal Intelligence Service offices were located on the third floor of the Munitions Building in the rear section of the third wing. Above, construction workers banged and shouted while the walls shook from the incessant vibration of jackhammers as a fourth floor was being added. Nevertheless, the small team of codebreakers plodded ahead through the summer of 1940, alternately closing the windows and sweltering or opening them and risking deafness. Finally, as the summer was ending and the construction was near completion, fire broke out overhead and the offices were nearly drenched with water.

Despite it all, the team managed to put together a spaghetti-like maze of multicolored wire, contacts, and switches and come up with a magical contraption that, on September 25, 1940, issued its first totally clear, ungarbled text of a Purple message. The band of cryptologists had accomplished the impossible — they had created a perfect clone without ever having seen its twin.

By now the SIS consisted of the Signal Intelligence School; the 2nd Signal Company, which conducted the intercept operations; Section A (Administration), which took care of the paperwork and tabulating; Section B (Cryptanalytic), the largest, which turned out the finished intelligence product; Section C (Cryptographic), which designed the Army codes and conducted communications security operations; and Section D (Secret Ink), a small unit that was also known as the Laboratory Section.

Just down the street, in Room 1649 of the Navy Department building, OP-20-G performed its similar functions under the direction of the man regarded as the father of the naval cryptologic organization, Laurance Safford, now a commander. Under him were three subsections that formed the core of his operations: GX, which conducted interception and direction finding; GY, which handled the cryptanalysis; and GZ, which was responsible for translation and dissemination.

In all, the combined forces of Friedman's SIS and Safford's OP-20-G were very considerable, but they were also very unharmonious, each sacrificing the collective good in a race for the "credit" for a particular solution or the recovery of a particular key. Because both organizations very often shared the same intercept material as well as the means for breaking it, whenever an important message was read each would immediately rush a copy of the translation to the White House in an effort to impress the President. "The method of processing and disseminating the diplomatic messages that were read," reported a secret, high-level review board years later, "was both duplicative and unseemly."

At last, after lengthy negotiations and several tries, a compromise was reached between the Army and Navy whereby they agreed to exchange all diplomatic traffic from their ten or twelve listening posts so that both services could work on the traffic. But to prevent duplication of effort, it was resolved that the Navy would translate all Japanese diplomatic intercepts originating on odd days and the SIS would handle the even days. The Navy would send the results to the President; the Army would service the State Department.

Later, as the threat of hostilities in the Pacific grew more intense, the Navy decided to focus its entire cryptanalytic efforts on Japanese naval ciphers. It therefore hastily concluded a gentleman's agreement with the SIS, transferring to the Army COMINT (communications intelligence) unit its entire interest and capacity in all cryptanalytic fields other than naval and related ciphers. The idea was that the SIS would accept stewardship of the Navy's excess cryptanalytic cargo, exploit it to the best of its ability during the war, and return it, presumably enriched, when the war was over.

In December 1941 American COMINT more closely resembled a medieval feudal state than the empire it is today. The SIS was responsible for military traffic, although no military traffic was being produced. OP-20-G secretly handled naval traffic. Together, on a daily odd-even basis, they were responsible for diplomatic traffic. Both the Coast Guard and the FBI claimed authority for "spy" or clandestine traffic, and the Federal Communications Commission's Radio Intelligence Division considered itself responsible for radio interception and direction-finding.

With regard to the finished, translated product, the diplomatic traffic was being furnished in full to the War, Navy, and State Departments; the clandestine traffic was being furnished in full to the War and Navy Departments and in part to the State Department and FBI. The Navy traffic was available in full only to the Navy Department, but summaries were furnished to the War Department for use on a high level only.

Equally cumbersome was the slow and complicated method of delivering the products, which involved having a courier hand the message to the official and then take it back with him once it had been read. Briefings were entirely oral so that no COMINT material on paper would ever be left behind. The system was designed to ensure a hermetic seal of security, but at the sacrifice of speed and understanding.

The system was a hodgepodge. No one was responsible for a continuous study of all material. Recipients would read their portion of intercepts, and then it would then be whisked away, never to be seen again. There was very little that could be done to put together all the pieces in a cohesive form, or to correlate them with information available from other sources. Though the technical side of COMINT, particularly in the breaking of Purple, had been performed with genius, the analytical side had become lost in disorganization.

In the early morning hours of the first Sunday in December 1941, the Navy's listening post at Bainbridge Island in Puget Sound, Washington, intercepted several messages transmitted between Tokyo and Washington, D.C., over the commercial circuits of Mackay Radio & Telegraph Company. Bainbridge in turn retransmitted them to OP-

20-GY in Washington, where watch officer Lieutenant (junior grade) Francis M. Brotherhood was heading toward the end of his 11:00-to-7:00 shift.

It had been a busy weekend. Less than twenty-four hours earlier, Bainbridge had snatched from the ether thirteen parts of what appeared to be a fourteen-part message from Japan's Foreign Office to its Washington embassy. The long, rambling message, encrypted in Purple, was a reply to a U.S. diplomatic note transmitted eleven days earlier, in which Secretary of State Cordell Hull called on Japan to withdraw all its forces from China and Indochina in return for a U.S. promise to release Japanese funds and resume trade.

Throughout the long night, Brotherhood wondered whether there really was a fourteenth section. Now, as he watched the Purple machine transform the intercept into English, he had his answer: Japan had decided to break off negotiations with the United States.

With the recovery of the last section, Brotherhood typed the second, shorter intercept into the Purple machine, but this one emerged in Japanese, which called for translation next door at the Signal Intelligence Service. The clock on the wall was now reading a few minutes past 5:00 A.M.

At seven-thirty, Lieutenant Commander Alwin D. Kramer, chief of OP-20-GZ, the translation section, arrived after a short night's sleep. He had been up until past midnight delivering the previous thirteen sections of the Tokyo message, and now he saw what he had hoped for — the final section. A short while later, he slipped the message into his well-worn, double-locked briefcase and began his rounds, which included the White House and Secretary of the Navy Frank Knox.

Over at SIS headquarters, the Army messenger had also begun his rounds with the fourteenth section. His list included such officials as Secretary of State Hull and Secretary of War Stimson. Soon after he departed, Colonel Rufus Bratton, chief of the Far Eastern Section of Military Intelligence, arrived at his SIS office and immediately spotted the final section. As he was reading the message, he was handed a copy of the second, shorter message.

Bratton's dark eyes widened. "Will the Ambassador please submit to the United States Government," the message read, "(if possible to the Secretary of State) our reply to the United States at 1:00 P.M. on the 7th, your time." The significance struck him at once. Japan had ordered its ambassador to break off negotiations with the United States precisely at 1:00 P.M. on a Sunday afternoon. It was the penultimate act before war. It was now about 9:00 A.M.

Nine o'clock in the morning in Washington was 3:30 A.M. in Hawaii. A scant 250 miles north of Diamond Head, Admiral Nagumo's strike force of six carriers, supported by battleships and cruisers, drifted gently at anchor.

Bratton began a frenzied attempt to locate Army Chief of Staff General George C. Marshall. He picked up the telephone and called his quarters at Fort Myer, but his orderly told him that the general had gone horseback riding.

"Please go out at once," Bratton frantically told the orderly, "get assistance if necessary, and find General Marshall, ask him to — tell him who I am and tell him to go to the nearest telephone, that it is vitally important that I communicate with him at the earliest practicable moment." The orderly, Sergeant Aguirre, left at once, but the search was in vain.

It was some time later that Marshall arrived back at his quarters and found the message to call Bratton. In urgent tones, Bratton told Marshall of an important message he should read, and, since it was now between ten and ten-thirty, he offered to drive out with it immediately. Marshall, however, preferred to drive down to the office himself.

At about the same time, Lieutenant Commander Kramer returned from his courier rounds, where he had displayed the final part of the Tokyo message. Now, for the first time, he saw the translation of the second message, and its meaning became instantly clear. Magnifying his alarm were several other messages, particularly No. 910, which ordered the embassy to destroy all remaining cipher equipment and machine codes.

By now Kramer was almost running out the door. Before he left, he had determined that zero hour for the attack, or 1:00 P.M. in Washington, would be the middle of the night in the Far East and would be just after dawn in Hawaii. He first headed down the passageway to Admiral Harold Stark's office. The chief of Naval Operations was already in conference discussing the ramifications of the final section of the Tokyo message he had received just a short time before. Kramer pointed out to an aide the significance of the deadline and then raced down Constitution Avenue toward the ornate State Department building, which also housed the War Department. The Secretaries of State, War, and Navy were also conferring, and Kramer hurriedly indicated the import of the final messages. Then he rushed down the long steps and across the lawn to the White House.

Marshall had finally arrived at his office and slowly, carefully, began reading the fourteen pages, starting with page one. Bratton tried to get the general to go immediately to the one o'clock delivery message, but Marshall could not be budged.

It was now about 11:00 A.M., almost six hours after the giant ear on Bainbridge Island had first snared the prophetic message, and all of Washington's senior elite had read it. There were two hours to go.

As Marshall finished the last message, its ominous impact finally struck him. Less than an arm's reach away was a "scrambler" phone by which he quickly could have been in contact with Major General Walter Short in Hawaii. But Marshall considered this method too risky when dealing with information as sensitive as Purple intercepts. Scrambling was far from a totally secure procedure; it had in the past succumbed to interception.

Instead, the warning message was sent to the War Department's Message Center, where the communications officer indicated that it would be in the hands of the recipients in less than half an hour. But as a result of poor atmospheric conditions, the circuit to Fort Shafter in Hawaii was out, and the message was instead sent by considerably less direct commercial channels, finally appearing on a printer in RCA's Honolulu office at 7:33 A.M.

The message General Marshall had instructed to be sent by "the fastest safe means" was then slipped into an envelope marked simply "Commanding General Hawaiian Department Fort Shafter, T.H." and placed unceremoniously in its proper pigeonhole for later delivery.

At 7:55 A.M., the first bomb smashed into a seaplane ramp on Ford Island in Pearl Harbor. Before the last bomb whistled down through the black and orange sky two hours later, Americans would give their lives at the rate of almost thirty a minute.

Nearly two hours after that final fatal explosion, Tadao Fuchikama, a young Japanese messenger for RCA, entered Fort Shafter. A few minutes later, he handed the envelope marked "Commanding General Hawaiian Department" to an officer in the Signal Division, got back on his motorcycle, and headed home, his last delivery of the day now completed. At 2:40 P.M. the signal officer passed the message to the decoding officer, and twenty minutes later, fifteen and a half hours after the ominous one o'clock delivery message was first liberated from the heavens over Bainbridge Island, Marshall's warning at last reached a devastated General Short. It was now yesterday's news.

Disorganization and divided responsibility had cost America dearly. It was up to the Secretary of War to turn chaos into order and discord into teamwork.

It is one of cryptology's supreme ironies that the man who now
believed that too little attention had been shown the intercepted Japanese diplomatic traffic was the same man who a dozen years earlier
had slammed closed Herbert Yardley's Black Chamber with the statement "Gentlemen do not read each other's mail": Henry L. Stimson.
The situation, however, had changed. "In 1929," Stimson later wrote,
"the world was striving with good will for lasting peace, and in this
effort all the nations were parties." Then, speaking in the third person,
he continued, "Stimson, Secretary of State, was dealing as a gentleman
with the gentlemen sent as ambassadors and ministers from friendly
nations." Now, as Secretary of War, the gentleman had turned warrior.

Within a few weeks after the Pearl Harbor disaster, Stimson had
concluded that the entire field of communications intelligence was
in need of a total re-evaluation, and he offered the task of performing
it to Alfred McCormack, a prominent Brooklyn-born lawyer and one
of the leaders of the New York Bar. On January 19, 1942, six days
after his forty-first birthday, McCormack was appointed special assistant to the Secretary of War, with a mandate to examine closely the
entire spectrum of COMINT, from the moment of intercept to its
use in the hands of the final consumer, and to determine how best
to squeeze from it every ounce of benefit.

Among the most immediate problems, McCormack soon discovered
that:

- intercept facilities were extremely limited;
- arrangements for transmitting material from the point of intercept to
  the cryptanalytic center were hit-or-miss;
- there was a critical shortage of translators;
- there were neither sufficient personnel nor adequate procedures for
  studying and checking the translated product to derive the maximum
  degree of intelligence;
- the method of presenting the intelligence to the responsible authorities
  in Washington was ineffective; and
- there was no arrangement for getting such intelligence to commanders
  in the field promptly and in a manner that would ensure security.

By March McCormack had reached a number of broad conclusions.
The upshot was the formation of a separate branch of the War Department's Military Intelligence Service to take the raw intercepts, synthe-
size them with information from all other sources, and put everything
together in clear, concise, and timely reports. The key words would
be *evaluation* and *analysis*.

Named chief of the Special Branch, as the top secret unit was called, was Colonel Carter W. Clarke, a Signal Corps officer who had assisted McCormack in his research on COMINT. McCormack himself was given a direct commission as a full colonel and entered active duty as deputy chief under Clarke.

The new chief's first few months were spent trying to urge the Signal Corps to expand the Signal Intelligence Service and broaden the coverage by increasing the number of intercept stations. The effort was successful, and the SIS soon moved from its cramped quarters in the Munitions Building to a secluded, spacious former girls' school across the Potomac in Arlington, Virginia. Known as Arlington Hall both before and since, the quiet estate was made up of several dozen brick and wood-frame buildings that rambled in every direction. It was, however, ideally suited to accommodate a rapid expansion concealed from the prying eyes of foreign agents.

Several months later, the intercept arm of the SIS, the 2nd Signal Service Battalion, moved even farther south, to the tree-covered Vint Hill Farms in Warrenton, Virginia. In October 1942 the Cryptographic School, successor to the Signal Intelligence School, also moved to Vint Hill Farms Station, where for the rest of the war it trained Army men and women in all phases of cryptology.

During this period, as the reorganization was taking place, the SIS began suffering from acute identity crisis; its name changed almost weekly. From 1929 until 1942 it had been called the Signal Intelligence Service, but in July and August it went from SIS to Signal Intelligence Service Division, then Signal Security Division, then Signal Security Branch, and finally the Signal Security Service, which it managed to keep until July 1943, when it became the Signal Security Agency. When the war ended, the name was changed again, to Army Security Agency.

Soon after the SIS reorganization began, Clarke turned his attention to organizing his Special Branch, which would turn the intercepted, deciphered, and traffic-analyzed products of the SIS into finished intelligence.

Clarke organized the branch into a small headquarters staff and several Area Sections, which divided along broad geographical lines. They collected, studied, and analyzed the intercepts and other information, and developed the results into spot reports and long-term studies. Also added was a Reports Section, which was formed to scan all incoming traffic, assign it to the appropriate Area Sections, and assist in producing the reports.

By far one of the most significant contributions of the Special Branch was the development of a carefully prepared daily publication carrying all of the important spot intelligence gleaned from each day's batch of messages. Its name reflected the sorcery required to produce it: the Magic Summary.

During the summer of 1943 a breakthrough was at last made into the Japanese military traffic. Until then, no Japanese Army system had been broken, only the Navy codes and the Purple diplomatic system. The first break, in March, was made by the Wireless Experimental Center, the British COMINT unit in India. By June the first decoded and translated messages were available for study.

Because of the increased flow of traffic, Clarke revamped his Special Branch into three streamlined sections. The A Section took over responsibility for the diplomatic and clandestine material and for the production of the Magic Summary. Among the items produced were reports of personal interviews with Hitler and Mussolini in which the Axis leaders discussed the future of the war effort and whether they were prepared to extend an olive branch to one or another of the Allied powers.

Development of intelligence derived from the Japanese Army traffic went to B Section; C Section, originally code-named Bunker Hill, studied German military traffic obtained from the British.

Despite the accomplishments of Clarke's Special Branch, which were manifold, the organization suffered a serious handicap: it was not able to exercise any real operational control over the Signal Security Agency. Such matters as what circuits were to be monitored, in what order the traffic was to be sent for cryptanalysis, which systems were to be attacked first, and the priority of material chosen for translation were not within its domain. The brain of America's COMINT giant had no control over its body.

The adverse results of this administrative malfunction were numerous. The SSA, which was under the Signal Corps, was never able to view the "big picture," since its role consisted primarily of intercepting, solving, and translating the material. The Special Branch, on the other hand, was under G-2 and was principally an analytical organization with no operational control. Therefore, the SSA would often concentrate its intercept facilities on circuits that were already covered, like transmitters in Southeast Asia, Malaya, and South China, instead of on potentially more productive areas, like the Japanese Home Islands, Korea, Manchuria, and North China. Likewise, the SSA continually ignored Special Branch recommendations to give a high priority to the solution of certain medium- and low-level systems believed important in Japanese shipping, instead of emphasizing only the high-level systems.

In June 1944 the Special Branch was reorganized into a more homo-geneous organization within G-2, and in December, in a major power grab, G-2 wrested operational control of the prized Signal Security Agency from the Signal Corps.

As the war began grinding to a close, attention turned to the role of COMINT during peacetime. In early August 1945, W. Preston Corderman, now a brigadier general and for the past eighteen months chief of the SSA, created a postwar planning board to chart the future of the organization. The timing proved appropriate. Two days later "Little Boy," a long, black, nine-thousand-pound device with a square tail, hurtled down through the sky over southern Japan. At exactly fifteen minutes past eight o'clock on the morning of August 6, 1945, Little Boy reached critical mass, and the city of Hiroshima vaporized. Three days later, "Fat Man," another heavy, square-tailed device, this one with an obese, bulbous shape, turned the city of Nagasaki from a solid into a gas.

It has been estimated that the cost of COMINT during World War II was approximately a half billion dollars annually. Yet even if that figure were tripled, COMINT still would rank as possibly America's best-paying investment. Admiral Chester Nimitz rated its value in the Pacific as equivalent to another whole fleet; General Thomas Handy is reported to have said that it shortened the war in Europe by at least a year.

In the Pacific, COMINT located the Japanese fleet on its way to the Coral Sea and again en route to Midway in 1942, enabling the U.S. fleet to mass the carriers for the battles that are generally re-garded as the turning point of the war against Japan. In 1942 COMINT also revealed the critical Japanese decision not to join Germany in its war on Soviet Russia. In 1944 it helped pick the soft spots for the island advance, often showing where the Japanese expected to be attacked and where their troops were massed.

Throughout the war, COMINT told how many ships Japan had, where they were, and when they were lost. While the Germans contin-ued to blame an imaginary direction-finding device for their high U-boat losses, COMINT craftily plucked the subs' locations from the ether when the U-boats carefully reported their positions each night to the German Admiralty.

In the land war, COMINT read Rommel's intentions in Africa so well that the Desert Fox, finding himself often outmaneuvered, guessed the truth. But when he confided his suspicions to Berlin, he was summarily informed by the German High Command that such things were not possible. And before D Day in France, COMINT told where Von Rundstedt assumed the main Allied attack would come, as well as some of Berlin's replies brushing off his good advice, presumably in favor of Hitler's intuition.

Even before Pearl Harbor, COMINT drawn from Japanese sources had contributed to the Allied effort in Europe by giving advance warning of the German decision to attack Russia. Baron Hiroshi Oshima, Japan's ambassador in Berlin, proved a veritable mine of information as he faithfully communicated to Tokyo what was confided to him by the German leaders.

COMINT also provided the only reliable measure of how fast the Japanese were losing their will to resist. It supplied a thorough and immediate record of the peace feelers that the Japanese asked Ambassador Naotake Sato in Moscow to send to Washington through the Russians, as well as their explanations to him of how the decisions were being reached and on what points further concessions would be made. Throughout 1945, COMINT provided the United States with Japan's instructions to her principal negotiator, often before the Japanese code clerks in Moscow could put the message on Sato's desk.

Finally, COMINT's value stretched even beyond the Instruments of Surrender. On August 11, 1945, Major General Clayton Bissell, chief of G-2, sent a memorandum to General Marshall advising him that the long-range interests of both the United States and Great Britain would be best served by avoiding any physical compromise of Japan's diplomatic systems, especially their Purple system, during the postwar period. It was hoped that Japan, in splendid ignorance, would continue to use the same systems, thus allowing the United States and Britain to maintain uninterrupted surveillance through their cryptanalytic keyhole.

On September 2, as the final drama of the war took place aboard the battleship *Missouri,* America's COMINT giant was suddenly placed on a crash diet. Most seriously affected was the Navy, which, through the gentleman's agreement made at the beginning of the war, had awarded temporary custody to the Army of all interest in worldwide intercept and cryptanalysis in order to concentrate on Japanese naval traffic and codes. Now that the war was over the Navy was, in effect, out of business, and it sought repossession.

As viewed by the Army, however, the trusteeship had gradually ripened over the years into full ownership, and it considered absurd any shifting of pieces of the worldwide COMINT set-up merely for the purpose of "giving the Navy something to do." Nevertheless, the two services eventually adopted a compromise policy.

Although the size and budget of America's COMINT community was rapidly shrinking, the top-heavy bureaucracy that attempted to control it was rapidly enlarging. In 1942, as the Coast Guard, the Federal Communications Commission, and other agencies attempted to enter the codebreaking business, the Joint Chiefs of Staff recommended to President Roosevelt that he issue a presidential memorandum limiting cryptanalytic activites to the Army, Navy, and the FBI. Such an action, they argued, would both conserve COMINT resources and promote security. Roosevelt agreed, and, following the issuance of the memorandum, a standing committee was established for coordinating and defining the spheres of responsibility of the ever-feuding Army and Navy.

As the war progressed, the need for even closer relationships became obvious, and in May 1944, an informal Army-Navy Communications Intelligence Coordinating Committee (ANCICC) was established. In March 1945 this matured into the formal Army-Navy Communications Intelligence Board (ANCIB), which had as its desired purpose further cryptanalytic cooperation. But the Navy, always fearful of any effort that might encroach on naval COMINT, offered little assistance.

Meanwhile, the State Department had set up its own Special Projects Staff to handle the flow of COMINT into the department, so it, too, sought admission to the fraternity. By December, then, the group had once again changed its name, this time to the State-Army-Navy Communications Intelligence Board (STANCIB).

Next at the door were the FBI and the newly formed Central Intelligence Group, and in June 1946 STANCIB became the United States Communications Intelligence Board (USCIB). The following year the Air Force became the sixth and final member.

On July 1, 1948, the board promulgated the first "charter" for the COMINT community, National Security Council Intelligence Directive (NSCID) No. 9. Established by the National Security Council, the NSCIDs function as top secret bylaws for the intelligence community. NSCID No. 1, for example, sets out the basic responsibilities for the director of Central Intelligence. The NSCIDs are, in turn, supplemented by Director of Central Intelligence Directives (DCIDs).

Titled "Communications Intelligence," NSCID No. 9 formally established the USCIB "to effect the authoritative coordination of Communications Intelligence activities of the Government" and "to advise the Director of Central Intelligence in those matters in the field of Communications Intelligence for which he is responsible." But the directive also stated that unanimous agreement of all twelve members (two from each agency) was required for decisions and that the board must keep hands off the internal workings of member COMINT agencies. Thus, the USCIB was nearly impotent from birth.

By far the most amazing section of the NSCID, however, dealt not with organizational structure but with the unique status of COMINT within the government:

> The special nature of Communications Intelligence activities requires that they be treated in all respects as being outside the framework of other or general intelligence activities. *Orders, directives, policies, or recommendations of any authority of the Executive branch relating to the collection . . . of intelligence shall not be applicable to Communications Intelligence activities, unless specifically so stated and issued by competent departmental or agency authority* represented on the [United States Communications Intelligence] Board. Other National Security Council Intelligence Directives to the Director of Central Intelligence and related implementing directives issued by the Director of Central Intelligence shall be construed as non-applicable to Communications Intelligence unless the National Security Council has made its directive specifically applicable to COMINT. [Emphasis supplied.]*

Thus, should an Attorney General or even the President issue a public ban on all forms of electronic surveillance by the federal government, for example, the COMINT community would be free to ignore it, since it was never "specifically so stated" that the order applied to the supersecret COMINT community.

Also significant were the definitions. Although communications intelligence was defined as "intelligence produced by the study of foreign communications," the term "foreign communications" was defined in the broadest of contexts. It took in "all telecommunications and related materials . . . of the [foreign] government and/or their nationals or of any military, air, or naval force, faction, party, department, agency, or bureau of a foreign country, or of any person or persons acting or purporting to act therefor . . ."

But the definition did not stop there. It also embraced virtually all communications entering or leaving the United States, as long as they could be connected in any way with certain very broad subject areas. The definition of "foreign communications," the NSCID continued, will also include "all other telecommunications and related material of, to, and from a foreign country which *may* contain information of military, political, scientific or economic value." (Emphasis supplied.)

---

* The words "Communications Intelligence" were inserted by the author because they were deleted from the original. See notes.

Since nearly all communications — telephone calls, telegrams, telexes, facsimiles, or any other form — *may* logically contain information in at least one of the general categories, the NSCID gave the COMINT community the power to eavesdrop at will on the entire U.S. international telecommunications system. It was an authorization clearly at odds with Section 605 of the Communications Act of 1934, which provided for secrecy of communications.

Despite the reorganizations, the directives, and the high-level boards, the COMINT community was as fractionized in 1948 as it ever was. The Army, with its large civilian component and vast experience with the nonmilitary aspects of COMINT, was generally in favor of some sort of consolidation; the Navy, on the other hand, was as reluctant as ever to surrender any of its COMINT sovereignty; and the Air Force wanted only to be left alone to build up its network of far-flung listening posts.

In August of 1948, Secretary of Defense James V. Forrestal finally created a board, under the chairmanship of Rear Admiral Earl Everett Stone, then director of Naval Communications, to study the COMINT situation within the defense establishment and recommend a solution. Composed of representatives of all military interests in the COMINT family, the Stone Board went round and round for several months, but wound up submitting a divided report — the Navy and Air Force both opposed to consolidation, the Army advocating it with the exception of interception and decentralized field processing stations. Unhappy with the results, Forrestal simply locked the report in a safe and hoped the problem would go away.

With Forrestal's resignation in March 1949, Louis A. Johnson assumed the office — and, along with it, the problem of the Stone Report. To help him resolve it, he brought in General Joseph McNarney, who eventually decided on a middle way. His plan required a merger but left each of the three services the right to maintain its separate COMINT organization.

On May 20, 1949, therefore, Secretary Johnson issued a top secret directive establishing the Armed Forces Security Agency and placing it "under the direction and control of the Joint Chiefs of Staff." Its mission was "to provide for the placing under one authority the conduct of communications intelligence and communications security activities . . . within the National Military Establishment, except those which are to be conducted individually by the Departments of the Army, Navy and Air Force."

Four days after they received the Secretary's directive, the JCS set up an ad hoc committee to lay out plans for the formation of the new agency. One of its first actions was to find a director; they settled on Admiral Stone, who had chaired Forrestal's COMINT review panel. The fifty-three-year-old Milwaukee native had spent almost his entire thirty-two-year career in communications and held a master's degree in communications engineering from Harvard.

Stone's selection to head the new agency, however, presented certain problems, especially for the Navy. Because even the fact that such an agency as AFSA existed was considered top secret, no announcement could be made of Stone's appointment. He was, for all intents and purposes, expected to disappear officially from public view. But he had to be replaced as chief of Naval Communications, a not insignificant position, and it was highly likely that someone might just wonder what had happened to the last chief.

After several months of nervous haggling between the services, the final recommendation on release of the information was sent by General Omar Bradley, head of the JCS, to Secretary of Defense Johnson on August 31. It called for a statement by the director of public information containing the not very informative phrase "Rear Admiral Stone has been assigned to duty with the Joint Chiefs of Staff." The information director was further advised that even that simple statement was not to be released unless someone actually inquired about Stone. A few days later Johnson stamped his approval on the recommendation, and AFSA thus became the first government agency to be formed in total secrecy.

By the time the order took effect, however, the issue had already become moot. Stone quietly assumed office on July 15, after being relieved as DNC by Rear Admiral John R. Redman without the slightest notice.

The directive that created AFSA also created its governing board, the Armed Forces Security Agency Council (AFSAC), made up of the two USCIB members from each of the services and one additional member from each service. The director of AFSA, who acted as permanent chairman, brought the total membership to ten.

Although the directive never gave AFSAC any control over AFSA except to make recommendations to the JCS regarding COMINT and to coordinate joint cryptologic military requirements, the council immediately set out to grab as much power as it could from the newborn agency. On September 1, the council submitted to the JCS a draft directive establishing AFSAC as "the agency of the Joint Chiefs of Staff charged with insuring the most effective operation" of AFSA and giving the council the responsibility to "determine policies, operating plans and doctrines" for the agency as well as authority to forward to the director of AFSA "for implementation, without reference to the Joint Chiefs of Staff, its unanimous decisions on matters which it determines not to involve changes in major policies." As a high-level review later declared, "For all practical purposes the directive made AFSAC . . . the boss of AFSA."

Within a short period the directive was approved, and COMINT was placed, in essence, back at square one — under the three-headed control of the services. The goal of unification under a single control had once again succumbed to interservice rivalry.

Probably nowhere was the confusion and disarray of America's COMINT establishment more evident than in the method used for selecting targets. Initially, all targeting originated with the USCIB's Intelligence Committee, a group made up of representatives of the CIA, FBI, State Department, and the intelligence units of the Army, Navy, and Air Force. Once a month the representatives would receive a chartlike form known as the USCIB Intelligence Requirements List, which was divided by countries and under each country listed a variety of target items (advanced weapon systems, troop movements, and so on). The members would then rate the priority of each target on a scale of 1 to 5, with 5 being the highest. The results of the voting would then be forwarded directly to the office of the director of AFSA, where they would be tabulated and assigned to the various intercept stations.

The major problem with the system, though, was its use of overly broad target items and the lack of any mechanism to allocate them to specific communications channels. The system also failed to convert intelligence needs into clear COMINT targets. The most dramatic evidence of these weaknesses was the failure of COMINT to warn of the Korean invasion.

During the seven months that preceded the June 25, 1950, attack, the various intelligence agencies were becoming increasingly concerned about the possibility of a Soviet move against South Korea. On April 12, at a meeting of the Watch Committee, a secret inter-agency group set up to examine all sources of intelligence for warnings of Soviet moves against the non-Soviet world, one of the six items studied was a report relayed by the Commander-in-Chief, Far East Command, which stated that "the North Korean Peoples' Army will invade South Korea in June of 1950."

The minutes of the meeting held on June 14, less than ten days before the attack, showed the committee's continuing interest in Korea:

A list of sensitive areas for consideration by the Watch Committee as potential sources of conflict with the USSR was presented by the Chairman (a CIA man). These areas, arranged in the Chairman's estimate of the order of their explosiveness in the near future (six months to one year) are: Indo-China, Berlin and West Germany, Iran, Yugoslavia, South Korea, the Philippines and Japan. Members of the Watch Committee were asked to present alternative lists or rearrangements of this list at the next meeting, 28 June 1950.

Despite the definite indications that Korea was a highly likely area of conflict, and the fact that the CIA apparently considered South Korea to be the fifth most volatile area in the world, these concerns were never communicated to AFSA through the USCIB's Intelligence Requirements Lists.

During the same seven months, for example, the USCIB submitted nine separate lists. On the highest-priority list (List A), Korea was mentioned only once out of 124 specific priority items, and ranked twelfth and last in frequency of mention among the areas of the world. On the second-priority list (List B), Korea was mentioned only 5 times out of 277 separate items and ranked fifteenth out of eighteen areas mentioned. Even on the lowest-priority list (List C), Korea came up only once out of ninety separate items and was tied for thirteenth and last place in frequency of mention.

Thus, as a result of the failure by the intelligence agencies to communicate to AFSA the true extent of their growing concern over the Korean problem, the agency was poorly prepared to handle Korean traffic when the invasion took place.

The failure and general dissatisfaction with the list procedures forced Admiral Stone to protest to AFSAC on August 18 that he was in a position of having to direct the intercept and processing effort of AFSA without formal integrated guidance from the services as to their intelligence requirements. On October 2, therefore, AFSAC agreed to establish the Intelligence Requirements Committee, comprising the representatives of the military intelligence offices: Office of Naval Intelligence (ONI), Army Intelligence (G-2), Air Force Intelligence (A-2), and AFSA itself. The new AFSAC Intelligence Requirements Committee (AFSAC/IRC) assumed the responsibility for targeting and setting priorities primarily for military traffic, and the United States Communications Intelligence Board's Intelligence Committee (USCIB/IC) confined itself primarily to nonmilitary traffic.

Under the new procedures, both AFSAC/IRC and USCIB/IC were to submit their recommendations to AFSA. They would then go to an Intercept Priorities Board (IPB) made up of the heads of the various branches of AFSA's operations organization, AFSA-02, and always chaired by the chief of AFSA-02.

The IPB, in turn, had about ten Special Intercept Priorities Groups (SIPGs) set up within the various branches of AFSA-02. Before each monthly IPB meeting, the SIPGs would prepare and submit their own recommendations, based on the interests and needs of the various processing units.

After it had received the recommendations of the two intelligence committees and the various SIPGs, the IPB would lay out the actual intercept plan for the coming month. At this point the requirements went to AFSA-28, the Intercept Division of the Collection Group of AFSA, which translated them into circuits and links to be intercepted and monitored by the numerous listening posts.

Once the traffic had been intercepted, the general rule was that processing that could be accomplished effectively within twenty-four hours after intercept was to be done at the point of intercept within the theater, further processing that could be done within forty-eight hours was to be done at the theater level, and all other processing normally would be done back in Washington at AFSA. But regardless of where the processing was done or which service did it, one copy of everything intercepted would be sent back to AFSA.

At AFSA, the reams of cleartext and cryptanalyzed ciphertext would first be attacked by low-grade personnel with little or no knowledge of the language. They were trained merely to scan the traffic for various words or patterns of words, and then, almost by reflex, to file the message in the appropriate bin.

Following the initial scan, expert linguists in eleven reading panels would make the second sort, reducing the bulk again by some 20 to 25 percent and cross-filing what remained into about ninety general categories. It was this group which would also select the individual texts to be translated verbatim and disseminated to consumers — a final distillation of less than 1 percent. Nothing, however, that resulted from the second sort was destroyed; these messages would be kept available for further study or for subsequent translation.

Finally, there were the "beachheads." These were groups of intelligence analysts and liaison personnel stationed at AFSA by the COMINT consumers. They would study the intercepts in their un-published state both for the sake of speed and to help reduce the bulk of finished COMINT. Among the consumers were the three service intelligence agencies — ONI, G-2, and A-2 — each with about a hundred people. Another was the FBI, which would submit long watch lists and which received about seven thousand items a month (or about half of the total AFSA product). One copy of each item would be delivered to FBI headquarters. Other consumers were, of course, the CIA and the State Department.

Although the beachheads were physically within the AFSA compound and the personnel attached had full access to all levels of
the AFSA operation, they were not under AFSA control.

On July 14, 1950, the United States Communications Intelligence
Board met for the fifty-third time. Under the chairmanship of State
Department code chief W. Park Armstrong, Jr., the board took up
the invasion of Korea and unanimously agreed that "the present scale
of communications intelligence effort falls far short of meeting total
requirements or even enabling the United States to exploit available
communications information to its full potential."

As a result, Admiral Stone easily won authorization to increase
AFSA's civilian manpower by fully 50 percent, bringing the total to
4,921. The number of military personnel attached to AFSA also rose,
from 1240 to 1948, and the number of intercept positions doubled,
from 903 to 1821. One year later, AFSA civilian strength had risen
to 6613 and the overall strength to over 8500, with a budget of $60.9
million. But despite the numbers and the dollars, the agency spent
most of the war trying to catch up.

Disappointment over the quality of COMINT during the war
reached all the way to the White House. President Truman, on December 13, 1951, directed Secretary of Defense Robert A. Lovett and
Secretary of State Dean G. Acheson to establish a committee to survey
America's communications intelligence resources and to take whatever
corrective actions they found necessary. Fifteen days later the two
secretaries appointed George Abbott Brownell, fifty-three, a Harvard-
educated lawyer, former minister to India and Mexico, and most recently a special assistant to the Secretary of the Air Force, to head
a panel of distinguished citizens with a mandate to find a cure for
the ailing COMINT establishment.

Over the next six months the Brownell Committee interviewed
forty-three witnesses, held fourteen days of executive hearings, and
poked its head deeper into the super hush-hush community than had
ever been attempted before. In a 239-page report issued on June
13, 1952, the committee pointed a finger directly at the services and
the Joint Chiefs of Staff for the disarray of the COMINT community
and the failure of AFSA:

> In theory the Joint Chiefs of Staff exercise direction over AFSA. In prac-
> tice this direction is taken over almost entirely by their agency AFSAC,
> which is an interservice committee acting under the rule of unanimity.
> Its members devote much of their time in frustrating detail to safeguard-
> ing individual Service autonomies. The Director of AFSA is obligated

to spend much of his energy on cajolery, negotiation, and compromise in an atmosphere of interservice competition. He has no degree of control, except by making use of such techniques, over the three COMINT units operated by the Services. In fact, he is *under* the control of the three Service units, through their representation on AFSAC. His only appeal is to the same three Services sitting as the Joint Chiefs of Staff. [Emphasis in original.]

Among the numerous proposals the committee studied for strengthening the COMINT system was the CONSIDO plan. Originated several years earlier but never acted on was a plan that would have assigned to AFSA all responsibilities for both the collection and processing of COMINT, but created an entirely separate agency to analyze, evaluate, and disseminate the product — a Consolidated Special Information Dissemination Office, or CONSIDO.

Under the CONSIDO proposal, the new, independent organization would be composed of analysts of the various COMINT consumer agencies reporting to a chief of CONSIDO, who would have absolute control over all evaluation and distribution of COMINT. Although the committee rejected this two-headed concept, it did show considerable interest in the idea of a single, central agency combining all aspects of the COMINT operation: collection, processing, evaluation, and distribution. Such a system, the committee noted, had been used by the British since 1920. Among the advantages would be better control and more limited distribution of the intelligence: "It would drastically cut back, for example, the current practice of monthly printing of some two million sheets of code-word paper to gratify the 'minimum' demands of the customers."

The committee also looked with favor on a CONSIDO variation that would make the head of a centralized COMINT agency the nation's true intelligence chief by having collateral intelligence from consumer agencies flow *into* the final COMINT product rather than having the bulky raw COMINT flow outward to the consumers. Such an idea, however, would most likely have found little support from the director of Central Intelligence.

Although the committee saw merit in various aspects of the CONSIDO plan, it settled instead on a less radical, yet still strongly centralized approach. Its recommendations called for the director of AFSA to be given almost total operational control over all United States COMINT collection and processing activities. He would be authorized, though, to delegate portions of that control to the various services for their close support of forces in the field. The key was that the control would flow downward from the director of AFSA.

With regard to the selection of an AFSA chief, they recommended that initially the position be held by a career military officer of at least three-star rank appointed, preferably, for a term of six years but not less than four years, and that his deputy be a career civilian. But the committee also made it clear that it saw no problem with a civilian holding the top spot: "If, as things develop, it should ultimately appear that a civilian could better qualify for the position, it is strongly recommended that no sense of tradition or vested military interest be allowed to stand in the way of his appointment."

From the very beginning the committee realized that the major problems affecting the nation's COMINT system originated not from within AFSA but from above, and it was there that they looked for the most drastic restructuring.

In the belief that COMINT authority should emanate from the highest office, the committee recommended that the President issue a presidential memorandum appointing the Secretary of Defense as the executive agent of the government for COMINT and making the director of AFSA responsible directly to the Defense Secretary rather than to the Joint Chiefs. The memorandum was to leave no doubt as to the authority of the director of AFSA: "This memorandum should provide that . . . the Director of AFSA is responsible for accomplishing the mission of AFSA, and that for this purpose all COMINT collection and technical processing resources of the United States are placed under his operational control."

Then the committee turned its attention to its number one target — AFSAC: "AFSA is now under the Joint Chiefs of Staff. The Joint Chiefs as a body pay little direct attention to the organization and leave its supervision almost entirely to their agent, AFSAC. Control of AFSA is thus under three bosses (the three services represented in AFSAC), whose principal energies and loyalties are elsewhere, and to make matters worse, three bosses who must act by unanimous agreement."

The committee recommended that AFSAC be disbanded and replaced with a special committee under the National Security Council and a revitalized United States Communications Intelligence Board, which had been nearly emasculated by the creation of AFSAC.

Under this complex reorganization, the Secretary of Defense, as executive agent for COMINT, would report directly to a Special Committee of the National Security Council for COMINT, consisting of himself and the Secretary of State — and the President, as circumstances might require. A new NSCID No. 9 was to be drafted, abolishing AFSAC and reorganizing the USCIB under the chairmanship of the director of Central Intelligence. The new board would be composed of representatives of the Secretary of Defense and Secretary of State, the director of AFSA, the chairman of the Joint Intelligence Committee of the JCS, and a representative of the director of the FBI.

The director of AFSA would be required to bring to the attention of the board any new major policies or programs before they were adopted, as well as any reports the board might ask to see.

The board, in turn, would be responsible for advising and making recommendations regarding COMINT and AFSA to the Secretary of Defense. On a vote of not fewer than four members, each member having one vote, decisions of the board would be binding on the Secretary. Any dissenting member of the board, however, would have seven days to file an appeal to the Special Committee, whose determination would be final.

It was a complicated formula but one designed to accomplish the major goals of the committee. By placing far greater authority in the hands of the director of AFSA, it would be creating a stronger, more efficient organization. The scuttling of AFSAC and the resurrection of the USCIB would break the military's iron grip on COMINT and give the various civilian consumers a say in its collection. And the appeal process to the Special Committee would eliminate the USCIB's cumbersome requirement for unanimity in voting.

On October 24, 1952, four months after the committee had submitted its final report, President Harry S Truman attached his signature to the bottom of a top secret–code word, seven-page presidential memorandum addressed to Secretary of Defense Lovett and Secretary of State Acheson.* Contained in those seven pages was an almost verbatum iteration of the Brownell Committee's recommendations translated into a presidential order and mandated to take effect secretly on November 4.† But there was one added surprise for the supersecret organization. It had a new name to reflect its new role — the National Security Agency.

* The memorandum was most likely given to Secretary of Defense Lovett, Undersecretary of State David K. E. Bruce, and Everett Gleason of the National Security Council, during a 3:30 P.M. meeting in the Oval Office. (President Truman's schedule for October 24, 1952, Papers of Harry S Truman, Files of Mathew J. Connelly, Harry S Truman Presidential Library, Independence, Missouri.)

† On December 29, 1952, in one of his last acts as President, Truman quietly stamped his approval on a newly revised NSCID No. 9 incorporating the recommendations of the *Brownell Committee Report*. If the Truman memorandum was NSA's birth certificate, the new NSCID was its baptism.

3

ANATOMY

IN THE FIFTY YEARS since Friedman hired his first three assistants for the fledgling Signal Intelligence Service, America's cryptologic empire had grown from back room to boom town. By 1980 the Puzzle Palace had become the largest single espionage factory the free world had ever known or could ever imagine. It had become a bizarre Klondike on the Severn, where thousands of modern-day prospectors sift through endless streams of intercepts with computerized tin pans searching for that elusive nugget — the word, the pattern, the anomaly — that will lead to a golden vein of exposed secrets.

Once small enough for a single office in the old Munitions Building, the lineal descendant of the SIS today requires a virtual city just to process the mountains of intercepts constantly flooding in from its worldwide electronic dredging operation.

SIGINT City, as one might without exaggeration name the NSA's sprawling complex, lies halfway between Washington and Baltimore on a thousand acres of Fort George G. Meade. With a resident population of about thirty-five hundred, SIGINT City would in fact be larger than more than 130 other cities and towns in the State of Maryland. As in most major cities, however, that figure is increased fifteenfold by the early morning clog of nine-to-five commuters pouring off the Baltimore-Washington Parkway toward the nearly twenty buildings of downtown SIGINT City.

In many respects, the town is much like any other — you can get a haircut, do your banking, visit a travel agency, take books out of a library, buy cosmetics, or see a doctor about hemorrhoids. It has its own bus service, its own police force (with salmon-colored patrol cars), its own college (enrollment, eighteen thousand), its own television station, and even its own studio, which has produced such thrillers as *Stranger Unchallenged.* Its post office handles more than eighteen thousand pieces of mail per day; its telephone exchange connects thirty thousand calls a month. Energy to power SIGINT City comes from its own power station, which supplies the community with 106,668 KVA of electricity — or enough to run a city of fifty thousand people.

There are some differences, however, between SIGINT City and Fargo. Before climbing into the barber's chair and asking for a razor cut, for instance, you first must have survived months of rigorous background checks, been strapped to a lie detector, received a top secret sensitive compartmented SIGINT security clearance, and signed numerous forms agreeing never to mention a word about the city, its occupants, or their professions. Also unlike Fargo, SIGINT City offers no Welcome Wagon, no Chamber of Commerce, and no Gray Line tours. Tourism, one can safely say, is at least an eon away.

Choice of the Maryland site for NSA's expansive city was far from accidental, and the drama that led up to the selection sparked a near-mutiny among the agency's civilian work force.

With the formation of the Armed Forces Security Agency, all of the nation's major SIGINT (signals intelligence) and COMSEC (Communications Security) activities were, to a limited extent, consolidated into a single organization for both efficiency and economy. To increase these desirable qualities, it was decided to concentrate all SIGINT operations at Arlington Hall and all COMSEC activities at the Naval Security Station on Nebraska Avenue, with research and development divided between the two.

This worked well for organizational structure and as a means of keeping the agency close to official Washington, but there was one recurring nightmare: the possibility that an enemy attack on Washington, or even sabotage, could completely and totally annihilate America's entire cryptologic reservoir — SIGINT as well as COMSEC, personnel as well as computers. Such a disaster would place the state of the art back before World War II, back more than a decade. Compounding the fear was the realization that a mere nine thousand yards separated the two facilities, hardly enough space to provide either one with adequate protection.

Nonetheless, the JCS in its joint wisdom decided that "the increase in efficiency due to concentration justified the temporary acceptance of the hazards involved as a calculated risk." But they began searching for a distant location to store duplicates of some of the more vital records and equipment.

Both before and during World War II, American SIGINT activities were so dispersed that, from a practical standpoint, there was no real risk of complete disruption. In addition, close collaboration with the British SIGINT organization provided additional insurance against such a hazard. Yet what would have happened had such a misfortune taken place? A top secret JCS memorandum explains: "In the Pacific, loss of COMINT information for as few as ten critical days might have resulted in the occupation of Port Moresby instead of the Battle of the Coral Sea. Seven days' interruption would have denied the information on which our victory in the Battle of Midway was based." But the sentence that most burned into the minds of the Joint Chiefs was the conclusion that loss or prolonged interruption "immediately preceding or during the initial phases of war . . . might be fatal to the nation."

Therefore, on March 14, 1950, the JCS requested authority from Secretary of Defense Johnson to begin making plans to relocate AFSA outside the Washington area, beginning with the SIGINT activities at Arlington Hall, considered the most irreplaceable because of the computers. Ten days later approval was granted, and on April 21 AFSA director Stone appointed an ad hoc site board to find a suitable location, preferably on existing government-owned property in Texas, the Tennessee Valley, or the Denver area.

After seven long months and thirty-five on-site inspections, the board finally announced the decision: Fort Knox, deep in Kentucky's Bluegrass Country. Captain Thomas H. Dyer, one of the Navy's top codebreakers and chairman of the site board, and his four associates felt pleased with the choice; after all, Fort Knox certainly provided "security in depth," was well removed from other probable targets, and had adequate land for construction. There was, however, one factor that the board members, all military officers, unfortunately never took into consideration: the possible reaction of AFSA's five thousand civilian employees.

AFSA was not just an ordinary military organization, and its employees were not just the run-of-the-mill paper-pushing Washington bureaucrats. They were, for the most part, the cream of the scientific and mathematical crop, cipher brains and then some. Many had had to be wooed or even shanghaied from top jobs in industry and academe; others had spent years turning their peculiar craft into art. Even the clerks and secretaries were a special breed, all having passed the government's most rigorous security investigations. Losing even 10 percent would be a total disaster, and a move to the backwoods of Kentucky threatened a loss far greater than that. While the military were by nature transients, the civilians were by nature settlers, and the place they were settled was Washington.

Despite the protests and pleas for reconsideration, however, the decision stuck, and when the Secretary of Defense gave his blessing to the move on April 10, 1951, many at Arlington Hall began scanning the help-wanted ads. The 2.05 percent attrition rate the agency had managed to maintain promised to go straight through the roof.

By now AFSA had changed hands. Admiral Stone had been replaced by Major General Ralph Canine, who recognized the seriousness of the situation almost at once. Yet he knew that the die had been cast, and he was prepared to live with the result. It was with much surprise, therefore, that he picked up the telephone on the morning of December 10 and found that Rear Admiral W. G. Lalor, the secretary to the Joint Chiefs, was calling to get Canine's personal feelings on the matter.

"As the director out here," Canine told Lalor, "I do not agree with that, if I am given a free hand; as a matter of fact, quite the contrary. I would say that from my standpoint that's a very poor decision and . . . if I am given the opportunity, I will say so . . . I don't agree [with] the decision as recommended to the Joint Chiefs of Staff. If they want me to tell them that I will be glad to."

Two days later he did just that, and Secretary of Defense Lovett on January 4, 1952, rescinded his order and directed that a new site be found within a twenty-five-mile radius of Washington. Canine became a hero.

Within less than a month, the possible locations had been narrowed down to eight, one of which was the Bureau of Public Roads Laboratory in Langley, Virginia, later to become the home of another set of spooks, the CIA. Of the choices, the hands-down favorite was Fort George G. Meade. Twenty-two miles from Washington's zero milestone, it had more than enough land, facilities for logistic support, and low vulnerability. The only disadvantage was that it would still require a large number of civilian employees to move, but only to the other side of Washington at most. The advantages clearly outweighed the disadvantages. The location, halfway between Washington and Baltimore, meant that both cities could be used as sources of personnel and utilities.

The selection of Fort Meade was a good one. Within hours of receiving the recommendation from General Canine, JCS chairman Omar Bradley sent a memorandum to Secretary Lovett granting his approval. Lovett quickly gave the green light to begin planning for the massive relocation of the top secret agency, an operation that was given the code name Project K.

In July 1954, the $19,944,451 contract for the construction of Project K was awarded to the Charles H. Tompkins Company of Washington. It called for a three-story glass and reinforced-concrete structure in the shape of a large, boxy, squared-off **A**. The exterior walls were to be fabricated of precast insulated concrete panels with a sickly green stone-chip facing. In addition to the 1.4 million-square-foot main building, which included a vast basement for the massive computers, Project K called for a 60,000-square-foot supply building, sidewalks, bituminous parking lots, access roads, guardhouses, and a power substation.

By the time the secret project was completed in the fall of 1957, the $20 million cost had almost doubled, to $35 million. But within less than six years the building was already bursting at its pea-green seams, and on June 24, 1963, steam shovels of the J. W. Bateson Company began scooping out the foundation for a new Headquarters Building. Located between the jutting wings of the A-shaped Operations Building and connected to it by a central corridor, the nine-story, $12 million tower was built primarily to house the analysts and codebreakers of NSA's Production Organization. It gave to the Puzzle Palace an additional 512,000 square feet, 140,000 of them for a basement labyrinth of computers and data-processing equipment that would completely fill the area between the stretched-out arms of the original Operations Building. Three years after the first bucket of dirt was pulled from the front yard of the Operations Building, NSA director Marshall Carter opened the new addition by cutting the ceremonial ribbon.

Almost the size of the CIA building with the United States Capitol sitting on top, the NSA's joint Headquarters-Operations Building is the Taj Mahal of eavesdropping.* Inside are 7,560,000 linear feet of telephone wire, 70,000 square feet of permanently sealed windows, 16,000 light fixtures, a cooling tower capable of handling eleven million gallons of water a day, and the nation's longest unobstructed corridor — 980 feet — casting the 750-foot central corridor of the Capitol into a distant second place.

Driving north on the peacefully truckless Baltimore-Washington Parkway, past miles of rolling, tree-covered Maryland countryside, the visitor to the Puzzle Palace catches his first glimpse of the tan, nine-story monolith, with its surrounding green three-story A-shaped building, as he makes a right turn onto Savage Road. At first glance it looks as though the structure might belong to the Social Security Administration or some other elephantine bureaucracy. But the innocence of first impression gives way as one gradually gets nearer.

The entire complex is surrounded by a ten-foot Cyclone fence

---

* The CIA building is 1,228,000 square feet; the Capitol is 718,740 square feet. Total: 1,946,740 square feet. The NSA is 1,912,000 square feet.

crowned with multiple rows of barbed wire. Attached to the fence every few dozen feet are warnings against taking photographs or making so much as a sketch, under the penalties of the Internal Security Act. Inside this is another fence, consisting of five thin strands of high-voltage electrified wire attached to wooden posts planted around the building in a bed of green asphalt pebbles. Finally, there is another tall Cyclone fence reinforcing the others. The area within is occasionally patrolled by armed guards with snarling attack dogs. On the roof, almost unseen, closed circuit television cameras with telephoto lenses peer downward as they slowly rotate to scan all the area surrounding the building.

Also littering the roof is a multitude of strange antennas. Resting on either end of the rectangular Headquarters Tower are two enormous radomes, one with an angular, pock-marked surface like a giant golf ball, the other smooth, like a Ping-Pong ball. Elsewhere are long-wire antennas, parabolic microwave dishes, log-periodic antennas, and a large white satellite dish hidden inside a mammoth green shell.

One enters the building through a set of glass doors at the top of a dozen steps. This is Gatehouse 1, one of four such gatehouses around the complex, but the only one leading directly into the Tower. Straight ahead, two armed Federal Protective Service guards in blue uniforms make sure each entering face corresponds to the matching picture on the color-coded, computer-punched, plastic-laminated security badge dangling below each employee's neck.

Before passing the checkpoint, the visitor must turn to the right through another set of glass doors and enter a modern, brightly appointed reception room, where his or her NSA "sponsor" processes the outsider through one of two receptionists. A visitor without security clearance must be signed for by the sponsor and accompanied at all times. Once signed in, the visitor is issued a 4½-by-2½-inch red and white striped badge marked in large bold letters ONE DAY on the front and with a warning against misuse on the back. Nowhere, however, does the laminated badge make any reference to the National Security Agency.

Once properly tagged and escorted, the visitor passes the initial checkpoint and walks along a corridor into the Headquarters Building lobby. Along the way one passes a wall-sized, thirty-three-foot acrylic mural depicting actual Agency employees engaged in a variety of activities, from listening through earphones to collecting signals from a satellite. The long mural was specifically designed for "ambulatory viewing" (viewing while one walks).

Straight ahead, dominating the wall at the end of the passageway, is a huge, shimmering mosaic of the Agency's seal. It is four feet in diameter, contains over twenty thousand hand-cut cubes of Byzantine smalt glass, and has a stern eagle standing guard in the center. Clutched tightly in its talons is a large, ancient skeleton key — a key for unlocking the secrets of others while jealously guarding its own. Around a sparkling, cobalt-blue background, blue letters on white spell out the name of the occupant the eagle seeks so fiercely to protect: NATIONAL SECURITY AGENCY.

A sharp left at the seal, and one is in the Tower lobby, decorated with oil paintings of each of the Agency's former directors. Here, past another armed guard, six automatic elevators can take you one floor below to a twenty-first-century world of superadvanced computers, or straight up to the ninth-floor executive offices, nicknamed Mahogany Row.

At the far end of Mahogany Row, behind a bright blue door set in a matching wall decorated with the Agency seal, is Room 9A197, the office of the director — DIRNSA (pronounced dern-za) to the initiated. Past the outer office of executive registry secretaries and a turn to the right, DIRNSA's office is comfortable but not exceptional. In front of his highly polished desk are two leather armchairs facing a matching leather couch. In between is a low coffee table; to the right, windows overlook the green Maryland countryside. An enormous world globe rests below the venetian-blind-covered windows, and, at least when Vice Admiral Bobby Inman was director, a model schooner sat on a ledge.

Back down in the lobby, a brief walk through the glass-enclosed hallway connecting the Headquarters Tower with the three-story Operations Building brings the visitor to the NSA equivalent of Main Street. A jaunt down C Corridor, longer than three football fields, will take you past a branch bank of the Equitable Trust, the Tower Federal Credit Union, the Globetrotter travel desk, the Drug Fair drugstore, the Commuter Transportation Center, the Blood Donor Center, a ticket service booth, a shop to repair your shoes, another to clean your clothes, and a barber shop, where Walter Aiken will trim your sideburns or give you "the works."

Nearby is the cafeteria, where 180 people sweat over fifteen ovens twenty-four hours a day, seven days a week, preparing codfish cakes and chicken pot pies. On warm sunny days, employees can eat in a sheltered outdoor courtyard near an old-fashioned gazebo.

Should the vichyssoise contain a touch of botulism, however, there would be small need for alarm. Within the complex is a full-service medical center capable of treating everything from the toenail to the psyche and complete with emergency unit, X-ray and operating rooms, and one room containing a dusty skeleton with a VIP security badge dangling below its bony neck.

Elsewhere in the Puzzle Palace are the five-hundred-seat Friedman Auditorium, named after William F. Friedman, whose bust is encased at the entrance, and the NSA library, probably one of the most unusual in the world, where one can pick up a book on Mycenaean documents or watch a tape of a Saudi Arabian television program while following along with an accompanying transcript.

At the center of C Corridor, also guarded by pistol-packing FPS officers, escalators carry employees to the second- and third-floor operational areas. Here, along broad hallways, heavy steel doors bear color-coded round seals to indicate the level of sensitivity of the work going on behind them. Red, for example, means the project is compartmented, and thus off limits to those without a specific "need to know." Other hallways have warning signs prohibiting unauthorized entry. If someone without the proper badge should miss the sign and continue walking, warning bells will go off and red lights begin to flash. A voice from a speaker will ask the intruder to identify him or herself to an overhead camera.

The doors to some of the most sensitive offices, such as the communications center in the Operations Building, can be opened only by inserting one's hand into a cipher lock, a black box containing ten buttons, and pressing a certain number of them in the proper sequence.

Inside the offices, some people work at standard, gray, government-issue desks; others scribble on the green chalk boards that line the pastel walls in virtually every office in the Operations Building. Used by the Research and Engineering Organization, the Operations Building also contains numerous laboratories. On top of the desks are two types of telephones: "black" phones for unclassified conversations connect into the outside telephone network; "gray" secure phones are for classified conversations. In addition, there is a system of "security conveyor belts," which can move documents from one end of the complex to another in fourteen minutes without their having to pass through a central control point. For faster delivery, a German pneumatic-tube system can whisk documents from one office to another at the touch of a dial in less than ninety seconds.

During the 1966 dedication ceremony for the new Headquarters Tower, Director Marshall Carter quipped to the crowd: "You will notice in the Operations Building lobby we have the details of its construction immortalized in bronze and a portrait of General Canine.

Today, we have this [new] construction immortalized in bronze and across the lobby a portrait of [former director] General Blake." Then, with the flash of a smile, he added, "Now you see why I'm pushing for another building."

There was more prophecy than humor in General Carter's comments. Within two years he had his own name "immortalized in bronze" on an attractive $5.7 million three-story building of steel and glass. Known as the S Building, the 261,516-square-foot, bronze-colored facility was designed as the home for the Agency's Communications Security Organization, referred to internally as the S Organization. COMSEC, which until 1968 had maintained its headquarters and offices at the Naval Security Station on Nebraska Avenue in Washington, was the last of the major divisions to make the move to Fort Meade.

Sharing the building with COMSEC is the Agency's massive printing facility, one of the largest and most diversified printing plants in the United States government, employing several hundred people. The pressroom equipment ranges from a fifty-inch two-unit Goss web press to a computer cathode-ray tube phototypesetting machine capable of putting out more than a million pages of material annually.

Building after building, the Puzzle Palace continued to expand its empire. What had started out as a Black Chamber was turning into a Black City. To house the increasing numbers of single military people assigned to the Agency, new dormitories were added and expanded. By the early 1970s there were five buildings housing about thirty-five hundred men and women. Also added were a mess hall that can seat a thousand people, an $844,000 recreation building, and a $2 million Troop Support Building to house the administration activities of the three service cryptologic agencies.

In 1972 the construction continued with a $2.6 million Sensitive Materials Center to contain the millions of miles of intercept tapes produced yearly by the Agency's worldwide net of listening posts. Until then, they had been stored throughout half a dozen other buildings in the Baltimore-Washington area. Because of their delicate chemical nature and the frequent need to reuse a particular tape — it may present a particularly difficult codebreaking problem or contain information of continuing importance — the new building was needed to keep the tapes at a constant temperature and humidity. Also, since some of the tapes are simply erased and reused, the new 100,000-square-foot facility could house a centralized tape-rehabilitation center.

Another function of the Sensitive Materials Center, housed in a building known as SAB 3 (for Support Activities Building 3), is to serve as headquarters for the Agency's mail and courier services. From SAB 3, NSA couriers head toward Washington each morning, transporting and picking up cargoes of supersensitive documents on seventeen different runs, five days a week. Constantly arriving and departing, too, are military couriers from the Armed Forces Courier Service (ARFCOS) and diplomatic couriers from the State Department.

One year later, in 1973, the Agency decided to consolidate its storage and logistic functions in still another new building, the $3.5 million Logistics Building, known as SAB 4. Once the 125,400-square-foot building was completed, the Agency spent another $53,000 moving in approximately seven hundred vanloads of paper and office supplies. Half a million cubic feet of the building are used to store the paper on which the intercepts eventually appear.

Storing the mountains of paper, however, is the least of NSA's problems. The major difficulty is what to do with it once it has been read, analyzed, shredded, and burn-bagged. It is almost impossible for anyone to comprehend how much secret information is actually produced each day by the NSA. According to a 1980 report by the Government Accounting Office, the NSA classifies somewhere between fifty and a hundred million documents a year. "That means," the GAO report concluded, "that its classification activity is probably greater than the combined total activity of all components and agencies of the Government." More secrets than the Army, Navy, Air Force, CIA, State Department, and all the other government agencies combined!

Translated into pounds, the Puzzle Palace's production of classified waste is almost forty tons a day, two hundred tons in an average week. Such statistics led one senator to question an NSA official, "Is the National Security Agency literally burying itself in classified material?" To which the NSA assistant director, seemingly resigned to his fate, responded, "It would seem that way."

The problem of how to get rid of its secrets has plagued the NSA for decades. At one point the Agency tried to have it all turned into pulp, but this meant that the material had to be sealed in plastic bags and trucked to the Halltown Paperboard Company (apparently the only company that would have anything to do with the scheme), several hundred miles away in Halltown, West Virginia, where the NSA would have to take over the plant for twenty-four hours. Dumped into a macerator, what were once the nation's deepest secrets would suddenly become material for someone's egg carton. But the problem with this system was that some paper was just not acceptable, and the Agency was left with twenty thousand square feet of warehouse space full of paper that had to be burned.

Finally, out of desperation, the Agency's Installations and Logistics (or L) Organization turned to the American Thermogen Corporation of Whitman, Massachusetts, for the construction of what came to be known as White Elephant No. 1.

In late 1972, members of NSA's L Organization journeyed up to the Bay State to view a pilot model of a $1.2 million "classified waste destructor" and came away impressed. According to the company, the three-story machine was supposed to swallow the Agency's mountains of secrets at the rate of six tons an hour and cremate them with temperatures up to 3400 degrees Fahrenheit.

To transport the huge heaps of burn bags from the various buildings into the fiery monster, the Puzzle Palace turned, appropriately enough, to Florida's Disney World. Just as the trash accumulated in Fantasyland and the rest of the Magic Kingdom is transported automatically by underground conveyor belt to a central waste disposal facility, the burn bags from all the buildings of SIGINT City would be sucked into a $2 million pneumatic-tube system in steel pipes buried ten feet underground and would be shot directly into the incinerator.

When the elaborate incinerator was finally completed, in the summer of 1973, the marvel of modern pyrotechnics had only one problem: it didn't work. Instead of the top secret trash becoming converted into gases and liquids, which could be piped off, it would occasionally congeal into a rocklike mass and accumulate in the belly of the Elephant, where jackhammers were needed to break it up. On at least one occasion, horrified security personnel had to scurry around gathering up bits and shreds of undigested intercepts, computer printouts, and magnetic tapes that had managed to escape through the stack. Twenty-ton Army trucks had to be drafted into service, along with armed guards, to cart the undigested secrets to secure storage at Army Intelligence headquarters at Fort Holabird, just outside Baltimore.

In all, the destructor managed to operate for a total of fifty-one days out of its first seventeen months. By the time the Agency canceled its contract, in December 1974, it had already paid off all but $70,000 of the $1.2 million construction price. Said one red-faced NSA official, "Our research will continue."

When SIGINT City could no longer absorb any more buildings, the people of the Facilities and Planning Staff had to look elsewhere to lay their bricks and mortar. The site selected was Elkridge Landing Road, a dozen miles north of Fort Meade and a stone's throw from the runway lights of Baltimore-Washington (Friendship) International Airport. Here the Agency leased two seven-story towers and two two-story buildings (one of which is now used by the National Aeronautics and Space Administration), all securely wrapped in NSA's standard triple fence of barbs and sparks.

Officially known as FANX (for Friendship Annex) I, II, III, and IV, the facility has been given a less arcane name by spooks assigned there: Friendship Leper Colony. Explained one employee: "We are like the people of a leper colony. We do belong to NSA, but are socially second class to NSA." He added, "It really wouldn't hurt so badly if the people at NSA didn't reply like 'Oh, so *you're* from the Annex at Friendship,' in a more-holy-than-thou voice, when they ask where you work. That really smarts!"

Nor is that the only complaint about the way station. In explaining why the seven-story FANX III does not have piped-in Musak like its sister up the road, the same employee said, "It's probably that the government doesn't want to invest too much money in FANX III, since it's only a matter of time until it is wiped out by one of Friendship's jets on a bad-weather approach to the airport — which just happens to be one hundred yards out from my sixth-floor office, and sometimes one floor down!" Then there is the parking lot dubbed Cardiac Hill: "Water doesn't stand on Cardiac Hill — it runs. Ankle deep! And after you find that parking place, you don't worry about being dry when you get to work; you won't be and you know it."

Even with its FANX suburb, SIGINT City continues to strive to become America's fastest-growing city. Under way is another $6.5 million project to house an additional six hundred military personnel, a $5 million Facility Control Center, a $2.5 million Logistics Support Center, and a $2.5 million addition to the Troop Support Facility. Two million dollars are earmarked for road improvements, and $3.5 million for other projects ranging from underground communications to a beefed-up security control point.

But the *pièce de résistance* is a mammoth $92 million (at last estimate), one-million-square-foot addition to the Headquarters-Operations Building complex. The construction will add two nine-story towers to the existing Headquarters Tower, which is connected to the Operations Building. NSA would thus become the possessor of the largest government building in the Washington area, with the sole exception of the Pentagon. Still, this cement and glass monument to eavesdropping will likely remain off the tourist maps for many years to come.

•

As invisible as the Agency itself are the SIGINT czars who direct its far-flung operations.

Portly, white-haired Major General Ralph Julian Canine, the Agency's first director and considered by some the father of NSA, actually came to the position by default. On January 19, 1951, before the changeover from AFSA to NSA, the Joint Chiefs stated the method by which the new director would be picked. An ad hoc committee of the AFSA Council, composed of two flag officers of each service, would convene on or about February 1 and select a director from among the list of candidates supplied by the Army and the Air Force (the Navy was excluded because one of its officers, Admiral Stone, had just held the position). When the committee met on January 29, however, the Army had supplied only one candidate, Canine, and the Air Force had not bothered to submit any! So Canine was a shoo-in and assumed command of AFSA in August 1951.

At fifty-five, the two-star general had spent most of his career as a ground soldier; he had commanded artillery units in France in World War I and again in World War II, at the Battle of the Bulge. In between, his assignments ranged from teaching military science at Purdue to being mess officer at Fort McDowell to serving as chief of staff of the XII Corps at Fort Jackson. In the thirty-four years since his graduation from Northwestern, however, the Indiana-born general's only experience in communications was as a part-time communications officer and acting brigade adjutant at Camp Funston, Kansas, in 1919. His experience with intelligence was more substantial, because his arrival at AFSA followed ten months as deputy assistant chief of staff for Army Intelligence at the Pentagon.

Despite his nonscientific background, however, Canine seemed to hit it off immediately with the military and the civilians, as well. "The people who make up this Agency," he said, "are its most important asset. It is by means of their hands and their brains that we will succeed. I am convinced that the way to insure that our job is done successfully is to hire the best people and to give them a work climate that favors the development of ideas." By deciding that that work climate should be Maryland instead of Kentucky, he managed to win the hearts and minds of nearly all employees.

Canine and the newborn NSA seemed a near-perfect match. He managed to maintain the respect of the civilians without alienating the brass-buttoned military. His greatest asset lay not in his technical expertise but, apparently, in his ability to unify an agency of inflated egos, hard-boiled militarists, and a myriad of special-interest groups. One of his first directives dealt not with the war then going on in Korea but with the color scheme of the furniture. Canine ordered that the furniture be rearranged so that all oak would be in one wing, all maple in another, and so on, until the previously haphazard arrangement took on a look of harmony.

"Lady, I know you've had that chair since 1942," he is supposed to have remarked on one occasion, "but it is the wrong color for this wing. Let's compromise — let the chair go to Wing 3; then you and the cushion can stay here in Wing 5." The effect of the resulting orderliness was a greatly improved efficiency. Canine later admitted, however, that he had issued the directive because he didn't know what else to do to get the people to know him.

In November 1956, after more than five years as head of AFSA-NSA, Canine retired and was succeeded by John Alexander Samford, a fifty-one-year-old Air Force lieutenant general whose weathered good looks seemed to betray his early years as an open-cockpit pilot. The West Pointer, one of the Army's early birds in aviation, was awarded his gold wings in 1929. After a number of assignments in both the United States and Panama, he took part in a history-making 1939 mercy mission to Santiago, Chile, which had suffered a devastating earthquake.

During World II, Samford spent most of his time in England, serving in a number of positions in the Eighth Air Force, including chief of staff. In 1944 "Sammy" Samford returned to Washington and received his first taste of the blacker arts as deputy assistant chief of staff for Air Force Intelligence in the Pentagon. This was followed by a thirty-month return to the academic life, first as commandant of the Air Command and Staff School and later, briefly, as commandant of the Air War College at Maxwell Field in Montgomery, Alabama.

In October 1951, during the Korean War, the veteran command pilot became director of Air Force Intelligence, a post that gave him a good background for his next assignment, NSA vice director (as the deputy director's job was designated until the fall of 1956). Appointed to that post on June 1, 1956, he spent the next six months trying to learn as much as he could about the strange world of SIGINT while interning under General Canine. Finally, on November 24, he took over the reins of the Puzzle Palace from the retiring director.

Samford continued the expansion of NSA's worldwide listening posts begun earlier by Canine. His four-year tour at the NSA ended with considerably more attention than it began. Several months before his scheduled November 1960 retirement, the Agency suffered the worst scandal in its history when two employees decided to make a permanent change of address to Moscow.

Entering in the middle of the firestorm was Vice Admiral Laurence Hugh (Jack) Frost, a 1926 Annapolis graduate with a well-rounded career in both communications and intelligence. The thin, silver-haired naval officer had spent two years studying applied communications at the Navy's graduate school in Annapolis before undertaking a series of shipboard assignments, which included service as communications officer on the flagship U.S.S. *Dallas.*

During World War II Frost won a Bronze and two Silver Star medals while commanding the destroyer U.S.S. *Waller* through the Japanese-controlled Solomon Islands. Afterward, he returned to communications and a variety of assignments in Naval Intelligence until 1953, when he picked up his two stars as a rear admiral and became chief of staff at NSA for two years. In May 1956 the fifty-three-year-old admiral was appointed director of Naval Intelligence, and four years later re-entered the Puzzle Palace.

Frost's brief twenty months as director were consumed mostly by the various inquests into the double defection. Among his reforms was the shifting of the Agency's civilian personnel from regular civil service to excepted status, a move that permitted the Agency to fire an employee in the interests of national security without the employee's having any recourse. Frost's own cryptologic career was terminated prematurely following a dispute with the Pentagon. On June 30, 1962, he left the NSA to become commandant of the Potomac River Naval Command, a sort of halfway house for admirals on the brink of retirement.

Replacing Frost was fifty-one-year-old Gordon Aylesworth Blake, an Air Force lieutenant general and avid square dancer, who, like his predecessor, had spent a considerable portion of his career in communications. During World War II he commanded the Army Airways Communications System in the Pacific, and in 1953 he was appointed director of Air Force Communications. From 1957 to 1959 the tall, balding general commanded the NSA's air arm, the U.S. Air Force Security Service. Following brief tours as Vice Commander-in-Chief and Chief of Staff, Pacific Air Forces; and Commander, Continental Air Command, Blake entered the Puzzle Palace as the Agency's fourth director. There, he concentrated on establishing closer relations between the NSA and the three service cryptologic agencies.

One of his innovations was the development of the NSA's own hush-hush version of the Oscar — the Travis Trophy. As indicated by the inscription on the silver, two-handled cup, the trophy is TO BE AWARDED ANNUALLY TO THE U.S. CRYPTOLOGIC AGENCY WHICH HAS MADE THE MOST SIGNIFICANT CONTRIBUTION IN THE FIELDS OF OPERATIONS, MANAGEMENT, ADMINISTRATION OR SUGGESTIONS.

Established in 1945 by Sir Edward Travis, the first director of the Government Communications Headquarters (GCHQ), the British counterpart of NSA, the Travis Trophy's original purpose was to serve as a prize for competitive games, such as chess and softball, between the Army and Navy SIGINT organizations. Blake discovered the cup, forgotten since the establishment of the Armed Forces Security Agency, collecting dust at Arlington Hall Station, and decided to revive it as a competitive award among the three service cryptologic agencies for outstanding contributions in cryptology. GCHQ director Sir Clive Loehnis, as the cup points out, fully concurred with the idea, and on September 10, 1965, the incumbent NSA director, Marshall S. Carter, awarded the shiny bowl to its first winners, the 6988th Security Squadron of the Air Force Security Service. The British were represented at the ceremony by Reginald H. Parker, the properly mustachioed representative to the NSA from GCHQ.

Blake's successor as DIRNSA was Lieutenant General Marshall Sylvester (Pat) Carter, a third-generation Army officer and one of the best qualified of all NSA directors in breadth of experience. A graduate of West Point with a master's degree in engineering from MIT, Carter had spent his early Army years in antiaircraft artillery units and, during World War II, in Army logistics. In 1946 he was named special representative in Washington for former Chief of Staff George C. Marshall while the general was on his China mission as ambassador. The following year, when Marshall became Secretary of State, he managed to get Carter promoted to brigadier general and took him along as a special assistant, thereby giving the future NSA director a firsthand look at American foreign policy. Later, when Marshall was named Secretary of Defense, he brought his protégé with him as his executive assistant. In April 1962, after a number of air defense assignments, Carter returned to Washington to become deputy director of the CIA under John A. McCone, picking up his third star along the way.

At the "pickle factory," or "McConey Island," as the irreverent general would occasionally call the agency, he wound up spending almost 25 percent of his time running the show as acting director in McCone's absence. It was Carter, for example, who first received the U-2 photos indicating the presence of Soviet offensive missiles in Cuba and it was he who first showed the "pornography" to President Kennedy.

But despite the heady challenges and responsibilities of being the nation's number two spook, he found the job to be not without its hazards. On three occasions Carter tangled with Defense Secretary Robert S. McNamara and, unfortunately for his military career, managed to win each round. Once, during a meeting at the White House with JFK, McNamara came up with what he thought was a piece of hot intelligence but which was actually eight hours old. Carter had

gotten new information from the NSA, just before he left CIA headquarters, that completely changed the picture. "I had the word of
Isaiah . . ." Carter recalled, so "I had to correct McNamara right
there — and he didn't like that worth a damn!"

According to Carter, "McNamara could never understand that I
was working directly for the President [as deputy director of Central
Intelligence] and the government by law, and was not just another
lieutenant general to be overridden as a subordinate in his chain of
command." When Carter entered the CIA he had replaced Charles
P. Cabell, a four-star Army general, and after he had spent three
years on the job, McCone decided to recommend him for his fourth
star. But McNamara opposed the promotion, and, instead of gaining
a star, Carter ended up losing one — and, along with it, his job.

When President Johnson replaced McCone with retired Vice Admiral William F. Raborn on April 11, 1965, Carter was left out in the
proverbial cold. According to the National Security Act of 1947, which
set up the CIA, the military was forbidden to occupy the top two
positions at the same time. No longer in a three-star billet, Carter
was demoted to major general but, in a face-saving move, was allowed
to continue wearing his three silver stars. The fig leaf, however, helped
little. As he confided in a letter to a friend:

> When Admiral Raborn was selected to be the Director of Central Intelli-
> gence, I contracted an immediate and virulent case of instant unemploy-
> ment. It is now the Army's problem — not mine — and I dare say that
> before I totally rot on the vine they will find a gainful task for me some
> place in this embittered, tired world.

Left without an assignment for about a month or more, Carter
was tempted to turn in his greens. Nevertheless, he decided to hold
off in the hope that a real job might turn up. At about that time,
one of his former West Point classmates — NSA director Gordon
Blake — decided to retire, and Cyrus Vance, McNamara's deputy,
asked Carter to take over the Puzzle Palace.

The proposition was appealing to Carter, but it had the taste of
a demotion. "I was in effect stepping down . . . because I was getting
back into the Department of Defense machine."

The NSA, Carter believed, had become an overlooked stepchild,
mindlessly channeling its flood of intercepts to the analysts at Langley. Director after director had come and gone, and though most
were competent in terms of collection and technical knowledge, few
put much emphasis on analysis of the data. Even in general policy
discussions at United States Intelligence Board meetings, some di-

rectors apparently felt intimidated because they lacked the "big picture."

Admiral Frost once described the feeling as "sometimes quite awkward." While the SIGINT and COMSEC subcommittees generally presented no problem, the general meetings frequently did. "In the case of the U.S. Intelligence Board, the posture of the director of NSA is a bit different in the evaluation field than it is in the production field," Frost commented after he left his post, adding that, although this did not deny him a vote in certain areas, it "may well lead to deferring to those responsible for evaluating *all* sources of information."

Carter was well aware of these problems when he was approached by Vance, and had no illusions about the job. He told Vance that he would take the post only under one condition — that he be responsible solely to either Vance or McNamara. The condition was agreeable and, to Carter's relief, freed him from coming under the thumb of Dr. Eugene G. Fubini, the assistant secretary of defense in charge of intelligence. The condition was based on a personal dislike for Fubini and also, apparently, on Carter's distaste for the prospect of having to answer to a group of middle-level bureaucrats after being the number two man in the entire intelligence community for the previous three years.

Finally, on June 1, 1965, Pat Carter, fifty-three, took charge of what he would frequently call "Anagram Inn." Stocky and bald on top, Carter had a infectious sense of humor that could appear at almost any time. Once while deputy director of the CIA he sent a personal letter to a rather reluctant potential recruit with " 'peculiar' types of attributes," declaring: "What I was thinking of was perhaps your availability at various times for varying periods to do special jobs, in some cases out of the country." He added, "It would not, repeat not, involve shooting spies, bugging telephones, and organizing coups or running around bare-ass naked like Mata Hari. You should know we don't do that sort of stuff!!"

Carter was also an avid outdoorsman, and weekends were frequently spent hunting quail and deer in what is without doubt America's most exclusive game preserve: Camp Peary, Virginia. Better known as "the Farm," the several thousand wooded acres outside Williamsburg are the CIA's secret training base for its recruits as well as senior spies. Both while at CIA and later at NSA, Carter enjoyed guest privileges at the Farm (code-named Isolation), where he sported around in a jeep named Baby Doll or hunted for doves while a short distance away future CIA officers learned the latest techniques in sabotage and infiltration. So frequent were Carter's pilgrimages to Isolation that it led his assistant, Henry Knoche (himself deputy director of CIA during the late 1970s), to comment in a letter, "Should you ever opt to run for office or even COS [Chief of Station] at 'the Farm,' please know you'll have my vote."

From the start, Carter knew that the NSA had an image problem, inside as well as outside its confines. He hoped to change the external situation by a more aggressive presence on the USIB as well as the other intelligence boards. Inside, it was a different matter.

Whereas people at the CIA can at least derive some inner satisfaction from an occasional book, article, or news report about their agency, the innominate workers in the Puzzle Palace are sentenced to almost total oblivion by the Agency's enforced policy of anonymity. Because he believed that a modicum of recognition was essential for morale, Carter began inviting senior government officials out to the Agency itself for an NSA version of the pep talk.

Until Carter became director, few officials had even known where the NSA was hidden, let alone visited the location. Even Moscow appeared to know more about Carter and his Agency than most of official Washington. One Soviet magazine dubbed him "Pat — the Electronic Ear" and wrote of "Carter's 'skill' in shady, backstage machinations." The article went on: "They say that the better the secret agent, the less one hears about him. If this is so, Pat Carter should take pride of place over his colleague Helms."

By bringing senior policy-makers out to the Puzzle Palace for a tour around the building and a talk in the Friedman Auditorium, Carter hoped to boost the Agency within the intelligence community and at the same time present his workers for a pat on the back. By far his greatest coup took place on September 26, 1967, when Vice President Hubert H. Humphrey arrived at Gatehouse 1 amid ruffles and flourishes for a tour and address. One of the most senior officials ever to enter the Puzzle Palace (Vice President Bush paid a visit on February 23, 1981), Humphrey told the assembled spooks that, although "most of you labor long and productively with little expectation of public recognition . . . there are people on the highest levels of government who do know what you're doing and appreciate your efforts. I came here to tell you that and to thank you on behalf of a grateful nation."

Others invited to lead NSA in a cheer at one time or another were former CIA director Allen Dulles; James Rowley, director of the Secret Service; Bromley Smith, executive secretary of the National Security Council; James Lay, executive secretary of the USIB; and J. Patrick

Coyne, executive secretary of the President's Foreign Intelligence Advisory Board.

Noticeably excluded from Carter's invitation list was anyone in uniform. Although technically the NSA is "a separately organized agency within the Department of Defense," Carter preferred to put the emphasis on the word *separately* rather than *Defense.* There was a constant tug of war between the military, who wanted the Agency under its total domination, and Carter, who wanted to preserve and increase the Agency's national role.

"You know I was fighting, the whole four years I was there; I was fighting to keep the military from taking over NSA," Lieutenant General Carter later recalled. "I wanted to at least hold the fort on what we had." The military, more specifically, was the Joint Chiefs of Staff. What they wanted for the Agency was more brass and fewer civilians, more tactical and less strategic SIGINT, and stronger lines of control to the military establishment.

Despite an occasional defeat, Carter managed to win his share of the battles with the Pentagon in his efforts to nationalize the NSA. One of his victories was the battle of the seal. Sitting around the big, oblong conference table at the weekly United States Intelligence Board meetings, Carter would occasionally glance up at the seals of the member agencies on the wall and would invariably frown. There was the handsome CIA seal framed at the top by the words CENTRAL INTELLIGENCE AGENCY and at the bottom by UNITED STATES OF AMERICA, then the seal of the AEC, again ATOMIC ENERGY COMMISSION at the top and UNITED STATES OF AMERICA at the bottom. When he came to his own seal, his frown would deepen. It was a masterpiece of symbolism. It bore the Defense Department eagle with wings outstretched, resting on top of a shield containing a lightning bolt crossed by a skeleton key and bisected by three links of chain, together with two more bolts of lightning jutting from each side of the shield. But what bothered Carter so much was not the symbols but the words: NATIONAL SECURITY AGENCY at the top and DEPARTMENT OF DEFENSE at the bottom. It was time for a change.

Back at the Puzzle Palace, one day he called to his office Richard Nachman, NSA's artist-in-residence, and instructed him to come up with three or four different insignias. "I want United States of America, I want National Security Agency, I *don't* want Department of Defense," Carter told Nachman, emphasizing, "I want something unique, not a whole lot of goddamned arrows and lightning bolts and everything coming out of the eagle's rear end."

The design finally selected combined simplicity with elegance. Pictured was a stern, powerful, almost three-dimensional eagle with wings drawn to its side in a proud, protective stance. Grasped tightly in its sharp talons was an ancient key. But most important, the new insignia replaced DEPARTMENT OF DEFENSE with UNITED STATES OF AMERICA, thus symbolically declaring the NSA's independence from the Pentagon.

To Carter the new artwork represented independence, but he realized that to John O'Gara, head of the Pentagon's Office of Special Intelligence, it would represent sedition. Though there was nothing on the books actually forbidding the action, Carter decided his best move would be to present O'Gara with a fait accompli. First the seal went on internal stationery; then, after three months during which there was no reaction, he ordered it on the internal newsletter. Still no reaction. "So then," Carter recalled, "I said we'll go balls out, do the whole damned smear, and we did and the first time it hit over there I got a phone call from O'Gara."

"Who approved it?" O'Gara asked.

"I did," Carter replied.

Carter heard nothing more about it until O'Gara called again a month later and said, "I think you'd better put in a request for permission to use this."

Carter answered, "It's too late, Jack; we've already been using it for six months . . . We've used up all the old correspondence paper, we've used up everything that has the old seal on it, and we've already printed the new seal on everything, all of our paper."

Replied O'Gara: "How much do you have into that?" To which Carter answered, "Oh, probably about a hundred and twenty-five thousand, I imagine, altogether, but . . . if you want to change back, why just send me a directive and a hundred and twenty-five thousand and I'll see that it's done." Carter finished his account with a loud chuckle. "That's the last I heard from him."

Some of Carter's problems with the Pentagon stemmed from the fear of the senior brass that NSA was headed down a one-way road toward total civilian domination — and that Carter was helping to accelerate the pace. Understandably, there were probably few tears shed in some quarters when Carter announced plans to retire, effective August 1, 1969, after more than four years as DIRNSA.

Picked to become the sixth NSA director was Vice Admiral Noel Gayler, a handsome, salt-and-pepper-haired naval aviator. Born on Christmas Day, 1914, in Birmingham, Alabama, Gayler graduated from the Naval Academy and spent the better part of his career as a fighter pilot. During World War II he became the first person in history to be awarded three Navy Cross awards. In 1957 he was selected to be aide to Secretary of the Navy Thomas S. Gates, Jr., and in August 1960, after a tour as commanding officer of the aircraft carrier U.S.S. *Ranger,* he went to London as the naval attaché. After several other fleet and Pentagon assignments, Gayler became deputy director of the Joint Strategic Planning Staff at Offutt Air Force Base in Nebraska, where his duties included selecting the targets for the strategic strike forces. From there he went to NSA.

In many respects, Gayler's background was the exact opposite of Carter's, which may have been the reason he was chosen. Whereas Carter had been influenced by civilian attitudes during his tours at the State Department and the CIA, Gayler's background, with the exception of London, had been uncontaminated by civilian influence. Also, his lack of prior intelligence experience may have been seen as an advantage by those who felt Carter had tried to turn the Puzzle Palace into another CIA. Finally, unlike Carter, who knew he was on his final tour and therefore could not be intimidated very easily, Gayler was young enough to have at least one more assignment, which could earn him a fourth star. He could be expected, then, to toe the line when it came to military versus civilian decisions.

If those were the reasons behind Gayler's selection, it seems that, at least initially, the planners must have been disappointed. In October 1971, more than two years into Gayler's tour at the NSA, the Army Security Agency chief, Major General Charles J. Denholm, told his tale of woe at a classified briefing for the Army vice chief of staff. "At the end of World War II," Denholm told General Bruce Palmer, Jr., "NSA was about 99 percent military. Now at NSA within the top 2000 spaces, you will find that there are perhaps 5 percent military. There are many GG-17s and above. There are about 650 GG-15s and above. There are about thirteen military men among the three services out of about 275 super grades that are running the show. So the military has gradually disappeared from the higher echelons at NSA." Denholm concluded, in the not-for-NSA's-ears briefing, "I fear that in about five years there probably will be no more military at NSA. All the key NSA slots are disappearing."

At the heart of the battle between the military and civilians was control of the budget. Known as the Consolidated Cryptologic Program (CCP), it combines into a single, gargantuan budget submission America's entire SIGINT and COMSEC resources, including, to an extent, targeting. Estimated by some to be as high as $10 billion, it includes everything from the cost of a set of headphones at a desert listening post in Morocco to NSA's CRAY-1 computer in the basement of its Headquarters Building.

By 1969 NSA's cryptologic community had grown to a whopping

ninety-five thousand people, almost five times as many as the CIA personnel. So large was the CCP that even NSA director Carter called it "monstrous." To emphasize the point, one day he called into his office one of the employees from the NSA printing division who happened to moonlight as a jockey at nearby Laurel racetrack. The man stood about four feet six. Carter had the jockey get behind an Agency pushcart, on which was piled the CCP and its supporting documentation, and called in the NSA photographer to snap the picture. The photo, according to Carter, was worth a thousand explanations, especially since "you couldn't tell whether [the jockey] was four feet six or six feet four."

Another time, Carter decided to impress Deputy Secretary of Defense Cyrus Vance with the amount of work that went into the CCP by delivering it to him personally. To make the point, Carter plopped the entire program in the middle of a big, green G.I. blanket, tied the four ends together, and had his two biggest security men put it in a car and accompany him to the Pentagon.

"I just took it into Vance's office, these two big guys carrying it," Carter recalled with a laugh. "Vance said, 'What the hell is that?' and I said, 'I wanted you to see the total effort of the National Security Agency and its operations control services — what they had to do to meet the requirements of your staff as to what we in the cryptologic community are doing.' And I had the guys untie this and here's this massive bundle of paperwork. I just thought he was going to fall out of his chair." The former DIRNSA added, "The damned thing just kept building, building, building!"

By the early 1970s, with the winding-down of the war in Vietnam and the corresponding reduction in defense and intelligence spending, the Puzzle Palace began to feel the pinch. As a result, control of the CCP within NSA became of the utmost importance, since it determined just where and how the dollars would be cut. Although both sides contributed to the final version of the CCP, at some point in the review process it had to come down to one person speaking for both groups.

In what one former NSA official termed a "declaration of war," a strategy paper was submitted to Director Gayler, arguing that that one person should be a civilian. Written by Milton S. Zaslow, then the assistant deputy director for Operations and the second most powerful civilian in the Agency, and Robert J. Hermann, chief of W Group, the intercept unit in the Operations Organization, the paper argued that because it is the civilian leadership at NSA that represents the continuity, it is in a better position to determine the needs of the SIGINT community. Said the former NSA official: "The strategy paper was written saying 'We're the ones who know all about this stuff, we'll control it and we'll tell you what you can have, and we'll see that you get the support you need when you need it.' "

But the military argued that since they were the ones operating the listening posts, the aircraft, and the submarines, they should have final authority over the CCP.

Eventually Gayler had to make the choice — and the decision went to the military. In the view of one of the civilians: "He wasn't a ball player until the end. From what I saw, he [Gayler] was really good for NSA, up until the end, and then I think he sold out; he went along with the military."

On August 24, 1972, after three years as America's chief electronic spy master, Gayler was promoted to full admiral and awarded one of the choicest assignments in the military: Commander-in-Chief, Pacific (CINCPAC), based in Hawaii. Gayler's ascent to four-star rank and promotion to bigger and better things marked a turning point in the history of the NSA that has, thus far, not been reversed. Before Gayler, DIRNSA was generally acknowledged to be a final resting place, a dead-end job from which there was no return. Beginning with Gayler, however, NSA has been a springboard to four-star rank and major military assignments.

Gayler's successor was Lieutenant General Samuel C. Phillips, an officer who had spent the past twelve years in the Air Force space and missile program and, probably, the National Reconnaissance Office, which operates America's fleet of spy satellites. He stayed barely a year. The man chosen to finish out his assignment was his former deputy in Los Angeles, Lieutenant General Lew Allen, Jr.

Allen, tall and professorial-looking, with rimless glasses and a few wisps of fine dark hair across his crown, arrived at the Puzzle Palace on August 15, 1973, following an assignment of only five and a half months with the CIA. Born on September 30, 1925, in Miami, Florida, Allen graduated from West Point and later earned his master's and doctorate in physics from the University of Illinois. His early career was spent mostly in the nuclear weapons field, where he specialized in the military effects of high-altitude nuclear explosions. In December 1961 he was assigned to the Space Technology Office of the Director of Defense Research and Engineering, both within the Office of the Secretary of Defense. From that point, his career was centered in the supersecret National Reconnaissance Office. After serving as assistant to the director of Special Projects, he was named director of Special Projects within the Office of the Secretary of the Air Force as well as deputy commander for Satellite Programs, Space, and Missile Systems Organization. These two positions, in combination, presumably formed a third: operational head of the NRO.

The assignment of the space-age spy, used to keeping as far from the limelight as possible, to the Puzzle Palace seemed to be a matter of the wrong person in the wrong place at the wrong time. Among the hot potatoes Allen found dumped in his lap on taking over the Agency was a legal case being prosecuted by the Justice Department that threatened to expose one of the NSA's most secret operations. On top of that, the greatest part of General Allen's four years as director was spent defending his palace against the onslaught of Executive Branch, Senate, and House intelligence investigations. In the process, he became the first director ever to testify publicly before a congressional hearing.

As bloody as the battles were, however, they were no doubt worth the reward: promotion to four-star general and, after a brief assignment as head of the Air Force Systems Command, control of the entire Air Force as chief of staff.

Succeeding Allen as the occupant of Room 9A197 was Vice Admiral Bobby Ray Inman, who, at forty-six, was the youngest DIRNSA in the Agency's history. Inman is thin, with a boyish face and a gap between his two front teeth. He was born in the dusty Texas town of Rhonesboro and graduated from the University of Texas at the young age of nineteen. After dropping out of law school, he taught in public schools for a year and then, with the draft board hot on his tail, joined the Naval Reserve. Assigned at first to an aircraft carrier for about two years, he planned to do three years in the Navy and then get out, but he happened to be transferred to Paris and then stayed in for an assignment to London as an aide.

Having decided to make the Navy his career, in 1957 Inman applied for naval postgraduate training and received it in the field that was his third choice, Naval Intelligence. "They were obviously desperate," Inman later joked. Course completed, he was assigned as a watch officer for the chief of Naval Operations. "I stood my first watch one early July evening in 1958," he recalled. "A few hours later the coup in Iraq came. Nuri Said and Faisal were overthrown, killed, and dragged through the streets. A few hours later the decision was made to accept a request that we land Marines in Lebanon." It was a dramatic start to what was to become a remarkable career.

In 1961 Inman became an operations intelligence analyst at the Navy Field Operational Intelligence Office at NSA. "I was an analyst for thirty-three months looking at the Soviet Navy as my prime occupation in a complete all-source environment," Inman said of the NSA assignment. "That means no categories of intelligence were restricted in their flow for my consideration, so long as they dealt with the general topic of the Soviet Navy. I was watching them at a time when they rarely sent any ships two hundred miles beyond their waters, and when they did the units frequently broke down and had to be towed back. By the time I left three years later I had seen them develop a permanent presence in the Mediterranean and off West Africa, and they were building a framework for their presence in the Indian Ocean."

Following a tour as an assistant naval attaché in Stockholm, Inman became the chief of the Current Intelligence Branch at Pacific Fleet Headquarters in Hawaii. From here he had a close-up view of such intelligence disasters as the capture of the U.S.S. *Pueblo* and the loss of the EC-121 off Korea. In September 1974 Inman was appointed director of Naval Intelligence and two years later became vice director for Plans, Operations, and Support at the Defense Intelligence Agency.

Inman was the first NSA director after the spate of intelligence investigations, and his approach, therefore, can be described as modified enlightened. Unlike many of his predecessors, Inman was a skilled diplomat when it came to dealing with Congress; he had acquired the talent while suffering through the various congressional investigations as director of Naval Intelligence. His tenure seems to have been divided between trying to ensure an NSA monopoly in the field of cryptography and working out protective legislation for NSA's SIGINT operations with the Senate and House Intelligence Committees.

In his efforts to eliminate outside competition in the cryptographic field, Inman took the unprecedented step of going public in a number of lectures and interviews. Most of these, however, were low-key affairs, intended to attract little attention and to produce even less substance. "I try to do it out of any glare of publicity, because of my conviction that the heads of the intelligence agencies should not be public figures," he told one group. "If they are, if the work force sees their profiles day after day on the front page of the paper, on television, on the weekly magazine cover, and sees them getting all the credit for what they're doing, it's a little hard for them to enforce the discipline of protecting secrecy."

One of the more enlightened reforms during Inman's stay at NSA dealt with a phobia that had plagued the Agency for twenty years: the fear of homosexuality within its ranks.

The worst scandal ever to hit the Agency took place in 1960, when the two analysts, who many believed were homosexuals, defected to Moscow. In the McCarthy-type purge that followed, dozens of NSA employees suspected of homosexuality were forced to resign or were fired. Since then, any hint of homosexual behavior has resulted in either the person's not being hired or, if the fact is revealed later, being forced to resign.

Then, when it was discovered in early July 1980 that a GG-11 linguist, on temporary assignment for some special schooling in Rosslyn, Virginia, was probably a homosexual, the first reaction by the Agency was to lift his clearance and begin an investigation. During questioning, the six-year employee of the Agency candidly admitted that he was, in fact, gay. Several days later a supervisor called him into his office, told him that he would certainly be fired, and strongly urged him to resign.

Instead, the employee contacted Franklin E. Kameny, a gay rights crusader in the Washington, D.C., area. Kameny in turn called the NSA supervisor and advised him that there would be no resignation under any circumstances, that the case would be fought both administratively as well as judicially, and demanded the immediate restoration of the employee's security clearance and his job. In addition, Kameny, a skilled bureaucratic street fighter who spits out his words, told the supervisor that "if the case had to be fought, it would be fought to the accompaniment of a torrent of publicity of our making . . . which would not be of the Agency's liking."

The words struck the right nerve in the reclusive, publicity-shy Agency, and on September 15, NSA general counsel Daniel C. Schwartz telephoned Kameny and asked him to "lower the heat." Schwartz, a former Federal Trade Commission lawyer, said that the case had sparked a high-level reconsideration of Agency policies regarding homosexuality and that it appeared as though the final decision would be favorable.

There the matter rested until the middle of October when Schwartz contacted Kameny, who was acting as counsel for the employee, and asked him to come with his client to the Agency on Wednesday, October 29, to discuss a settlement. Greeted and given badges at Gatehouse 1, the two were escorted by Schwartz up to his ninth-floor office, where they were joined by Assistant General Counsel William Hamel and Deputy Director of Administration Louis J. Bonanni. Schwartz opened the conversation by saying that the Agency had decided to reinstate the employee and restore his clearance. The incredible catch, however, was that the employee would be required to sign a prepared agreement in which he promised that he would tell his family (mother, two sisters, and five brothers) of his homosexuality and that he would not succumb to blackmail.

CONDITIONS FOR RETENTION OF EMPLOYMENT IN A CRITICAL SENSITIVE POSITION AND FOR RETENTION OF ACCESS TO SENSITIVE CRYPTOLOGIC INFORMATION

MEMORANDUM OF AGREEMENT

I, , in recognition of the critical importance of the sensitive cryptologic mission and activities of the National Security Agency to the defense and national security of the United States, understand and accept the need for extraordinary security measures and high standards of personnel security in the Agency. I acknowledge my obligation to comply with the Agency standards of conduct and the Agency policy relating to safeguarding of information regarding Agency organization, activities and functions deemed by the Agency to require protection in the national interest. As conditions of retention in employment in a critical sensitive position in the National Security Agency and to having access to classified information, including Sensitive Cryptologic Information, I agree:

1. I will report to the Director of Security or his representative and not succumb to any attempt to blackmail me or subject myself to coercion or duress because of my sexual preference or behavior related to that preference. I will take steps, within the next 60 days, to reduce my vulnerability to blackmail or extortion by informing the members of my family of my sexual preference. When this has been done, I will inform the Director of Security or his representative.

2. I will not violate the laws of any jurisdiction in which I find myself as they relate to conduct in public.

3. I will not condone, support or participate in any activity not consistent with the Agency's policy on anonymity or which may bring disrepute or notoriety to the Agency.

4. I will agree to cooperate with such investigation as may be required from time to time to update my background investigation or to confirm my compliance with these conditions.

_____

(Date)

_____

WITNESS   (Date)

Both the employee and Kameny agreed to the conditions, but they had one of their own. Because both felt the decision was an important one, they wanted to publicize the case, at least within the gay press. The NSA officials at first objected but later relented, on the condition that the employee's name not be mentioned, an acceptable condition. The agreement signed, the employee was scheduled to return to his job the following Monday.

Once Kameny and the employee left, however, Schwartz, and, presumably, Inman, began having second thoughts about the idea of publicity. About ten o'clock that night, Kameny received a call at his Washington town house from Schwartz, asking him to hold off on the publicity for between thirty and sixty days; he wanted to "mend fences" with others in the government, and he felt it would be better if they learned of it from him rather than from a newspaper story. Specifically, he wanted to consult with the Senate and House Intelligence Committees, some sections of the Defense Department, and the CIA. By then Kameny had already reserved space in *The Blade*, the local gay newspaper, but he nevertheless agreed.

Six weeks later, about the middle of December, Schwartz called Kameny and requested that no publicity at all be released regarding the agreement. In the intervening month and a half, Ronald Wilson Reagan had been elected President, and the political winds had suddenly shifted sharply to the right. "They had read the election returns and they felt that there would be a lot of people who would not be very happy about this," Kameny said of Schwartz's comments. "They were concerned about a backlash from the Moral Majority, and he specifically used the phrase 'Moral Majority,' and asked that we not publicize at all. I said that's a much graver decision to make."

Adding to the drama was the fact that Inman was seriously being considered for the number two job at CIA. Until William J. Casey was named the new CIA boss, Inman had also been in the running for that position. Although Kameny wanted very much to run the gay story, he believed that having Inman at the CIA would further ensure fair treatment for gays throughout the intelligence community, and he did not want to do anything that might hurt the NSA director's chances.

On the other side of the coin, however, according to one NSA official, "there remain people throughout the intelligence community who really do feel deep in their guts that homosexuals are not appropriate people to be given security clearances. There are a lot of that ilk who are upset by the decision." Apparently as a result of these feelings, and perhaps in an attempt to embarrass Inman, anonymous callers began leaking the story to the *Washington Post* shortly after Christmas. Ironically, the first story broke on December 30, the day after the gay NSA employee reported to Security that the terms of the agreement had been complied with and his family had been notified. Security said it would verify the information, but told him that, as far as it was concerned, his job was absolutely safe. Within about two weeks he was promoted to GG-12.

Undoubtedly to the disappointment of the leakers, Inman came through the whole affair like a breath of fresh air. After a month or so of playing hard to get, saying he was going to retire from the Navy to make money in the corporate world, he accepted Casey's offer to become deputy director of the CIA and, along with it, a promotion to full admiral — a rarity for someone who was not an Annapolis graduate. His confirmation hearing was the congressional equivalent of a love-in, with both liberal and conservative senators tripping over each other to heap compliments on him. "If ever there was unanimous consent and enthusiasm, this is it," said Senator Richard Lugar of the Senate Intelligence Committee.

Named on March 10, 1981, to fill Inman's chair in the Puzzle Palace was his old friend Lincoln D. Faurer, a fifty-three-year-old Air Force lieutenant general. A native of Medford, Massachusetts, Faurer graduated from West Point and picked up a master's degree in engineering management from Rensselaer Polytechnic Institute, as well as a second master's, this one in international affairs, from George Washington University. He spent most of his career carrying out intelligence and strategic reconnaissance assignments, commanding RB-47s in the 1950s, and taking over a surveillance squadron on the frigid Aleutian island of Shemya during the late 1960s.

In July 1964 Faurer was assigned to the Defense Intelligence Agency in the Directorate of Scientific and Technical Intelligence, eventually becoming chief of the Space Systems Division in the Missiles and Space Office, until his departure in 1967. Seven years later he returned to the DIA as deputy director for Intelligence and in July 1976 he took over one of the two vice director posts as vice director for Production. That same year, Inman came to DIA and moved into the other office as vice director for Plans, Operations, and Support. Under this arrangement, Faurer was responsible for current intelligence, estimates, scientific and technical intelligence, and research. Inman, on the other hand, ran the Defense Intelligence School, the collection operations, the Defense Attaché System, and counterintelligence and security.

In the summer of 1977, when Inman was transferred to the Puzzle

Palace, Faurer was sent to Germany as chief of intelligence for the U.S. European Command, and two years later, on receiving his third star, became deputy chairman of NATO's Military Committee in Brussels.

Unlike Inman, Faurer has determined to keep out of the spotlight and apparently has begun rebuilding the Agency's wall of anonymity.

•

Speaking of his role as director of NSA, General Marshall Carter once said, "I sure as hell was no codebreaker." The comment was not intended as a put-down but simply a statement of fact. DIRNSAs, as can be readily seen by their backgrounds, are not selected to be codebreakers or codemakers but senior bureaucratic managers who are supposed to balance budgets, settle squabbles, crack whips, pat backs, extinguish fires, and coordinate the Agency's relations with the Executive Branch, Congress, and numerous policy boards. The day-to-day running of the Puzzle Palace is left to the deputy director, who is traditionally the senior cryptologist in the United States government.

The first vice director was Rear Admiral Joseph Numa Wenger, who was named deputy director of the Armed Forces Security Agency in 1948. He stayed on after the agency became the NSA. In the fall of 1953, he was followed by Brigadier General John B. Ackerman, who came from the Air Force Directorate of Intelligence. His successor was General John Samford, who served only six months in 1956 before becoming DIRNSA. Samford was the last man to hold the vice director title and the last of the number two men to come from the military.

The first to hold the title deputy director, or D/DIRNSA, was Joseph H. Ream, a Yale man and a Wall Street lawyer who became an executive vice president of CBS. When Ream left the NSA to return to CBS, after less than a year, he kept silent about his association.

Ream was the last of the outsiders to fill the job. His successor was an old SIGINT hand, Dr. Howard Theodore Engstrom, who had established himself in NSA Research and Development as a deputy director in charge of that branch. Engstrom, who was fifty-five at the time, had rather more professional background than most of his predecessors. During World War II he had been a captain in the Navy SIGINT organization, and after his discharge he had helped found Engineering Research Associates. That company specialized in the development of advanced cryptologic equipment, including Atlas, the SIGINT community's first computer. When E.R.A. was bought out by Remington Rand in 1952, Engstrom became a Remington Rand vice president. It was another short tenure. After ten months in the deputy director job, Engstrom returned to Remington Rand.

His exit, however, was the last of the fast turnovers, and it opened the way for what can only be described as the reign of Dr. Louis Tordella, who ran the Puzzle Palace for the next sixteen years as seven DIRNSA appointees came and went. Never before or since has any one person held so much power for so long a time within the American intelligence community. Yet even within that community, he managed to remain a man hidden in shadows.

Louis William Tordella was born on May Day, 1911, in the small Indiana town of Garrett. His university was Loyola in Chicago, where he excelled in math and chemistry, took a master's degree, and became a member of the faculty after getting his doctorate at the University of Illinois. When he joined the Navy in 1942, just after Pearl Harbor, he was assigned to cryptologic duties, and he ended the war as Lieutenant Commander Tordella, commanding officer of the Navy Security Group listening post on Skaggs Island, California. It was a short step to a Navy Department job in Washington, where Tordella helped develop operational policy for the Armed Forces Security Agency and, later, blueprints for the future NSA.

From the very beginning, Tordella was the golden boy of the Puzzle Palace. He was the first employee selected to attend the National War College in 1953–1954. The next year, he represented NSA as senior liaison officer with the Office of the Secretary of Defense. In August 1958, Tordella was appointed to succeed Engstrom in the highest civilian job in NSA. That year he was forty-seven, and he was the youngest NSA deputy director to date.

Undoubtedly one of Tordella's greatest contributions to the Agency was a massive research and development program to advance the computer capabilities of both SIGINT and COMSEC. When Tordella cut the ceremonial ribbon on Harvest in 1962, he had brought to NSA what was then "the world's largest computing system."

Another major contribution was simply continuity. As a parade of directors came and went, serving an NSA tour en route to retirement or another assignment, Tordella stayed on, a familiar presence, reassuring the British, Canadians, and other cooperating governments that the fragile, supersensitive relations between NSA and its foreign counterparts would not be disrupted. General Carter later remarked about his D/DIRNSA that "to [Tordella], the director was a transient," and Tordella's main worry was "Let's don't let him screw up the operation." (Despite the irony, Carter's respect was deep and real; before he retired as director, he secretly nominated Tordella to succeed him.)

When Tordella retired in 1974, he was laden with honors. CIA director William Colby presented him with the CIA's Distinguished Intelligence Medal, and Secretary of Defense James Schlesinger awarded him the highest intelligence decoration of all, the National Security Medal. After his retirement, he stayed on as a sort of cryptologist emeritus and consultant.

Following Tordella as D/DIRNSA was Benson K. Buffham, a man who has spent most of his professional life as a communications intelligence specialist. Buffham lasted four years in the job, and his successor, Robert E. Drake — another professional who had worked his way up through the ranks — served for two.

By this time, the appointment of able and seasoned professionals from within the Agency had become the established tradition, and the next appointee altered the tradition in one way only. She is Ann Z. Caracristi, who, at fifty-nine, had spent most of her adult years as a top SIGINT analyst and manager. She got a job with the Army Security Agency in 1942, almost immediately after graduating from Russell Sage College. She spent the war attacking Japanese cryptographic systems, and, after a brief postwar detour in journalism, she returned to cryptography in ASA. She moved steadily up the ladder in ASA and later NSA. In 1959, she was named chief of the Office of SIGINT Research, and from 1972 to 1975 served as deputy chief of A Group, the major SIGINT analysis group. She was its chief until 1980, when she was appointed D/DIRNSA by Director Inman.

Like many of the other successful managers in NSA, Caracristi is thoroughly dedicated to her profession. She is single and lives alone in a bright red house in the heart of Washington's elegant Georgetown section. In her turquoise Dodge Omni, she commutes the twenty miles north to Fort Meade each morning. Caracristi is one of the very few women to attain high rank in the defense establishment — as witnessed by the fact that, in 1975, she was the first woman in the history of NSA to win promotion to the top rank of GG-18 (the NSA equivalent of the civil service grade of GS-18), and only the second in the entire Defense Department to reach the top of the ladder.

Below the level of deputy director, NSA's organizational structure has always been one of the Agency's closest-guarded secrets. Unlike the CIA, which has never hidden most of its upper framework, the NSA quietly arranged to have Congress pass, in 1959, a statute forever sealing this information under a blanket of secrecy. Section 6 of Public Law 86–36 provides: "Nothing in this Act or any other law . . . shall be construed to require the disclosure of the organization or any function of the National Security Agency, of any information with respect to the activities thereof, or of the names, titles, salaries, or number of the persons employed by such Agency." Thus, under the little-known law, NSA has the unusual authority virtually to deny its own existence.

Basically, the NSA is made up of ten "key components": four primarily operational "organizations," five staff and support activities, and one training unit.

Office of Signals Intelligence Operations (DDO): In the NSA's pecking order, this office, under the deputy director for Operations, has always been looked on as first among equals. Formerly known as the Office of Production, or simply PROD, it has a legion of eavesdroppers, codebreakers, linguists, traffic and signals analysts who constitute the largest single organization within the Puzzle Palace. At the helm of PROD from 1963 to 1968, first as deputy assistant director and later as assistant director, was Oliver R. Kirby, a chunky, crew-cut, NSA veteran who was given the Pentagon's highest civilian award in 1963, the Distinguished Civilian Service Award. In the spring of 1968, Kirby succumbed to the temptations of private industry and went to work for LTV Electrosystems, Incorporated, in Greenville, Texas, as vice president of advanced planning, a position he holds today with the successor company, E Systems, apparently one of the NSA's major suppliers of SIGINT hardware. It is E Systems, for example, along with IBM, that reportedly built the computers for NSA's massive listening post at Pine Gap, Australia, in the late 1960s.

Taking Kirby's place was Air Force Major General John E. Morrison, Jr., one of the Agency's most vivacious public speakers. Carter had picked the general for the post primarily to lessen the pressure from the Joint Chiefs and the military, who wanted to fill some of the top slots with a few of their own people. Morrison headed PROD until March of 1973, when he retired from the Air Force after thirty-two years of service.

Retired along with Morrison was the title of assistant director for Production. The successor, Army Major General Herbert E. Wolff, became the first deputy director for Operations (DDO). Known as a "wheels-up, ballsy character, a tough-ass," who "made no bones about it to anyone," Wolff decorated his office wall with a chrome-plated machine gun and, according to one former official, "ate civilians alive." His assignment seems to have been the result of a military victory in a top-level power struggle with the civilians. When Wolff arrived, he reportedly locked the door that connected his office and that of his civilian assistant DDO, Milton Zaslow.

In July 1975, to the dismay of the generals, DDO reverted back to civilian control, when Director Lew Allen, Jr., appointed Robert Drake to the post. Three years later, on Drake's elevation to deputy director of the entire agency, DDO was again handed back to the military when Army Major General George L. McFadden, Jr., took over the post. McFadden had served as deputy director for Field Management and Evaluation (DDF) for the previous three years. As head of this office, which oversaw the operations of the worldwide listening posts, McFadden was the nominal deputy chief of the mostly paper Central Security Service, NSA's military alter ego. (The DDF position was eliminated in 1980, and some of its functions were assigned to DDO and several other organizations.)

Replacing McFadden in August 1979 was Rear Admiral Henry J. Davis, Jr., USN, the first naval officer to head the office since the early 1960s, when Rear Admiral Jefferson R. Dennis, after whom one of the streets of SIGINT City is named, was chief of PROD. As is required, his deputy is a civilian, Robert E. Rich, an old hand at the Agency who started out with the AFSA in 1950. Rich had previously served in Room 2A256 of the Pentagon as NSA's representative to the Department of Defense.

DDO encompasses the entire spectrum of signals intelligence, from intercept to cryptanalysis, traffic analysis to analysis of cleartext, high-level diplomatic systems to low-level radiotelephone. Its brief covers the analysis of systems belonging to friend as well as foe, democracies as well as dictatorships, microcountries as well as superpowers. It is the Black Chamber's Black Chamber.

Soon after he became director, General Canine split PROD into four operational divisions and three support divisions. ADVA (advanced Soviet) concentrated on high-level Soviet cipher problems and specialized mostly in developing new methods of attack. GENS (general Soviet), on the other hand, was primarily responsible for the lower- and medium-level systems and concentrated on exploitation. The third operational division was ACOM (Asian Communist), which studied the systems of Korea, China, and the rest of Communist Asia. Finally, there was ALLO (all others), which analyzed the systems of all other areas of the world, including those of America's allies and neutral nations. ALLO-34, for example, was responsible for Middle East traffic analysis.

Computer support for the four codebreaking sections was provided by the programmers and computer experts of MPRO (machine processing), and TCOM (telecommunications) relayed the worldwide traffic. The final division, Collection, was responsible for managing the far-flung intercept network.

After the two analysts defected to Moscow in 1960, PROD was reorganized into three large SIGINT analytical groups and two support groups. As before, the three codebreaking groups were set up along geographical lines, and each handled all the analysis of its particular target. The groups were themselves divided, in descending order, into offices, divisions, and branches.

With the shake-up, ADVA and GENS were combined into A Group, largest of the three, which was now responsible for all analysis of the Soviet Union and its satellite countries. Named chief of A Group was Arthur J. Levenson, the former chief of ADVA, who would later leave the Puzzle Palace, apparently, for IBM. From 1975 to 1980, when she became the Agency's deputy director, Ann Caracristi was the top Russian codebreaker.

B Group took over from ACOM responsibility for China, Korea, Vietnam, and the rest of Communist Asia. Named chief was Milton Zaslow, a long-time Agency veteran and a specialist in Chinese.

Francis A. (Frank) Raven, the former chief of GENS, headed the final operational group, G Group, made up of the former ALLO. Responsible for attacking the traffic of much of the Third World, G Group during the 1960s and 1970s also began analyzing international telecommunications to and from the United States. By 1972 G Group had grown to 1244 civilian employees (608 female and 636 male) and about 600 military, scattered among five offices, four divisions, and fourteen branches.

In terms of support, MPRO became C Group, and the Collection Division became W Group, responsible for coordination and management of all intercept operations.* TCOM remained the same until about 1976, when it was merged with C Group to become the Office of Telecommunications and Computer Services.

In addition to the groups, DDO also has a number of staff components, among the most important of which is PO5, the Agency's consumer staff liaison, which is NSA's point of contact for all other federal intelligence agencies. Until she retired in February 1976, after thirty-three years in the business, the position was held by Juanita M. Moody. Through her office passed the watch lists and other SIGINT requests from the CIA, the DIA (Defense Intelligence Agency), the FBI, and the other intelligence community members. And it is through this office that the collected intercepts are transmitted to the community.

* At one time all electronics intelligence was concentrated in a separate organization, K Group. Later, K Group was merged with W Group. (Interview with Raymond T. Tate, former deputy director for COMSEC.)

PO4 is the DDO staff component responsible for the formulation of operational policy and plans.

Swelling DDO's ranks are vast numbers of engineers, scientists, and mathematicians engaged in the esoteric craft of signals analysis, itself composed of four of the blacker arts: communications signals analysis, the study of any emission that could transmit information; electronic signals analysis, primarily ELINT (electronics intelligence) and RADINT (radar intelligence); telemetry analysis; and signals conversion, which attempts to locate signals hidden by such techniques as spectrum-spreading, where the signal virtually disappears into the noise, or frequency-hopping, where the signal jumps from frequency to frequency at rapid-fire speed.

Once the elusive signal has been netted, classified, and reconstructed, it then goes, if encrypted, to the modern Merlins of DDO's cryptanalytic division. There, where analysts once bent over stacks of quarter-inch graph paper, today they coordinate their paper and colored pencils with their desk-mounted computer terminals, using both the old and new tools of the trade to ransack the upper reaches of theoretical mathematics in search of a common link between yesterday's message and today's.

Should the cryppies run short on sorcery, the traffic analysts may still be able to salvage a sizable chunk of intelligence. Working with only the "externals" of the message — where it came from, its apparent destination, the priority, grade of cipher system used, as well as the frequency and volume of other messages — the traffic analysts can often supply the missing piece of a much larger puzzle. A sharp increase in traffic to and from Tyuratam, for example, may indicate an imminent space launch; a sudden switch into a high-grade cipher system or unusual jump in priority by units stationed along the border with Afghanistan may mean an outbreak of hostilities. But some patterns are not so easy to recognize; they require the study of tremendous amounts of communications data, as well as of related information, if any relationship between them is to be discerned.

Not all SIGINT, however, is wrapped in code or hidden in the radio spectrum. Much of the traffic flowing into the Puzzle Palace consists of unencrypted voice and text from telephone, cable, and telex. To turn about fifty foreign languages into English the NSA employs, according to Raymond Theodore Tate, former deputy director for COMSEC, "the largest single population of foreign-language experts in the United States, and one of the largest in the world outside the Soviet Union."

In addition to both standard and scientific translation of most languages and most dialects, a special breed of language expert known as a crypto-linguist attacks secure voice systems and develops such advanced tools as computer-assisted voice translation. Because the Agency maintains that it constantly strives to stay at least five years ahead of the state of the art, there is every reason to believe that it has developed, or at least is close to perfecting, the ultimate computer, one that can listen to clear voice and automatically translate or transcribe. For years the NSA has used a form of machine translation known as "automatic look-up," which identifies words in a text, locates the meaning in the target language, and prints out the definition. The device can also be used to flag target words, including those on a watch list, or to count the frequency of particular words or characters in a text as an aid to breaking a cryptographic system.

Office of Communications Security (COMSEC): "The Soviets today have the capability to intercept and locate the sources of United States communications frequencies. They maintain the largest signal intelligence establishment in the world . . . operating hundreds of intercept, processing, and analysis facilities, with heavy exploitation of unsecured voice communications." So reported Assistant Secretary of Defense Gerald P. Dinneen in an eye-opening admission before the House Appropriations Committee. Hoping to limit the USSR's take, or at least render it useless, are the cryptographers of COMSEC.

The ability of foreign nations to exploit American communications through SIGINT is not limited to the sophisticated eavesdroppers of the Soviet Union, however. The Vietnam War demonstrated to NSA the ease with which even an electronically unsophisticated nation could take advantage of unprotected communications. Former COMSEC chief Tate said:

We have ample evidence that the North Vietnamese and the Vietcong effectively evaded air and artillery strikes because of advance information gained through monitoring unsecured United States and Allied communications. In addition, we have evidence that in a significant number of cases the enemy was able to exploit our communications to their advantage in carrying out operations against United States and Allied forces. From prisoners of war, defectors, and captured materials, it was obvious that the North Vietnamese and Vietcong, having made only modest investments in relatively unsophisticated monitoring equipments, achieved a valuable COMINT capability against unencrypted voice communications.

Better known within the walls of the Puzzle Palace as the S Organization, or simply COMSEC, NSA's Office of Communications Security provides the methods, principles, and equipment to protect the entire panoply of classified U.S. communications, including command and control, voice, data, teletype, and telemetry; it also prescribes the way in which the systems are to be used. This encompasses everything from the scrambler phone in the President's limousine to the banks of chattering crypto machines in the State Department's sixth-floor code room — and a great deal in between.

National COMSEC policy is formulated by the National Security Council's highly secretive United States Communications Security Committee. Until recently, it was known as the U.S. Communications Security Board and had as its executive secretary Robert E. Sears,* chief of NSA's Policy and Foreign Relations Staff. The purpose of the committee is to establish national COMSEC objectives, develop standards for the other departments and agencies of the federal government, and establish policies for COMSEC cooperation with foreign governments and such organizations as NATO. Policies established by the COMSEC Committee are passed on to the Secretary of Defense, who acts as the federal government's executive agent for COMSEC, and are then transmitted to NSA.

Making up the COMSEC Committee are the Secretary of Defense, the Secretary of State, all the service secretaries, and the Secretaries of Commerce, Treasury, and the Attorney General. The chairman is normally the Pentagon's deputy under secretary of defense for command, control, communications, and intelligence (C³I). In 1982 the post was held by Donald C. Latham, a former deputy chief of NSA's Office of Microwave Space and Mobile Systems. But the full committee, at least when it was the COMSEC Board, met no more than once a year, and then only to ratify the decisions of various working groups. And these working groups were dominated by the executive secretary — always from the NSA. Thus, the board was little more than an extension of the Puzzle Palace.

Should an issue fail to be resolved by the full board, it then, as with the old U.S. COMINT Board, would go up to a special committee made up of the Secretary of Defense and the Secretary of State. If they could not agree, then it would go to the President for a decision. Thus far, no decision has ever reached that level, and only two have ever gone up to the special committee. The last time was in 1975, when, strangely, the NSA took the issue directly to the special commit-

---

* Sears was awarded the NSA Exceptional Civilian Service Award on July 24, 1979, for his service as chief of the NSA Policy and Foreign Relations Staff and as executive secretary of the United States Communications Security Board. He was cited for "his outstanding personal dedication, initiative, leadership and professional competence which have enabled the Department of Defense to establish and carry on Communications Security relationships throughout the world."

tee without ever notifying the board, because it felt the subject was too sensitive even for them. Hand-carried by the deputy director for COMSEC, Ray Tate, the supersensitive matter was approved by Secretary of State Henry A. Kissinger.

The process by which NSA's S Organization turns out its crypto equipment is both long and expensive. The first step is an in-depth study of the new communications system for which the crypto protection is requested. It concentrates particularly on the system's potential vulnerability to interception. Once the weaknesses have been identified, engineers go to work, either adapting an existing crypto machine or designing an entirely new device to overcome them. The speed at which a new cryptographic system is developed depends on priorities set, for the most part, by the U.S. COMSEC Committee.

Despite this drawn-out procedure, which may take years and cost tens of millions of dollars, the S Organization occasionally turns out a cryptographic lemon. One such occasion came to light when a subcommittee of the House Appropriations Committee discovered millions of dollars' worth of the NSA's most advanced crypto gear stashed away unused in Air Force bunkers, collecting dust and rust. The equipment, known as the KY-28, was rushed into production during the Vietnam War to give fighter pilots a secure means of conducting close air-support operation. To the pilots, however, the black boxes represented at the least a nuisance and at worst a hazard, because there was a required synchronization time between the time a transmission was attempted and the time it was actually received. Said one Air Force general: "A fighter pilot does not like to wait that long when he is in a very heated kind of combat situation . . . You can put anything in a fighter airplane you want, and if you cannot convince the fighter pilot that it will satisfy his needs, he is not going to use it."

So after upward of $110 million was spent to modify twenty-two hundred fighter aircraft, the black boxes went to the bunkers, and the engineers at NSA went back to the drawing boards.

Both the codemaking COMSEC and the codebreaking DDO are supposedly involved in new code systems. All codes devised by COMSEC are submitted to DDO so that they can be tested for their resistance to cryptanalytic attack. "We operated on the alleged mystique that anything COMSEC did was ground through the operational side of the cryptologic branch to see if they could get into it," said former NSA director Carter. Whether testing was fact or fancy, however, even Carter himself was not quite sure. "That was what we were supposed to do; that was what we said we were doing," but, he added, "I wasn't technically oriented enough to know whether in fact we did do it."

Deputy director for COMSEC from 1973 to 1978 was Ray Tate, an Alabama native who served as a combat air crewman on B-24s and B-17s during World War II. After a stint with the Electronics Division at the Air Proving Ground Command in Orlando, Florida, Tate again strapped on his crash helmet and flew with the Navy during the Korean War. In 1954 Tate joined the NSA as an electronics engineer in the S Organization and later earned his B.S. and M.S. degrees. After working in PROD on special collection, processing, and signals analysis programs, he took over the number two spot in COMSEC in September 1972. Ten months later he was promoted to GG-18 and named to the top COMSEC position. He retired from the Agency in January 1978 at the age of fifty-three.

Office of Research and Engineering: Turning the art of eavesdropping into a science is the goal of the third of NSA's original "big three" organizations. From their laboratories and blackboard-lined offices the scientists and engineers of R and E constantly push at the limits of possibility in their development of technological wonders ranging from electronic components so small that it takes a scanning electron microscope to perform diagnostic tests on them, to designing a dish-shaped antenna, large enough to hold two football fields end to end, in order better to hear the Russians. One of the innovative ways that R and E (named the Office of Research and Development in the early 1960s) proposed to intercept very directional microwave transmissions was to have silvery metallic barium salts shot into the sky by rockets. The signals would then bounce off the salt layer and return to a location where they could be intercepted.

Originally, R and E was divided into three divisions. REMP (for research, engineering, mathematics, physics) specialized in broad, across-the-board cryptanalytic problems, rather than attacking the systems of any one particular nation.

Scientists and mathematicians in REMP would concentrate on the upper reaches of theoretical statistics and mathematics for codebreaking possibilities. REMP later became the Mathematical Research Techniques Division.

RADE (for research and development), on the other hand, directed its efforts toward building increasingly sophisticated intercept and signals analysis hardware. This included new forms of magnetic tapes, each of which could hold hundreds of intercepted microwave communications channels. RADE was later renamed the Intercept Equipment

Division and was at one time headed by Arthur H. Hausman, who left the Puzzle Palace in 1960, after twelve years, to lend his knowledge of magnetic tapes to the giant Ampex Tape Company, as vice president for research. In 1971 he was named president and chief executive officer.

STED (for standard technical equipment development) was the section that would assist COMSEC in the research and development of advanced cryptographic equipment. It later became the Cryptographic Equipment Division and was headed by Howard Barlow, who later went on to head NSA's COMSEC Organization from the late 1960s until the appointment of Ray Tate in 1973.

The reorganization that resulted in the name changes also added a new section, the Computer Techniques Division, in which all the computer research was carried out.

Assistant director for Research and Development for the better part of a decade was Mitford M. Mathews, Jr., a soft-spoken man in his forties who had the ability to translate the most complex theory into its simplest form — a quality especially appreciated by General Carter. "I could talk to him and understand just what he meant," the former director recalled. "Talk to another guy and they were so far over my head and out of my competence to understand that sometimes I got the idea they were confusing me on purpose."

Ironically, though he was in charge of an army of Ph.D.s, Mathews himself had but a bachelor's degree, earned in 1943 from the University of Illinois. Added to this, however, were two decades of experience, starting with his assignment to the R and D Division of the Signal Intelligence Service in the 1940s, extending through service with the Armed Forces Security Agency and ten years with NSA. He succeeded Dr. Solomon Kullback (one of Friedman's original trio of recruits back in 1931) as head of R and D. In May of 1966, Mit Mathews was awarded the Pentagon's Distinguished Civilian Service Award and a year later won NSA's own highest honor, the Exceptional Civilian Service Award. His career ended tragically on January 18, 1971, when, at forty-eight, he died suddenly while on a business trip in Rochester, New York.

Taking over as deputy director for Research and Engineering was Howard E. Rosenblum, who in January 1978 replaced Ray Tate as head of COMSEC. Rosenblum was succeeded that month by James V. Boone.

Office of Telecommunications and Computer Services: Whereas most government offices or large corporations measure in square feet the space taken up by their computers, NSA measures it in acres. "I had five and a half acres of computers when I was there," said General Carter. "We didn't count them by numbers; it was five and a half acres." Even though the emphasis today is on increased capacity and decreased size, one NSA employee, when recently told the statistic, commented, "It's double that today."

Resting today in the cavernous subterranean expanses below the National Security Agency's Headquarters-Operations Building is probably the greatest concentration of computers the world has ever known. It is a land where computers literally talk back and forth to each other and where, using what is known as "brute force," they are able to spit out solutions to complex statistical problems in nanoseconds rather than the decades it once might have taken.

NSA, like its predecessors, has been a silent partner in America's computer growth from the very beginning, yet because of what one NSA computer expert called its "policy of anonymity," NSA's role has been almost totally hidden. When the Association for Computing Machinery sponsored an observance in honor of the twenty-fifth anniversary of its founding, NSA simply observed in silence. Likewise, when the "pioneers" gathered at COMPCON-76, the quarter-century anniversary meeting of the Institute of Electrical and Electronic Engineers' Computer Society, NSA again exhibited an advanced case of shyness. Apparently, the fact that America uses computers in its SIGINT and COMSEC activities is still a national secret.

Despite the anonymity, NSA's role in computer development has been enormous. As far back as the mid-1930s, the Army and Navy SIGINT organizations were using complex machinery in both cryptanalysis and cryptography. The machines, using high-speed digital circuits and a punched-card format, were the forerunners of the modern computer. The major problem with them, however, was their overspecialization. A number of the expensive devices were built to attack a specific code or system, so if the system was changed or abandoned, the machine was of little value.

During World War II the Naval Security Group contracted with Eastman Kodak, National Cash Register, and several other firms to design and build these machines. The Signal Security Agency, on the other hand, worked closely with Bell Laboratories. Another major contractor during the war was IBM, which built a specialized attachment for its IBM tabulator, thereby increasing the power of the standard punched-card systems by several magnitudes.

After the war, both the Army and Navy sought to continue the development of sophisticated cryptologic equipment, but with no war to fight, it found outside contractors less willing to undertake the research. The rigorous security clearances, oppressive physical security, and the limited usefulness of the equipment in the marketplace caused many companies to shy away from the field. Because of this, a group of former Navy officers, familiar with cryptography and SIGINT, banded together to form Engineering Research Associates, Incorporated, which took on some of the Naval Security Group's most complex assignments.

At about the same time, a group of engineers and mathematicians at the University of Pennsylvania's Moore School of Electrical Engineering completed an electronic marvel named ENIAC (for electronic numerical integrator computer), and thus gave birth to the computer era. ENIAC was an ungainly giant whose body was a good deal larger than its brain. Its total storage capacity was only twenty numbers, yet its eighteen thousand electron tubes took up the better part of a room thirty feet by fifty.

The development of ENIAC led to a series of lectures on the theory of computers presented at the Moore School and sponsored jointly by the Office of Naval Research and the Army's Ordinance Department. Among those attending the lectures, given between July 8 and August 31, 1946, was Lieutenant Commander James T. Pendergrass, of the Naval Security Group, whose assignment was to assess the potential of computers in the fields of cryptography and signals intelligence. Pendergrass came away from the lectures excited. Computers appeared to offer the flexibility that machines lacked. Where many of the machines were designed to handle one particular problem, such as breaking one foreign crypto system, computers could handle a whole range of problems.

Soon after Pendergrass returned with his favorable report, negotiations began between the Security Group and Engineering Research Associates for the formation of Task 13 and the design and construction of the SIGINT community's first computer, Atlas. Named after the mental giant in the comic strip "Barnaby," Atlas lived up to its namesake. By the time it was delivered to the Security Group in December 1950, Atlas had an impressive capacity of 16,384 words and became the first parallel electronic computer in the United States with a drum memory. A second, identical computer was delivered to NSA in March 1953.

About the time ERA was putting the final touches on Atlas, engineers of the Army Security Agency were busy building their own codebusting computer. Nicknamed Abner, the machine was completed in April 1952 and became the most sophisticated computer of its time. One could enter or extract information from Abner not only with the standard key-punched computer card but also with punched paper tape, magnetic tape, parallel printer, typewriter, or console.

One of the most costly as well as far-reaching research programs ever undertaken by NSA was born not on a chalk-covered blackboard in R and E but at a cocktail party in July 1956. Over cocktails, several high-level NSA equipment planners began discussing with Director Canine one of the Agency's perennial problems: the race between the insatiable requirements of the codebreakers for new and better ways to attack ever-increasing volumes of data and the efforts of NSA engineers to design and build bigger and faster computers to meet these needs. No matter how powerful the new equipment, the engineers never seemed to catch up.

At the time, a new computer known as Harvest was being designed to fill such requirements with an estimated hundredfold improvement over the best current computers, but a completion date was still several years away. Exasperated by the situation, Canine exploded: "Dammit, I want you fellows to get the jump on those guys! Build me a *thousand-megacycle* machine! I'll get the money!" Within the next few days, Project Lightning was under way, with a budget of $25 million for a five-year effort to develop "thousand-megacycle electronics."

Backed by President Eisenhower, Lightning research began in June 1957. Contractors on the project, believed to be the largest government-supported computer research program in history, included Sperry Rand, RCA, IBM, Philco, General Electric, MIT, University of Kansas, and Ohio State. Though the primary goal of the project was to increase circuitry capability by 1000 percent, the end results in actuality went even further, extending the state of the art of computer science beyond any expectations.

One of the most rewarding by-products of Lightning was the boost it gave to the development of NSA's mammoth Harvest complex. In 1955 IBM began planning its most ambitious computer, the Stretch. So huge was Stretch that IBM designers believed the market contained only two possible customers: the NSA and the Atomic Energy Commission. The AEC signed up for the computer primarily because of its advantages in high-speed multiplication, but NSA, looking for more flexibility as well as the manipulation of great volumes of data, sent the engineers back to the drawing board for a more customized version. In April 1958 a final design was approved, and in February 1962 the Puzzle Palace took delivery of its long-awaited Stretch, now modified and considerably faster.

Once in place as the heart, or, more appropriately, brain, of NSA's enormous Harvest complex, even Stretch began to look somewhat diminutive. Attached was a variety of unusual, complex accessories that more than doubled the computer's original size. One was a unit known as Tractor, which was capable of automatically locating desired information from a magnetic-tape library of 160 cartridges, then mounting, positioning, and threading the correct tape, and transferring the information at a mind-boggling 1,128,000 characters per second. Whereas most magnetic tape contained a hundred bits to the inch, NSA managed to pack three thousand in the same space, and then whisk them past the reading heads at 235 inches per second. So successful was Harvest that NSA used it for the next fourteen years, finally switching to a more advanced system only in 1976.

Today the NSA's enormous basement, which stretches for city blocks below the Headquarters-Operations Building, undoubtedly holds the largest and most advanced computer operation in the world. Like that of a human, NSA's brain is divided into right and left hemispheres, code-named Carillon and Loadstone. Carillon, at one time made up of IBM 360s, today consists of four enormous IBM 3033s linked together and attached to three IBM 22,000-line-per-minute page-printers.

Even more powerful, however, is Loadstone. Dominating the center of a yellow-walled, gold-carpeted hall of computers, front-end interfaces, and mass storage units, is a decorative 4½-foot-wide, 6½-foot-tall hollow semicircle of narrow gold and deep green panels surrounded by a black, vinyl-upholstered bench-type seat. It appears to be an ideal resting place for lunch or a midmorning coffee break. It is, however, probably the world's fastest, most powerful, and most expensive computer.

Built by Cray Research of Mendota Heights, Minnesota, the $15 million CRAY-1 may be the ultimate testimony to the old proposition that looks are deceiving. Housed within what one wag once called "the world's most expensive love seat" are more than 200,000 integrated circuits, each the size of a thumbnail, thirty-four hundred printed circuit boards, and sixty miles of wire. So compact is the five-ton, seventy-square-foot unit that enough heat is generated per cubic inch to reduce the machine to a molten mass in seconds were it not for a unique Freon cooling system using vertical aluminum and stainless steel cooling bars that line the wall of the computer chassis.

The supercomputer is the brainchild of Seymour Cray, an electrical engineer who began his career by building codebreaking machines in the early 1950s with Engineering Research Associates, then headed by future NSA research chief and deputy director Howard Engstrom. Cray's dream was to build a number-cruncher capable of 150 to 200 million calculations per second. It would have between twenty and a hundred times the capacity of current general-purpose computers — or the equivalent of half a dozen IBM 370/195s.

In the spring of 1976 the first CRAY-1 rolled out of the firm's production plant in Chippewa Falls, Minnesota, and, apparently, directly into the basement of the Puzzle Palace. A second was quietly delivered to NSA's think tank, the Communications Research Division of the Institute for Defense Analysis at Princeton University.

With a random access semiconductor memory capable of transferring up to 320 million words per second, or the equivalent of about twenty-five hundred 300-page books, NSA could not have been disappointed. And when it was hooked up to the computer's specialized input-output subsystem, the machine could accommodate up to forty-eight disk storage units, which could hold a total of almost 30 billion words, each no farther away than eighty millionths of a second.

On top of this, NSA in 1983 plans to put into operation secretly an enormous worldwide computer network code-named Platform, which will tie together fifty-two separate computer systems used throughout the world. Focal point, or "host environment," for the massive network will be NSA headquarters at Fort Meade. Among those included in Platform will be the British SIGINT organization, GCHQ.

But even with the power of the CRAY-1, the Puzzle Palace is still searching for more speed, more power, and more memory capacity with such concepts as digital applications of Josephson Junction technology, optical logic elements, magnetic bubbles, and laser recording. Currently, NSA is conducting advanced research in analog optical computing technology as well as both light-sound interaction devices and charge-transfer devices for achieving more than one quadrillion (or 1,000,000,000,000,000) multiplications per second.

Until the mid-1970s, NSA's telecommunications and computer services were handled by two separate organizations. The Agency's communications functions were centralized within the Office of Telecommunications, but computer services were somewhat decentralized within the various organizations. The largest computer capability was controlled by DDO's C Group, which ran Harvest and provided the codebreaking organization with its computer support. About 1976, C Group was eliminated and all Agency computer functions were transferred to the newly reorganized Office of Telecommunications and Computer Services, known generally as the T Organization.

After the reorganization, in August 1976, Rear Admiral Eugene
S. Ince, an eighteen-year cryptologic veteran and former director of
the Naval Security Group, Europe, became chief of the T Organization. At one time the newly appointed Ince ventured down into the
basement to take a look at Loadstone but was halted at the entrance
by a security guard who could not find his name on the access list.
"It's all right," he reportedly assured the guard. "I'm Admiral Ince
and I'm in charge of this organization." Still, his name was not there,
and he was sent packing. Needless to say, his name was promptly
added to the list and the guard received a letter of praise for her
security alertness.

In June 1978 Ince became head of the Naval Security Group and
was replaced by Milton Zaslow, the former assistant DDO, who was
just returning from London as NSA's senior United States liaison
officer (SUSLO). Assistant deputy director of the T Organization since
May 1977 is Kermith H. Speierman, a former top scientist for Bur-
roughs Laboratories and later chief of NSA's Information and Computer Services Division. "K" Speierman was one of the principal figures in the telecommunications–computer services consolidation.

Several floors above and to the rear of Gatehouse 3, behind a solid
steel-gray door pasted with warning signs and controlled by cipher
lock, is the center of NSA's worldwide eavesdropping net. If NSA is
America's giant ear, the T Organization's massive Communications
Center is the ear's drum. Inside, row after row of rat-a-tat-tatting
crypto machines bare the world's secrets on multicolored, six-ply carbon paper, each sheet repeating the word CLASSIFIED on one side
while the other side repeatedly warns against disclosure under penalties specified by the espionage laws.

The chatter of Soviet transport pilots, the latest home communiqué
from the Kuwaiti ambassador to Algeria, the singsong of a Chinese
merchant telephoning an order for spare parts to a supplier in Kuala
Lumpur — whatever the net snares crackles back to the Puzzle Palace
over the Agency's own supersecret communications network, SPINT-
COM, which is short for special intelligence communications. The
intercepts make their way via SPINTCOM to a synchronous satellite
22,300 miles over the equator and are then beamed down to a pair
of giant dish antennas hidden in a wooded area behind NSA. From
there the intelligence flows via a $500,000, three-quarter-mile-long
underground cable past a $2.2 million antenna control facility and
into the COMM Center to be distributed to analysts, linguists, and
codebreakers.

Also zapping in to the Puzzle Palace via the twin earth terminals is another worldwide circuit, this one reserved for the most important and immediate of intelligence messages. The Critical Intelligence Communications network, or CRITICOM, is designed to flash to the President and a handful of other senior officials intelligence alerts and warnings of the highest priority — an imminent coup in a Middle East sheikdom, for example, or the assassination of a world leader, or the sinking of a Soviet sub. It is the goal of NSA to have such a CRITIC message on the President's desk within ten minutes of the event.

Because of the speed required to initiate a CRITIC, mistakes in separating good intelligence from bad occasionally occur. One such error took place several years ago, when an analyst at an Air Force listening post on the Greek island of Crete traced a Soviet bomber to a landing on a lake in central Russia. From his intercept equipment he knew that the aircraft had not crashed, so he shot off a CRITIC to the effect that the Soviet Union had apparently developed a new generation of bombers capable of landing on water. What he failed to realize, however, was that Lake Baikal is covered with a thick layer of ice during most of the year.

Once a CRITIC has been issued, further reports on the same subject often take the form of spot reports, one rung lower on the priority ladder. Still another level in the CRITICOM system are PENREPs, or penetration reports, issued whenever a Soviet strategic aircraft appears over non-Soviet territory.

In 1973 NSA's CRITICOM/SPINTCOM network was transformed into the Digital Network–Defense Special Security Communications System (DIN/DSSCS), which fully integrated the message traffic into the Defense Department's general service AUTODIN network (automatic digital network). A further advancement, known as Streamliner, was added in 1976. An automated communications system, Streamliner was designed to reduce writer-to-reader time through the reduction or elimination of many formerly time-consuming tasks, such as message-routing, filing, and formating, which previously had to be performed manually by communications personnel.

Office of Administration: Just down the hall from the Railroad Retirement Board in Boston's aging McCormack Post Office and Court House building stands the door to Room 406. Unlike the rest of the office doors lining the fourth floor, however, the door to 406 bears no name and is made not of glass but of solid, reinforced wood. Above, its transom is covered with plywood and nailed tightly shut. Beside the door, which is permanently locked on the outside, is a

small black button, which, when pushed, alerts an employee to open
the door just a crack to question the visitor. Opening the door any
farther would reveal the large, round seal on the opposite wall, a
seal bearing the words NATIONAL SECURITY AGENCY–UNITED STATES OF
AMERICA.

Officially opened on November 7, 1980, Room 406 contains NSA's
Northeast Recruiting Office. As with almost everything else connected
with the NSA, it is shrouded in secrecy. Chief head-hunter in the
college- and university-saturated city is Charles Raduazo, who spends
a considerable amount of his time on the road, going from college
to college, quietly whispering the virtues of Anagram Inn. What he
is hunting for, principally, are engineers, and of those the choicest
of the lot are the double-E's, the electrical engineering wizards who
may someday build a better signals trap. Mathematicians, especially
at the master's or Ph.D. level, are also high on Raduazo's wanted
list, along with a smattering of language majors, primarily those with
Chinese, Slavic, Near Eastern, and Asian skills. Occasionally the need
will arise for a particular exotic language — such as, for example,
an Indonesian dialect called Sana.

Once they've got the candidates' attention, the recruiters then leave
them with an 11-by-8½-inch glossy giveaway that manages to go its
entire twenty pages without ever once informing the reader that he
or she is being asked to work for an intelligence agency. The pamphlet
even makes an Orwellian attempt to rewrite history, by declaring in
its opening paragraph: "Some time before the second world war, a
cabinet officer closed down a U.S. codemaking operation with the
admonishment that 'Gentlemen do not read each other's mail.' " By
transforming the Black Chamber from a code*breaking* organization
into a code*making* organization, the NSA managed not only to change
history but to create a nonsensical paragraph.

The next step for the future and would-be spooks is the standardized
Professional Qualification Test (PQT) administered under contract
by the Educational Testing Service. The exam is designed not just
to test the candidates' academic knowledge but to spot the "cipher
brains." One question, for instance, asked the applicant to imagine
that he or she was an anthropologist on a high cliff overlooking a
series of islands. From the perch the anthropologist could see messengers in canoes zigzagging between the islands. In addition he or she
could see smoke signals sent from island to island. After reading
about a half-page of information like "Canoe A goes to island 3 then
to island 7 then to island 5 and so on while Canoe B goes to island
12 then island 1 . . . In the meantime smoke signals are sent from

island 6 to island 3 . . ." the applicant must answer questions like "Which island is the chief of the group?" and "Which island controls communications?" and "Which island is the least important?"

Another question may deal with a company scattered throughout a large office building that communicates between offices by means of an unreliable intercom system. The applicant is again given information: "Because of faulty wiring, in order for a person in office A to communicate to someone in office E, he must go through office C, but those in office C can only communicate with persons in office E by first going through office J . . ." This account goes on for about half a page; then the applicant is asked "How would one get a call from office J to office B?" and "What if no one was in office A, how then would a person call from office Y to office H?" and about ten more such questions.

Those who leave the examination room without having suffered a severe breakdown probably assume NSA installs intercoms on South Sea Islands. But this portion of the test is designed to ferret out those few with the rare ability to become masters of traffic analysis, to search through reams of messages and come up with patterns.

Throughout March, those who are finally selected — usually about 150 of the two thousand or so who apply each year from around the country — come down to the Agency's Friendship Annex (FANX) for preemployment screening. There, in the NSA's new four-story Airport Square Building, the new recruits spend their first day going through personnel interviews, filling out forms, and getting a medical checkup. Then they go down a narrow passageway to a set of swinging doors opposite a small sign listing the name of Robert Bates and his title: Chief of Polygraph Services.

Through the doors are numerous small offices painted in pastel hues, each with a glass window on one side and a large two-way mirror on the other, which is used by polygraph personnel to monitor sessions occasionally. The machines, sixteen in all, are built into oversized, well-polished, wood-grain desktops and look something like a new electronic game. Behind the machines in the small rooms, the Agency's twenty certified examiners study the slow, back-and-forth movements of the four or five thin, red-ink pens and make notes after each question. On the other side of each desk, the applicant sits in a large, heavily padded, executive-type swivel chair. What keeps a recruit from being mistaken for a corporate tycoon, however, are the electrodes attached to his or her fingers; thick, black belts strapped around the chest; and bulky blood pressure pads around the upper arm.

The polygraph program began early in 1951 with the hiring of six examiners at annual salaries of $6400, and it remains the most dreaded part of NSA's admission ritual. Originally conducted in a well-guarded, ominous-looking building at 1436 U Street, N.W., in Washington, before the office moved to the Operations Building and then to FANX III, the sessions earned a black eye during the 1950s and early 1960s because of the heavy dependence on the EPQ, or embarrassing personal question. These questions are almost inevitably directed toward intimate aspects of a person's sex life and bear little relationship to the person's honesty or patriotism. Following a congressional investigation and an internal crackdown, the personal questions are now somewhat tamer. "Have you ever had an adult homosexual experience?" for example, is one of the standard questions today.

Following the polygraph, applicants undergo a battery of psychological tests to determine their suitability for both employment and access to the Agency's highly classified materials. Ninety percent of all applicants are interviewed by a clinical psychologist. The results of the psychological tests, together with the polygraph report, are forwarded to the Pentagon's Defense Investigative Service (DIS), where an intensive special background investigation (SBI) is begun.

Unlike a routine background investigation — which includes a check of all federal investigative agencies for derogatory information (called a National Agency Check), verification of birth and citizenship, a check on college education and full-time employment within the previous five years, a check of local criminal justice records, and a credit check — the SBI goes even further: it covers fifteen years and includes a neighborhood check. Passing a BI is required for a top secret clearance, but a successful SBI is necessary for the highest of all Defense Department clearances, the sensitive compartmented information, or SCI clearance, which is a prerequisite for employment at the Puzzle Palace.

After the SBI is completed (it often takes more than a year), the results are sent back to NSA for evaluation. All information obtained about an applicant from the poly, psychological testing, and the full field investigation is then put together and brought before NSA's Applicant Review Panel, comprising representatives from the personnel, medical, and security offices. The board examines each applicant on the "total person" principle and gives the candidate a thumbs-up or refers the case to the director of personnel for a "we regret to inform you" letter.

The second day of the two-day program, for which another one-day badge is issued, consists mainly of more briefings, including a security briefing, an unclassified operational briefing, and, for a few of the most desirable prospects, possibly even a tour of an operational area. This, however, requires the sanitizing of the entire area — everything classified must be removed — so it is seldom given.

Following their forty-eight hours at FANX, the recruits head back to school to finish their last semester and, in the meantime, to sweat out the background investigation, which takes about four or five months. Those who pass the SBI and decide to try out the Puzzle Palace generally come on board as GG-7s, which at the beginning of 1981 stood at $15,193 a year. Engineers were paid annual bonuses and could even start off at $22,000 a year if employment chief Robert A. Dedad felt the potential employee was worth it.

Once cleared and on the payroll, the employee may be given further tests to determine which particular field he or she is best suited for. Some of the tests are clearly designed to pick out the cipher brains; they include such esoteric titles as "Garbled Telegrams," which requires answers to questions based on "telegrams" distorted by typographical errors. Another is "Matrices," which involves identifying or reconstructing a letter or number pattern in order to find the missing entry or original pattern. "Digit Identification" requires one to determine a designated missing digit in an arithmetic computation in which asterisks have been substituted for many of the digits. In "Number Series" the person must first determine the principle on which a number series is based and then indicate what the next number in the series will be.

Depending on the results of the exams and other considerations, the employee will be assigned to one of twenty-three professions in fourteen different career fields (see the Appendix), usually starting off as an intern. The Traffic Analysis Intern Program, for example, is three years long and consists of formal courses, such as Basic and Intermediate T/A, Computer Aid to T/A, and Advanced Traffic Analytic Disciplines, interspersed with six or eight on-the-job assignments, each from three to six months long. Once the internship is completed, the person can rise only to about the GG-11 level. Beyond that, he or she must first "professionalize," which means meeting the requirements established by a Traffic Analysis Career Panel. After being certified as a professional traffic analyst, he or she is eligible to compete, at appropriate stages, up to the supergrades.

The path is somewhat different for those who enter without a college degree or do not go through the internship program. A typical employee may start off in DDO as an analytic assistant and then become a cryptanalysis technician, with a grade range of GG-5 to GG-12.

Beyond that, just as with a cryptanalysis intern, he or she would have to professionalize as a cryptanalyst in order to rise any higher.

In addition to hiring and firing, the Office of Administration also runs the Agency's security force, issues countless personnel management letters, and enforces the Agency's voluminous internal rule book: the *NSA Personnel Management Manual.* Keeper of the rule book from 1976 until October 1980, when he was sent to London as senior United States liaison officer, was Dr. Don C. Jackson. He was replaced by Louis J. Bonanni, the former assistant director for Installations and Logistics.

Office of Installations and Logistics: Hidden beneath the same heavy blanket of secrecy that covers the Agency itself is a cozy fraternity of electronics, communications, and computer suppliers. They could aptly be termed the Crypto-Industrial Complex. Some — like IBM, Motorola, and RCA — are household words; others — like Ultra Systems, Harris Corporation, and Sanders Associates — are considerably less well known outside the SIGINT-COMSEC community. Nevertheless, they all have one thing very much in common: a desire to get as many of NSA's cryptologic contracts as possible.

Because NSA depends almost entirely on outside contractors to build its SIGINT and COMSEC equipment as well as to carry out a large chunk of the research and development that goes into it, cryptology has become a billion-dollar business. By January 1977 the number of active contracts maintained by the Agency had risen to over seven thousand, with an aggregate contract dollar value of about $900 million. Yet, because only 8 percent of those seven thousand contracts account for more than 86 percent of the $900 million, competition for the big, complex projects, such as Rainmaker, Silkworth, and Maroon Shield, is fierce.

Until the mid-1970s, all NSA contracting had been handled by the Army under the cover name "Maryland Procurement Office." When NSA was originally formed, General Canine was advised by the Pentagon to use his billet strength strictly for operational activities and to depend on the Army to do his buying for him. This, it was argued, would also have the advantage of avoiding duplication.

The major problem with the system, however, was that 90 percent of the people doing the contracting had not much in the way of security clearance, and thus their role was limited to little more than that of a bystander. In addition, the technical expertise needed to deal with the supersophisticated crypto devices was well beyond the reach of most of the Army military and civilians involved in the contracting process. In fact, according to Richard P. Floyd, former chief of NSA's Procurement Policy and Support Division, "the people that do that professional business for the Army are ninety-eight percent non–college graduates. They are old-timers who have been shuffling papers since they got out of high school. They know the jargon and they know contract law — they've lived it — but they can't in any way stand up to the doctoral, academic brains out at NSA who make machines. First of all, they didn't even have a right to because they didn't have a clearance — and that's the way they liked it!"

As the system developed, engineers from PROD/DDO or COMSEC would get together with their counterparts in the Office of Research and Engineering and present them with a particular problem. R and E, the Agency's connection with the outside world, would then go to a particular contractor and work up a possible design solution for the problem. Finally, after a handshake, R and E would turn to Army procurement and say, according to Floyd, " 'Hey, I want to buy this — rubber stamp this contract.' What I'm saying to you," Floyd emphasized, "is that the way the system evolved, systematically, the commitments were made long before they legally should have been made."

Toward the mid-1970s, the Army inspector general took notice of the situation and began questioning procurement officials. He wanted to know how they could award contracts for equipment and systems about which they were, by and large, uninformed. As a result, the Army happily washed its hands of the whole business and allowed NSA to take over the entire Maryland Procurement Office.

On June 30, 1975, the Army moved out, and the NSA moved in twenty contracting officers, sixty-three negotiators, and about twenty administrative and clerical workers. Head of Procurement was Elizabeth R. Haig, an NSA veteran who had previously served as the general counsel for R and E.

But despite the change in faces, the old-boy network of contract awards apparently continued to thrive. That, at least, is what Floyd told Director Lew Allen during a classified briefing on January 19, 1977. At forty-seven, Floyd had spent more than half his life with the Agency. Joining the old AFSA in June 1951, the Boston College graduate began as a linguist and in 1957 was named chief of ALLO-34, responsible for Middle East traffic analysis. In 1963 he devised the Far East ELINT policy for B Group and two years later was appointed inspector general. Following a year on Capitol Hill as a Congressional Fellow, Floyd took over responsibility for developing collection policy, third party collaboration, and field support for B Group.

After several more assignments in DDO and R and E, Floyd, who had managed to pick up his law degree along the way, moved over to the Installations and Logistics Organization as chief of Procurement Policy and Support.

In his briefing, Floyd told Allen of the Agency's proclivity for non-competitive, sole-source contract awards. He identified the major violators within the NSA, the contractors, and the amounts of money involved. To overcome the problem, Floyd asked for authority to recruit a team of lawyers and accountants who could learn the business and become fully involved *before* commitment and thoroughly review and constructively oppose sole-source procurement.

As sensible as the idea was, to many in the Agency — particularly those in R and E and others in Procurement — it amounted to nothing less than heresy. "Within two weeks after the briefing," Floyd later said, "systematic harassment . . . was commenced." He noted, "If you control the procurement process and the people who administer it in an agency the size of NSA, you're talking about a lot of power."

The "harassment" began when Procurement chief Haig requested that Floyd undergo a medical and psychological evaluation because of "a number of explosive and argumentative incidents" that were adversely affecting his productivity and relationships with co-workers and superiors. Floyd is a burly man with thick black hair and a strong determination. He was insulted by Haig's statements, which he called false and defamatory, and he requested a grievance hearing before an outside examiner. In the meantime, he reported to the Agency's chief in-house psychiatrist, Dr. Robert L. James, who reported that Floyd "did not show sufficient evidence to make a diagnosis of psychiatric disorder," but nevertheless recommended that he see a mutually acceptable outside psychiatrist, Dr. S. Eugene Long, for a "fitness for duty evaluation."

Long's report, issued on May 14, said that, though Floyd's exhaustion from overwork and, possibly, his high blood pressure may have exacerbated matters, the doctor could "find no indication of psychiatric disorder, nor of significant anxiety felt as such by Mr. Floyd."

Less than two weeks later, Charles W. Matthews, the grievance officer who investigated the case, issued a generally favorable report, pointing to Floyd's "exceptional talents and potential," and noting as the root cause of the conflict "the blatant, potentially explosive understaffing conditions." Matthews recommended that Floyd be reassigned "to a position where his talents can be employed to the best advantage of the agency."

Instead, the Agency's new director, Vice Admiral Bobby R. Inman, after giving "full consideration" to the case, decided that Floyd's grievance "is not sustained" and promptly fired him from his $38,293-a-year post. Floyd, in turn, brought a $3.5 million damage suit.

The protest that sparked Floyd's troubles apparently had little effect on Procurement's rubber-stamp activities. Two months after Floyd gave his briefing to Director Allen, an $18 million modification for a contract code named Silkworth came up for review. The formal review consisted of two procurement officers, at about three-thirty one afternoon, scrounging up a third at the last minute, then talking over the contract for about forty-five minutes before stamping their approval and, apparently, rushing out the door to beat the four-thirty traffic jam.

Only because of a formal complaint by Floyd, an inspector general looked into the contract award and concluded

> that the amount of time (45 minutes) spent by the board was, in this instance, insufficient for the members to feel confident in their recommendation for approval. Also a feeling of resentment was expressed by the board members for what was claimed to be a practice of "hurry up" in a process that requires methodical attention. In conclusion, the IG recommended that management planning provide sufficient time for the review process.

Although probably the most important division within the Office of Installations and Logistics, or L Organization, Procurement is not the organization's only function. Other responsibilities include growth planning for SIGINT City and NSA installations overseas, as well as the usual assortment of household maintenance chores — such as what to do with the NSA's flux of classified waste.

Run by military officers for many years, the L Organization went civilian in April 1977 with the appointment of Louis J. Bonanni as assistant director for Installations and Logistics, following the sudden death of his predecessor, Air Force Brigadier General Charles E. Shannon.

Office of Plans and Policy (DDPP): Unlike the other NSA offices, DDPP (deputy director for Plans and Policy) is primarily a staff position. Its origins date back to the mid-1960s, when General Carter established the executive for Staff Services to function as a sort of chief of staff. In March 1977 Director Allen upgraded the position to assistant director for Policy and Liaison (ADPL) and in January 1980 the office was eliminated and replaced with an even more powerful one, the DDPP, a position filled by Richard N. Kern.

Office of Programs and Resources (DDPR): Like DDPP, DDPR is basically staff-oriented. Known in the 1960s and early 1970s as the Office of the National Cryptologic Staff, its chief, until he left to head up NSA's Pacific command in 1968, was Rear Admiral Lester R. Schulz, who, a dozen hours before the bombs began raining on Pearl Harbor, handed the thirteen-part Purple intercept to President Roosevelt in his White House study and heard him say, in effect, "This means war." As assistant director for the National Cryptologic Staff, Schulz had the unenviable position of liaison between NSA and the service cryptologic agencies. It was a job that required a significant amount of diplomacy and tact in dealing with the parochial interests and clashing personalities of the three military groups and the basically civilian organization.

During the early 1970s the functions were taken over by an Office of Plans and Resources, which, like its predecessor, prepared the SIGINT community budget, the Consolidated Cryptologic Program. After a succession of Navy rear admirals, Air Force Major General Howard M. Estes, Jr., was appointed assistant director for Plans and Resources (ADPR) in August 1979. Five months later his office was reorganized, and Estes became deputy director for Programs and Resources (DDPR).

Office of General Counsel: When the Agency's first general counsel, a civilian by the name of Smith, was about to retire, he made the surprising suggestion to General Canine that the post of general counsel be abolished because it was unnecessary. Canine took his advice and did away with the office, much, no doubt, to the chagrin of Smith's assistant and heir apparent, Roy R. Banner, who became merely the NSA's legal assistant rather than its general counsel.

This changed in 1965, however, when General Carter upgraded the post and named the fifty-year-old Banner his general counsel. Apparently downgraded again in a later reorganization shuffle, Banner's office was placed under Gerard P. Burke, who was named assistant director for Legal and Legislative Affairs (ADLA) in March 1977. Burke had served an earlier tour in NSA and had then become executive secretary to the President's Foreign Intelligence Advisory Board. He returned to NSA in July 1976 as special counsel and eight months later was named ADLA.

Believing that outside lawyers, uninfluenced by years in the intelligence business, might better keep NSA clear of the array of illegal abuses that had marked its past, Admiral Inman appointed Daniel B. Silver general counsel in February 1978. Inman did away with the title of assistant director for Legal and Legislative Affairs and made the post of general counsel a full key component, responsible directly to him through the deputy director of the Agency.

Silver, a thirty-seven-year-old Harvard Law School graduate, left the Puzzle Palace in October 1979 to become the new general counsel for the CIA. He was replaced by Daniel C. Schwartz, a former Federal Trade Commission lawyer.

National Cryptologic School: "The magnitude of their education, of their mental capacity was just overwhelming to me," Carter recalled of the people he found himself surrounded with when he became director. "I made a survey . . . when I got there and it was just unbelievable, the number of Ph.D.s that we had at the operating levels — and they weren't sitting around glorying like people do."

To channel the mental power in the right direction, the NSA established what must be the most selective institution of higher learning in the country: the National Cryptologic School. The NCS was the final metamorphosis of the Training School that had started out on the second floor of a rambling wood-frame building known as Temp "R" on Jefferson Drive between 3rd and 4th streets in southwest Washington. Here, in the early 1950s, the students would clamber up the creaking stairway between wings 3 and 4, past the guard post, and disperse into the five wings of the school.

Today, the NCS occupies a modern, seven-story tower at NSA's FANX location. Opened on November 1, 1965, the school offers a wide range of both technical and analytical courses, ranging from the basic eight-week Cryptologic Orientation Course (CY-001), which details the role of the NSA in the U.S. intelligence community, to Introduction to SIGINT Technology (EA-010), to the advanced National Senior Cryptologic Course (CY-600), a seven-week, full-time course for senior managers in the SIGINT community. For the forty-five students taking the spring 1976 CY-600 course, the schedule included such things as a four-day seminar entitled Cryptologic Issues in National Security, and a politicomilitary simulation called Kappa-76.

But of all the courses, none can compare with the one titled Intensive Study Program in General Analysis. Offering the equivalent of a Ph.D. in codebreaking, the seminarlike eighteen-week course is designed for the career, senior-level analyst. It is given once a year, from February to June, and is limited to a select twelve students, who study over sixty books and documents, attend lectures and group discussions, and do more than four hundred practical exercises that inculcate them with an understanding of both theory and application.

Although the course has definite advantages in terms of career advancement, for those lucky enough to graduate it has a most prestigious side benefit: admission into the supersecret Agency's own supersecret fraternity, the Dundee Society.

Attired in a fitted beige Nehru jacket with an odd-looking ecclesiastical decoration around his neck, white trousers said to be woven from the hair of virgin llamas, and white leather shoes reputedly crafted by reformed anthropophagi from the Andaman Islands, the mysterious "Guru and Caudillo" presided over a secret society symbolized by a Dundee marmalade jar containing the world's first codebreaking machine: four well-sharpened pencils.

Similar marmalade jars are on each student's desk along with a card bearing the first cardinal rule of the course: "You break jar, you eat marmalade" (to empty a jar to replace the broken one). Once the course is underway, the dozen students begin attacking the maddening code systems of the mystical kingdom of Zendia and attempt to read the traffic of its prime minister, Salvo Salasio.

Also known as the Nameless One and His Cerebral Phosphorescence, the Guru and Caudillo was Lambros D. Callimahos, an NSA legend. For twenty-two years the white-haired Mr. C. with the gentle blue eyes and natty bow tie taught the Intensive Study course with a rare combination of wit and brilliance. (His more elaborate attire was reserved for meetings of the Dundee Society.)

Born of Greek parentage in Cairo on December 16, 1910, he came to the United States at the age of four. By the time he was twenty-four, after studying the flute at the Juilliard School of Music and in Paris, Callimahos had become a world-renowned flutist.

While he was earning his reputation as a first-class musician, Callimahos was also learning all he could about cryptology, a subject that had fascinated him since he first read Edgar Allan Poe's story "The Gold-Bug" when he was eight. On his concert tours through Europe, he would ransack libraries for books on the subject. Fluent in seven languages, Callimahos would jot down notes in black loose-leaf notebooks, using a different language every day of the week in order to maintain his fluency.

On February 11, 1941, the flutist volunteered for the Army's Signal Intelligence Service dressed as his virtuoso status demanded: waxed mustache, goatee, black hat — the biggest one he could find in Paris's Latin Quarter — long black Chesterfield coat, black suit, black gloves, ebony cane, black spats, black shoes, black briefcase, and a white silk scarf. "I looked just like a spy out of a Viennese operetta, or perhaps an advertisement for Sandeman port — it really shook them up," he recalled many years later.

Receiving a commission despite his outfit, Callimahos served in the China-Burma-India Theater as an assistant theater signals intelligence officer. Following the war he took up residence at Arlington Hall, where he became technical assistant to William F. Friedman, and continued as a civilian with the Armed Forces Security Agency and NSA. He was a prolific writer and the author of more classified technical books and monographs than any other government cryptologist. Among his works, written with William F. Friedman, are three massive volumes on military cryptanalysis (MC I, II, and III), as well as articles on codes and ciphers for the *World Book Encyclopedia, Collier's Encyclopedia,* and the *Encyclopaedia Britannica.*

On October 28, 1977, Lambros Callimahos, sixty-six, died of cancer at Walter Reed Army Medical Center.* Three months earlier, wearing his finest Nehru jacket, the Guru and Caudillo had presented Dundee certificates to the students in his thirty-second class of General Analysis, along with an honorary membership to CIA director Stansfield Turner.

Named as the first "dean" of the National Cryptologic School was Frank B. Rowlett, Friedman's first employee (after his secretary) in the newly formed Signal Intelligence Service in 1930. In 1958, after five years with the CIA, he replaced the retiring Friedman as special assistant to the director, a position he held for eight years under four directors. Rowlett led the study group that prepared the way for the National Cryptologic School's founding and stayed on as commandant to give it some direction. He retired two months later, on December 30, 1965. On March 2, 1966, Rowlett became the third NSA employee to win the intelligence community's top award when President Johnson presented to him the National Security Medal during a ceremony at the White House. If the surroundings looked familiar to him, it was because he had been there a brief nine months earlier to receive the President's Award for Distinguished Federal Civilian Service, the highest award given to a civilian in the federal government. "His brilliant achievements," read the presidential citation, "ranging from analyses of enemy codes to technological advances in cryptology, have become milestones in the history of our Nation's security."

Commandant of the National Cryptologic School and assistant di-

* NSA's Bruce W. Fletcher took over as director of the Intensive Study Program and also as head of the Dundee Society, albeit with the title Guri-ji, or Little Guru.

rector for Training (ADT) from July 1979 until April 1981 was Eugene
J. Becker, who holds an M.A. from Harvard in Middle Eastern studies.
Following his tour at the NCS, Becker became the NSA representative
to the Pentagon and was replaced by Robert L. Prestel, a one-time
chief of the school's cryptology department. In 1979, at various times,
close to 19,000 students were enrolled in five hundred different
courses. About 13,500 of these were NSA civilians, 2500 were NSA
military, and the remaining 2800 were from other government agencies or military services.

In addition to the NCS, the Puzzle Palace also offers a broad selection of rather esoteric professional associations, known as Learned
Organizations. One of the first established was the Crypto-Linguistic
Association, which itself has a number of subgroups. The members
of the Special Interest Group on Lexicography (SIGLEX), for example, strive to push ahead the state of the art of dictionary- and glossary-
making, including dictionaries for unwritten languages! Two other
Special Interest Groups are SIGVOICE, concentrating on topics ranging from accents to spoonerisms, and SIGTRAN, dedicated to the
art of translation.

Lectures sponsored by the association have covered such subjects
as the status of research in the field of computerized translation of
the human voice (one of NSA's ultimate goals), to a talk by Professor
Ernst von Glasersfeld, of the University of Georgia, on Yerkish, a
symbolic language for communicating by computer with chimpanzees.

Also sponsored by the association is an award program named in
honor of its first president, the late Dr. Sydney Jaffe. The award is
presented to those "whose achievements in the field of languages
have contributed to the mission of the cryptologic community"; the
two recipients who shared the first award, in 1973, commanded between them seventeen languages.

Other Learned Organizations are the Crypto-Mathematics Institute,
the Computer Information Sciences Institute, and the International
Affairs Institute. The traffic and signal analysts have their Communications Analysis Association, the cryptanalysts have their Kryptos Society, and the intercept operators have their Collection Association,
which presents an award to the best eavesdropper ("communications
processor") of the year.

PENETRATION

LIKE A HEAVY FOG, secrecy and security inside the Puzzle Palace permeate the air. Staring down from pastel walls, security posters declare: YOU ARE A SECURITY TARGET and SAFEGUARD CLASSIFIED INFORMATION. Others are less subtle. One depicts a man with gun in hand, noose around his neck, his feet embedded in a concrete block, a chain around his ankle attached to a five-hundred-pound weight, and his mouth taped shut. Below is the inscription "You don't have to go to extremes . . . JUST DON'T TALK!" Another pictures a wastebasket, containing copies of the *New York Times, Newsweek,* and other news sources, below the caption SNOOPER BOWL. Underneath are the words "Every litter bit hurts." The slogans also appear throughout the buildings, flowing across moving electronic signs. At one point even placemats for the cafeteria had security slogans printed on them.

For many years, until December 1977, the Agency's first line of defense, beyond the triple fence, in an overall program known as "security in depth" was the Marines. Activated on October 15, 1954, as the first (and only) Marine Guard unit ever assigned to a national intelligence orgranization, they manned the gatehouses surrounding SIGINT City, checking badges and sorting through briefcases, purses, and lunch bags. For five hours before they took up their guard positions each day, they would form what was known as an Alert Force and remain quartered in a Marine barracks three hundred yards behind the Operations Building. In the event of a threat to security, they would grab their helmets and weapons and rush to the trouble spot.

Beyond the gatehouses, a dizzying system of magnetic, color-coded, key-punched badges determines where in the buildings a person is allowed to go. Those fully cleared and with the requisite "need to know" wear the green badges granting them access to all but specially compartmented spaces. Yellow is reserved for non-NSA employees, such as the representatives of the foreign SIGINT organizations with offices in the Agency. For those holding anything less than a full clearance, red badges are issued.

Emblazoned on the front of the badge is the bearer's name and social security number, along with a full-face picture. The reverse, like that of the visitor's badge, contains a warning against improper use and a post office box address in the event of loss, but no mention of the Agency.

Still other badges are used for specific purposes. For example, anyone transporting documents from the building must first obtain a Courier badge from his or her section's security officer.

There are a dozen or more badges in the different colors of the spectrum marked with a variety of designs, from solids to diagonal stripes. Further access control is provided by "tabs" attached to the chain above the badge. Some denote a particular function, such as NSA Photographer; others grant special access to the wearer.

At times the system can be bewildering. For instance, when the Agency was in the process of moving, bag and baggage, from Washington to its present location at Fort Meade, additional badges had to be issued. Green was for cleared NSA personnel, white for moving supervisors, pink for uncleared contract laborers, blue for uncleared military and civilian truck drivers, and yellow, when worn with a red picture badge, for the management representatives of contractors.

But color is not the only security indicator built into the system. Each badge is also key-punched like an IBM card, so that by inserting it into a reader one can instantly determine the holder's current status.

Just as bewildering as the chromatic system of security badges is an Alice-in-Wonderland system of code words,* caveats, and security classifications that are, in fact, themselves classified.

While most in government are familiar with the standard confidential, secret, and top secret security classifications, few outside the inner circles of the intelligence community are aware of a supersecret dual system designed for the handling of SIGINT information.

The keystone of this system is the warning HANDLE VIA COMINT CHANNELS ONLY. Once a document is so marked, it is automatically elevated to a status higher than top secret; it is restricted to those

---

* It is interesting to note that there is a distinction between code words and nicknames. A code word is a single word selected from an arcane document known as the JANAP 299 (for Joint Army, Navy, Air Force Publication) and is always assigned a classified meaning; a nickname consists of two words and is assigned an unclassified meaning. (Department of Defense Regulation 5200.1R, D-1.)

few holding a final top secret special intelligence clearance and indoctrinated into the tight-lipped world of SIGINT. Few messages, letters,
or reports leave the Puzzle Palace without the injunction.

Once the document has been removed from the more plebeian
security classifications, an arcane assortment of code words further
limit access to it. TOP SECRET UMBRA, for example, indicates that the
information is of the highest SIGINT sensitivity. Previously the code
word for this was Trine and before that, during the early 1960s,
Dinar. Still others have included such exotic designations as Vipar,
Harum, Froth, and Canoe. One step below, paralleling the conventional Secret, is Spoke, always written SECRET SPOKE.

Though words like Umbra and Spoke indicate a general level of
sensitivity, other five-letter code words are more specific in their meaning. Gamma, for instance, was reserved for Soviet intercepts of the
very highest importance and also, ironically, starting in 1969, for
the monitored conversations of American antiwar leaders like Jane
Fonda and Dr. Benjamin Spock.

Additional code words, always beginning with the letter *G* and containing four letters, narrowed the source of the Soviet communication
even further. Gupy, for example, was used to indicate that the source
of the information was the intercepted conversations of top Soviet
officials, including party leader Leonid Brezhnev, President Nikolai
Podgorny, and Premier Alexei Kosygin, as they conversed over their
limousine radiotelephones. Another four-letter code word in the
Gamma series referred to information about Soviet-Arab communications, and still others to mail openings and information from foreign
code books. In all, about twenty different code words were assigned
to the Gamma series, among them such unlikely ones as Gilt, Gout,
Gult, Gant, Gabe, and Gyro.

Designating a somewhat less sensitive area of Soviet intercepts was
the Delta series of code words. These referred to information on
Russian military operations, such as the location of Soviet submarines
or Russian aircraft operations. Among the Delta words were Dace,
Dice, and Dent.

In addition to code words indicating the level of sensitivity and
source of the information, there are code words for specific operations.
Holystone and Desktop, for instance, designate several highly sensitive
undersea operations.

Essentially, each code word is a separate, highly specialized entity.
Access to Gamma Gilt does not give one access to Gamma Gout,
just as access to Holystone does not automatically grant access to
Desktop. Each requires separate briefings, indoctrination, and oaths.

Often a document contains references to a number of operations and sources and carries a stupefying classification like TOP SECRET UMBRA GAMMA GANT HOLYSTONE DESKTOP. In such a case the reader would have to be cleared and certified for each category.

Though most code words "retire" because of the loss of a particular source or the end of a particular mission, some remain unchanged for decades. Occasionally, the code word has to be changed because it has been compromised. This is what happened on March 28, 1965, when the *New York Times Magazine* ran a story by Max Frankel profiling President Johnson's assistant for national security affairs, McGeorge Bundy.

With the article there was a photograph of Bundy speaking with Johnson on the White House lawn, and, although little appeared out of the ordinary about the seven-month-old file photo, to the trained eye it was a most revealing picture. Captured by the photographer's lens, and clearly visible in print, was a spiral-bound document in the presidential assistant's left hand bearing the boldly stamped words TOP SECRET DINAR.

The compromising picture instantly created a flap at both the CIA and the Puzzle Palace. A CIA employee was dispatched to New York to request the negative, which, if blown up, might reveal even more of the document. Meanwhile, Lieutenant General Carter, then deputy director of the CIA and soon to become director of the NSA, got on the phone to Bundy to brief him on the photo and the consequences of its publication.

"Hey, Mac," Carter remembers asking a surprised Bundy, "you got two hundred and fifty thousand dollars in your confidential account over there?" When asked the reason for the question, Carter informed Bundy of the compromised photo and the high cost of changing a SIGINT code word — a cost, the general said, he hadn't budgeted for.

It was an expensive and time-consuming proposition. Unlike Defense Department code words that are used strictly by the U.S. military, many SIGINT code words, including Umbra, are used throughout the supersecret international SIGINT community. If any of these become compromised, thousands of rubber stamps bearing the old word have to be recalled, and new stamps with the revised code word must be made and then transported by courier to every listening post. Carter added, "We've got to get the British and the Australians and the New Zealanders and the Canadians and everybody in the act."

Because of what has become almost a fetish of rubber stamps and

red ink, even many unclassified letters leaving the Puzzle Palace are
tattooed with warnings and restrictions. Responding to a Freedom
of Information Act request with a copy of an unclassified, innocuous
internal memorandum, the Agency saw fit to decorate the envelope
with RESTRICTED DELIVERY, DELIVER TO ADDRESSEE ONLY, and POSTMAS-
TER: DO NOT FORWARD OUTSIDE AREAS SERVED BY U.S. CIVIL POST OF-
FICES. It also sent the memo by certified mail, with return receipt
requested. And this despite the fact that the original request specifically stated the information was to be used for publication.*

Yet for all the barbed wire and electrified fences, the cameras, the
badges, and the armed guards, NSA's greatest threat comes not from
without but from within. Even during the protest-ravaged sixties and
early seventies, few demonstrators had ever heard of the NSA, let
alone knew where to protest against it. The one exception, and the
only "confrontation" in its entire history, took place on March 22,
1974. Veteran activist and former Catholic priest Philip F. Berrigan
and his wife, in one of their typically small antiwar demonstrations,
led a group of twenty-one protesters to the Agency's main gate, where
they proceeded to pour a gallon of human blood over a wooden
cross while decrying the "American war machine." Twenty minutes
and three arrests later, the demonstration was over and the gathering
trooped back down Savage Road. The Puzzle Palace had at last had
its brief brush with the world outside.

But it is not the Berrigans whom security officials fear; it is the
turncoats, the employees who, because of money, blackmail, or ideology, have decided to switch sides. And it is toward their early elimination that the Agency's security clearance program is directed.

The first step in NSA's clearance process is also the most dreaded —
the polygraph. Despite Pentagon directives that state, "The polygraph
shall be employed only as an aid to support other investigative techniques and be utilized generally only after the investigation by other
means has been as thorough as circumstances permit," NSA uses
the lie detector as an initial security screening measure.

Unlike the CIA, NSA explicitly uses the poly as a primary tool
for the collection of adverse information on potential employees. According to the Agency, at least 95 percent of all negative information
on applicants comes from the polygraph, and 85 to 90 percent of
this information is considered significant enough to warrant investiga-

* So frustrated was the Carter administration over the loose way in which intelligence
information was being handled that the President created still another category: Royal.
This was to be used primarily on highly sensitive intelligence documents when disclosure of the material contained in them could also result in disclosure of the source.

tion. Out of 2531 applicants for whom security processing was completed during fiscal year 1978, 775 were rejected.

Although security at the Puzzle Palace appears close to hermetic, much of it is little more than illusion. Triple-wrapping in chain link and electricity notwithstanding, access to the front lobby and plush reception area is easier than walking into a Greyhound bus station. Although the Agency is located on an Army base, there are no guardhouses or MPs checking passes; in fact, were it not for a WELCOME sign on Savage Road, one would not even realize he or she had entered a military base.

Once on the base, anyone from the Soviet ambassador to Yassir Arafat can walk up the dozen or so steps and into the reception area, no questions asked, take a seat, and begin listening to some very interesting conversations. Actual examples include several members of Britain's ultrasecret GCHQ comparing security at NSA with that "in the Cotswolds" while waiting for their security badges to be issued, a member of Canada's equally secret Communications Branch of the National Research Council (the Canadian Puzzle Palace) swapping stories with his NSA sponsor, and an assortment of COMSEC contractors speaking over the internal telephones.

Within the Puzzle Palace, little is considered more sensitive than the names, faces, and titles of its thousands of employees, each of whom is looked on as a potential target for a hostile intelligence service. Congress recognized this as far back as 1959, when it enacted the extraordinary Public Law 86–36, proclaiming, "Nothing in this Act or any other law . . . shall be construed to require the disclosure of the organization or any function of the National Security Agency, or any information with respect to the activities thereof, or the names, titles, salaries, or number of persons employed by such agency."

According to Daniel Schwartz, NSA general counsel, the reason for this overwhelming concern with names is that numerous employees are posted overseas on "covert assignments" and that the "lives or safety" of these persons "might be endangered" by the release of their names.

In spite of these serious concerns, for almost three decades NSA has published a chatty, twenty-page monthly newsletter containing exactly those names, along with their faces, titles, internal organizational codes, and other supposedly "sensitive" information. Although the newsletters today are still unclassified, readers are supposed to burn them after reading. "*Newsletter* copies received in the mail or taken from Agency buildings should be given special care and should be destroyed as soon as they have been read," reads the instruction on each issue.

Yet even without the newsletters, obtaining information on NSA employees is easier than converting beets into borscht for any KGB agent worthy of his cloak and dagger. Considerately, the upper crust of the Puzzle Palace, consisting of the two or three hundred most senior officials together with the representatives of the foreign SIGINT organizations, all park side by side in the Agency's prestigious, reserved-space front parking lot. Should Moscow wish a dossier on the NSA's most senior spooks, all an agent need do is drive through the parking lot collecting license numbers and then get the names and addresses from the local Registry of Motor Vehicles.

Inside, the brawny, no-nonsense Marine force has been replaced by beer-bellied civilians of the General Services Administration's Federal Protective Service. They plow dutifully through each exiting briefcase looking for classified documents, but according to one guard, they are forbidden to search one's clothing "unless something is showing." An employee seeking to smuggle out documents can simply place them in a coat pocket to avoid detection.

But of all the weaknesses in NSA's vaunted security, none is more glaring than the way in which the polygraph is used. Unlike the CIA, which uses the polygraph on each and every potential employee, from janitor on up, the NSA exempts all military personnel on the theory that their assignment to the Agency is not voluntary. Since submission to a polygraph examination must be a voluntary act, NSA argues that requiring it of military personnel would violate their rights. The CIA, however, does require it of military employees assigned to the agency, noting that their association with the CIA is voluntary.

The effects of this double standard can be clearly seen in the history of those members of the military seeking to switch to civilian status. During fiscal year 1978, sixty-eight military assignees sought to trade in their uniforms for tweed and double knit. Of that number, approximately 20 percent were eventually judged unfavorable by the Applicant Review Panel. In fully 90 percent of these cases, information obtained through the polygraph contributed to the decision. The results: thirteen people who had been working in the Agency as military employees never would have gotten through the front door as civilians.

•

Heading NSA's Office of Security, or M5, as it is known within the Agency, during its first decade was soft-spoken S. Wesley Reynolds, a former FBI agent with a square jaw and straight black hair. A native of New Jersey and a graduate of St. John's Law School, Reynolds had joined the FBI in 1942 and spent the better part of his early career chasing spies and maintaining liaison with the various military intelligence services.

Unhappy at the prospect of continual transfers, Reynolds turned in his badge in March of 1952 and, after a brief stint outside the government, joined the infant NSA as deputy to Colonel Leslie Wyman, the security director. At the time, internal security consisted of a cabal of undercover informants who would spend most of their time listening for rumors and peering around corners. Every so often an employee would be called down to the security office and never be heard from again. Reynolds soon took over as security chief and abolished the cabal, relying instead on frequent security briefings and a program of security education.

Although Reynolds managed to remove some of the repressiveness from the Office of Security, there was an occasional return to the black bag. In all, four instances of electronic surveillance without a court notice occurred during the late 1950s. Three of these incidents took place at the homes of either current or former employees and included the bugging of a young, black, female employee, who, it was believed, was having contacts with an official of an unfriendly foreign embassy. The fourth instance occurred when the gumshoes planted a bug in the young woman's New York City hotel room during a weekend rendezvous with her embassy friend. In the end, it was determined that the two were interested simply in sex, not in secrets.

Following the double defection in 1960 of two Agency employees, Wes Reynolds was forced to resign.

•

Replacing Reynolds was Leonard P. Bienvenu, a lawyer from the Justice Department with a degree from Stanford in Chinese. At Justice, Bienvenu had served directly under Attorney General Robert F. Kennedy as his security officer and also as the executive secretary to the National Security Council's Interdepartmental Committee on Internal Security. Before that, he was with the CIA, and during World War II he served as an intelligence officer in North China and Manchuria.

Unlike his predecessor, Bienvenu managed to survive his own spy scandal and its ensuing shake-up. But as a result, in an effort to strengthen the office's counterintelligence program, he came close to returning the Agency to the undercover, cabal style of security Reynolds had ended ten years earlier.

Under Bienvenu's External Collection Program, begun in October 1963, M5 agents would make periodic visits to the watering holes, restaurants, and other establishments in the vicinity of the Puzzle Palace in order to determine where NSA employees gathered after work, whether they discussed classified information, and whether foreign espionage agents also frequented the same places. When the program was in effect, one would always have to assume that the stranger sitting on the next stool was from M5.

In addition, the program involved encouraging persons working in these establishments — the bartenders, hostesses, and waitresses — to report back to NSA any "suspicious incidents" involving Agency people. Local police were also made aware of the "sensitivity of NSA's mission," should the need for cooperation arise.

Ill-conceived from the start, and lacking adequate personnel to accomplish its objectives, the program died a quiet death somewhere between 1966 and 1967.

M5's External Collection Program, though possibly the most blatant, was far from being the only example of paranoia and overreaction during the 1960s. As worrisome to the Agency as loose-lipped spooks were those few outsiders who dared to write about it. To keep track of this small fraternity, M5 set up a special file called "Nonaffiliates of NSA Who Publish Writings Concerning the Agency."

The sharpest thorn in NSA's side was David Kahn, a reporter for *Newsday* and an amateur cryptologist. In 1961 the thirty-one-year-old journalist signed a contract with the Macmillan Company to write a book on cryptology, a subject to which the Puzzle Palace felt it controlled the exclusive rights.

After two years of part-time work on the project, Kahn quit his job with the Long Island daily and began devoting all his time to researching and writing on the topic that had fascinated him for twenty years.

At about the same time, however, the NSA became aware of Kahn's forthcoming book — eventually titled *The Codebreakers* — which included a chapter on the Agency, and began a frantic effort to prevent its release, or, if they failed in that, at least to lessen its impact. Innumerable hours of meetings and discussions, involving the highest levels of the Agency, including the director, were spent in an attempt to sandbag the book. Among the possibilities considered were hiring Kahn into the government so that certain criminal statutes would apply if the work was published; purchasing the copyright; undertaking "clandestine service applications" against the author, which apparently meant anything from physical surveillance to a black-bag job;

and conducting a "surreptitious entry" into Kahn's Long Island home.

One by one the options, ranging from the absurd to the downright illegal, were suggested and rejected for one reason or another. At one point the director suggested planting in the press disparaging reviews of the author's work, and such a review was actually drafted. Also suggested and carried out was the placing of Kahn's name on the NSA watch list, enabling the Agency's vacuum cleaner to sweep the airwaves for his phone calls and telegrams. This task was made all the easier when Kahn moved to Paris to take over as a news-desk editor for the *International Herald Tribune*.

Unilateral action was rejected, however, and the matter was brought before the United States Intelligence Board in early 1964 and assigned to the board's SIGINT Committee, chaired by the NSA director, Air Force Lieutenant General Gordon Blake.

Calling the book "a possibly valuable support to foreign COMSEC authorities," the committee recommended to the board "further low-key actions as possible, but short of legal action, to discourage Mr. Kahn or his prospective publishers" from releasing the book. In addition, the USIB report noted that John A. McCone, chairman of the board and director of the CIA, "would discuss the subject with Mr. Dulles, consider what CIA might be willing to do, and get in touch with Navy, in an effort to prevent publication of the book or at least to review the manuscript."

Just what actions the CIA actually took to halt publication or procure the manuscript are unknown, as is the role played by former CIA director Allen Dulles. What is known, though, is that Macmillan agreed to turn over to the Pentagon two chapters at first, and later the entire manuscript, without the author's permission, just as it had done a quarter of a century earlier with another manuscript — Herbert O. Yardley's *Japanese Diplomatic Secrets*.

After receiving the entire manuscript on March 4, 1966, the Pentagon shipped it over to NSA, which in turn brought it before the USIB's SIGINT and Security Committees for review. A letter was then sent from the Department of Defense to Lee C. Deighton, Macmillan's chairman of the board, advising him that the department "deplored" the book and that "it would not be in the national interest to publish the book," but if the publishers were going to go ahead with it, the national interest required the deletion of certain specified sections.

By now the Agency realized that there was no way it was going to keep the book out of the bookstores; the best it could hope for was to limit the damage by having Deighton agree to the reduced deletions. But after a month with no reply, it seemed that even this approach was doomed to failure.

There remained one final option. In early July, Richard Helms, newly appointed CIA director and chairman of the USIB, met with Blake's successor as NSA director, Marshall S. Carter, and suggested that the general make a quiet journey to New York and appeal to Deighton personally.

Carter, Helms's former boss, agreed. As the deputy director of the CIA, Pat Carter had been through it all before. That time it was with *The Invisible Government,* a revealing narrative by David Wise and Thomas B. Ross. Several years earlier, when that book was about to come out, he had tried working through the authors themselves and, he felt, had been burned in the end. According to Carter, "We blew it!"

Nevertheless, even this approach involved considerable risk. If the press learned that the chief of the nation's most shadowy spy agency was paying a secret call on one of the nation's largest publishers, the whole effort would explode in NSA's face. Defense Secretary McNamara had this in mind when, while approving the idea, he refused to put anything in writing to the publisher. Carter had originally drafted a letter of introduction for McNamara's signature, stating simply yet mysteriously, "This will serve to introduce Lt. Gen. Marshall S. Carter, USA, who has a matter to discuss with you. I am aware of what Gen. Carter has to say and his remarks have my endorsement and approval." But McNamara "chose not to sign anything" and placed the whole matter back in Carter's lap.

So on July 22, 1966, his stocky frame tucked into a civilian suit, and without the advice of his general counsel, Carter boarded a Friday morning commuter flight from Baltimore to New York's La Guardia Airport for an appointment with Deighton. By now, what had started out as an effort to eliminate several hundred pages, including the entire chapter on NSA, had been reduced to the bare-bones minimum — the deletion of a handful of paragraphs dealing with the most sensitive subject of all: NSA's relationship with its supersecret British partner, GCHQ.

In fact, the subject was considered so sensitive that GCHQ was putting pressure on Macmillan in London. At the request of Brigadier John H. Tiltman, for many years one of GCHQ's most senior cryptologists and a top-ranking liaison officer between the two agencies, GCHQ official Geoffrey Evans interceded with the publisher in London.

Deighton, originally uncertain about the purpose of the meeting, was surprised to learn of Carter's affiliation with NSA. He called in the book's editor and the company's outside legal counsel, who informed Carter, in essence, "that when a publisher contracts to print a book, he has to get permission of the author to make changes in the manuscript."

"I pointed out," Carter informed a few of his top deputies several days later, "that Kahn's reputation as a cryptologist was suspect; that he was an amateur; that he had never been employed by the Government; that, fortunately, there were enough errors in the book to denigrate the substantive documentation of cryptology in the eyes of the community; that under no circumstances, regardless of how we came out with Kahn, would we give security clearance to the book; that the book by itself, while perhaps it could not be characterized as sensationalism, was sufficiently wrong in sufficient areas to depreciate its validity as the final anthology of cryptology."

Despite the undeserved attack on Kahn, the trio sympathized with Carter's "national security" arguments and agreed to approach the author with the suggested deletions. In addition, at the NSA director's request, "they said that they would not make a memorandum for the record or have anything in their files on the fact of my meeting with them or of what transpired."

To the profound relief of the organizations on both sides of the Atlantic, Kahn, in a transatlantic telephone call, which he took in a small room at the *Tribune* office in Paris, reluctantly agreed to delete the requested material, consisting of the following paragraphs:

> Another agency outside the U.S. government with which NSA maintains close contact is the Government Communications Headquarters — the cryptanalytic agency of Great Britain. NSA's United Kingdom Liaison Office exchanges cryptanalyzed material, techniques of solution, and so on, with GCHQ. The two agencies sometimes divide the work of solution, one agency taking one country and the other another, and trade their results to save duplication of effort; but more often both work independently. In addition, they exchange personnel on a temporary basis to broaden the men's cryptologic experience. (British cryptanalysts in NSA are, naturally, kept away from the areas where NSA is probably trying to break British ciphers.) A similar but much smaller liaison program is maintained with Canada and Australia.
>
> Whereas NSA is in the Defense Department, Britain's GCHQ is a department of the Foreign Office. Like NSA, though, it apparently handles the strategic cryptanalysis for both military and diplomatic agencies. GCHQ is located on Priors Road, Cheltenham, in Gloucestershire, about 85 miles west of London, in a cluster of low buildings where it moved from Bletchley Park, apparently shortly after World War II.

Sir Clive Loehnis, a graduate of the Royal Naval colleges and a former naval officer qualified in signal communications, was named director in 1960 at age 58. A member of the Institute of Electrical Engineers, Loehnis served in the Admiralty's Signal Division and then in the Naval Intelligence Division in World War II, entering the Foreign Office in 1945. He had been deputy director since 1952 under Sir Eric Jones, a textile merchant who never went to college and who served in the Royal Air Force Volunteer Reserves, presumably in cryptology, during the war. Jones apparently served in GCHQ starting in 1946, and six years later, aged 45, became director. Named deputy director in 1960 under Sir Clive was Leonard J. Hooper, then 46, a graduate of Oxford with honors in modern history, who was transferred to GCHQ from the Air Ministry in 1942. He served as assistant director from 1952 to 1960. Among GCHQ's best cryptanalysts are Brigadier John H. Tiltman, perhaps England's outstanding expert in the field, who has spent the last few years at NSA, Dr. I. J. (for Irving John) Good, a fellow of the Royal Statistical Society, a brilliant mathematician, and a prolific writer,* and C. H. O'D. Alexander, one of England's chess champions.

---

* His papers, on probability, evidence, philosophy of science, and mathematical statistics, are usually rewarding, but sometimes he turns in some with less substance than usual. A wag may have had these in mind when he told an NSA colleague, who had asked why Jack Good had published no papers recently, that "It's an ill Good that Blows no wind."

To be sure, neither the NSA nor the GCHQ found any humor in the footnote. However, Kahn may have had the last laugh in spite of his censors. Though the above material was deleted from the text, buried in the notes at the back of the book and overlooked by the censors were the references to the very material that had been deleted. By looking up the references, anyone could acquire almost half of the above information!

•

On October 9, 1954, shortly before noon, a carload of FBI agents pulled up to a modest apartment building in Arlington, Virginia, and arrested a gangling, forty-year-old physicist. Less than an hour later Joseph Sidney Petersen, Jr., neatly clad in a double-breasted wool suit and tightly knotted tie, became the first person ever to be arraigned on charges of violating Section 798 of Title 18 of the United States Code — the COMINT statute. By doing so, the recently fired NSA employee managed to spark the young Agency's first full-blown spy scandal.

A native of New Orleans, the tall, myopic Petersen spent his undergraduate years at Loyola University before taking a master's degree

in science at St. Louis University. In mid-1941, after several years
of teaching at Loyola and at Ursuline College in New Orleans, and
after successfully passing the Army correspondence course in cryptanalysis, he joined Friedman's SIS and spent the war at Arlington
Hall, solving Japanese diplomatic code messages.

Seated next to Petersen at the hall, also working on Japanese systems, was Colonel J. A. Verkuyl, a Dutch liaison officer and a renowned
cryptologist. The two rapidly became close friends, and Verkuyl introduced Petersen to another colleague who shared their interest in
codes, Giacomo Stuyt, communications officer at the Dutch embassy
in Washington.

When the war came to a close, and the United States and the Netherlands ended their cryptologic cooperation, Verkuyl returned home,
and Petersen involved himself in training programs for the newly
formed Army Security Agency and later the Armed Forces Security
Agency. Also, without authorization, he began sending Verkuyl ideas
for methods that he thought might be useful in helping his Dutch
friend set up a cryptology corps in the Netherlands. Then, strangely,
in 1948 he started passing on to Stuyt, who had remained at the
embassy after the war, copies of top secret notes and highly classified
documents he smuggled out of the agency. Included were details of
America's success in breaking the Dutch codes and a 1939 SIS document entitled "Analysis of the Hagelin Cryptograph, Type B-211,"
which was the device the Netherlands government was using for its
diplomatic communications. Exactly why Petersen turned informant
for the Dutch — whether out of a twisted sense of friendship or a
unilateral desire to protect Holland's code systems, has never been
adequately explained. What does appear likely, however, is that Petersen's generosity stretched over a period of almost six years.

Petersen's behavior was brought to the attention of NSA's Office
of Security in 1954 almost by accident. During the course of a routine
security clearance update, one of the M5 agents mentioned to GENS
chief Frank Raven that he had come across some information indicating that Petersen was maintaining a correspondence with a person
in Holland named Verkuyl. "Verkuyl!" Raven said. "Verkuyl was head
of Dutch COMINT in the U.S. during the war. You better check
that out — something stinks."

M5's worst fears were confirmed when investigators, making a surreptitious entry into Petersen's apartment, discovered a large cache
of very highly classified documents. There was one bit of luck, however. It was also discovered that whenever Stuyt had returned documents to Petersen after photocopying them, the rounded, American-

type staples had been replaced by squared-off Dutch staples. A massive
search was then made throughout the Agency, and many of the other
compromised documents were identified.

NSA Director Ralph Canine was notified immediately, and on October 1, 1954, Petersen was dismissed from his $7700-a-year job. The
question then became whether to prosecute, and thus risk revealing
to the world the very secrets that the Agency was seeking to protect,
or whether to handle the matter quietly. The problem was brought
before the United States Intelligence Board, with Allen Dulles arguing
that the potential harm in terms of publicity greatly outweighed any
possible good. Canine, on the other hand, was strongly in favor of
making an example of Petersen. In the end, he was given the green
light, with the proviso that only the least sensitive, least damaging
items be introduced into evidence.

At the arraignment following his arrest, Petersen pleaded innocent
and refused both a preliminary hearing as well as an attorney. Unable
to raise the $25,000 bond, he was marched off to the Alexandria
City Jail and ordered held for a federal grand jury session, beginning
on December 6.

The hearings that followed were a mixture of both public and private
sessions; Federal District Court Judge Albert V. Bryan heard the sensitive testimony in chambers and shifted to open court for the nonsensitive. Although the government had a stack of highly classified documents to base its prosecution on, it followed the rule laid down by
the USIB and instead chose several of the most innocuous to go
into court with. Among them was a document entitled "Chinese Telegraphic Code SP-D," dated July 1, 1945, and classified as secret. Another was a traffic analysis known as A.F.S.A.230763;KC037, "Routing
of North Korean Political Security Traffic as Indicated by Group A2,"
dated February 20, 1951, and stamped top secret. Also included was
the analysis of the Hagelin B-211 Cryptograph.

The choice of documents proved an embarrassment to the prosecutors, however. Charging that the material was "grossly overclassified,"
David B. Kinney, Petersen's attorney, pointed out that the Chinese
code was commercial and easily available to anyone, and also that
the Hagelin machine was sixteen years old and could be purchased
in Sweden by private buyers.

Nevertheless, Kinney knew that the best hope of salvaging his client
from the stiff ten years in jail and $10,000 fine lay in a compromise
plea. On December 22, Petersen pleaded guilty to "knowingly and
willfully [using] in a manner prejudicial to the safety and interest of
the United States classified information concerning communications

intelligence activities of the United States and foreign governments." In return for Petersen's not forcing the government to disclose confidential information at a public trial, the prosecution dropped the two more serious espionage charges.

But the plea helped little. Calling the documents that Petersen had pilfered "gravely important" and warning that their disclosure "could have led to very, very serious consequences to the security of the United States," Judge Bryan socked Petersen with a seven-year prison sentence. "The pith of this offense is not *what* the defendant withdrew, but *that* he withdrew, records from the National Security Agency," the judge concluded.

After the sentencing, Petersen, who had claimed all along that he had merely taken the documents home for use in preparing a training session, was sent to the Federal Medical Center at Springfield, Missouri, for psychiatric observation and was later transferred to a federal prison to serve the remainder of his term.

With Petersen under lock and key, life for the gumshoes of the Office of Security returned to normal. But four years later, in 1958, the mild-mannered physicist was due for release on parole, and his ghost came back to haunt them.

Broke, out of work, and possibly bitter toward the government, Petersen, Agency officials feared, might fall prey to Soviet recruiters. As a precaution, Wes Reynolds ordered another surreptitious entry into Petersen's home in order to plant a listening device that would either confirm or dispel the Agency's fears. Without bothering with the legal requirement of a court order, the security people installed the bug and turned on the tape recorders. As weeks turned into months with no indication of anything bordering on treason, additional break-ins were made to service the battery-operated device. Finally, after three months during which there was not the slightest hint of dishonorable activity, the bug was removed and the Petersen case closed once and for all.

•

Seated at a long table on a raised stage in front of rows of TV cameras, blinding Klieg lights, and a dozen microphones, two NSA analysts began fielding questions dealing with NSA's innermost secrets.

Such a nightmare was enough to make even the most fearless security officer break out in a cold sweat. Nevertheless, on September 6, 1960, that nightmare came true in the worst of all possible places: Moscow's gilded House of Journalists.

The drama that led up to the worst scandal in the history of the

NSA had its origins almost a decade earlier and half the earth away, when Bernon F. Mitchell, a trim, brown-haired sailor assigned to the Naval Security Group's listening post in Kamiseya, Japan, first met William H. Martin, newly assigned from an intercept station in Alaska.

Born on March 11, 1929, in San Francisco, Mitchell grew up in the Northern California coastal city of Eureka. The youngest son of a Eureka attorney, Bernon, who in later years would insist that his name be pronounced with the accent on the last syllable, first became interested in mathematics when he spotted a number on the last page of a picture book and inquired if that was the end of the numbers.

In high school the precocious youth was so frustrated by the slow pace of his science class, particularly since his teacher either couldn't or wouldn't delve deep enough into Einstein's relativity theory, that he decided to turn in his books and transfer to another school a good eighty miles away.

Following graduation, Bernon enrolled at the California Institute of Technology, where, after a brief fling at languages, he studied statistics. More bookworm than BMOC, his light reading consisted mainly of tomes on the philosophy of mathematics, interspersed with a sprinkling of Freud. Quiet and shy with girls, he preferred the piano to panty-raids and enjoyed endless hours of debating, especially when the debate offered him an opportunity to expound on his strong agnostic beliefs.

At the end of the first semester of his sophomore year, the C+ student enlisted in the Navy — not to see the world, but to beat a rapidly approaching draft call. Though it may have occurred to Bernon to apply for a student deferment, as most of his classmates had done, his father had been a strict World War II draft board chairman and pressured his son to sign up.

He was assigned to the heavily guarded Kamiseya intercept base, and it was here that Mitchell first met "Ham" Martin, like himself an introspective, thoughtful young man who shared a passion for debating and an intolerance toward religion.

Martin was born on May 27, 1931, in Columbus, Georgia. In 1937 his father, John H., packed up six-year-old Ham and the rest of the family and moved them diagonally across the country to Yakima, Washington, and, eight years later, to Ellensburg, a cow town in the heart of the Kittitas Valley, forty miles to the north. Here the boy caught the attention of Dr. Loretta Miller, a psychology professor at nearby Central Washington University. Miller was impressed by his quick intelligence and set up a series of special tests to determine whether he could skip high school altogether and, instead, enroll in a special program for gifted students at the University of Chicago.

Although his test scores were high, young Martin's principal believed that he was not yet mature enough to jump right into college, and he worked out another arrangement. Under this plan, Martin studied college subjects during his summers while receiving high school credit, which enabled him to finish three years of high school in two.

After a year at Central Washington, where his interests focused on mathematics, Martin enlisted in the Navy. Because of his math background he was selected for cryptologic duties with the Naval Security Group and was shipped first to Alaska and later to Kamiseya.

Neither Martin nor Mitchell enjoyed Navy life enough to sign up for another hitch, but both remained fascinated by mathematics, and particularly its applications to cryptanalysis, even after their enlistments expired in 1954. Martin stayed in Japan for an extra year as a civilian with the Army Security Agency.

Mitchell returned to Eureka and, after a brief rest, enrolled at Stanford in order to finish his degree in mathematics. The choice of Stanford was a natural one. Both his father and mother were graduates, and his younger brother, Clifford, had spent his undergraduate years there as a star fullback before going on to the law school.

By the time his senior year rolled around, Bernon began thinking of the future. Ever since his Navy days the thought of going to work for the NSA, where mathematicians often work a good five years ahead of the state of the art, had appealed to him; he began the application procedure.

He seemed to be the ideal candidate for the Puzzle Palace: bright, with a degree in math and experience in cryptanalysis. In addition, he had already been granted a tough Naval Security Group cryptologic clearance, which made his chances of passing the NSA clearance hurdle decidedly good.

On February 25, 1957, Mitchell was interviewed on campus by one of the Agency's recruiters, who came away impressed. A week and a half later and several hundred miles to the north, another NSA recruiter began interviewing another candidate with almost identical credentials: William H. Martin, now in his last year as a straight-A math major at the University of Washington, in Seattle. Both apparently had kept in touch after their discharge from the Navy, and on July 8, 1957, the two reported for duty at NSA's Gatehouse 1 as GG-7s.

Despite the fact that they had previously received a final top secret clearance for their work in the Navy, NSA required that they go through the entire clearance process once again. On July 23, Mitchell was called to one of the tiny rooms used for the polygraph interviews, strapped to the machine, and asked a long series of questions. He showed little reaction until the questions began turning to sexual perversion and blackmail. All of a sudden his cooperation ceased, and he refused to answer any further questions.

Eleven days later he was back in the little room, and once again the questions turned to his sex life. This time Mitchell gave in and told his interrogator about certain "sexual experimentations" with dogs and chickens he had done when he was between the ages of thirteen and nineteen.

At this point, the results of the tests, together with a favorable report by the various federal intelligence and law enforcement agencies and the results of Mitchell's Navy background investigation, went to a middle-level evaluator in the Agency's Office of Security. He felt that Mitchell's farm animal "experimentation," when considered in the context of his age at the time, its lack of recurrence, and the favorable reports from the other checks, did not warrant denial of a clearance. Five days later Mitchell was granted an interim security clearance.

Martin received his interim clearance about a week later, after floating through the lie detector and National Agency Check without any problem.

On September 4, 1957, even though NSA had not yet requested renewed background investigations on the two buddies, Bernon F. Mitchell and William H. Martin held up their right hands, took the Security Indoctrination Oath, and were awarded their green badges, which confirmed them into the fraternity and granted them access to cryptologic materials through top secret code word.

Over the next five months the military agencies designated to conduct the background investigations on the two employees (the Air Force Office of Special Investigations for Mitchell and the Office of Naval Intelligence for Martin) rang doorbells and wore out shoe leather. The results, turned over to NSA between January and April of 1958, showed that, though acquaintances had variously rated Martin as an insufferable egotist, subject to flattery, and somewhat irresponsible, there was no reason to block his final clearance. Mitchell fared a bit better. But the gumshoes were to some extent handicapped by NSA's Office of Security rule that kept the results of the polygraph from the personnel department and the investigators conducting the BI. They were unable to take a closer look into Mitchell's adolescent animal fetish.

On Monday morning, January 27, 1958, having spent a number of months at George Washington University and the NSA Training School preparing for their duties, Mitchell and Martin reported to the Office of Research and Development, then under Dr. Solomon Kullback, and began applying their mathematical skills to the art of cryptology.

During this first year neither showed any ill feeling toward his work or the Agency. They took up separate residences in the company town, Laurel, Maryland, and joined the Washington Chess Divan. Mitchell, captain of the NSA chess team, began lifting barbells; Martin chased bar girls.

For close to a decade now, the NSA had been engaged in a secret and bloody air war with the Soviet Union. In April 1950, a Navy patrol bomber with a crew of ten was attacked and destroyed by Soviet fighters while flying over the Baltic. A year and a half later another Navy bomber on a reconnaissance mission off Siberia was shot down, with the loss of all ten on board. That year an Air Force Superfortress on another reconnaissance flight met the same fate over the Sea of Japan. Neither the crew nor any wreckage was ever found.

One of the luckier missions took place on March 15, 1953, when a four-engine American reconnaissance plane flying twenty-five miles off the Soviet coast, a hundred miles northeast of the giant Soviet naval base of Petropavlovsk on the Kamchatka Peninsula, was set on by two MIGs. One of the two opened fire on the American aircraft, which immediately returned fire. Neither of the planes suffered damage, and the ferret made it safely back to Elmendorf Air Force Base in Alaska.

Six months later there was still another attack. This time the ferret was protected by sixteen Sabrejets while it collected signals over the Yellow Sea. Nevertheless, eight MIGs swooped in for an attack; they were successfully repelled. One MIG was reportedly downed. By September 1954, American luck again began running out. On the fourth day of that month a Navy bomber on a reconnaissance flight from Atsugi, Japan, was shot down by two Soviet jets forty miles off the coast of Siberia with the loss of one flier. Only two months later another was shot down near the northern Japanese island of Hokkaido. The eleven crew members managed to bail out, but by the time rescuers arrived, one had died. The men aboard a Navy ferret attacked by Soviet aircraft over the Bering Sea on June 22, 1955, were more fortunate. They managed to crash-land on St. Lawrence Island with no loss of life.

In 1958, little more than two months apart, two American aircraft were shot down after crossing the Soviet border into Armenia. Several months later two more attacks occurred, one over the Baltic and one over the Sea of Japan. Both crew and aircraft returned unharmed.

For the crew and technicians of the ferrets, hopscotching along the Soviet coast, daring the Russian bear to snatch them out of the sky, the term "Cold War" was a serious misnomer.

Mitchell and Martin had known of the spy flights since their Naval Security Group days at Kamiseya in the early 1950s. Now, as NSA analysts working on foreign code problems, they learned of another type of ferret operation, one that troubled them greatly. These were the ELINT missions, in which the aircraft would not only skirt the Soviet borders but actually penetrate them in order to trigger otherwise inactive radar equipment and thus capture their telltale signals for later analysis by the Puzzle Palace.

The two first learned of the highly secret, highly compartmented missions early in 1959. The previous September an Air Force EC-130 had crashed inside Soviet Armenia; six crew members were killed and eleven others declared missing. Five months later, after numerous futile attempts to have the Soviet Union shed more light on the fate of the eleven lost airmen, the State Department released a verbatim transcript of the voices of Soviet MIG pilots in the process of shooting down the unarmed American aircraft. This showed as fraudulent earlier Russian statements to the effect that the plane simply crashed. (A more detailed account is in the next chapter.)

The same day as the State Department released the transcript — a move that top officials of the NSA probably objected to strongly — NSA director John Samford took to the Agency's public address system to suggest that employees refrain from discussing the subject of the EC-130. He apparently hoped this would keep the lid on the operation. The suggestion, however, had the opposite effect; employees throughout the Puzzle Palace began talking among themselves about the possible consequences of the incident. One high official mentioned to Martin that this particular aircraft "had been carrying electronics specialists and special equipment for receiving at close range the signals of Soviet radar transmitters" and that the plane had deliberately crossed the border "in order to get into immediate proximity of Soviet radar installations."

That America engaged in such dangerous and provocative activities shocked both Martin and Mitchell. While not averse to intelligence collection per se, they felt that by sending aircraft across foreign borders and into hostile territory, the American government was foolishly risking igniting a spark that could set off World War III. Even worse was the fact that very few government officials appeared to be aware of the true nature of the missions. Senator Hubert Humphrey's attacks on the Soviet Union for its unprovoked actions against the EC-130 seemed to indicate that Congress also had been kept in the dark about the policy of border penetrations.

Although Martin and Mitchell felt that someone should let Congress in on the operation, they were well aware of the COMINT statute that called for a ten-year prison sentence for anyone revealing just such information. Regardless, they decided to take the chance, and a few weeks later made an appointment with Congressman Wayne Hays, who, they knew, had publicly expressed concern about the State Department's concealing from Congress the pertinent facts of the incident.

After briefly reminding the Ohio Democrat of Senator Humphrey's most recent comments about the EC-130, and telling him of their concern over the failure of the Executive Branch to keep members of Congress correctly informed, the two began describing the aircraft's true mission and their fears that such border crossings were a danger to world peace. Before they were finished, however, the phone rang. Ironically, it was William Macomber, the assistant secretary of state for congressional relations, asking Hays to refrain from further public discussion of the EC-130 incident.

Hays jotted down his visitors' names on the back of his checkbook and told them he thought that perhaps Congress should make an investigation of the matter, "but that what he could do would depend mainly on the reaction of his seniors in Congress." Before leaving, Martin and Mitchell cautioned the representative about the risk they had taken under the COMINT statute and asked him to keep the fact of their visit strictly confidential.

Hays, never accused of being one of Congress' brightest members, briefly mentioned the meeting to Representative Tom Morgan, chairman of the Foreign Affairs Committee, but never spoke of it again because he suspected that the two men had been sent from the CIA to see whether he could keep a secret!

To Mitchell and Martin, rapidly becoming disenchanted with American society as a whole, the lack of even a letter of acknowledgment from the congressman on an issue as important as the illegal ELINT flights was the last straw. As they grew increasingly bitter toward the government, they also began feeling more and more estranged from a society that, they believed, was alien to their own values and beliefs.

To fill the void, they began looking toward the Soviet Union as a society where they would be more accepted, where their intellects would be respected instead of overlooked, where they would not be looked down on for their strong agnostic views, and where such hostile and illegal actions as overflights were not condoned.

It was a view that smacked of gross naïveté; unrealistic and, in large part, illogical. It was a view of Russia they had picked up from the pages of the English-language propaganda magazine *Soviet Life*. But to them it represented a favorable alternative.

By midsummer 1959 they had made their decision to defect, but they were in no hurry and planned to spend the next year exploring how to go about it. There was another good reason for postponing the flight: because of the high recommendations and letters of praise for the excellence of his work from his boss, R and D chief Kullback, Martin had been awarded a full-time academic scholarship to study for his master's degree in mathematics. It was a significant honor; of all the applicants, Martin was the only one chosen for the full-time program. Later, after winning approval for a second year, he became the first employee to be given a two-year scholarship. He was one of the Puzzle Palace's up-and-comers.

In September 1959 Martin left for the University of Illinois, at Urbana, where he excelled. Earning straight A's in such courses as abstract algebra and mathematical logic, he also had time to earn an A in a course he had begun taking while a student at the University of Washington, one that was not required under his NSA scholarship — Russian.

At Urbana he began associating with members of the Communist Party, and in December he and Mitchell took the first overt step toward their goal: against NSA regulations they flew to Cuba, where, most likely, they got in touch with Soviet officials.

Following the trip, Martin returned to Illinois. Mitchell returned to NSA and proceeded to have an unhappy love affair with a married woman. Later, he secretly sought counseling from Dr. Clarence Schilt, a Bethesda, Maryland, psychiatrist. In Schilt's office at the Silver Spring Medical Center, Mitchell told the doctor that he would like to discuss some of his theories about sex. Because he feared that the NSA might learn of his visits and assume he was a patient, he asked Schilt whether he might simply use him as a sounding board for his ideas.

During the three one-hour meetings in May and June 1960, Mitchell's conversations ranged from his feelings of superiority, to his bisexuality, to his agnosticism. At the conclusion of his third meeting,

Mitchell told Schilt cryptically, "Maybe I'll see you again and maybe I won't."

Also in June his friend Ham returned from Illinois and they began planning their annual leave together. They requested two weeks, from June 24 to July 11, to visit their parents on the West Coast, and within a few days the request was approved, along with permission to extend the visit an additional week, to July 18, if they needed more time. Neither had seen his parents for more than a year, although they both telephoned home quite regularly. On Father's Day, three days before the leave was to begin, each called home once again. Bernon complained to his mother that his woman friend had left for Greece, returning to her husband. "Keep your chin up," Mrs. Mitchell encouraged her son, as she told him to keep up with his visits to the psychiatrist. She unexpectedly triggered an acrimonious conclusion to the conversation when she told Bernon she would pray for him. Instead of feeling comforted, Bernon was enraged: "Why don't you do something for humanity instead of praying?"

The following Wednesday they packed, and on Thursday morning, June 25, they drove the twenty-five miles south to Washington's National Airport, where Bernon and Ham climbed into the silver fuselage of Eastern Airlines flight 307. A few minutes before noon, their seat belts fastened and their adrenaline beginning to race, Bernon F. Mitchell and William H. Martin lifted into the air on the first leg of a journey that had as its final destination, not the West Coast and family, but the Soviet Union and a new way of life. They were about to become the two most important defectors in American history.

Landing in Mexico City after a brief stopover in New Orleans, the pair registered at the Hotel Virreyes and told the clerk that they would be staying about two weeks, but the next morning they abruptly checked out and boarded a Cubana Airlines plane bound for Havana. There they were quietly hustled aboard a Soviet freighter — possibly the 5865-ton *Ilya Mechnikov* or one of the other Russian ships secretly hauling heavy artillery and, later, offensive missiles to Cuba — for their long voyage to their new homeland.

At NSA it was more than a month before they were missed. On July 26, a week and a day after their leave extension had expired, their supervisor tried to reach them at their numbers in Laurel and then at their parents' homes out west. When it seemed that they had simply disappeared, the supervisor contacted Maurice H. Klein, director of personnel, who, in turn, got in touch with security director Wes Reynolds, who was then out at UCLA, supervising security for an NSA symposium (known as SCAMP). Reynolds returned on the next available plane and immediately began a quiet investigation. A check of the various airline manifests turned up their names on the flight to Mexico and the later flight to Cuba.

Without bothering to seek a warrant, agents from NSA's Office of Security broke into the small shingle house Mitchell rented at 1010 Eighth Street in Laurel. Still parked in front was his 1959 Ford with its Fort Meade parking sticker on the bumper and, inside, a tennis racquet, a chessboard, and a copy of the skin-diving magazine *Underwater Adventure*. The agents found the house a shambles. One item that intrigued them was a key to a safe deposit box, which was apparently left for them to find. The agents quickly got in touch with the Maryland State Police, who obtained a court order to open the box, and then proceeded to the State Bank of Laurel. There they slipped the key into box number 174, rented under the name of Bernon F. Mitchell, and pulled out a sealed envelope, which bore on the top a request that the contents be made public. It was signed by both Martin and Mitchell.

Whatever hopes the NSA may have had that things were not so bad as they seemed were shattered by the first sentence of the multiple-page statement: "We hope to explain to our relatives, friends, and others who may be interested why we have sought citizenship in the Soviet Union." The writers went on to list, in a well-written, articulate fashion, their principal grievances against the government of their former homeland, especially their disillusionment over America's practice of knowingly making "false and deceptive statements both in defending its own actions and in condemning the actions of other nations" (undoubtedly a veiled reference to the ELINT ferrets) and also over the government's occasional habit of secretly manipulating "money and military supplies in an effort to bring about the overthrow of governments which are felt to be unfriendly to the United States."

Finally, they cited one more example to indicate that "the United States Government is as unscrupulous as it has accused the Soviet Government of being." This involved an apparent NSA–CIA Division D operation, in which "the United States Government gave money to a code clerk working in the Washington embassy of a United States ally for supplying information which assisted in the solving of that ally's coded messages." (Later, in the USSR, they identified that ally as Turkey.)

But why the Soviet Union? Here, they argued, their main values and interests would be shared by a majority of the people, and, consequently, they themselves would be accepted socially. Another reason was their belief that "the talents of women are encouraged and utilized to a much greater extent in the Soviet Union than in the United States." This, they felt, "enriches Soviet society and makes Soviet women more desirable as mates."

But their reasons, as set out in the statement, were as much economic and ideological as social. Under capitalism, they charged, science and technology are used to the disadvantage of the masses, causing needless suffering "by contributing to technological unemployment." Such was not the case in the Soviet Union, argued Martin and Mitchell.

Despite the statement, an embarrassed Pentagon decided to pretend ignorance. According to one individual, "Officials vainly hoped the note would never have to be made public."

On August 1, the Pentagon released the news that two employees of the National Security Agency had failed to return from a vacation and that they were missing and unaccounted for. Five days later, after their trip to Cuba had been discovered and the statement secretly had been retrieved, the department revised its statement, adding, "It must be assumed that there is a likelihood that they have gone behind the Iron Curtain." Incredibly, hoping to hide the magnitude of the loss, which one high Defense Department official confidentially called "possibly the worst security breach since Klaus Fuchs gave the Russians the secret of the atom bomb," the Pentagon went on to say that the information available to the two in their work "could in no way be prejudicial to the security of the United States communications. They had no access to classified documents about American weapons and defense plans." It was a little like saying that Klaus Fuchs did not harm the Western powers because he had had no access to Los Alamos and Harwell.

The statement, in the best Pentagonian double-talk, was designed to deceive. But it infuriated other members of the intelligence community who knew of the farewell note. One high-ranking intelligence official decided to reveal to House Majority Leader John W. McCormack the true facts surrounding the double defection. In a confidential meeting in the congressman's office, the official told the Massachusetts Democrat that the Defense Department's pronouncements were entirely misleading and that the United States had, in fact, sustained one of the worst security breaches in its history.

The day after the meeting, on August 30, McCormack went public with his new information and called on Pennsylvania Democrat Francis E. Walter, chairman of the House Un-American Activities Committee (HUAC), to begin an inquiry into the incident.

"Information furnished me from usually reliable sources," McCormack declared, "leaves no doubt that the two employees have defected to Russia and that they took valuable cryptographic information with them, and its loss is far more serious than any official has publicly admitted." He added that there was a "possibility" that the two employees had been in contact with Soviet agents as early as December, "and could easily have turned over valuable information to the Communists in Mexico months before they turned up missing." To make matters worse, Walter learned that one of the two had requested and received information about the U-2 flight of Francis Gary Powers before he was downed on May 1 and that both men had worked on Soviet communications about the U-2 and other reconnaissance flights.

One week later, McCormack's charges were confirmed in excruciating detail.

As Moscow's large, theaterlike House of Journalists began filling to capacity with newspeople from both the Communist and non-Communist world, Martin and Mitchell took turns reading a long, prepared statement. Again they indicated that their main dissatisfaction concerned a number of dangerous and unethical intelligence-collection activities carried out by their former employer, the NSA. Topping the list were the ferrets. "A single incident or misinterpretation," Martin and Mitchell warned the crowd from behind Cyrillic-lettered name plates, "concerning the purpose of planes involved in these flights could be the cause of war." As an example, they described in detail the flight of the ill-fated EC-130 over Soviet Armenia.

One of the other NSA activities that disenchanted them was the practice "of intercepting and deciphering the secret communications of its own allies." Later, in reply to a question from an *Izvestia* correspondent, Martin identified a few of those countries: "Italy, Turkey, France, Yugoslavia, the United Arab Republic, Indonesia, Uruguay — that's enough to give a general picture, I guess."

At least half of the ninety-minute press conference was spent giving the world its first look inside the Puzzle Palace. The two described everything from the number of manual intercept positions (more than two thousand) to the subdivisions of PROD to NSA's very secret partnership with Britain's GCHQ. Almost as an afterthought they added that NSA regularly read the secret communications of more than forty nations.

At the conclusion of their prepared statement, the two men, dressed neatly in dark Western business suits, agreed to take questions. One correspondent asked for details about how they had reached Moscow.

Martin, with a broad grin, declined to answer, saying, "Others may want to use the same route."

After an exhausting hour and a half, Mikhail A. Kharlamov, chief of the press department of the Soviet Foreign Ministry, indicated an end to the questioning, but Martin, obviously enjoying the spotlight, protested and was allowed one more swing at the NSA.

Back in the United States the reaction to the press conference ranged from disbelief to outrage. Emery Mitchell, Bernon's father, said of the defection, "This thing was not voluntary." Martin's father, a vice president of the Schaake Meat Packing Company in Ellensburg and president of the local Chamber of Commerce, shared the elder Mitchell's opinion and said his son was in Moscow "under duress." Eisenhower branded Martin and Mitchell "self-confessed traitors," the Pentagon called them turncoats, and former President Truman said "they ought to be shot."

At least three inquests were begun into the scandal, the most ambitious that of Walter's HUAC, which had as part of its mandate an investigation into NSA's hiring practices. Thirteen months, two thousand man-hours, and sixteen executive session hearings later, Chairman Walter issued the committee's report. It seemed to indicate that the primary reason for the defection was homosexuality. Never once did the committee bother to look into what might have been the deeper reasons for the defection, the political or ideological motivations.

To many in the Puzzle Palace, the thirteen months between the defections and the final report of HUAC had been like waiting for the other shoe to drop. To personnel director Maurice H. Klein, however, it had been more like waiting for an ax to fall.

At forty-eight, Moe Klein had been in the business for close to twenty years, first as a lieutenant during World War II, assigned to Arlington Hall, and later as a major, when he was an assistant chief of the Army Security Agency's Operations Division. In 1949, as the ASA was changing over to the Armed Forces Security Agency, Klein decided to turn in his uniform and join the new organization as a civilian. It was a wise move, since the new agency was going to become largely civilian in personnel, but it also involved submitting a new application and once again filling out innumerable forms, chief among which was the standard Government Employment Application, or Form 57, in bureaucratese.

Klein had been through it all before. In February of 1942 and again in May of that year he had put pen to paper and logged his past. But starting in September, something began to shift. Although the forms remained basically the same, his past underwent slight changes. His date of birth was switched from March 24 to April 12, 1912, his mother's birthplace from Russia to the United States, his name was transformed from Morris Harry to Maurice Harold, and, more seriously, the graduate of New Jersey Law School became an alumnus of Harvard Law — a school he had attended for one year only. In 1949, hoping to win a place in the new agency, the Army officer filled out another Form 57 and another Personal History Statement, again with the now-familiar misinformation.

After a short wait and with little difficulty, Klein received his appointment and, along with it, his top secret cryptologic clearance, which, to his relief, was based on the background investigation carried out years before for his military clearance. That eliminated the need for a new check.

His luck changed for the worse, however, when President Eisenhower entered the White House and issued an order directing that all civilian government employees occupying sensitive positions be reinvestigated. The resulting BI, in 1955, turned up Klein's wayward information and it was reported to the Agency's security chief, Wes Reynolds. Reynolds interrogated the personnel director but, having known Klein for a number of years, and believing that the errors on the application form had no security significance, took no action.

It was a close call. To make sure there would not be another, Klein allegedly pulled out his personnel file and removed the Form 57 containing the false information and replaced it with a newly prepared form, this one with accurate information.

All went well until Martin and Mitchell decided they wanted to visit Red Square. After the defections, NSA went into a collective state of panic. The House, the Senate, the Pentagon, all began investigations — and they all wanted documents. When HUAC investigator Donald Appell showed up at the main gate to request a number of employment applications, including Form 57s, Klein refused to turn them over. He was then served with a subpoena.

Klein's unusual reaction to the committee's request raised suspicions in the mind of Frank S. Tavenner, Jr., chief investigator for the committee. After all, it was a fairly reasonable request, in light of the committee's mandate to examine the Agency's hiring practices. In fact, the committee had bent over backward in order to know as little as possible about the Agency's actual operations.

Now attention began turning toward Klein himself, and he was requested to transmit his personnel file to a HUAC investigator at the Pentagon. Realizing that the investigator would surely discover that the substituted Form 57 had been printed by the Government Printing Office later than the form's supposed date of execution (June 15, 1949), Klein, according to the committee, pulled another switch. He searched through stacks of his old papers and located a Form 57 dated before June 1949; it was one he apparently had used as a trial sheet, and it still contained some penciled entries, which, the committee concluded, he erased. He then typed in the correct background information, along with the date June 15, 1949.

It was a sloppy job; the erasures quickly caught the eye of investigators, who shipped the document over to the sleuths at the Veterans Administration's Identification and Detection Division. They determined from a photocopy of the document that the typewriter used was an IBM Electromatic with elite type, but without the original of the document, then in the possession of the Department of Defense, they could make no accurate guess about the year the machine had been made.

The committee next sent the results of the investigation to Secretary of Defense Robert McNamara, who called on the FBI to examine Klein's document. The determination was: "The form 57 in question could not have been filed by NSA's director of personnel when he became a civilian employee of the Agency in 1949." In fact, the Pentagon's own probe clearly established that the form had not been filled out until the time Klein's records were requested by the Defense Department for review by HUAC.

When Klein was called before the committee, meeting in executive session, he ignored the evidence and flatly denied the charges that he had done any switching. He explained that the mistakes about his law school career were simply the result of carelessness. As to the other discrepancies, he said that there had long been a question in his family as to whether his mother was born abroad or in this country, and that his birth certificate had been filed by a doctor who gave his name and birth date incorrectly.

Nevertheless, as a result of the investigation, Klein was ousted on November 10, 1961, less than three months before he could have retired with his pension. Commenting on his ordeal, Klein later said: "I am not a Communist. I am not an un-American. I had nothing to do with Martin and Mitchell. My problem," he concluded sadly, "has been a form."

Two days after Klein cleaned out his desk, Reynolds, forty-seven, was also asked to step down. Ostensibly he resigned for violation of the Pentagon's new "standards of conduct" directive, relating to the acceptance of gratuities by military personnel. But in reality,

Reynolds' departure was final restitution for the sins of Martin and Mitchell.

As the months passed, and the reality of Soviet life gradually became clear, the once-fiery passions of the two defectors slowly burned down to disillusionment. During a chance encounter with an American in a Leningrad café two years after his debut in the House of Journalists, Ham Martin confessed that his decision to flee to Russia had been based on a view of Soviet life derived mostly from the English-language Soviet propaganda magazines, *USSR* and *Soviet Life*. Like all propaganda journals, Martin said sadly, *USSR* was apt to paint the situation in somewhat rosy terms.

Though disillusioned, Martin — who had changed his name to Sokolovsky shortly after Truman declared that he and Mitchell should be shot — said he nevertheless intended to make the best of his new situation.

He was now married to a Russian woman whom he met while vacationing at the Black Sea resort of Gagra a few months after the defection. He complained of the Soviet government's failure to keep its promise that they would be free to live wherever they chose. Recently, he said, he had applied for a change of residence to Moscow because of his wife's health. He explained that she was from the south and suffered from asthma in Leningrad's humid climate. Despite the promise, however, the request was turned down.

On the other hand, the Russians did keep their promise to provide him with approximately the same salary that he received at NSA, a handsome 500 rubles (about $555) a month.

The alumnus of the Puzzle Palace, now a Soviet citizen, was studying for his candidate's degree, which is similar to a Ph.D. Having passed his orals with an average grade, he was working on his dissertation in statistics at the Institute of Mathematics. Yet even here there were reminders of the differences between what was and what is, like libraries with rooms containing material not approved ideologically or politically by the Soviet government and open only to research specialists.

Even more disillusioned is Mitchell. In late 1979 the Leningrad computer specialist began requesting information from the American consulate about the possibility of returning to the United States. The inquiry triggered a State Department review of his status, and in February 1980, almost twenty years after the Klieg lights had been turned on in Moscow's Hall of Journalists, he was formally stripped of his American citizenship. "We found him to have expatriated himself by becoming a Soviet citizen," said one State Department official.

Next, Mitchell applied to the consulate for permission to return to the United States as an immigrant, but this request was also turned down. The basis for the rejection was the section of the immigration laws barring people affiliated with the Communist Party. Although it could not be determined for certain whether he actually had joined the party, the State Department based its decision on the fact that when he left, "he gave valuable information to the Soviet Government which is part and parcel of the Communist Party." Under such a determination, there is no appeal.

Persistent, Mitchell then applied for a tourist visa, but this too, not surprisingly, was rejected. This left him, apparently, with two choices. Someone in his family could lobby a member of Congress to have a private bill passed, in effect overruling the State Department, or Mitchell could apply to immigrate to a third country, such as Canada. Yet even if he did win a new homeland, there is always the matter of a Soviet exit visa.

But according to his father, who hears from Bernon on the telephone somewhat regularly, the problem is not with the Soviet Union trying to keep him in, but with the American government wanting to keep him out. When asked about his son's second thoughts over the defection, the senior Mitchell said, "I don't think there is any doubt about that — I think he had some very soon."

•

In the weeks and months that followed the defection of Martin and Mitchell, the Puzzle Palace began taking on the atmosphere of a lonely outpost under siege. Under increasing pressure from Chairman Walter and his HUAC to cleanse itself of anyone even remotely suspected of "sexual deviancy," the Agency launched a massive purge, quietly ousting "deviates" at the rate of more than one every other week.* Any man exhibiting the slightest effeminacy became an instant suspect.

With the Office of Security on full alert for limp wrists and telltale lisps, it was little wonder that no one happened to notice a $100-a-week Army sergeant arriving for work each morning in his baby-blue Jaguar or one of his two late-model Cadillacs. After all, Sergeant Jack E. Dunlap, a womanizing, beer-drinking "family man" with a wife and five children, hardly fitted the pattern the purifiers were looking for.

It was an unfortunate oversight. In their manic search for homosex-

* A total of twenty-six individuals were dropped from the rolls of the Agency because of "indications of sexual deviation." (U.S. House of Representatives, Committee on Un-American Activities, *Security Practices in the National Security Agency*, Report, August 13, 1962, p. 18.)

uals, they completely overlooked Moscow's replacement for Martin and Mitchell.

On paper, Jack Edward Dunlap was the ideal security risk. When first assigned to NSA in April 1958 as a chauffeur for Major General Garrison B. Cloverdale, an assistant director and the Agency's chief of staff, the thirty-year-old sergeant had already accumulated an impressive record. After enlisting in the Army in June 1952, following eight years in the Merchant Marine, Dunlap served heroically with the 36th Infantry in Korea and was awarded the Purple Heart and Bronze Star for "coolness under fire and sincere devotion to duty." Nor did his personal life show anything that would call into question his honesty or loyalty. The tall, lanky native of Bogalusa, Louisiana, had quit high school after three years for a life at sea and had picked up three Good Conduct Medals while in the Army. He could easily have been nominated for "soldier of the year."

Although the exact date is somewhat uncertain, there is no doubt that by June of 1960, as Martin and Mitchell were packing their bags to see the lights of Moscow, Staff Sergeant Jack Dunlap, now elevated to the position of clerk-messenger at the Agency, had become a highly paid employee of the KGB.

At the NSA, just as at the CIA or any other highly sensitive government agency, those employees with the greatest access to secret information are not the department heads or project chiefs, who, under the uniform "need to know" policy, are knowledgeable only about their particular operations. Instead, the system works in such a way that, oftentimes, the lower a person is on the ladder of responsibility, the greater is his or her access to sensitive information. Before the director can send an "eyes only" message to the President, for example, it first has to be typed by a secretary, who then most likely hands it to someone to deliver to the message room, where a teletype operator punches it into a crypto machine. At the White House it is first torn off the machine, handed to another messenger, who probably turns it over to someone else for eventual delivery to the President. By the time it reaches his hands, the message destined for his eyes only has come under the possible scrutiny of at least six other pairs of eyes. With most messages and documents, that number is increased many times.

Dunlap, who acted as a courier for highly classified documents between various parts of the Agency, was now in a position to be of that number.

Although the how of Dunlap's conversion from war hero to traitor may remain forever locked away in some Moscow file cabinet, the when and the why have become much less opaque. He was a political neuter, and his motivation was purely economic. Strapped financially, trying to support a family of seven on his meager Army wages plus whatever he could pick up on the side by pumping gas for a dollar an hour, Dunlap may have initially sold his soul and the NSA's secrets more out of necessity than greed, but it was not long before the order was reversed. In fact, it is the greed that serves to signal the start of his entrepreneurship.

In June 1960, the same man who the month before could barely afford a secondhand station wagon slapped down a cool $3400 in cash for a thirty-foot cabin cruiser fully equipped with galley and bar. Later, in what became an orgy of high living and fast spending, Dunlap took on a blond mistress; picked up a record-setting hydroplane skimmer; joined the Stoney Creek Racing Boat Club; traded in his station wagon for a Cadillac convertible, a yellow Caddy sedan, and a hot little Jaguar; and began hobnobbing with Maryland's landed gentry at some of the most exclusive resorts. Where months before he had hardly enough money in the bank for a ticket to a boat show, he now could afford to send two of his friends to New York, all expenses paid, to select the finest of Italian handmade speedboat propellers for his racer. In his very first year as NSA's only salesman, he took home a sum estimated to be between $30,000 and $40,000 — an enormous commission from a normally stingy customer. (A few years ago the Soviets paid a mere $3000 for a copy of the CIA's top secret KH-11 spy satellite operations manual.)

Any questions about the source of his newfound wealth were quickly turned away with a variety of explanations, depending on his mood and the situation. To some, he said that he owned land on which a precious mineral powder, valuable to the cosmetic industry, had been found. Others he told that he had inherited a large plantation in his home state. To his mistress he simply said he made trips to "the bookkeeper."

But interest in the enlisted man's sudden affluence was only by his friends and neighbors, and not, incredibly, by his employer, even though, because of Martin and Mitchell, security was supposedly at its most vigilant. Even when the Agency, fearful of what he might disclose under sedation, sent an ambulance to transport him to the Fort Meade Army Hospital following a spill during a yacht club regatta, no one bothered to wonder where his sailing money came from.

For almost three full years Jack Dunlap worked as the Soviet Union's resident mole in the nation's supersecret, supersecure agency. His tenure as a spy during the early 1960s, in fact, was slightly longer than John Kennedy's tenure as President of the United States. The damage to America's SIGINT and COMSEC operations during those years cannot even be estimated, for no one except his KGB handlers will ever know exactly which documents were sold. One Pentagon official later commented that Dunlap's treason was "thirty to forty times as serious as the Mitchell and Martin defections."

Just as it was greed that got him his fancy cars and his high-powered boats, it was greed that caused his downfall. Afraid of being transferred into some nonsensitive, overseas assignment at the end of his tour of duty at the Puzzle Palace, he decided to leave the Army and apply to the Agency as a civilian so that he could continue his highly profitable avocation.

But unfortunately for the sergeant, security screening for civilians was far stricter than for members of the military. As is still the case, NSA waives the polygraph test for members of the armed forces assigned to the Agency, but tests each and every civilian applicant. Twice in March 1963 Dunlap was strapped to the box and admitted to instances of "petty thievery" and "immoral conduct." A few months later, his background investigation started turning up indications of his high living, and on May 23 the Army quickly relieved him of his security clearance and transferred him to a job in a Fort Meade orderly room.

As the investigation continued into June, Dunlap could feel the vice tighten, squeezing out any possibility of hope. He checked into a nearby motel on June 14 and two days later washed down several containers of sleeping pills with a couple of beers. The next morning his friends found him sprawled across his bed, still alive but burning with fever. Rushing him to a hospital, they left behind his two suicide notes — one to his wife, the other to his girl friend — for investigators to find later. Still, there was no mention of espionage in the notes, and the investigators found nothing to charge him with formally, though the investigation now took on added urgency.

Dunlap was released from the hospital on July 2, cured of the overdose but still determined to take his life one way or another, a fact he himself made clear to his Army Security Agency company commander. Nevertheless, no attempts were made to alter his thinking, and on July 20 he once again attempted to end it all, this time with a revolver. But also once again a friend intervened, wrestling the gun away from him, and the attempt failed.

It was a brief reprieve. Two days later, on a warm Monday evening, Dunlap parked his car on a lonely dirt road, strung a length of radiator hose from his exhaust pipe into his right front window, started his engine, and bade a final farewell to the Puzzle Palace. On July 25,

1963, Sergeant First Class Jack Edward Dunlap was buried with full military honors at Arlington National Cemetery.

The story, as well as the investigation, might have ended there had not Dunlap's widow, Diane, come across a cache of highly classified documents in their Glen Burnie home almost a month after her husband's death. On learning of this, the NSA's Office of Security called in the FBI, and the investigation switched from third gear into overdrive. But by now it was too late. The only person who knew the details behind one of America's worst spy scandals was resting six feet beneath a hill overlooking Washington and the Potomac River.

•

With Dunlap's death, it was hoped that the spy- and defector-wracked Agency had seen its last scandal. Such, however, was not to be. Incredibly, on the very day that fishermen discovered Dunlap's lifeless body slumped in the front seat of his car near Markey's Creek, another former NSA employee turned up in Moscow and told the world his story on the front page of *Izvestia*.

This time it was Victor Norris Hamilton, a former cryptanalyst assigned to the Agency's codebreaking Production Organization. A naturalized American citizen, Hamilton had come to the United States with his wife, an American whom he had met in Libya, some time during the 1950s and settled in Georgia after changing his name from Hindali. His failure to get a teaching job he attributed to his Arab origins, although he was a graduate of the American University in Beirut. He resigned himself to working as a doorman and bellhop until an American colonel recruited him for the Puzzle Palace.

Starting, on June 13, 1957, as a $6400-a-year "research analyst," he was placed in the Near East Sector of PROD's ALLO (all other countries) division, which, according to Hamilton, "concerns itself with the U.A.R., Syria, Iraq, Lebanon, Jordan, Saudi Arabia, Yemen, Libya, Morocco, Tunisia, Turkey, Iran, Greece, and Ethiopia." Continued Hamilton in his statement to the Russian newspaper:

> The duties of my colleagues in ALLO included the study and breaking of military ciphers of these countries, and also the deciphering of all correspondence reaching their diplomatic representatives in any part of the world . . . NSA reads the ciphers of all these countries by applying cryptanalysis . . .
>
> I knew for a fact that the State Department and Defense Department systematically read, analyzed, and utilized in their own interests the enci-

phered correspondence between the U.A.R. embassies in Europe and
the U.A.R. government in Cairo.

For example, I had in my desk all the deciphered communications
between Cairo and the U.A.R. embassy in Moscow relating to the visit
of the U.A.R. government mission to the USSR in 1958 for the purpose
of purchasing petroleum in the Soviet Union. NSA sent all these communications to the State Department, just as it continually sends it the
deciphered instructions of the U.A.R. Ministry of Foreign Affairs to its
embassy in Washington . . .

It is especially important to note that American authorities take advantage of the fact that the UN headquarters is located on American soil.
Their highhandedness has reached the point where the enciphered instructions of the governments of the U.A.R., Iraq, Jordan, Lebanon, Turkey, and Greece to their missions to the UN General Assembly fall into
the hands of the State Department before arriving at their proper address.

For about a year and a half things went well for Hamilton at NSA,
but then he began showing signs of deep-rooted psychological problems. By February 1959 the Agency pronounced him "mentally ill"
but decided to retain him in his position because of his superior
proficiency in Arabic. Four months later, however, it regretted that
decision, and Hamilton, "approaching a paranoid-schizophrenic
break," was forced to resign. According to Hamilton himself, the
real reason for his firing was his desire to re-establish contact with
relatives in Syria. Whatever the reason, the Arab codebreaker shipped
off to Moscow and in so doing inflicted another body blow to the
already black-and-blue Agency.

Infested by moles and potential defectors for more than twelve
of its first fifteen years, AFSA-NSA managed the distinction of becoming not only the most secretive and most hidden member of America's
growing intelligence consortium, but also the most thoroughly penetrated.

PLATFORMS

LAND

Rumors began to spread in the tight-knit, northern Maine border town soon after the newcomer arrived. Early November was long past tourist season, and he did not look like a logger.

The mystery deepened when the quiet young man in his mid-twenties suddenly rented a house on the old Gillin farm, near where Houlton's first settlers were buried. Within days, a half-dozen others had joined him; some speculated that they were with the Secret Service.

Then passersby saw thousands of feet of wire being strung, and soon a huge, strange-looking antenna system began taking shape. In less than a week it was up, and a fortnight before the close of World War I, Signal Corps Lieutenant Arthur E. Boeder flipped a switch and brought to life America's first transatlantic eavesdropping station.

•

More than sixty years later Lieutenant Boeder's intercept post has long since disappeared, replaced by a parking lot and a Kingdom Hall, where Jehovah's Witnesses come to listen for celestial messages of a different sort.

Although wireless telegrams are no longer snared from the ether above the Gillin farm, land-based American SIGINT platforms stretch from glaciated islands in the Bering Sea to snake-infested swamplands in Virginia, and from Turkish poppy fields to the ragged peaks of the Himalayas.

Before NSA can attack a code or read a message, it first must be able to capture and record the elusive signal. Such is the job of the Central Security Service, an invisible organization virtually unknown beyond Fort Meade.

Made up of the Army Intelligence and Security Command (the old ASA), the Naval Security Group, and the Air Force Security Service, the CSS is the eyes and ears of America's cryptologic empire. They are the soldiers, sailors, Marines, and airmen who sit in long rows with earphones, turning dials, activating tape recorders, and tapping out messages on six-ply, multicolored carbon paper.

Chief of the forty-five-thousand-member CSS is the same person who runs the fifty-thousand-employee Puzzle Palace: the director of NSA. Quietly established by President Nixon in 1972 "to provide a more unified cryptologic organization within the Department of Defense," the CSS was more an accident than the result of a well-thought-out plan.

Conceived in the course of discussions leading up to the 1971 reorganization of the intelligence community, the original idea was to create, in essence, a fourth branch of the armed services. While the members of the "cryptologic" branch would wear the same uniforms as their counterparts in the Army, Navy, Marines, and Air Force, they were to specialize solely in SIGINT and COMSEC areas and would follow an entirely separate chain of command — one leading ultimately to the director of NSA.

As might be expected, however, the military brass sounded battle stations and eventually torpedoed the idea. Out of the rubble appeared the Central Security Service, which, according to one of its drafters, "was a half-assed, last-minute job" to destroy the original fourth-service proposal.

"I was in on the writing of the goddamned thing and I don't know what the hell it is," the former senior intelligence official declared. "Never did understand what it was."

Eventually established by Nixon's executive order, the CSS managed to compound the one problem it was originally designed to correct. Rather than consolidating the cryptologic community, it drove the wedge even deeper by creating a system of "dual staffs." The result was so disastrous that the entire organization was, in effect, scrapped, leaving only the chief (DIRNSA) and deputy chief, a second position filled by NSA's deputy director for Field Management.

Calling the organization a "tower of babel," a one-time assistant to several of the CSS deputy chiefs pointed out how far the confusion reached: "I can assure you that, having been their deputy . . . we talked about that all the time and couldn't figure out what the hell it was."

Even the author of the executive order, then the director of the Office of Management and Budget, James Schlesinger, hoped to avoid the subject when it came up during hearings before a subcommittee of the House Appropriations Committee. He was pressed by Florida congressman Robert L. F. Sikes, who asked, "Since the elimination of the dual staff of CSS within NSA, leaving only one man in that organization other than the Chief, is there justification for maintaining the fiction of a separate organization?" Schlesinger, who by the time of the hearings was Secretary of Defense, simply demurred, saying, "I think it would be desirable to get General Allen here."

Whether CSS was a fictional organization or not, DIRNSA's real control over the legions of uniformed analysts and intercept operators reposes in the supersecret NSCID No. 6, revised on February 17, 1972:

> The Director of the National Security Agency is authorized to issue direct to any operating elements engaged in SIGINT operations such instructions and assignments as are required. All instructions issued by the Director under the authority provided in this paragraph shall be mandatory, subject only to appeal to the Secretary of Defense.

By-passing not only the Joint Chiefs but even the secretaries of the branches of the armed forces, the NSCID devolves incredible authority and responsibility on the NSA director, giving him, at least where SIGINT is concerned, his own Army, Navy, Marines, and Air Force.

Of the three service cryptologic agencies, or SCAs, as they are known, the Army's is the oldest, tracing its roots back to MI-8 in the First World War. Still headquartered in the aging, ramshackle former girls' school, Arlington Hall, the ASA merged in the late 1970s with Army Intelligence to become the U.S. Army Intelligence and Security Command (INSCOM).

Like its sister, the Naval Security Group also remains housed in the stately, red brick former girls' school on Nebraska Avenue that it occupied during World War II.

Youngest of the group, the U.S. Air Force Security Service, recently renamed the U.S. Air Force Electronic Security Command (AFESC), was founded in 1948 and bases its headquarters in a sprawling H-shaped complex at Kelly Air Force Base in San Antonio, Texas. Its main building, Ardisana Hall, was named after the late Brigadier General Bernard Ardisana, who was serving as NSA's assistant deputy director for Operations at the time of his death.

Using platforms ranging from satellites to submarines, the SCAs envelop the globe in an electronic web, the main strands of which are the land-based, antenna-strewn intercept stations, descendants of Houlton's Gillin farm.

Completed two weeks before the Armistice, the Houlton station had a life span of less than a year. Without a war and with censorship dead and buried, the War Department saw little need to continue patrolling the ether, a fact that was particularly upsetting to Herbert O. Yardley, now left to his own devices to acquire the needed messages for his Black Chamber.

The situation changed in 1930, however, when the SIS took over and was given, among other responsibilities, the authority to locate, interpret, and solve "enemy communications" — but only in time of war. The implementing order did authorize the establishment of a radio intercept service and the construction of listening posts, but, again, their purpose during peacetime was to be limited solely to training of personnel and development of equipment.

Toward the end of 1931, construction had begun on an experimental intercept station at Fort Hunt in Battery Cove, Virginia, twenty-five miles southeast of Washington, which concentrated on developing high-speed receivers but also gathered actual intercept material for "practice" by the student cryptanalysts.

By February 1938 the Signal Intelligence Service had six listening posts in full-time operation. In the United States, stations were plucking signals at the Presidio in San Francisco, California; Fort Sam Houston, Texas; and, to take care of traffic between Washington and the major cable companies in New York, Fort Monmouth, New Jersey. Overseas units were set up at Manila in the Philippines and Fort Shafter in Hawaii; and concentrating twenty-four hours a day on the Rome, Berlin, and Tokyo circuits was the monitoring station at Quarry Heights in the Canal Zone.

At the same time, the Navy was fishing for signals from intercept stations located at Cheltenham, Maryland; Winter Harbor, Maine; Bainbridge Island in Puget Sound, Washington, which covered the Tokyo-to-Washington traffic; Oahu in Hawaii; and a blockhouse on Corregidor in the Philippines. Smaller listening posts were located at Guam; Imperial Beach, California; Amagansett, Long Island; and Jupiter, Florida.

Because of the thickening clouds of possible hostilities from the Far East and growing tensions in Europe, the ban on peacetime interception was secretly lifted on March 26, 1938, and the signal snatchers began spinning their dials with unrestrained vigor. After Pearl Harbor, eavesdropping posts began springing up like mushrooms, and by the time the war ended, earphone-clad men and women were operating stations from the Aleutians to Australia, and from India to Africa. Having learned the value of mastery of the airwaves, America's slowly unifying SIGINT community marked the postwar and Cold War years by turning their antennas toward the menacing Russians and their neighbors to the east. Hardly had the dust begun settling over war-ravaged Japan when the island nation suddenly switched from being America's chief SIGINT target to its chief SIGINT platform. At Wak-kanai on the island of Hokkaido, northernmost city in the empire, the Army Security Agency took over 184 acres and began tuning in the Soviet Union, a mere forty miles farther north. Like tall gray weeds, more ASA antennas began sprouting from a 1229-acre stretch of southern Hokkaido, four miles southwest of Chitose.

At Sakata, on the main island of Honshu, a third intercept post directed its ear 550 miles across the Sea of Japan toward the intriguing geographic confluence of China, Korea, and the Soviet Union. Still another appeared at Kakata on the southern island of Kyushu. The Naval Security Group, meanwhile, concentrated at Kamiseya in the port area of Yokohoma and at Hanza, Sobe, and Futema on Okinawa.

Following the Korean War, NSA pushed closer still to its principal targets with ASA listening stations at Seoul, fifty acres at P'Yong T'Aek, the Red Cloud Compound twelve miles from Uijonabu, and a small base at Toegeuag.

To watch the underbelly of the Russian bear, particularly the missile and space activity at Tyuratam, the Puzzle Palace turned to strate-gically located Turkey. Selected as the site for the major listening post was the small city of Karamursel, a few miles from the Sea of Marmara and thirty-seven miles southeast of the mosque and minaret skyline of Istanbul. Apparently known as Main Site by the major ten-ant, the Air Force Security Service, the 697-acre barbed-wire-encircled compound in Asian Turkey was actually manned jointly by the USAFSS and the Naval Security Group.

Shortly after Karamursel sprang to life, other, smaller units began setting up shop on dry mud flats and in poppy fields along the rugged Black Sea coast. Operating at first out of green, antenna-sprouting vans and small windowless blocks of cement, these field stations homed in on Soviet air and naval traffic, commercial communications, and radar signals bearing such peculiar names as Wiff, Token, Mush-room, and Neptune.

Closest to the target was the intercept station at Trabzon, a small coastal village in the shadow of Turkey's Kuzey Anadolu Dağlari Mountain Range and a mere seventy miles from the Russian border. Two hundred miles to the west, on the road to Carsamba, a handful of Air Force SIGINT specialists manned an almost identical station at Samsun. From here, since at least the summer of 1955, America has kept close watch on the Russian launch site at Kapustin Yar, northwest of the Caspian Sea. By late 1963 or 1964 a longer-range radar had been installed at Diyarbakir, about sixty miles north of Syria, enabling the monitoring of missiles launched from the newer Soviet test center at Tyuratam, east of the Aral Sea. Still another intercept post was established at Sinop on Cape Ince, a jut of land on the Black Sea coast pointing like a stubby finger toward Soviet Georgia and the Caucasus Mountains.

Like cannabis, the NSA eavesdropping stations continued to flourish. One appeared in the capital city of Ankara, and another turned up in the small town of Anadolu Kavak, fourteen miles south of Istanbul, where twenty-three Security Group sailors captured signals in a dilapidated 870-square-foot operations building and lived in "highly rat infested" Quonset huts, according to one official.

In 1975 the Turkish government pulled down the shade on NSA's SIGINT window when the United States embargoed arms to Turkey after its invasion of Cyprus. Beginning in July of that year, all intercept operations were suspended, but the various listening posts continued to be guarded and manned in the hope of a quick resolution to the stand-off. There was none, and in September 1976 the American personnel slowly began pulling out. Four months later the once heavily guarded and highly sensitive operations compound at Karamursel was taken over by Turkish Navy personnel. "The 'OPS' Compound from this day forward," said a Naval Security Group notice to the few remaining Americans, "is no longer a 'CONTROLLED' area. Access to the compound, and movement within, is no longer dependent upon security clearance, nor are escorts required for uncleared personnel."

In 1978 Washington lifted the arms embargo, and Karamursel and the other listening posts seem to have been reclaimed by the American spooks. The price, however, was unlimited access for Turkey to the reams of intercepted communications. This was provided for in a secret "supplementary agreement" to the public Agreement for Cooperation on Defense and Economy, signed on March 29, 1980. Article II of that secret supplement states, in part, "All intelligence information, including raw data, produced at intelligence collection installations in the Republic of Turkey shall be shared by the two Governments in accordance with arrangements determined jointly by the competent technical authorities of the two Governments."

Like Japan, Germany switched from cryptologic worry to cryptologic window, serving as an excellent base for American eavesdropping on European Russia and the Eastern bloc countries. In Bremerhaven, a port city on the Weser River near the North Sea (and a few years earlier a major German naval base), the Naval Security Group began planting antenna fields and strapping on earphones. The ASA, meanwhile, moved SIGINT equipment into Frankfurt, Augsburg, and Gablingen and the Air Force set up SIGINT stations at Zweibrücken and the Rhein-Main airbase and COMSEC operations at Berlin and Darmstadt.

By the mid-1950s the NSA's supersecret Intercept Deployment Plan (IDP) called for the establishment of a total of 4120 worldwide, round-the-clock intercept positions. The plan was part of NSA's Peacetime Communications Intelligence (COMINT) Radio Intercept Requirements. The numbers on the IDP continued to grow throughout the balance of the decade and into the next. By September of 1965 the ASA alone had 26,233 people scattered through the world in ninety-nine separate units. The high point was reached in 1969, during the height of the war in Vietnam.

•

Reduced to its most simple state, an intercept station is little more than a radio receiver — an ultrasophisticated and hypersensitive radio receiver, but nonetheless a receiver. A station can be a vaultlike van on the back of an Army truck or a network of Wullenweber antennas, each capable of holding three football fields, end to end.

Typical of the large, Wullenweber-type stations is the Naval Security Group Activity at Edzell, Scotland. Established in July 1960, when one U.S. Navy officer and eight enlisted cryptologic technicians reported for duty, the listening post grew rapidly and by August of 1976 had accumulated approximately fifteen hundred military and dependents. Located amid the rolling farmland, thick woods, and heather-clad hills of Kincardineshire, in eastern Scotland, the 490-acre station takes its name from the village of Edzell, about three miles away.

The contrast between the green, fertile countryside, where few things grow taller than tomato plants, and the gargantuan Wullenweber is shocking. At first sight the antenna appears to resemble either a frightening prison out of a Kafka-esque nightmare or possibly a leftover set from the latest sci-fi thriller.

Actually, the antenna is more a twentieth-century Stonehenge. The forty-acre Wullenweber site consists of a two-story, boxlike cement operations building surrounded by four concentric circles of poles and wires almost a thousand feet in diameter and from eight feet to over a hundred feet in height.

Also known as a circularly disposed antenna array (CDAA), the system is designed to locate and intercept signals ranging from the low band, such as submarine traffic, to the high band, such as radio-telephone. Because of its omnidirectional design, the system is capable of plucking the signal from the sky regardless of its origin.

The outermost ring, shortest of the four, is the high-band antenna array. Approximately 875 feet in diameter, it consists of 120 equally spaced antenna elements (each resembling a thick, upright tube with a pole sticking out from the top), one for each three degrees of azimuth. Behind it is the taller second circle, the high-band reflector screen, composed of vertical wires suspended from pole-supported horizontal braces. Its purpose is to shield the high-band antenna from signals arriving from any direction other than the one it is monitoring.

Still taller is a third ring, the low-band receiving array, consisting of forty equally spaced "folded monopoles," similar to the first ring of "sleeve monopoles." The innermost of the rings is the giant low-band reflector screen, which looks like an enormous circle of ten-story-high telephone poles with thin copper wires stretched vertically between them and suspended from above.

To locate the source of the transmission, each antenna element is connected to a separate, buried coaxial cable that terminates inside the operations building at the center of the array. Because every cable is electrically the same in length, this permits a device known as a goniometer to determine which receiving element was the first to be struck by an incoming signal. That, in turn, indicates from which direction the signal arrived, since the first receiving element to be struck by a signal is the one nearest the transmitting station.

This procedure, however, will give the intercept operator only a vague idea of where the target transmitter is located, since there most likely will be many possible transmission sites along the route of the signal. Therefore, in order to "fix" the target, numerous Wullenwebers over a wide geographic area are linked together, forming a high-frequency direction-finding net (HFDF, or Huff Duff, as the British used to call it in World War II). The network of HFDF stations simultaneously plots the direction of the same signal. The point at which all lines intersect is the location of the target. Appropriately, the Navy's code name for its HFDF operations is Bullseye.

Thirty miles south of Washington, D.C., Fauquier County, Virginia, serves as a refuge from the steel and cement, the crowds and the crime, of the nation's capital. Along the winding back roads, four-wheeled Mustangs must coexist with four-legged stallions, and property is purchased by the acre rather than the square foot. Small farms dot the landscape in a gentle patchwork, sending forth from the rich, moist soil corn, soy, and, at a 720-acre secluded estate ten miles east of Warrenton, antennas.

Vint Hill Farms has been growing antennas since 1942. Although expensive to plant, the rhombics and the log periodics, the broadbands and the monopoles, produce some of the choicest SIGINT in the eastern United States. Each day several thousand men and women dressed in green and khaki harvest the crop, process it through expensive machines, and ship it off to a customer in southern Maryland, who will take all the farm can produce.

For forty years Vint Hill Farms and its sister station on the opposite coast, Two Rock Ranch, north of San Francisco, have been the Army Security Agency's principal intercept stations in the continental United States. Among Vint Hill's likely targets is Washington's Embassy Row, a brief forty-five minutes' drive north, and the flood of international U.S. telecommunications constantly flowing in and out of the country. Apparently not even the British are spared in the embassy monitoring, as one former Vint Hill employee secretly confirmed to the House Government Operations Subcommittee on Government Information and Individual Rights. "We had a whole bank of machines," the Vint Hill farmer revealed. "I was one of a whole team of men whose only job was to read and process intercepted British communications."

If Vint Hill is Washington's giant ear, its tympanic membrane is an antenna system known as a rhombic array. Unlike the monstrous Wullenweber, the rhombic is the essence of subtlety. Each antenna consists of a wire several feet off the ground attached to four posts spaced in the shape of a diamond. Each side is roughly ten feet in length, and at one end the wire is connected to a coaxial cable that runs underground to a centrally located operations building. The entire array is made up of a series of between thirty and forty rhombics scattered over several hundred acres.

Whereas the circular Wullenweber, like a fishnet, is designed to pick up any signal regardless of its direction, the rhombic, like an arrow, is designed to intercept very specific, very directional circuits. "We built them with the idea of a particular circuit," recalled Brigadier General W. Preston Corderman, one-time head of the ASA and a pioneer in telecommunications interception, "and when we wanted to intercept a particular circuit we would first find out . . . what directional antenna would get the best results on a theoretical basis and then we would build the antenna to meet that specification."

With a rhombic array, intercept operators sitting in an operations building can continuously monitor dozens of specific circuits, such as long-distance, high-frequency telephone channels, twenty-four hours a day. Also, the array need not be situated in a direct line between the two communicants to pick up a circuit as long as one rhombic is pointing toward one station and another rhombic is pointing toward the other. "Take for instance if it's Rio, Brazil, and Berlin," said Corderman. "Well, you would have to have one going south to get the Rio end and you would have to have one going east to get the Berlin end."

Regardless of rhombic or Wullenweber, however, directional or omnidirectional, the center of the action is inside the windowless box of cement known as the ops building. Like a mutant, the intercept station consists only of an ear and a brain connected by a coaxial auditory nerve.

Typically, as at the Naval Security Group listening post at Kamiseya, the Operations Department is divided into four divisions:

Collection: Made up of those copying messages sent in Morse code and those copying voice, such as telephone.

Processing and Reporting: The codebreakers and analysts, consisting of Surface, Weather, Shipping, Data Processing, and Collection Management Branches.

HFDF or Bullseye: Conducts direction-finding operations and manages a Net Control Branch.

COMSEC: Monitors U.S. military communications to ensure compliance with transmission security regulations.

A similar organizational structure is probably used at the large, joint Air Force–Navy intercept station at Karamursel, southeast of Istanbul. There, according to one former analyst, about twenty-five Morse and five voice operators are set to work against the Soviet tactical and long-range air forces. Sitting in front of their receivers, the collection specialists first check out their assigned targets on the latest TEXTA, a computer-generated digest of up-to-the-minute intelligence collected from nearly every communications facility in the world. Published by NSA and known as the bible of the SIGINT community, it stands for technical extracts of traffic, and gives the intercept operator such vital information as how, what, and to whom each transmitting station communicates. Next, they go over lists of likely locations, frequencies, and the call signals that may be used. Finally, they reach up to the frequency dial and "roll onto" their target.

Close to the top of the list in terms of targets is Soviet Navair, the system by which Russia keeps track of its own military aircraft, and Civair, the radio messages to and from the air control centers at the myriad civilian airports. Information from these intercepts is correlated with traffic picked up from air-to-ground broadcasts by Russian aircraft and signals from air defense radar — occasionally triggered by a U.S. aircraft on a "provocative" mission.

Aiding the intercept operator, people from the IIFDF Division are also busily tracking the Russian fliers through triangulation plots in cooperation with other Net stations.

Several desks away, other SIGINT specialists keep close watch over Soviet submarine activity, hoping to catch the split-second "burst" as a sub radios a supercompressed message back to base. Once the burst is recorded on several large tape drops, the tape will be slowed down, the signal demodulated, analyzed, and perhaps broken.

Another high-priority target for the signal chasers at Karamursel is the Soviet space program. On April 23, 1967, a number of analysts were routinely copying the return of Soyuz 1, bringing Soviet cosmonaut Vladimir Komarov back from twenty-six hours in space, when problems suddenly developed on re-entry. Recalled one of the intercept operators:

> They couldn't get the chute that slowed his craft down in re-entry to work. They knew what the problem was for about two hours . . . and were fighting to correct it. It was all in Russian, of course, but we taped it and listened to it a couple of times afterward. Kosygin called him personally. They had a video-phone conversation. Kosygin was crying. He told him he was a hero and that he had made the greatest achievement in Russian history, that they were proud, and that he'd be remembered. The guy's wife got on too. They talked for a while. He told her how to handle their affairs and what to do with the kids. It was pretty awful. Toward the last few minutes he began falling apart, saying, "I don't want to die, you've got to do something." Then there was just a scream as he died. I guess he was incinerated.

As is true of any large organization with numerous branch offices scattered hither and yon, the Puzzle Palace must deal with the nagging problems of duplication of effort, interservice rivalry, and breakdowns of communication. To help cure these organizational headaches and provide central coordination to the listening posts in the hinterlands, the Agency established a hierarchy of regional and local offices and combined centers for intercept processing and analysis.

The Pacific regional office, Headquarters NSAPAC, is in Hawaii. On June 1, 1965, as the war in Vietnam became increasingly explosive, ribbon-cutting ceremonies were held to inaugurate the opening of the NSAPAC Operations Group (NOG), a sort of Pacific command post for the Agency. The activity, which was to coordinate all SIGINT in the Pacific, was housed in the Commander-in-Chief, Pacific

(CINCPAC), Command Center at Camp Smith, north of Pearl Harbor. Chief of NSAPAC during the hottest part of the Vietnam War, from June 1968 until June 1971, was Rear Admiral Lester R. Schulz, the former NSA assistant director for the National Cryptologic Staff.

Subordinate to HQ/NSAPAC are a number of local offices, such as that of the NSAPAC Representative to CINCPAC, who at one time was Robert E. Drake, later NSA's deputy director during the late 1970s. Another is the office of the NSAPAC Representative, Taiwan. One of the most important posts is the NSAPAC Representative, Japan, with headquarters at heavily protected Camp Fuchinobe, a 592-acre site a dozen miles west of Tokyo.

In addition to its NSA offices, the Agency has a large and very secret codebreaking-and-analysis center on Okinawa. Concerned about the possible repetition of effort by the three military SIGINT organizations, Secretary of Defense Neil H. McElroy in January 1957 established a special ad hoc committee to study the matter of greater efficiency and economy in national SIGINT. Among the recommendations submitted by the committee a year later was the establishment of a consolidated triservice processing center, to be located at Sobe, Okinawa. Formally opened in 1961, the Joint Sobe Processing Center (JSPC) is manned by personnel from the NSA, the Army Security Agency, the Naval Security Group, and the Air Force Security Service. The facility permits the sharing of expensive computers for traffic analysis and other cryptologic activities that support the theater commander in the Pacific.

A similar facility was built several years later to consolidate the U.S. SIGINT effort throughout Europe. Located on 21,000 square feet of floor space in the I. G. Farben building in Frankfurt, West Germany, the same building in which the Headquarters NSA Europe is located, the Joint Operations Support Activity Frankfurt (JOSAF) enabled the Agency to close down the listening post at Zweibrücken.

A secret NSA underground facility at Kunia, Hawaii, is currently undergoing more than $2 million worth of alterations to house a third triservice processing operation. This may replace Okinawa's JSPC when the island reverts to full Japanese control.

The establishment of these joint centers reflects the long-standing belief that codebreaking and other processing functions should be carried out at the most forward locations at which the required speed can be achieved. Processing that can be done effectively within twenty-four hours after intercept is handled at the point of intercept within the theater, such as at the Navy intercept station at Kamiseya. The more difficult traffic, that which can be successfully attacked within

forty-eight hours of intercept, is referred to the joint processing centers, like the JSPC at Sobe. The remainder is attacked at Fort Meade.

Of all the intercept stations built during the 1950s' boom, the ultimate in both ambition and failure was in the remote Allegheny hollow
of Sugar Grove, West Virginia, population forty-two. Nestled deep
in the wooded and mountainous South Fork Valley of Pendleton
County, Sugar Grove sits at the heart of one of the most extraordinary
natural preserves in America, a refuge not for vanishing wildlife or
eroding landscape, but for something even more endangered: quiet.

Enacted into law by the West Virginia State Legislature on August
9, 1956, the Radio Astronomy Zoning Act provides for a one-hundred-
square-mile National Radio Quiet Zone, providing a sanctuary from
the electromagnetic interference normally found in abundance in
more urban areas. The closest city of any size, Harrisonburg, Virginia,
with a population of about seventeen thousand, is separated by mountain ranges that shield Sugar Grove from any interference. There
are no high-powered radio or television stations, and only a few elec-
tric-power transmission lines crisscross the rugged landscape. Nor
are the skies above frequented by commercial airlines, which elimi-
nates interfering radar signals. Even heavy trucks and buses are prohibited; they are confined to the Shenandoah Valley on the opposite
side of the mountains.

To a handful of officials at NSA, the Naval Security Group, and
the Naval Research Laboratory, the static-free site seemed perfect
for translating into reality a theory that even today would boggle
the mind. Planned for the backwoods of Sugar Grove was the world's
biggest bug.

For years scientists and engineers in NSA's Office of Research and
Development toyed with the idea, scratching equations and formulas
on the long green chalk-boards that lined their offices. If a radio
telescope could be built large enough, they hypothesized, they should
be able to turn the moon into a sort of SIGINT relay station by
listening to Soviet radio communications and radar signals reflected
from its surface.

By 1959 the Puzzle Palace and Office of Naval Research had sold
the idea to enough moon-struck congressmen, chagrined by the Russian space coup with Sputnik 1, and were awarded a hefty $60 million
for the project. Nevertheless, one year later, with barely the foundation
laid, they were back behind the same witness table pleading for an
additional authorization of almost $18 million.

Almost from the start the cost overruns were as staggering as the
project itself. What was being built was the largest movable structure

that had ever been created. Thirty thousand tons of steel welded into the shape of a dish sixty-six stories tall and six hundred feet in diameter — wide enough to hold two football fields. The giant ear would rest on mammoth drives capable of swinging it up, down, sideways, and 360 degrees around a fifteen-hundred-foot track so that it could be aimed at any point above the horizon with pinpoint accuracy.

The mathematical calculations required for the project were, in the words of one engineer, "almost beyond comprehension." As many as thirteen components had to be joined together at one point, which demanded up to ninety-two separate formulas to be worked out simultaneously, a feat that would have taxed the capability of even the largest commercial computer then available.

Despite the fact that an IBM 704 computer had been working on the design specifications for more than half a year, by 1961 the construction still had advanced no farther than the rotating tracks and pintle bearings. So once again the engineers went back to the Congress and pulled out their pocket linings. But by now Congress was beginning to realize just how much it had been oversold on the moontap, and put a ceiling of $135 million on the project, a sum that only a few months later was determined by the Navy to be in the neighborhood of $65 million short of what was needed.

By the summer of 1962, Sugar Grove had become a solid steel albatross, and the administration began taking a closer look at the project. In a memo to President Kennedy, Science Adviser Jerome B. Wiesner pointed to his long involvement with the project and noted that both he and CIA director John McCone felt that "from the intelligence point of view it is a very marginal project." Telling Kennedy that he expected Secretary of Defense McNamara to cancel the operation in a very short time, the future president of MIT indicated his agreement: "In view of the sad history of the project, I believe that this is the proper thing to do."*

Eventually it was decided that Sugar Grove would be the ideal replacement facility for the Naval Radio Station at Cheltenham, Maryland. The Quiet Zone, it was felt, would be an excellent location for the Navy's receiving antennas, which could be connected by underground cable to the transmitting station left at Cheltenham. The switch was approved on May 10, 1969.

Since its beginnings in the mid-1950s, the secrecy surrounding

---

* Dr. Wiesner also noted, "This project was started a decade or so ago by intelligence specialists in the Navy who proposed listening to Soviet radio communications and radar by means of reflections from the moon."

Sugar Grove has been intense. The cover story throughout the entire life of the project was that the six-hundred-foot dish was purely for research and radio astronomy, permitting scientists "to tune in on radio signals as far as 38 billion light years away," according to the local newspaper. The timing was appropriate; Sir Bernard Lovell had completed the world's first radiotelescope just the year before. This was the giant 250-foot Mark I at Jodrell Bank.

Even today, twenty years after the enormous steel ear received its death notice, the blanket of secrecy around the project remains as tightly drawn as ever. The reason is that Sugar Grove continues to be one of the NSA's most important — and secret — listening posts.

When a series of documents indicating the antenna's original eavesdropping requirement was uncovered in an unclassified file in the Naval Operational Archives, the material was immediately summoned back to NSA and stamped SECRET. As justification, the Agency cited the COMINT statute (18 U.S.C. 798), the law allowing NSA to withhold any information regarding its activities and personnel (Public Law 86–36), and the law protecting intelligence sources and methods (50 U.S.C. 403[d][3]).

What the documents showed was that after the original Big Ear had been abandoned and the site turned into a naval receiving facility, the Naval Research Laboratory (NRL), the organization that originally helped plan and build the antenna for the NSA, continued to operate on the station — a station that now included a huge and unique double set of Wullenwebers. More significantly, the NRL continued to operate a sixty-foot microwave receiving antenna built in 1957 as a prototype for the original Big Ear.

On the first day of July 1975, the Naval Security Group officially relieved the NRL and took over a two-story underground operations building known as the UBG. Since then, the now-classified documents show, top NSA officials have been making frequent trips to the isolated compound. On March 23, 1978, for example, Deputy Director Benson K. Buffham led a group on an inspection tour of the UBG, which was scheduled to house a highly secret new project. Other groups followed in May, September, and November.

The secret visits continued throughout much of 1979. On September 11, Air Force Major General Howard M. Estes, Jr., NSA's assistant director for Plans and Resources, arrived with a group to inspect construction for the new projects. Two months earlier the facility was paid a very unusual visit by Michael J. O'Neil, chief counsel for the House Intelligence Committee.

What was quietly being constructed in the secluded forests near

Sugar Grove was a spectacular array of satellite microwave receiving antennas. They ranged in size from thirty feet across to an enormous 150-foot dish, one of the largest ever built and constructed partly from materials left over from the Big Ear project. Also added was the Raymond E. Linn Operations Building, or LOB, a windowless, white cinder-block structure named after a chief petty officer in the Naval Security Group who was killed when the Israeli Navy torpedoed the U.S.S. *Liberty,* an NSA SIGINT ship.*

Did the Puzzle Palace discover a new, more economical way to tune in on the Russians from the backwoods of West Virginia? Or are its targets closer to home? The answer may be found in the title of one of the key NSA visitors to Sugar Grove: chief of G Group, the official whose organization is responsible for eavesdropping on all communications to and from the United States. Nowhere among the visitors, however, was the chief of A Group, the Russian expert, or, for that matter, any other group chief.

Nor is that the only indication of what Sugar Grove's true mission is.

Less than sixty miles from Sugar Grove, in Etam, West Virginia, three other large, dish-shaped microwave antennas are surrounded by forest. In contrast to Sugar Grove, however, there is nothing secret about these satellite antennas. They belong to the Communications Satellite Corporation (COMSAT) and serve as the doorway through which passes more than half of the commercial, international satellite communications entering and leaving the United States each day.†

Flowing in and out of Etam's 62-, 97-, and 105-foot dishes at the speed of light are thousands of telephone calls, telegrams, and telex messages arriving from or destined for 134 countries around the globe. Over many of Etam's 4943 half-circuits (each half-circuit is a two-way communications link between the earth station and an INTELSAT satellite) computers talk business with other computers at the rate of seventy thousand words a minute. The four earth stations — there is a sister station at Andover, Maine, and there are two stations on the West Coast — control nearly all nongovernmental

---

* Chief Linn was scheduled to retire in June 1967, but having spent thirty years in the Navy, he persuaded officials to allow him "just one more trip, one more liberty port." It was his last voyage. (James M. Ennes, Jr., *Assault on the Liberty* [New York: Random House, 1979], p. 18.)

† Of COMSAT's 9663 half-circuits in the continental United States, Etam handles 4943. (*COMSAT Guide to the INTELSAT, MARISAT, and COMSTAR Satellite Systems,* Office of Corporate Affairs, Communications Satellite Corporation, Washington, D.C., page 27.)

international satellite communications entering and leaving the continental United States.

From their secret site five miles north of Sugar Grove, the NSA dishes should be able to pick up every earthbound whisper destined for Etam, as well as every pulse sent skyward. According to James Warren, general manager of the Etam station, the busiest earth station in the world, all that is needed to intercept the COMSAT signals is an equivalent-size satellite antenna. "The trick, of course," said Warren, "would be to hide a 105-foot dish antenna."

In fact, NSA has done just that. Completed early in 1980 was a shining, white 105-foot dish antenna complementing the previously constructed 150-, 60-, and 30-foot dishes. Yet despite the size of the massive antennas, what is probably NSA's main domestic vacuum cleaner is extremely well hidden. Not even the hint of an antenna is visible from the lonely two-lane public road that passes about a mile away. Only by driving down the restricted and guarded government access road leading to the site can one see the valley of antennas. Even aircraft are forbidden to overfly the area.

Technically, the whole operation should be child's play for the Puzzle Palace. "Interception of microwave signals can be done rather easily," concluded a study done by the Federal Communications Commission several years ago, "since the technical parameters of the microwave stations (e.g., station location, frequencies, directional azimuths, etc.) and the nature of the associated multiplex equipment are public information." The only requirement, the report pointed out, was "appropriate technical know-how and financing," hardly problems for the wealthiest of American spy agencies, which boasts that "the Agency's mission requires that our professionals strive to stay as much as five years ahead of what is considered the state of the art outside NSA." In addition, one could hardly find someone with more "technical know-how" than William O. Baker, head of AT&T's Bell Laboratories and at the same time a member — perhaps the most important member — of the very secret NSA Scientific Advisory Board. After all, it was Bell Labs under Baker that, to a great extent, developed and perfected the very system that the NSA hoped to penetrate. And according to Dr. Solomon Kullback, the former head of research and development at NSA, "the actual interception of microwave communications has never been a problem." The problem, he said, was in developing a system capable of recording the massive amounts of information.

Finally, the FCC study went on to state that microwave eavesdropping is undetectable "unless the receiving antenna . . . is spotted."

It also noted that of the possible locations for intercepting international microwave traffic, the ideal spot would be near the commercial earth terminal, and that it would require an antenna of some thirty feet in diameter, the size of Sugar Grove's smallest dish.

Since COMSAT's Etam earth station represents only one (the largest) of the four satellite "gateways" into the continental United States, it would seem logical that NSA would attempt to cover the other three earth terminals as well.

The Naval Security Group Activity at Winter Harbor, Maine, for example, buried deep in Acadia National Park, sixty miles from Bangor, would likely serve as an excellent platform from which to intercept signals to and from COMSAT's Andover station, 125 miles to the west.

On the West Coast, COMSAT's northern earth station is located in Brewster, on the Columbia River halfway between Seattle and Spokane in north-central Washington. Curiously, in the early 1970s the NSA opened a very secret installation a hundred miles to the south on an isolated tract of land in the Army's enormous 261,057-acre Yakima Firing Center. So secret is the $3,564,000 installation that few people even in the NSA are aware of its existence.* Nor, for that matter, do the local residents have any notion of this facility. In the city of Yakima neither the Chamber of Commerce nor Jim McNickey, city editor of the local *Yakima Herald,* had ever heard of such an installation or its cover name, the Yakima Research Station. Only at the post office had the research station ever come to be known. "They're a real top secret–like place," said one postal employee. "They bring in their own mail to us and pick it up and stuff — they don't even have their own mail go out with the other Firing Center mail. They are on their grounds but they're, apparently, a separate entity. We really don't know much about them except that they're out there."

One person who does know much about them is Tom Land, the NSA chief of station. When asked what agency his research station was attached to, he replied that it was "sensitive information" and that his station was engaged in "classified research." After more prodding, however, Land eventually admitted that the station was, in fact, attached to the NSA, but added, "I'm not used to talking on a open phone like this" and "It's not the kind of thing you would go around talking about, especially from here."

* At approximately the same time as the Yakima Research Station was built, Congress appropriated this amount to NSA for "Classified location: Operational facilities" within the United States. (U.S. House of Representatives, Committee on Appropriations, *Military Construction Appropriations,* Hearings for 1970, Part 3, 91st Cong., 1st Sess., p. 577.)

Finally, there is COMSAT's fourth earth station, at Jamesburg, California, a tiny village on the edge of Monterey's Los Padres National Forest in central California. A possible location for an NSA tap is the Army Security Agency intercept station at Two Rock Ranch, 130 miles to the north.

But what if the message happens to go by undersea cable? At first blush this would seem to complicate the process of interception, since there are six transatlantic lines, and tapping a cable is a far greater technological feat than simply snatching it from the air. A submarine would have to lay a long cable right alongside the commercial cable and then pick up the traffic by induction. The real problem, however, comes in trying to relay the information back to the NSA — or to Moscow, depending on the tappers.

Addressing the problem several years ago before a Federal Communications Commission hearing was J. Randolph MacPherson, a telecommunications expert and chief trial attorney for the Defense Communications Agency:

> To intercept a cable transmission requires physical access to the cable. This is something which is much more difficult than physical access to a satellite transmission. To intercept a cable also requires maintenance of the hardware which performs the interception. This means that whoever is intercepting the cable has to take care of the means by which he is doing it. This is something that is also not present in satellite transmissions because one need not be up in space monitoring any particular pieces of equipment to perform that interception.
>
> Thirdly, to intercept a cable, especially in the case of an undersea cable, assuming you've accomplished the first two goals, you have to transmit it to where you want to listen to what you're intercepting.
>
> This is something that is not necessary with the interception of a satellite transmission because it can be performed, as I stated, given the right equipment, very simply in your backyard or on a boat or any place else where you have access to that satellite transmission line.
>
> It is also much easier to detect interception of cable facilities. This is something that technically can be performed. It is very difficult if not impossible to detect the interception of a satellite transmission.
>
> The net result of this is that it is a much more risky undertaking and much less attractive for anyone to try and intercept cable transmissions as opposed to satellite transmissions.

Nevertheless, even cable has its Achilles' heel. There were six submarine cables resting on the Atlantic seabed, but TATs 1 and 2 (Trans Atlantic Telephone cable), out of Nova Scotia, consisted of a scant 165 circuits, so they were retired in 1978. TATs 3 and 4, both of which stretch from Tuckerton, New Jersey, to England and France, also have a small capacity (350 voice channels) and handle little more than 6.5 percent of the cable traffic. Handling more than 90 percent of all transatlantic undersea communications are TATs 5 and 6, with a combined capacity of 4845 circuits. Communications from much of Europe and even the Middle East funnel into TAT 5 in Spain and TAT 6 in France, where they begin a thirty-four-hundred-mile undersea transit to a building in Green Hill, Rhode Island, buried almost three stories underground, wrapped in five feet of concrete, and sealed with a ten-ton vault door capable of withstanding pressures up to twenty-five pounds per square inch.

At the cable head the signals are demultiplexed, and most are converted to microwaves, shot out of their heavily protected cocoon up a tower, and beamed thirty miles away to an AT&T Long Lines relay station in Montville, Connecticut. During the course of that brief millisecond of travel, the communications are just as susceptible as the signals to and from Etam.

Those not transmitted out of Green Hill via microwave go by buried cable to Cheshire, Connecticut, seventy miles away, and there most enter the terrestrial microwave network.

Thus, by having four strategically placed satellite antenna fields located near the COMSAT earth terminals and several average microwave receiving horns stuck on a rooftop or hanging on the side of an obscure tower near the various cable heads, the NSA should be able to monitor continuously nearly every international telephone conversation or message to or from anyone in the United States. Such a power could have been fantasized only by Orwell — and never dreamed of by Hoover.

Because of the limited number of gateways, the international communications network will probably always be easier to monitor than the massively large and complex domestic network. But the increasing use of microwaves and the corresponding decrease in land lines throughout the United States are gradually closing the gap. In addition, a rapidly growing domestic satellite system may eventually permit domestic eavesdropping on a scale almost unimaginable. In 1981 COMSAT orbited the fourth of its domestic COMSTAR satellites, which it leases to AT&T. This brought to fifty-four thousand the number of simultaneous domestic telephone conversations that can be beamed down to COMSAT's seven COMSTAR earth stations.

The ease with which domestic microwave channels can be intercepted was made graphically clear in an extraordinary how-to manual quietly produced several years ago by the MITRE Corporation at the request of the Ford White House:

4.2.1. *Microwave Radio Signal Acquisition*

A possible strategy for intercepting the calls on the radio route is as follows:

1. Locate the microwave repeater sites for the route of interest.
2. Acquire the use of a small farm along the route with sufficient line-of-sight access to the radiated energy.
3. Set up radio interception equipment including a sufficiently large antenna . . . in a barn to avoid being observed.
4. Place call between accomplices and put tracer signals on the circuit.
5. Scan the microwave channels to find tracer signals.
6. Telephone accomplice from farm either when tracer is found or no tracer tone can be found (accomplice must have second main station telephone to receive such a call) and have him end call and place a new call with the tracer tone.
7. Begin monitoring the channels on which tracer signals were found.
8. Continue search for trunk circuits until the portion of the trunk group carried by the microwave route has been approximately identified.
9. Terminate use of tracer calls and continue to monitor the circuits for desired information.
10. Program micro-computer equipped with inband signaling decode device to automatically scan the groups of interest. In the event either of the two targeted telephones is dialed, the scanning device will either signal the interceptor to listen, or automatically connect a recorder to the conversation.
11. Recorded conversations can either be analyzed for relevant communications in situ or transported to an information extraction facility.

So common are the small, gray, cone-shaped microwave antennas that dot city rooftops and shoot skyward from hills and fields, they have become as unseen as crocuses in springtime. Nevertheless, it is this network of inverted tops, small saucer-shaped dishes, and cornucopia-like antennas that has transformed our domestic telecommunications system from the wire to the wavelength.

Spaced between twenty-five and thirty miles apart and in line of sight of each other, each of the antennas can transmit, receive, and relay up to 61,800 simultaneous calls with the addition of the new single sideband equipment. It is over such broadband microwave links, which blanket the country like an electronic net, that the vast majority of long-distance telephone communications travel.

Because this net is so large, however, and the variables so great, it is likely that the NSA confines its domestic monitoring to the foreign diplomatic traffic flowing between Washington and New York. This may be done with large microwave receivers concealed in white golf ball–like radomes high atop the Agency's nine-story Headquarters Building and seven-story Friendship Annex (FANX III), both ideally located directly in the path of the microwave links.

Others, though, see a more sinister domestic microwave "tap" implanted by the NSA. David L. Watters, a telecommunications engineer once attached to the CIA's communications research and development branch, pulls out a microwave routing map of the greater Washington area and jabs his index finger at a small circle with several lines entering it and the letters RCV. Just below the circle are three more letters: NSA. "There's your smoking pistol right here," Watters indicates with a second jab.

The circle is actually a large microwave tower with nine cones pointing in five directions. It is located several hundred yards behind NSA's main Operations Building at Fort Meade. What makes the tower suspect, says Watters, is that it is tied into the local telephone company circuits, which are interconnected with the nationwide microwave telephone system owned by AT&T. While this in itself, he indicates, may have little significance, the key is in the letters RCV, which stand for Receive Only Station.

"The only thing that you can [infer] from that is that it is an extremely broadbanded capability that they have," Watters says in a soft Georgia accent. "They would not need to have a receive only circuit capability to the extent that this provides if they were simply receiving messages over Western Union or telex or whatever. This implies that they are scanning, continuously, thousands of circuits all over the country."

The telecommunications specialist, who had at one time worked for AT&T's engineering arm, Western Electric, made the same point when he was a witness, on February 8, 1978, before the Senate Intelligence Committee. "It is understandable that radio and television, weather and press wire communications services, would require only one-way circuits," he said. "It is not understandable that the National Security Agency would require thousands of times the circuit capacity of the world's press services combined, AP, UPI, Reuters, et cetera, except that these one-way circuits are thousands of remote wiretaps!"

Another indication of NSA's "broadband sweeping of multicircuited domestic telecommunications trunk lines," Watters told the senators, lies in the Agency's request for an amendment to the wiretap law that would permit NSA to engage in warrantless wiretapping "for the sole purpose of determining the capability of equipment" when such "test period shall be limited . . . to . . . ninety days." Continuing, he warned:

Let there be no misunderstanding here. There is only one category of wiretapping equipment or system which requires up to ninety days for test and adjustment, and that system is broadband electronic eavesdropping equipment, the vacuum-cleaner approach to intelligence gathering, the general search of microwave trunk lines. I make this assertion on the strength of actual experience in the electronic intelligence trade and on the strength of over twenty-five years' experience in the telecommunications profession. An ordinary, single-line wire tap requires only five minutes to adjust and test.

Although some microwave testing may be done by engineers in NSA research and development spaces in the floors below the big white golf ball at FANX, most of it, apparently, is conducted in the utmost secrecy at a mosquito-filled swamp on Kent Island in the Chesapeake Bay.

Using the Army Corps of Engineers as a go-between, the NSA in January 1961 negotiated a five-year lease for the 210 acres on Cox Neck Road with the Diamond Construction Company of Savannah, Georgia, at a rent of $4500 per year. Four years later, on February 24, 1965, the NSA executed its option and purchased the site for $48,500.

Considered a "classified facility" by NSA, the location consists of a one-story, white, windowless NSA Propagation Research Laboratory, which houses between $250,000 and $350,000 worth of automatically operating, unattended equipment. Also on the site is a small, white, cinder-block control building inside a barbed-wire-topped chain-link fence. Near the control building are a number of unusual antennas. One is an awkward-looking radio direction finder — a large, steerable, rectangular antenna resting on top of an air-conditioned, windowed control room raised one story above the ground. Another appears to be a satellite transmitting antenna built atop a two-story platform. Others are a round, white radome raised about a dozen feet above the ground; a high-frequency, broadband, rotatable log-periodic antenna on top of a seven-story tower with a small, dish-shaped microwave parabolic reflector at its base; a low-frequency long wire antenna; numerous high-frequency antennas atop sixty-foot telephone poles; and, finally, what seem to be several microwave horn radiator antennas resting on the ground inside the fence and, apparently, another horn-type antenna on top of another seven-story tower.

Known within the R and E spaces of the Puzzle Palace as the Kent Island Research Facility, its purpose was explained by former NSA deputy director Louis Tordella during a closed-door hearing before a Senate subcommittee. The Agency established the facility, said Tordella, "for the conduct of research and evaluations on very-high-frequency and microwave antenna systems. These systems are peculiar to the Agency's mission. The area utilized to conduct this type of research and evaluation must have a low radio noise interference level. The types of antennas used in these systems require a wide, unobstructed view of the horizon. The size of the Kent Island tract (210 acres) is adequate to allow experimentation and development of several compatible projects simultaneously." More specifically, as Tordella elaborated at another time, "we are on Kent Island . . . examining anomalous propagation effects and other peculiarities associated with our problem of intercept of communications."

Although the facility is largely automatic and unmanned, it does have one resident engineer, Harry (Link) George, a burly island resident. "I'm the chief and crew," George said when asked how many people work there, adding, "It's a crew of one." With regard to the owner of the facility, however, all he would say was that it was part of the Department of Defense: "Anything other than that I can't say."

Finally, when questioned as to why the NSA had selected the isolated tract, Tordella made what an Agency detractor might consider a classic Freudian slip: "It happens to be ideally suited for our business; namely, very low and swampy."

OVERHEAD

"I am 201. I can see the fence well."

Thirty-two thousand feet above the rocky landscape of Soviet Armenia, the MIG pilot had just spotted the Turkish border. A few minutes before, Russian radar had picked up the first blips of an unidentified intruder heading southeast across the "fence" from eastern Turkey. From their base near the Armenian capital of Yerevan, 201 and four other fighters scrambled off the tarmac for a rendezvous with the unwelcome visitor.

"To the south there is 2–3 balls," 201 radioed his base after glancing below at the 20 to 30 percent cloud cover. Then, a few seconds later, MIG 582 made visual contact. "I see the target, a large one," he informed 201, his group leader. "Its altitude is 100 [10,000 meters], as you said."

That very moment 201 also spotted the lumbering, four-engine propeller-driven aircraft and, without hesitation, gave the order, "Attack," as he himself opened fire.

The pilot of MIG 218 also had the unarmed target in his sights but, probably never having downed an actual aircraft before, was reluctant to shoot. Noting this, 201 again shouted his command into his radio: "Attack, attack, 218, attack."

The trespassing pilot knew that the only way he could save himself and his crew members was to make it back across the border into Turkey. It was a distance of little more than a few dozen miles but with an air speed of 180 miles per hour and five MIGs attacking from his rear, he would need a miracle.

"Target speed is 300 [kilometers]. I am going along with it. It is turning toward the fence." There would be no miracles.

"The target is burning."

"There's a hit."

"The target is banking."

"It is going toward the fence . . ."

"Open fire . . ."

"218, are you attacking?"

"Yes, yes, I . . ."

"The target is burning . . ."

"The tail assembly is falling off the target."

"82, do you see me? I am in front of the target . . ."

"Look!"

"Oh?"

"Look at him. He will not get away. He is already falling."

"Yes, he is falling. I will finish him off, boys, I will finish him off on the run."

"The target has lost control, it is going down."

"Now the target will fall."

"82, a little to the right."

"The target has turned over . . ."

"The target is falling . . ."

"Form up . . ."

"82, I see. I am watching the target. I see."

"Aha, you see, it is falling."

"Yes . . . form up, go home."

Shortly after two o'clock on the afternoon of September 2, 1958, the target, an American EC-130 ELINT aircraft on assignment for the National Security Agency, crashed in the mountainous terrain of Armenia, thirty-five miles northwest of Yerevan.

The most violent incident in the history of Soviet-American relations had just taken place. In the cloudy skies above the Russian town of Leninakan, the Cold War had suddenly turned white hot.

For many years the NSA had been "ferreting" the Soviet borders with aircraft jam-packed with the latest in electronic and communications eavesdropping gear. Flying parallel to the Russian border, the aircraft would pick up the faint emissions of air defense radar, ground communications, and microwave signals. Once captured, the signals would be sent on to NSA for analysis.

It was an effective and efficient method of collecting the needed intelligence, and supplemented the ground-based intercept platforms by helping to fill in the blanks. But there was one major handicap: only that radar which is activated can be captured, and some of the most important radar became activated only by a border penetration. For this reason pilots occasionally engaged in the dangerous game of "fox and hounds"; they would fly directly toward the border, setting off the radar, and then pull away at the last minute. Once in a while pilots would actually penetrate Soviet airspace, intentionally or unintentionally.

The EC-130, piloted by Air Force Captain Rudy J. Swiestra, of Compton, California, had taken off earlier that day from Incirlik, a small American field outside of Adana, Turkey, and was to fly northeast to Trabzon, a dusty town on Turkey's Black Sea coast, where an Air Force Security Service listening post maintained a round-the-clock watch on Soviet communications and other signals. Once over Trabzon the ELINT aircraft was to turn east and head for the Soviet border and then parallel the fence down to the area of Lake Van, near the Iranian border. Once there, the plane would reverse direction and return to Adana along the same route. It was as the craft was returning north along the border that it veered into Russian territory.

As was the standard practice, SIGINT personnel at Trabzon were continuously monitoring Soviet air traffic. It was with growing horror, therefore, that they listened as the MIG pilots began blasting away at their fellow spooks. Word of the downing certainly must have been flashed almost immediately to President Eisenhower and other top officials over NSA's special CRITICOM network. But in order to maintain a cover for the operation, the Air Force initially listed the aircraft as missing and its fate unknown. Rescue planes, though, began searching the area along the border. The cover story was that the aircraft's mission was part of a worldwide Air Force project to study radiowave propagation, the usual story to cover NSA eavesdropping operations.

On September 12, ten days after the downing, the Soviet Union revealed that the plane had crashed in Soviet Armenia and that six crew members had apparently died. No mention was made of the other eleven persons on board and no mention of how the aircraft had crashed.

The following day Richard H. Davis, the American chargé d'affaires in Moscow, delivered a note to the Foreign Ministry, demanding information about the remaining eleven airmen and details surrounding the crash. Replying, the Soviets charged that the EC-130 had deliberately violated Soviet airspace but gave no further details.

It was a Catch-22 situation. Eisenhower knew exactly what had happened and why; he had probably even read the intercepted conversations of the MIG attackers. But to reveal this knowledge would be to tell Russia and the world that American intelligence continuously eavesdrops on the Soviet Union.

Instead, the Air Force released details of what it called an "investigation" of the incident. The investigation turned up several "witnesses" who had observed the plane being escorted eastward by Soviet fighters from the Soviet-Turkish frontier near the Turkish city of Kars. These witnesses had heard an explosion and seen a column of smoke rise from behind a range of hills in Soviet territory. Anyone who had read the intercepts, however, knew this was not the case; that the MIGs had not even seen the ELINT aircraft until it was well inside Soviet territory.

In Washington there was growing speculation that the eleven missing crewmen had bailed out before the aircraft crashed and either were taken prisoner or were still wandering somewhere in southern Russia.

Whatever the fate of the Americans, top officials of the Eisenhower administration felt certain that the Russians knew more than they were telling. It was decided, therefore, to take an unprecedented and calculated risk: to reveal secretly to Soviet officials the intercepted conversations of their own MIG pilots.

On November 13, Deputy Under Secretary of State Robert Murphy met in his office with the Soviet ambassador, Mikhail A. Menshikov, and with Major General Mikhail N. Kostiouk, the Soviet air attaché in Washington. Murphy had specifically requested that Menshikov bring Kostiouk with him.

After reviewing the diplomatic exchanges about the EC-130 incident, Murphy informed the ambassador that the United States government believed that the American pilot had probably made a navigational error as the result of signals transmitted by radio beacons in Soviet Georgia and Armenia. Then, having accidentally flown into Soviet airspace, the plane had been shot down by Soviet fighters "without regard to the rules of civilized international practice as though it was an enemy aircraft."

Ambassador Menshikov, as expected, denied the involvement of Soviet aircraft, and with that, Secretary Murphy launched into what must be one of the most remarkable and dramatic offers in the history of the department. He offered to have played for the Russian ambassador the actual tape of the intercepted conversations between the Soviet pilots who shot down the EC-130. A startled Menshikov declined to listen to the recording, saying that he was not competent to assess it from a technical point of view. But Murphy had already taken that into consideration; he explained that it was for just that reason that General Kostiouk, an expert in aviation, had been invited to attend the meeting. In addition, he told Menshikov that it was his responsibility as the Soviet ambassador to the United States to listen to the recording. When Menshikov again refused, he was handed a transcript in Russian of the recording.

Before the two Russian diplomats departed, Murphy made it clear that the United States was serious in its determination to get to the bottom of the disappearance of the lost fliers. He mysteriously referred to "evidence" in the possession of the United States government, indicating "that additional and very important information was available" and that it was the intention of the government to pursue the case further.

What the "evidence" was, whether decipherments of Russian messages, interceptions of telephone conversations, or information from agents, has never been revealed. What does appear certain, however, is that the United States government, with this evidence, was convinced that the eleven had not perished in the crash.

Finally, Murphy emphasized that "some" of our men had been killed, that there were certain rules of conduct in the civilized world, and that the United States hoped and desired that information regarding the missing men would be forthcoming.

The dramatic episode in Murphy's office failed to produce the hoped-for response. Also, as expected, the Russians kept silent about the intercepts of their air communications, most likely out of embarrassment.

In separate meetings in January with veteran Soviet diplomat Anastas I. Mikoyan, then first deputy chairman of the Council of Ministers, both Vice President Nixon and Secretary of State Dulles pleaded for a statement about the missing men. Nixon cited the potential for reducing tensions between the two nations. Mikoyan's reply was short and to the point: all information had been released previously.

Incredibly, apparently convinced that the Soviet Union knew either the whereabouts or the fate of the airmen, the State Department continued to press the matter. Almost from the beginning, the initiatives and overtures to the Soviet Union had been quiet and behind-the-scenes and the results uniformly negative. Now the State Department decided to reverse its tactics, and on February 6 it went completely public. Almost certainly against the advice of the NSA, Dulles released a complete translation of the intercepted conversations between the MIG pilots just before, during, and immediately after the attack on the aircraft. The transcript showed without a doubt that the attack not only took place but was in fact deliberate. But though Dulles was prepared to show Russian culpability in the incident, he was not prepared to admit that the aircraft was on a spy mission. Nor, for that matter, would Dulles reveal how the United States had acquired the recording or why the government had waited five months to make it public.

Surprised and shocked, the Soviet government would have none of it. Calling the recording a "fake" and a "gross forgery," Moscow issued a statement charging that the material released was "concocted by the American intelligence service."

Prodded by relatives of the missing men, Eisenhower finally decided to take his appeal directly to Premier Nikita S. Khrushchev. On May 4, the U.S. ambassador to Moscow, Llewellyn E. Thompson, on instructions from the White House, met privately with the Russian leader at the Kremlin and again pressed for information. Whether Thompson brought with him any of the "evidence" that the State Department had referred to earlier is unknown. What is known is that Thompson came away empty-handed, and on November 20, 1962, the missing men were officially pronounced "presumed dead."

Whatever became of the Americans who took off on that early September morning to collect signals for the NSA may remain forever a mystery. If the State Department or the NSA knows the answer, neither is telling. But there was one more strange bit of information that turned up almost two and a half years after the aircraft took to the sky that may contain the answer. Buried deep in a January 1961 issue of the popular Soviet magazine *Ogonek* was the second installment of a long article by East German writer Wolfgang Schreir, dealing with American espionage. In that article, which was reprinted and translated from the East Berlin magazine *Neue Berliner Illustrierte,* Schreir referred to the flight of the American aircraft and then indicated that even before the Soviet fighters closed in on the plane, "eleven of the seventeen members of the crew dropped by parachutes on Soviet territory." Then Schreir added, "They were caught in the outskirts of Yerevan."

At first overlooked by the Soviet government, the article was later denounced as in error. But the fact remains that the information as originally printed bore the stamp of authority, in that the magazine was itself published in the printing house of *Pravda,* the official organ of the Communist Party, and presumably had been approved for publication. Since the Schreir article, no further word has ever been released about the men or their fate.

Despite the downing of the EC-130, the Puzzle Palace continued to send its ferrets aloft. In July 1959, a Navy P4M Mercator, specifically rigged for electronic surveillance, was strafed by North Korean MIGs while sniffing the air for signals thirty-eight miles off the North Korean coast.

In that incident, the twin-engine turbo-prop aircraft, with two auxiliary jet engines capable of being switched on for an extra burst of speed, was on a routine ELINT patrol at seven thousand feet. Suddenly there was a yell: "Sighted two swept-wing jets . . . They're firing at us!" A few seconds later, tail gunner Eugene Corder, a twenty-year-old Navy petty officer, collapsed with more than forty shrapnel wounds.

Normally, the P4M, a Navy antisubmarine warfare aircraft, could have relied on other weapons, such as a pair of 20-mm guns in a forward turret and a 50-mm pair mounted in a turret atop the fuselage, but these had been removed in order to squeeze in the special reconnaissance gear and five extra crew members to operate it.

To escape his attacker, Navy Lieutenant Commander Donald Mayer, pilot of the stricken craft, dived from seven thousand feet down to fifty feet above the whitecaps of the Sea of Japan. On the way down his copilot could see the big red stars painted on the fuselages of the fighters as they made six more passes, three of them with guns blasting. Mayer eventually made it back to Japan with only Corder wounded. He later recovered.

The thirty-third air incident involving Communist and United States aircraft since the early 1950s had ended. "This is the first time in one of these murderous attacks the crew has come home," Rear Admiral Frederick S. Withington, the top U.S. Navy commander in Japan, said after the plane returned. Eleven times previously, American and Communist aircraft in the Far East had been involved in similar brushes. Some of the Air Force crews had made it back, but all the Navy planes had been lost.

The bloody electronic air war continued throughout the 1960s, with the most serious incident taking place in the spring of 1969. On April 15 of that year, shortly after dawn, thirty Navy men and one Marine boarded an unarmed, four-engine EC-121 at Atsugi Air Base near Yokohama, Japan. The flight plan called for them to head northwest until they reached a point off North Korea's Musu Peninsula. From there they were to make a number of elliptical orbits, each about 120 miles long, running from the northeast near the juncture with China and the Soviet Union, along the coast toward the southwest.

As the Navy SIGINT specialists turned dials and scanned frequencies, their flight was being monitored seven hundred miles away at the chief Naval Security Group base at Kamiseya, a few miles from Camp Fuchinobe, the NSA's headquarters in Japan.

Prior to any reconnaissance flights along the North Korean, Chinese, or Soviet Far Eastern borders, a top secret message would be transmitted to Kamiseya and other SIGINT stations, detailing the flight time and course that the plane would follow. Then, at the designated flight time, technicians would start adjusting switches and flipping on recorders to begin monitoring the various frequencies used by the radar and air defense stations in the target country. At the same time, other personnel attached to Operation Bullseye would begin homing in on the transmitters with their sensitive high-frequency direction-finding receivers in order to pinpoint their exact location.

One hour and seventeen minutes after the EC-121, with its six tons of eavesdropping equipment, left the runway at Atsugi, it transmitted a routine voice message. Four hours and forty-three minutes later the aircraft transmitted another routine message, this one by teletype. Then at 1:50 P.M., a little less than seven hours after it took off, the aircraft disappeared from the radar screen, shot down by North Korean fighters some ninety miles southeast of Chongjin, North Korea. All aboard were lost.

Immediately after the incident, all further surveillance flights in the Sea of Japan, which had been averaging more than sixty per month, were halted. Three days later, however, President Nixon ordered that the reconnaissance missions be resumed and that they receive adequate protection.

Besides serving as flying listening posts, airborne SIGINT platforms are also frequently used in tactical direction-finding operations. Known as airborne radio direction-finding (ARDF) platforms, their greatest role was during the Vietnam War, directing artillery and air strikes toward North Vietnamese ground units.

Typical of the ARDF missions was Combat Cougar, in which Air Force SIGINT personnel, snug in the bellies of EC-47 "gooney birds" and huddled over $4 million worth of receiving equipment, electronically combed through the jungles eight thousand feet below. As soon as an enemy unit was located, its "fix" would be transmitted to one of several major NSA Direct Support Units (DSU) on the ground, like that at Pleiku or Phu Bai. Once the fix was received, the personnel on the ground would triangulate the target by feeding the data into a computer, along with information received from other air, land, or seaborne DF stations, then pass it on to commanders in the field.

"The first bombing that ever occurred from ARDF data occurred in 1968," recalled one Combat Cougar veteran. "There was an area about 19 kilometers southwest of Hue that we'd been flying over. Some of the communications we collected and a pattern analysis that was performed on it indicated that there were quite a few NVA or VC units concentrated in a small area, about a mile in diameter. General Abrams personally ordered the largest B-52 raid that had ever taken place in Vietnam at that time. There was one sortie an hour for thirty-six hours, thirty tons dropped by each sortie on the area." So devastated was the site that it was afterward called Abrams Acres.

•

Those are the workhorses — the plodding EC-47s, the fat EC-130s, and the hunchback EC-121s. Miles above, in the blue-black curve of space, the superstar of winged espionage makes its home. Faster than a speeding bullet, more powerful than a fleet of locomotives, and able to leap wide continents in a single two-thousand-mile-per-hour bound is the SR-71 Blackbird. Named for its sooty, heat-resistant titanium skin, which glows cherry-red as it flashes across the heavens at Mach 3.32, the successor to the ill-fated U-2 can photograph 100,000 square miles of the earth's surface in less than an hour from a height of more than 85,000 feet. At the same time, its package of superadvanced SIGINT sensors can chart electronic battlefields and peer deep over a border with side-looking radar.

In November 1978 President Jimmy Carter ordered the reconnaissance jets over Cuba to help determine whether recently arrived Russian MIG-23 fighters had a nuclear capability. (They did not.) One year later they were again ordered high over Havana to keep an eye and ear on growing numbers of Soviet troops taking up residence on the island.

As crafty as the Blackbirds are, however, they are mostly stand-ins for the true overhead sentries, the spy satellites. A Blackbird will cover a hot spot until a satellite is in place, or will lend an eye with cloud-penetrating infrared sensors, but more than on any other platform, the Puzzle Palace relies on its growing space force of orbiting ferrets.

On a crystal-clear day in mid-August 1960, a C-119 transport flying eight thousand feet over the South Pacific near Hawaii managed to catch in its trailing **Y**-shaped net a three-hundred-pound capsule ejected minutes before by the Discoverer 14 satellite. Snared in the aircraft's trapezelike mitt as it parachuted toward the Pacific waves, the recovered orb symbolized the opening of the latest frontier in espionage: space.

A few days before the midair save, another orb had been successfully recovered after a gentle landing in the sea. The successes, after eighteen months and twelve tries, proved that space indeed was a suitable platform for espionage; that photos snapped over the most forbidden territories could be ejected from the satellites and recovered for processing.

The first steps in what has eventually become a Soviet-American "black" space race were actually taken six years earlier, in 1954, when CIA director Allen Dulles appointed Richard M. Bissell, an economist and brilliant innovator, as his special assistant for Planning and Coordination. What Bissell was planning and coordinating was a new form of reconnaissance platform, one that need not skirt alongside a hostile border or hopscotch in and out, but could fly completely over it with impunity: the U-2. In July 1955, just eighteen months after the contract with Lockheed was signed, the Black Lady became operational, and a fleet of twenty-two was deployed at a cost of $3 million below the original cost estimate.

As the U-2s began winging their way over the Soviet Union, Bissell set up the informal Ad Hoc Requirements Committee (ARC) to coordinate collection requirements for the program. Originally the membership was limited to representatives of the CIA, the Army, Navy, and Air Force, but later, as SIGINT packages were added, NSA joined the group.

With the successful recovery of the Discoverer ejection capsule in 1960 and the subsequent race to provide the United States with a functioning and efficient satellite intelligence system, Bissell's ARC was replaced by a formal U.S. Intelligence Board committee, the Committee on Overhead Reconnaissance. Known simply as COMOR, the committee was responsible for coordinating collection requirements for the development and operation of all overhead reconnaissance systems.

The following year, in 1961, the CIA and the Air Force jointly formed a centralized administrative office to run the spy satellite program. This was the National Reconnaissance Office, an organization so secret that even today its very name is considered classified information. Similar to the NSA during the early 1950s, the NRO is considered a "black" agency, one whose very existence is denied by the government.

Under the NRO arrangement, the Air Force and CIA informally agreed that the Air Force would provide the launchers, the bases, and the recovery capability for the satellite program, and the CIA would be responsible for the research, development, contracting, and security. It was also agreed that the director of the secret organization would come from the Air Force and report to the Secretary of Defense but would accept intelligence requirements from the USIB and its COMOR.

Shortly before the formal establishment of NRO, the Air Force made its first successful launch of the second generation of spy satellite: Samos. Launched aboard an Atlas-Agena A on January 31, 1961, Samos delivered its images not by ejecting capsules but by processing the photos on board and then transmitting the signals back to earth. Because such a procedure produced a picture of much lower quality, the system was used mainly for looking at the big picture or "area" surveillance, and capsule ejection satellites were used on lower orbits, taking the "close look" at targets selected from the area transmissions.

Photo intelligence, however, was only one of the treasures NRO hoped to mine from space. Equally important were the possibilities of using space for both SIGINT and early warning, both familiar subjects to the scientists at NSA. Among the warning satellites sent aloft during the early and mid-1960s was the Midas series, which was packed with sophisticated infrared sensors capable of detecting the heat from a ballistic missile on liftoff. The most controversial of the Midas launches involved a plan to have a satellite eject a canister that would spew 350 million hairlike copper dipole antennas around the earth in an orbital belt two thousand miles high, five miles wide, and twenty-four miles deep. It was theorized that the Midas belt would serve as a passive reflector for the relay of defense communications. After one failure, the mission reportedly succeeded with Midas 6 in May 1963.

Another of the early-warning series launched during this period was Vela, a twenty-sided satellite with eighteen detectors designed to detect nuclear explosions.

But of all the hardware sent aloft, the most secret were the SIGINT platforms. Known as ferret satellites, they often rode into space piggyback aboard a photo satellite and then were projected into a higher orbit.

As the systems became more sophisticated and more expensive, there were major battles throughout the intelligence community over which sensors would be launched, where they would be targeted, and how the intelligence would be processed and distributed.

The most bitter fighting took place between the Air Force and the CIA over control of NRO. Although the Air Force technically ran the Reconnaissance Office, in reality it was little more than a deliveryman, launching systems designed, produced, and programmed by the CIA. Because of this, senior Air Force officials in the program protested that far too much effort was being directed toward national intelligence priorities at the expense of tactical Air Force objectives.

In 1965, after two years of battles that consumed a large amount of his time, CIA director John McCone buried the hatchet with the Air Force and agreed to a partnership arrangement known as EXCOM. Standing for Executive Committee, EXCOM was made up of the director of Central Intelligence, the assistant secretary of defense in charge of intelligence, and the Scientific Adviser to the President.

Under this system, the director of NRO would still be chosen by the Air Force, but now he or she would report directly to the EXCOM troika. EXCOM, in turn, would report to the Secretary of Defense, who was given the primary administrative authority for overhead reconnaissance systems. The arrangement also recognized the authority of the DCI, as head of the intelligence community, to establish the collection requirements in consultation with the USIB. In the event the DCI could not agree with the Defense Secretary, he had the right to appeal to the President.

The EXCOM arrangement was apparently successful in establishing a decision-making mechanism, but a serious problem remained in the area of analysis.

Since 1958, when the CIA established the Photographic Intelligence Center, the agency has been responsible for processing photo intelligence for the entire intelligence community. With the creation of NRO in 1961, the office was upgraded to the National Photographic Interpretation Center (NPIC) and housed in a tall, nearly windowless yellow cement building at the Washington Navy Yard (where it remains today). The new facility was staffed by both CIA and DIA analysts, which led to much duplication as analysts from both agencies studied the same photo for the same objective. As a result, DCI Richard Helms and Secretary of Defense McNamara set up a special joint review group to look into the problem.

The solution was to make the NPIC more of an intelligence community organization by giving the CIA its own in-house photo intelligence unit — the Imagery Analysis Service in the Directorate of Intelligence. And the USIB replaced COMOR, its satellite intelligence committee, with a new committee responsible for coordinating both collection *and* analysis — the Committee on Imagery Requirements and Exploitation (COMIREX).

Just as the CIA has always been responsible for the imagery side of satellite espionage, NSA, with certain small exceptions, has always been responsible for the SIGINT side. Unlike the CIA, however, with its Photographic Intelligence Center and, later, its National Photographic Interpretation Center, the NSA during the early part of the spy satellite program, possibly for security, had no similar community-wide center for the analysis of SIGINT.

This was changed somewhat in September 1966 with the creation of the Defense Special Missile and Astronautics Center at NSA. Standing in front of a long ribbon, appropriately fashioned of teletype tape, newly appointed DCI Richard Helms, mouth open in the middle of a laugh, took a snip with his scissors and formally opened the intelligence community's newest addition: DEFSMAC (pronounced deaf-smack). Joining in both the laugh and the cutting were NSA director Marshall Carter and DIA director Lieutenant General Joseph F. Carroll. Behind, the full membership of the United States Intelligence Board applauded in approval. To symbolize the occasion, the USIB had decided for the first time to journey across the Potomac and hold a formal meeting at NSA headquarters.

So secret is DEFSMAC that it has never been officially revealed; even within the intelligence community it remains surrounded in mystery. It functions, apparently, as the electronic-spy world's early-warning nerve center. "If we start at NSA," says Raymond Tate, NSA's former deputy director for COMSEC, "we have a system like this: the Defense Space and Missile Activity [sic], (DEFSMAC), located at NSA, is a combination of the DIA with its military components and the NSA. It has all the inputs from all the assets, and is a warning activity. They probably have a better feel for any worldwide threat to this country from missiles, aircraft, or overt military activities, better and more timely, at instant fingertip availability, than any group in the United States."

Like a physician listening to a heart, DEFSMAC listens to the earth through a SIGINT stethoscope, hoping to detect the first sign of an irregular beat. Once such a sign is detected, the word would be passed instantly over DEFSMAC's direct CRITIC circuits to the White House Situation Room, the National Military Command Center at the Pentagon as well as the alternate War Rooms, and, most important, to the spacetrack and early-warning analysts at the North American Air Defense Command (NORAD) Headquarters, buried beneath 1450 feet of granite at Colorado's Cheyenne Mountain. This warning can range from a few minutes to as much as a day and may include such valuable intelligence as the type of missile or spacecraft to be launched or its likely trajectory.

Once the launch has taken place, an early-warning satellite in geosynchronous orbit will spot the rocket plume within one minute of liftoff and signal back to earth that a launch has occurred. From then on, watch officers at NORAD track closely the vehicle's flight profile to ensure that it is not on a "threat azimuth."

In the meantime, DEFSMAC notifies all potential listening posts and SIGINT sensors in the range of the vehicle to begin telemetry interception.

DEFSMAC's stethoscope depends, more than on any other input, on NRO's fleet of spy-in-the-sky ferrets and watchdogs, and for that reason the cooperation between the NSA and NRO has always been very close. NRO's most recent director, Dr. Robert J. Hermann, for example, spent most of his career at NSA.

Fresh out of Iowa State University, Hermann joined the Air Force in 1955 as an electrical engineer and was assigned to the Puzzle Palace. After two years he returned to Iowa State as an instructor in the Electrical Engineering Department but remained tied to NSA as a "consultant." In September 1959, after picking up his master's degree, he was selected for the NSA Fellowship Program and in 1963 received his Ph.D. from Iowa.

Back at NSA, Hermann rose rapidly through the ranks, serving as an electrical engineer on the Technical Planning Staff, then briefly at the Pentagon in the Defense Research and Engineering Office. In 1965 he became chief of NSA's Office of Systems Engineering and by February 1969 was deputy assistant director for Science and Technology and acting chief of the Office of Systems Management. A little less than two years later he became chief of W Group in PROD, and in July 1973, at the age of forty, the dark-haired, bespectacled Hermann took charge of one of the Agency's three major organizations when he was named deputy director for Research and Engineering.

After he had been head of R and E for only a year, NSA director Lew Allen assigned him as a special assistant to the director for the purpose of studying SIGINT support to military operations. This assignment led to his being selected in 1974 by Alexander Haig, newly appointed U.S. NATO commander in Europe, as his chief of Strategic Warning and Combat Information Systems staff, where his major responsibility was attempting to provide Haig with a system of direct early-warning and tactical SIGINT support. The system apparently would allow Haig to receive time-sensitive SIGINT and other intelligence at near real-time speed, rather than having it first go to Washington for processing. This way both Haig and Washington would receive the warning indicators and tactical-and-combat-related intelligence simultaneously.

Two years after joining Haig, Hermann returned to Washington to become the principal deputy assistant secretary of defense for Communications, Command, Control and Intelligence (C³I), the Pentagon's deputy intelligence czar. After a year of so with C³I, Hermann achieved "his lifetime ambition," according to former COMSEC chief Ray Tate, when he was selected by President Jimmy Carter as assistant secretary of the Air Force for Research and Development and, more important, director of the clandestine National Reconnaissance Office.

With the coming of the Reagan administration, however, Hermann was told to clean out his desk. Because he still had a year or so until his retirement, he was kept on temporarily as a special assistant to the Pentagon's under secretary for Research and Engineering, Richard D. DeLauer. Appointed by President Reagan to take over the spy satellite organization was Edward C. Aldridge, who was also named under secretary of the Air Force.

Although details of the NRO's organizational structure have never been revealed, its framework may be pieced together from various sources. Apparently, the director is normally cloaked with the title of assistant secretary of the Air Force for Research and Development, as with Dr. Hermann, or with that of under secretary of the Air Force, as with Aldridge.

Because of the large number of other responsibilities faced by the holders of those two offices, day-to-day operation of the NRO most likely falls to the director of Special Projects, a directorate within the Office of the Secretary of the Air Force. Head of this office, which does not appear in either the *Government Organization Manual* or the Air Force Pentagon telephone directory, doubles as deputy commander for Satellite Programs of the Air Force Space and Missile Systems Organization (SAMSO), based in Los Angeles. Here, close to the major contractors for the spy satellites, such as TRW at Redondo Beach, California, and also the major launch site, Vandenberg Air Force Base, the NRO is principally headquartered. Liaison and coordination, but not direction, probably come through the Air Force Secretary's Office of Space Systems.

Among the pioneers in aerial espionage was Lieutenant General Lew Allen, Jr. In 1965 he became deputy director for Advanced Plans in the Directorate of Special Projects and was stationed in Los Angeles. Three years later he was assigned to be deputy director of the Office of Space Systems and became its director in 1969. In September 1970 he became assistant to the director of Special Projects and seven months later took over as director of Special Projects, with additional duty as deputy commander for Satellite Programs at SAMSO in Los Angeles. On March 1, 1973, newly appointed CIA director James Schlesinger picked Allen as his deputy for the Intelligence Community. As we have seen, it was a brief assignment; a few months later he took over the Puzzle Palace.

•

About the same time that Richard Helms, scissors in hand, sliced through the yellow ribbon of teletype tape, officially opening NSA's DEFSMAC, the NRO was taking bids on an ambitious new satellite program designed to serve as a platform, not for just one sensor system, as before, but for multiple eavesdropping packages. Under the cover name of the Defense Support Program (DSP), and quite possibly the code name Byeman, this new generation of space bird was to be the principal element in America's ballistic missile early-warning system and, on a not-to-interfere basis, was to carry additional sensors, including, possibly, a SIGINT package.

In mid-December 1966 the contract for the satellite was awarded to TRW, and the sensor kit went to Aerojet Electrosystems. Twenty months later, on August 6, 1968, the first of the series, designated DSP Code 949, was secretly shot aloft from the Eastern Test Range at Cape Canaveral, Florida. Resembling a large, ten-foot oil drum from which drooped a noselike twelve-foot Schmidt infrared telescope, the satellite was placed in an extremely high, 22,300-mile geosynchronous orbit. At this height, the speed of the satellite would be almost exactly that of the earth, thus allowing it, in effect, to hover over a single spot on the earth's surface near the equator. Perched over Singapore, the long-nosed bird could "see" almost half the earth, including most of China and western Russia, but missing northernmost Siberia.

To overcome this problem, the orbit chosen for the satellite was slightly off center. Inclining the orbit 9.9 degrees enabled the craft to drift about ten degrees above and below the equator. It was thus allowed to trace out a figure-eight ground tract, bringing into its vision the higher latitudes of the Soviet Union. On this tract, during each twelve-hour period, the satellite would drift as far east as the South China Sea and as far west as the Indian subcontinent. To the north, the craft would pass almost directly over Saigon, and then to the south over Jakarta. Due to the slight ellipticity of the orbit, the satellite was able to maintain a somewhat greater "dwell-time" in the more critical northern areas than in the south.

Although the spacecraft could, from this orbit, peer down on the northernmost reaches of the Russian continent, it was unable to view large portions of the land mass during its southern sojourns. To compensate, another 949 satellite was sent skyward on April 12, 1969, and placed in the same orbit, but synchronized so that it patrolled the north while its twin rotated south.

In addition to the satellite's long snout, which is designed to detect ballistic missile launches, presumably from infrared energy emitted by the rocket booster plumes and the high temperature of their re-entry vehicles, the bird also carried Vela-type detectors for monitoring above-ground nuclear explosions.

The success of the twin Code 949 satellites was considerable, and they served as prototypes for an even more advanced series launched under the Defense Support Program's aegis: the Code 647 satellite. After one failure, the first 647 was launched on May 5, 1971, from Cape Canaveral, which is better located for a near-equatorial orbit than is Vandenberg, and parked over the Indian Ocean between the Maldives and Seychelles Islands. Another was launched on March 1, 1972, and stationed over the Panama Canal, where it could detect a submarine-launched ballistic missile attack from either the Atlantic or East Pacific Ocean.

Almost identical to the 949 craft, the DSP 647 satellites are reportedly the most important of all elements in the U.S. missile early-warning system. Three such satellites can provide full coverage of all potential ICBM and SLBM launch areas. According to another report, the red-eyed spycraft has observed more than a thousand ballistic missile launches by the Soviet Union, China, France, and the United States.

Although early warning is the number one priority for the 949–647 series, it is quite likely that later launches may have included a large amount of SIGINT equipment. In his book *The Technology of Espionage*, Lauren Paine claims that one of the integrated satellites was an "orbiting laboratory in miniature."

It could pick up, record, and transmit emanations from all land communication systems, including radio and microwave telephonic transmissions. It was also rigged with other varieties of electronic surveillance equipment which were sensitive enough to do the work of the hundreds of secret listening posts the United States Intelligence community had in such places as Turkey, Iran, and West Germany. It was capable of duplicating everything those listening posts could do.

What Mr. Paine may have been describing was an experimental prototype of a new DSP satellite code-named Rhyolite. Launched on December 20, 1972, the prototype may have carried aloft an experimental test package for the most advanced bug ever invented.

Unlike their photo and infrared sisters, SIGINT satellites have always been cloaked under the heaviest of security blankets. Whereas photo and the other forms of imagery sensors have applications outside the intelligence community — such as for weather and for geologic surveys — there is no such demand for a commercial satellite whose sole purpose is to eavesdrop on the world below.

Known as ferret satellites, the SIGINT craft were originally developed during the late 1950s primarily to supplement the lumbering four-engine ferrets that prowled the Soviet and Chinese borders — and occasionally didn't return. Although the manned airborne listening post, crammed with tons of sophisticated hardware, was obviously preferable to an oil drum–sized bug high in the heavens, the winged intercept station had numerous handicaps. Topping the list was geography. While the border radar along the route of the SIGINT patrols was relatively easy prey, the total amount of border area accessible to the aircraft was minute compared with the actual borders of the landed giants. More important, since one of the primary reasons for mapping and analyzing the radar installations is to enable the United States to develop countermeasures for bomber and missile penetration in the event of war, it would be of high importance to eavesdrop on the various defenses deep within the nation's interior. The satellite, therefore, with its celestial impunity was the perfect platform.

Although some experimental SIGINT equipment may have been built into a few of the early Discoverer spacecraft, true ferret launches seem to have begun early in 1962. On May 15 of that year, a secret launch sent a satellite into a near-polar orbit ranging from 180 to 401 miles. One month later a second satellite was launched into a somewhat higher orbit, of between 234 and 244 miles. As some speculation indicates, this may have been a sort of team approach to eavesdropping, whereby, as with the photo satellites, one spacecraft was designed for a sort of wide-area, search-and-find mission in which it would locate and log the approximate positions of the various radars as well as determine their frequency, and a second, larger and more complex, would be used to follow up with a more comprehensive examination of those signals.

Reportedly, the altitude of three hundred miles would also be ideal for the interception of high-frequency communications. At that altitude a satellite would be within line-of-sight range of radar stations and radio transmitters up to twelve hundred miles away. In one day, then, as the satellite orbits north to south and the earth rotates east to west, the ferret would come within receiving range of virtually all radars and high-frequency transmitters in the world.

The satellite is apparently designed so that, as it passes over its preprogrammed targets, it can capture the various signals on tape and then, when over friendly territory, like Australia, transmit the intelligence back down to an earth station in highly compressed bursts.

During the mid-1960s, as fewer and fewer new radar sites were being discovered, some of the ferrets became compact enough to simply ride into space piggyback aboard a larger photo mission. When the photo satellite reached its normal operating height, usually under a hundred miles, the ferret would be dropped off, and a self-contained rocket would shoot it into a nearly circular, three-hundred-mile-high orbit. From here, the relatively small (about three feet and 125 pounds) satellite would conduct merely an inventory, rather than an examination, of the radars in its path. The information, once collected on earth, would be processed through a computer, and any irregularities or new stations would appear. During much of the 1960s and 1970s the SIGINT beach balls were launched piggyback into space at the rate of about three to five per year.

Although the orbs apparently performed admirably on some signals, such as radar and high frequency, other important signals were beyond their hearing. Chief among these were signals in the microwave frequencies that carried such important intelligence as telephone conversations and telemetry information. Microwaves, it was felt by NSA scientists during the mid-1960s, were too highly directional to be monitored from anywhere outside a relatively short and very narrow area.

Despite this skepticism, the decision was made to begin building what would, in effect, become the ultimate bug, Rhyolite. Under the National Reconnaissance Office framework, the CIA awarded the contract to TRW, which put together the satellite in its windowless M-4 building at Redondo Beach. It was the same facility that built the early-warning DSP Code 949–647 satellites, but, unlike its predecessors, Rhyolite was pure SIGINT. According to one account:

Each satellite carried a battery of antennas capable of sucking foreign microwave signals from out of space like a vacuum cleaner picking up specks of dust from a carpet: American intelligence agents could monitor Communist microwave radio and long-distance telephone traffic over much of the European landmass, eavesdropping on a Soviet commissar in Moscow talking to his mistress in Yalta or on a general talking to his lieutenants across the great continent.

First launched operationally on March 6, 1973, the satellite was placed into a geosynchronous orbit and parked above the Horn of Africa. From this aerie, Rhyolite could eavesdrop on microwave transmissions from western Russia as well as intercept telemetry signals transmitted from liquid-fuel ICBMs launched from the Tyuratam missile-testing range and solid-propellant missiles, like the SS-16 and intermediate-range SS-20, launched from Plesetsk.

A second Rhyolite was hoisted into geosynchronous orbit on May 23, 1977, and reportedly was positioned above Borneo, where, according to a former CIA official who was initially involved in the project, it is capable of "sucking up" a vast amount of both Soviet and Chinese military communications and radar signals. Also from this location, Rhyolite is better able to pick up telemetry intelligence from Soviet missiles that are fired from the eastern test ranges and smash into the Kamchatka Peninsula impact zone or in the North Pacific area northwest of the Midway Islands.

Two more of the satellites were sent into orbit on December 11, 1977, and April 7, 1978, and placed close by the original duo to act as spares in case of a malfunction.

In its role as a telemetry sensor, Rhyolite serves as one of America's chief "national technical means of verification" of Soviet compliance with the strategic arms limitation agreement (SALT I). As part of this agreement, signed in Moscow in May 1972, the United States and the Soviet Union both agreed "not to interfere with" or "use deliberate concealment measures which impede verification by national technical means of compliance with the provisions of this Treaty."

Through the use of Rhyolite for the interception of telemetry intelligence, or TELINT, the United States attempts to ensure Soviet compliance with such agreed points as the numbers and types of antiballistic missile launchers, ICBMs, and SLBMs. In addition, TELINT provides valuable information about Soviet ballistic missile development and targeting.

Apparently believing that satellites at extreme geosynchronous orbits were incapable of intercepting signals as directional as their very-high-frequency (VHF) and microwave band used for the transmission of telemetry data, the Soviet Union never bothered to encode telemetry. This reportedly changed in mid-1977, about six months after the USSR learned about Rhyolite from a spy working at TRW. Since then, the Soviets have begun encrypting the data on one-time pads and have even gone a step further by trying to come up with a "tape bucket" system, whereby the information is tape-recorded on board the missiles and then parachuted back to earth, thus frustrating the codebreakers. This denial of telemetry data became one of the major sticking points in the SALT II negotiations.

As advanced as Rhyolite is, it is still only one element in America's "verification" efforts. Of even greater importance are the land and sea platforms that peer into the Soviet Union from a half-dozen "windows," the most valuable of which was in Iran. Code-named Tracksman 2, the intercept station, located in the remote, mountainous village of Kabkan, forty miles east of Meshed, was *the* most important listening post America had for monitoring Russian missile and space launch activity. From this listening post, surrounded by nomads and described by one former CIA official as "a 21st-century operation of advanced equipment," intercept operators could easily monitor every detail of the liftoff and early flight of missiles launched from Tyuratam, a short seven hundred miles away. Its proximity to the test site also allowed the post to serve a "tip-off" function; it could signal satellites to switch on their cameras and recording equipment, and alert air crews in Alaska to take to the skies to monitor the end of a test trajectory.

Rhyolite, with its limited size and 22,300-mile distance above the test range, was slim competition. Even if the satellite were equipped with antennas as enormous as the ones at Kabkan, the laws of physics would prevent the telemetry signals reaching Rhyolite from being more than one one-thousandth the magnitude of those that had been received in Iran. In addition, many consider the intelligence gathered during the earliest moments of flight to be the most critical, because it reveals details about the boosters and throw-weights of the missiles. Even the low-flying SIGINT beach balls are just partially effective, since they pass overhead only briefly at various times throughout the day, times that the Russians could easily adjust their schedule to avoid.

Because of these limitations, the intelligence community during the mid-1970s began drawing up plans for a new generation of SIGINT satellites to replace Rhyolite. Code-named Argus, this new system was to provide for a "fallback" intelligence capability that could be used if SIGINT facilities in Iran, Turkey, or elsewhere were ever lost. Because of its sky-high price tag, though, the new system sparked a bitter — and very secret — battle in the intelligence community, the administration, and the Congress. The first confrontation was apparently between the SIGINT experts of NSA and the imagery specialists of the CIA. Referring to his schedule for the following day, former CIA director William Colby once noted: "Carl Duckett for Science and Technology said that tomorrow's meeting of the Executive Committee of the National Reconnaissance Office (which I would chair) would see a big fight over whether to delay an electronic sensor system in order to find the funds to keep one of our photo systems functioning at peak schedule with the increased costs that inflation had brought."

Eventually approved by the NRO, the system was submitted to Secretary of Defense James Schlesinger, Colby's predecessor at the CIA and now the official with the ultimate authority over all overhead reconnaissance operations. Known for the bloody budget-cutting ax he had used at CIA, Schlesinger let it swing once again, vetoing Argus even over the positive recommendation of his own Defense Intelligence Agency. Reportedly, he felt that the new system was simply not needed, since the United States had the Iranian posts and other land-based sensors.

Colby, however, was just as strongly in favor of the satellite program and, exercising his prerogative under the NRO procedures, took the matter directly to the President, with the recommendation that the National Security Council sit in judgment on the matter. President Ford agreed, and the Security Council came back in full support of Argus. That left the matter up to the House Appropriations Committee, which, taking note of the cost of the program and of the conflict within the Executive Branch over its worth, turned thumbs down on the proposal.

Despite the defeat, Argus was apparently reincarnated both in 1977 and 1978, but neither time did the $200 million proposal make it past the desk of CIA director Stansfield Turner. At about the same time he was nixing Argus, his agency came out with a report expressing confidence that the Shah of Iran would keep his nation well under control for many years to come. Less than a year later, with the violent ouster of the Pahlavi monarchy, the CIA had reason to regret both the optimistic report and the rejection of Argus.

Within weeks of the coup, the American government put out word that it had ceased operation at the Kabkan listening post and at its

sister station at Behshahr, on the Caspian coast. The intercept operators at Behshahr, in fact, had pulled out in December 1979. But Kabkan was not only vital; it was irreplaceable. For that reason the United
States decided to take the dangerous step of continuing to operate
the base in total secrecy even from the government of the host country.
It was hoped that once the dust of the revolution had settled, new
agreements could be worked out and the eavesdropping could continue uninterrupted.

But the convulsion that had seized the Iranian empire was growing
more rather than less severe. Believing that all former American monitoring stations had been abandoned, the new Iranian chief of staff,
Major General Mohammed Wali Qaraneh, in a brave assertion meant
for local consumption, told a news conference in late February that
his government would not tolerate American listening posts on Iranian
soil.

On hearing the broadcast, Iranian airmen working with the Americans at Kabkan suddenly mutinied, took over the base, and held the
foreigners hostage. Eight months before they themselves would become Iranian hostages, officials of the American embassy in Tehran
worked out a settlement whereby the United States agreed to pay
the airmen $200,000 in severance and back pay on the condition
that they set the Americans free. The bargain was accepted, and the
SIGINT specialists headed for home.

The true loss from the seizure of Kabkan, however, was not measured in dollars; it was measured in opportunity. "Kabkan is not replaceable," said one official. "No tricks are going to overcome that
in the short run, and the short run could be three or four years. It
is going to affect our capability on verification. I don't think people
realize how important that base was, not just for SALT, but generally
for keeping up with the Soviet missile program. It provided basic
information on Soviet missile testing and development. You're talking
about a pretty big loss. It's serious."

Rhyolite could make up only in part for the closing of the Iranian
window. Had the more advanced Argus been given the go-ahead,
some argue, the situation might have been brighter. The loss of the
posts in Iran meant that NSA in particular and the intelligence community in general have been forced to make do with less. They have
had to beef up existing systems while searching for other vantage
points. Suggestions included the use of specially equipped U-2 aircraft
to fly from bases in Pakistan along the Soviet Union's southwestern
border recording the telemetry, and the assigning of a larger role
to the listening posts in Turkey. Both of these, however, were criticized

as inadequate by former DIA chief Daniel Graham. Basing monitoring stations in Turkey, said the retired Army lieutenant general, would be virtually useless because of the topographical interference created by the Caucasus Mountains. As for the U-2s, Graham said, "Sending airplanes would be fraud because they're not up for twenty-four hours and they can't carry the tons of equipment we had in Iran."

Partly because of these problems, the United States turned to an unlikely source to assist it in building a new SIGINT spy base: China. Because they had as much to gain by sharing in the intelligence as the Americans, the Chinese agreed, and in 1980 construction began on the listening post to be located in a remote, mountainous region of the Xinjiang Ulghur Autonomous Region in western China, near the Soviet border. China thus managed to become as important a platform as it is a target.

Supplementing Rhyolite in the heavens, in addition to the SIGINT beach balls, are two low-flying satellite systems that serve a combined photo and SIGINT function and could be modified to play a larger role in telemetry coverage.

The first is the Code 467 satellite, better known as Big Bird. Built by Lockheed and first launched on June 15, 1971, the satellite is a massive twelve-ton, fifty-five-foot-long spy station built around an extraordinary, superhigh resolution camera capable of distinguishing objects eight inches across from a height of ninety miles. On one mission, Big Bird reportedly snapped the make, model, wing markings, and ground support equipment of a group of planes stationed near Plesetsk. Infrared cameras on board are capable of detecting hidden, underground missile silos because the silos' temperature is warmer than that of the surrounding earth. Other sensors include multispectral photography, which aids in spotting camouflage, and an array of SIGINT listening devices.

Launched at the rate of about two per year, the Big Birds were the first satellites capable of both search-and-find surveillance and close-look detection. The major handicap of the Code 467 is its short life span, which started out at about 52 days but by 1978 was extended to 179 days.

The second of the low-altitude surveillance platforms (LASPs) is the Code 1010, or KH-11 satellite, code-named Keyhole. Even more sophisticated than Big Bird, Keyhole incorporates a real-time capability, permitting it to send back to earth high-quality, telephoto television signals as well as SIGINT information. Confirmation of the satellite's SIGINT capability came during a trial several years ago in which it was revealed that Section 2 of the sixty-four-page KH-11 systems technical manual was classified TOP SECRET UMBRA, the overall code word for high-level SIGINT information. Nearby were the words "Spool Label Color-Coded for DP" and the word "canisters." This may mean that, like Big Bird, Keyhole can store exposed film and tape in canisters that are periodically ejected into the earth's atmosphere, descend by parachute to a point in the Pacific Ocean north of Hawaii, and are recovered in midair or float on or just under the surface of the ocean, giving off radio and sonar signals for eventual recovery by frogmen. The SIGINT spools, as opposed to the film spools, can then be sent for data processing (DP).

Keyhole was first launched on December 19, 1976. Later launches were on June 14, 1978, and February 7, 1980. It could achieve a three-hundred-mile-high orbit, almost twice as high as Big Bird's highest orbit, and thus had a life expectancy of about two years, a considerable improvement over the previous generation.

But despite the technological wonders of Big Bird and Keyhole, the satellites had problems in monitoring telemetry because they were low-altitude orbiters and thus easy prey for the Soviet test engineers, who would simply plan the more critical missile activities, such as liftoff, during times when the satellites were out of view. What was needed was an advanced, geosynchronous follow-on system to Rhyolite.

Argus was just such a system, but after three years of continuous defeats, it seems to have been abandoned for a new system, one considerably larger and far more sophisticated. Code-named Aquacade, the supersatellite was made possible by a new method of getting the SIGINT bug into orbit: the space shuttle. Unlike the past workhorse, the Titan III rocket, the shuttle promised to carry far bigger payloads, not only in terms of weight but also in size.

Such increased capability, though, was not without a price. What had to be sacrificed was time, since it would be years before the shuttle would be fully operational. But at the time, with the Iranian listening posts operating at full steam and Rhyolite backed up with in-orbit spares and showing no signs of quitting, it looked to the intelligence planners like a good risk. That was before anyone ever heard of a bearded religious zealot called Ayatollah Ruhollah Khomeini.

With the loss of the secret Tracksman stations, a loss only partly correctable by Rhyolite, DEFSMAC's primary intelligence source for Soviet space and missile activity vanished. Equally serious, the planned orbiting of Aquacade, which could help make up for the loss, had run into delay after delay because of difficulties with the space shuttle. The orbiting delivery truck was rapidly becoming NASA's answer to the C-5A, with mammoth cost overruns and postponements measured in years.

To the Senate Intelligence Committee, however, increasingly concerned over the intelligence gap, the oversold shuttle began looking more like an Edsel. In early 1980, for example, the committee was told that the first operational launch of the spaceplane would take place in December 1981. Nevertheless, only six months later that flight had been pushed back to September 1982. Even worse, it now appeared that the shuttle would not be able to handle some of the spy satellites that had been designed for it. Addressing a closed congressional hearing, Air Force Secretary Hans M. Mark admitted that "the Shuttle may not perform up to its completely full payload capability . . . In other words, even though the Shuttle exists, we may not be able to use it to launch all of these spacecraft."

Faced with such problems, and worried about their effects on the SALT treaty and America's verification efforts, the Intelligence Committee cancelled Aquacade's shuttle reservation and ordered the SIGINT bird to be sent up atop an expendable rocket instead.

But now there were even more problems. Originally designed for the shuttle, the satellite was too big to be put on top of a rocket. This would force a scaling-down of the design, which might have an adverse effect on the entire mission. And not only that. Since both the Pentagon and the National Reconnaissance Office had put so much confidence in the space shuttle, the production lines of the larger launch vehicles, such as the giant Titan III booster, were on the verge of shutting down. This meant that, although the Air Force had planned for enough launch vehicles to cover the twelve "vital national security launches" (as they euphemistically term the NRO spy flights) planned between 1980 and 1985 in the event of shuttle problems, the costs would run to a stratospheric $100 million per rocket. Conceded Air Force Secretary Mark, himself a former NRO chief, the price tag "would probably make them the most expensive rockets in history."

Launching the Aquacade series and some of the other oversized supersatellites would undoubtedly exceed even that amount, since it would require going back into production with still another booster in the process of being phased out in anticipation of the shuttle. This is the Atlas-Centaur's high-performance upper stage, which, when strapped onto the Titan III, will provide the extra push needed to get the satellites up to where the shuttle was supposed to carry them.

Yet, as costly as the rockets are, it is the bird itself that eats up the major share of the NRO budgetary dollar, a point emphasized by former NSA director Marshall Carter. Speaking of the NRO launch process, Carter noted, "That technique was pretty well established there and they would just light up another at Vandenberg. The big expense was in the research and development of the satellite body itself, what it contained, all the various collection things."

Thus, with the cost of a single satellite sometimes exceeding $100 million, according to some officials, added to the $100 million or so for the rocket, plus the combined reconfiguration costs, a single Aquacade SIGINT satellite could easily hit a quarter of a billion. Nevertheless, even though the satellite was built primarily for the NSA, none of its costs would ever, apparently, appear in the Agency's budget. Instead, they are secretly hidden in the classified budget for the Air Force, which serves as a cover for the NRO. This was confirmed by General Carter, a veteran of the early NRO organization when he served as deputy director of the CIA before leaving to head NSA. When asked whether the NRO budget was incorporated into the CIA budget, Carter replied: "No. They were knowledgeable of it when I was there of course because we had a great part of the participation, but as I recall, the NRO budget was within the Air Force budget. But a lot of the CIA stuff was in the NRO budget when I was there." Were the Puzzle Palace to be assessed for the full costs of its space program, its budget would most likely double or even triple. Shielded behind the oppressive secrecy of an agency whose very existence is a national secret, however, what minimal accountability there might have been simply vanishes. Referring to the spy satellite program, the late Allen Ellender, former chairman of the Senate Appropriations Committee, is reported to have lamented, "If you knew how much money we waste in this area, it would knock you off your chair. It's criminal."

Once the satellite achieves orbit, responsibility for both the operation of the ground collection stations and their costs is assumed by the NSA, although actual control of the spacecraft is retained by the NRO through its operations center in Sunnyvale, California, near San Francisco.

Planning for these ground terminals began in 1966, the same year that the Agency formed DEFSMAC and began taking bids on the DSP Code 949 early-warning satellite. Today there are at least three and possibly four of the supersecret SIGINT satellite ground terminals.

•

"It's a long way from Frankfurt." Staring down at the endless expanse of wind-swept earth, reddened like a Martian desert by whirling dust storms of iron-oxide sand, the comparison surely must have passed through the mind of the American with the dark, receding hairline and the heavy, black-framed glasses. The flight from South Australia's modern capital of Adelaide, lush with vineyards and olive groves, to Alice Springs, at the heart of the island continent's wild and fierce outback, is more than a journey of miles and hours; it is a journey of the senses.

Making the trip in January 1967, at the height of central Australia's hot, dry summer season, was Richard Lee Stallings, a mid-fortyish NSA official whose previous assignment had been at NSA's European headquarters, in Frankfurt. He was on his way to supervise the construction of the ground terminal that would serve as a way station between the planned SIGINT and early-warning satellites and NSA.

Stallings arrived down under in October 1966, a few weeks after the DEFSMAC ribbon-cutting ceremonies, and spent his first few months in Canberra, the Australian capital, working out the final niceties with government officials. These negotiations culminated in a secret agreement, signed on December 9 by Paul Hasluck, the Australian Minister for External Affairs, and E. M. Cronk, an American embassy official. The agreement was to run for a period of ten years and thereafter until terminated by either side, but on October 19, 1977, this was formally extended for nine more years, after which either government can request termination on one year's notice.

Smack in the center of Australia, "the Alice," as it is called by its population of white and aborigine ranchers and cattlemen, is the only town in a vast and untamed geographic void known to some as the outback and to others as the Center. One and a half times the size of Texas, the raw Australian interior is made up mostly of drifting desert and dry riverbeds. Like a never-ending series of smooth, graceful ripples, the Macdonnell Ranges cut across 250 miles of the heart of the outback, offering occasional patches of shelter and soil. A water hole in an elbow of the ranges served as a likely spot in 1872 for the establishment of a telegraph station. In honor of the wife of the superintendent of telegraphs, nearly a thousand miles south in Adelaide, the outpost was named Alice Springs.

By the time Richard Stallings stepped off his plane in January 1967, the population of Alice had grown to six thousand. Surrounding the town were massive cattle "stations," or ranches, some the size of Rhode Island. Although there is never an abundance of rain, when it does come it is usually enough to produce feed to fatten the cattle until the next cloudburst. But the previous eight years had been the worst in local memory. The drought, during which there had been just over an inch of rain in the first ten months of 1965 and less than five the year before, had reduced the area to a dust bowl of starving cattle.

But the conditions that were so disastrous to the local population were precisely those considered ideal by the NSA. Less rain meant less chance of a signal being washed out and less possibility of interference from an electrical storm. The isolation of the area brought with it the advantage of freedom from interference caused by spurious signals and lowered the chance of being detected.

Six months before the formal United States–Australian agreement for the NSA base was signed, construction crews began laying a new road southwest of town. It was in the direction of Temple Bar Creek and the Mereenie water bores. Such a road had long been sought by the local residents, who depended almost entirely on the deep wells for their water, but the government had stubbornly resisted building it. It was therefore with both surprise and delight that they read the June 1966 announcement that such an access road was being laid. What they could not understand, however, was why the road kept going for miles past the water bores to nowhere.

Nowhere was eleven and a half miles southwest of Alice Springs at Laura Creek in a valley formed by the rocky foothills of the Macdonnell Ranges. Known as Pine Gap, it was shortly to be transformed from a Stone Age wasteland into a twenty-first-century spy base.

Today Pine Gap looks like an advance moon colony in the Sea of Tranquillity. Hidden in the valley is a secret community of 454 people, eighteen single-story concrete buildings, some the size of supermarkets, and, most startling, a futuristic array of six silvery-white igloolike radomes containing dish antennas ranging in size from less than 20 feet to about 105 feet. Others are about 70 and 55 feet, and two are 40 feet.

To decrease the possibility of both penetration and electrical interference, the planners have surrounded Pine Gap with a seven-square-mile "buffer zone" encircled by a double fence and have established twenty-four-hour-a-day patrols. Even aircraft are forbidden from flying closer than two and a half miles from the Gap. Its cover, as the sign next to the first checkpoint indicates, is a "Joint Defense Space Research Facility" sponsored by both the American and Australian Defense Departments.

In reality, the base serves as a terminal for a number of spy satellites and also as a highly sophisticated intercept station. Code-named Merino, Pine Gap was completed just before the launch of the first in the series of DSP 647 early-warning satellites, the first two of which were parked in geostationary orbit over Singapore, where they could peer down on China and northern and western Russia.

Beamed down to Pine Gap from the spacecraft are signals from infrared warning devices designed to detect ballistic missile exhausts during the powered stages of their flight. In order to prevent any false warnings, televisionlike signals from a visible-light sensor (VLS) are also transmitted back to Merino for analysis by NSA personnel. Complementing these are most likely other sensors, including, possibly, a limited SIGINT capability. Once the data have been received at Pine Gap, notice of any significant situation or threat would apparently be transmitted instantly to DEFSMAC, where a real-time hookup might be instituted.

Additional radome-enclosed antennas were added in the early 1970s to collect signals from the orbiting Rhyolite satellites. The SIGINT data would apparently be recorded on tape as the satellite overflies the Soviet Union and China and then be transmitted at a high rate of speed to Pine Gap. A similar system is probably used for the small SIGINT beach balls; however, here the intelligence is probably first transmitted to the more powerful Big Bird photo satellites for relay to Merino.

Australia also serves as an ideal platform for direct nonsatellite interception of Soviet communications, according to one former NSA official:

> Pine Gap is described as a "window" in internal NSA communications. Both Exmouth Gulf [a Naval Security Group intercept station on Australia's North West Cape] and Pine Gap have electronic interception missions along with other communications functions. Pine Gap and the antennas subordinate to it are quite important. They are ideally situated from a global "bounce back" point of view to monitor Russian high-frequency telemetry originating in the testing area near the Caspian Sea and in the down range at Tyura Tam [sic]. Australia is peaceful, quiet, and all that, and an ideal place for some kinds of NSA installations.

In November 1969 construction began on another highly secret American satellite terminal, this one code-named Casino. Smaller than Pine Gap, it was built at an equally isolated site on the Woomera Prohibited Area, a 73,000-square-mile tract of rugged and unpopulated land six hundred miles southeast of Alice Springs. Used for joint British and Australian weapons testing, the entire area is under heavy guard. Anyone granted permission into the forbidding territory is first issued a list called "Conditions of Entry to Prohibited Areas," which includes such warnings as "You shall not, unless duly authorized in writing by the proper officer, by letter, orally, or any other means, disclose any information relating to . . . the Prohibited Areas."

Located in a small valley of the Prohibited Area known as Nurrungar (136.46°E and 31.19°S), Casino reportedly concentrates on processing imagery from photo satellites like Big Bird and the KH-11 Keyhole orbiter, and is therefore of primary interest to the CIA rather than the NSA. According to one report, Nurrungar receives photos transmitted from the reconnaissance satellites shortly after the spacecraft pass over China. It is needed to supplement other ground stations because the low-altitude orbiters are in transmission range for only ten minutes. The added station allows for more snapshots of the targets.

While construction crews were pouring blacktop past the Mereenie water bores toward Pine Gap, NSA was making plans to open another secret location on the other side of the earth. Harrogate, England, is exactly opposite Pine Gap, Australia, in more ways than its location on the globe. Instead of deserts pock-marked by dry lake beds and rugged, treeless mountain ranges, there are gentle hills, green rolling pastures, and mile upon mile of desolate moorland. Slightly less than two hundred miles north of London, the small quiet Yorkshire town, like its distant relative down under, was about to become a key player in a futuristic war of twenty-first-century espionage.

Throughout the summer of 1966, dozens of civilian NSA employees began quietly turning up at Harrogate's Grand Hotel. By June the number of spooks registered at the hotel had reached seventy, and by the beginning of July they had commandeered the entire building with a six-month lease. Before their arrival they had been briefed extensively never to admit their relationship with the NSA, but the presence of the new arrivals stirred rumors in the town that the secret American Army base eight miles to the west was about to be taken over by civilians.

"Well, we're not happy about it, but if they want it, I suppose they'll take it." Eleven years earlier, in the middle of February 1955, S. Robinson, owner of Nessfield Farm in the Kettlesing area west of Harrogate, received the surprising news that the British War Department wanted his 246-acre farm. No reason was given for the government's wanting 562 acres of rural moorland, but a year later four American Army officers and three enlisted men arrived, and construction began on a strange "communications" station.

Finally, on September 15, 1960, after five years and $6.8 million worth of cement and antennas, the 13th U.S. Army Security Agency Field Station formally opened. Named Menwith Hill Station, the four-hundred-man base, virtually free from urban electromagnetic interference, was ideally suited for eavesdropping.

As the American civilians continued to flow into town during the summer of 1966, the rumors of their imminent takeover were continually denied by both governments. Nevertheless, on August 1, the formal transfer from ASA to NSA officially, yet secretly, took place. Eventually, the sole military person on the base was a junior lieutenant recruited as commissary officer.

Soon after the changeover, the triple-fenced listening post started taking on an appearance strikingly similar to Pine Gap's. Giant dish-shaped antennas began going up, some accompanied by enormous eggshell-like radomes set on concrete nests. By 1980 the number of antennas had grown to eight. Beyond the fences were placed signs, in case there was any doubt, warning: MINISTRY OF DEFENCE / PROHIBITED PLACE / OFFICIAL SECRETS ACT / 1911–1939.

According to Frank Raven, chief of G Group until 1975, the major reason for the NSA's taking charge was the failure of the Army to allocate sufficient intercept spaces and resources for the much-needed strategic intelligence, such as diplomatic and economic targets. "The Army fought like hell to avoid intercepting it," said Raven. Until NSA moved in, the Army had been using the station primarily for tactical coverage. Also, NSA was upset because no resources had been devoted to intercepting the newer forms of communications, like satellite microwave.

Principal targets of Menwith Hill, according to Raven, are western Europe, eastern Europe, and the Soviet Union east of the Urals. "It wouldn't be any good on Siberia," he added. Most of the signals intercepted are too sophisticated to be attacked at the station and are therefore forwarded by satellite back to Fort Meade for analysis.

Some of Menwith Hill's strategic intercept capabilities were probably inherited from a U.S. Air Force Security Service listening post at Kirknewton, near Edinburgh — which just happened to cease operations the very day before NSA began operating the Yorkshire station. Some reports indicate that many of the operations formerly performed by Kirknewton were simply transferred down the road to the new NSA base. One former employee of the Kirknewton listening post explained the routine:

> Intercepted telegrams came through on telex machines. I was provided with a list of about 100 words to look out for. All diplomatic traffic from European embassies was in code and was passed at once to a senior officer. A lot of telegrams — birthday congratulations for instance — were

put into the burn bag. I had to keep a special watch for commercial traffic, details of commodities, what big companies were selling, like iron and steel and gas. Changes were frequent. One week I was asked to scan all traffic between Berlin and London and another week between Rome and Belgrade. Some weeks the list of words to watch for contained dozens of names of big companies. Some weeks I just had to look for commodities. All traffic was sent back to Fort Meade in Washington.

Like Pine Gap, Menwith Hill has both a strategic intelligence collection mission and also an early-warning mission. And like the Australian station, it was transformed into an advanced satellite activity only a few weeks before the formal inauguration of DEFSMAC. It is probable, then, that at least part of its function is to serve as a ground station for one of the DSP early-warning satellites, possibly parked over the South Atlantic. Other antennas are most likely used to receive data transmitted by orbiting SIGINT satellites. A new antenna array, in fact, was added in 1973, the same year in which the first Rhyolite SIGINT bird became operational. The location of Menwith Hill would appear to be ideal for the collection of data from orbiting satellites passing over the Soviet Union's northern and coastal areas. Covered by such a satellite trajectory would be Russia's Plesetsk missile test site, as well as the sensitive Murmansk and Arkhangelsk seaport areas.

Still another satellite apparently associated with Menwith Hill is Big Bird. Evidence of this is the large number of employees from Lockheed Corporation, builder of Big Bird, attached to the station.

It is considered a choice assignment within NSA, and personnel are generally sent to Menwith Hill for three-year tours. Some live on station, where there is a recreation center, a club, a commissary, and a branch of the Tower Federal Credit Union — a credit union limited to employees of NSA or those associated with the Agency. According to one former Menwith Hill official, the station conducts its operations round the clock, with virtually all operational personnel assigned as shift workers, or, in Menwith Hill parlance, "trick trash." Nonshift workers, mostly office personnel, are in turn labeled "day ladies."

Security at the station is reported to be extremely tight. "All employees have to work under rigid security control," said one report. "Family members are ordered never to mention 'NSA,' and all, including children aged twelve and over, are instructed to report all contacts with 'foreign nationals.' Officials and their families have been quickly sent home for even minor indiscretions of teenage children."

The security briefings are apparently conducted before the employees and their families leave the United States and again, once they have arrived at the station, in the Mission Briefing Conference Room in the operations building.

Sharing seats alongside the NSA operators, at least in some areas, are SIGINT specialists from Britain's Government Communications Headquarters (GCHQ). According to the former Menwith Hill official, the two groups work very closely together. "In fact," he said, "the cooperation was so smooth that when the Brits would put down their earphones for their ten A.M. tea break, the Americans would simply cover their positions." He added that the GCHQ people were especially good in the computer software area and especially well adapted for attacking the European code systems, because of their extensive experience during World War II.

Chief of Menwith Hill Station for about five years, until the fall of 1980, was Albert Dale Braeuninger, a self-described "technician" in his mid-fifties who wears a lapel pin of joined American and British flags. When asked the mission of the base, Braeuninger gives his stock response: it is simply a relay station. Any connection to NSA is routinely denied. Despite this, when Braeuninger left Harrogate in 1980 he moved back to a home near Fort Meade and took over a senior position at the Puzzle Palace — an unusual transfer for the head of a simple relay station.

Finally, a third highly secret satellite receiving station was opened at Buckley Air National Guard Base, a heavily guarded facility in Aurora, just outside Denver, Colorado. Known as an Aerospace Data Facility of the Air Force Space and Missile Systems Organization (SAMSO), it appears to be a joint NSA-NRO operation and may control and receive data from the DSP 647 early-warning satellite launched into orbit over Panama on March 1, 1972, as well as other intelligence from such SIGINT orbiters as Rhyolite. One 1974 report indicated that the intelligence data flowing into Buckley through its five radome-covered satellite dishes was processed by powerful dual IBM 360–75J computers.

An indication of the secrecy surrounding Buckley is an episode that took place in September 1977. Forty-eight employees of the installation were fired for having smoked marijuana on occasion. Told by Air Force investigators that they were looking for evidence in an espionage investigation, the employees were questioned repeatedly about their use of marijuana or other drugs. Throughout the questioning, the interrogators from the Office of Special Investigation barred lawyers from the sessions on the grounds that they lacked the proper security clearance. Eventually the case came to the attention of James

H. Joy, local director of the American Civil Liberties Union, who termed the incident a "witch hunt" and brought pressure on the Air Force to reinstate the fired employees. Realizing that it had overstepped legal bounds, the Air Force relented and allowed back thirty-nine of the people, mostly contract employees of the Hughes Aircraft Corporation and the Lockheed Aircraft Division, builders of the Big Bird.

The NSA, however, was not so forgiving with four of its employees caught in the fishing expedition, and ordered them to resign or be dismissed. Said the wife of one sixteen-year veteran of the Puzzle Palace: "We were just shanghaied."

SEA

When Frank Raven took over the newly formed G Group in 1960 he underwent the NSA equivalent of culture shock. As the chief of GENS (general Soviet), he had been responsible for attacking the medium-level cipher systems and reading the unencrypted traffic of one major country, the Soviet Union, and a handful of satellite nations. Under the reorganization of PROD, however, the two Russian cryptanalytical divisions, GENS and ADVA (advanced) were merged into a single unit: A Group, under former ADVA chief Arthur Levenson. At the same time, ACOM (Asian Communist) became B Group and ALLO (all others) was transformed into Raven's new G Group.

Now instead of one country and a few satellites, Raven was responsible for, conceivably, more than a hundred nations speaking a score of different languages, including allies, neutrals, and the entire Third World. But there was an even more significant difference between GENS and G Group: a severe lack of intercept coverage and thus a lack of raw traffic. Whereas the Soviet Union was nearly circled by intercept stations and monitored round the clock by ELINT aircraft, the United States had only two listening posts in all of Africa — near Asmara on the wind-swept Eritrean plateau in Ethiopia and in Sidi Yahia in the sun-baked Moroccan desert. Thus there was virtually no coverage south of the Sahara. South America was even worse — there were no listening posts there, although there were several in Panama and one in Puerto Rico. To overcome this problem, the NSA decided to copy the Russians and build its own fleet of eavesdropping ships.

For years the Russians had been sending antenna-laden trawlers into waters close to sensitive U.S. military facilities and activities, hoping to pick up revealing signals. In April 1960, for example, the *Vega,* a short, stubby, six-hundred-ton Soviet trawler with eleven antennas protruding from a huge electronics van mounted on the bridge, cruised down the East Coast of the United States and chugged within twelve miles of Cape Henry, Virginia. With a range of "hundreds of miles," according to one intelligence official, the electronic gear could easily pick up signals from the Navy's enormous naval base at Norfolk, as well as from nearly a dozen other smaller military facilities in the area.

Before arriving off Virginia, the *Vega* had swung through an area eighty-five miles east of Sea Girt, New Jersey, where the Navy was conducting maneuvers with the nuclear submarine U.S.S. *George Washington,* the first sub to be equipped with the twelve-hundred-mile-range Polaris missile. At one point, the Russian spy ship even reversed its engines in what appeared to be an effort to ram a Navy tug assigned to pick up dummy missiles that the sub was firing.

Another prime target of the trawlers during the early 1960s was the U.S. nuclear weapons' testing program in the South Pacific. In the spring of 1962 a number of Russian intelligence collection vessels dangerously traversed the restricted nuclear testing area north of Johnston Island and patrolled ten to fifteen miles outside the boundaries. Largest of the ships was the modern 3600-ton hydrometeorological research ship *Shokal'skiy,* which was equipped with sixteen laboratories, a pad for launching meteorological rockets to study the effects of nuclear explosions on the upper atmosphere, and equipment to pick up and analyze debris from the explosions. This nuclear refuse could provide intelligence on such things as bomb design and yield. The time and approximate location of the explosions could also be determined from electromagnetic pulses received on board, and still other data were obtainable from optical observations of high-altitude bursts and from hydro-acoustic devices measuring sound waves from the explosion.

The idea of building an NSA navy at first met with considerable resistance within the Pentagon, but the go-ahead was finally received in 1960, and the Agency began scouting for a spy fleet. "What we wanted was a slow tub," recalled Frank Raven, "that was civilian, that could mosey along a coast relatively slowly, take its time, and spend time at sea."

First selected was the U.S.N.S. *Private Jose F. Valdez* (T-AG 169) (for General Auxiliary 169), a rusting veteran salvaged from the mothball fleet of the U.S. Maritime Administration. But to Raven and the personnel of G Group, "the *Valdez* was a dream boat." Originally named *Round Splice* and then the *Private Joe P. Martinez, Valdez* was

built at the Riverside Yard in Duluth, Minnesota, in 1944 and spent
most of her life as a coastal transport with the Military Sea Transportation Service (MSTS), hauling troops one place and paper clips another.

Picked to be the sister ship of the *Valdez* was the U.S.N.S. *Sergeant
Joseph E. Muller* (T-AG 171), almost a twin, which pushed supplies
around the Far East until she retired in December 1956 after a few
chilly months of Arctic resupply work.*

They were slow, unglamorous, seagoing delivery trucks, but they
were also ideal as electronic snoopers. Because they were run by
the MSTS instead of the Navy, they could be home-ported far from
a U.S. naval base. And because they were civilian-manned, they would
be able to spend more time conducting operations and less time making liberty calls. Also, the slow speed was ideal for copying the maximum amount of traffic without the ship's appearing to be deliberately
loitering.

Following commissioning and sea trials, the *Valdez* was sent off to
Africa and home-ported at Capetown. From the South African port,
the ship could easily cruise up and down either the east or west coast.
Although the fact that she was a spy ship was almost an open secret,
most of the African nations swallowed the cover story — that her
mission was to cover Soviet missile testing. In fact, she did spend a
small amount of time in the South Atlantic off Namibia, monitoring
the landing of Russian missiles fired from Kapustin Yar. But her principal mission was to keep a close ear on the newly emerging nations
of postcolonial Africa and on the internal struggles of the colonies
that remained.

As the *Valdez* crawled up and down Africa, sometimes so slowly that
someone once suggested painting a wave on her bow to give the
impression that she was moving, the *Muller*, home-ported in Port Ever-
glades, Florida, directed her antennas toward Fidel Castro's Cuba.

Shortly after the NSA began laying plans for its eavesdropping
flotilla, the Navy became interested in the program, and a heated
battle for control soon erupted. The resulting compromise eliminated
much of NSA's autonomy and produced the second generation of
spy ships. The ships to come after the *Valdez* and the *Muller* would
no longer be civilian-manned or operated by the MSTS. Instead, the
Navy would man and run the ships, and the Naval Security Group

* There was, apparently, a third such ship, the U.S.N.S. *Lieutenant James E. Robinson*
(T-AG 170), in operation at least during 1963–1964. However, little information about
her is available. (Department of the Navy, Office of the Chief of Naval Operations,
OPNAV Notice 5030, "Reclassification of Certain Naval Ships," October 30, 1962.)

would conduct the intercept operations. This meant that the Navy would be able to conduct some of its own targeting, but only on a not-to-interfere basis. Whereas the NSA was interested in national and strategic targets, such as diplomatic and political intelligence, the Navy was interested in foreign naval communications.

On July 8, 1961, the first of the second-generation spy ships was commissioned. Named the U.S.S. *Oxford* (AGTR 1 — for Auxiliary General Technical Research), the vintage World War II Liberty ship at 441 feet was more than a hundred feet longer than her two predecessors. She was also faster, which gave her the advantage of being able to get someplace in a hurry but the disadvantage of creating suspicion by cruising well below her maximum speed.

Throughout 1961 and 1962 the *Oxford* patrolled the eastern coast of South America and would occasionally relieve the *Muller* on her Cuban watch. In October, one of the two ships picked up the first indications that the Soviet Union was in the process of installing offensive missiles in Cuba. Armed with this tip, the CIA sent a U-2 aircraft high over the island and returned with the proof.

In 1963 two more of the second-generation seaborne listening posts were commissioned. These were the U.S.S. *Georgetown* (AGTR 2) and the U.S.S. *Jamestown* (AGTR 3).

Manned by a crew of 18 officers and 260 enlisted men, the *Georgetown* took over South American monitoring operations and relieved the *Oxford,* which set sail for the coast of Vietnam. In 1964, following a six-week assignment off Cuba relieving the *Muller,* she picked her way down the coasts of Venezuela, Brazil, Uruguay, and Argentina before returning to her home port of Norfolk.

On January 5, 1965, the *Georgetown* steamed through the Panama Canal and down the Pacific coast of South America, where she spent about three months eavesdropping off the coast of Chile. The second half of the year was spent on the Atlantic side of the continent.

In 1966 the SIGINT ship concentrated her eavesdropping operations in the southwest Caribbean and along the Pacific coast of Latin America. During her now annual *Muller* relief operations, the *Georgetown* managed to pluck from the sea three fleeing Cubans on an innertube raft twelve miles north of Havana, a common activity of the *Muller.*

As the *Georgetown* concentrated on the Caribbean and Latin America, her sister ship, the U.S.S. *Jamestown,* assisted the *Valdez* in patrolling Africa. Passing through the Strait of Gibraltar on her first operational cruise in April 1964, she monitored North African communications as she slowly traversed the Mediterranean Sea and then collected

Middle East signals as she transited the Suez Canal and cruised down the Red Sea to the British Protectorate of Aden (now South Yemen). Following a brief port call, she continued around the Horn of Africa, down to Cape Town, and then up the West African coast, circumnavigating the continent. The 31,011-mile journey ended on August 17, when the ship steamed back into Norfolk.

Two and a half months later, on November 2, she again headed back across the Atlantic for SIGINT operations along the western and southern African coasts, making port calls in Cape Town and at Dakar in Senegal (now Senegambia). In the spring of 1965 the *Jimmy T*, as she was affectionately known by her crew, was reassigned to the Pacific coast of South America, and in October she headed to the Far East to aid the *Oxford* in monitoring the rapidly expanding war in Southeast Asia.

The final two ships of the second-generation sea-based platforms were commissioned in late 1964. Unlike the previous three, however, the U.S.S. *Belmont* (AGTR 4) and the U.S.S. *Liberty* (AGTR 5) were reconverted Victory hulls and were about fourteen feet longer and slightly more powerful than the *Oxford, Georgetown,* and *Jamestown.*

After several shakedown cruises in the Caribbean, the *Belmont* departed for Africa on April 26, 1965, to replace the *Jamestown.* Two days later, however, partway across the Atlantic, the ship received an emergency order to reverse course and proceed to an area just off Santo Domingo and begin monitoring operations. On April 28, presumably to protect American citizens caught in the middle of a sudden rebellion, President Lyndon Johnson dispatched 405 Marines to the Dominican Republic. The *Belmont* arrived two days later, and the following day was ordered to La Romana to evacuate 250 Americans. After some confusion, however, the *Belmont* returned to its operations area without the evacuees. By May 5, the United States had placed 22,289 troops on the island with a new purpose: "to help prevent another Communist state in this hemisphere."

The *Belmont* remained on station off Santo Domingo, monitoring internal and international Dominican communications until July 13, when she returned to her home port, Norfolk. She spent much of the remainder of 1965 and a large portion of 1966 picking up signals off Chile and Peru, and made a brief cruise down the coast of Venezuela in the fall.

At exactly 4:43 on the afternoon of October 17, 1966, while cruising a few miles off the Peruvian coast north of Callao, the *Belmont* began to suffer severe vibrations; they lasted about twenty seconds. The ship was immediately stopped and the crew was sent to general quarters. The enemy, however, turned out to be Mother Nature: the *Belmont* became one of the few ships in history (if not the only one) to find itself 155 fathoms above the epicenter of an earthquake. Although the *Belmont* was not damaged, the city of Callao and the surrounding area suffered heavy destruction.

On February 1, 1967, the *Belmont* steamed out of Norfolk on a long journey that took her down the east coast of South America, through the Straits of Magellan, where she encountered fifteen- to twenty-foot waves, and then slowly past Chile, Peru, Ecuador, and Colombia, collecting miles of intercepted communications. Finally, on June 9, more than four months and 17,154 miles later, the tired ship pulled into Pier 4 at Norfolk.

Five weeks before the *Belmont* arrived back in home port, her sister ship, the *Liberty*, had sailed out of the same port on its fourth deployment along the West African coast. On May 22 she pulled into the Ivory Coast capital of Abidjan for what was to be a four-day port call.

But as the spring of 1967 was turning into summer, the focus of G Group's attention rapidly began shifting from Africa to another area of the world. "I do not wish to be alarmist," United Nations Secretary General U Thant cautioned the Security Council on May 19, "but I cannot avoid the warning to the Council that in my view the current situation in the Near East is more disturbing, indeed, I may say more menacing than at any time since the fall of 1956."

The day before, Egyptian President Gamal Abdel Nasser had ordered the UN peacekeeping force to leave Egypt and the Gaza Strip. Israel refused to allow the force to relocate on its side of the frontier. On May 20, Israeli tanks were reported on the Sinai frontier, and the following day Egypt ordered mobilization of 100,000 army reserves. On the 22nd, Nasser announced the blockade of the Gulf of Aqaba, and the Israelis followed up the next day by declaring the blockade "an act of aggression against Israel."

Anticipating the possibility of such a crisis, G Group several months earlier had drawn up a contingency plan. It would position the *Liberty* in the area of "LOLO" (longitude o, latitude o) in the Gulf of Guinea, concentrating on targets in that area, but actually positioning her far enough north so that she could make a quick dash for the Middle East should the need arise.

But G Group also had to do something about the *Valdez*. After more than four years of patrolling the tropical waters off the east coast of Africa, her bottom had become so encrusted with sea life that her top speed was down to between three and five knots, thus requiring her to be brought back to Norfolk, where she could be beached and scraped. It was decided to take maximum advantage of the situation and bring the *Valdez* home through the Suez Canal, mapping and charting the radio spectrum as she crawled past the Middle East and the eastern Mediterranean. "Now, frankly," recalled Raven, "we didn't think at that point that it was highly desirable to have a ship right in the Middle East; it would be too explosive a situation. But the *Valdez* obviously coming home with a foul bottom and advertising that she was coming home with a foul bottom and pulling no bones about it and being a civilian ship could get away with it."

It took her about six weeks to come up through the canal and limp down the North African coast — past Israel, Egypt, and Libya. But as she got about halfway between Greece and Italy, on May 23, Washington pushed the panic button. Following the announcement of the Egyptian blockade and the buildup of troops on both sides of the border, NSA decided it was time to send the *Liberty* up to the Mediterranean. As was the standard procedure, the request was submitted to the Joint Chiefs of Staff's Joint Reconnaissance Center, which would make the final decision and initiate the order. At 8:20 P.M. (EDT) the Pentagon dispatched a flash (highest precedence) message to the *Liberty*, instructing her to get underway immediately for Rota, Spain, where she was to take on supplies and await further orders.

The message was received on the *Liberty* about three and a half hours later, at 3:45* on the morning of the 24th, and by 7:00 A.M. she was steaming east and then north at full speed (seventeen knots).

At NSA, G Group began rounding up all available Arabic linguists and packing them off to back-up listening posts in Greece, Turkey, and other stations around the Mediterranean. "By God," said Raven, "if you could speak Arabic and you were in NSA, you were on a plane."

The need for Arabic linguists was especially critical on the *Liberty*, which, because of her West African targets, carried only French linguists. So six Arabic linguists — three enlisted Marines and three NSA civilians — were flown to Rota to rendezvous with the *Liberty*. Also scheduled to rendezvous in Rota was the *Valdez*, which contained all the critical information on Middle East traffic: "who was communicating on what links — teletype, telephone, microwave, you name it," according to Raven.

* Unless otherwise indicated, all times quoted are U.S.S. *Liberty* time.

On the morning of June 1, the *Liberty* pulled into Rota and took on 380,000 gallons of fuel and a supply of food and dry goods. Already waiting for the ship were the linguists and the reams of SIGINT data from the *Valdez,* which had headed back to Norfolk.

According to the original NSA plan, the *Liberty* was scheduled to depart that same day and steam for the eastern end of the island of Crete, where she would remain "parked." As a result of a hearability study conducted by the *Valdez,* it was determined that, because of what amounted to a "duct" in the air, that particular location off Crete was ideal for eavesdropping on the entire Middle East. "You can sit in Crete and watch the Cairo television shows," said Raven. "If you're over flat water, basically calm water, the communications are wonderful."

Within hours of her arrival at Rota, the *Liberty* had loaded all her fuel, supplies, linguists, and intercept data — but now there was a problem with the ship's unique but troublesome TRSSCOMM system. Short for Technical Research Ship Special Communications (and pronounced triss-comm), the system consisted of a sixteen-foot, dish-shaped antenna mounted on a movable platform and capable of bouncing a 10,000-watt microwave signal off a particular spot on the moon and down either to the receiving station at Cheltenham, Maryland, or to one of the other Navy SIGINT ships. The TRSSCOMM had the advantage of being able to transmit large quantities of intelligence information very rapidly without giving away the ship's location to hostile direction-finding equipment or interfering with incoming signals. But its major disadvantage was that it seldom worked properly.

The problem was with the complex hydraulic systems needed to keep the antenna pointed directly at the moon despite the bucking and rolling of the ship. Activated by an elaborate system of sensors and sophisticated computers, the various hydraulic mechanisms were never quite sufficient to twist and turn the massive dish. Purple fluid would gush from beneath gaskets, and the antenna would become useless. Another disadvantage was that, regardless of the hydraulic system, in order to communicate, both the ship and the receiving antenna had to have a clear view of the moon.

This time the problem was that the shipyard in Norfolk had mistakenly installed low-pressure fittings in the system where high-pressure fittings were called for. Throughout the night a crew on a nearby submarine repair ship put together some new fittings and managed to get the system working, but they warned that the repairs were only temporary.

The following morning the *Liberty* passed through the Strait of Gibraltar and steamed at top speed toward her operational area. Three days later, on June 5, she was passing the south coast of Sicily when Israel lashed out with air strikes against Egypt, Jordan, and Syria, annihilating their air forces on the ground while pushing its tanks deep into the Sinai.

At 8:49 on the bright, sunny morning of June 8, the *Liberty* reached what was known as Point Alpha. According to the top secret operational order received when she arrived in Rota, the ship was to proceed not to Crete, but to a point thirteen nautical miles from the eastern coast of Egypt's Sinai Peninsula (Point Alpha), where she would change course to the southwest and begin a slow, five-knot patrol along a ninety-mile dogleg ending at Port Said (Point Charlie), retracing the tract until new orders were received. Because Egypt claimed a territorial sea of twelve miles and Israel only six miles, the *Liberty* was ordered not to approach closer than 12.5 and 6.5 miles to the respective shores.

Nearly ten hours before the *Liberty* arrived off the Sinai, an NSA analyst rushed into the office of G Group chief Raven and asked incredulously, "For God's sake, do you know where the *Liberty* is?" Raven, believing she was sitting off the east end of Crete as originally planned, had barely begun to answer when the analyst blurted out, "They've got her heading straight for the beach!"

"At this point," recalled Raven, "I ordered a major complaint to get the *Liberty* the hell out of there! As far as we [NSA] were concerned, there was nothing to be gained by having her in there that close, nothing she could do in there that she couldn't do where we wanted her . . . She could do everything that the national requirement called for [from the coast of Crete]."

But the Navy, apparently, had other ideas for the *Liberty*. "Somebody wanted to listen to some close tactical program," said Raven, "or communications or something which nobody in the world gave a damn about . . . We were listening for the higher echelons."

Reluctantly, the Navy agreed to pull the ship back. A message was sent from the JCS Joint Reconnaissance Center (JRC) at 6:30 P.M. (EDT) (12:30 A.M., June 8, *Liberty* time), ordering the ship not to approach Egypt closer than twenty miles and Israel closer than fifteen miles. An hour and twenty minutes later an official of the JRC telephoned the duty officer at the Command Center of the Commander-in-Chief, U.S. Naval Forces, Europe, directing that the ship proceed no closer to the coasts than 100 nautical miles. This oral order was followed up with a written message dispatched from Washington at

9:10 P.M. (3:10 A.M. *Liberty* time), more than five and a half hours before the *Liberty* reached Point Alpha.

Yet, in what a congressional committee later called "one of the most incredible failures of communications in the history of the Department of Defense," none of those warnings ever reached the *Liberty*. Thus, on reaching Point Alpha, the ship began her slow crawl along the Sinai toward Port Said and the mouth of the Suez Canal.

Throughout much of the morning the *Liberty* had been buzzed by low-flying Israeli reconnaissance aircraft. The boxy, French-built Nord 2501 Noratlas transports were normally used to move cargo and troops. Several, however, had been converted into SIGINT ferrets and were also fitted with lens openings for photo coverage. Resembling the American C-119 "flying boxcar" with its double tail, the aircraft would circle the ship several times and then return in the direction of Tel Aviv. On several other occasions, high-flying jet fighters circled briefly and then departed.

At 1:10 P.M. Commander William L. McGonagle, commanding officer of the *Liberty*, sounded General Quarters. "This is a drill! This is a drill! . . . All hands man your battle stations," he shouted into the ship's general announcing system. The drill, the third in four days, had been prompted by news reports of poison gas being used in the fighting on shore. Although the reports later proved erroneous, the drill offered Commander McGonagle an opportunity to reinforce the seriousness of the almost unseen war, now in its fourth day. Directing the crew's attention to a large fire and tall spirals of thick, black smoke coming from the shore about twenty miles west of El Arish, he insisted that everyone keep his eyes wide open and his mind alert.

By now the war had dissolved into a one-sided slaughter. From the earliest moments of its surprise attack, the Israeli Air Force had owned the skies over the Middle East. Within the first few hours, Israeli jets pounded twenty-five Arab airbases ranging from Damascus in Syria to an Egyptian field, loaded with bombers, far up the Nile at Luxor. In the Sinai, Israeli tanks and armored personnel carriers pushed toward the Suez along all three of the roads that crossed the desert. Then, using machine guns, mortar fire, tanks, and air power, the Israeli war machine overtook the Jordanian section of Jerusalem as well as the west bank of the Jordan River, and torpedo boats captured the key Red Sea port of Sharm El Sheikh. One Israeli general estimated that in the Sinai alone, Egyptian casualties ranged from 7000 to 10,000 killed, compared with 275 of his own troops.

By Wednesday, June 7, nearly all resistance had been eliminated. Nevertheless, an essential element in the Israeli war plan was complete secrecy about all details of the true extent of the Israeli penetration into Arab territory as well as the size and scope of its military victories. Vital to the Israeli strategy was the prevention, for as long as possible, of any cease-fire imposed by any of the superpowers. The longer it took to end the war, it was reasoned, the more territory Israel could capture — and Israel still had definite plans for Syria. Thus, "any instrument," wrote American naval historian Dr. Richard K. Smith in the *United States Naval Institute Proceedings,* "which sought to penetrate this smoke screen so carefully thrown around the normal 'fog of war' would have to be frustrated."

At 1:50, Commander McGonagle secured from General Quarters and checked the ship's position on the radar screen: she was still in international waters fourteen miles off the shoreline of the Sinai. At 2:00 lookouts reported a jet aircraft about five miles off the starboard quarter, cruising at about five thousand feet on a parallel track with the ship.

A moment later, like a bolt of lightning, more jets swooped in from astern, barely clearing the masthead, and the *Liberty* was converted into a seagoing inferno. Deafening explosions rocked the ship, and the bridge disappeared in an orange and black ball. Seconds later they were back — Israeli Mirage and Mystère fighter bombers. Flesh fused with iron as rockets were followed by napalm, which was followed by strafing.

Back they came, crisscrossing the ship almost every forty-five seconds. Designed to punch holes in the toughest tanks, the Israeli shells tore through the *Liberty*'s steel plating like bullets through cardboard, exploding into jagged bits of shrapnel and butchering men deep in their living quarters. Then more napalm — silvery metallic canisters of jellied gasoline that turned the ship into a crematorium.

Then, as suddenly as it began, it was over. Scattered along the decks and on the ladders, eight men lay either dead or dying, including both the executive officer and the operations officer. More than a hundred more were wounded, many seriously. Commander McGonagle's right leg was torn wide open by shrapnel.

Gone was the radar and most of the radio equipment, along with the antennas, apparently one of the prime targets. Also destroyed was the critical gyro compass. Perforated by over a thousand holes, more than eight hundred large enough for a man's fist to go through, the bulkheads and decks took on a look of gray Swiss cheese.

In the moments after the attack, sailors lifted mutilated shipmates onto makeshift stretchers of pipe frame and chicken wire, damage control crews pushed through passageways of suffocating smoke and blistering heat, and the chief petty officer's lounge was converted into a macabre sea of blood-soaked mattresses and shattered bodies.

At 2:24, minutes after the air attack, horror once again washed over the crew as three Israeli motor torpedo boats were sighted rapidly approaching the ship in attack formation. A signal flashed from the center boat but was obscured by the smoke. The air strikes had destroyed the *Liberty*'s signaling lamps, making a return message impossible, in any event.

Suddenly the boats opened up with a barrage of fire from 20-mm and 40-mm guns. One armor-piercing bullet slammed through the ship's chart house and into the pilot house, coming to rest finally in the neck of a young helmsman, killing him instantly. Three other crewmen were slaughtered in this latest shower of hot lead.

Now the Israelis were ready for the kill. "Stand by for torpedo attack, starboard side!" Commander McGonagle shouted into the announcing system. At 2:31 a torpedo passed off the stern, and a moment later a second struck the *Liberty* forward of her starboard side, immediately below the waterline — the precise location of the ship's SIGINT spaces.

BOOM!!! In an instant a forty-foot hole opened in the side of the ship, and twenty-five more Americans, mostly highly skilled technicians attached to the Naval Security Group, were either blown to bits or drowned as the black sea rushed in and flooded the compartment.

Now dead in the water, the *Liberty* began to list to starboard as the French-built, sixty-three-ton torpedo boats began to circle, firing at men attempting to extinguish fires. At 3:15, following a "prepare to abandon ship" order, one sailor located three of the last surviving rubber life rafts and, after securing them with heavy line, dropped them over the side in the event of a final order. Seeing this, the Israelis mercilessly opened fire, peppering two of the boats with holes and cutting the line on the third. When it drifted past their torpedo boat they pulled it aboard, apparently as a grotesque souvenir of their cold-blooded massacre.

A few minutes later, more than an hour after the attack began, the three forty-two-knot torpedo boats turned and raced in the direction of their base at Ashdod. Almost at the same moment, as if awaiting official orders to begin the final act of the bloody drama, two jet fighters once again appeared off the stern, and two large Israeli Hornet assault helicopters, loaded with armed troops, hovered on either side of the wounded ship. "Stand by to repel boarders!" came the shouted order over the *Liberty*'s loud-speakers, but after several tense minutes the four aircraft departed as mysteriously as they had arrived, leaving the *Liberty* to descend slowly into her watery grave.

But the *Liberty* was not yet ready to die. During the height of the assault, radiomen had patched together enough equipment and broken antennas to get a distress call off to the Sixth Fleet. Despite intense jamming by the Israelis, the transmissions reached their destination, and four "ready" F-4 Phantom jets of the U.S.S. *America,* cruising near Crete, catapulted into the air toward the *Liberty,* four hundred miles to the east. But as ready aircraft, the four apparently carried only nuclear weapons, and a short time later were recalled on orders of Secretary of Defense Robert McNamara.

Crew members of the *America,* as well as the carrier U.S.S. *Saratoga,* which was cruising nearby, then began the time-consuming process of off-loading the nuclear armament and switching to conventional bombs and rocket pods. Conversion completed, four F-4B Phantoms armed with Sparrow and Sidewinder missiles, along with four A-4 Skyhawks carrying Bullpup missiles tucked under their wings, scrambled off the deck of the *America* while four piston-driven Douglas A-1 Skyraider bombers with a fighter cover shot off from the *Saratoga.* Included in the pilots' orders was the authorization "to use force including destruction as necessary."

Shortly after the Sixth Fleet swung into a crisis mode, a fact that would have been readily apparent to any Israeli traffic analysts monitoring the sudden, sharp increase in U.S. fleet communications, the Israeli government launched a diplomatic offensive aimed at convincing Washington that the attack had been a mistake. At about 4:10 the Israelis informed the U.S. embassy in Tel Aviv that its defense forces had "erroneously" fired on a U.S. ship off the Sinai, and sent its apologies. Four minutes later the information was flashed to Washington and the Sixth Fleet, which immediately recalled the fighters and bombers.

At 4:32, words of ultimate terror again rang through the *Liberty.* "Aircraft and torpedo boats approaching, starboard side. Stand by for torpedo attack, starboard side." Panic immediately broke out in the makeshift hospital set up below the main deck. Men who were treating the injured, recalling the destruction of the earlier torpedo, clambered up the ladder, and those they were treating yanked loose IV tubes and reopened ugly wounds in a mad scramble not to be left to die. Seeing the pandemonium, Lloyd Painter, a junior officer who was himself injured, took command of the situation and managed to return the men and restore relative calm.

But the jets zoomed by overhead without incident, and the torpedo boat 204T *Tahmass* appeared to be attempting to communicate with its signal lamp. The message, however, made no sense, and finally the Israeli commander shouted over a bullhorn in English: "Do you need assistance?" Commander McGonagle, enraged, gave his quartermaster an appropriate response to relay back to the *Tahmass*, one the Israelis were not likely to find in their phrase book.

Another attempt to contact the *Liberty* was made at 6:41, when an Israeli Sikorsky helicopter appeared overhead and dropped a message package to the deck. Inside was the card of Commander Ernest C. Castle, the U.S. naval attaché at the American embassy in Tel Aviv, with the note: "Have you casualties?" The answer could have been found by looking down at the rivers of blood crisscrossing the deck and the two bodies still lying in full view near machine-gun mount 51. An attempt was made to reply with the Aldis lamp, but the message was apparently not understood, and after about ten minutes the machine departed.

Despite a forty-foot hole in her twenty-two-year-old skin, a heavy list to starboard, most of her equipment destroyed, thirty-two of her crew dead and two thirds of the rest wounded, a dead executive officer, and a commanding officer whose life blood was overflowing his shoe, the *Liberty* was heroically brought back to life and slowly made her way toward safer waters.

Throughout the long night, propped up in a chair on the port wing of the bridge, Commander McGonagle continued to conn his ship, using the North Star ahead and the long wake behind for direction. Shortly after dawn, the *Liberty* rendezvoused with the American destroyers *Davis* and *Massey,* and, after eighteen continuous hours on the bridge, the weary skipper finally headed to what was left of his cabin.

Helicopters soon arrived and began lifting scores of wounded to the deck of the *America,* where the more seriously hurt were transported by plane to Athens and then to the naval hospital in Naples. Commander McGonagle, however, remained with the ship until she docked in Malta. After she spent five weeks in drydock for temporary repairs, he sailed her back across the Atlantic to Pier 17 at the Little Creek amphibious base near Norfolk, arriving on July 29.

On June 9, the day after the attack, the Israeli government presented its explanation of the incident to the U.S. embassy in Tel Aviv. It claimed that the 10,680-ton, 455-foot *Liberty* had been mistaken for the thirty-eight-year-old Egyptian troop transport *El Quseir,* a 2640-ton, 275-foot coastal steamer designed to hold four hundred men and forty horses.

Yet before the attack, the *Liberty* had been under close Israeli surveillance for more than six hours. On four occasions, specially converted aircraft packed with SIGINT gear and photo equipment made low circles over the ship, sometimes coming as low as two hundred feet and barely skimming the masthead. On two other occasions, jet fighters flew over the ship and circled several times.

Given the extent of that surveillance, it would seem utterly inconceivable that the Israelis could have confused the *Liberty* for the *El Quseir*. The superstructure of American SIGINT ships, bristling with antennas and a large microwave moon-bounce dish, was totally unlike anything in the Egyptian Navy, or almost any other navy in the world, for that matter. Also unmistakable were the giant "GTR 5" identification symbols painted on her bow and the sides of her stern, each in white accentuated by black shadowing. Only ten days before the attack, the nearly ten-foot numeral "5" on the *Liberty*'s bows had received a fresh coat of white paint. Also, the *Liberty* wore her name on her stern in English, not in the Arabic script of the Egyptian naval vessels. Likewise, it was not Arabic communications that the Israelis skillfully managed to jam, but English.

And then there was the flag. Five feet tall and eight feet across, the standard size 9 ensign was flapping gently in nine-to-twelve-knot winds during most of the morning, plainly visible atop the huge tripod-shaped foremast that towered nearly a hundred feet above the flying bridge. Yet despite the fact that the flag was continually checked each time there was an overflight, the Israelis limply claimed that the ship was not flying a flag when sighted. This became true only after the Israeli Air Force shot it down. And then in its place, at least five minutes before the torpedo boat took aim, the huge seven-by-thirteen-foot holiday ensign was raised.

Israel, boasting one of the most successful intelligence services in the world, the Mossad, could hardly have been unaware that the *Liberty* was an American SIGINT ship. It is even more unlikely that the Mossad, on the eve of war, did not know that the ancient *El Quseir* was, in fact, rusting alongside a pier in the port of Alexandria, 250 miles from where the *Liberty* was attacked, where she remained throughout the entire Six Day War.

"The Israeli government," former *Liberty* officer James M. Ennes, Jr., noted in his book, *Assault on the Liberty,* "must have been desperate for a scapegoat to have singled out *El Quseir.* The entire Egyptian Navy consists of a few converted Soviet and British destroyers, frigates, and submarines, some minesweepers, several boats, two yachts, and a single transport — *El Quseir* . . . No one could pretend that *Liberty* was mistaken for a destroyer, a submarine, or the former royal yacht, so she would simply have to be mistaken for the El Quseir, which was, after all, the only scapegoat around."

Dr. Richard Smith agreed. "Indeed," he wrote in his analysis of the attack on the Liberty, "it is likely that the Israelis just picked out the Egyptian ship which most resembled the Liberty, even though this was a remarkable exercise in imagination."

If, as the overwhelming evidence seems to indicate, the Israeli explanation was manufactured and the attack was both premeditated and deliberate, what could have been the reason for such a ruthless assassination? One possibility is that the Liberty was attacked precisely because of what she was: a floating eavesdropping factory that was penetrating Israel's smoke screen and capturing on magnetic tape the telltale battle whispers of a lopsided war.

Far more threatening to Israel than a tub full of foot soldiers and a herd of horses were the Liberty's sleeve monopoles and parabolic reflectors, her YAGIs and log periodics, the strange antennas and the men with their bulging earphones. Did senior Israeli officials fear that captured signals would indicate that the war was not started by Egyptian land and air forces moving against Israel, as Israel had originally claimed, but by a belligerent Israel itself?

It may have been just a coincidence that the final thrust of the war, the invasion of Syria, originally scheduled to take place on Thursday, June 8, was suddenly postponed as the Liberty steamed into the eastern Mediterranean. Or that the often faulty TRSSCOMM had just begun transmitting to Washington a few moments before the initial air strike against the ship. Or that the first targets attacked, after the four token .50-caliber machine-gun mounts were wiped out, were the antennas — cutting TRSSCOMM communications in midsentence. Or that the torpedo happened to hit precisely between frames 53 and 66, the number two hold, which contained the SIGINT spaces. Or that the postponed Syrian invasion finally took place less than twenty-four hours after the last shots were fired into the Liberty.

Or they may not all have been coincidences.

Nearly as bizarre as the attack itself was the reaction of the American government to the incident. A foreign nation had butchered American servicemen, sending thirty-four to their graves and more than a hundred others into hospitals and later, possibly, psychiatric wards. A virtually unarmed American naval ship in international waters was shot at, strafed with rockets, torpedoed, set on fire with napalm, then left to sink as crazed gunners shot up the life rafts. The foreign nation then says, sorry about that, and offers an explanation so outrageous that it is insulting, and the American government accepts it, sweeps the whole affair under a rug, then classifies as top secret nearly all details concerning it.*

Curiously, among those details were several intelligence reports that directly contradicted the Israeli claims. According to a July 27, 1967, CIA report, a confidential informant, presumably within the Israeli government itself, stated that there was no question that the Israelis knew what the ship was prior to the attack and implied that the attack was no mistake:

> He said that "you've got to remember that in this campaign there is neither time nor room for mistakes," which was intended as an obtuse reference that Israel's forces knew what flag the *Liberty* was flying and exactly what the vessel was doing off the coast. [The source] implied that the ship's identity was known at least six hours before the attack but that Israeli headquarters was not sure as to how many people might have access to the information the *Liberty* was intercepting. He also implied that there was no certainty or control as to where the information was going and again reiterated that Israeli forces did not make mistakes in their campaign. He was emphatic in stating to me that they knew what kind of ship U.S.S. *Liberty* was and what it was doing offshore.

Corroboration of this report appeared several months later when other confidential sources stated unequivocally that the attack was deliberate and had been ordered personally by Defense Minister Moshe Dayan:

* On April 28, 1969, almost two years after the attack, the Israeli government finally paid $3,566,457 as compensation to the wounded crewmen of the *Liberty*. This was obtained, however, only after the men retained private counsel to negotiate with a team of top, Israeli-hired, Washington lawyers. A substantial portion of the claim, therefore, went to lawyers' fees. (Richard K. Smith, "The Violation of the *Liberty*," *United States Naval Proceedings* [June 1978], p. 70.)

Ten months earlier, the Israelis issued a check to the U.S. government for $3,323,000 as settlement to the families of the thirty-four men killed during the attack. (Department of State press release, May 13, 1969.)

Finally, the U.S. government asked a token $7,644,146 for Israel's destruction of the ship, even though $20 million had been spent several years earlier to convert her into a SIGINT ship and another $10 million had gone for the highly sophisticated hardware.

Despite the modest amount requested, the Israeli government refused to pay. By the winter of 1980, the interest on the original figure had reached $10 million, and Israeli ambassador Ephraim Evron, following the American elections, suggested to outgoing Vice President Mondale that if the United States dropped the $7.6 million down to $6 million and eliminated the interest entirely, his country might be willing to pay the more-than-thirteen-year-old claim. President Jimmy Carter agreed, and in December accepted the $6 million, absolving Israel of any further damages. (Bernard Gwertzman, "Israeli Payment to Close the Book on '67 Attack on U.S. Navy Vessel," *New York Times* [December 19, 1980], pp. A1, A4.)

[The sources] commented on the sinking [sic] of the U.S. Communications ship *Liberty*. They said that Dayan personally ordered the attack on the ship and that one of his generals adamantly opposed the action and said, "This is pure murder." One of the admirals who was present also disapproved the action, and it was he who ordered it stopped and not Dayan.

Whatever the truth may be, it is clear that the incident, a most violent act of terrorism committed against the United States government, deserves to be more fully explained by both governments.

•

Two years before the attack on the *Liberty*, in the spring of 1965, plans were underway for a third generation of spook ships. Although by now the United States already had seven in its eavesdropping fleet, these were all directed against strategic targets — inland governmental, commercial, and military communications — and were responsible almost exclusively to the NSA.

For years this situation had been a sore spot for the Navy, long used to sharing command with no one when it came to matters of the sea. Therefore, when the NSA began laying plans for the civilian ships *Valdez* and *Muller*, the Navy quickly fired off a salvo of protests and insisted that all future SIGINT ships be traditional naval vessels manned by naval crews.

But now the Navy had become little more than seagoing chauffeurs and hired hands for the NSA, permitted to go after its own targets only when doing so could not in any way interfere with the primary mission — monitoring NSA's targets. Thus, when it came to its own SIGINT operations, primarily against foreign naval signals, the Navy had to stick its analysts in awkward, antenna-covered mobile vans, place them aboard destroyers and destroyer escorts, and then pull the ships out of normal service to patrol slowly along distant coasts. It was a highly inefficient operation, combining the minimum collection capacity of a crowded steel box with the maximum costs of using a destroyer to cart it around.

The destroyers and escorts were also very provocative. Where few nations would notice an old, converted supply ship slowly cruising up and down a shoreline, they would have ample reason to be alarmed if it was an American warship. The destroyers *Maddox* and *Turner Joy* were cruising on just such missions, known as "DeSoto patrols," in the Gulf of Tonkin in 1964 when they were allegedly attacked by enemy torpedo boats, an incident that led to the first U.S. bombing of North Vietnam.

Among those most troubled by this situation was General Carter's nemesis, Dr. Eugene G. Fubini, then fifty-one, an assistant secretary of defense and also the deputy director of Defense Research and Engineering. As the Pentagon's electronic spy chief, he had been particularly concerned about the Soviet Union's extensive fleet of about forty SIGINT trawlers, which would not only loiter off such sensitive areas as Norfolk and Cape Kennedy, but frequently would tag along with American naval forces operating in the Mediterranean and Pacific.

"These trawlers were following our fleet," Fubini once recalled, "bothering us, listening to us, copying everything we said. They knew our tactics and the technical parameters of our equipment. They probably knew more about our equipment than we did. So I began to wonder: Why can't we take a leaf from their book? Why can't we do the same thing? If we could mingle with them, we'd know what they were up to."

Fubini's idea for an American version of the Russian spy fleet was readily acceptable to Admiral David L. McDonald, the chief of Naval Operations, who was well acquainted with the problem from his previous assignment as commander of the U.S. Sixth Fleet. On April 20, 1965, Fubini and McDonald sat down with Vice Admiral Rufus L. Taylor, director of Naval Intelligence, and Rear Admiral Frederic J. Harlfinger II, assistant director for Collection for the Defense Intelligence Agency, and discussed the various ways to approach the problem.

Originally, Fubini's dream was on the grandest of scales. He envisioned the program broken down into three phases, the first two of which called for thirty reconverted "tuna boats," at a cost of about $1 million each. The third phase would add forty more, these built from scratch. Once the dream passed through the sobering reality of the budget process, however, phase one and two had been slashed to three ships, and phase three was cut to a dozen, or fifteen at most. At the same time, the idea of using tuna boats was scrapped because they were considered too light for the heavy SIGINT equipment. Instead, AKLs (for Auxiliary Cargo Light), tiny tramp steamers, some smaller than many tugs, were substituted.

A few days after the meeting, a feasibility study was initiated, resulting, about six weeks later, in a two-phase recommendation. First, the Navy would start off with one ship operating in the Western Pacific, then add two more ships in the same area about a year later. If these two missions were successful, the Navy could then proceed to build a small flotilla of the ships for use in trouble spots around the world.

The plan quickly received the approval of Fubini's boss, Harold Brown, the director of Defense Research and Engineering, as well as Cyrus R. Vance, the deputy secretary of defense.

Chosen as the maiden vessel for the Navy's spy fleet was the U.S.S. *Banner*, a humble little craft that had spent most of her life bouncing from atoll to atoll in the Mariana Islands and was now on her way back to the United States to retire in mothballs. At 935 tons and 176 feet, the twenty-one-year-old ship was a dwarf compared with the 10,680 tons and 455 feet of the *Liberty*.

Throughout much of August and September, the *Banner* underwent modifications at the Puget Sound Naval Shipyard in Bremerton, Washington, transforming her into AGER-1, for Auxiliary General Environmental Research, a euphemism for a third-generation seaborne listening post.* On October 1, a brief seven weeks after she entered the yard, the *Banner* steamed out of Bremerton directly to Yokosuka, Japan, arriving seventeen days later for the initiation of her first patrol.

Code-named Operation Clickbeetle, the *Banner*'s mission called for a series of four- to six-week patrols in the Sea of Japan to "conduct tactical surveillance and intelligence collection against Soviet naval units and other targets of opportunity," according to her top secret orders, which continued:

> C. Upon sailing for patrol station, *Banner* will check out of the movement report system, and will proceed to her assigned patrol areas in strict electronic silence. Silence will be maintained until *Banner* is detected and comes under surveillance by Soviet bloc forces, at which time *Banner* will break silence and submit periodic reports. When surveillance of *Banner* by Soviet bloc forces ceases, *Banner* will resume electronic silence.
>
> D. Upon arrival in the assigned patrol areas, *Banner* will be authorized freedom of movement within her assigned patrol areas to monitor lucrative Soviet naval deployments or exercises.

The order also contained a number of restrictions, including the warning to the ship to "remain a minimum of one mile outside the Soviet bloc–claimed territorial waters, a total distance of thirteen miles."

After arriving at Yokosuka, the *Banner* departed almost immediately on her first patrol, a hazardous mission scheduled to take her within four miles of Siberia's Cape Povorotny Bay. For many years the Soviet

* The AGER designation actually took effect on June 1, 1967. Prior to that she was designated AKL-44. (Department of the Navy, Office of the Chief of Naval Operations, OPNAV Notice 5030, "Reclassification of Naval Ships," May 2, 1967.)

Union had maintained that her territorial waters extended twelve miles from the mouth of the bay, a claim the United States disputed on the grounds that it violated the "baseline" concept of international law. The *Banner*'s assignment was to find out just how serious the Russians were about the claim.

As the *Banner* chugged north toward Siberia, a frigid storm began caking ice forward and on the superstructure. Still closer — and Soviet destroyers and patrol boats began harassment exercises by darting in and out toward the bobbing trawler, sometimes closing to within twenty-five yards before veering away. But as a fresh storm began brewing, the fear of capsizing under the weight of the ice predominated, and the *Banner*'s skipper, Lieutenant Robert P. Bishop, radioed his headquarters in Yokosuka and then swung 180 degrees back toward Japan. Several hours later a reply came through, ordering him back and warning him not to be intimidated. Bishop obeyed and turned back into the storm, but finally gave up after progressing a total of minus two miles over the next twenty-four hours.

In the three years that followed, the *Banner* conducted a total of fifteen similar missions. Of these, the first seven were in the Sea of Japan, primarily monitoring the major Soviet naval base at Vladivostok. Three of the remaining eight were off the coast of mainland China in the East China Sea, and the final five were back in the Sea of Japan. There was harassment during ten of the *Banner*'s sixteen patrols, the most serious in the East China Sea off Shanghai, when eleven metal-hulled Chinese trawlers began closing in on the *Banner*. Lieutenant Bishop, however, skillfully managed to maneuver away from the danger without incident.

According to Trevor Armbrister, in his book *A Matter of Accountability*, the Navy had originally wanted to operate the *Banner* only off the coast of the Soviet Union, theorizing that there would be a minimal risk involved since it would be merely countering similar surveillance by the Russians. No such quid pro quo existed with the Chinese or North Koreans, however, and it was feared that they might retaliate against the ship. Nevertheless, according to Armbrister, the Navy agreed to task the *Banner* against those countries only after considerable pressure from the NSA, which found the Clickbeetle program exceeding their expectations and were hungry for more.

Under the original plan, Clickbeetle was designed to free the Navy from the "sharecropper" role it had suffered on the five large NSA ships. Now the situation would be reversed, and the Navy would pick the targets and allow NSA tasking only on a not-to-interfere basis. But the NSA found the program far too valuable to leave entirely to the admirals, and it forced a compromise whereby some missions would be available to NSA for "primary tasking" and others would go primarily to the Navy.

Shortly after the *Banner* left Bremerton for Yokosuka, the Navy began to implement phase two of the SIGINT program and located two more coastal freighters to convert into AGERs. Their names reflected the monotony of their tasks as Army supply ships: FS-344 and FS-389, soon altered to the U.S.S. *Pueblo* (AGER 2) and the U.S.S. *Palm Beach* (AGER 3). In April 1966 they were towed to Bremerton and, because of numerous modification problems as well as budget cutbacks, spent the next year and a half undergoing extensive conversion. Finally, on December 1, 1967, the *Pueblo* sailed into Yokosuka harbor to join the veteran *Banner*.

Throughout the fall of 1967, as the *Pueblo* was undergoing sea trials, a six-month schedule for the *Banner* and *Pueblo* was drafted. It called for nine separate missions, including one off North Korea, two off the Soviet port of Petropavlovsk, two in the East China Sea, and four in the Sea of Japan. Of these, the NSA demanded primary tasking on at least five.

The first mission, this one Navy-sponsored, went to the *Pueblo*. It called for the ship to "sample electronic environment of east coast North Korea" and to "intercept and conduct surveillance of Soviet naval units operating Tsushima Straits." The estimate of risk: "minimal." After all, said one official, "based upon 150 years of never having [anything] happen," what was the chance of something happening this time?

Following standard procedure, the request for final approval of the *Pueblo* mission worked its way up the chain of command and into a fat notebook with "Monthly Reconnaissance Schedule for January 1968" written in bold letters across the front. Maintained by the Joint Chiefs of Staff's JRC, the loose-leaf binder contains brief summaries of the several hundred surveillance operations during the coming month. These may range from SR-71 overflights of China to submarine snooping in the White Sea.

Once complete, the notebook, "the size of a Sears, Roebuck catalogue," according to one former official, is sent off to the various concerned agencies for approval, disapproval, or comment. On Friday, December 29, the notebook with the *Pueblo* proposal was sent out and received back the same day, duly approved by the JCS, CIA, NSA, and the State Department. Later that day it was also approved by Paul H. Nitze, the deputy secretary of defense, and by the National Security Council's secret 303 Committee. There were no comments and no disapprovals.

Yet there was one lingering doubt. It was in the mind of a retired

Navy chief petty officer at NSA who was very uneasy over the *Pueblo*'s "minimal" risk assessment. This assessment, he knew, was the job of the Defense Intelligence Agency, and NSA had no responsibility in the matter, especially since this was a Navy mission. Nevertheless, the uneasiness grew, so he brought his concerns to the attention of his superiors, and eventually the deputy assistant director of PROD agreed. Even though he had never contradicted a DIA assessment before, he felt in this case that a "warning message" was justified, and he addressed it to the JCS "for action":

> The following information is provided to aid in your assessment of CINCPAC's estimate of risk . . . The North Korean Air Force has been extremely sensitive to peripheral reconnaissance flights in the area since early 1965 . . . The North Korean Air Force has assumed an additional role of Naval support since late 1966. The North Korean Navy reacts to any ROK naval vessel–ROK fishing vessel near the North Korean coast line . . . internationally recognized boundaries as they relate to airborne activities are generally not honored by North Korea on the east coast of North Korea . . . The above is provided to aid in evaluating the requirements for ship protective measures and is not intended to reflect adversely on CINCPACFLT deployment proposal.

The message arrived at the DIA's Signal Office in the Pentagon at 10:28 that night and was sent over to the National Military Command Center, where the watch officer decided to refer it to Brigadier General Ralph Steakley, the chief of the JRC. He also decided to send a copy to the chief of Naval Operations but mistakenly attached the wrong designator — and the message was to be lost for a month. But there was still the message sent to the JRC.

When General Steakley arrived back in his Pentagon office on January 2, he saw the NSA warning message but never brought it to the attention of either the JCS or the DIA. Instead, he changed the priority of the message from "action" to "information" and sent it off to the headquarters of the Commander-in-Chief, Pacific, in Hawaii, not bothering to designate any particular office. As a result, when the message reached CINCPAC headquarters it was simply routed to some junior officers, who, noticing the "information" tag, took no action except to read it, file it, and promptly forget it.

Once again, just as with the *Liberty*, the NSA had sent out a warning, and the military communications system had swallowed it up. On January 5, 1968, the unprotected *Pueblo* set sail for Korea, and eighteen days later, once again, a terrified radioman flashed a vain signal into the ether: "We need help. We are holding emergency destruction.

We need support. SOS SOS SOS. Please send assistance. Please send assistance. Please send assistance. Please send assistance. SOS SOS SOS. We are being boarded."

By nightfall one sailor was dead, the rest of the crew captured, and America had lost its second SIGINT ship in a little over seven months. But it had actually lost even more. Within eighteen months the paperwork began, and six months later what was left of America's SIGINT fleet had been quietly decommissioned and, still later, was sold for scrap.

TARGETS

I have been informed that the Secretary of Defense has decided that we must terminate the operation known as Shamrock. Effective 15 May 1975 no data from this source will be processed and all activities will cease as soon as possible. The two smaller volume locations will stop operations by 16 May 1975. Their respective equipments will be removed by 26 May 1975. The larger volume location will be disestablished in a rapid manner consistent with sound security procedures.

Records and files which are revealing of the operation will be assembled and secured; destruction (other than duplicates) is prohibited at present. Personnel who have been briefed or who otherwise know of the operation will be debriefed and reminded of their continuing obligation regarding protection of the compartmented source.

Fearing exposure by a persistent press and increasingly aggressive congressional committees, NSA director Lew Allen, Jr., in a May 12, 1975, handwritten memorandum for the record, at last ended what Senate Intelligence Committee chairman Frank Church once labeled "probably the largest governmental interception program affecting Americans ever undertaken."

Slightly less than thirty years earlier, as the last pages of the Second World War were being written, Operation Shamrock had its beginnings. In August 1945, as the radioactive dust was still settling over Hiroshima and Nagasaki, those who were in charge of America's signals intelligence empire looked toward an uncertain future. The end of hostilities also brought the end of censorship and thus the end of access to the millions of cables entering and leaving the country each year. On August 15, President Truman issued a directive instructing the director of censorship to declare an end to the activities of his office. Executive Order 9031 of September 28, 1945, made the instruction formal and provided that the office should be totally abolished by November 15.

SIGINT had now reverted to the position it held following World War I, when Yardley was left to beg, borrow, or steal the needed cables. Faced with the problem this time was Brigadier General W. Preston Corderman, the redheaded chief of the Signal Security Agency. Tutored in his craft by Friedman as the second student in the infant Signals Intelligence School back in the early 1930s, Corderman knew what it meant to attempt signals intelligence without access to the cables. He felt it was of the utmost importance to establish, in some way, a very secret, very intimate arrangement with the three major cable companies in order to have access to the all important telegrams.

On August 18, 1945, therefore, Corderman sent two trusted representatives to New York City for the delicate purpose of making "the necessary contacts with the heads of the commercial communications companies in New York, secure their approval of the interception of all [foreign] Government traffic entering the United States, leaving the United States, or transiting the United States, and make the necessary arrangements for this photographic intercept work."

Their first overture, to an official of ITT Communications, met with complete failure. He "very definitely and finally refused," Corderman was informed, to agree to any of the proposals.

Next, they approached a vice president of Western Union Telegraph Company, who agreed to cooperate unless the Attorney General of the United States ruled that such intercepts were illegal.

Armed with this agreement, the two went back to ITT the next day and suggested to a vice president that "his company would not desire to be the only non-cooperative company on the project." The implication was that to refuse was to be less than patriotic, so the vice president went to see the company president about the matter. A short while later he returned and indicated that ITT would be willing to cooperate with the Agency provided that the Attorney General decided the program was not illegal.

Later the same day the two SSA officers shuttled across town to RCA corporate headquarters. With two thirds of America's cable industry already in their pocket, they met with RCA's president and asked him to join in the "patriotic" effort. The executive indicated his willingness to cooperate with the Agency but withheld his final approval until he, like the others, had heard from the Attorney General.

A few days later, as the three communications executives met with their corporate attorneys, who uniformly advised them against participating in the intercept program, the SSA officers indicated in a memorandum to General Corderman the extent of the cable companies' worry over the illegality of the program:

> Two very evident fears existed in the minds of the heads of each of these communications companies. One was the fear of the illegality of the procedure according to present FCC regulations. In spite of the fact that favorable opinions have been received from the Judge Advocate General of the Army, it was feared that these opinions would not be protected. If a favorable opinion is handed down by the Attorney General, this fear will be completely allayed, and cooperation may be expected for the complete intercept coverage of this material. The second fear uppermost in the minds of these executives is the fear of the ACA which is the communications union. This union has reported on many occasions minor infractions and it is feared that a major infraction, such as the proposed intercept coverage, if disclosed by the union, might cause severe repercussions.

Within a matter of weeks, despite the fear of prosecution and the warnings of their legal advisers, all three companies began taking part in what, for security reasons, was given the code name Operation Shamrock. By September 1, 1945, even before the Articles of Surrender were signed by Japan, the first batch of cables had been secretly turned over to the Agency.

Although all three communications companies agreed to participate in Shamrock, the degree of involvement and methods of cooperation varied greatly.

ITT agreed to give the Agency access to all incoming, outgoing, and transiting messages passing over the facilities of its subsidiary, ITT Communications (now ITT World Communications). It was agreed that "all traffic will be recorded on microfilm, that all [foreign] Governmental traffic will be recorded on a second microfilm in addition to the original one, that these films will be developed by the SSA, and the complete traffic will be returned to ITT."

Western Union, however, apparently limited its cooperation initially to providing traffic only to one country and also insisted that "Western Union personnel operate the [microfilm] camera and do all the actual handling of the messages." The agreement stipulated that the SSA would furnish all the necessary cameras and film "for the complete intercept coverage of Western Union traffic outlets" not only in New York but also in San Francisco, Washington, and San Antonio. In New York, company employees selected the targeted messages and then processed them through a microfilm machine on the transmission room floor, where, at four o'clock each morning, they would be picked up by an SSA agent in civilian clothes.

Probably the most complete cooperation was that given by RCA Communications (now RCA Global), a subsidiary of the Radio Corporation of America. On October 9, 1945, W. H. Barsby, vice president of RCA Communications, notified General Corderman of his company's agreement to cooperate with his agency. To handle the necessary arrangements for the cooperation, Barsby picked William Sidney Sparks, the traffic manager and also a vice president.

As a lieutenant colonel in the Army Signal Corps Reserve, Sidney Sparks appeared to be the ideal man for the assignment. In his current position he was responsible for the company's traffic operations throughout the world and also for maintaining contacts with foreign communications companies. In addition, Sparks was thoroughly familiar with the operations of the SSA, or Arlington Hall, as he knew it. Until July 1945, he had been in charge of the War Department Signal Center, where he had worked extensively with Arlington Hall in the development of a streamlined, "packaged," militarized version of the newly developed teletypewriter.

When Sparks was first approached by the SSA in October, he was not informed that cooperation had already been approved by Barsby. Nor did Barsby ever inform Sparks of his meeting with the SSA. He assumed, then, that no higher officials within the company knew of his secret meeting with the agency's representatives.

During the meeting, the men from the Army Security Agency (changed from the Signal Security Agency on September 15) told Sparks of the continued need, in the national interest, to scrutinize traffic passing through his company. He was also told that the operation had to be conducted with the utmost secrecy because of its possible illegality. When Sparks agreed to cooperate, the ASA officers suggested that electrical connections be attached to certain tie-lines in the operations area and that these connections terminate in a secure place, where they could be monitored by ASA personnel. Sparks, however, pointed out that this would involve setting up complex repeaters, which would require twenty-four-hour expert technical attention, and that "everybody and his brother would know just exactly what we were doing and why."

The officers agreed and then suggested that RCA itself segregate and turn over to the agency the telegraph tapes originating and terminating at certain private tie-lines. Again Sparks disagreed on security grounds, saying that it would involve people going around and picking out all of those tapes and putting them away somewhere. This, he believed, would have attracted a great deal of undesirable attention, and he rejected it as infeasible.

He told the officers that probably the most secure and efficient way to handle the problem would be to turn over to the agency *all* traffic entering, leaving, or transiting the company. The suggestion was music to the ASA officials' ears, and they quickly agreed.

At the time, when a message was received in the telegraph office, it came through in the form of a coded, five-hole tape, which was then put through another machine to produce a hard copy. The ASA people suggested that the hard copies of the telegrams be turned over to the agency, but here, Sparks felt, they were going too far. By reading the first inch or so of the tape, which contains the address information, they could easily determine whether or not the message would be of interest. But the officials raised the possibility of an embassy worker going outside to the telegraph company itself to send the telegram in order to avoid any possible monitoring of the embassy's communications. Still, Sparks was unconvinced, and the officials agreed to the conditions before heading back to Washington.

Sidney Sparks understood the potential consequences of his action. Should the arrangement be discovered by his superiors, he knew very well that, at the least, it would be the end of his career. But he also felt strongly that America did not exist in a vacuum and that the nation was on the verge of a different type of war, a war of nerves and of tension. "I knew in my own mind that the Cold War was heating up at this time," he later recalled. "I was impressed by it, and I was under no illusion at all that any responsible Government has to monitor, to some degree, the traffic of the other [foreign] Government agencies as far as it can get hold of them . . . I was prepared to cooperate in doing this at what I knew to be great personal risk to myself." It would be more than thirty years before Sparks learned that the burden of cooperation had already been accepted by RCA before he was ever approached.

Later that month Captain Ahern of the ASA, in charge of the New York operation, met with Sparks to go over the final details of the cooperative enterprise. The RCA executive had already made arrangements with the company's real estate office to take over additional space near the telegraph office on New Street. Then he went down to the real estate manager, picked up the key, and brought it back to the captain.

Sparks told Ahern that he had already informed his six supervisors, who rotated on shifts in the telegraph office, of the operation, and the superintendent of the telegraph office as well. The procedure, he explained, was that every night close to midnight, near the end of the shift, a supervisor would pick up the tapes of the day's traffic and place them in a secure location to be picked up by the ASA people, who would take them to their own office for sorting. After selecting the ones of interest, they would transmit copies of the telegrams to another ASA office in midtown New York and then, presumably, to Arlington Hall. After they had finished with the tapes, according to the agreement, the tapes were to be returned to the telegraph office for destruction.

The procedure appeared acceptable to both sides, and within a few days Operation Shamrock had begun. The ASA people would arrive each morning in civilian clothes between the hours of three and five and begin the job of sorting. The fact that they were in the military, however, was an open secret, since they arrived each day in a military green vehicle and constantly referred to each other as "sergeant" and "corporal."

Within less than a year, the restrictions on hard copies had fallen by the wayside, and the ASA began receiving full, complete copies of each and every telegram — regardless of whether it was to or from an American citizen, a corporation, or an embassy — which they were at liberty to keep or destroy. In addition, Shamrock was not limited to the borders of New York. ASA personnel in both Washington and San Francisco made daily pickups of traffic from all three communications companies, and, in San Antonio, an Army signal officer from Fort Sam Houston was charged with picking up the messages from the local Western Union office each day.

By March of 1946, with Shamrock fully underway, both Western Union and RCA again expressed concern over the illegality of their participation. This concern, increased because of the apparent lack of any approval by the Attorney General, was relayed to General Dwight David Eisenhower, the Army chief of staff, by the head of ASA:

> It can be stated that both [Western Union and RCA] have placed themselves in precarious positions since the legality of such operations has not been established and has necessitated the utmost secrecy on their part in making these arrangements. Through their efforts, only two or three individuals in the respective companies are aware of the operation.

In a somewhat feeble effort to pacify the nervous executives, Eisenhower later that month forwarded to each of them a formal Letter of Appreciation.

Again, throughout 1947, the fear of criminal prosecution continued to hound the executives of all three companies. They were now demanding assurances, not only from the Secretary of Defense and the

Attorney General, but also from the President himself, that their participation was in the national interest and that they would not be subject to prosecution in the federal courts. To ease their concern, Secretary of Defense James Forrestal asked them to meet with him on Tuesday, December 16, 1947. It was an extraordinary meeting, attended by Sosthenes Behn, chairman and president of ITT, and General Harry C. Ingles, president of RCA Communications. Joseph L. Egan, president of Western Union, was invited but could not attend.

At the meeting, Forrestal, telling the group that he was speaking for President Truman, commended them for their cooperation in Operation Shamrock and requested their continued assistance, "because the intelligence constituted a matter of great importance to the national security." Forrestal then said that "so long as the present Attorney General [Tom C. Clark] was in office, he could give assurances that the Department of Justice would also do all in its power to give the companies full protection." One official was still unclear as to Shamrock's level of authorization, however, and asked Forrestal if he was speaking not just for the Office of Secretary of Defense, but in the name of the President of the United States. Mr. Forrestal replied that he was.

With an eye to the national elections, coming up in less than a year, Forrestal made it clear that "while it was always difficult for any member of the Government to attempt to commit his successor, he could assure the gentlemen present that if the present practices were continued the Government would take whatever steps were possible to see to it that the companies involved would be protected."

The next month, Western Union president Joseph L. Egan and the company's operating vice president were briefed on the December meeting.

Forrestal's assurances that Shamrock had the full backing of the President as well as the Attorney General appeared to satisfy the three for the time being, but there was no guarantee just how long this would last. Almost out of desperation, therefore, the Defense Secretary decided to reveal the existence of Shamrock to a few selected members of Congress in an attempt to obtain legislation that would at last put to rest the legal worries of the communications companies.

In early June 1948, several members of Forrestal's staff met secretly with Senate Judiciary Committee chairman Alexander Wiley and Representative Earl Cory Michener, chairman of the House Judiciary Committee, and quietly informed them of the administration's delicate, unwritten agreement with the three communications companies. They were asked to introduce legislation in their respective committees to relax Section 605 of the Communications Act of 1934, which prohibited the interception of communications. The proposed amendment to the act would authorize the President to designate certain agencies to obtain the radio and wire communication of foreign governments. This would have had the effect of giving legal sanction to the Shamrock operation as originally conceived. Once the meeting ended, the Defense Department representatives again reminded the senator and the congressman of the top secret nature of the information that had just been revealed.

On June 16, in a closed-door executive session, the Senate Judiciary Committee considered and approved the bill, but the support was less than unanimous. Because of this, the committee voted to leave to the chairman's discretion whether or not to release the bill to the Senate floor. At this point Forrestal's representative interceded and effectively killed the bill by telling the committee that "we [do] not desire an airing of the whole matter on the Floor of the Senate at this late date in the session." Even without the passage of the bill, Forrestal was happy with the vote of confidence from the committee. As one of the Pentagon officials explained, they "thought a great deal had already been accomplished and that the administration had sufficient ammunition to be able to effect a continuation of the present practices with the companies."

Among the promises Forrestal made to the communication companies' executives in the December meeting was that Congress would consider in its forthcoming session legislation that would make it clear that such activity was permissible. He never promised them, however, that such legislation would pass. As a result, no further attempts were ever made to authorize Shamrock by statute. If the activity was to continue, it would have to continue both secretly and illegally.

A little more than nine months after the Judiciary Committee's hearing, on March 28, 1949, James V. Forrestal resigned from office and within less than a week he was admitted to Bethesda Naval Hospital, suffering from severe depression, anxiety, and acute paranoia. He believed he was the victim of "plots" and "conspiracies" and talked of unidentified people "trying to get me." For the next seven weeks, Forrestal underwent treatment for what his doctor described as involutional melancholia psychosis.

In the early morning hours of Sunday, May 22, Forrestal sat alone in his hospital room, copying onto sheets of paper the brooding lines from Sophocles' *Ajax*. "No quiet murmur like the tremulous wail," he wrote, "of the lone bird, the querulous night——" The word *night-ingale* was left unfinished. Forrestal walked across the hallway into a small kitchen, tied one end of his dressing gown sash to a radiator just beneath a window, and knotted the other end around his neck. Seconds later, his body plunged from the hospital's sixteenth-floor window.

Among those stunned by Forrestal's death were the company chiefs he had secretly assured fifteen months earlier. On hearing of Forrestal's resignation and hospitalization, they had sought a renewal of the assurances against prosecution from his successor, Louis Johnson. On Wednesday, May 18, 1949, only four days before Forrestal's suicide, Johnson met with these officials and stated that President Truman, Attorney General Tom Clark, and he endorsed the Forrestal statement and would provide them with a guarantee against any criminal action that might arise from their assistance.

Confirming the fact that the knowledge of Shamrock went well beyond the Office of Secretary of Defense were two handwritten notes penned on the memorandum of the meeting. One approval bore the initials T.C.C., those of Attorney General Tom C. Clark; the other, signed by Secretary Johnson, stated, "OK'd by the President and Tom Clark."

The May 18 meeting was the last time any of the companies ever sought assurances against prosecution from the government.

In 1949 when the ASA changed into the Armed Forces Security Agency it inherited Shamrock, which three years later became the stepchild of the newborn National Security Agency. Taking over the New York operation in 1950 from Captain Ahern was a former master sergeant named Joseph Wolanski. In 1956, NSA's Bob Sage became the local man. From the very inception, however, the person in charge of the New York agents was a mysterious Mr. Feeney.

The first major change in Shamrock did not take place until early 1963, when NSA was notified by RCA Global that it was getting ready to switch from the old system of paper tapes and hard copies to a revolutionary computerized system in which all incoming and outgoing messages were recorded on round magnetic journal tapes.

Unknown to all but a handful of spooks at NSA, the change in technology was also about to enable America to make a quantum leap forward in its ability to snoop. By the time RCA's new computer telegraph system was in full operation the following year, NSA's Harvest computer was ready for it. Now, instead of sorting manually the daily batches of hard copies and paper tapes in the NSA room at RCA, couriers would simply pick up the ten to twelve tape disks each morning, fly them down to Fort Meade to be copied, and, with luck, get them back to New York the same day.

Once copied, the tapes would be run through Harvest, which could be programmed to "kick out" any telegram containing a certain word, phrase, name, location, sender or addressee, or any combination. It might be a name from a watch list, any message containing the word *demonstration,* or any cable to or from the Israeli UN delegation. In microseconds the full text of any telegram containing selected material could be reproduced. America's Black Chamber had suddenly gone from Yardley to Orwell.

The following year, ITT World Communications also converted to magnetic tapes, and by 1966 the cost and logistics of the NSA courier operation was beginning to worry the man in charge, Dr. Louis Tordella. From his earliest days as deputy director, Tordella took personal charge of every detail of the operation. So secret was Shamrock that, besides Tordella and the various directors, only one lower-level managerial employee had any responsibility for the program. Both were instructed to report directly to Tordella if any problems arose with the communications companies. Below the program manager were the couriers.

What must have worried Tordella constantly was the ever-present risk of losing the tapes in the process of transporting them between New York and NSA and back to New York. A plane crash or simple carelessness; it really didn't matter. If for any reason the original tapes were lost or destroyed, it would almost certainly mean the end of the operation. So on August 18, 1966, a hot Thursday in Washington, Tordella met with Thomas Karamessines, then the CIA's acting deputy director of Plans, and requested the CIA's assistance in setting up a small cover office in downtown Manhattan. Tordella explained that NSA needed the "safe" space so that NSA employees could copy the international communications received from the commercial carriers.

The CIA agreed, and in November, after assigning the cryptonym LPMEDLEY to the operation, settled NSA in a commercial office building in lower Manhattan under the guise of a television tape-processing company.

After almost seven years of sinful cohabitation, however, the NSA was evicted. Unlike NSA, the CIA has a charter, which subjects it to legal dos and don'ts. One of the don'ts is a prohibition against conducting operations within the United States, so when the CIA's general counsel, Lawrence Houston, discovered the illicit hideaway, he sent the tape processors packing. Tordella was told that Houston was "concerned about any kind of operation in which the CIA was engaged in the continental United States." According to Tordella, the words were short and sweet: "Get out of it."

Undeterred as well as unencumbered by similar legal restraints, Tordella quickly found other suitable accommodations in Manhattan, and Shamrock continued.

In Washington, Shamrock had begun life under slightly different circumstances. Faced with ever-increasing threats posed by Japan and Germany in the months preceding Pearl Harbor, FBI director J. Edgar Hoover began working with the Justice Department on a proposed executive order that would permit the Bureau to obtain necessary cable traffic from the private telegraph companies. Before the order could be completed, however, Pearl Harbor was attacked.

Congress, acting with uncharacteristic swiftness, enacted the censorship law, and on December 22, 1941, the Solicitor General told the Bureau that the proposed executive order would no longer be necessary, since the newly created Office of Censorship would have full authority over international communications, and the FBI could obtain any that it needed from that office.

While all this was taking place, though, the Bureau was moving ahead on its own. Shortly after December 7, Hoover was asked by the State Department to request the cable companies to hold up the transmission of messages to certain countries for twenty-four hours, and then to make copies of the cables so that they would be available for review. The request was made, and the companies all agreed without a fight. Hoover notified the Attorney General that the program had begun.

A short time later, the Censorship Office, under an agreement worked out with the Bureau, began sending to the FBI copies of those messages which it felt might pertain to national defense. But the arrangement proved unsatisfactory, and the Bureau expanded its own "drop copy" program over the following five years. By the fall of 1946, the FBI was covertly obtaining, directly from the cable companies, cable traffic to and from some thirteen countries.

Following the war, and under the secret agreements worked out by the SSA with the cable companies, the FBI acted as a go-between, picking up copies of cable traffic to and from the various Washington offices and forwarding about half of it to NSA while keeping the rest for itself. At RCA the local FBI man would make his daily pickup in mid to late morning. By then, the requested telegrams had already been sorted out by the company's chief bookkeeper, who received the modest sum of $50 per month for her services (increased to $100 in 1965). Welcome as the secret payments were, they did present a bit of a problem when it came to income tax time. One could hardly list "secret FBI payments" on a tax form. To resolve this problem, the Bureau, in 1966, began withholding 20 percent for income tax purposes, then reviewed the 1040 at the end of each year in order to make appropriate changes, which took the form of IRS credits and adjustments for the deductions.

•

Besides the change in technology in the early 1960s, there was another development that had an even more significant effect on the future of NSA operations. When Robert F. Kennedy entered the Justice Department as Attorney General in 1961, he brought with him a suitcase full of leftover business from his days on the Senate subcommittee investigating racketeering and turned organized crime into Public Enemy Number One. But where crime had no problem organizing, the investigators did.

"When we got there we found that there was no central repository for information concerning individuals with a known criminal background," recalled Herbert J. Miller, Jr., chief of Kennedy's Criminal Division. "IRS would have information, SEC would have information . . . and there were some . . . twenty-nine or thirty investigative agencies that gathered intelligence." Kennedy's idea was to bring all of those resources together for the first time and exchange known information. His vehicle was a small "intelligence unit," set up in the department's Organized Crime Section, that essentially, according to Miller, "consisted of a filing system which correlated all of the information the federal government had on organized racketeering. Suppose Al Capone was still operational in those days," Miller said; "we'd find out what every one of the investigative agencies knew about Al Capone and put it in one file instead of each of them having a piece of information."

One of the first courses of business, therefore, was the establishment of a watch list of leading racketeers, which was distributed throughout the interested agencies, among them the NSA. Starting in 1962, the Criminal Division began sending to NSA the names of hundreds of racketeers, requesting any information about them that the Agency might have or might obtain in the future. The resulting intelligence secretly contributed to numerous prosecutions.*

* In *Robert Kennedy and His Times* (Boston: Houghton Mifflin, 1978, at p. 267), noted historian Arthur M. Schlesinger, Jr., writes:

A second area of major concern for the Kennedys was Cuba. Just as the Criminal Division sent the NSA its lists of racketeers, the FBI began submitting to NSA the names of U.S. citizens and business firms that had dealings with Cuba. In turn, the NSA provided the FBI with intelligence on American commercial and personal communications with Cuba gleaned from Shamrock and the interception of international telephone calls.

In an effort to find ways for the FBI to make better use of the NSA intercepts on Cuba, a meeting in May 1962 was set up between Raymond Wannall, chief of the Bureau's Nationalities Intelligence Section of the Domestic Intelligence Division, and officials of the Puzzle Palace. "Of the raw traffic now available," wrote Wannall in a memo following the meeting, "the material which would be most helpful to us would consist of periodic listing of firms in the U.S. which are doing business with individuals in Cuba and the Cuban government . . . With regard to personal messages, we feel that those relating to individuals travelling between Cuba and the U.S. would be the most significant . . . We will furnish NSA a list of persons in whom we have an investigative or an intelligence interest."

Now, for the first time, NSA had begun turning its massive ear inward toward its own citizens. To Harvest would now go Miller's reincarnated Al Capone as well as Vito Genovese and Meyer Lansky and most likely Jimmy Hoffa. Snatched from the air and cables would be the messages and telephone calls of Cuban relatives separated by miles and ideology, of American businessmen and union officials.

With no laws or legislative charter to block its path, the ear continued to turn. What racketeers and Cuba were to the Kennedys, protesters and drug dealers were to Presidents Johnson and Nixon. The systematic inclusion of American names and organizations in NSA's watch lists, which began in 1962, took a major swing upward in 1967. On October 20 of that year, Major General William P. Yarborough, the Army's assistant chief of staff for Intelligence, sent a TOP SECRET COMINT CHANNELS ONLY message to NSA director Marshall Carter, requesting that NSA provide any available information about possible foreign influence on civil disturbances in the United States.

For the first time all the federal groups that knew anything about the underworld came together in the same room and exchanged information.

Kennedy gave the job of coordination not to the FBI but the department's Organized Crime Section. There researchers compiled a roster of leading racketeers, circulated the list among the investigative agencies, and used the result as the basis for prosecutions.

I would appreciate any information [the Yarborough message said] on a continuing basis covering the following:

A. Indications that foreign governments or individuals or organizations acting as agents of foreign governments are controlling or attempting to control or influence the activities of U.S. "peace" groups and "Black Power" organizations.
B. Identities of foreign agencies exerting control or influence on U.S. organizations.
C. Identities of individuals and organizations in the U.S. in contact with agents of foreign governments.
D. Instructions or advice being given to U.S. groups by agents of foreign governments.

To one senior NSA official, the receipt of such a request was "unprecedented . . . It is kind of a landmark in my memory; it stands out as a first."

Pressured by the White House, the FBI, and the Attorney General, who were growing increasingly nervous over the mounting civil unrest in the country, the Department of the Army established a civil disturbance unit and assigned Yarborough to direct its operations. Among Yarborough's most immediate worries was the massive March on the Pentagon, which was scheduled to take place the day following his message to Carter.

According to the Yarborough message, "the 'big' question" was "determining whether or not there is evidence of any foreign actions to develop or control these anti-Vietnam and other domestic demonstrations."

The day after receiving the message, Carter sent a cable to Yarborough, DCI Richard Helms, and each member of the USIB, informing them that the NSA was "concentrating additional and continuing effort to obtain SIGINT" in support of the Army request. Nevertheless, despite this notification that NSA's domestic watch list effort was about to be greatly expanded, there is no record that the matter was ever discussed at a USIB meeting nor that the USIB ever validated a requirement for monitoring in support of the civil disturbance unit.

As the Army began sending over its pages of protesters' names, other agencies did the same — some individually, some on preprinted forms, and some simply over the telephone.

The Secret Service delivered a watch list containing names of individuals and organizations active in the antiwar and civil rights movements, presumably believing that picking up their phone calls and messages might in some way help protect the President.

The CIA was interested in "the activities of U.S. individuals in either civil disorders, radical student, or youth activities, racial militant activities, radical antiwar activities, draft evasion/deserter support activities, or in radical related media activities, where such individuals have some foreign connection." The FBI and the DIA followed suit.

The names on the various watch lists ranged from members of radical political groups to celebrities to ordinary citizens involved in protest against their government. Included were such well-known figures as Jane Fonda, Joan Baez, Dr. Benjamin Spock, Dr. Martin Luther King, Jr., the Reverend Ralph Abernathy, Black Panther leader Eldridge Cleaver, and Chicago Seven defendants Abbie Hoffman and David T. Dellinger.

A frightening side effect of the watch list program was the tendency of most lists to grow, expanding far beyond their original intent. This multiplier effect was caused by the inclusion of names of people who came in contact with those persons and organizations already on the lists. Because of NSA's vacuum cleaner approach to intelligence collection — whereby it sucks into its system the maximum amount of telecommunications and then filters it through an enormous screen of "trigger words" — analysts end up reviewing telephone calls, telegrams, and telex messages to and from thousands of innocent persons having little or nothing to do with the actual focus of the effort. Thus, if an organization is targeted, all its members' communications may be intercepted; if an individual is listed on a watch list, all communications to, from, or even mentioning that individual are scooped up. Captured in NSA's net were communications about a peace concert, a communication mentioning the wife of a U.S. senator, a correspondent's report from Southeast Asia to his magazine in New York, and a pro–Vietnam War activist's invitations to speakers for a rally.

Focal point in the Agency for the watch lists was Juanita Moody, the consumer staff liaison officer. Moody quit college in 1943 to enlist in the Army's Signal Security Agency as a clerk and over the decades ascended the cryptologic ladder in NSA's Production Organization.* Known internally as PO5 (PROD's fifth staff element), the consumer staff liaison officer serves as the Agency's principal point of con-

---

* Moody retired in February 1976 and on December 16, 1977, during a ceremony held at CIA headquarters, CIA director George Bush presented her with the first National Intelligence Medal of Achievement. The award, one of three awards conferred by the director of Central Intelligence at the recommendation of the National Foreign Intelligence Board (formerly the USIB), honors the recipient for service to the entire intelligence community. Following the recommendation of Lieutenant General Lew Allen, Jr., Moody was presented with the medal "in recognition of exceptional service to the intelligence community." ("Juanita M. Moody Honored by CIA, Receives National Intelligence Medal," *National Security Agency Newsletter* [February 1977], page 4; "Postscripts," *National Security Agency Newsletter* [August 1977], page 14.)

tact with the rest of the intelligence community. On receiving the watch lists, she would forward most of them to Frank Raven, chief of PROD's G Group, which was responsible for processing SIGINT from all non-Communist areas of the world, including the United States.

A 1934 graduate of Yale, Raven had been analyzing ciphers and breaking codes since before Pearl Harbor. In 1940, as a newly commissioned Navy ensign, he was assigned to be the Navy's bagman with the telegraph companies. "An official would leave the stack of traffic on a desk and then go to lunch," Raven recalled. "I would have to pick up the traffic, take it to the Navy Building for copying, and then get it back before they came back from lunch." This way, he said, the official could deny any knowledge of the operation. Following the SIS victory over Purple, Raven added the crowning touch by discovering, in effect, the "key to the keys" of the system, thus enabling the United States to shear away the code more rapidly than the Japanese code clerks themselves. In the 1950s he took charge of the Russian military and medium-level cipher systems as chief of GENS, before he became head of G Group in the early 1960s.

Deputy chief of G Group during the late 1960s and early to mid-1970s was Mary (Polly) Budenbach, a graduate of Smith College who began her career as a novice analyst in World War II.

As the watch list requests began pouring in during the late 1960s and early 1970s, Raven's problems mounted. He was well aware that NSA's mission was supposed to be limited strictly to foreign intelligence, yet the names and organizations passing across his desk in swelling numbers were going farther and farther over the line.

In May 1968, one month after the Memphis assassination of Dr. Martin Luther King, Jr., a frustrated FBI was still unable to locate the man they believed responsible, James Earl Ray. A proposal was made to institute both wiretap and microphone surveillance against the brother and sister of the suspect at their homes as well as at their business, the Grapevine Tavern. At the time, however, Attorney General Ramsey Clark was strongly opposed to all electronic eavesdropping, with the exception of a few very narrow national security areas. Also, a number of recent Supreme Court decisions placed strict limitations on the techniques. Finally, an internal FBI memo suggested that such actions would probably be unconstitutional, and the idea was eventually dropped.

Nevertheless, Frank Raven received a direct order to place Ray's name, along with about a dozen of his aliases, on the watch list. But what was so unusual about the request was that it came not from the FBI nor the Justice Department, but directly from the office of Secretary of Defense Clark M. Clifford, though Clifford himself has no memory of such a request. "I tried to object to that on constitutional grounds as to whether or not it was legal — as to whether or not we should do it," Raven recalled, "and I was told at that time that you couldn't argue with it — it came from the highest level." But the NSA search apparently turned up little, and Ray was eventually picked up in London on June 8, 1968. "We just wasted computer money on that one," Raven concluded. "It didn't cost NSA a dollar that they wouldn't have spent anyway, but it probably bumped out three or four other problems which were, in my opinion, more important."

The existence of NSA's involvement in the James Earl Ray investigation seems to have been one of the Agency's best-kept secrets. Not only were the NSA's actions never revealed in any subsequent court proceedings involving Ray; they were apparently never revealed even to the House Assassinations Committee, which spent months attempting to examine every detail of the murder.

Although some of the watch list names arguably could fall in the large gray area between foreign and domestic intelligence, others, said Raven, were downright "asinine." "When J. Edgar Hoover gives you a requirement for complete surveillance of all Quakers in the United States, when Richard M. Nixon is a Quaker and he's the President of the United States, it gets pretty funny." What caused the Quakers to be sucked into NSA's vacuum cleaner, apparently, was Hoover's belief that the religious group was shipping food and supplies to Southeast Asia.

The conflict over how to handle the flood of questionable watch lists streaming into NSA was becoming more and more divisive. "There's one school of thought that argues that when a customer levies a requirement on NSA, you note it [and] you try to give him whatever you can on the subject," Raven pointed out. "That doesn't necessarily mean you're going to do anything, but you will note any requirement that comes in from a consumer — the Army, the FBI, or CIA, or things of that sort." But then there was the other side of the issue:

> The other school of thought was the school of thought of G Group, which was that if you consider a requirement coming in to be illegal or out of line or you can't do it for any reason — you simply don't have the resources . . . you tell the customer square to his face that we thank you for your requirement but we're sorry we can't do it because we don't have the resources; it's outside of our mission; it's outside of our

authorization; or what have you. Now how to handle these two questions is a very major policy fight — and you can argue who's right and who's wrong even today — I don't know . . . You see Juanita Moody was of the school, right or wrong, that you just note it and file it — don't stir the customer up. We were of the opinion that if it were obviously an asinine requirement, or we weren't going to do anything about it, we would tell the guy.

As a result, Raven would note in a memo to Moody that G Group was planning to disregard various watch list entries, and Moody, according to Raven, would occasionally send the. memo on to the customer but most often would not.

Once Moody passed the latest watch list additions on to G Group, they would be incorporated into various "scan-guides," which would be used by the analysts to pick out the requested information. According to Raven, "A scan-guide is: in the traffic which you are reading, report any reference to [for example] Secretary of State Haig. You don't go out and do any intercept . . . but in the [traffic] that you are processing, if you see any reference to Haig, either favorable or unfavorable, you report them to somebody in the State Department."

The scan-guides would then be distributed to the various offices in G Group, such as G1, G2, G3, and so forth, each of which would cover a specific geographic area — the Middle East, Africa, South America, or another area.

From the very beginning, the domestic watch list program was treated within the Puzzle Palace with the strictest secrecy. Any message containing watch list material was stamped TOP SECRET and HANDLE VIA COMINT CHANNELS ONLY, and also bore the code word Trine (later Umbra), indicating that the material was in the highest of the three COMINT categories. On top of that, a second code word was added, placing the message in the same category as the most sensitive Soviet intercepts. This was in the Gamma series, which included such hush-hush programs as the interception of radiotelephone communications to and from the limousines of senior Soviet officials, code-named Gamma Gupy.

Despite this tight security, however, the civil disturbance watch list program became even more restricted and compartmented on July 1, 1969, when it received its own code word and charter:

CHARTER FOR SENSITIVE SIGINT OPERATION MINARET (C)

1. MINARET (C) is established for the purpose of providing more restrictive control and security of sensitive information derived from communications as processed . . . which contain (a) information on foreign

governments, organizations, or individuals who are attempting to influence, coordinate, or control U.S. organizations, or individuals who may
foment civil disturbance or otherwise undermine the national security
of the U.S *An equally important aspect of MINARET will be to restrict the
knowledge that information is being collected and processed by the National Security
Agency.*

2. MINARET specifically includes communications concerning individuals or organizations, involved in civil disturbances, antiwar movements/
demonstrations and Military deserters involved in the antiwar movements . . .

3. MINARET information will not be serialized, but will be identified
for reference purposes by an assigned date/time. Information will be
classified TOP SECRET, stamped "Background Use Only," and addressed to named recipients. *Further, although MINARET will be handled
as SIGINT and distributed to SIGINT recipients, it will not . . . be identified
with the National Security Agency.* [Emphasis added.]

Accompanying the Minaret charter was a brief approval message
signed by an assistant NSA director, most likely Major General John
Morrison, head of PROD. Until 1969, only the intercepted communications that were specifically between *two* Americans received such
special treatment. Now, with the adoption of Minaret, all communications to, from, or mentioning an American were so classified.

What made Minaret so sensitive was not the importance of the
intelligence; far less security was afforded much more important Soviet
intercepts. Minaret became ultrasensitive only because it bordered
on illegality and therefore had to be masked to shield the Agency.
Removed from the messages were any indications that they had originated within the Puzzle Palace, even the HANDLE VIA COMINT CHANNELS
ONLY caveat that accompanies virtually everything leaving the Agency
related in any way to SIGINT.

Also with the charter came more formal procedures for submission
of the names. No longer could one simply pick up a scrambler phone
and call a GG-12 in PROD and have a name added. All submissions
now had to be in writing and were subject to a tighter chain of command. Said one senior NSA official, "From 1969 on [the watch list]
was handled in a very careful, reviewed, and systematic way."

•

"I consider keeping dangerous drugs out of the United States just
as important as keeping armed enemy forces from landing in the
United States . . . We are going to fight this evil with every weapon
at our command." On October 24, 1969, President Nixon designated

international narcotics control a concern of U.S. foreign policy and established the White House Task Force on Heroin Suppression. Members included representatives from the White House staff, State Department, Treasury, Bureau of Narcotics and Dangerous Drugs (BNDD), and the Department of Defense. Also named was DCI Richard Helms, who was instructed by the President "to contribute to the maximum extent possible." His contribution consisted of establishing an Office of Narcotics Coordinator under the agency's Deputy Directorate of Plans (now the Deputy Directorate of Operations), which provided the task force with narcotics intelligence reports and studies concerning trafficking in Turkey and Southeast Asia, as well as any European connections between Latin American traffickers and Turkish opium suppliers.

A second responsibility of the office was to act as liaison with other agencies on narcotics problems. This the CIA took quite seriously, and within a short period of time the ONC was supplying the BNDD with training, was lending it "flash rolls" for overseas operations, and was providing it with sensitive intelligence reports. These included OO Reports, compiled by the Domestic Collection Division exclusively from interviews of people who had traveled to foreign countries; analytical reports, such as one entitled "Cocaine Trafficking Network in Colombia"; and the Director of Operations Narcotics Control Reports (DONCS), which were sent directly to BNDD's chief of Strategic Intelligence.

Most important, however, the CIA, probably through its Division D, also began conducting overseas interceptions specifically for the collection of international narcotics intelligence. When this activity produced information concerning the narcotics-trafficking activities of U.S. citizens, however, the local CIA officer would reportedly bow out, surrendering his information to his local BNDD counterpart, who would continue the investigation, most likely with similar, NSA-supplied eavesdropping equipment.

Pleased as the Bureau was to receive the CIA's help, there was one flaw in the arrangement. The CIA was forbidden by law from conducting eavesdropping operations within the United States. This presented a major problem for the BNDD, since a large portion of the traffickers it was interested in operated, at least a large part of the time, within the United States. One particularly frustrating case involved information it had received indicating that arrangements for certain South American drug deals were being conducted by telephone from a booth in New York's Grand Central Station.

Because the CIA was forbidden from monitoring domestic telephone conversations and also because, under the law, BNDD felt that it could not tap public telephones, BNDD director John E. Ingersoll turned to an agency that had, from its birth, never been handicapped by such mundane considerations: the NSA. In fact, Roy Banner, the Agency's top lawyer for many years, had secretly helped draft the wiretap legislation contained in the 1968 Omnibus Crime Control and Safe Streets Act, making sure to insert an inconspicuous loophole for NSA's operations. In a July 24, 1968, memorandum, Banner boasted of the coup, telling his director that the effect of the NSA-added exception to the act (§2511(3)) "is to remove any doubt as to the legality of the SIGINT and COMSEC activities of the Executive Branch of the Government." He then added that the language of the law "precludes an interpretation that the prohibitions against wiretapping or electronic surveillance techniques in other laws applies to SIGINT and COMSEC activities of the Federal Government."

In early April 1970 an official from BNDD journeyed up to Fort Meade and met with Deputy Director Tordella, who assured the official that NSA could handle the bureau's request to start a watch list and even fulfill its requirement for coverage of the public pay phones in Grand Central. On April 10, Director Ingersoll dispatched a memorandum to Director Gayler, thanking him for Tordella's help and attaching a general statement of his bureau's watch list requirements.

After first establishing the fact that BNDD's "primary responsibility . . . is to enforce the laws and statutes relating to narcotic drugs, marihuana, depressants, stimulants, and the hallucinogenic drugs," the memorandum went on to list the bureau's requirements:

1. The BNDD has a requirement for any and all COMINT information which reflects illicit traffic in narcotics and dangerous drugs. Our primary interest falls in the following categories:
   a. organizations engaged in such activities
   b. individuals engaged in such activities
   c. information on the distribution of narcotics and dangerous drugs
   d. information on cultivation and production centers
   e. international agreements and efforts to control the traffic in narcotics and dangerous drugs
   f. *all violations of the laws of the U.S. concerning narcotics and dangerous drugs.*

2. To assist NSA in the selection of pertinent COMINT information, the BNDD will provide a list of organizations and individuals with a history of illicit drug activities. This Watch List will be updated on a monthly basis and any additions/deletions will be forwarded to NSA.

Any COMINT information developed on these individuals/organizations should be brought to the attention of the BNDD. [Emphasis supplied.]

Instituting the BNDD's watch list was no simple matter, according to Frank Raven, who, as chief of G Group, was responsible for processing the traffic. "That requires special intercept. That requires covering telephone circuits from New York to Venezuela," he recalled. Although processing data communications on that link was quite economical, not so the telephone circuits. "Not voice," according to Raven. "We don't have that kind of resource. I mean, these people have the idea that NSA covers all the communications in the world — they don't cover a tenth of one percent of the communications in the world. As a matter of fact, that's probably a high estimate."

With the implementation of the BNDD watch list and special domestic targeting requirements, the NSA had taken its most dangerous step. Not only had the Agency clearly begun supporting domestic law enforcement agencies; it was also preparing to begin the specific targeting of American citizens within the United States. Until then, all intelligence provided through the Minaret program had been "byproducts," information on watch-listed persons picked up during the course of monitoring *foreign* targets for *foreign* intelligence collection. The giant ear had suddenly turned directly inward.

By June the first watch list intercepts began flowing to the BNDD, and in September the special domestic targeting had begun. Initially, the monitoring was conducted from one NSA intercept site, but in December 1970 that station was closed. The operation began again in March at an NSA East Coast facility operated by the military, probably the Naval Security Group listening post just outside the little town of Northwest, Virginia, a swampy, snake-infested site bristling with $10 million worth of antennas. In 1975 the Security Group moved from the fourteen-hundred-acre site on the Virginia–North Carolina border to Sugar Grove, West Virginia.

Although only six South American cities, in addition to New York and Miami, were of primary interest in the drug monitoring, this is somewhat misleading, since these are transit points: calls are routed through them to other cities. For example, by monitoring one New York–South American city link, NSA could pick up calls from other South American cities to other cities in the United States. The calls, once received either at the Etam or Andover earth station, would simply be routed through New York City to other United States destinations. Likewise, a call from St. Louis to Caracas will likely go first to New York and then be transmitted down to Etam. In all, NSA

monitored nineteen separate United States–South American links for
voice traffic at the two sites between 1970 and 1973.

Though the procedures NSA set up for Minaret and the drug monitoring were, at times, quite informal, the normal method by which
the Agency sets targets and priorities is standardized and formal.

Of all the superclassified documents within the Puzzle Palace, few
come close to matching the secrecy of the one known as the IGCP.
Instituted about 1966, and possibly standing for Intelligence Guidelines for COMINT Priorities, the IGCP is NSA's bible for targeting.
Prepared by an IG staff made up of representatives of the member
agencies of the intelligence community, and issued by the DCI in
his role as chairman of the USIB, the document provides the NSA
director with specific priorities and guidelines for the NSA's overall
SIGINT collection responsibilities.

In the IGCP, the world is divided into numerous "subelements."
Western Europe, for example, is Subelement 27; other Asian countries
(such as India), are 24; Latin America is 26; the Middle East and
North Africa are 28; and the sub-Saharan countries are 29.

Listed directly below each subelement are the various methods of
SIGINT collection. Interception of international commercial communications, for example, such as telephone, telegram, and telex, is identified as Group B. Another group, most likely Group A, is for foreign
internal communications. Finally, listed numerically under the groups
are the specific NSA targets, known as "line items." A line item may
be a requirement for all information relating to weapons systems
or military construction. In addition to identifying the specific target,
the line item also includes information on when the desired information is needed, such as "within 48 hours after recognition," and the
information's level of completeness. Level 1, for example, would be
the most complete.

As a general rule, when an agency submits a new requirement to
NSA that falls within an existing line item, like additions to a watch
list, and does not require additional resource allocations, NSA would
normally honor that requirement without further review. However,
when in NSA's view a new requirement does necessitate additional
collection or processing efforts, or constitutes a significant change
in scope, completeness, or time specification of an existing line item,
then the requesting agency would be informed that it must first submit
the requirement for approval to the IG staff. Once it is approved,
the IG staff would submit it to the SIGINT Committee, one of the
USIB's three intelligence committees. This committee, always chaired
by the NSA director, would then approve the changes in the IGCP

as appropriate, unless further action by the USIB is required.

But a serious problem with the document was that many of the requirements listed were far too broad to be of much assistance to the analysts sifting through the reams of intercepted traffic. The Army at one point, for example, simply asked for "all information on the veneral disease rate in East Germany," because it might reflect on the capabilities of the East German troops. One of the major critics of the IGCP was Frank Raven, who labeled it "a worthless piece of paper." "The first priority would be as to whether or not the Russians are going to attack you," said Raven. "Well, you would be astonished by the things that you can justify under evidence of a Russian attack." One of those requirements called for reporting the disappearance of any senior Communist official — but never specified what was meant by a "disappearance." "We were required to report this world-wide within something like fifteen minutes. Now you report within fifteen minutes that Brezhnev is missing — but at what point is he missing? . . . Hell, if he goes to the john, he's disappeared!"

When BNDD's John Ingersoll submitted his bureau's drug watch list to NSA in April 1970, no line item existed for international narcotic trafficking. Nevertheless, NSA began processing this intelligence without first going through the normal USIB procedures. The Agency did informally notify the IG staff of the program, but advised it "that such effort should not be given visibility."

Declaring that drug abuse had grown to crisis proportions and that it was "imperative that the illicit flow of narcotics and dangerous drugs into this country be stopped as soon as possible," President Nixon, in August 1971, upgraded the priority of the drug control effort. In a memorandum to Secretary of State William Rogers, he disbanded the White House task force and directed the establishment of the Cabinet Committee on International Narcotics Control (CCINC), naming as members the Secretaries of State, Defense, and Treasury, the Attorney General, the director of Central Intelligence, and the ambassador to the United Nations.

The major objective of the CCINC was the "formulation and coordination of all policies of the Federal Government relating to the goal of curtailing and eventually eliminating the flow of illegal narcotics and dangerous drugs into the United States from abroad." Named as executive director of the committee on September 7 was Egil (Bud) Krogh, Jr., who, under his other hat as head of Nixon's leak-plugging "plumbers' unit," had approved the infamous burglary of Daniel Ellsberg's psychiatrist's office, conducted only three days earlier.

One of Krogh's first actions was to appoint an Intelligence Subcommittee, chaired by the CIA narcotics coordinator. Now for the first time the CIA, DIA, NSA, State Department, Treasury Department, and the White House were brought together as one force in the war against drugs.

Earlier that summer the CIA finally decided to "legitimate" its drug watch list by processing it through the USIB mechanism. Writing of the program in a memorandum to the other members of the IG staff, the CIA member noted: "During the past year this effort was increased in scope, with most of the work done on the basis of informal requests for information from the various agencies involved in the problem. COMINT produced has been of great value to the CIA production offices and has been used as a principal source of information in several intelligence reports and memoranda. We understand that it has also bee [sic] of considerable value to operational components, such as the Bureau of Narcotics and Dangerous Drugs."

Following approval by the USIB, the new narcotics requirement was added to NSA's IGCP as Line Item 8 of Group B, Subelement 32:

> 8. International Narcotics activities.
>   a. Report information relating to the international trafficking in narcotics and dangerous drugs.*

Time specification of the item was to be "within 72 hours after recognition" and reporting to be at an estimated completeness level of "2," the level at which the NSA had been reporting all along.

Throughout 1972 the Nixon administration's drug war continued. On June 12 the CIA reorganized its Office of Narcotics Coordinator into the more unified Narcotics Coordination Group, or NARCOG.

---

* This line item applied only to Subelement 32, possibly North and Central America. Later, however, NSA "developed its processing effort" against the international, internal, and external communications of much of the world and, therefore, on July 22, 1974, added a new line item to Subelements 24, 26, 27, 28, and 29. Generally, the language of this additional line item was identical in each subelement and in all cases provided for the various watch lists and referred to travel. For example, the 1974 IGCP provided:

> Subelement 27 [Western Europe]
>   Group B [ILC traffic (international licensed
>   carriers)]
>   Line Item 6
>   d. Travel of selected indi-
>   viduals. *a/*
>   (1) Travel of individu-
>   als related to nar-
>   cotics trafficking. *b/*

---

a/ As specified by or through CIA.
b/ As specified by BNDD, ONNI, Customs, and/or CIA.

The following month the White House issued Executive Order 11676, providing for the establishment, within the Justice Department, of the Office of National Narcotics Intelligence (ONNI), whose major goal was to be "the development and maintenance of a National Narcotics Intelligence System." And in September the President told an International Narcotics Control Conference: "We are living in an age, as we all know, in an era of diplomacy, when there are times that a great nation must engage in what is called a limited war. I have rejected that principle in declaring total war against dangerous drugs . . . We are going to fight this evil with every weapon at our command."

By now, the names of U.S. citizens on NSA's many watch lists had grown from the hundreds into the thousands, presenting increasing worries for the Agency's chief keeper of the secrets.

More and more, during his thirteen years as the Puzzle Palace's de facto head, Dr. Louis Tordella began resembling *Webster's* definition of one of the Agency's highest code words, Umbra: "the dark cone of shadow from a planet or satellite on the side opposite the sun." If NSA was the darkest part of the government, Tordella was the darkest part of the NSA. Even General Carter, DIRNSA for the longest period of time, could never be *totally* sure he knew all of the Palace's secrets; he believed there may have been times when, "because of the sensitivity they felt, well, why burden [me] with it?"

When Noel Gayler took over as director in August 1969, Tordella waited a year or so before briefing even him on the NSA watch list program. The DIRNSA, however, was not the only one kept in the dark about the operation. The fact that NSA had begun devoting additional resources to the specific purpose of targeting U.S. citizens had never been approved by, or even formally brought before, the USIB. Although the board did approve the drug watch lists, it was only when the information was picked up as a by-product of NSA's normal foreign intelligence collection. As one senior official familiar with the mechanics of the Agency's operations pointed out, "Consumers and NSA are often in direct contact and USIB cannot maintain complete oversight. Consequently, NSA may, without the knowledge of USIB, embark upon a new collection requirement."

That the USIB was completely unaware of the NSA's specific U.S. targeting programs, like the one directed at the pay telephones in Grand Central Station, is evidenced by a report prepared by the USIB's Critical Collection Problems Committee (CCPC). On January 31, 1972, DCI Richard Helms asked the CCPC to conduct a review of intelligence efforts against narcotics, looking into such problems as the coordination of collection, dissemination, and production of national intelligence information on narcotics. The final report was

issued in October 1972, more than two years after NSA had secretly
begun directing programs against American citizens. Under the heading "SIGINT Information on Narcotics and Dangerous Drugs," the
report opened its first paragraph with the declaration: "1. No SIGINT
resources are dedicated solely to the intercept of narcotics information. The SIGINT which is now being produced on the international
narcotics problem is a by-product of SIGINT reporting on other national requirements."

Another group that Tordella and Gayler mistrusted with the watch
list information was, incredibly, their own intercept operators. Though
using the three service cryptologic agencies (ASA, NSG, AFSS) to
perform the Agency's worldwide intercept operations had the advantage of providing a cheap labor force, it also had a number of definite
disadvantages. One of them was that most of the operators were
young military personnel on short tours of duty. Because their turn-
over was high, the risks that one might someday decide to blow the
whistle on the operation was greatly increased.

Tordella and Gayler's fears were realized in August 1972, when a
twenty-five-year-old former staff sergeant in the Air Force Security
Service decided to bare his top secret soul to the magazine *Ramparts*.
A latent Vietnam War protester and former traffic analyst at listening
posts in Turkey, West Germany, and Vietnam, Perry Fellwock wove
a tale of much fact and some fancy in a question-and-answer session
with the magazine, using the pseudonym Winslow Peck. The Joplin,
Missouri, native's claim that NSA was able to break all Soviet code
systems ("We're able to break every code they've got"), was most
likely an exaggeration, but the majority of the sixteen-page article
was, unfortunately for the Agency, quite accurate. Once the magazine
hit the stands there was little the red-faced officials of the Puzzle
Palace could do except hold their tongues in embarrassed silence.
Prosecution, they must have reasoned, would only serve to confirm
all that Fellwock had said.

The information released by the disenchanted sergeant, Tordella
most likely concluded, was severely damaging to the Agency. Had
Fellwock known of the drug watch list program, however, the results
would have been devastating, which was why Tordella had withheld
the most sensitive names and telephone numbers from the intercept
operators at the East Coast listening post. In October, he sought the
help of his sister agency, and, without protest, the CIA accepted and
turned the mission over to Division D. On November 17 the chief
of the Special Programs Division of the CIA notified his agency's director of Communications of the new requirement: "NSA had tasked [the
East Coast site] with this requirement [to monitor for drug traffic] but

were unwilling to provide the site with the specific names and U.S. telephone numbers of interest on security/sensitivity grounds . . . To get around the problems mentioned above NSA requested the Agency [CIA] undertake intercept of the long lines circuits of interest. They have provided us with all information available (including the 'sensitive') and the [CIA] facility is working on the requirement."

Again, the tightest security was wrapped around the project, and even the CIA's own drug coordination unit, NARCOG, was uninformed of the new operation.

One who did discover the project, however, was CIA general counsel Larry Houston, and in a January 29, 1973, memorandum to the acting chief of Division D he made it clear that he didn't like what he found. In Houston's opinion the activity possibly violated Section 605 of the Communications Act of 1934, prohibiting the unauthorized disclosure of private communications. He concluded, too, that, since the intercepted messages were eventually given by NSA to BNDD, the activity was for law enforcement purposes, which was also outside the CIA's charter. As a result of Houston's memorandum, the CIA suspended any further collection.

According to Tordella, however, the major reason for the CIA pullout was that the phone calls were being intercepted from U.S. soil. "I was told that if they could move a group of Cubans up to Canada," Tordella later recalled, "it would be quite all right, but they would not do it in the United States." Rebuffed by the CIA, the Puzzle Palace took back its names and telephone numbers and continued the operation itself, once again unaffected by the burdens of federal law or the restraints of a charter. But six months later the risk of exposure became too great even for the NSA, and the drug program was shut down once and for all.

"Five or six years before we retired we did some very nice drug busts," recalled Frank Raven. "We demonstrated that we could follow drug transactions and drug dealers. We could do it quite economically — it wasn't a high-budget item." One such bust involved tipping off the BNDD about the impending arrival on American shores of an automobile that was so lined with cocaine that the drug authorities believed that the car had actually been built around the cocaine. Concluded Raven: "NSA could really have cleaned up the drug business — drug-running and such . . . But it got so screwed up in American law and American red tape that it wasn't worth the effort."

•

Although the science of codebreaking has undergone tremendous changes in the years between the pencil and the CRAY-1 computer, one principle has remained constant: it is always far easier to steal a code — and much less costly — than to attempt to break it.

This was where the black-bag experts of the FBI fitted into the cryptologic puzzle. A midnight break-in at the offices of the Syrian legation in New York City or the Iraqi embassy in Washington could provide an invaluable aid to the codebreakers of PROD. A photographed code book, the diagram of a new piece of crypto equipment, or the attachment of a bug to a scrambler phone could save millions of dollars and years of work.

But with a brief stroke of the pen, former gangbuster J. Edgar Hoover ended it all on July 19, 1966. On the bottom of a DO NOT FILE memorandum from his assistant director for Domestic Intelligence, William C. Sullivan, the subject of which was black-bag jobs, Hoover scratched, "No more such techniques must be used." In case the point was missed, he made his decision even more clear six months later. In a memo dated January 6, 1967, Hoover declared:

> I note that requests are still being made by Bureau officials for the use of "black bag" techniques. I have previously indicated that I do not intend to approve any such requests in the future, and, consequently, no such recommendations should be submitted for approval of such matters. This practice, which includes also surreptitious entrances upon premises of any kind, will not meet with my approval in the future.

The switch in attitude by Hoover upset no one more than it did Lou Tordella. He believed that the director was simply growing old and more wary about preserving his established reputation — a wariness nurtured by the protective instincts of his close friend and number two man in the Bureau, Clyde Tolson. At one point Tordella speculated, in a conversation with chief FBI spook Sullivan, who also strongly disagreed with the new policy, that Tolson had probably told Hoover something to the effect: "If these techniques ever backfire, your image and the reputation of the Bureau will be badly damaged."

Growing impatient with the "new" Hoover, and hoping they could change his mind, Tordella and General Carter, in 1967, scheduled a brief meeting with the FBI director. The fifteen-minute appointment slowly stretched into two and a half hours as the two codebreakers sat through reruns of Hoover's past exploits against the likes of John Dillinger, "Ma" Barker, and the "Communist Threat." At last they were able to get across their point that the break-ins should continue, and it appeared that Hoover might have been moved; he told them that their reasoning was persuasive and that he would consider re-establishing the earlier policies.

Delighted, Tordella and Carter headed back to Fort Meade. A few days later they congratulated each other when the news came that Hoover would allow FBI agents to resume the collection methods asked for by NSA. But that elation turned into anger three days later, when the FBI liaison to NSA brought the word that Hoover had changed his mind: the restrictions would remain. Sullivan then called Tordella to tell him that "someone got to the old man. It's dead." That someone, Sullivan surmised, was Tolson.

In his note to Tordella and Carter, Hoover indicated that he would conduct black-bag jobs for the NSA only if so ordered by the President or the Attorney General. Tordella, however, was reluctant to approach either. "I couldn't go to the chief law enforcement figure in the country and ask him to approve something that was illegal," he later explained — despite the fact that both he and Carter had already asked the director of the FBI to approve an identical policy. As for the President, this was "not a topic with which he should soil his hands," said Tordella. For the time being, at least, the matter would have to rest.

On January 20, 1969, Richard Milhous Nixon was sworn in as the thirty-seventh President. He had won with less than 1 percent of the total popular vote following what was probably the most violent presidential election campaign year in history.

In March and April, student riots erupted in San Francisco, Cambridge, and Ithaca; in Chicago, police and ghetto blacks began battling in the streets. In May, Assistant Attorney General Richard Kleindienst declared: "When you see an epidemic like this cropping up all over the country — the same kind of people saying the same kinds of things — you begin to get the picture that it is a national subversive activity." On November 15, over 250,000 people massed in Washington to protest the war in Vietnam while President Nixon and his close friend Charles (Bebe) Rebozo watched football on TV in the White House.

As the smoke from the April riots began dissipating, Nixon ordered his top domestic aide, John Ehrlichman, to have the intelligence community help him put together a report on foreign Communist support of campus disturbances. Because of what both men felt was a lack of substantial intelligence, however, the report was inconclusive, and two months later Ehrlichman decided to have a second and more thorough report prepared on the subject.

Assigned to the task was a twenty-nine-year-old Hoosier on Pat

Buchanan's research and speech-writing staff, Tom Charles Huston. A lawyer and recently discharged Army intelligence officer, the young White House counsel had drawn the assignment chiefly because of his keen interest in the subject and because he seemed to know more about New Left politics than anyone else on the White House staff.

On June 20, 1969, Huston dispatched a memorandum to the NSA, the CIA, the DIA, and the FBI, declaring that the "present intelligence collection capabilities in this area may be inadequate," and requesting, on behalf of the President, information about "what resources we presently have targeted toward monitoring foreign Communist support of revolutionary youth activities in this country." Huston also asked the agencies to indicate what gaps existed in intelligence on radicals and what steps could be taken to provide maximum possible coverage of their activities. Ten days later all the reports had been received, and once again Ehrlichman and the others in the White House were disenchanted by the results and the quality of intelligence.

Throughout the rest of 1969 and into 1970 the dissatisfaction continued. This, together with the growing number of riots and bombings, especially the explosion of a Weatherman "bomb factory" in a Greenwich Village town house in March, led White House chief of staff H. R. Haldeman to call a meeting in his office to discuss ways for improving coordination between the White House and the intelligence community. Also discussed at the April 1970 meeting was "whether — because of the escalating level of the violence — something within the Government further needed to be done."

The decision was to ask the President to meet with the directors of the four intelligence agencies and request from them reports on what could be done to curb the growing violence. Among those at the meeting — held, after several postponements, on Friday afternoon, June 5 — was Tom Huston, newly promoted to a high staff position in the White House and given responsibilities for internal security affairs.

In a sense, the meeting in the Oval Office represented a major coup on the part of Huston, who had long advocated the conference and was responsible for arranging it, and for William Sullivan, who had over the past year shared with Huston the belief that the best way to combat violence in America was to cast off the yoke of restrictions from the intelligence agencies. Lacking any in-depth background in intelligence matters, Huston continuously relied on Sullivan for guidance. Sullivan would point out what was desirable in terms of changes, and Huston would then attempt to convert the desirable into the possible.

Present at the meeting, besides Huston, Ehrlichman, and Haldeman, were Noel Gayler of the NSA, Donald V. Bennett of the DIA; CIA chief Richard Helms; Hoover of the FBI; and, incongruously, Robert H. Finch, Secretary of the Department of Health, Education, and Welfare.

According to Bennett, "The President chewed our butts" because of the lack of worthwhile intelligence on domestic violence. "Based on my review of the information which we have been receiving at the White House," Nixon told the gathering, "I am convinced that we are not currently allocating sufficient resources within the intelligence community to the collection of intelligence data on the activities of these revolutionary groups." To obtain the "hard information" he wanted, the President told the directors that they were to form a special committee to review the collection efforts of the intelligence agencies in the internal security area and then recommend steps that would strengthen the capabilities of the government for collecting intelligence on radicals and others who protested against government policy.

Concluding the meeting, Nixon asked that the intelligence chiefs work with Huston on the committee report. He appointed Hoover to serve as chairman of the committee, which was to be known as the Interagency Committee on Intelligence (Ad Hoc). Named to head the staff group that would be responsible for the actual drafting of the Special Report was Hoover's deputy for domestic intelligence, William Sullivan.

At Fort Meade, Tordella and Gayler looked on the ICI with joy and optimism. It could prove to be the perfect vehicle to force Hoover back into the black-bag business while giving presidential support to many of the Agency's very questionable collection activities. It also provided a perfect opportunity to expand NSA's domestic targeting operation. To head up the Agency's effort in support of the committee, Gayler picked Benson K. Buffham, the deputy assistant director for PROD under General Morrison and the top civilian in NSA's Production Organization.

Hoover wasted no time in starting the ball rolling. The first meeting was scheduled for eleven o'clock the following Monday in the FBI director's office. Gayler brought Buffham with him, though Helms and Bennett decided to come alone. After first reminding the chief spooks of the President's dissatisfaction with the current state of intelligence on domestic radicals, Hoover made it clear that what he felt the President wanted was a historical summary of unrest in the country up to the present.

Astonished by Hoover's interpretation of the President's charge, Huston objected, saying the report was not to be a historical summary at all but an assessment of current and future threats, a review of intelligence gaps, and a summary of options for changes in operations.

Gayler was next to object, seconding Huston's comments and adding that it was his understanding, too, that the purpose of the committee was to concentrate on the shortcomings of current intelligence collection. Bennett and Helms also agreed with Huston's view of the purposes of the ICI, and Hoover, who considered Huston a "hippie intellectual," reluctantly agreed and then abruptly adjourned the meeting.

The following day, around the large, oblong conference table in Room 7E-26 at CIA headquarters, the committee staff met for the first of four drafting discussions. Reading from an outline stamped TOP SECRET, Huston reiterated the purpose of the committee and then added that "operational details will be the responsibility of the chairman [Sullivan]. However, the scope and direction of the review will be determined by the White House member [Huston]." In other words, Sullivan would provide the expert guidance for picking out which collection barriers the counterintelligence experts wanted removed, and Huston would make sure the committee did not stray from the goal of suggesting ways to remove these barriers.

Among the "objectives" of the committee, Huston added, was the "maximum use of all special investigative techniques" and "clarification of NSA's role in targeting against communications traffic involving U.S. revolutionary leaders and organizations."

After Huston's presentation, Sullivan asked for comments on the level of classification for papers or reports prepared by the committee. Buffham spoke up, suggesting the adoption of a code word, and after some discussion it was agreed to stamp everything TOP SECRET, followed by NSA's caveat, HANDLE VIA COMINT CHANNELS ONLY. In addition, Helms recommended the establishment of a "Bigot List," "reflecting the names of all persons in each member agency or department who will work on or have knowledge of the work of the Committee." Both suggestions were unanimously adopted.

Next, the committee turned to the heart of the matter: the methodology of intelligence collection. One by one, around the table, the representatives discussed the numerous restraints on collection that hampered their ability to obtain the intelligence desired by the President. Buffham, who was accompanied by two of his top aides — Raymond James Gengler, a twenty-two-year Agency veteran who was representing G Group; and Leonard J. Nunno, representing Juanita Moody's

Consumer Liaison Office — called attention to the outline circulated by Huston in which the committee was called on "to define and assess the existing internal security threat." He said that such a study would require immediate attention from the counterintelligence specialists in each member organization. Huston agreed and suggested that the FBI prepare an assessment from the domestic point of view and the CIA from the foreign point of view. All members concurred, and the two agencies were asked to have the papers ready for distribution at the next meeting, scheduled for Friday, June 12, back at CIA headquarters.

The second meeting, like the first, was basically preparatory, consisting of general discussions and establishing the groundwork for the third, and most important, meeting. On June 17, the committee was ready to examine thoroughly the first draft of the report, a process that began at two o'clock and lasted for four hours.

As the draft session began, Buffham immediately brought up the matter of resuming FBI black-bag jobs in support of NSA's activities, saying that millions of dollars could be saved by such operations. The topic figured so prominently throughout the afternoon that it led staff chairman William Sullivan to draw the impression "that Admiral Gaylor [sic] of National Security Agency may have been a moving force behind the creation of this committee."

As the report finally evolved through the late afternoon, for each of the intelligence collection methods the President would be presented the option of (1) continuing the present restrictions, (2) asking for more information, or (3) accepting one of the listed relaxations.

Under Category One, "Interpretive Restraint on Communications Intelligence," the committee took up COMINT, and Buffham launched into a discussion of NSA's authority under the top secret National Security Council Intelligence Directive Number 6 (NSCID No. 6). Under the directive, considered by the Agency to be its "charter," the NSA has always interpreted its mission to be one of *foreign* intelligence collection. Thus, the Agency believed that it was barred from such activities as monitoring communications between U.S. citizens and targeting specific U.S. citizens.

Because of this, Buffham, Tordella, and Gayler saw in the Special Report a chance to obtain explicit approval to do what, in fact, they had already been doing for close to a decade. Such approval from the President for this practice would also allow them to expand the number of American names on the various watch lists. Buffham therefore proposed the following as ways to relax restrictions on COMINT collection:

— Present interpretation should be broadened to permit and [probably should read "a"] program for coverage by NSA of the communications of U.S. citizens using international facilities.

— Present interpretation should be broadened to permit and [probably should read "a"] program for coverage by NSA *at the request of the FBI* of the communications of U.S. citizens using international facilities. [Emphasis in the original.]

Category Two was entitled "Electronic Surveillances and Penetrations." Here again Buffham made the point that NSA "has been particularly hard hit by this limitation." Hoping to force the FBI back into the business of wiretap assistance to NSA, the deputy chief of PROD pointed out in the report that acquisition of important intelligence "from COMINT without benefit of the assistance which electronic surveillance techniques can provide, if possible at all, would be extremely expensive. Therefore, this approach could result in considerable dollar savings compared to collection methods."

Category Three dealt with mail coverage and thus was of primary concern to the FBI and CIA.

Category Four, "Surreptitious Entry," was probably the restriction NSA most wanted abolished. Of all the agencies involved in the ICI, NSA was the one with the greatest interest in removing the restraints on surreptitious entry. It was Tordella's golden opportunity to return to the days of diplomatic black-bag jobs.

The remaining categories were of primary concern to the other members of the committee.

Once the draft report was completed, Buffham and the representatives from the other agencies showed the document to their superiors. Gayler and Tordella both liked what they saw, as did Helms and Bennett, but Hoover blew his stack. "For years and years and years I have approved opening mail and other similar operations," the seventy-five-year-old FBI director fumed, "but no. It is becoming more and more dangerous and we are apt to get caught. I am not opposed to doing this. I'm not opposed to continuing the burglaries and the opening of mail and the other similar activities, providing somebody higher than myself approves of it."

Hoover wanted the entire report rewritten to eliminate the more extreme options, but Sullivan persuaded him simply to add his objections in the form of footnotes. Below the section dealing with electronic surveillances, for example, Hoover added that the FBI did not wish to change its current procedures but "would not oppose other agencies seeking authority of the Attorney General for coverage re-

quired by them and thereafter instituting such coverage themselves."
In other words, if the NSA wanted a bug planted in the residence
of some diplomat, it would have to do the planting itself.

The fourth and final meeting of the ICI staff took place on June
23. It was supposed to be used to polish up the final report, which
was due to be signed two days later, on Thursday, June 25. But once
the staff members took a look at Hoover's footnotes, they knew there
were going to be problems.

Buffham reported back to a hopping-mad Gayler, who immediately
got on the phone to Huston, demanding either another meeting of
the directors, at which he would insist that the footnotes be withdrawn, or that he be allowed to add his own footnotes. Huston, hoping to avoid any more problems with Hoover, tried to calm the NSA
director. He told Gayler that he would set forth the director's views
in his cover letter to the President. Huston himself was considerably less concerned about the footnotes, feeling quite confident that
in the end what the White House wanted, the White House would
get.

At three o'clock on the afternoon of June 25, Gayler met with Bennett, Helms, and Huston in Hoover's office for the official signing
ceremony..Following a few introductory remarks, the FBI chief turned
to the first page and, addressing each member individually, asked
whether he had any comments. He then did the same for the second
page, and so on through the whole forty-three-page document. Each
time Hoover came to Huston, however, he'd throw in an intentional
jab by referring to him by a different name: "Any comments, Mr.
Hoffman? Any comments, Mr. Hutchinson?" And so on. Nevertheless,
Huston hoped the meeting would end before anyone raised objection
to the footnotes. "We got down to about 'X' number of pages," Huston recalled later, "and, finally, it was just too much for Admiral
Gayler, and so, sure enough, there he goes." Gayler began to com-
plain about one of the footnotes, and he was soon echoed by DIA's
Bennett.

The criticism took Hoover by surprise, and, clearly upset, he rushed
through the remainder of the report. Once the four directors had
signed the Special Report, Hoover reminded them to have all working
copies of the document destroyed, then thanked them for their participation, and dismissed the committee for the last time, its assignment
completed.

The following day Huston received the report at the White House
and initiated his plan of action for getting the President to approve
the strongest possible options contained in the Special Report. His

first step was to draft a memorandum for Haldeman, outlining what the President should do with the report. Dated simply "July 1970" and titled "Domestic Intelligence Gathering Plan: Analysis and Strategy," the memorandum would eventually become known by a much simpler name: the Huston Plan.

The memo was Huston's ultimate revenge on Hoover. Calling the FBI director "the only stumbling block" to the ICI, and referring to his objections as "generally inconsistent and frivolous," Huston recommended that Nixon pacify Hoover with a "stroking session" and an autographed picture. "Mr. Hoover is set in his ways and can be bull-headed as hell, but he is a loyal trooper," the memo concluded. "Twenty years ago he would never have raised the type of objections he has here, but he's getting old and worried about his legend. He makes life tough in this area, but not impossible — for he'll respond to direction by the President and that is all we need to set the domestic intelligence house in order."

Following his denunciation of Hoover, Huston, in an attachment entitled "Operational Restraints on Intelligence Collection" and labeled TOP SECRET/HANDLE VIA COMINT CHANNELS ONLY, set out his recommendations on which restraints the President should lift. Of the first four, three dealt, significantly, with the NSA:

A. Interpretive Restraint on Communications Intelligence.
    Recommendation:
        Present interpretation should be broadened to permit a program for coverage by NSA of the communications of U.S. citizens using international facilities.
    Rationale:
        The FBI does not have the capability to monitor international communications. NSA is currently doing so on a restricted basis, and the information it has provided has been most helpful. Much of this information is particularly useful to the White House and it would be to our disadvantage to allow the FBI to determine what NSA should do in this area without regard to our own requirements. No appreciable risk is involved in this course of action.

B. Electronic Surveillances and Penetrations.
    Recommendation:
        Present procedures should be changed to permit intensification of coverage of individuals and groups in the United States who pose a major threat to the internal security.
        Also, present procedures should be changed to permit intensification of coverage of foreign nationals and diplomatic establishments in the United States of interest to the intelligence community.

Rationale:

At the present time, less than 65 electronic penetrations are operative. This includes coverage of the C.P.U.S.A. [Communist Party, U.S.A.] and organized crime targets, with only a few authorized against subjects of pressing internal security interest.

Mr. Hoover's statement that the FBI would not oppose other agencies seeking approval for operating electronic surveillances is gratuitous since no other agencies have the capability.

Everyone knowledgeable in the field, with the exception of Mr. Hoover, concurs that existing coverage is grossly inadequate. CIA and NSA note that this is particularly true of diplomatic establishments, and we have learned at the White House that it is also true of New Left groups.

. . .

D. Surreptitious Entry.

Recommendation:

Present restrictions should be modified to permit procurement of vitally needed foreign cryptographic material.

Also, present restrictions should be modified to permit selective use of this technique against other urgent and high priority internal security targets.

Rationale:

Use of this technique is clearly illegal: it amounts to burglary. It is also highly risky and could result in great embarrassment if exposed. However, it is also the most fruitful tool and can produce the type of intelligence which cannot be obtained in any other fashion.

The FBI, in Mr. Hoover's younger days, used to conduct such operations with great success and with no exposure. The information secured was invaluable.

NSA has a particular interest since it is possible by this technique to secure materials with which NSA can break foreign cryptographic codes. We spend millions of dollars attempting to break these codes by machine. One successful surreptitious entry can do the job successfully at no dollar cost.

Surreptitious entry of facilities occupied by subversive elements can turn up information about identities, methods of operation, and other invaluable investigative information which is not otherwise obtainable. This technique would be particularly helpful if used against the Weathermen and Black Panthers.

The deployment of the Executive Protection Force has increased the risk of surreptitious entry of diplomatic establishments. However, it is the belief of all except Mr. Hoover that the technique can still be successfully used on a selective basis.

On July 14, a week or so after he had submitted the memo and recommendations to Haldeman for delivery to the President, Huston received the good news that Nixon had approved the entire package. The only thing that bothered him now was that the President had decided against the Hoover "stroking session."

Just over a week later, on July 23, Huston put the final touches on the plan and sent it off via courier to the various agencies. When Gayler, Tordella, and Buffham received their copies, there was, no doubt, a victory celebration. From the very first, Tordella had regarded Huston and the ICI meetings as, in his own words, "nothing less than a heaven-sent opportunity for NSA." Now they had, in black and white, the presidential authorization to do what they had been doing all along. In addition, Tordella could once again order embassy buggings and break-ins from the FBI.

"The President has carefully studied the Special Report," the Huston memorandum to Admiral Gayler began, "of the Interagency Committee on Intelligence (Ad Hoc) and made the following decisions:

> 1. *Interpretive Restraint on Communications Intelligence.* National Security Council Intelligence Directive Number 6 (NSCID No. 6) is to be interpreted to permit NSA to program for coverage the communications of U.S. citizens using international facilities.
> 2. *Electronic Surveillances and Penetrations.* The intelligence community is directed to intensify coverage of individuals and groups in the United States who pose a major threat to the internal security. Also, coverage of foreign nationals and diplomatic establishments in the United States of interest to the intelligence community is to be intensified.
>
> . . .
>
> 4. *Surreptitious Entry.* Restraints on the use of surreptitious entry are to be removed. The technique is to be used to permit procurement of vitally needed foreign cryptographic material and against other urgent and high priority internal security targets.

If there was jubilation in Gayler's office over the Huston Plan, there was outraged fury in Hoover's office. According to Sullivan, the FBI director "went through the ceiling." Hoover stormed out of his office with his assistant, Cartha DeLoach, and straight into the nearby office of Attorney General John Mitchell. Mitchell was totally surprised. It was the first time he had ever heard of the Interagency Committee on Intelligence, let alone the Special Report or the Huston Plan, and his immediate reaction was to agree with Hoover: the illegalities spelled out in the memorandum could not be presidential policy.

Mitchell, also angry at having been by-passed by everyone on the whole affair, told Hoover to "sit tight" until President Nixon returned from San Clemente, when he would have the chance to take the matter up with him.

When Nixon returned from the Western White House, one of his first visitors on July 27 was John Mitchell. The proposals contained in the Huston Plan, the Attorney General declared, were, in toto, "inimical to the best interests of the country and certainly should not be something that the President of the United States should be approving." In addition, Mitchell said, "the risk of disclosure of the possible illegal actions, such as unauthorized entry into foreign embassies to install a microphone transmitter, was greater than the possible benefit to be derived."

Convinced, Nixon decided to withdraw his approval of the plan. Haldeman told Huston that, because of the meeting with Mitchell, the President had decided to revoke the memorandum immediately so that he, Haldeman, Mitchell, and Hoover could "reconsider" the recommendations.

Upset, angered, and embarrassed at having to recall his memorandum, Huston walked down to the Situation Room and into the office of Sit Room director David Y. McManis. After mumbling something about Hoover's having "pulled the rug out" from under him, he handed McManis the presidential order to rescind the decision memorandum dispatched from that very office only four days earlier. McManis then sent a memorandum to Hoover, Gayler, Helms, and Bennett, recalling the document. By the close of business the following day, July 28, each agency had complied, and the Huston Plan was placed securely under lock and key in the White House. But, as the markings on the returned documents indicated, each agency had removed the staples, undoubtedly so that it could photocopy the plan for its records and, possibly, for its own future protection.

Equally perturbed over the sudden revocation of the Huston Plan were Tordella, Gayler, and Buffham. Suddenly they were back to square one. Still, they had been conducting their domestic intelligence targeting without authorization for many years before the Huston Plan, and just because the President had formally withdrawn his approval, they saw no reason to stop. In fact, the watch lists of American names were flowing into the Puzzle Palace faster than ever.

What really bothered the NSA threesome about the loss of the Huston Plan was not that they would have to continue such massive operations as Shamrock, Minaret, and the drug watch lists without authority, but that the FBI's wiretappers and second-story men remained beyond their reach.

A few days after his humiliating visit to the Situation Room, Huston went to Haldeman's office and tried to persuade him to convince the President that the objections raised by Hoover should be overridden. He urged a meeting between Haldeman, Mitchell, and Hoover and, in anticipation of the meeting, submitted a memorandum to Haldeman, laying out various rebuttals to arguments that Hoover might make. "I don't object to NSA conducting surreptitious entry if they want to," went one Hoover argument, followed by Huston's response: "The answer is that NSA doesn't have the people, can't get them, has no authority to get them, and shouldn't have to get them. It is an FBI job."

More memos followed, but Huston knew that the game had already been won — and not by him. "I was, for all intents and purposes, writing memos to myself," he recalled. What Tordella had told Gayler when the new director first moved into the Puzzle Palace had apparently been lost on the young White House assistant: on matters relating to domestic intelligence, no one challenged Hoover.

Less than two weeks after Nixon rescinded the Huston Plan, its author was called into Haldeman's office and informed that a new White House aide would be taking over responsibility for internal security matters and that from now on he would be on the new aide's staff. The following day Huston met his new boss, a young lawyer who had worked under Mitchell at the Justice Department and had been transferred to the White House only a few days earlier — John Wesley Dean III. Demoted and frustrated, Huston resigned from the White House staff less than a year later and returned to Indiana to practice law.

Although Huston may have found his way to the White House graveyard, his plan was still very much alive and well. By late August, Haldeman had approached Dean and instructed him to see what he could do to get the plan implemented. On September 17, Dean paid a visit to his old boss, Mitchell, and explained Haldeman's request, but the Attorney General simply reiterated his opposition to the plan — with one exception. The original Huston Plan had called for the establishment of a permanent interagency committee for intelligence evaluation, and Mitchell said he now felt that such an organization might be useful.

Dean returned to Haldeman and suggested that the establishment of an evaluation committee could be viewed as a first step, with the lifting of collection restraints to come later. "A key to the entire operation," he wrote in his memo to Haldeman, "will be the creation of an interagency intelligence unit for both *operational* and evaluation purposes . . . *and then to proceed to remove the restraints* as necessary to obtain such intelligence." (Emphasis added.)

Haldeman concurred, and throughout the fall the interagency Intelligence Evaluation Committee (IEC) was set up, housed under a Justice Department cover, and placed under the charge of Robert C. Mardian, the assistant attorney general for Internal Security. The first meeting, on December 3 in Dean's office, looked like a reunion of Huston's old Interagency Committee on Intelligence. Buffham and Jim Gengler of PROD were there, representing the NSA; James Angleton of the CIA; George Moore from the FBI; and Colonel John Downie of Defense. The focus of the IEC, it was decided, would be on "intelligence in the possession of the United States Government respecting revolutionary terrorist activities in the United States and to evaluate this intelligence to determine (a) the severity of the problem and (b) what form the Federal response to the problem identified should take."

Underlying this "evaluative" aspect of the committee, however, was a firm desire to reinstate the ill-fated Huston Plan. This was made clear in one of the committee's first publications, an unsigned memorandum for Mitchell, Haldeman, and Ehrlichman. "All those who have been involved in the project," the January 19, 1971, memo began, "firmly believe that the starting point for an effective domestic intelligence operation should be the implementation of the Special Report of the Interagency Committee on Intelligence."

Several days after the memo was issued, NSA began preparing a memorandum of its own on the contributions it was prepared to make to the IEC. Entitled "NSA Contribution to Domestic Intelligence," the top secret, eyes only memo was addressed to Attorney General Mitchell and Secretary of Defense Melvin Laird and was signed by Gayler. Under "Scope" the January 26 memorandum listed: "Intelligence bearing on: (1) Criminal activity, including drugs (2) Foreign support or foreign basing of subversive activity (3) Presidential and related protection." The source of the intelligence was to be "telecommunications with at least one foreign terminal." And the procedures included:

1. Compartmented reporting to FBI or BNDD for criminal activity, to FBI and CIA for foreign-related subversive activity, and to the Secret Service for Presidential protection.
2. No indication of origin.
3. No evidential or other public use under any circumstances.
4. Screening at source (NSA) to insure compliance with the above criteria.

The memo concluded with the comment "It is further understood that NSA will insure full availability of all relevant SIGINT material by competent and informed representation in the Justice working group."

A week later, Buffham hand-carried the memo to Laird's office, passed it to the Secretary's military assistant, and received it back a few minutes later with the comment that Secretary Laird had read and agreed with it. That same day, at five minutes past noon, he entered Mitchell's office, showed him the document, and departed about five minutes later.

For the first time, NSA had formally revealed its watch list operation to higher authority; ironically, though, the memorandum was written in the future, not the past or present tense.

Just as the Huston-sponsored ICI was a front-door approach to the initiation of a virtually unrestricted domestic espionage program, the Dean-sponsored IEC, in Hoover's view, was a back-door approach to the same problem. The FBI director wasted no time in informing IEC chairman Mardian that the Bureau would refuse to supply staff support to the committee, a prospect that worried Mardian enough to make him warn the Attorney General that they might as well close up shop without it. Eventually Hoover did send over two analysts, but they were little more than tokens.

Given Hoover's truculent attitude toward any effort designed to bring down barriers on domestic collection, Gayler, Tordella, and Buffham saw little hope in the IEC as the vehicle to bring the FBI back into the business of diplomatic break-ins and embassy buggings. The only avenue left was a direct appeal to the Attorney General.

With Helms along for support, Gayler met with Mitchell on March 29, 1971, and explained that the NSA was "most desirous" of having the black-bag coverage resumed. Hoover, who was also at the meeting, then turned to the two intelligence chiefs and told them that he "was not at all enthusiastic about such an extension of operations insofar as the FBI was concerned in view of the hazards involved."

Mitchell had known of the NSA-FBI feud for some time now. Earlier that year, on February 5, he had mentioned it at a meeting of the President's Foreign Intelligence Advisory Board (PFIAB). When questioned about increasing electronic surveillance on foreign embassies, the Attorney General told the group "that NSA and FBI Director Hoover are having a running battle on this very point." He added that "NSA is also urging resumption of physical entry." Then, in defense, Mitchell commented, "We have more taps on now than when the Republicans came to Washington."

Once Hoover said his piece during the meeting in Mitchell's office, the AG asked both Helms and Gayler to prepare "an in-depth examination" of exactly what the two wanted. After reading the report, he said, he would reconvene the group "and make the decision as to what could or could not be done."

Although no record exists of the Helms-Gayler report or the outcome of Mitchell's decision, CIA director Helms did eventually propose to Hoover a very sensitive bugging operation against a specific embassy, quite possibly that of South Vietnam. But a week later Hoover once again rejected it. A few hours later Helms sent a letter to Mitchell, requesting that Hoover be overruled, and the following day he received a positive response. Within two days the bugging equipment had arrived at FBI headquarters from the CIA, and over the course of three weeks, beginning on April 27, the FBI bagmen installed it. On May 18 the CIA was informed that the bugs "were tested and all were working." Hoover at long last had suffered a defeat.

Helms, however, had not heard the last from the old G-man. In early February 1972, the CIA was informed that Hoover was about to testify in Congress and planned to tell the congressmen that the bugging operation had been initiated at the request of the CIA. The agency immediately requested that the operation be halted.

Ten months later, on the eve of a massive bombing campaign against Hanoi and Haiphong, the CIA asked the Bureau to reinstate coverage of the embassy. But by December 20, two days after the bombs began dropping and twelve days after the CIA asked for the coverage to be renewed, the FBI still had not acted. As a result, the State Department sent its own request to the Bureau, asking that it "institute all possible coverage" of the target. Finally, two days later, coverage was partly re-established, and by December 26, the day after Christmas, all the bugs were back in working order.

FISSURES

Physically, the Puzzle Palace is protected by a moat of steel, high-voltage electricity, and barbed wire, but this is little more than window dressing. Its real protection is an invisible fourth barrier, a wall more formidable than all of the Cyclone fences and armed guards in Washington put together. It is a wall of anonymity, of mystery, and of silence, and it has seldom been breached.

Since first erected in front of MI-8 and the Black Chamber, the wall has managed to hide from public view not only almost all activities and details concerning the NSA and its predecessors, but, for their first four decades, until 1958, any official confirmation that such an agency existed at all. Even in the late 1950s, when NSA's name at last appeared in an official, unclassified government document, its listed functions were simply a vacuous cover story. Until then its name, the identity of its director, and even its existence were considered more sensitive than top secret and were known only to a handful in government.

Even today one can find more public information on the Soviet KGB, the NSA's closest competitor in terms of size in the world of espionage, than on the NSA itself. Harrison E. Salisbury, for nearly forty years an editor and foreign and domestic correspondent for the *New York Times,* candidly admitted that during most of his long career he himself had never even heard of the Agency. "I should have," he confessed. "So should every American. This is the behemoth of U.S. security outfits . . . In many ways it makes the CIA and the FBI look like country cousins."

The Pulitzer Prize–winning journalist, who learned of the Agency only after discovering that for decades it had been reading his cables and monitoring his communications, added that he was hardly alone in his surprise: "Those initials are not exactly your household acronym. If I ask my neighbor what is the country's biggest security agency, he will say the CIA or the FBI. He will be wrong. The National Security Agency is the biggest, and not one American in 10,000 has even heard its name."

It is only slightly less than extraordinary that in a nation that has turned investigative journalism into an art form, where the government is dissected daily by an army of news-hungry media people, and that boasts of having the most informed populace in the world, only one person in ten thousand has ever heard of its largest and most expensive spy agency. Such is the effectiveness of NSA's wall of anonymity.

Just as the most enduring architecture is the product of great amounts of time and craftsmanship, so too is the wall surrounding the Puzzle Palace. Its foundation is built on granitelike statutes, like the COMINT law, considered by many to be the American equivalent of Britain's harsh Official Secrets Act, and Public Law 86–36, the amazing, little-known loophole that virtually excludes NSA from the burden of the Freedom of Information Act and allows the Agency to almost deny its own existence. Some Washington wags have been known to say the initials stand for No Such Agency; those inside the wall have another definition: Never Say Anything.

Resting on the foundation is what NSA refers to as its "policy of anonymity," a sort of reverse public relations plan, under which employees are forbidden from saying any more about their jobs than that they work for the Department of Defense. It is probably the only agency in government without a public information officer; the few inquiries received are simply met with a brisk "no comment." So pervasive is the policy that even officials in other government departments generally refer to the Agency in hushed tones, and then only when necessary.

But perhaps the most important element in the wall's construction is a large underpinning of mystic ritual and superstition. Few aspects of America's military and diplomatic past conjure up as much intrigue and romance as codebreaking. The Zimmermann telegram, the Black Chamber, the breaking of the Japanese Purple code, the Battle of Midway, Magic, Ultra — they lend an almost supernatural aura to the field, an aura hardly in keeping with today's computerized supercodes and vacuum cleaner approach to private and commercial microwave interception, but one that the NSA wants people still to believe in.

For decades the NSA has managed to elude anything vaguely resembling close congressional scrutiny, or even a journalistic peek, by spreading out its black cloak of codes and ciphers and repeating the warning that the slightest inquiry could gravely jeopardize America's fragile cryptologic efforts. The real fear, however, is not that of compromising "the American code," which, in a sense, is changed thousands of times a second, but of revealing the existence of such massive illegal operations as Shamrock and Minaret. After the defections of Martin and Mitchell, for example, Chairman Walter made it clear that, although his House Un-American Activities Committee intended to investigate the circumstances surrounding the affair, it would conscientiously keep its eyes averted from all activities of the Agency while doing so:

> The specific functions of the National Security Agency and the role they play in the security of the United States are so highly sensitive that they are carefully guarded, not only from the public, but from other Government agencies as well.
>
> The sensitive nature of the operation of the National Security Agency was recognized and respected by the Committee on Un-American Activities during its investigation and hearings. The committee did not attempt to learn the details of the organizational structure or the products of the Agency, feeling it had no need for knowledge in these areas.

David Kahn, for many years the only outsider skillful enough to snatch a glimpse over the wall, commented on NSA's constant attempts to play on Congress' fear and ignorance. In *The Codebreakers* he wrote, "Often the agency enshrouds its secrets in fearful gloom, awing Congressmen with sacred mysteries that are no more to be uttered than is the tetragrammaton."

For more than fifty years the wall of anonymity NSA inherited stood with only the slightest of cracks, represented by Yardley's book and the defections of the early 1960s, but even those originated mainly inside. As the 1970s began, however, a number of unprecedented attacks threatened not only to shake the wall to its foundation, but actually to send it tumbling down on those within. The first fissure appeared on June 13, 1971, when the *New York Times* started publishing excerpts from a top secret history of U.S. decision-making in the Vietnam War: the Pentagon Papers.

In the White House, President Nixon, already nearly consumed with paranoia over earlier leaks, viewed the breach of security with concern and anger. Compounding his distress was the news from the FBI that one of its most important national security informers, a turncoat KGB agent working for the United Nations in New York, had informed them that a complete set of the Papers had been passed to the Soviet embassy. Although the agent, code-named Fedora and said to be Soviet diplomat Victor Lessiovski, had been reporting to the FBI for more than a decade, some in the intelligence community, particularly the CIA, questioned his bona fides. CIA spy hunter James Angleton, for example, believed the Russian to be an *agent provocateur* rather than an authentic informer, an opinion the FBI rejected but years later would agree with.

Where Nixon was furious over the leak of the Papers, officials at the Puzzle Palace were stunned and horrified. If the Russians had, in fact, obtained their own set of the Papers, then along with them may have gone the key to one of NSA's most prized, as well as most secret, intelligence sources.

Code-named Gamma Gupy, the operation involved eavesdropping on Soviet government leaders by intercepting their scrambled radiotelephone conversations as they traveled around Moscow in their limousines. It was accomplished, apparently, from the American embassy by an Army Security Agency unit, USM-2. Once captured, the intercepts would be stamped TOP SECRET VIPAR GAMMA GUPY and transmitted back to the Puzzle Palace for unscrambling.

One former intelligence official who had access to the transcripts described the system as one of the most valuable intelligence pipelines the United States had in the Soviet Union. Among the conversations being read in the Agency were those of party boss Leonid Brezhnev, President Nikolai Podgorny, and Premier Alexei Kosygin. Although the Russian officials were wise enough not to speak of high-level strategic affairs over the minimum-security phone system, Gamma Gupy "gave us extremely valuable information on the personalities and health of top Soviet leaders," the former intelligence officer declared. "But we didn't find out about, say, the invasion of Czechoslovakia. It was very gossipy — Brezhnev's health and maybe Podgorny's sex life."

What started teeth rattling at NSA was that some of Brezhnev's conversations had been referred to, without their origin being identified, in one of the volumes that was reported to have been given to the Soviet embassy but was never printed in the *Times.*

The fears seemed to be confirmed when, immediately after the Papers were reported to be in Russian hands, the intercepts became much more mundane. The intelligence experts speculated that the Soviet Union had deduced the United States capability and had sent warnings to its top officials.

While possibly the most serious problem, Gamma Gupy was not the only worry. Peppered throughout the forty-seven-volume study, NSA officials believed, were numerous other references that could tip off foreign governments, particularly that of North Vietnam, that their communications were being intercepted and their codes broken.

Even before the Pentagon Papers, the subject of leaks to the press had become white hot in the Nixon White House; now with the latest spectacular revelations, lead was beginning to melt. The administration, the President decided, would begin an immediate counterattack on two fronts, one through the courts and the other, much less visible, with a small unit later to become known as the plumbers.

The opening shot on the legal front was fired shortly after the first excerpts began rolling off the presses. The Department of Justice applied for and received a temporary restraining order, halting any further publication of the documents until a hearing before a federal judge could determine whether future publication should be permanently banned.

For the hearing, Pentagon general counsel J. Fred Buzhardt recruited what he felt were three of his biggest guns to testify about the validity of the top secret classification of the documents. The only problem was that two of them had never even read the material, and the third was not considered a very good witness to begin with. It was a distressing situation for Michael Hess, the assistant U.S. Attorney who was about to argue the case for the government.

Surprised by Hess's reaction, Buzhardt reluctantly began to speak of another possible witness, one who could most authoritatively address the matter of the sensitivity of the Pentagon Papers — but there was a catch. Because not only the identity of the witness was considered top secret but even the agency he represented, the only way his testimony could be taken would be for him to be closeted in a private room with no one else present except the judge.

After Hess said that was impossible because it violated every rule of judicial procedure, Buzhardt suggested that his secret witness submit a sealed affidavit exclusively for the judge's eyes. Again Hess had to remind the Pentagon lawyer that the *Times* had just as much right to any statements introduced in court as it did to cross-examine a witness.

"Then we can't do anything," an angry Buzhardt shot back. "It is such a secret matter that it must be given to the judge alone."

As Hess surmised, and as Buzhardt years later confirmed, the only official capable of commanding such intense cloak-and-dagger secrecy was Vice Admiral Noel Gayler, director of the Puzzle Palace.

There was still more to worry about than revelation of NSA's codebreaking successes. Scattered throughout the documents were numerous verbatim copies of classified and previously encrypted messages,

complete with date-time-groups; that is, the series of numbers identifying the exact time and date the message was sent. The fear was that
once the plain text of the messages was revealed, an adversary might
be able to compare them to intercepted encrypted versions, one of
the oldest techniques in cryptanalysis, and thereby break the code.

Such a problem had been anticipated by the *Times*. To help resolve
the dilemma, the newspaper brought on as a consultant David Kahn,
who assured them that any injury to American cryptographic systems
would be negligible.

Another argument to be used should the government decide to
bring up the matter of codes was that of the congressional hearings
into the loss of the U.S.S. *Pueblo,* the ill-fated SIGINT spy ship captured by North Korea. Contained in the unclassified transcript of
the hearings, and open to the public, are almost a dozen once-classi-
fied messages that, like those in the Pentagon Papers, were completely
unaltered and unparaphrased and contained the original date-time-
group.

Once the hearing was under way, Judge Murray Gurfein, himself
a World War II veteran of the OSS, brought the issue of codes to
life when he spoke of his concern about the lack of paraphrasing
for the messages. Alexander M. Bickel, the Yale Law School professor
who was representing the *Times,* attempted to allay the judge's concern
by arguing that there had never been an allegation by the government
that "anything the *Times* put in print broke a code, compromised a
code, came within five miles of an existing code." But Gurfein was
still not convinced. Looking at Bickel, he exclaimed: "Neither you
nor I nor the *New York Times* is competent to pass on that subject,
as to what will lead to the breaking of a code."

Bickel then raised the argument that "the security of codes is insured
by their being changed with extreme rapidity in very short order."
But Gurfein brushed aside the argument, saying that the history of
the Vietnam conflict could be discussed "without reprinting verbatim
a code message."

The debate, until now in open session, became *in camera* when
the sensitive subject of codes came up again, Gurfein still expressing
unease over release of the messages in unparaphrased form. But after
more squabbling, the issue was at last buried when Vice Admiral
Francis J. Blouin, deputy chief of Naval Operations and one of the
government's three main witnesses, rose from his seat. "Judge Gurfein," the decorated veteran of three wars said, "you and I are probably the only people in this room old enough to remember when verbatim texts compromised a code." Bickel was smiling from ear to ear.

"The security of the Nation is not at the ramparts alone. Security also lies in the value of our free institutions. A cantankerous press, an ubiquitous press must be suffered by those in authority in order to preserve the even greater values of freedom of expression and the right of the people to know." With those eloquent words Judge Gurfein, on June 19, 1971, decided the historic case in favor of the *Times,* though continuing the restraining order to give the government time to appeal.

At the Puzzle Palace the decision caused fear and gloom. It was an outcome dreaded by Director Gayler, but one that he had recognized as a possibility and for which he had already established a contingency plan.

On the Saturday morning the decision was released, the ink had hardly dried when Buzhardt informed Whitney North Seymour, Jr., the U.S. Attorney for New York City who had argued the case, that a high official from the NSA by the name of Milton Zaslow wanted to meet quietly with someone from the upper management of the *Times* to discuss certain security matters. Zaslow, a former chief of B Group, had taken over from Benson K. Buffham the choice post of Deputy Assistant Director for Production. As the top civilian in PROD, just below Major General John E. Morrison, Jr., chief of the Production Organization, Zaslow was the Agency's second-highest professional cryptologist, second only to Deputy Director Tordella. "Milton was the most powerful civilian there; he was Gayler's right-hand man," said one former NSA official. "Gayler wouldn't poop without him."

Seymour passed on the request to *Times* attorney Bickel, who was apprehensive about such a meeting, fearing NSA might attempt to trap the newspaper by telling it something and then prohibiting it from responding or even revealing what was said. Nevertheless, the *Times* agreed to the meeting, and it was decided that Vice Chairman Harding Bancroft would represent the paper, because he had at one time held a sensitive security clearance when he worked at the State Department, and NSA had requested someone with such a clearance.

In order to waste as little time as possible, the meeting was first scheduled for the next day, Sunday, but was later changed to Monday afternoon at three. When it turned out that Seymour's office in the Federal Building was not secure enough for Zaslow, the U.S. Attorney suggested a small, private, out-of-the-way room in a building occupied by the Bar Association of New York. The building had the added advantage of allowing Zaslow to enter from one side and Bancroft to enter from another.

Zaslow, a rather short, pudgy-faced man with thick, wavy, black hair, reportedly arrived wearing a pistol strapped across his chest and accompanied by a security agent from M5 wearing two revolvers at his sides. The melodrama gave one *Times* official the impression that the two had been sent over by central casting for a remake of *Gang Busters.* After an introduction, Seymour left Bancroft and Zaslow alone in the room and waited outside, along with the M5 agent and a *Times* lawyer.

Once they were alone, Zaslow wasted no time in saying why he was there: he wanted the *Times* to agree to delete from the Pentagon Papers anything that might alert foreign governments to the fact that their communications systems had been penetrated. This meant that any information regarding successes, the means employed in interception, or any reference to time of interceptions was to be strictly excised. The necessary deletions could be made, Zaslow said, if the *Times* agreed not to print details that would reveal intelligence sources, that would identify specific movements of North Vietnamese troops or supplies, or that in any way referred to a specific intercept.

Bancroft, to Zaslow's relief, saw no problem in abiding by the guidelines but pointed out that an editor might occasionally have some difficulty in certain gray areas. Recognizing that possibility, Zaslow offered Bancroft both his NSA and home numbers to call for assistance if the need arose, but cautioned that he would have to get an OK from his superiors and pointed out that only two or three other people even knew of this meeting.

After the meeting, Zaslow and his security agent headed back to Fort Meade, and Bancroft returned to the *Times,* where he reported his conversation and received assurances that the documents had already been edited with NSA's considerations in mind.

•

If the Russians had not learned of Gamma Gupy through the pages of a purloined copy of the Pentagon Papers, they definitely knew about it three months later after reading the September 16, 1971, *Washington Post.* Tucked into the top right-hand corner of page F7, Jack Anderson's "Washington Merry-Go-Round" column confirmed what the Kremlin may have already suspected. Without indicating exactly how the conversations are intercepted, Anderson reported on the government's ability to eavesdrop on "the kingpins of the Kremlin." He told of transcripts indicating that Brezhnev "sometimes drinks too much vodka and suffers from hangovers," and that Kosygin "is in poor health, and his complaints are more authentic," and that they both frequent a private clinic to get their aches soothed.

This compromise of COMINT reverberated like a sonic boom throughout the upper reaches of the intelligence community as well as the White House. Not knowing how much more damning information Anderson had up his sleeve, and hoping to build a firewall against any further damage, DCI Helms quietly invited the columnist to lunch and pleaded with him not to divulge the means by which the interception was made or ever again refer to the project.

In defense, Anderson insisted that his original source had told him that the Russians already realized their phone traffic was being monitored (possibly through their own set of Pentagon Papers), but he agreed not to mention any further details of the system. He specifically promised not to allude to the operation in his book, *The Anderson Papers.*

Despite his numerous defeats in the courts over the Pentagon Papers — first in the district court, then in the appeals court, and finally in the Supreme Court — Richard Nixon remained in the battle. Shortly after the Papers first appeared in the *New York Times,* Nixon called John Ehrlichman to his office and instructed him to form a White House Special Investigations Unit with the sole purpose of plugging up the administration's security leaks. Ehrlichman picked his assistant, Bud Krogh, and former Kissinger aide David Young for the assignment. To round off the four-man unit, Krogh and Young turned to G. Gordon Liddy, a special assistant to the Secretary of the Treasury for organized crime who spent most of his time preaching the virtues of gun ownership throughout the government, and E. Howard Hunt, a former CIA spook with a so-so track record who was now an employee of a Washington public relations firm working as a consultant to Nixon hatchetman Charles Colson on anti-Kennedy propaganda. Operating out of Room 16 on the first floor of the White House, the plumbers were a study in right-wing mania, and their chief target was Pentagon Papers' leaker Daniel Ellsberg.

To drum up support for their cabal, Liddy crashed a staff meeting of the secret Justice Department Intelligence Evaluation Committee (IEC) and told the members, including the NSA representative, that his unit had been set up because of the President's deep concern over the many leaks and that "the President wants this sort of thing stopped." He went on to explain that his role in the plumbers' unit was as an "expediter," with the responsibility "to break down bureaucratic problems by applying either grease or dynamite." Despite Liddy's bravado, the secretary of the meeting recorded that "Mr. David Young can speak for Mr. Ehrlichman and is 'heavier' than Mr. Liddy; therefore, any requests from Mr. Young should be honored without checking with Liddy."

Liddy also told the August 4, 1971, gathering that he "intends to use the Staff members for direct and rapid access to their own Agencies in order to get over and minimize bureaucratic problems." He added that, although each agency would be officially charged through its respective head, "Mr. Ehrlichman was not prepared to wait until agencies had polished their contributions and sent them back through channels, but rather wanted to have access to information when and as it is developed." Liddy, therefore, according to a summary of his remarks at the meeting, expected "to be able to ask for things," from NSA as well as the other intelligence agencies, "through the IES [Intelligence Evaluation Staff] members and have them vested with the authority to get them and release them to the White House." To make sure the members took their new responsibilities seriously, Liddy informed them that he would sit with the IEC staff and audit the full IEC meetings.

Thus Liddy installed an underground pipe direct from the back door of the Puzzle Palace, as well as the rest of the intelligence community, via the secret IEC staff to the plumbers' unit. What, if anything, flowed through that pipe from NSA is unknown. What is known, though, is that during the investigations that followed the Watergate break-in, one of the arguments put forth by the White House, in an effort to limit inquiry into the plumbers' unit, was that continued investigation might endanger an operation involving codebreaking and COMINT. To this day there is still at least one plumbers' mission that has never been declassified or revealed.

•

As the fissure created by the Pentagon Papers was sending tremors through the Puzzle Palace, several other hairline cracks were beginning to form.

On a cold day in the preceding December, a federal grand jury in Detroit handed out secret indictments against fifteen members of the radical Weatherman organization, a militant faction of the left-wing Students for a Democratic Society (SDS). The group, which included such revolutionary superstars as Bernardine Dohrn, Mark Rudd, and William Ayers, were charged with plotting a campaign of bombing and terrorism during a Weatherman "war council" in Flint, Michigan, a year earlier, in 1969.

The indictments set off a massive hunt by the FBI, which placed Dohrn on the ten-most-wanted list and forced most members of the group to go underground. During mid-1971, as the White House began putting more pressure on the federal law enforcement and intelligence community to crack down on radicals, the FBI and the

Secret Service added the Weathermen to their NSA watch lists. In short order they began receiving copies of communications to, from, or about members of the group, communications that had been intercepted by the Puzzle Palace.

By the summer of 1973, four of the militants had been captured and began standing trial. Ironically, that same summer the administration also went on trial as the Senate Watergate Committee took center stage.

In the Puzzle Palace, Lou Tordella, who as deputy director and chief mason of NSA's wall of anonymity for the past fifteen years, was worried. He knew the Agency's fingerprints were on many questionable activities and that the committee had the scent of blood. When committee chairman Sam Ervin pounded his gavel on the first morning of public hearings, Tordella could see the outline of yet another new fissure.

On June 7, 1973, the fissure broke through. That morning the *New York Times* revealed for the first time the existence of the Huston Plan and published its full text, including the revelation that NSA was "currently" monitoring international communications and wanted restrictions lifted on embassy black-bag jobs "to permit procurement of vitally needed foreign cryptographic material." Nevertheless, because the plan was so broad and revealed such a wide spectrum of illegal activities by the whole intelligence community, only a small amount of attention was directed at the Puzzle Palace.

But out of public view, as a side effect of the Watergate hearings, another pressure was threatening to send the wall tumbling. Shortly before the Huston Plan became known, lawyers representing the Weathermen, then on trial in Detroit, took a shot in the dark. Knowing the propensity of such groups as the plumbers to engage in buggings and burglaries, and hoping to find some evidence of governmental misconduct against their clients, the attorneys filed a motion requesting disclosure of all illegal federal surveillance directed against the defendants. This included any and all use of burglary, sabotage, electronic surveillance, *agents provocateurs,* or other "espionage techniques" against their clients by the White House plumbers, CIA, NSA, and the Departments of Justice, Treasury, and Defense.

On June 5, Federal District Court Judge Damon J. Keith approved the motion and ordered the agencies to comply. Two days later, Assistant U.S. Attorney William C. Ibershof returned to court to ask for reconsideration of the motion, saying, mysteriously, that "there were other considerations" involved, but refusing to elaborate. The plea rejected, Ibershof later that month offered an affidavit by the FBI absolving itself of any illegal or "unauthorized" activity in investigating the Weathermen. As to the other agencies, said Ibershof: "The Government doesn't believe this is a proper forum for a trial of Government misconduct."

Judge Keith was unimpressed. Calling the denial a "perfunctory" response that "failed to go to the crux of the matter," he ordered the prosecution to produce, by September 3, "sworn statements from a person or persons with full knowledge of the actions of each specified group or agency" and set for later a hearing on the question of whether any of the evidence had been "tainted" by the government.

The order rocked the NSA. A public affidavit by the Agency admitting the interceptions would expose the Minaret and Shamrock operations as well as the watch list procedure. Compliance was unthinkable. On August 28, therefore, NSA officials at last informed Assistant Attorney General Henry Petersen of the problem, telling him that communications involving the Weathermen defendants had been intercepted, but strongly opposing "any disclosure of this technique and program."

By the time Lieutenant General Lew Allen, Jr., took charge on August 15, the Puzzle Palace seemed under siege. Abandoned by the CIA to carry on alone the illegal BNDD drug-targeting program, the Agency, fearing exposure, had reluctantly dropped the project in June. Now that its once-impregnable wall of secrecy was further threatened by court scrutiny, it decided to bury the evidence. Although the Agency ordinarily keeps its material for at least five years, the decision was made in late August or early September to destroy everything related to the drug operation — not only the product, but all internal memoranda and administrative documents. By the middle of September not a single piece of paper remained to link the Puzzle Palace to the operation.

The immediate problem now was how to handle Judge Keith.

Following his eye-opening meeting on August 28 with NSA officials, Assistant Attorney General Petersen, on September 4, notified Attorney General Elliot Richardson of the operation, "of which we had no previous knowledge." In the meantime, prosecutors asked for an extension of time on the judge's order for sworn statements from the various agencies, citing the court's unusual requirement for affidavits from sensitive federal agencies not under Justice Department jurisdiction.

The continuance granted, Petersen next directed a memorandum to FBI director Clarence M. Kelley, requesting to be advised by September 10 of "the extent of the FBI's practice of requesting information intercepted by the NSA concerning domestic organizations or persons for intelligence, prosecutorial, or any other purposes." In addition, Petersen wanted Kelley's thoughts on how NSA's intercept program was affected by the decision in a relevant case, *United States* v. *United States District Court* (commonly known as the *Keith* case) handed down more than a year earlier. In the *Keith* decision, the Supreme Court, while recognizing the President's constitutional duty to "protect our Government against those who would subvert or overthrow it by unlawful means," held that the power inherent in such a duty does not extend to the authorization of warrantless electronic surveillance deemed necessary to protect the nation from subversion by *domestic* organizations. Still at issue, however, was whether the Executive has the constitutional power to authorize electronic surveillance without a warrant in cases involving the activities of *foreign* powers or agents.

Because Minaret did entail warrantless electronic surveillance against some domestic organizations, including the Weathermen, *Keith* appeared to cast doubts on the legality of the operation, unless it could be shown that the groups were acting in concert with a foreign power.

On September 10 Kelley responded, informing Petersen that the FBI had requested intelligence from NSA "concerning organizations and individuals who are known to be involved in illegal and violent activities aimed at the destruction and overthrow of the United States Government." With regard to *Keith,* the FBI director engaged in semantic somersaults: "We do not believe that the NSA actually participated in any electronic surveillance, per se, of the defendants for any other agency of the government, since under the procedures used by that agency *they are unaware of the identity of any group or individual* which might be included in the recovery of national security intelligence information." (Emphasis supplied.)

Kelley seemed to have conveniently forgotten that the FBI and the other agencies had, in fact, submitted to NSA those very names and identities as part of the watch lists.

Petersen next advised Richardson that the current number of individuals and organizations on NSA watch lists submitted by the FBI was "in excess of 600" and warned of the numerous legal problems involved. He recommended that

the FBI and Secret Service be immediately advised to cease and desist requesting NSA to disseminate to them information concerning individuals and organizations obtained through NSA electronic coverage and that NSA should be informed not to disclose voluntarily such information to Secret Service or the FBI unless NSA has picked up the information on its own initiative in pursuit of its foreign intelligence mission.

Four days earlier, on September 17, NSA director Allen had decided himself to warn the FBI and the other watch list agencies of the "ever-increasing pressures for disclosure of sources by the Congress, the courts, and the press." Adding "Naturally I am concerned ultimately for the protection of highly vulnerable SIGINT sources," Allen asked each watch list supplier to "review the current list your agency has filed with us in order to satisfy yourself regarding the appropriateness of its contents."

After reviewing the Petersen memorandum, Attorney General Richardson, on October 1, directed FBI director Kelley and the Secret Service to cease requesting information obtained by NSA by means of electronic surveillance and also requested that his approval be sought before either agency renewed requests to the NSA for foreign intelligence or counterespionage information.

Then he turned to General Allen. "It has recently come to my attention for the first time," Richardson wrote, "that your Agency is disseminating to the Federal Bureau of Investigation and the Secret Service information obtained by NSA by means of electronic surveillance." Citing the *Keith* decision, he indicated that he found the watch list activity to be of questionable legality, and requested that NSA "immediately curtail the further dissemination" of watch list information to the FBI and Secret Service, although "relevant information acquired by you in the routine pursuit of the collection of foreign intelligence information may continue to be furnished to appropriate Government agencies."

Three days later Allen responded, saying that he had "directed that no further information be disseminated to the FBI and Secret Service pending advice on legal issues." As might be expected, he made no effort to inform the Attorney General that the Agency had, only four months earlier, abandoned an even more questionable eavesdropping operation, the BNDD drug-targeting program. Nor did he happen to mention that the Agency was continuing an operation that was almost certainly illegal — Shamrock.

Meanwhile, as Allen, Richardson, and Petersen were exchanging worried notes, the prosecution in Detroit was in a shambles. On September 12, U.S. Attorney Ralph B. Guy, Jr., notified Judge Keith that the government wished to submit for *in camera* inspection an affidavit from an unspecified federal agency. After pointing out that the interception referred to in the affidavit involved a sensitive national security matter and had no effect on the prosecution of the case, Guy then shocked attorneys for the Weathermen by declaring that if the court ruled that the affidavit must also be shown to the defense, then the government would request return of the document and "the liberty to exercise their option to dismiss the proceedings." But after consideration, the prosecution decided that even this was too dangerous an option, and on October 15, as Judge Keith was still considering the *in camera* issue, the government threw in the towel and moved to dismiss the case without argument, rather than risk exposure of NSA's involvement.

Once again the NSA managed to remain unseen, but the cost of maintaining its wall of anonymity was growing very expensive. Not only had the Justice Department been forced to drop a case it had spent almost three years building, but for the first time an Attorney General had become involved in an Agency operation — and his reaction had been decidedly unenthusiastic. Closer to home, the Puzzle Palace was again forced to drop an operation; Minaret was terminated shortly after the confrontation with Richardson.

•

No one knew the high cost of anonymity better than Lou Tordella. As deputy director for the past fifteen years — so long a tenure was unheard of in the intelligence community — the lanky, soft-spoken mathematician had led the fight to keep the letters N-S-A from the pages of the *New York Times* and the lips of Walter Cronkite. It was his trowel that would apply mortar to the slightest crack in the wall and his sword that would send inquisitors scurrying. Where a magician might be able to make a rabbit disappear, Tordella made an entire federal agency disappear.

But the times were slowly changing. The buffeting by the courts and the Attorney General had taken the shine from his sword; even dulled it a bit. Worse, the once lip-sealing incantation "national security" had been stripped of much of its magic by the Senate Watergate Committee. Even the all-powerful chant "codes and ciphers" had been shown to be somewhat hollow by the Pentagon Papers case. Tordella was running out of mortar.

He was also running out of time. Shortly after the scuttling of Minaret, the sixty-two-year-old master cryptologist announced his plans to retire, effective December 31, 1973, but agreed to remain on the job until a successor was chosen. That happened on April 21, 1974, when Benson K. Buffham was selected to become deputy. One month earlier, on March 22, during ceremonies held quietly at the Pentagon, Tordella became the seventeenth person to receive the coveted National Security Medal.* Since it was first established by executive order in 1953, only three other NSA officials have received the top intelligence award: SIS founders William F. Friedman and Frank B. Rowlett; the Agency's first vice director, Joseph N. Wenger; and, in ceremonies on February 23, 1981, former director Bobby Inman.

Although retired, Tordella followed the pattern set by many senior Agency officials and simply turned around and became an NSA consultant. The number of such transitions once led an Agency old hand to observe, "Old NSA officials never die; they simply become consultants."

Known as "Buff" to his old friends in PROD, Benson Buffham started out, like many others in the business, with the Army Security Agency shortly after the start of World War II. He then spent most of his career working his way up in the Production Organization and became its deputy chief in the mid-1960s. During the early Nixon years he represented the Agency on such dubious committees as the Interagency Committee on Intelligence and the Intelligence Evaluation Committee. In 1971 he was appointed deputy director for Plans and Programs and was replaced in PROD by the gun-toting Milton Zaslow.

Along with his corner office next to the director on Mahogany Row, Buffham also inherited Tordella's trowel and sword. Neither was needed, however; the assaults that were so frequent in the early part of the decade appeared to have ceased. But the calm was deceiving. On December 22, 1974, hairline cracks again began forming in the protective wall surrounding the Puzzle Palace.

On that day, Seymour Hersh lifted the lid on intelligence abuses when he reported in the *New York Times* details of Operation Chaos, the supersecret and highly illegal CIA spying program directed against Americans. The storm of outrage that followed sent Congress screaming for investigations and the spook community running for cover.

Hoping to blunt any Capitol Hill offensive and at the same time show token concern over the abuses, President Gerald R. Ford, on January 4, 1975, set up a milktoast commission headed by Vice President Nelson A. Rockefeller. The Commission on CIA Activities Within the United States, better known as the Rockefeller Commission, gave the CIA a one-eyed lookover. The seriousness and vigor of the com-

* Among the other winners were General Walter Bedell Smith, J. Edgar Hoover, General William Donovan, Ambassador Robert Murphy, Allen Dulles, John McCone, Admiral William Raborn, Desmond FitzGerald, Arthur Lundahl, and Lawrence R. Houston. ("Dr. Louis W. Tordella Honored with National Security Medal," *National Security Agency Newsletter* [April 1974], p. 4.)

mission was demonstrated by one member, former governor Ronald Reagan, who, after leaving before the conclusion of the opening session, managed to miss three of the next four weekly meetings. Busy stumping the rubber-chicken circuit, he could not afford even a visit to commission headquarters for more than a month after the panel's creation.

Focusing on the narrow issue of whether or not the CIA had violated specific laws, the commission left the Puzzle Palace almost untouched. On the few occasions where the CIA and the NSA operations overlapped, the final report simply glossed over the issues. In a brief paragraph devoted to the watch list program, the NSA was obliquely referred to as "an international communications activity of another agency of the government." On another occasion, referring to CIA support of the NSA drug watch list operation, the commission wrongly reported that "the Director and other CIA officials instructed involved personnel to collect only foreign intelligence and to make no attempt — either within the United States or abroad — to gather information on American citizens allegedly trafficking in narcotics." As the Senate Intelligence Committee later discovered, the CIA had, in fact, directly targeted American citizens on the drug watch list for the NSA.

Less kindly disposed toward the Puzzle Palace was the select committee set up in the House, under New York Democrat Otis Pike, with a mandate to look into the whole intelligence community.

As a starting point in its brief examination of NSA, the committee requested the Agency's "charter," National Security Council Intelligence Directive No. 6. Immediately, there was resistance. When Albert C. Hall, an assistant secretary of defense and the Pentagon's intelligence czar, showed up before the committee on August 7, 1975, minus the NSCID, Pike exploded. "It seems incredible to me, very frankly," he said, "that we are asked to appropriate large amounts of money for that agency which employs large numbers of people without being provided a copy of the piece of paper by which the agency is authorized." The committee then voted 10 to 0 to subpoena the document.

More forthcoming was beleaguered CIA director William E. Colby when he testified the following day. Under questioning by Wisconsin Democrat Les Aspin, Colby, almost by inadvertence, let slip the first public acknowledgment of NSA's eavesdropping on international communications. Replying to Aspin, Colby agreed that NSA listens in on "communications that go abroad from the United States or are abroad."

"Does that involve American citizens on one end?" pressed Aspin.

"On some occasions," Colby admitted, "that cannot be separated from the traffic that is being monitored. It's technically impossible to separate it."

Possibly feeling he had gone too far already, Colby turned aside further questioning on the subject by saying, "I really think we would do better to discuss this in executive session."

But Colby and Hall were teasers; the main event was scheduled for August 8. At six minutes past ten o'clock on that Friday morning, a tall, bespectacled, ramrod-straight Air Force lieutenant general stood up behind the witness table and raised his right hand. For the first time in history an NSA director was about to testify publicly, before an open congressional hearing. Lew Allen, Jr., was about to give the world its first tantalizing peek into the Puzzle Palace.

After pointing out to the committee that "no director of the National Security Agency has ever before been required to come before a congressional committee in open session," Allen read a seventeen-page statement consisting mainly of a brief history of the Agency and a listing of congressional and Executive Branch studies and reports NSA had participated in. Calling the Agency's SIGINT and COMSEC operations "uniquely vulnerable to compromise," and recalling that several years earlier McGeorge Bundy, in testimony before the Senate, identified SIGINT as "one of six activities which he believed constituted 'real secrets,' " Allen concluded by requesting that all questions relating to NSA's operations be held for closed session.

It was the question-and-answer session that the administration feared the most. Just two days earlier Colby had acknowledged NSA's international eavesdropping. Hoping to avoid another such disclosure, White House emissary John O. Marsh, Jr., met with Chairman Pike only a few minutes before the session was to start and advised him that the area they were getting into "involves extremely sensitive information" and that Allen's testimony should be treated as "top national security."

Despite the White House plea, there was a brief round of questions. NSA general counsel Roy Banner, accompanying Allen, was asked whether he felt that, although wiretapping is prohibited by law, interception of telephone calls of American citizens heading overseas is not prohibited. Banner's answer: "That is correct."

During four hours in closed session in which the NSA chief was asked specifically about the Agency's eavesdropping activities, Allen consistently took the position that "at the present time" the Agency was not listening in on domestic or overseas calls placed by Americans.

But the testimony was unconvincing and caused Chairman Pike to comment "I do not fully accept that" and point to Colby's statements of the previous Wednesday.

The real problem was actually one of casuistry. The NSA has always maintained that eavesdropping occurs only when a person is "targeted," not merely when his or her communications are intercepted, even though that same nontargeted intercept may eventually be recorded, transcribed, and disseminated to other agencies.

Despite his debut before the Pike Committee, Allen knew that the real test would be in the tug of war the Agency was waging with the Senate Intelligence Committee and its chairman, Senator Frank Church. During the summer and early fall, the Church Committee had been hearing testimony in executive session from both current and former Agency officials, and the mood was growing less and less cordial. Of the witnesses to be called, probably the most sensitive was to be the chief of G Group, the organization that ran most of the Agency's domestic operations. But the current chief of G Group had been on the job for barely six months, and the Agency, feeling that he lacked the background to field the committee's tough questioning, sent him on a "panic" trip to Europe.

Six months earlier Frank Raven had retired from the Agency after heading G Group since its inception almost fifteen years before. Now Director Allen needed him back. "We have a real problem with our testimony for the Church Committee," he told Raven in a telephone call, and then asked him to appear as the witness for the questions about G Group's activities. Raven reluctantly agreed.

Throughout his thirty-five-year career in NSA and its predecessors, Frank Raven had suffered from a syndrome that remains endemic in the Puzzle Palace — a reluctance to comment on world events out of fear of inadvertently revealing information picked up through SIGINT. When conversations at social events turned to the Middle East or the latest coup in South America, he would suddenly clam up — which would inevitably provoke his wife, who called him by a family nickname, to issue the gentle admonition: "Philly, talk!"

Now, as he was getting out of his car to begin his first day before the closed Church Committee hearings, his wife issued a new admonition: "Philly, keep your damned mouth shut!"

Throughout the first day, as he sat in the rear of the hearing room waiting to be called, Raven had a chance to listen to the testimony of other NSA officials, and he was growing increasingly perturbed. "They were *hanging* NSA," he recalled. "NSA was getting deeper and deeper in trouble, and NSA didn't deserve it. They were on the defensive. Instead of trying to cooperate with the committee, and trying to find out what had happened, and who had done what, they had a chip on their shoulder and they were fighting the committee every inch of the way."

Seated at the witness table as each official was called to testify were Roy Banner and Juanita Moody, who was responsible for liaison with the rest of the intelligence community as well as the distribution of all SIGINT. "Now, as I sat there that afternoon," Raven recalled, "the guy who was the witness knew the answers to the questions that they were asking. Roy Banner and Juanita Moody *didn't*. If the guy had been permitted to give the answers — the truth — there wouldn't have been any problems . . . but the two of them [were] putting in all kinds of . . . asinine legal objections and questions and quibbling over the questions and quibbling over answers, and they didn't know what they were talking about."

Frustrated by the Agency's attempt to muzzle the witnesses, Raven, who was due to take the stand the next day, called General Allen's office and issued an ultimatum: if the Agency wanted his testimony, it first would have to issue a direct order from General Allen forbidding anyone else from NSA from speaking unless he — Raven — asked him or her for advice. He would answer all direct questions from the committee, and if he needed help or a legal opinion, he would ask for it. "I wasn't going to have staff types," said Raven, "who didn't know what my answer was going to be, cutting in and quibbling over the legal technicalities of the NSA charter and the CIA charter and such, when they had no idea of what I was going to say."

Raven got his order, and the next day neither Banner nor Moody appeared; rather, they sent assistants, who remained silent during the former G Group chief's testimony. The result, apparently, was unexpected candor. At one point, Senator Walter F. Mondale asked Raven how long he had been familiar with Operation Shamrock. "Well, you might consider me a Johnny-come-lately," he responded. "I was on the problem in 1940, and I had been off and on it since 1940." Later Raven recalled, "I thought Mondale would choke! . . . He said I was the first person he had met who would admit they had known any of these problems over five years."

In looking back on the experience, Raven believed that NSA had been wounded badly in the committee hearings primarily because it had "too defensive an attitude and [was] trying to fight the committee rather than get the truth on the table."

In early October, that fight intensified when Senator Church announced that the committee intended to hold two days of public hearings on NSA improprieties and abuses — and that among the witnesses to be called was General Allen.

On Tuesday, October 7, the day before the hearings were to begin, the administration flew into a panic and launched an intense, last-minute campaign to get the committee to halt the hearings. That morning President Ford personally telephoned Senator Church to explain the dangers of public disclosure of NSA operations. Ford then followed up the phone call by dispatching Attorney General Edward H. Levi to a closed committee meeting with a more detailed appeal. Next, Senator Barry M. Goldwater, vice chairman of the committee, proposed that the public hearings be dropped completely. The Goldwater proposal was narrowly defeated by a vote of 5 to 4. At last, against the wishes of the committee chairman, the members voted, 6 to 4, simply to "defer" the hearings, pending further meetings with administration officials.

The reprieve was brief. On October 23 the committee reversed itself and voted in favor of public hearings on NSA, to begin six days later. On October 29, accompanied by General Counsel Roy Banner and Deputy Director Benson Buffham, General Allen entered through the carved double doors of Room 318 in the Russell Senate Office Building and gave the senators, a hushed audience, and the world their first public look at an NSA SIGINT operation. So implausible was the scene that it led Allen at one point to the conclusion that by his giving public testimony he was committing a felony in violating the COMINT statute.

Allen limited NSA's *mea culpa* to the watch list program and Operation Minaret, which, he admitted, eventually had a "significantly reduced" intelligence value because of the very restrictive controls placed on the handling of the material. Nevertheless, he did point out that as a result of the programs "a major terrorist act in the U.S. was prevented" (presumably a plot, involving Palestinian terrorists, aimed at American Jews) and "some large drug shipments were prevented from entering the U.S." In all, the NSA director told the panel, the BNDD watch list contained about 450 Americans and over 3000 foreign individuals; the Secret Service, about 180 American people and groups and about 525 foreign individuals and groups; the FBI, about a thousand U.S. and about 1700 foreign; the CIA, about 30 Americans and 700 foreign individuals and groups; the DIA, about 20 U.S. individuals.

Over the six-year period between 1967 and 1973, Allen estimated, the Agency had issued about 3900 reports concerning the approximately 1680 watch-listed American citizens, and about 10 percent of these involved Americans on both ends of the circuits, but in all cases at least one terminal was on foreign soil.

In the questioning that followed, the most eye-opening admissions had to do with the way in which the NSA officials viewed the legal system as it applied to the Agency.

Leading off the questioning, chief counsel for the committee, F. A. O. Schwartz, Jr., pressed the director about the effect of the wiretap statutes on NSA eavesdropping. "You believe you are consistent with the statutes," the committee lawyer said to Allen, "but there is not any statute that prohibits your interception of domestic communications."

Allen replied, "I believe that is correct."

Later, Senator Mondale, questioning Deputy Director Buffham about his role in the Huston Plan, asked whether he had ever been concerned about the legality of the portion of the plan that would have authorized NSA to expand greatly its targeting of American citizens.

"Legality?" Buffham asked, perplexed. "That particular aspect didn't enter into the discussions."

Turning to the Agency's chief lawyer, Roy Banner, Mondale asked whether, in his opinion, the watch list was legal. "I think it was legal in the context of the law at the time," responded the general counsel.

When Chairman Frank Church interrupted with the suggestion that all questions regarding legality be reserved for the committee's questioning of Attorney General Levi, Mondale said: "I think that is important to the determination of this committee of how these laws are interpreted. I believe they still think it is legal. That is what worries me."

"May I make just one comment, Mr. Chairman?" Banner interrupted. "There is one court decision on the matter. It was held in that decision to be lawful."

"Then you think it is lawful? That is what it held?" pressed Mondale.

"I think it was lawful at the time," Banner responded.

"That is just my point," Mondale shot back. "They still think it is legal."

Finally, Church cut off the discussion once and for all.

The fact that the top three officials of the Agency all agreed that NSA exists somewhere in an extralegal limbo, unrestrained by the same laws and statutes that govern the rest of the nation, was made all the more significant when weighed alongside an earlier question by Pennsylvania senator Richard Schweiker. Asked whether it would be possible to use NSA's watch list and massive technological capability "to monitor domestic conversations within the United States if some person with malintent desired to do it," Allen replied, "I suppose that such a thing is technically possible."

Once the questioning came to an end, the trio was excused, and the committee turned to another NSA operation, of which the Ford administration vehemently opposed any public mention: Shamrock. Although the White House had reluctantly agreed to allow Director Allen to appear as a witness with regard to the watch lists and Minaret, Shamrock was a whole other ball game. Nevertheless, the committee voted to release a report on the project, a report considered SECRET/ COMINT CHANNELS ONLY by NSA, and on November 6, 1975, Senator Church read it into the record.

•

Unfortunately for the Puzzle Palace, the Church Committee was not the only body interested in Shamrock. Prompted by a July 22, 1975, article in the New York *Daily News,* charging that for at least five years the FBI and the NSA routinely monitored commercial cable traffic to and from the United States, the House Government Operations Subcommittee on Government Information and Individual Rights began an investigation. Authority for the inquiry was based on the subcommittee's oversight responsibilities "for matters concerning the rights of privacy of American citizens and for the operations of the Federal Communications Commission."

The Ford administration and the NSA may have looked at the Pike and Church Committees with considerable apprehension; they viewed the Government Information Subcommittee and its behatted chairwoman, Bella S. Abzug, with downright horror. Where the two intelligence committees were somewhat predictable in their investigations, the Abzug Subcommittee was like an ammunition-laden cargo plane out of control. It had decided, shrewdly, not to seek information directly from the Puzzle Palace but, instead, to call on the testimony of officials from the international communications companies who either knew about the operation or had participated in it. Whereas the NSA might be able to hide behind the shields of classification and executive privilege, the same protection was not available to private corporations.

Initially, the subcommittee received considerable cooperation from both the companies and Joe Craig, a former FBI agent identified as one of the alleged bagmen. But on October 21, two days before the first public hearings were to begin, the support began crumbling. It was apparently on that date that the administration first became aware of the Abzug investigation, and it launched a massive counterattack. A letter from FBI director Kelley said that, because the matter in question "is under investigation," he had forbidden former agent Craig from testifying. At the same time, RCA Global and ITT World Communications suddenly informed the subcommittee that they would refuse to send officials unless so ordered by a subpoena.

On the day before the start of the scheduled hearings, a platoon of officials from the White House, NSA, Pentagon, and Justice Department converged on the chairwoman in an effort to change her mind about holding public sessions. In the delegation were NSA director Allen, Pentagon intelligence chief Albert Hall, Deputy Attorney General Harold Tyler, Special Counsel to the President John Marsh, and White House congressional liaison Charles Leppert. Their argument was that such hearings would jeopardize either a current Justice Department criminal investigation or the national security.

Unimpressed, Abzug refused to cancel or postpone the hearings. So in a last-ditch effort, only moments before the congresswoman gaveled the hearing to order, Attorney General Levi came to the hearing room and tried his own appeal. He fared no better than the others, and at eleven o'clock on October 23, 1975, the hearings began as scheduled — but without the main witnesses. With Craig and the cable companies awaiting subpoenas, the only testimony came from two representatives of AT&T and one of its subsidiaries, Chesapeake & Potomac Telephone Company.

Conceding the first round to the administration, the combative New York Democrat offered both Allen and Levi a chance to come before the committee and state their case for the record. Both refused. In the meantime, the Church Committee had released its findings on Operation Shamrock, but, feeling that the report did not go far enough, the Abzug Subcommittee decided to continue its own inquiry.

On February 4, 1976, subpoenas were issued to three FBI special agents, one former FBI special agent, one NSA employee, and executives of ITT World Communications, RCA Global, and Western Union International.

Two weeks later, on February 17, in an extraordinary and unprecedented expansion of the doctrine of executive privilege, President Ford notified Defense Secretary Donald Rumsfeld and Attorney General Levi that, because the subpoenas also called for records "containing the most sensitive national security information," he was instructing them to notify the subpoenaed parties that they should "decline to comply."

The following day Rumsfeld instructed the NSA employee, and

Levi instructed the present and former FBI agents, that, inasmuch as President Ford has asserted executive privilege in the matter, the subpoenas were not to be complied with. Then, for the first time in history, the concept of executive privilege was extended to a private corporation: Attorney General Levi, in a letter to the attorney for Western Union, wrote, "On behalf of the President, I hereby request that Western Union International honor this invocation of executive privilege."

With the stage set for a major battle between the Congress and the Executive Branch, on February 25 the Manhattan congresswoman once again called the hearings to order. Joe Craig was the first to be called. After first requesting that he not be subjected to radio, television, or still-photography coverage, he told the panel that, because the Attorney General had instructed him not to testify in response to the subpoena, "I must respectfully decline to testify before your subcommittee at this time."

The pattern was repeated by the next three witnesses, all current FBI employees. Finally, the subcommittee turned its attention to Joseph J. Tomba, a dark-haired, middle-level NSA employee in his mid-thirties. An engineer with sixteen years of service at NSA, he had been recruited during his senior year at West Virginia University in 1960. Assigned to the C1 Group in PROD during the mid-1960s, he eventually was promoted to a supervisory position after completing the Agency's General Organization Management, Supervisory Level Course (MG-110). In 1970 he may have taken over management of Shamrock from Mr. Feeney, who had held the position for eighteen years, from the time NSA inherited the program from the Armed Forces Security Agency in 1952. So compartmented was the program that besides the middle-level manager, the only other persons exercising responsibility over the operation were the director and deputy director.

Like his predecessors, Tomba sought refuge behind executive privilege, but not before he drew the ire of the subcommittee with a brief opening statement. "General Allen has asked me to convey to you," he told a surprised Abzug, "his willingness to attempt to meet the requirements of your subcommittee along with the necessary safeguards applicable to any classified information. To this end, his staff is available to work with your people to define more precisely your exact information requirements."

"I certainly appreciate your bringing that message to us personally," the chairwoman responded after stating that the subcommittee already had invited the general on several occasions, "particularly since it is quite obvious that apparently no telephone communication can be made without interception."

A few minutes later, by a vote of 6 to 1, the subcommittee voted to recommend to the full committee that all five witnesses be cited for contempt of Congress.

Stonewalled by the government, the subcommittee next turned to the telegraph companies. On March 3, Thomas S. Greenish, executive vice president of Western Union International, testified before the panel and turned over an eight-year-old list of NSA targets, an action that President Ford had vigorously attempted to block by asking the corporation to honor his all-embracing claim of executive privilege.

Following Greenish to the witness table was Howard R. Hawkins, chairman of the board and chief executive officer of RCA Global Communications, along with several of his subordinates. Their testimony represented still another defeat for the administration. Attorney General Levi had earlier asked, "on behalf of the President," that representatives of the corporation neither testify before the subcommittee, nor produce documents, "until procedures can be agreed upon to assure that the President's invocation of executive privilege is not effectively undone." Defying the President and Attorney General, Greenish and his associates went ahead with their testimony and also produced an assortment of records.

About a week later, George Knapp, president of ITT World Communications, and several other employees testified about Shamrock. The administration seems to have thrown in the towel; it made no attempt to prevent their appearance.

After the hearings, the subcommittee staff began work on a draft report, to be issued by the Government Operations Committee, which examined the NSA's eavesdropping activities on communications entering and leaving the country. But a controversy soon arose over whether the report should be released, and, following its completion in the fall of 1977, the decision was made to bury it quietly.

Entitled "Interception of International Telecommunications by the National Security Agency," the draft report pointed to the NSA's "extraordinary capability to intercept" and concluded that "no other agency of the federal government undertakes such activity on such an immense scale." Calling the enormous secrecy surrounding the Agency "obsessive and unfounded," the report went on to charge that NSA's appeal to the Congress and the public that they simply "trust us" was totally unjustified when viewed in light of the Agency's long record of privacy violations.

The report was particularly critical of the Agency's constant attempts to hide behind semantics. Pointing to a statement by Vice Admiral Bobby Inman, General Allen's successor as DIRNSA, in which he stated: "Let there be no doubt . . . there are no U.S. citizens now targeted by NSA in the United States or abroad, none," the report called the declaration "misleading." It added that, "while an American citizen or company might not be targeted by name, by virtue of his international activities, his communications might be selected by the NSA on the basis of its 'foreign intelligence' criteria. The NSA has not denied that it, in fact, 'selects' U.S. messages of this nature."

Although spared the final indignity of a public report on Shamrock by the Abzug Subcommittee, the Puzzle Palace was not yet out of the fire. Prompted by the Rockefeller Commission's allegations of questionable activities on the part of the intelligence community, Attorney General Levi established a top secret task force to investigate the commission's findings and determine whether any other questionable electronic surveillances may have been conducted. Among the areas looked at were several NSA operations, including Shamrock and Minaret.

It was the first time that any law enforcement agency had ever been charged with investigating the legality of SIGINT operations, and the reaction within the intelligence community was predictably hostile. Noting that "attitudes ranged from circumspection to wariness," Dougald D. McMillan, author of the task force's final report, wrote that "one typically had to ask the right question to elicit the right answer or document." He pointed out that "it is likely, therefore, that we had insufficient information on occasion to frame the 'magic' question. One also had to ascertain the specific person or division to whom the right question should be addressed, since compartmentalization of intelligence-gathering often results in one hand not knowing what the other is doing."

Nevertheless, over the course of twelve months, the hand-picked, specially cleared team of Justice Department lawyers gradually pulled back layer after layer of secrecy cloaking some of the NSA's most advanced eavesdropping technology and supersecret processing techniques. The final report of the task force, classified TOP SECRET UM-BRA/HANDLE VIA COMINT CHANNELS ONLY, and excluded from declassification, was considered so sensitive that only two copies were ever printed. On its completion, on June 30, 1976, the 175-page legal-size document was delivered to George W. Calhoun, chief of the Special Litigation Unit, who drafted the equally sensitive fifty-page "Prosecutive Summary" for Benjamin R. Civiletti, the assistant attorney general in charge of the Criminal Division, and his assistant, Robert L. Keuch.

In the end, despite the fact that the task force had managed to uncover no fewer than twenty-three different categories of questionable electronic-surveillance activities involving the NSA, CIA, and FBI, the report concluded with the recommendation that "the inquiry be terminated in all respects for lack of prosecutive potential." Acquittal.

Of the twenty-three categories of "questionable activities," five were barred from prosecution by the statute of limitations and seven "clearly possess no prosecutive potential." As for the rest: "There is likely to be much 'buck-passing' from subordinate to superior, agency to agency, agency to board or committee, board or committee to the President, and from the living to the dead."

In addition, calling the subject matter of the report "an international *cause célèbre* involving fundamental constitutional rights of United States citizens," the task force pointed to the likelihood of graymail and the possibility that defense attorneys would probably subpoena "every tenuously involved government official and former official" to establish that authority for the various operations emanated from on high. "While the high office of prospective defense witnesses should not enter into the prosecutive decision," the report noted, "the confusion, obfuscation, and surprise testimony which might result cannot be ignored."

Rather than point a finger at any one official or any one agency, the task force instead indicted the national security system as a whole, a system that granted the agencies "too much discretionary authority with too little accountability . . . a 35-year failing of Presidents and the Congress rather than the agencies."

While on the one hand charging that those NSA, FBI, and cable company employees who participated in Shamrock apparently violated several sections of the Communications Act of 1934, the "Prosecutive Summary" pointed to NSA's highly secret Executive Branch "charter," NSCID No. 9 (later NSCID No. 6), which gave the Agency virtual carte blanche to disregard legal restraints placed on the rest of the government. "Orders, directives, policies, or recommendations of any authority of the Executive branch relating to the collection . . . of intelligence . . ." the still top secret document reads, "shall not be applicable to Communications Intelligence activities, unless specifically so stated." The summary concluded: "Its birth certificate (which was, by the way, top secret) said it did not have to follow the limitations in the NSES [National Security Electronic Surveillance] area that limited other agencies unless it was expressly directed to do so."

Another reason for recommending against prosecution with regard to Shamrock was far less complex: "It is not illegal to 'ask' a company to give out copies of cables. If the company complies, it may be violating the statute but the recipient would not."

Thus, the invaders were once again driven off. In the six years since Daniel Ellsberg fired the opening volley with the Pentagon Papers, to the March 4, 1977, Justice Department recommendation against prosecution, the Puzzle Palace had undergone attacks from the press, the courts, the House, the Senate, the White House, the Attorney General, and the special Justice Department task force. In the process the Agency had been forced to abandon several operations, make its first public statements, and at last acknowledge that its functions include more than "protecting the security of U.S. communications." But to those inside the triple fence, worst of all was the sudden realization that their wall of anonymity was no longer impregnable.

"We may as well get used to it," one long-time senior official wrote in an article published in a TOP SECRET/COMINT CHANNELS ONLY inhouse publication; "used to feeling exposed and unprotected at moments when our accustomed and familiar anonymity seems to be snatched away." Hoping that their "time of indecent exposure" had at last come to an end, but realizing that they may have seen only the beginning, she concluded: "Packs of hungry animals of various breeds, having caught the scent, are out there gnawing at the foundations of the storehouses, sniffing and rooting for more beans."

PARTNERS

"DEPENDENCE is so great and co-operation so close that I am convinced security chiefs would go to any lengths to protect the link-up . . ."

The "link-up" that veteran British journalist Chapman Pincher referred to is quite likely the most secret agreement ever entered into by the English-speaking world. Signed in 1947 and known as the UKUSA Agreement, it brought together under a single umbrella the SIGINT organizations of the United States, Britain, Canada, Australia, and New Zealand. Under the pact, the five nations carved up the earth into spheres of cryptologic influence, each country assigned specific targets according to its potential for maximum intercept coverage. Britain, for example, was assigned various Chinese frequencies to cover from its Little Sai Wan station in Hong Kong, and the United States was responsible for other frequencies from its listening posts in Taiwan, Japan, and Korea.

The UKUSA nations also agreed to standardize their terminology, code words, intercept-handling procedures, and indoctrination oaths, for efficiency as well as security. Vipar, Trine, and Umbra, therefore, would appear on the TOP (or MOST) SECRET documents and intercepts, regardless of which member originated them. The voluminous loose-leaf binder that contains these rules and procedures is known as the IRSIG — for International Regulations on SIGINT.

The UKUSA Agreement, whose existence has never been officially acknowledged by any country even today, had its beginnings in the violent summer of 1940. France had collapsed under the weight of Hitler's mechanized war machine, and by August the Luftwaffe had begun pounding the airfields of southern England. The Battle of Britain had begun, and Winston Churchill could offer his countrymen nothing but "blood, toil, tears, and sweat" as the Royal Air Force put up its magnificent defense.

Churchill's words were gallant, but he knew that it would take more than blood and sweat if England were to survive. It was a far different kind of war from any that had ever been fought before, one that he would later call a "Wizard War," a war fought as much with science as with gunpowder.

It was for this reason that Churchill directed the British ambassador to Washington, Lord Lothian, to undertake negotiations of the utmost delicacy with the American President. On July 8 the Ambassador met with President Roosevelt and offered to reveal highly secret technical information about England's latest developments in radar and several other scientific fields in which America was considerably behind. The offer was made formal two days later in a letter from Lord Lothian to the President. "Should you approve the exchange of information," the letter read, "it has been suggested by my Government that, in order to avoid any risk of the information reaching our enemy, a small secret British mission consisting of two or three Service officers and civilian scientists should be despatched immediately to this country to enter into discussions with Army and Navy experts."

In the world of diplomacy, magnanimous offers are the rarest of things. It was therefore no surprise that the letter included an implied quid pro quo. "His Majesty's Government," the letter concluded, "would greatly appreciate it if the United States Government, having been given the full details of any British equipment or devices, would reciprocate by discussing certain secret information of a technical nature, which our technical experts are anxious to have, urgently."

Lothian undoubtedly would have liked to underline the last word.

Roosevelt brushed aside a number of objections by a few high-ranking military officers, including General George C. Marshall, and opened the door for the arrival in late August of Sir Henry Tizard, adviser to Britain's Ministry of Aircraft Production. In his briefcase were MOST SECRET details on such advanced projects as radar, radar countermeasures, sonar, proximity fuses, and radio interception.

But one project was notably absent from Sir Henry's brown leather case: a project that was as important and vital to the ultimate survival of the island nation as its code name implied: Ultra. It was Britain's secret of secrets.

As the war was beginning to turn from lukewarm to hot, Britain had managed to acquire a working model of Germany's highest-level cipher machine, the Enigma. Although there are several versions of exactly how it was acquired, there is no debate that by August 1939 it was in the hands of a short, fiftyish Scotsman, Commander Alastair C. Denniston. He was one of Sir Alfred Ewing's original quartet of cryptologists who became the charter members of Britain's legendary

World War I codebreaking outfit known as Room 40 O.B. The taciturn commander was now in charge of England's equivalent of America's Signal Intelligence Service, the Government Code and Cypher School.

It was in August that Denniston and his tweedy band of intellects moved from Broadway, in the London borough of Westminster, to a gaudy, ornate red-brick mansion in Bletchley, a rural market town fifty miles north of London. With them they had taken Enigma — a small metal device that looked more like a cross between a switchboard and an old portable electric typewriter — and a mandate to find a way to determine which of a myriad combination of settings might have been used in any given batch of intercepts. The answer was an awe-inspiring lady known as "the Bronze Goddess."

The goddess was a bronze-colored column surrounded by a larger bronze-colored face and was quite probably the world's first electronic computer. Denniston and his Bletchleyites, particularly A. Dillwyn (Dilly) Knox, a tall, gangling young man with dark unruly hair, and Alan Turing, a brilliant young mathematician, had created the goddess; now they must teach her to speak.

Early in April 1940, four months before Sir Henry Tizard arrived in Washington with his stuffed briefcase, the Bronze Goddess uttered her first syllables: a few short Luftwaffe messages dealing with some personnel changes. They were of little immediate importance, but they had a significance then beyond imagination.

That Tizard made no mention of Ultra to his American counterparts on his journey was no oversight. The secret was Britain's greatest, and Tizard himself may not have known how successful Bletchley had been. In any case, Churchill saw no need to include cryptologic information in the Tizard exchange, since it was logically assumed that America had very little to offer in exchange.

By October, Churchill's attitude had changed. It was in that month that he learned for the first time of America's success in breaking Japan's high-level diplomatic code. He was duly impressed. Whereas his team at Bletchley had Enigma, a working model, to go on, William Friedman and his crew had had nothing but imagination.

Exactly how Churchill first became aware of the American achievement has never been revealed by either side, but by November a highly secret agreement had been signed by the neutral United States and a Britain fighting for her life. The agreement provided for "a full exchange of cryptographic systems, cryptanalytical techniques, direction finding, radio interception, and other technical communication matters pertaining to the diplomatic, military, naval, and air services of Germany, Japan, and Italy."

Picked to head an American mission to Bletchley was the dean of American cryptology, William F. Friedman. Together with one of his Army assistants, First Lieutenant Leo Rosen, and two naval officers, Friedman was to deliver to England not only two of America's seven Purple machines, but also two Red machines and a mixed variety of codes, including the U.S. Navy's radio intelligence manual.

The mission was to take place late in December, and on December 23, 1940, Friedman was placed back on active duty as a lieutenant colonel. He had successfully passed his medical exam several days earlier, although, fearing rejection for the mission, he had failed to inform the physicians of some psychological problems that had plagued him during his attack on Purple. It was a serious oversight.

Now, faced with a mission of tremendous importance, the delivery to war-torn England of America's most vital secret in return for Britain's most closely held secret, Friedman grew increasingly nervous and apprehensive.

On December 26, his orders were cut, directing him to report to the assistant chief of staff for G-2, and then to "proceed to London, England, reporting upon arrival to the Military Attaché for temporary duty, for the carrying out of the instructions of the Secretary of War." Then there was a delay in the mission, and Friedman's tension and anxiety became excruciating. He felt that once he arrived in England, he would be unable to function properly, and this exacerbated his depression. He began to consider suicide.

On Sunday, January 5, 1941, Friedman was admitted to the neuro-psychiatric ward of Walter Reed Hospital with a diagnosis of psycho-neurosis, a nervous breakdown.

The mission to England could not wait for Friedman's recovery, and his orders were officially cancelled on January 24. Taking his place was his long-time assistant, Abe Sinkov, now an Army major. Sinkov, accompanied by Captain Leo Rosen of the Army Signal Corps, and Navy Lieutenant Robert H. Weeks and Ensign Prescott Currier of Op-20-G, sailed to England with the two Purple machines as January began turning into February.

By the time the foursome were set to return, it appeared that the United States had given up a swordfish to catch a herring, though Sinkov and his associates may not have been aware of it.

They returned with an assortment of advanced crypto equipment, including the revolutionary Marconi-Adcock high-frequency direction finder, but no Enigma. In fact, the British probably did not even inform the Sinkov delegation of the extent of their successes against the German code. The problem was with the Foreign Office. Because of instructions from Lord Halifax, the delivery of Enigma had been vetoed on the grounds that it was against British policy to divulge high-level cryptologic secrets to anyone, regardless of the reason. Since the Foreign Office exercised supervisory powers over the intelligence and cryptologic agencies, the veto stuck.

Despite the imbalance in the trade, cooperation between the two countries continued to increase, climaxing in April 1943 when Colonel Alfred McCormack of the Special Branch, accompanied by Colonel Telford Taylor of Military Intelligence and a now fully recovered William Friedman, left for England on another extremely secret mission — this time for a two-month survey of British COMINT operations.

Now, for the first time, Britain decided to lift fully the thick veil that had long shrouded its deepest secret. As a result, America's Military Intelligence Service at last became completely aware of the amazing successes achieved by the British in their exploitation of German military traffic, their Ultra secret. Intelligence derived from this source had for some time been made available to both British and U.S. field commanders through a complex and highly secure procedure involving British intelligence liaison officers, known as special liaison officers, or SLOs. Ultra, however, had never been made available to Washington, which greatly hindered the work of the Special Branch in both short-range and long-range intelligence planning in the European theater.

The American trio was greeted at Bletchley by Royal Navy Commander Edward W. Travis, who had taken over the reins of a newly reorganized COMINT organization from Commander Denniston a year earlier. Travis, a bespectacled, stocky figure, was himself an enigma. Commanding a team of Oxford dons, Ph.D.s, and scientific marvels was a man who himself had never been to college. Travis had joined the Navy at the age of eighteen and had spent the better part of his career in the Signals Division. Now, at forty-five, he was leading England's greatest intellectual battle.

Under the reorganization, the Government Code and Cypher School became the Government Communications Headquarters, GCHQ, the name by which Britain's SIGINT organization is still known today, and all previously semi-independent departments, including the Naval Section and Air Section, were placed under one head.

Denniston returned to London, where he took charge of the diplomatic branch from an office "above Peggy Carter's hat shop," as the 7–9 Berkeley Street location was commonly known.

During their two-month stay at Bletchley, the team led by Colonel McCormack was given complete briefings on Enigma and Ultra. Displaying a 3-by-5-inch card captioned PERMIT TO ENTER BLETCHLEY PARK GROUNDS and stamped NOT VALID AFTER 30 JUN 1943, the three men would enter the secluded estate each day and discuss with their British counterparts the best ways to utilize the products of Enigma and Purple to their collective advantage.

The results of their efforts reached a climax on May 17 with the signing of a formal agreement of cooperation between the COMINT agencies of Britain and the United States, the BRUSA Agreement. The significance of the pact was monumental. It established for the first time intimate cooperation on COMINT of the highest level. It provided for exchange of personnel, joint regulations for the handling of the supersensitive material, and methods for its distribution. In addition, paragraph eight of the agreement provided that all recipients of high-grade COMINT, whether British or American, were bound to the severely strict security regulations that were appended to the document. The cooperation, procedures, and security regulations set out in the BRUSA Agreement serve as landmarks in the history of communications intelligence. Even today, they form the fundamental basis for all SIGINT activities of both the NSA and GCHQ.

In October 1943, the War Department issued its formal regulations conforming to the mandate of the BRUSA pact, which meant, among other things, the establishment of an entirely new lexicon of code words. Until the October regulations, COMINT was divided into three groups, depending on the importance of the enemy cryptographic system used. Intercepted messages enciphered in the enemy's highest code system were given the code name Dexter, the American equivalent of the British code word Ultra. Intercepts of a lesser importance were assigned the code word Corral, and the rather frightening Rabid was reserved mainly for T/A intelligence, or traffic analysis.

Now, however, because of the BRUSA Agreement, Britain and the United States sought to standardize both code words and terminology. Having at one time or another used such bizarre code words as Zymotic, Swell, and Sidar, the British had early in the war settled on Ultra, Pearl, and Thumb as the three mystic passwords in their descending order of importance.

The War Department contributed to the standardization at first simply by adding the British Ultra before each of the three U.S. code words and later by adopting Ultra, Pearl, and Thumb for its own COMINT material. (Pearl and Thumb were later dropped and replaced by the single code word Pinup.)

The seriousness with which the department regarded its most sensitive form of intelligence can be seen in an October 1943 memorandum entitled "Security of Ultra Dexter Intelligence." The document, which before each paragraph contained the phrase "Burn After Reading," spoke of Ultra Dexter's "extreme importance." "If the enemy were to learn of the existence of this source," the memorandum warned, "it would probably be lost forever, and this would vitally affect operations on all fronts." Similar warnings were given for Ultra Corral and Ultra Rabid information.

The success of BRUSA quickly led to a series of conferences involving not only Britain and the United States, but the codebreaking agencies of Canada and Australia as well. At the second Joint Allied Conference, held at Arlington Hall Station on March 13, 1944, the participants included Colonel W. Preston Corderman, William F. Friedman, Abe Sinkov, and Solomon Kullback of the Signal Security Agency, and Carter Clarke and Telford Taylor of G-2. From GCHQ there was Commander Edward Travis, Leonard James Hooper (a future director), and Colonel John H. Tiltman, liaison officer to the SSA. Representing the Canadian Examination Unit was Lieutenant Colonel Edward M. Drake, who would head Canada's SIGINT organization until the early 1970s. Australia's Central Bureau, Brisbane, was represented by Captain S. R. I. Clark. In all, there were thirty-five persons attending what was surely one of the most secret conferences of the war.

By the time the long-awaited V-E Day arrived, the depth of the Anglo-American friendship could be seen in the dinner enjoyed by Friedman and the now-knighted Sir Edward Travis at Bletchley Park, a dinner whose menu included Potage Ultra, Poulet Arlington, Légumes à choix random, and, for dessert, Dolce Americo-Britannique à la mode Brusa.

After two years of compromising and negotiating, BRUSA was supplemented in 1947 by the five-power UKUSA Agreement, which, according to one report, established the United States as a first party to the treaty, and Britain, Canada, and Australia–New Zealand as second parties. NATO nations and such other nations as Japan and Korea later signed on as third parties. Among the first and second parties there is a general agreement not to restrict data, but with the third parties the sharing is much less generous.

Charged with keeping the delicate gears of cooperation well oiled throughout the 1950s was Friedman, who helped draw up the postwar blueprint of UKUSA as he had of the earlier BRUSA. Friedman's friendship with his British "cousins," as he would call them, was of particular importance in March of 1952, when Sir Edward retired, at the age of sixty-four, after more than a decade at the top of Britain's cryptologic pyramid. "Leaving GCHQ with all that it means will naturally be a heart wrench," he wrote his old friend during his last few days, adding that it was "softened considerably by the fact that I know I am leaving behind me a first-class team and all things being equal the organization should continue to prosper." One of his sorrows, he told Friedman, was that he never expected to visit Washington again, primarily because of Britain's depressed economic state: "I see no hope in my lifetime of the U.K.'s financial position allowing me to pay visits to the dollar area at my own expense."

He was, unfortunately, right. Four years later, on April 18, 1956, Sir Edward died after an operation. He had victoriously led Britain's most secret and most important battle, a battle for which his King awarded him a knighthood, France made him a Chevalier de la Légion d'honneur, the Italians made him an Officer of the Crown of Italy, and the American President gave him his grateful nation's highest civilian award, the Medal of Merit. Yet he would remain as anonymous in death as he had been in life.

Taking over from Travis as head of GCHQ was Eric Malcolm Jones, C.B.E., who had sold textiles until he was thirty-three. In 1940 he joined the Royal Air Force Volunteer Reserves, where, presumably, he got his first taste of cryptology. After the war he transferred to GCHQ and now, one month before his forty-fifth birthday, the handsome flier with dark hair and pencil-thin mustache was about to become its chief.

As his deputy, Jones appointed Royal Navy Commander Clive Loehnis, forty-nine. The son of a barrister, Loehnis chose the sea rather than the law. A graduate of the Royal Naval Colleges of Osborne, Dartmouth, and Greenwich, he became qualified in signals in 1928 and left the Navy in 1935 as a lieutenant commander. In 1938 he returned to the Signals Division of the Admiralty, where he earned the silver oak leaves of a commander before retiring in 1942 and going into the Naval Intelligence Division. When he was demobilized after the war, he entered the Foreign Office, presumably the GCHQ, of which it is a division.

Friedman had known both Jones and Loehnis for years, and they were on the best of terms. Thanking him for a note of congratulations, Jones wrote to Friedman about his selection: "It is a fascinating prospect; in fact I can think of none I would like better. And with so many able and nice people about me the burdens should not be too heavy." Then he came to the important part. "As you know,

BRUSA is to me terribly important and I admit to a certain pride in having been so closely connected with its birth. A prospering BRUSA in the midst of friendly relations is right in the forefront of my aims for the future." Friedman and the NSA could breathe a sigh of relief; the cooperation would continue uninterrupted.

Among the terms provided by the BRUSA-UKUSA Agreements was the exchange of COMINT personnel among the United States, Britain, Canada, and Australia. Soon after NSA was formed, therefore, it secretly began sending people to London to work with the codebreakers of GCHQ. Using the cover name "Office of the Senior United States Liaison Officer," or simply SUSLO, the team moved into Flat 507 at 7 North Audley Street, a handsome building just north of Grosvenor Square. A few blocks to the east lay the greenery of Hyde Park; a few steps south lay the American embassy.

About the same time that AFSA became the NSA, GCHQ moved from the London suburb of Eastcote into its new headquarters on Priors Road in Cheltenham, Gloucestershire, eight-five miles to the west. The move to Cheltenham, a quiet city among the green rolling pastures and rural country roads of the Cotswolds, where one is as likely to encounter a heifer as another human being, was undoubtedly prompted by the same concerns that caused AFSA-NSA to consider moving to Fort Knox. With both COMINT and COMSEC concentrated in London since the end of the war, an attack on the city during another war would virtually wipe Britain off the cryptologic map. The move of GCHQ and COMINT to the Cotswolds left the London Communications Security Agency, another branch of the Foreign Office, at 8 Palmer Street, just down the road from Buckingham Palace.

NSA soon followed GCHQ to Cheltenham, setting up an operations branch there while maintaining its main office in London. SUSLO during the mid-1950s was Navy Captain Prescott C. Currier, who was picked to be executive secretary of the United States Communications Intelligence Board during the summer of 1958. It was Currier who, as an ensign a decade and a half earlier, was a member of the Sinkov delegation that had delivered the two Purple machines to England. Deputy SUSLO, in charge of the Cheltenham unit until he sailed back to the United States aboard the S.S. *America* on July 10, 1957, was John J. Larkin.

The British, likewise, set up their Senior United Kingdom Liaison Office in Washington during the same period. In the mid-1950s it went under the cover name of the British Joint Services Mission and was located in the main Navy Building. SUKLO at the time was Colonel Freddy Jacob.

Another part of the top secret agreement dealt with control of the special radio circuits linking NSA and GCHQ. Under BRUSA, the United States was to have control over the U.S. end of the circuit, and the British were to exercise control over their end. By 1954, however, the United States was beginning to have second thoughts about that part of the agreement and sought to take control of both ends of the circuit. "It is toward this end," the Joint Chiefs of Staff indicated in a memorandum to the director of NSA, "that efforts are being made to modify the arrangements resulting from the BRUSA Agreement so that the United States would have control of both terminals of the GCHQ-NSA communications." The British had other ideas, however, and so indicated in a memorandum to General Ralph Canine. As a result, a meeting to discuss the possible change in the agreement was set up for June in England, to coincide with a meeting already arranged in connection with discussions on establishing a Centralized COMINT Communications Center (CCCC).

The CCCCs were designed as special relay centers for the exclusive handling of NSA's traffic, traffic considered too secret to be sent on normal military channels, even though they were certified for top secret. Only specially COMINT-cleared personnel were allowed access to the CCCCs that contained the special NSA-supplied on-line cryptographic equipment. For increased security, the CCCCs were located in entirely separate buildings, away from any military relay center. If for some reason a CCCC had to be in the same building, it was totally segregated.

Among the most critical elements of cooperation between the two nations, especially with regard to the United States, was the right to establish listening posts on each other's territory. This appears to have been a lopsided agreement, since by March 1951 the United States had a total of seven units in the United Kingdom or on U.K.-controlled territory, but there is no evidence of reciprocation. For that matter, even during the Korean War a plan for the possible emergency evacuation of a British COMINT unit in Hong Kong met with resistance.

It had been originally agreed that if there was an emergency evacuation, the unit would be allowed to relocate and set up shop on American-controlled Okinawa. A directive to this effect was therefore sent to the commanding general of the Army's Far East Command in Tokyo. Unfortunately, the Army Security Agency had already made plans to more than double its proposed intercept station on the island from about 300 to 674 people, and this was to be done in the facilities planned for the British. The general, consequently, wired back to

Washington that "it would appear, therefore, undesirable if not altogether infeasible to plan to locate the British unit on Okinawa" and as a result recommended Guam.

Back in Washington the Joint Chiefs rejected Guam and instead suggested that the British unit go to Singapore, British North Borneo, or Australia. Eventually, however, apparently under British pressure, the JCS assented to the move and directed that the Far East commander provide emergency accommodation on Okinawa "any time the Air Commander-in-Chief British Far East Air Force considers that conditions warrant removal of the unit to a more secure site." Nothing was said about comfort, however, and the Army began breaking out tents, next to the ASA's 111 Signal Service Company in Okinawa's Sukiran area, for the British to for quarters, messing, and administration facilities. The intercept gear was to go in a number of steel-and-wood prefabricated buildings nearby.

Among the areas of the world being listened to most closely by the Puzzle Palace during the mid-1950s was the oil-rich Middle East. In 1952 the Egyptian monarchy was overthrown by the military, and since 1954 the nation had grown increasingly nationalistic under the leadership of Colonel Gamal Abdel Nasser. Seeking to project himself as the leader not only of his own poverty-stricken nation but of the entire Arab world, Nasser set as his three main goals modernization, the elimination of the newly formed state of Israel, and the bodily eviction of the British from the Suez Canal.

In Washington, the Eisenhower administration, believing that the preceding administration had overcommitted itself to the safety and security of Israel, embarked on a new policy of "impartiality" in the region, a move that particularly worried Britain and France. Meanwhile, Nasser was becoming more friendly with Moscow, which had offered to subsidize the building of a high dam across the Nile at Aswan. Distressed, Washington countered with an offer to arrange Western financing for the construction project, but on July 19, 1956, after it appeared likely that the Russian offer would fall through and Egypt would have to turn to the United States, Secretary of State John Foster Dulles withdrew the offer. It was an embarrassing humiliation for the Egyptian president, and he retaliated by nationalizing the Suez Canal.

The seizure sent shock waves through London and Paris. Britain feared a cut-off of oil from the Middle East; France viewed Nasser as influential in prolonging the Algerian revolt. Both immediately began thinking in terms of military action, action in which British Prime Minister Sir Anthony Eden fully expected American cooperation. But Dulles feared that any show of force against Egypt would be interpreted by the newly emerging nations of Asia and Africa as renewed evidence of Western imperialism, and therefore refrained from joining with Britain in any use of force.

As Britain turned a cold shoulder to its ally across the Atlantic, Israel began expressing fears over the shifting balance of power in the Arab world. During October, therefore, British, French, and Israeli officials met secretly in France to discuss the situation. Within a few short weeks the discussion turned into action, and on October 29 Israel lashed out with a violent attack against Egypt. Two days later Britain and France joined Israel in the invasion, launching troop carriers by air and sea from Cyprus.

Fearing that the Soviet Union would make good on a threat to use force to crush the invasion — with long-range missiles, if necessary — and wishing to avoid a return to prewar colonialism, Eisenhower put intense pressure on the Eden government to end the fighting. Within a week Eden conceded and on November 6 ordered a cease-fire. The crisis was over, but the effect on Anglo-American relations was traumatic.

Throughout the weeks and months that followed the crisis, the inevitable question was whether Washington was in fact caught off guard by the surprise Anglo-French-Israeli attack. According to Secretary Dulles, it was. Testifying before a joint meeting of the Senate Foreign Relations and Armed Services Committees, Dulles stated, "We had no advance information of any kind." Yet this was contradicted by his brother, CIA director Allen Dulles, years later. "Here intelligence was well alerted to what Israel and then Britain and France were likely to do," Allen Dulles wrote in his book *The Craft of Intelligence.* "In fact," he added, "United States intelligence had kept the government informed but, as usual, did not advertise its achievement."

That the NSA was reading the secret traffic of all three belligerents seems unquestionable. Responsibility for solving the coded messages of Britain, France, and the Middle East nations was the responsibility of PROD's ALLO section (now G Group).

Britain appears to have been aware of NSA's successes in breaking its codes shortly after the ill-fated invasion. George Wigg, a Labour member of Parliament and a former Army colonel, publicly stated several weeks after the British withdrawal that the United States had recently "cracked" the British, French, and Israeli Foreign Ministry and armed forces' codes, and thus had prior knowledge of the planned attack.

Ironically, at the same time as the British were putting the final touches on the invasion plan, a plan that most likely depended heavily on SIGINT, GCHQ director Eric Jones was meeting with NSA officials in Washington. Whatever the reason for the peculiarly timed mission, it appeared at least somewhat successful, since Jones later termed it "profitable."

On Wednesday, October 31, just as the first Anglo-French troops began hitting Egypt's sandy coast, Jones boarded the R.M.S. *Queen Mary* for a six-day journey back to England. At three-thirty that afternoon, as the triple-stacked Cunard superliner pulled away from its berth just off New York's West 50 Street, Jones must have been troubled by the reaction the invasion might have on the delicate GCHQ-NSA relations. Two days out at sea, the SIGINT chief addressed a letter to his old friends the Friedmans, in which he expressed sadness at the imminent retirement of General Canine and of the course of events. "Needless to say," Jones wrote, "the differences between our two countries over the Middle East are rather marring my trip home."

NSA was equally concerned about the possible adverse effect on joint SIGINT cooperation caused by the cooling-off of relations between the two countries. In addition, concern was most likely expressed over possible changes in the crypto systems of Britain and the other NATO countries because of the widespread feeling that America had broken their codes. The situation was complicated by the fact that newer, more complex cryptographic devices were being produced in Europe, devices that could set NSA codebreakers back many years.

Because of these worries, Air Force Lieutenant General John A. Samford, who had replaced General Canine as DIRNSA, turned to Friedman and asked him to undertake a series of ultrasensitive missions to England and the continent. These missions, the details of which are still considered top secret by the Agency, probably were directed at reasserting the need for close cooperation between GCHQ and NSA and at establishing some sort of agreement with Europe's largest manufacturer of cryptographic devices, Crypto A.G.

Despite his age, despite his history of psychological problems, and despite three heart attacks, which had brought him within a whisper of death, on August 5, 1957, Friedman, after several months of briefings, picked up his maroon-jacketed special passport and two weeks later was airborne toward England. The trip was ostensibly a spur-of-the-moment decision having to do mostly with an upcoming book on Shakespeare. Even his wife, who was traveling with him, apparently did not know he was on a mission for the NSA.

After a week in London devoted mainly to matters related to his book, Friedman officially re-entered duty status at eight o'clock on Monday morning, August 26. He was picked up at his hotel by official car and driven the eighty-five miles through the countryside to the familiar buildings of GCHQ in Cheltenham, where he no doubt met with Sir Eric Jones, who had been in the honors list in January 1957, only a few months after the Suez fiasco.

Jones had celebrated his knighthood into the Order of St. Michael and St. George by taking a vacation in the snow-covered mountains of the Italian Alps. Among the mail forwarded to him there was a letter of congratulations from Friedman. Writing from his room in the Grand Hôtel Principe in Limone Piemonte, Jones thanked his old friend for the words of encouragement. The honor, said Sir Eric, "has been won by a lot of hard work by very many people within the circle and on the fringes of it, and it has also been partly won by friendly cooperation from people such as customers." Chief among those "customers" were the British military and intelligence services. "At this time I am deeply conscious," Jones added, "that much of that work has been done on your side of the Atlantic, and that much of that cooperation has come across the ocean; and I am deeply grateful." Then he added a personal note: "To you, Billy, most notably, I am indebted, in so many ways over very many years. You indeed made a wonderful contribution to our joint endeavours and have been a good friend to me. All here, on this side, freely recognise that, none more than I."

Only Friedman could elicit such a feeling of friendship from the British, and it was only Friedman who could have secured from GCHQ the maximum degree of cooperation.

After a full day of meetings, Friedman spent the night in Cheltenham and engaged in further talks the next day, returning to London that night. On September 1, he was off to the Continent and the next, and perhaps most important, part of his mission.

In 1957, Crypto A.G. was to cryptography what General Motors was to automobiles. Based in Stockholm, the company was probably the world's largest supplier of crypto equipment to foreign governments. As many of the Third World nations began casting off the chains of colonialism, they turned to Crypto A.G. to protect their secret communications.

Heading the company was sixty-five-year-old Boris Caesar Wilhelm Hagelin, a Russian-born Swede who since the 1920s had been manufacturing crypto equipment and selling it to various governments. After the German invasion of Norway in April 1940, Hagelin packed his bags with blueprints and two dismantled ciphering machines and, together with his wife, made his way across Germany and down to Italy, where he boarded the *Conte di Savoia,* on its last outward-bound voyage, for the trip to New York. Once in the United States, Hagelin established the Hagelin Cryptographic Company and promptly made his million selling his machines to the United States Army. In 1944 Hagelin moved back to Sweden and again set up shop, but because of restrictive laws that permitted the government to appropriate inventions beneficial to the national defense, he moved his research and development facility to a hillside overlooking a lake in Zug, Switzerland, and in 1959 moved the entire firm there.

When Friedman left London, he headed for Sweden and then Switzerland, where, it seems likely, he met with the white-haired Hagelin. Close friends during the war, Friedman and Hagelin had a great deal in common. Both were born in Russia, within a year of each other, and both shared an almost fanatical passion for cryptology. Exactly what happened during their meetings may never be known, but it seems likely that some sort of "deal" was offered to Hagelin by Friedman on behalf of the NSA. What this deal may have involved can be only speculation, but it appears likely that Hagelin was asked to supply to the NSA details about various improvements and modifications made to the cipher machines his company had supplied to other governments, including, especially, the member countries of NATO. This would have greatly shortened the time needed by the United States to break their code systems.

Evidence of this can be found in a worried request made by the NSA to the British author Ronald Clark, who wrote a biography of Friedman in 1977. In his book, Clark made several references to Friedman's 1957 trip and to two other trips Friedman made to England and Europe during April and May of 1958. On learning of Clark's intention to mention these trips, officials of the NSA approached him and expressed their "serious concern" about what might be revealed. They made several unsuccessful attempts to read the manuscript, both in the United States and Britain. Finally, not knowing how much Clark actually knew of the mission — which was very little — the officials reluctantly explained to him that their reason for worry was that "the book might discuss the supply of cipher machines to NATO; and that this would deprive NSA of the daily information enabling the NSA to read the secret messages of other NATO countries."

With regard to the connection with Hagelin, evidence can be seen in a revealing letter dated August 8, 1958, from Friedman to Howard Engstrom, who had left office as deputy director of NSA only a few days before. In his letter, Friedman indicated his frustration over the handling of the "Boris" project and the fact that it was apparently being taken out of his hands:

> I have also to report to you, either with tears or laughter, I don't know which, that Sammy [NSA director Samford] made it crystal clear to me, in words of one syllable, that he did not want me to write any more to our friend Boris except on social matters. The thing is now in the hands of you-know-who and he thinks that *we* (including, especially, myself) should have absolutely nothing to do with it any longer. I am beginning to wonder, in connection with this project, whose ox is being gored? To whose interest is it that the project go through successfully? By the way, what became of the letter from Boris that I sent you from California? I asked Sammy if he had it and he said he didn't. I asked his secretary — she said she didn't. I would appreciate any info that you can give me as to its whereabouts. I want it — it was sent to me.

The "you-know-who" was most likely the CIA. Engstrom also made mention of the project in his reply to Friedman's letter. "I am very anxious to find out how the Boris deal is coming," he wrote, "and hope it doesn't die after all the effort you expended on it."

That it didn't die seems to be indicated by the NSA's response to Ronald Clark. In fact, it appears that Friedman's approach to Hagelin was merely the latest in a series of secret approaches to the crypto baron. Stuart Hedden, a Wall Street lawyer, had been the New York agent for Hagelin's company during the war, and in that capacity he formed a friendship with Friedman that lasted for decades. For a year, between 1952 and 1953, Hedden served as inspector general for the CIA, leaving when General Walter Bedell Smith stepped down as director. In a letter to Friedman written in 1955, Hedden referred to "Boris" and some of the approaches made to him. Noting that Boris "writes very rarely these days," Hedden commented, "After two wild goose chases which your shop and my old shop have brought him here on, I would not blame him a bit if he tried to weaken his ties here a little. I am sure it is not deliberate, but it may be subconscious."

•

The foundation of friendship and cooperation established with the BRUSA and UKUSA Agreements during the 1940s and reinforced by Friedman during the 1950s, continued to solidify during the 1960s and 1970s.

With the retirement of Sir Eric Jones in 1960, his long-time deputy, Clive (Joe) Loehnis, took over GCHQ. Two years later, like his predecessors, he was knighted, and in 1964, at the age of sixty-two, he retired.

Loehnis was succeeded in the £9,000-a-year post by Leonard James (Joe) Hooper, fifty, who had graduated from Oxford in 1936 with first-class honors in modern history. Following two years at the London School of Economics, he joined the Air Ministry and transferred to the Government Code and Cypher School in 1942, staying on with GCHQ. Six years after receiving his K.C.M.G., in 1967, Sir Leonard left office to take over Britain's top intelligence post, coordinator of Intelligence and Security in the Cabinet Office Joint Intelligence Committee, a position somewhat analogous to chairman of the U.S. Intelligence Board.

Heading GCHQ from 1973 to 1978 was Arthur Wilfred (Bill) Bonsall. Bonsall had graduated from Cambridge with second-class honors in modern languages and, like Hooper, joined the Air Ministry in 1940. Two years later he signed up at Bletchley Park and in 1977 he received his knighthood, at the age of sixty.

Director of GCHQ since 1978 is Sir Brian John Maynard Tovey, lover of sixteenth-century Italian art. The son of a minister, Tovey was born on April 15, 1926, and studied at St. Edmund Hall, Oxford, after which he transferred to the University of London's School of Oriental and African Studies. In 1945 he joined the Royal Navy and subsequently transferred into the Army Intelligence Corps. Starting off with the Foreign Service rank of junior assistant, the future director went to work for GCHQ in 1950. Seven years later he was promoted to principal, then assistant secretary in 1967, under secretary in 1975, and finally to the rank of deputy secretary in 1978.

Although the directors of NSA and GCHQ are the ones charged with the ultimate responsibility of ensuring continued harmony and cooperation between their agencies, it is the senior liaison officers, the SIGINT community's version of ambassadors, who control the day-to-day relations between the UKUSA partners. And it is for that reason that the post of SUSLO at NSA is both highly prized and carefully considered.

Just *how* carefully considered Deputy Director Lou Tordella discovered when he, without bothering to inform NSA director Marshall Carter, picked Cecil C. Corry, a twenty-five-year veteran of the Agency, to fill the post in England left vacant by the returning Dr. A. W. Hesse in the late 1960s.

Carter, who had other plans for the post, exploded when he learned that Tordella, without consultation, had taken it on himself to go ahead and advise Corry. At the time, Carter was in the process of gradually, if slightly, lifting the veil of secrecy that had long surrounded every aspect of NSA, and he wanted someone in London who he felt confident could express his feelings adequately to the British and its hypersecret GCHQ.

"Corry was very, very competent," Carter later explained, "but he just wasn't the personality I wanted representing me in London, under the circumstances, where I was more and more going open with the activities of NSA." Instead, Carter picked John J. (J.J.) Connelly, Jr., the affable assistant director for Personnel Management. Said Carter: "He was not a cryptologist, but he was the guy I wanted representing me at the Court of St. James's. Now when it was a low-level guy at Cheltenham, just there as a coordinator, liaison between NSA and GCHQ, then that was one thing. Where it was a guy representing me in the intelligence community of the British Empire — I wanted a different breed of cat."

Carter also objected to the fact that the representatives of the non-English-speaking collaborating governments were treated differently from the English-speaking partners. "We had a rule at NSA when I was there," the former DIRNSA revealed, "that only the British and Australians would be allowed in the main building . . . I'm talking about the whole number of English-speaking nations."

The hospitality changed, however, when it came to a meeting with officials of the South Korean government. Notified that the meeting would have to take place at another location, Carter protested. "We don't let them into the building," the director was informed by his senior staff. "I said: 'No way! If we are going to exchange information with the Koreans and they are going to look to us for guidance and everything, well they have a right to come in.' So I had them in for luncheons in my office and at the Maryland Club."

For more than twenty years the London home of NSA's SUSLO has been Flat 5 at 35 Bryanston Square, a stately building overlooking a green in the Mayfair section of the city. Ten minutes away by foot is Grosvenor Square and the American embassy, where the SUSLO offices are tucked away securely behind the door to Room 452 — one floor above the CIA offices.

Occupant of Flat 5 during the early 1970s was Benjamin J. Price, formerly deputy assistant director for Personnel Management and before that the NSA representative to the Commander-in-Chief, Pacific, in Hawaii. He was replaced by Milton Zaslow, the former deputy chief of PROD. When Zaslow returned to take over as deputy director for Telecommunications and Computer Services, Benson Buffham moved into Flat 5. Buffham, until then NSA's deputy director, apparently wanted a fling at the good life before retirement, although others saw the move as an effort at fence-mending. When Buffham retired in April 1980, he was replaced by the deputy director for Management Services, Dr. Don C. Jackson.

As serious as the NSA is about its SUSLO, so are the British with regard to their SUKLO. Representing GCHQ at NSA during the mid-1960s was Reginald H. Parker, a dashing Englishman with an infectious sense of humor. When "Reg" Parker first arrived at NSA, General Gordon Blake was DIRNSA, and, as Parker later confessed in a letter to General Carter, he had some apprehension when the new NSA director first arrived on board. "It is always a matter of concern to any senior liaison officer when there is a change of Director of the agency with which he spends most of his time. All I need say about your arrival at NSA in the summer of 1965," he wrote to Carter, "is that I rapidly found that I did not have to worry."

Like NSA, GCHQ hides its liaison officer under diplomatic cover. In London, Buffham was listed as a "political attaché." GCHQ's current (1982) SUKLO, George M. (Bill) Gapp, is simply listed as an "admin. officer" at the British embassy in Washington.

•

"It has long been known that during the eighteenth century the British government from time to time obtained valuable information from the interception of private and diplomatic correspondence passing through the post office."

So began a lecture on early mail-opening by Kenneth Ellis to his colleagues at GCHQ in Eastcote during the late 1940s. Official eavesdropping in Britain is steeped in tradition and shrouded in secrecy. Even Shakespeare made note of the practice when he wrote in *Henry V,* "The king hath note of all that they intend / By interception which they dream not of."

Although, as Ellis pointed out in his GCHQ lecture, "the interception of correspondence is as old as correspondence itself," the custom became organized in 1653, when Lord Thurloe created what was known as "the Secret Office," possibly GCHQ's earliest ancestor.

Housed in a series of three rooms adjoining the Foreign Office and Controller's House off Abchurch Lane, the Secret Office was directed originally by Isaac Dorislaus, who was known simply as "the Secret Man" by those few witting of the snooping. Later, his successors were given the cover of "Foreign Secretary" and, as one holder of the office once revealed, "ostensible employment about the Post Office the better to conceal the other important business."

The "other important business" consisted of opening and copying international, especially diplomatic, correspondence and sending the interceptions to the Confidential Under Secretaries in envelopes marked PRIVATE AND MOST SECRET. "Those *en clair,*" according to Ellis, "went straight to the King." Letters written in cipher, on the other hand, were sent by hand or special messenger to the Deciphering Branch for solution and then on to His Royal Highness, often arriving within twenty-four hours, sometimes even before reaching the hands of the intended recipient. After review by the King, the intercepts would be placed in a special envelope known as "the Long Packet" and sent off to selected ministers.

The staff of the Secret Office, paid out of a secret fund, consisted primarily of trained engravers, openers, decipherers, and translators. At the time, most of the diplomatic correspondence was secured with wax seals that required a great deal of technical skill to reproduce without detection. Three hours were regularly spent on the King of Prussia's mail alone.

Just as the Secret Office was established to intercept international correspondence, a "Private Office" was set up within the Office of the Secretary of the Post Office to concentrate on opening domestic mail. It was directed primarily by the First Lords of the Treasury and Admiralty, and no one was spared. The mail of private citizens was opened in order to catch crooks; ministers' mail to warn the King of impending resignations and security risks; the King's mail to observe his attitude and then alter it either by argument or well-placed leaks; opposition leaders' to undermine their policies; and even each other's to keep track of their conduct.

Britain's Royal Mail Openers managed a charmed existence. Their single public scandal occurred in 1844, when Joseph Mazzini charged Secretary of State Sir James Graham with opening his letters and passing the contents on to the Neapolitan government. A Secret Committee of the House of Commons was quickly formed to examine the government's mail-reading practices but ended up praising the officials for ingenuity. "In every case investigated," the committee concluded, "it seems to have been directed by an earnest and faithful Desire to adopt that Course which appeared to be necessary, either to promote the Ends of Justice or to prevent a Disturbance of the public Tranquillity, or otherwise to promote the best Interests of the Country." Wisely, the committee avoided any discussion of how or from where the government's authority to raid the mails derived, except to note that it had been doing it for a very long time.

That same "inherent" authority was later used to justify the interception of telegrams and, shortly after the first telephone exchange
was established in England in 1879, telephone conversations. Just
how far that authority extended was discovered December 16, 1920,
when Western Union President Newcomb Carlton shocked a Senate
subcommittee with the revelation that the British government secretly
required that his company turn over to Naval Intelligence every incoming and outgoing telegram received in Britain. The charge was subsequently confirmed in testimony by John Goldhammer of Commercial
Cable Company and Clarence H. Mackay of Commercial Cable Postal
Telegraph Company. "In July, 1919," explained Goldhammer, "when
British censorship ceased, we were ordered by the British Government
to turn over to them all messages passing between our own offices,
10 days after they were sent."

Minnesota senator Frank B. Kellogg, chairman of the subcommittee,
asked Carlton whether he had ever challenged the British on the
matter. "We thought that it would be misunderstood and we thought
it was a source of irritation to American cablers," the Western Union
chief responded. "They replied that they wanted those messages only
for such supervision as might give them an inkling of pending disorders within Great Britain, I assume having to do with Irish unrest,
and also to do with the bolshevik propaganda."

Chairman Kellogg then pressed Carlton as to whether there was
any way to prevent the British actions. "No; we cannot prevent it,"
he said, but added that it was not for want of trying:

> We took rather a firm stand about delivering them. We said that we
> would not be responsible for receiving and delivering messages destined
> to the United States unless we were certain that they are uncensored,
> so far as their contents are concerned, and we would prefer to shut
> down our cables as a protest if this thing was being done surreptitiously.
> We could not put it much stronger than that . . .
>
> And I went so far as to instruct our vice president in London not to
> deliver the messages to the British Government and see what would
> happen. The British Government then explained exactly what they did
> with the messages; they gave us their assurance that the messages would
> not be deciphered; the reason why they wanted to keep general track
> of who was cabling; and, furthermore, they guaranteed that no informa-
> tion of any kind would be issued.

Caught off guard by the embarrassing revelation, the British embassy sent off a letter denying the charges directly to Senator Kellogg
rather than through the State Department, a serious breach of diplomatic protocol. At the same time, the British government came up

with an amendment to the Official Secrets Act of 1911, requiring telegraph companies to turn over to the Secretary of State on demand "the originals and transcripts" of either all telegrams or any specified category of telegrams. Although the act required that the request must be made by "warrant," the term is misleading, since, unlike in the United States, where only an impartial judge may issue a warrant, the British term implies little more than an official directive. The British were even crafty enough to include a similar loophole in the landing license issued to the cable companies, authorizing "one of His Majesty's principal secretaries of state" to take over the telegraph facilities completely or to direct that the companies surrender "all telegrams tendered for transmission or arriving by the company's telegraphs." The sole requirement is for the official to consider that an "emergency" had arisen.

To the chagrin of the British, Newcomb Carlton was back before the subcommittee soon after the Christmas recess, but this time he was considerably less forthcoming. Asked by Senator Kellogg whether the messages turned over to British Intelligence included United States government communications, the cable chief buckled. "If you do not mind, I would like not to answer that," he pleaded. "It puts my company in a very embarrassing position with the British Government. We have large affairs with the British Government, and with various departments who treat us with every consideration. I was made to appear at the last hearing as being something of an informant; that I had informed this committee."

Kellogg brushed aside several further protests, and Carlton reluctantly acquiesced:

> It appears that the British Government was desirous of supervising in and out cable messages to certain European countries in the interest of British peace and quiet. In order to avoid an appearance of discriminating against these European countries, they decided to take charge, physical charge, of all in and out cable messages from every country, and they therefore adopted the plan of waiting 10 days, that is, to give 10 days between the handling of the message and the time that the Government called at the cable offices for the messages. The messages were then placed in large bags, sealed I believed, and put in wagons. Those wagons were driven away under the custody of the Admiralty, and lodged over night in a storehouse and returned to the cable offices the next morning.

Undoubtedly to Mr. Carlton's profound relief, the question of whether the American government engaged in similar shady practices never came up. One year earlier, after a conference with Herbert

O. Yardley and the Military Intelligence chief, Brigadier General Marl-borough Churchill, Carlton had instructed his vice president, J. C. Willever, to begin secretly supplying the Black Chamber with whatever it desired.

That tradition dies hard in the intelligence trade is evidenced by the fact that more than half a century after the Kellogg hearings, both the American and British cable-snooping operations were contin-uing as strong as ever and with barely a change. In London, the wagons had been replaced by Ministry of Works vans, the ten-day waiting period had been reduced to same-day pickup, and the over-night return had stretched to forty-eight hours. And in New York the hard copies had given way to magnetic tapes, and civilian couriers had replaced military messengers. The Admiralty had been supplanted by GCHQ, and the Black Chamber replaced by NSA.

Under the theory that two ears are better than one, the NSA and GCHQ, through their BRUSA-UKUSA pacts, agreed to share the wealth of each other's cable intercept programs. What this meant was that, in addition to collecting all the cable and telex traffic from the three U.S. telegraph companies under its Shamrock program, NSA would now also have access to the miles and miles of traffic flowing in and out of the British commercial telegraph system. Once received, the British tapes would be processed through NSA watch list–alerted computers. Thus, NSA would be able to ransack the entire United Kingdom telex and cable systems to locate a reference to Jane Fonda or Muammar Qaddafi, oil or drugs, IBM or British Petro-leum.

That the Agency was not above using the British intercepts to search for protesters in its domestic Minaret program was discovered by the special Justice Department task force that investigated the eaves-dropping policies of the intelligence community. Classified TOP SECRET UMBRA/HANDLE VIA COMINT CHANNELS ONLY, the task force report con-cluded that "MINARET intelligence, except one category of interna-tional voice communications involving narcotics, was obtained *inciden-tally* in the course of NSA's interception of aural and non-aural (e.g., telex) international communications, and the receipt of GCHQ-acquired telex and ILC [International Licensed Carriers] cable traffic (SHAMROCK)." (Emphasis in original.) Thus, wittingly or unwit-tingly, the British government became a co-conspirator in one of the NSA's most illegal operations.

Such a prospect, however, would likely cause little concern at GCHQ, since it almost certainly runs the cable and telex intercepts supplied by NSA through its own domestic watch list.

Just as UKUSA provides for the exchange of intercepted cable and telex, it also probably provides for the exchange of aural, or telephone intercepts. Duncan Campbell, an editor of the British magazine *New Statesman,* and Linda Melvern, a veteran reporter for the *Sunday Times* of London, suggested in a *New Statesman* article in July 1980 that one of the principal targets of the NSA's Menwith Hill Station in Harrogate, Yorkshire, is British international and domestic telecommunications.

The main thrust of the seven-thousand-word article was that a nearby Post Office Department (which until recently administered Britain's telecommunications as well as her mail services) microwave tower, known as Hunters Stones, was built for the specific purpose of filtering into Menwith Hill thousands of telephone conversations from all over the country. "The Post Office," the article said, "has built Menwith Hill into the heart of Britain's national communications system." The underground cable linking the tower to Menwith Hill five miles away, wrote the two journalists, "provides an umbilical link into the international telephone and telex system running through Britain."

The large number of microwave horns and dishes attached to the Hunters Stones tower in the lightly populated Yorkshire moors would seem to lend weight to the article's assumptions, along with the fact that another microwave tower, Tinshill, is only five miles away from Hunters Stones and thus would seem redundant. However, as Peter Laurie, another British writer who, like Campbell, specializes in electronics and security issues, pointed out in his book *Beneath the City Streets:* "The heaviest communications capacity is often in the most remote countryside. Partly this is because cities tend to be built in river valleys which are low and therefore unsuitable for microwaves."

Further, it would seem that domestic British communications would have little interest to the NSA, which uses Menwith Hill primarily to eavesdrop on Europe and the Soviet Union by way of SIGINT satellites. GCHQ, which also has a detachment assigned to Menwith Hill, would have considerably more interest in the subject, but it would appear unlikely that it would conduct its domestic eavesdropping from an NSA base.

A target that would be far more interesting to the NSA, and quite possibly the GCHQ, is the international communications entering and leaving England, much of them by satellite. The signals are transmitted and received by earth stations located at Madley in Herefordshire, about 130 miles northwest of London, and at Goonhilly Downs in Cornwall, near Falmouth. After the American stations at Etam, West Virginia, and Andover, Maine, the two stations are, respectively, the third and fourth busiest commercial earth stations in the world.

One of the world's first earth stations as well, Goonhilly Downs played a major role in the early TELSTAR experiments in 1962. That year, President John F. Kennedy signed into law the Communications Satellite Act, and in February 1963 the Communications Satellite Corporation (COMSAT) was formed. A year and a half later eleven countries signed agreements to form a single global satellite system: the International Telecommunications Satellite Organization, or INTELSAT, which put its first satellite, INTELSAT I, the Early Bird, into orbit on April 6, 1965. Activated two months later, it established the first satellite pathway between the United States and Europe, providing both transatlantic telephone and television service.

A key link in this system was Goonhilly Downs, then one of only five INTELSAT earth stations around the world. (By 1980, the number of earth stations in the system had grown to 263 in 134 countries.) In 1967 the international space consortium placed into orbit three of the more powerful INTELSAT II satellites, and over the next three years further upgraded the now worldwide satellite network with the third generation of communications satellite, INTELSAT III. Capable of handling all forms of communications simultaneously — telephone, telegraph, television, high-speed data, and facsimile, the satellites had a capacity of twelve hundred circuits each.

During this period, GCHQ secretly constructed its own pair of hundred-foot satellite dishes a short sixty miles to the north of Goonhilly, at Bude, also in Cornwall. With these dishes GCHQ would be able to eavesdrop on all communications flowing between the INTELSAT satellites and Goonhilly Downs in the same way that NSA is able to listen in on the Etam earth station from its secret site at Sugar Grove.

Apparently there was considerable resistance within the upper reaches of the British government to the costly project, so GCHQ director Sir Leonard Hooper resorted to a favorite and effective lobbying tactic: with NSA's support, Hooper stressed the importance of the project to UKUSA and especially to NSA. As usual, the magic worked, and Sir Leonard received his antennas. Later he sent his personal thanks to NSA director Carter, saying he was so grateful for the assistance that he thought the two dishes should be named after Carter and Deputy Director Louis Tordella: "I know that I have leaned shamefully on you, and sometimes taken your name in vain, when I needed approval for something at this end," the GCHQ director confessed. "The aerials at Bude ought to be christened 'Pat' and 'Louis'!"

It was a game Carter knew well, as he later explained when recalling the letter:

> I think what he's probably talking about is, he has difficulty getting money for something that he wants to do. He presents the British side, OK? [and gets] turned down. I'm just theorizing. And he says, "Well look, you can turn me down from the British viewpoint, but I'm in bed with Pat Carter on this thing — this is a joint requirement — he needs it as badly as I do. The product that he is going to develop for us will come right to us, so would you take another look at this because he wants it, it will help him in his business. We'll get the results of it."

And it was a game played on both sides of the Atlantic.

In 1967 Secretary of Defense McNamara appointed Frederick Eaton, a conservative New York lawyer and banker, to head a committee to review the U.S. SIGINT effort. For some time various senior intelligence and Pentagon officials had felt that some of the NSA's SIGINT activities were not meeting expectations and that this had resulted in a serious cost-effectiveness problem. Foremost among those who held this belief was Assistant Secretary of Defense Eugene Fubini, the Pentagon's electronic intelligence chief and a man with whom Carter continually bumped heads. Fubini, according to Carter, "had insisted that we were collecting too much on a particular target and that we were wasting money and wasting assets . . .

"Lou Tordella and I were just climbing the walls," Carter recalled of the formation of the committee. For one thing, he said, Eaton "came in bare-ass naked, didn't know anything about cryptology or anything — he hardly knew what NSA was doing." But Carter's main problem was Fubini: "It was a geared operation by Fubini, who had expected to control this committee and therefore get us directed to do things which he had [tried to] convince us should be done."

As the committee was nearing its deadline, a majority of the staff, made up largely of officials from the State Department, the CIA, and the Pentagon, reportedly had "accumulated substantial evidence that much of the NSA's intelligence collection was of little or marginal use to the various intelligence consumers in the community." Nevertheless, to the staff's surprise, Eaton "recommended no reductions and concluded that all of NSA's programs were worthwhile." Faced with this turn-around, many of the staff turned in their pens, and Eaton was forced to write the report's conclusion himself. Said Carter of the victory: "Fortunately, we had a couple of people who were smart enough to see what Fubini was trying to do, and they got to Eaton . . . and Eaton was able to tromp on Fubini."

Among those who had come to Carter's rescue was his old friend from Cheltenham. "But equally I hope that I have sometimes been of help to you," Sir Leonard wrote after thanking the NSA director for his assistance at Bude, "when the Eatons were around you for example."

As in any partnership, there are occasional differences and conflicts. One of the more nagging problems throughout the 1960s was a continuing feud between GCHQ and the London Communications Security Agency. Unlike the United States, where responsibilities for COMSEC come under the NSA, the British COMSEC organization had long been a separate department within the Foreign Office. Whereas GCHQ makes up the Signals Department, the London Communications Security Agency made up the Communications–Electronic Security Department and had its own director and staff. The battle was between those who wanted to see COMSEC placed under GCHQ and those who wanted to maintain its independence. The conflict made life difficult for NSA, which was trying not to take sides and to keep at arm's distance from the warfare.

By 1969 the decision had been made to merge the COMSEC organization into GCHQ, a not inconsiderable accomplishment, since, as General Carter noted, "they were a long time in pulling those two agencies together where they were even talking to each other. Joe Hooper alerted me to that."

Among the leaders of the pro-merger group was John Outhit Harold Burrough, C.B., C.B.E., who had joined GCHQ in 1946 after serving a dozen years in the Royal Navy. The son of an admiral and a graduate of Dartmouth, the Royal Naval College, Burrough was appointed GCHQ's SUKLO to Washington in 1965. In 1967 he returned to England and was assigned to the Cabinet Office as an under secretary, presumably on the Joint Intelligence Staff. After two years at Whitehall, Burrough was in line for one of the top two posts at GCHQ. "It could be Director of Plans, or conceivably Director of COMSEC — more likely the former, I think," he wrote to Pat Carter; "but one never knows until the decision is made!" Then he mentioned the merger: "In either case I shall be working once again for Joe Hooper, a fact which gives me great pleasure (in a small way I believe I have had some responsibility in my present post for the forthcoming 'merger,' which I have long advocated behind the scenes)." Burrough, a big, large-framed man, retired from GCHQ in 1976 at the age of sixty and became a director of Racal Communications Systems Ltd., one of the largest manufacturers of SIGINT equipment for both NSA and GCHQ.

But the differences, overall, were few and were greatly outweighed by common interests and personal friendships. So close was the friendship between Carter and Joe Hooper, in fact, that Hooper once wrote to Carter, "I have often felt closer to you than to most of my own staff — indeed closer than to any except perhaps John Rendle and John Burrough — and that is something I shall remember and cherish." Thus, when it came time for Carter to retire in 1969, there was a considerable amount of anxiety on the part of the GCHQ director: "As you can understand, I am pretty apprehensive about your successor, and whether I can strike up any kind of similar understanding with him. He is a completely unknown quantity to all of us. Put in a word for me."

The depth of the NSA-GCHQ relationship, a relationship that is continually denied on both sides of the Atlantic, can best be summed up in Sir Leonard's farewell letter to Carter (*opposite page*).

"Between us," Hooper wrote in another letter, "we have ensured that the blankets and sheets are more tightly tucked around the bed in which our two sets of people lie and, like you, I like it that way."

GOVERNMENT COMMUNICATIONS HEADQUARTERS,

OAKLEY. CHELTENHAM, GLOS.

Tel.: CHELTENHAM 55321.

D/8586/1003/11

22nd July 1969

Dear Pat,

Last week you told me that you were relinquishing your post as Director NSA from 1st August and going into retirement. Yesterday I was informed of the name of your successor.

This is simply to tell you how much we in GCHQ have valued your part in our dealings with NSA over the past four years. From the outset, though the extent of our working partnership was new to you, you showed an instinctive feeling for its nature and depth which was a great strengthener to those of us who had worked so long in it, and you have consistently gone out of your way to help us sustain and if possible improve our contribution to it. For this we are very grateful. You have given us practical help whenever we sought it but, more importantly, you have given every encouragement and made us feel that GCHQ really mattered to Director NSA. I think you believe, as I do, that the professional relationship between our two Agencies remains of great importance to our two countries and you have certainly made a very great personal contribution to its present strength and closeness.

You kindly received my senior staff whenever they came to Washington and they, like me, have benefited from your wisdom, kindness and hospitality. There are many who will remember you with respect and affection.

For myself I can truly say that my early years as Director GCHQ were made much easier by knowing that I had so good a friend and so understanding a colleague in the Director of NSA. No one could ask for more.

I do not yet know Admiral Gayler but I look forward to meeting him soon. Please tell him what you have found to be the worthwhile and the difficult parts of the UKUSA relationship and assure him that we in GCHQ will do our best to assist NSA in continuing its great and important mission under his leadership.

Thank you for all you have done, and for your way of doing it. You and your wife take with you into retirement the best wishes of myself and all my colleagues. May you have many years in which to enjoy a well-earned rest.

Yours very sincerely,

Joe Hooper.

Lieutenant General Marshall S. Carter,
  Director,
    NSA.

COMPETITION

"DEAR SIR," Earnest began with an overly large *D* and a small *s*, "I have in my possession a unsolveable code which I would like to sell." Noting his system's "superior power," the eleven-year-old Minnesotan firmly informed the government that he would "take not less than $20,000.00" for the code and advised that they write rather than come for it in person.

J. W. Hough also had a code he thought the government might like to consider. "It is, I believe, an improvement over any code system I have ever seen," he wrote, and to demonstrate, he enciphered the last portion of Lincoln's Gettysburg Address. Attached to the letter was a form entitled "Request for Extra Writing Privilege" with Mr. Hough's return address: United States Penitentiary, Leavenworth, Kansas.

For much of this century the only outsiders interested in the esoteric art of cryptography were a handful of hobbyists testing one another's skill with simple cryptograms, and a few entrepreneurs trying to make a business from selling commercial telegraph codes. Those code systems submitted to the government either for comment or for sale would inevitably wind up in a place known, according to one of the NSA's early pioneers, as the "nut file."

Such arrogance and contempt for those outside the barbed-wire fences was easily affordable in the early days of pencil-and-paper cryptology. There being no high technology involved nor any scientific interest in the subject, the government code experts were permitted a near-monastic existence. The ascetic life ended, however, when both codemaking and codebreaking became increasingly mechanized during the late 1930s. A decade later, with computers replacing punched-card machines, cryptology had developed into a full-fledged science. Where once outside interest was rejected, if not ridiculed, the constant need to push outward the boundaries of mathematics, engineering, and telecommunications now required the establishment of a close yet secret alliance with America's academic and industrial communities.

To forge this alliance, the NSA, soon after it was formed, established the National Security Agency Scientific Advisory Board (NSASAB), a ten-member panel of science wizards plucked from ivy-covered campuses, corporate research labs, and sheepskin-lined think tanks. Twice a year they would converge on Fort Meade, join with senior NSA scientists, and then split into groups like the SIGINT Exploitation Advisory Panel and the Electromagnetic Reception Advisory Panel, where they would discuss the application of the latest theories in science and technology to eavesdropping, codebreaking, and cryptography.

Among the early members of the board was Stewart S. Cairns, who had earned his doctorate at Harvard and was chairman of the mathematics department at the University of Illinois at Urbana (the same school where William Martin, not long before his defection, would be sent on a two-year scholarship). Chairman of the NSASAB during the mid-1950s was Dr. Howard P. Robertson, professor of theoretical mathematics at the California Institute of Technology and later a science adviser to President Kennedy.

When Vice Admiral Laurence Frost arrived at the Puzzle Palace in the fall of 1960, he found relations between the board and NSA strained and bitter. Agency officials were charging the board members with not putting enough time and effort into some of the projects; the board hit back at the NSA leadership for its lack of guidance and its declining support.

In an effort to reduce the acrimony and mend the fences, Frost, much to everyone's surprise, appointed Robert F. Rinehart to chairman of the NSASAB. A fifty-three-year-old mathematics professor at the Case Institute of Technology, Rinehart was the junior member of the board, having been appointed only a few months earlier. Yet, as he indicated in a letter to his fellow board members shortly after his selection, the "lack of previous NSA experience, implying absence of preacquired biases," was precisely the reason for his selection. "It is quite possible that the principle 'ignorance is beneficial,'" he added with tongue only slightly in cheek, "may have been carried to its ridiculous extreme."

Although some members remain on the board for only a year or two, others have stayed on for more than a decade. Among the latter, and dominating the advisory board during much of the 1960s and early 1970s, were Dr. William O. Baker of Bell Labs, Dr. Robert P.

Dilworth of Cal Tech, Arnold I. Dumey of the Communications Research Branch of the Institute for Defense Analysis at Princeton, Dr. Joseph J. Eachus of Honeywell, and Dr. Richard C. Raymond of General Electric. Another long-time member, and chairman from January 1967 until at least the mid-1970s, was Dr. Willis H. Ware, a research executive at the RAND Corporation. From 1951 to 1971 Ware was head of RAND's Computer Sciences Department and subsequently was named a deputy vice president. He first joined the NSASAB in 1964 as a member of the Data Processing Panel.

The Scientific Advisory Board was one of the NSA's earliest efforts to employ the talents of nongovernmental elements of the scientific and academic worlds, but it was far from the last.

In 1956 Dr. Howard T. Engstrom, a computer wizard and vice president of Remington Rand, took over NSA's research and development organization. The following year he was appointed deputy director of NSA and a year later returned to Remington Rand.

Joseph H. Ream, executive vice president at CBS, was imported to replace Engstrom as deputy director. He, too, left after a year; he headed up CBS's Washington office and later CBS-TV's programming department. Ream's interlude at NSA is listed on his CBS biography simply as "retirement."

Three months before Ream gave up codebreaking for "I Love Lucy," one of the most important meetings in the history of the Agency took place in a clapboard structure on Arlington Hall Station known as B Building. On July 18, 1957, a handful of the nation's top scientists crowded together in NSA's windowless Situation Room to present a blueprint for the Agency's future technological survival.*

Chaired by Dr. William O. Baker, forty-two, the brilliant research chief of Bell Labs, the committee had spent months analyzing the capabilities, direction, and potential of America's cryptologic resources. They concluded that the operations performed by NSA constituted one of America's most valuable assets and one of the most important weapons in the Cold War. To fall behind would be to invite another Pearl Harbor. They therefore recommended the initia-

* Present were Dr. Hendrik W. Bode, a physicist and communications engineering specialist from Bell Labs; Dr. David A. Huffman, an expert in information theory and signal design from MIT; Dr. Luis Alvarez, associate director of the University of California's Lawrence Radiation Lab at Berkeley and a future Nobel laureate in physics; Dr. Richard L. Garwin, a communications specialist from IBM's Watson Lab; mathematics professor Andrew M. Gleason of Harvard; Dr. John R. Pierce, Bell Labs director of communications research; Claude E. Shannon of MIT and Bell Labs, who pioneered the fields of information theory and speech privacy; and Oliver Selfridge, a computer specialist from MIT's Lincoln Labs. (Baker Committee, photo with attachments, Friedman Papers, photo file, George C. Marshall Research Library.)

tion of a Manhattan Project–like effort to push the USA well ahead of the Soviet Union and all other nations in the application of communications, computer science, mathematics, and information theory to cryptology. Such a goal, the Baker Committee suggested, could be accomplished only by a continuous transfusion of brainpower from the reservoir of scientific genius beyond Fort Meade.

NSA had now reached a crossroads. One year earlier, General Canine had begun laying the groundwork for Project Lightning, the five-year, $25 million program to increase computer speed a thousandfold. Research contracts had gone out to industrial and academic research groups. But this was to be open research, with the results reported in the literature and made freely available. In fact, research produced by Lightning contributed to over 160 technical articles, 320 patent applications, and 71 university theses.

Now the decision had to be made about whether to continue funding, as with Lightning, generalized, public research or to begin to direct those funds toward secret, specialized, cryptologic research. It was a choice between an open bridge or a hidden tunnel between the Agency and the outside scientific community. Following the Baker report, the decision was to use the tunnel. The vehicle would be Project Focus.

On the morning of October 22, 1960, a small group of invited guests sat quietly on folding chairs as they listened to Princeton University president Robert F. Goheen dedicate the latest building on his expansive campus. John von Neumann Hall was a contemporary, red-brick, two-story building with a pleasant, tree-shaded patio surrounded by an eight-foot-high brick wall. It might have been a new science building or possibly a student center.

It was neither.

Named after the brilliant mathematician who pioneered computer logic, John von Neumann Hall was, in effect, the academic world's entranceway into the NSA's secret tunnel.

A product of the Baker Committee, Project Focus involved the establishment of a private, independent think tank dedicated exclusively to aiding the NSA in discovering solutions to advanced cryptologic-related problems. One year earlier, in 1956, Secretary of Defense Charles E. Wilson had turned to James R. Killian, Jr., president of the Massachusetts Institute of Technology as well as chairman of the President's Board of Consultants on Foreign Intelligence Activities, and asked his help in bringing under one roof a permanent corps of civilians to assist the Joint Chiefs of Staff's Weapons Systems Evaluation Group in arbitrating the Pentagon's numerous internal battles over such problems as which missile system to fund. The result was the Institute for Defense Analysis, an academic think tank formed originally by MIT, the California Institute of Technology, the Case Institute of Technology, Stanford, and Tulane, and later joined by seven other universities.

Following the Baker Committee report, Killian, who was now the chairman of the board of IDA, was asked to establish a similar organization for the NSA. He agreed to do so; and following the receipt of $1.9 million in 1958, IDA's Communications Research Division was formed, and planning began for the building of offices and laboratories on Princeton's campus.

Despite the assertion of one official of the institute that IDA has always been "completely independent of the government" in order to ensure that the institute would be "able to carry out studies that don't merely support some preconceived idea of the government," the CRD has always had the most intimate ties with the NSA. Selected as CRD's first director was Dr. J. Barkley Rosser, fifty, a professor of mathematics at Cornell and a specialist in numerical analysis. Chosen as his deputy, however, was Dr. Richard A. Leibler, forty-four, a five-year employee of the Puzzle Palace and a chief architect of Project Focus. A former mathematician with the Sandia Corporation who had also taught, at various times, at the University of Illinois (where he became friends with another math professor, Dr. Louis W. Tordella), Purdue, and Princeton, Leibler was primarily interested in probability and statistics. He apparently enjoyed what he once referred to as "our lonely isolation in Princeton." In reference to NSA, he once wrote to William F. Friedman, "For reasons which you must appreciate, I try to get down there and back as soon as possible, so I usually manage to do all my work in a single day."

On September 12, 1961, A. Adrian Albert, aged fifty-five, chairman of the University of Chicago's mathematics department, replaced Barkley Rosser as head of the CRD. One of cryptology's earliest visionaries, Albert had seen the correlation between cryptography and higher algebra as early as 1941. In a paper entitled "Some Mathematical Aspects of Cryptography," he wrote, "It would not be an exaggeration to state that abstract cryptography is identical with abstract mathematics."

Like that of his predecessor, Albert's tenure at CRD was also short. In 1963 Deputy Director Leibler dropped the "deputy" from his title and moved into the director's office, thus tying the knot between the NSA and CRD all the tighter. The relationship must have been a good one. Leibler continued as director for the next fourteen years, leaving Princeton only in 1977 to return to the NSA as chief of the Office of Research within the Research and Engineering Organization.

Leibler was replaced by Dr. Lee P. Neuwirth, forty-three, who had served as deputy director for the previous twelve years. He had first joined CRD as a mathematician in 1961, two years after receiving his Ph.D. from Princeton.

Labeled "the most secret of the major think tanks" by Paul Dickson, in his book *Think Tanks,* IDA has its headquarters in a ten-story, concrete-and-glass high-rise across an acre of parking lots from the Pentagon. Eschewing even the smallest sign, IDA makes a point of not advertising its existence.

In the fall of 1967, partly as a result of this penchant for secrecy and the institute's heavy involvement in the Vietnam War, members of Princeton's chapter of the Students for a Democratic Society staged a demonstration in front of Von Neumann Hall, demanding that the university sever its ties with the institute. The students argued that Princeton's participation in IDA necessarily involved them indirectly in the war and also tended to compromise academic freedom by involving academicians in secret scientific projects whose findings could not be widely shared.

The protest against IDA spread to other campuses, and in the spring of 1968 it became one of the rallying cries of the students who staged the eight-day takeover at Columbia University.

The issue was finally resolved by the universities' agreeing to drop their official links with the institute while continuing to permit a representative of each school to serve in an individual capacity as a trustee.

Following the protests, the CRD quietly packed up and moved into a boxy, three-story brick building virtually hidden in an isolated wooded area off campus. Windowless except for the third floor, the building has, again, absolutely no signs indicating the name of the occupant.

By February 1970, IDA had grown into five divisions and three groups, comprising 285 professionals and a support staff of 274, with an annual income of a little more than $13 million. CRD, one of the smallest divisions, consisted of twenty-seven professionals (up only three from its first year) and thirty-three support personnel. The professionals, mostly mathematicians, were normally borrowed from universities on one-year contracts and were usually given far more latitude in attacking problems than their counterparts in NSA's Research and Engineering Organization.

The CRD's statistics are, however, a bit misleading. Shortly after the division's birth, several programs were launched to bring into the secret fraternity several dozen of the nation's most outstanding academic minds in mathematics and languages. The programs formed what must have been the country's most exclusive summer camp. Known as SCAMP, for Summer Campus, Advanced Mathematics Program, and ALP (the CRD wisely dropped the first two letters) for Advanced Language Program, the projects involved bringing together a wide variety of senior university scholars, introducing them to the mysteries of cryptology, and applying their collective genius to some of the NSA's most perplexing riddles.

Cleared and indoctrinated for top secret SIGINT and COMSEC material, the SCAMP and ALP participants, usually tenured professors from some of the nation's best schools, would arrive with their families in early summer and attend symposia and lectures in a specially built, heavily secured building on the campus of the University of California at Los Angeles. To avoid creating suspicion, the participants would be paid directly by UCLA, which in turn was reimbursed by IDA-CRD, which in turn was paid by NSA.

With the ending of Project Lightning in 1962, so too ended NSA's support of unclassified public research. Lightning had helped prime the scientific pump, and competition within private industry, it was felt, would ensure that the flow of technological advances in the computer and associated fields would continue to pour out. The Puzzle Palace, through CRD, SCAMP-ALP, and a select number of key consultants and contractors, could now focus its full attention, as well as its dollars, on a science where there was no competition, where NSA alone controlled a monopoly: cryptology.

But along came Lucifer.

"NSA," the Agency declared with all due modesty, "certainly hastened the start of the computer age." Among the early products of that age was the use of computers in the banking industry for everything from the massive transfers of money between banks and other financial institutions, to the simple recording of a midnight transaction at a remote automatic teller. But there was another product: computer crime. With sufficient knowledge and the access to a terminal, one could trick the computer into transferring funds into a dummy account or tickle a cash-dispensing machine into disgorging its considerable holdings.

To counter such possibilities, and realizing that data communications held enormous market potential, IBM board chairman Thomas Watson, Jr., during the late 1960s set up a cryptology research group at IBM's research laboratory in Yorktown Heights, New York. Led by Horst Feistel, the research group concluded its work in 1971 with the development of a cipher code-named Lucifer, which it promptly sold to Lloyd's of London for use in a cash-dispensing system that IBM had developed.

Spurred by the success of Lucifer, IBM turned to Walter Tuchman, a thirty-eight-year-old engineer with a doctorate in information theory, then working at the company's Kingston development lab. A sixteen-year veteran of IBM, Tuchman was asked to head up a data security products group that would transform Lucifer into a highly marketable commodity.

Aided by Carl Meyer, then forty-two, a German-born electrical engineer who had earned his doctorate from the University of Pennsylvania, Tuchman soon discovered that Lucifer would require considerable strengthening before it could withstand massive commercial use. The team spent the following two years tearing the cipher apart and putting it back together again, over and over, trying each time to give it more complex functions. The process included intense "validation," whereby experts would bombard the cipher with sophisticated cryptanalytic attacks. Finally, in 1974, the cipher was ready for market.

At about the same time that IBM was turning its attention to cryptography, another group was beginning to study the subject with great interest. In 1968 the National Bureau of Standards, charged since 1965 with developing standards for the federal government's purchase and use of computers, initiated a series of studies to determine the government's need for computer security. As a result of the studies, the NBS decided to search for an encryption method, or algorithm, that could serve as a governmentwide standard for the storage and transmission of unclassified data. Solicitation for such an encryption algorithm took place in May 1973 and August 1974.

The timing could not have been better for IBM, which submitted for consideration its Lucifer cipher. Labeled by David Kahn "the tiniest known 'cipher machine' ever produced," Lucifer actually consisted of a thumbnail-sized silicon "chip" containing an extremely complex integrated circuit. The "key" to the cipher was a long string of "bits" — o's and 1's — the combination of which would vary from user to user just as the grooves in front-door keys will vary from neighbor to neighbor.

Like the door key going into the lock, the cipher key goes into a series of eight "S-boxes," actually supercomplex mathematical formulas that, when combined with the particular key, transform intelligible data into indecipherable bits — and then perform the reverse magic on the other end.

Just as more grooves on the key usually means a more difficult lock to pick, more bits in the cipher key will decrease the chances of successful cryptanalysis. For this reason IBM developed Lucifer with a key 128 bits long. But before it submitted the cipher to the NBS, it mysteriously broke off more than half the key.

From the very beginning, the NSA had taken an enormous interest in Project Lucifer. It had even indirectly lent a hand in the development of the S-box structures. "IBM was involved with the NSA on an ongoing basis," admitted Alan Konheim, a senior employee at IBM's Yorktown Heights lab. "They [NSA employees] came up every couple of months to find out what IBM was doing."

For the first time in its long history, NSA was facing competition from within its own country. The outsiders were no longer mere hobbyists but highly skilled professionals, supported by unlimited funds and interested more in perfection than in speed.

Viewed from within the NSA's barbed and electrified fences, the dangers were real. For years the Puzzle Palace had been growing more and more dependent on the ever-widening stream of international data communications flowing invisibly through the air. That air was alive with messages about oil from the Middle East, financial transactions from Europe, and trade strategies from Japan. The NSA simply had to stretch out its electronic net and pull in the most valuable economic intelligence.

Of equal or greater importance was diplomatic and military intelligence plucked from the Third World. Encrypted, for the most part, on antique, inexpensive, or unsophisticated machines, most communications from Africa, South America, and Asia were easy pickings for the NSA. Through the back door would occasionally pass such jewels as a Third World minister's report to his Foreign Office of an intimate exchange with a Soviet or Chinese counterpart. "It goes on all the time," said G Group chief Frank Raven. "You'd be astonished the amount of information that you get on Communist targets from non-Communist countries."

But the development and widespread use of an economical, highly secure data encryption device threatened to turn the NSA's well-stocked stream into a dry riverbed.

Nervousness over competition from the outside was not limited, however, to the codebreakers of PROD. The cryptographers of COMSEC were just as worried, although for the opposite reason. For them, the major fear was that, by accident, the outside researchers might stumble across methods the NSA itself used, thereby compromising the Agency's codes.

As a result of closed-door negotiations with officials of the NSA,

IBM agreed to reduce the size of its key from 128 bits to 56 bits. The company also agreed to classify certain details about their selection of the eight S-boxes for the cipher.

After the company submitted the now-truncated cipher, the Bureau of Standards passed it on to the NSA for what it called a "deep analysis." The Agency, in turn, certified the algorithm as "free of any statistical or mathematical weaknesses" and recommended it as the best candidate for the nation's Data Encryption Standard (DES).

The decision set off an immediate firestorm within the scientific community. Some critics, pointing to the shortened key, charged the NSA with ensuring that the cipher was just long enough to prevent penetration by corporate eavesdroppers but was just short enough for the NSA's own codebreakers. Others pointed to the Agency's tinkering with the critical S-boxes and expressed fears that it may have installed a mathematical "trap door," enabling it to spring open the cipher with little difficulty. Hence the insistence on classification.

The reason for such actions, said the critics, was simple. Since the DES would eventually be manufactured commercially and installed on a wide assortment of equipment sold abroad, the NSA would not want to cut its own throat by permitting the foreign proliferation of an unbreakable cipher. Yet weaknesses in the cipher would still allow the Agency to penetrate every communications link and data bank using the DES, American as well as foreign.

Code expert David Kahn theorized that there was a secret debate within the NSA over the DES. "The codebreaking side wanted to make sure that the cipher was weak enough for the NSA to solve it when used by foreign nations and companies," he reasoned. "The codemaking side," on the other hand, "wanted any cipher it was certifying for use by Americans to be truly good. The upshot was a bureaucratic compromise. Part of the cipher — the 'S-boxes' that performed a substitution — was strengthened. Another part — the key that varied from one pair of users to another — was weakened."

Leading the charge against the DES were Professor Martin E. Hellman and researcher Whitfield Diffie of Stanford University. The two computer experts argued that a computer capable of breaking the code could be built using one million special search chips, each chip capable of testing one million possible solutions per second.

Known within the Puzzle Palace as a "brute force" attack, the method involves acquiring a number of deciphered messages from the particular target and then, using high-speed computers, matching them against intercepted, encrypted versions of the very same messages. If an encrypted message is attacked with every possible version of the code, at some point it will match its unencrypted counterpart. At that point the code evaporates, and all further messages are there for the taking.

How long it takes to break the code depends on the length of the key. For a 56-bit key, the number of possible combinations would be about seventy quadrillion. But using a computer with a million of the special-purpose chips, capable of testing one trillion possible keys per second, the entire range of possible keys could be searched in seventy thousand seconds — or less than twenty hours. On the average, however, Hellman noted, only about half of the keys would have to be tried before the appropriate key was found, making the average search less than half a day.

Then there is the matter of cost. According to the two Stanford scientists, the chips themselves could be produced for about $10 each, or about $10 million altogether. Allowing a factor of two for design, control hardware, power supplies, and the like, they concluded that such a computer could be built for about $20 million. Depreciated over five years, Hellman and Diffie maintained, the daily operating cost drops to about $10,000 a day, meaning that each solution would cost about $5000.

Looking further into the future, they noted that the cost of computation and hardware had decreased by a factor of ten every five years since the 1940s. Thus, if the trend continued, the machine would cost only $200,000 in ten years and each solution a mere $50.

But suppose IBM had ignored the NSA and instead submitted its original 128-bit key? The results, said Hellman and Diffie, would have been dramatically different. As opposed to the moderate $5000 price tag, each solution would cost an unimaginable $200 septillion, or $200,000,000,000,000,000,000,000,000.

Because of these concerns, the Bureau of Standards sponsored two workshops on the DES. At the first, in August 1976, NBS officials defended their choice for the DES and said that, given their existing machinery, a brute force attack would take seventeen thousand years. Yet the make-up of the NBS's DES team cast a shadow over the impartiality of the judgments. The leader of the bureau's computer security project was Dennis Branstad, a former employee of the NSA; Arthur Levenson, an NBS consultant on the project, had been, at least through the late 1960s, one of the NSA's most senior codebreakers as a group chief in PROD before he, apparently, left for IBM.

Other participants at the workshop disagreed on the costs, development time, and exhaustion time necessary to construct such a computer, with the majority suggesting ranges of two to ten years for construction, six months to ten years for exhaustion, and a price tag of from $10 to $12 million.

Also coming to the defense of the IBM algorithm were the cipher's inventors, Walter Tuchman and Carl Meyer. They said the cost of constructing a specialized DES codebreaking machine would be closer to $200 million and that DES-based devices could be designed to encipher messages twice using two different keys, thus effectively doubling the key size to 112 bits. But as a trio of experts from Bell Labs pointed out, "Most data terminals will not be set up to do this."

Finally, the Senate Intelligence Committee looked into the controversy and concluded that, although the "NSA convinced IBM that a reduced key size was sufficient [and] indirectly assisted in the development of the S-box structures," they could find no wrongdoing.

The controversy over the DES has, for the time being, ebbed. On July 15, 1977, it became the official government civilian cipher, and a half-dozen firms began turning it out for private industry. Some, such as the American Banking Association, have endorsed it, but others, like the Bell Telephone Company, have resisted it.

But there is one thing on which all sides in the debate agree: the issue will soon arise again. As new advances in computer speeds and capabilities, and new technologies, such as Josephson Junction, cryogenics, and bubble memory, come into play, the safety margin offered by the cipher will gradually disappear. Some give the cipher five years; others give it ten; few give it more. The intervening years will be decisive.

In the same way that companies today are beginning to market the DES, an enterprise known as the Code Compilation Company opened its doors for business in New York in the 1920s. Located in a tall, gray office building at 52 Vanderbilt Avenue, the company compiled and sold a wide assortment of codes to various trade and other businesses. In the back of the company offices was a heavy, locked door, through which only company employees were allowed to pass. The reason for such secrecy was that the back room held the headquarters for Code Compilation's parent: Herbert Yardley's Black Chamber, America's secret codebreaking organization.

The question the nation must resolve during the years before a second-generation DES is developed is whether, as in the Code Compilation Company, there will be a secret door between public and governmental cryptology.

•

Victorious in its battle over the DES, the NSA now set its sights on an even greater potential threat: academic research into cryptology.

Suddenly, on numerous campuses across the country, mathematicians and computer scientists began devoting substantial energies and resources to a subject that was once merely a strange word locked away in a dictionary. The research was both theoretical and applied; some scientists developed actual hardware, and others peered ever deeper into mathematical conundrums. So far had the interest gone that several colleges even offered courses in the subject, and in 1977 a scholarly journal devoted exclusively to cryptology was born.*

What must have come as NSA's biggest blow took place in 1976, when the two anti-DES scientists from Stanford, Hellman and Diffie, came up with what David Kahn called "the most revolutionary new concept in the field since polyalphabetic substitution emerged in the Renaissance." Later refined by three scientists at MIT, Ronald Rivest, Adi Shamir, and Leonard Adleman, the system was labeled public-key cryptography and offered a radical new twist to an old concept. Rather than using the same key, as with the DES, to encrypt and decrypt, the public-key system allows for two separate keys — one limited to encryption and the other to decryption. What this means is that a person can now freely distribute his computer's encryption key, such as in a national directory, permitting anyone to send secret information to him. But only he is able to decrypt the messages, since he alone has the decrypt key. An added bonus of the system is that it also permits the sender of the messages to sign, in effect, in indelible code, thus ensuring the authenticity of the author.

The problem faced by the NSA in trying to halt this research, and thus restore its own hegemony, was that, unlike the industrial world, with its heavy dependence on defense contracts and its conservative boards of directors, the university researchers were independent. The cozy relationship that the Agency had fostered with IBM would be impossible with the free-wheeling academics. Nevertheless, virtually all the researchers had an Achilles' heel: the National Science Foundation.

Set up as an independent government agency to foster research into basic scientific knowledge, the NSF accomplished its goals by awarding grants and contracts to universities and nonprofit research organizations. It was through such grants and contracts that most of the nongovernmental cryptologists received their funding. Thus, it was reasoned at NSA, if the Agency could wrest control of all cryptologic funding, it would effectively control almost all outside research

---

* One such course was taught by mathematics professor Cipher A. Deavours, Kean College of New Jersey, Union, New Jersey. The journal is *Cryptologia*, founded and edited by David Kahn, Cipher A. Deavours, Louis Kruh, and Brian J. Winkel.

in the subject. Such control could come to NSA if the NSF turned over to the Agency all responsibility for the cryptologic programs or, if this was not feasible, if it granted to the NSA the right to classify any program it deemed should be kept secret.

The first step in the NSA's power grab took place on April 20, 1977, when Assistant Deputy Director for COMSEC Cecil Corry (who by then had been with the Agency for thirty-five years) and one of his assistants, David G. Boak, journeyed down to Washington to meet with an NSF official at the foundation's G Street headquarters. The official was Dr. Fred W. Weingarten, the special projects program director of the Division of Computer Research, and the purpose of the meeting was to discuss the NSF's support of cryptographic research.

Corry, one of COMSEC's founding fathers and at this time the number two man in the organization, wasted little time in getting down to business. Soon after the meeting began, he suggested to Weingarten that an unspecified presidential directive gave the NSA "control" over all cryptographic work and that Weingarten and his foundation were operating outside that directive.

It was not the first time Weingarten had heard such a charge. Almost two years earlier, in June 1975, one of the NSF's grantees who also worked for the NSA told him that NSA "had sole statutory authority to fund research in cryptography, and, in fact, that other agencies are specifically enjoined from supporting that type of work." Weingarten, fearing that he may have been operating outside the law in awarding cryptographic grants, immediately suspended any new awards in the field and shot off a memo to NSF's general counsel asking for an opinion on the issue. Unable to find any such statute, Assistant General Counsel Jesse E. Lasken telephoned NSA's legal office, but no one there could find the supporting statute. The scare over, Weingarten's cryptographic funding continued.

Now he was hearing the threats again, but this time he told his two NSA visitors that his general counsel had looked into the matter nearly two years before and found no such directive involving research. The bluff having failed, Corry mumbled that they would have to get such a law passed and then resorted to his alternative strategy. Hoping to win for the NSA the power of the classification stamp over all cryptographic proposals, Corry suggested that the two agencies "coordinate" the review process for the proposals.

Because the NSA did have the only reservoir of expertise in the field, Weingarten agreed to send over the proposals, but only, he warned, so that NSA could provide its expert opinion on the technical quality of the work. Further, he told Corry, his division would continue to consider proposals in the field of cryptology, that it would operate in as open a manner as possible, that it would decline proposals only for fully documented scientific reasons, and that he would not permit any "secret reviews — reviews of the form 'Don't support this, but I can't tell you why.' "

Weingarten could see the beginnings of a major power play involving the open research policy of the foundation and the national security claims of the NSA. Several days after the meeting he recorded his views concerning the looming battle in an internal memorandum for the record:

> First — NSA is in a bureaucratic bind. In the past the only communications with heavy security demands were military and diplomatic. Now, with the marriage of computer applications with telecommunications in Electronic Funds Transfer, Electronic Mail, and other large distributed processing applications, the need for highly secure digital processing has hit the civilian sector. NSA is worried, of course, that public domain security research will compromise some of their work. However, even further, they seem to want to maintain their control and corner a bureaucratic expertise in this field. They point out that the government is asking NSA help in issues of computer security. However, unquotable sources at OMB tell me that they turned to NSA only for the short-term, pragmatic reason that the expertise was there, not as an expression of policy that NSA should have any central authority.
>
> It seems clear that turning such a huge domestic responsibility, potentially involving such activities as banking, the US mail, and cable television, to an organization such as NSA should be done only after the most serious debate at higher levels of government than represented by peanuts like me.
>
> Furthermore, no matter what one's views about the role of NSA in government, it is inescapable that NSF relations with them be formal. Informal agreements regarding support of areas of research or individual projects need to be avoided.

Apparently not having gotten the message, Corry wrote to Weingarten's boss, Dr. John R. Pasta, director of the NSF's Division of Mathematical and Computer Sciences, to say "We are grateful for your willingness to cooperate with us in considering the security implications of grant applications in this field."

Pasta sent the letter up through channels at the NSF, noting that his division had made no such agreement. Later he replied to Corry, "clarifying" the arrangements and adding that any review the NSA made on proposals would become part of the public record.

Meanwhile, on July 5, 1977, as each side continued to posture, Vice Admiral Bobby Inman moved into the Puzzle Palace, replacing newly promoted General Lew Allen, Jr. Inman's initiation into the battle was to be a quick one. The day after his arrival, one of his civilian employees, Joseph A. Meyer, having decided that the issue of public research into cryptology was destined to be as ignored under Inman as it was under Allen, took action. Without any authorization, he wrote a threatening letter to the Institute of Electrical and Electronic Engineers (IEEE), the nation's largest professional engineering society (of which he was a member), warning that those planning to participate in an upcoming IEEE symposium on cryptology might violate the law.

Among those who would be speaking and presenting papers at the October gathering were public-key originators Martin Hellman and Ronald Rivest. What bothered Meyer so much was not only that the meeting was going to be open to the public, but that a number of foreign guests would also be attending and participating. Worse, there were plans to send copies of the talks, before they were delivered, to the Soviet Union under a general umbrella agreement made by the IEEE several years earlier.

In his single-spaced, one-and-a-half-page letter, Meyer brought up the International Traffic in Arms Regulations (ITAR), through which the State Department controls the export of arms, ammunition, and "implements of war," like jet fighters and warships, which are listed in a document known as the U.S. Munitions List. Also on the list, under Auxiliary Military Equipment, were cryptographic devices, speech scramblers, privacy devices, and their associated specialized equipment.

What Meyer emphasized was that ITAR covered the export not only of actual hardware, but also of unclassified technical data associated with the restricted equipment. He claimed that holding symposia and publishing papers on cryptology were the same as exporting the information. Thus, he concluded, "unless clearances or export licenses are obtained" on some of the lectures and papers, "the IEEE could find itself in technical violation of the ITAR."

He had a point. The ITAR did cover any "unclassified information that can be used, or adapted for use, in the design, production, manufacture, repair, overhaul, processing, engineering, development, operation, maintenance, or reconstruction" of the listed materials, as well as "any technology which advances the state-of-the-art or establishes a new art in an area of significant military applicability in the United States." And export did include transferring the information both by writing and by either oral or visual means, including briefings and symposia in which foreign nationals are present.

But followed literally, the vague, overly broad regulations would seem to require that anyone planning to write or speak out publicly on any technology touching the Munitions List must first get approval from the State Department — a chilling prospect clearly at odds with the First Amendment and one as yet untested by the Supreme Court.

Nevertheless, the letter had its desired effect on the IEEE. Officials of the organization urged participants in the upcoming symposium to clear any questionable material with the State Department's Office of Munitions Control — thus, in effect, clearing it through the NSA.

Despite the fact that Meyer had penned his letter as a private citizen and a member of the IEEE, it was only a matter of days before it was discovered that he worked for NSA — which, of course, led many to believe that the letter was simply the NSA's covert way of stifling public cryptographic research.

Following a storm of embarrassing publicity over the incident, the Agency denied any connection with the letter, but for many the denial was insufficient. As a result, Inman sought help from a group he had come to know quite well during his years as director of Naval Intelligence and vice director of the Defense Intelligence Agency: the Senate Intelligence Committee. Inman asked the committee to conduct an impartial review of the Meyer affair and several other issues. The committee agreed, and in April 1978 it issued two reports, one classified and one unclassified, that acquitted the Agency of any involvement in the Meyer letter.

Possibly buoyed by the congressional vote of confidence, that same month the NSA took another giant step toward silencing the competition.

Six months earlier a foursome of inventors in Seattle, working in their spare time in the back of a garage, managed to develop a new type of voice scrambler. Led by thirty-five-year-old Carl Nicolai, a job-shopper, or technical "Kelly girl," the group called its new invention the Phasorphone and submitted a patent application in October 1977. In April 1978, Nicolai finally received a response from the Patent Office. But when he opened the letter, he was stunned. Instead of a patent, his hands held a strange form with the words SECRECY ORDER in large bold letters across the top.

Nicolai had suddenly been assaulted with one of the oldest weapons in the nation's national security arsenal: the Invention Secrecy Act. Passed in 1917 as a wartime measure to prevent the publication of inventions that might "be detrimental to the public safety or defense or might assist the enemy or endanger the successful prosecution of the war," the measure ended with the conclusion of World War I. The act was resurrected in 1940 and was later extended until the end of the Second World War. Then, like the phoenix, it once again rose from the ashes with the passage of the Invention Secrecy Act of 1951, which mandated that secrecy orders be kept for periods of no more than one year unless renewed. There was a catch, however. The act also said that a secrecy order "in effect, or issued, during a national emergency declared by the President shall remain in effect for the duration of the national emergency and six months thereafter." Because no one ever bothered to declare an end to President Truman's 1951 emergency, the emergency remained in effect until September 1978.

Nicolai's secrecy order told him little except that he faced two years in jail and a $10,000 fine for disclosing any aspect of his device "in any way to any person not cognizant of the invention prior to the date of the order." Nowhere on the order did it say why it was issued or who ordered the action.

Unknown to the Seattle inventor, the patent application for his backyard scrambler had traveled through one of the government's least-known bureaucratic labyrinths — one littered with such security classifications as SUPER SECRECY and BLUE SLIP. Once submitted to the Patent and Trademark Office, it, like all other applications, was sent to a unit called the Special Laws Administrative Group, better known as the Secret Group. Here, several dozen specially cleared examiners separate the applications into chemical, electrical, or mechanical inventions and then, using guide lists provided by the various defense agencies, determine whether any contain national security information. Those they suspect are passed on to the Pentagon's Armed Services Patent Advisory Board (ASPAB), a sort of clearinghouse for secrecy orders, which then requests an opinion from the appropriate agency and coordinates the decision to invoke secrecy.

When Nicolai's Phasorphone reached the ASPAB, there was disagreement. The middle-level official at NSA responsible for such decisions wanted the secrecy order issued (although others within the Agency disagreed), and he was supported by the Air Force and Navy representatives. But the Army saw no reason for such a move, so the decision was kicked up to NSA's Director Inman for a final decision. He gave the go-ahead to the order.

Nicolai had thus become, in the slang of the ASPAB, a "John Doe." Of the three hundred or so secrecy orders issued each year, all but a very few are either on inventions the government has originated itself and already classified, or on inventions somehow connected with the government. A John Doe is one of the few outside this circle. In this instance, John Doe was hopping mad.

The object of Nicolai's patent application and the NSA's anxiety was a voice privacy system that relied more, apparently, on the science of transmission security than cryptography. As opposed to cryptography, which merely renders the contents of a message unintelligible to those without the key, transmission security conceals the very existence of the message itself. The seed for the Phasorphone was planted in 1960 in an article on communications security by Alfred Pfanstiehl for *Analog* magazine. Pfanstiehl suggested that instead of the traditional method of transmission, where signals are sent between transmitter and receiver over a single frequency, a system of pseudorandom wave forms be used. Under such a system a code could be devised using pseudorandom alterations of the frequency spectrum exactly synchronized between transmitter and receiver. The system held promise for an area particularly vulnerable to eavesdropping: CB and marine band radio. But it could also be modified for telephone.

What was so worrisome to the NSA, it seems, was the movement by the private sector into yet another once-exclusive domain. For years the Agency had been putting strong emphasis on the marriage of cryptography and transmission security for hidden communications with submarines and clandestine agents in hostile foreign countries.* Such techniques included frequency-hopping, where messages are bounced from frequency to frequency at more than a thousand times a second; burst communications, where a message is supercompressed into a brief "squirt"; and spread spectrum techniques, where a signal is first diluted to a millionth of its original intensity and then intermingled with background noise.

To add insult to injury, Nicolai was planning to market his Phasorphone at a price most buyers could easily afford, about $100, thus increasing the interest in the technology.

That the NSA was suddenly attempting to flex its muscles in the patent area could be seen in the fact that the very day Nicolai's secrecy order was issued, another inventor was opening a secrecy order on

---

* In 1973, TRW began designing a satellite system for use by the CIA in communicating with agents in "denied areas." Code-named Pyramider, the system employed frequency-hopping. This provided the agent with large "safe areas" in cities, where the signals could be hidden among random urban radio transmissions. The system was also capable of reducing aircraft interception in remote areas to a radius of twenty nautical miles. (See Robert Lindsey, *The Falcon and the Snowman* [New York: Simon & Schuster, 1979], page 218.)

yet another invention. Dr. George I. Davida, a professor of electrical engineering and computer science at the University of Wisconsin, had submitted a patent application for a "stream" cipher device, incorporating advanced mathematical techniques, about the same time Nicolai submitted his Phasorphone application. Now, like his Seattle counterpart, Davida had also become a John Doe.

Whatever the NSA had hoped to accomplish by its rapid one-two punch was lost in the embarrassing public battle that followed. Soon after Davida received his secrecy order, Werner Baum, chancellor of the University of Wisconsin's Milwaukee campus, sent off a letter to the director of the National Science Foundation, which sponsored Davida's project, denouncing the secrecy order and calling for "minimal due process guarantees." He then told *Science* magazine that he regarded the order an invasion of his faculty's academic freedom and said it smacked of McCarthy-era tactics against universities.

After first winning the support of Senator Warren Magnuson, Nicolai also turned to *Science* and later charged that the order "appears part of a general plan by the NSA to limit the privacy of the American people." He added, "They've been bugging people's telephones for years and now someone comes along with a device that makes this a little harder to do and they oppose this under the guise of national security."

The warfare was soon publicized by the national media, and the NSA was forced to sound retreat. It rescinded Davida's secrecy order on June 15, blaming it on a "very well-meaning, middle-level bureaucrat" at NSA and an "attempt to hold the line that had clearly already been passed." Nicolai, however, did not have his secrecy order cancelled until October 11. "There I was, faced with a split decision inside NSA over whether the Nicolai invention represented a threat," Inman said later. "From dealing day by day with the Invention Secrecy Act, you have to make a quick, snap decision."

The bruises the Puzzle Palace had received in struggles over the DES, the Meyer letter, and the secrecy orders had taken their toll on both the Agency and its director. Inman believed the NSA had received a "bum rap" and was afraid the one-sided controversy was having a demoralizing effect throughout the Agency and that it would frighten away many promising recruits. Even worse, he told a closed-door meeting with employees in the Friedman Auditorium, some of the news stories were threatening to cause "immediate damage" to the Agency's sensitive "sources and methods."

The director's tactic was to launch a counterattack on two fronts — one in the open and the other behind the scenes. On the open front,

Inman decided to convert to his own use what he believed was his opponent's biggest weapon: the media. Both Nicolai and Davida, he felt, had used the press to manipulate the NSA. Now he himself would begin manipulating the press for the Agency's benefit.

The first round in Inman's public relations war was fired shortly after he rescinded Nicolai's secrecy order. For the first time in the NSA's twenty-six-year history, an incumbent director would grant an interview to a member of the press. Inman told *Science* magazine's Deborah Shapley that because of the "burgeoning interest" in cryptology, he felt it was necessary to

> find a way into some thoughtful discussion of what can be done between the two extremes of "that's classified" and "that's academic freedom" . . . Security has served the national interest with respect to the NSA extraordinarily well over a long period. So a whole series of directors have taken the view that "no comment" was the best response. But as we moved into burgeoning public interest in public cryptography, a substantial volume of unfavorable publicity has occurred with no counterbalance . . . to point out that there are valid national security concerns.

Despite the ballyhoo, Inman's "interview" was little more than a monologue; the only area he would discuss was NSA's side of the Davida-Nicolai controversy. With regard to Davida, Inman said, the order was a "bureaucratic error, because, as it turned out, the material had already appeared in the open literature and so could not be classified." In Nicolai's case, he admitted that there was disagreement among the reviewers and that he had opted to "err on the side of national security." As a result of the publicity brought on by the two cases, Inman said, he had instituted a new procedure whereby any pro-secrecy order decision is automatically reviewed by a high-level committee. Nevertheless, he noted, "we would . . . [classify] any application where we feel there is a valid national security use or concern."

But Inman's most telling comment was his statement to Shapley that he would like to see the NSA receive the same authority over cryptology that the Department of Energy enjoys over research into atomic energy. Such authority would grant to NSA absolute "born classified" control over all research in any way related to cryptology.

"A public address by an incumbent Director of the National Security Agency on a subject relating to the Agency's mission is an event which if not of historic proportions is at least, to my knowledge, unprecedented."

So began Admiral Inman's second venture into the spotlight. "Traditionally," he continued, "NSA had maintained a policy of absolute public reticence concerning all aspects of our mission." But now, he said, "the Agency's mission no longer can remain entirely in the shadows."

Speaking before a symposium of the Armed Forces Communications Electronics Association at the State Department in January 1979, Inman elaborated on the dangers inherent in "unrestrained public discussion of cryptologic matters" to which he had previously only alluded. Warned Inman:

> Application of the genius of the American scholarly community to cryptographic and cryptanalytic problems, and widespread dissemination of resulting discoveries, carry the clear risk that some of NSA's cryptanalytic successes will be duplicated, with a consequent improvement of cryptography by foreign targets. No less significant is the risk that cryptographic principles embodied in communications security devices developed by NSA will be rendered ineffective by parallel nongovernmental cryptologic activity and publication . . . All of this poses clear risks to the national security [and places the mission of the NSA] in peril.

Following his "sky is falling" address, Inman again called for increased governmental controls over outside cryptologic research. "While some people outside NSA express concern that the government has too much power to control nongovernmental cryptologic activities," he said, "in candor, my concern is that the government has too little."

As a result of Inman's call for a "dialogue" between the NSA and the academic community, the American Council on Education established a Public Cryptography Study Group to investigate, and recommend possible solutions to, the problems facing both groups. Cochairmen of the group were Werner A. Baum, the former University of Wisconsin chancellor who went to Davida's rescue and is now a dean at Florida State University, and Ira Michael Heyman, chancellor of the University of California at Berkeley. The seven other members were mostly professors of mathematics and computer science from various universities. Representing the NSA was General Counsel Daniel C. Schwartz.*

---

* The scientist-members were David H. Brandin, vice president, Computer Science and Technology Division, SRI International (nominated by the Association for Computing Machinery); Professor R. Creighton Buck, Department of Mathematics, University of Wisconsin (nominated by the American Mathematical Society); Professor George I. Davida, Department of Electrical Engineering and Computer Science, University

Inman proposed that the group consider the feasibility of a statute permitting the NSA to exercise prepublication censorship over a "central core" of nongovernmental technical information relating to cryptology. Such a statute, the group concluded, could be implemented either by making it a crime to disseminate cryptologic information or by requiring prepublication review by a government agency, such as the NSA. Under the first practice, the NSA would monitor virtually all published information and recommend criminal prosecution in any instances where restricted cryptologic information has been published. Under the second, anyone publishing cryptologic information without first having it cleared by the NSA would face a jail sentence.

Recognizing the constitutional questions involved in such drastic actions, the study group decided on a middle ground: a system of voluntary censorship. Under such a system, the NSA would reserve the right to notify anyone working on cryptologic writings — authors, researchers, publishers — of its desire to review such information before publication. The Agency would then request those individuals whose writings contained material that the NSA desired withheld to voluntarily refrain from publishing them. In case of disagreement, a five-member advisory committee appointed by the director of NSA and the science adviser to the President would make the ultimate recommendation.

The final vote on the voluntary system passed with near-unanimity on February 7, 1981. The sole dissenting voice was George I. Davida's, one of the only two specialists in data security in the group. Davida believed the decision of the study group was both unwise and dangerous and would set a precedent for future nonvoluntary intervention by the NSA in the academic community.

> Two years from now [he later wrote], if the NSA decides that it does indeed wish to impose restraints, the question will no doubt receive a hearing in Congress. It is easy to imagine the NSA offering the decision of our study group to Congress as evidence that academicians do indeed agree with the NSA — that our work could compromise the national security . . . It would be only too easy for us to lose our constitutional freedoms in bits and pieces . . . One gets the impression that the NSA is struggling to stand still, and to keep American research standing still

---

of Wisconsin (nominated by the Computer Society of the IEEE); Professor George Handelman, Department of Mathematical Sciences, Rensselaer Polytechnic Institute (nominated by the Society for Industrial and Applied Mathematics); Professor Martin E. Hellman, Department of Electrical Engineering, Stanford University (nominated by the IEEE); Professor Wilfred Kaplan, Department of Mathematics, University of Michigan (nominated by the American Association of University Professors).

with it, while the rest of the world races ahead . . . The NSA can best perform its mission in the old-fashioned way: Stay ahead of others.

Meanwhile, as the Agency continued its public campaign, it was also making significant headway on its second front — the quiet, behind-the-scenes effort to gain control from the National Science Foundation of all cryptologic funding. By controlling the dollars, the NSA would control the research.

Following a briefing on the NSA's operations in September 1978, NSF director Richard C. Atkinson suggested to Admiral Inman that one way to help alleviate the problem of the foundation's research impinging on the NSA's "sensitive areas" would be to have the Agency begin a small ($2 to $3 million), unclassified research support program at various universities. In this way, Atkinson suggested, the NSF could shift its effort away from the cryptologic area as the NSA took up the slack.

It was the opening Inman had been hoping for, and he quickly replied to Atkinson that his offer was "most attractive" but that before any program was implemented, "some homework needs to be done here."

If there was any doubt as to Inman's ultimate intentions, it was dispelled during the first meeting of the Public Cryptography Study Group on May 31, 1980. Among those attending the meeting as an "authorized observer" was Richard Leibler, who was listed simply as "Chief, Office of Research, Department of Defense." In fact, Leibler, having served as director of the Agency's think tank, IDA-CRD, for fourteen years, was now head of NSA's Office of Research. In a remark that was never included in the minutes of the meeting, Leibler noted that the "NSA would take over the funding of cryptographic research grants from the NSF, assuming there are no legal impediments to such transfer and the study group produces worthwhile recommendations on how to effect it."

Apparently the study group never considered the proposal. Still, Inman was just about ready to begin his coup; all he needed was the right research project to come along. Two and a half months later, that project appeared. On Thursday, August 14, Leonard Adleman, a theoretical computer scientist at MIT and one of the fathers of public-key cryptography, received a telephone call from Bruce Barns of the NSF. To his surprise, Barns told him that the NSF had decided not to fund part of his grant proposal. When asked why, Barns merely said something about an "interagency matter."

The following day, Adleman received another call, this one from

Inman himself, who explained that the NSA wanted to fund his proposal. It was an unsettling experience, and Adleman wanted nothing to do with the Agency. "In the present climate I would not accept funds from the NSA," he later told *Science*. He said that he was concerned about the terms the Agency might extract, whether his funds would be cut off if the NSA insisted on classification and he refused, and whether he would be denied due process. He added, "It's a very frightening collusion between agencies."

The sudden intervention of the NSA apparently caught the NSF off guard. NSF director Atkinson had resigned only six weeks earlier, and the acting director, Donald Langenberg, had become deputy director just a few weeks before Atkinson departed.

Following the incident, both Inman and Langenberg met with White House science adviser Frank Press. It was decided that, at least for the time being, all proposals for cryptographic research would go first to the NSF and then to the NSA for technical review. Should the NSA find a proposal it wished to fund, it would so notify the NSF, which would offer the researcher a choice of accepting funds from either agency.

In reviewing the three and a half years of bureaucratic footwork engaged in by the NSA and the NSF, a congressional committee concluded that the history reflected "not that of two agencies at loggerheads, but of the mission-oriented NSA having sent the NSF a message in bureaucratic code that the latter is still struggling to decipher. The record leaves little doubt about NSA's intentions."

On September 15, 1981, Lieutenant General Lincoln D. Faurer, Inman's successor as DIRNSA, transmitted another message, this one to America's computer industry. Unlike the message to the NSF, however, this one went unencrypted.

Two months earlier, the NSA had unveiled its newest addition: the Computer Security Technical Evaluation Center. Its purpose is to analyze computer hardware and software produced by private industry and rate the products in terms of their potential vulnerability to penetration. Although submission was supposed to be strictly voluntary, Faurer, addressing a meeting of the IEEE, left little doubt that to ignore the Center would be to risk saying good-by to lucrative government contracts. "Frankly," the NSA chief warned, "our intention is to significantly reward those DOD suppliers who produce the computer security products that we need."

By using this carrot-and-stick approach, the NSA hoped to rapidly push ahead the development of secure computer systems by private industry and at the same time, through the Center, encourage the

industry to share its innovations with the NSA. Lack of such cooperation, CIA Deputy Director Inman said at the Center's opening, "might
lead to a highly undesirable situation where private-sector users (e.g.,
banks, insurance companies) have higher integrity systems than the
government."

Despite their warnings, if the reaction of industry to the Center
proves anything like the reaction of the professional societies to the
Public Cryptography Study Group, Inman and Faurer are in for a
disappointment. As of the spring of 1982, the voluntary review system
of the Study Group had been all but officially ignored by its member
societies. Most have taken a position similar to the IEEE, which leaves
entirely up to the individual scientist the decision of whether or not
to submit and makes no recommendation one way or the other.

Such lack of enthusiasm for the program may have prompted Admiral Inman's blast, in January 1982, that if the scientists did not agree
to the voluntary review of their work by the intelligence agencies,
they would face a "tidal wave" of public outrage that will lead to
laws restricting the publication of scientific work that the government
might consider "sensitive" on national security grounds.

As a result of what he called the "hemorrhaging of the country's
technology," Inman warned a meeting of the American Association
for the Advancement of Science that "the tides are moving, and moving fast, toward legislated solutions that in fact are likely to be much
more restrictive, not less restrictive, than the voluntary" censorship
system of the Study Group.

Thus far, however, Inman's "tidal wave" of public outrage has yet
to dampen the soles of his shoes.

ABYSS

"THE PLO sends a man into New York, a terrorist, to place bombs
. . . An American organization is backing a revolution in Haiti . . .
A congressman is demanding money from a foreign government and
you discover that from their communications . . . What do you do
with it?" For fifteen years, G Group Chief Frank Raven struggled
with such conundrums. Where to draw the line between foreign and
domestic targets, legal and illegal interception, and foreign intelligence or law enforcement purposes?

"There was a big internal struggle within NSA on the question
as to whether or not we should work domestic targets," Raven recalled, "and this is not an easy question. There is no such thing —
and this is something I brought up before the Church Committee
and they were screaming on it — you cannot divide your problems
neatly and cleanly into internal U.S. and external U.S. . . . You have
intelligence which is entirely foreign and you have intelligence which
is entirely domestic. But then you have the third category which no
one will recognize, which is intelligence which moves back and forth
between them."

In this large gray area, where domestic and foreign intelligence
overlap, one of the most sensitive issues involves the handling of
communications of an "innocent" American — one neither targeted
nor watch-listed — that are scooped into the vacuum cleaner. This
happens with considerable frequency because of the way in which
names and phrases are jam-packed into the computers. Even though
NSA's specialized supercomputers have enormous storage capacities,
the tremendous number of targets forces the Agency to squeeze the
watch lists together as tightly as possible. Thus, according to Raven,
programmers would simply reduce Malcolm X to the last two letters
in his first name (lm) followed by a space and then the letter X.
Then any time an intercepted data communication containing that

particular combination of letters and spacing (lm X) streamed past the computer's reading head, it would automatically be kicked out for further analysis.

Part of the reason that the computers are swamped with watch list submissions is that many items require numerous entries. When searching for derogatory references to President Richard M. Nixon, for example, technicians would have to program a variety of possible key words, such as "Tricky Dicky." This, according to the former G Group chief, would be converted to "ky----ky."

Should this selection process still produce a considerable amount of traffic, the data could then undergo "secondary testing," such as the addition of the words "New York," to reduce the volume. Nevertheless, after all the narrowing-down, if the total number of intercepts relating to innocent Americans was reduced to only 10 percent, the final amount would still be staggering. From Operation Shamrock alone, the total number of messages selected for final analysis came to approximately 150,000 per month. This is readily understandable when one considers that there are about twenty-four million international telegrams and fifty million telex messages that enter, leave, and transit the United States annually, plus millions of additional messages transmitted on leased lines. Added to this are billions of words and numbers entering and leaving the country each year over computer terminals.

And then there is voice. Although computers have not, apparently, advanced to the stage where they can economically pick out words and phrases from spoken communications, they can very easily be programmed to start the tape recorders rolling when they "recognize" targeted multifrequency address codes — the *beedle-de-beep* sounds one hears after dialing a long distance call — which indicate who is calling whom. Once these calls are recorded, analysts could listen for watch-listed information contained on their scan-guides.

In the past, NSA has had an internal policy of not releasing to other agencies the names of innocent American citizens or corporations incidentally picked up in their electronic dragnet. Thus, if the Belgian ambassador wires to his Foreign Office a bit of political gossip picked up from an American at a Washington cocktail party, the NSA would most likely pass the gossip on to the State Department but delete the name of the original source.

The reason for the NSA's policy was, in part, the fact that its mission was limited to foreign intelligence. But it was also based on the well-reasoned fear that if it gave the consumer the name of the American, that agency would then turn around and act on the information —

and possibly blow the whole intercept operation. For example, if the State Department were advised that the source of the gossip was the department's chief of protocol, it would be highly likely that the official would be confronted with the sensitive information, and the possibility of an ensuing leak would be greatly increased.

But the most difficult problems were those concerning innocent Americans involved in illegal activities. "You get a guy who calls from phone booths in Grand Central Station," recalled Frank Raven, "and he's moving around Grand Central Station — it isn't always the same phone booth — and he's talking to people in South America; he's making the arrangements for shipping in drugs." Under such circumstances, said Raven, "you can [report] till you're blue in the face about the arrangements that are being made outside of the U.S. territory," but when it came to identifying the possible American, all NSA could report was that "an unspecified drug dealer in Grand Central Station is ordering drugs from Venezuela . . . You tell the foreign intelligence which is contained in the communication but you do not in any way indicate the precise identity of the possible American citizen who's involved."

Understandably, many of NSA's consumers found the nondisclosure policy frustrating and sometimes irrational. In fact, in one case where the Agency refused to give out the name of an American business firm, the FBI fought the action all the way to the director of Central Intelligence — and lost.

On the other hand, drug dealers were not the only ones who unwittingly found their way into NSA's magnetic-tape library. Also captured were the hungry demands of wayward congressmen insisting on bribes from foreign governments, a circumstance that, according to Raven, placed NSA "on a first-class spot!" He pointed out that "you don't get this on the Communist problems . . . but you get it all the time — as a matter of fact, it's a daily episode to the chief of G Group." The way out of the spot, said Raven, was simply to do nothing. The message was buried away in a file and considered domestic intelligence.

Another NSA official caught up in the no-win situation of handling evidence of congressional wrongdoing was, apparently, Juanita M. Moody, the consumer staff liaison officer in Operations who was responsible for the distribution of all SIGINT throughout government. In 1977 she was reportedly called from retirement to testify secretly before the House Ethics Committee concerning her knowledge of intercepted cable traffic to and from the South Korean embassy, which may have contained evidence of congressmen taking money from the South Korean government in exchange for influence.

Because South Korea came under B Group rather than G Group, Frank Raven was not involved in the "Koreagate" investigation. Nevertheless, there was little doubt in his mind as to how the possibly incriminating traffic was handled: "The fellow who decrypted them, the linguist who read them, would read them and file them."

One of the oldest, and probably most strictly followed, internal NSA guidelines was the prohibition against entirely domestic eavesdropping — where both terminals were located within the United States. It was possibly the rule that caused the most consternation, since it eliminated the possibility of collecting the communications between the foreign embassies in Washington and their consulates and UN missions in New York. "If the Russian [consulate] in New York calls the Russian embassy in Washington, that's domestic intelligence," complained Frank Raven. "If it's going to South America, it's all right . . . but if it's going between New York and Washington, you can't touch it."

For twenty-five years the NSA struggled in total secrecy over the questions of foreign versus domestic intelligence collection. Its power to eavesdrop, the Agency had always insisted, came under no earthly laws but rather emanated from some celestial "inherent presidential authority" reposed in the chief executive by the Constitution. But on March 23, 1976, in the wake of Watergate and the far-ranging intelligence abuses uncovered by the Church and Pike Committees, President Ford gave his blessings to a Senate bill that would have eliminated much of that "inherent authority" and, for the first time, required the NSA to submit to judicial review before initiating certain surveillances.

Known as the Foreign Intelligence Surveillance Act (FISA), the bill was introduced by Senator Edward M. Kennedy following months of closed-door negotiations with the Justice Department. For Kennedy, it was his fourth attempt in as many years to get legislation regulating warrantless eavesdropping — and the first time he had received administration support. Nevertheless, despite favorable endorsements by both the Senate Judiciary Committee and the Senate Intelligence Committee, the legislation was lost because the session ended before the full Senate could act.

There was a second unsuccessful attempt to get the bill passed in 1977, but the FISA was finally signed into law by President Jimmy Carter, who also backed the bill, on October 25, 1978.

For decades the technology of espionage had greatly outpaced the law. Now, with the FISA, the lawmakers were attempting to catch up. The statute would at last bring under the rule of law an area of surveillance that had heretofore been considered far too sensitive even to discuss with another branch of government: electronic eavesdropping within the United States on foreign embassies, diplomats, and agents of foreign powers.

The key to the legislation could have been dreamed up by Franz Kafka: the establishment of a supersecret federal court. Sealed away behind a cipher-locked door in a windowless room on the top floor of the Justice Department building, the Foreign Intelligence Surveillance Court is most certainly the strangest creation in the history of the federal Judiciary. Its establishment was the product of compromises between legislators who wanted the NSA and FBI, the only agencies affected by the FISA, to follow the standard procedure of obtaining a court order required in criminal investigations, and legislators who felt the agencies should have no regulation whatsoever in their foreign intelligence surveillances.

To settle the problem of where to draw the line between foreign and domestic intelligence, the legislation established a complex authorization procedure and added a strict "minimization" requirement to prohibit the use and distribution of communications involving Americans inadvertently picked up during the intercept operations.

A typical situation involving the NSA might originate with a CIA requirement to begin monitoring the Greek Tourist Information Offices in New York, Washington, and San Francisco as a result of a number of pro-Soviet and anti-American actions taken by the newly elected Greek Prime Minister, Andreas Papandreou.

After first being filtered through the intelligence community's National Intelligence Tasking Center and being placed on the IGCP, the CIA requirement would then go to NSA's consumer staff liaison officer, who would pass it on to the chief of G Group, the organization in Operations responsible for coverage of Greece. The chief of G Group would meet with the chief of W Group, responsible for intercept operations, and determine that coverage of the tourist offices would be regulated by the FISA because of the necessity to intercept wholly domestic communications links, such as those between New York, Washington, and San Francisco.

The intercept proposal would gradually work its way up the chain of command to the deputy director for Operations, the deputy director of NSA, and then to the general counsel, who would have to determine whether the target of the surveillance was either a foreign power or an agent of a foreign power, and also that the place or facilities to be monitored were in fact being used by the foreign target. This requirement constitutes one of the most important parts of the FISA law and was included to prevent the watch-listing of American citizens, which took place during the 1960s and 1970s.

The Greek Tourist Offices would qualify under the FISA as "foreign powers," since they would be official entities "directed and controlled by a foreign government." At the same time, the employees of the tourist offices would also become legitimate NSA targets as long as they were neither American citizens nor resident aliens, although even both of those groups would qualify as targets if they engaged in "clandestine" activities involving criminal acts on behalf of the Greek government.

Next, the general counsel would have to ensure that the necessary "minimization" procedures were adequate to eliminate, as much as possible, the chances of interception, retention, and dissemination of information concerning United States citizens, which might occur, say, when an American citizen simply called one of the offices to find out the requirements for a visa. The FISA prohibits the Agency from keeping or distributing such information unless it can be determined that the information concerning the American relates to the ability of the United States to protect itself against a foreign attack or sabotage, terrorism, or clandestine activities by a foreign agent.

However, if the American's telephone call or message falls into the vague, broad areas of providing for the "national security, defense, or foreign policy of the United States," then the NSA would be authorized to pass along the communication, with the identity of the American eliminated, unless the identity would be necessary for the consumer to understand the importance of the communication.

A final exception authorized the Agency to distribute the communication if it relates to criminal activity, thus clearing up the conflict of how to handle such matters as the inadvertent picking-up of evidence of bribe-taking congressmen.

From the NSA general counsel, the surveillance application goes to the NSA director, the Secretary of Defense, and then to the Justice Department's highly secretive Office of Intelligence Policy and Review, where staff attorneys put the final touches on the documents and submit them to the Attorney General for final approval. If it is granted, the attorneys, accompanied by an official from NSA's Office of SIGINT Operations, enter the tightly guarded Foreign Intelligence Surveillance Court and argue the merits of the case across a long table from one of the specially cleared FISA judges.

Presiding over the Star Chamber of the federal Judiciary is George L. Hart, Jr., a federal district judge in Washington, D.C. He and six other federal judges* from various parts of the country were hand-picked by Supreme Court Chief Justice Warren E. Burger to serve on the surveillance court for staggered terms, the first terms ranging from one to seven years. Trading in their robes and gavels for cloaks and daggers, they come to Washington on a rotating basis and hold court in a secure conference room at the main Justice Department building.

Almost unheard of outside the inner sanctum of the intelligence establishment, the court is like no other. It sits in secret session, holds no adversary hearings, and issues almost no public opinions or reports. It is listed in neither the *Government Organization Manual* nor the *United States Court Directory* and has even tried to keep its precise location a secret. "On its face," said one legal authority familiar with the court, "it is an affront to the traditional American concept of justice."

Inside the court, the judge would have to determine whether there was "probable cause" to believe that the Greek Tourist Offices are "foreign powers" and that the employees were "agents of foreign powers." Also, he would have to determine that the minimization procedures conformed to the statute and, if an American was the target, that the government's certification that the surveillance meets FISA terms is not "clearly erroneous." If these requirements are met, the judge *must* issue a warrant authorizing the intercept. There are no provisions for the judge to "look behind" the application to determine the necessity or propriety of the surveillance. As long as he finds that the target is "foreign" and that the proper application procedures have been followed, he has no choice but to approve it.

Under such circumstances, it is little wonder that the federal government has never lost a case before the court. In the court's first fifteen months, ending in December 1980, it approved all 518 applications, including one order that granted even broader authority than that sought by the Justice Department. The court has continued to maintain its perfect record through at least August 1981 — with one exception. Shortly after the creation of the court, Justice Department lawyers began seeking warrants from the judges for authorization to conduct surreptitious entries — black-bag jobs — into various "nonresidential premises under the direction and control of a foreign power." When the Reagan administration came into office, however, the Justice De-

---

* As of January 1982, they were Albert V. Bryan, Jr., son of the judge who had heard the case of Joseph Sidney Petersen, Jr. (Eastern District of Virginia), Frederick B. Lacey (District of New Jersey), Lawrence W. Pierce (Southern District of New York), Frank J. McGarr (Northern District of Illinois), William C. O'Kelley (Northern District of Georgia), and Frederick A. Daugherty (Western District of Oklahoma).

partment argued that the power for foreign intelligence black-bag jobs was vested not in the court, but in the inherent authority of the President. Presiding Judge Hart, in the court's only published opinion, agreed. Thus, in rejecting the administration's application for a new surreptitious entry, he was in fact going along with the argument of the Justice Department. As a result, the rejected break-in and all subsequent surreptitious entries need no court authorization, only presidential approval.

Given the fact that the top secret court has never said no to the government, it would be difficult to conclude that it has become anything other than a rubber stamp. How much of a rubber stamp may be judged by examining the way in which foreign intelligence surveillances were approved prior to the establishment of the court. Then the review was done by an interagency panel made up of the Secretaries of Defense and State and chaired by the director of Central Intelligence. The standards and methods of presenting the surveillance applications to the panel were substantially similar to the way they are handled by the court — but there was one key difference. Speaking of his experience with the review group, DCI Stansfield Turner once told the Senate Intelligence Committee, "I would point out there has been no meeting of the panel at which all of the requests before it were approved." It would appear that the surveillance requests were examined far more critically before the arrival of the court than since its creation.

Despite the court's tremendous emphasis on secrecy and security, there are several areas forbidden even from its review. One is the NSA's monitoring of telex and other data communications entering and leaving foreign embassies and other foreign-controlled properties, and the other is the monitoring of the dedicated, or leased, communications circuits used exclusively between foreign establishments in the United States. Thus, NSA would not have to seek an FISA warrant to intercept a radio or leased microwave circuit between the Soviet embassy in Washington and its UN mission in New York.

Because these two forms of eavesdropping, the House Intelligence Committee believed, included "some of the most sensitive surveillances which this Government conducts in the United States," the Congress excluded them from the jurisdiction of the spy court and placed the power to approve them exclusively in the hands of the Attorney General.

Even more disturbing than the apparent evolution of the surveillance court into an Executive Branch rubber stamp are the gaping holes and clever wording of the FISA statute, which nearly void it of usefulness. Such language, intentional as well as unintentional, permits the NSA to rummage at will through the nation's international telecommunications network and to target or watch-list any American who happens to step foot out of the country.

Once an American leaves the United States, he or she is stripped of any protection from the NSA. The Agency is permitted to target, record, transcribe, and disseminate any and all of his or her communications the same way it would the communications of the Red Brigades. There is no statutory requirement to seek approval from the surveillance court, the Attorney General, or any other authority.

Within the United States, the NSA is still free to pull into its massive vacuum cleaner every telephone call and message entering, leaving, or transiting the country, as long as it is done by microwave interception. And the Agency can program its high-speed computers and 22,000-line-per-minute printers to kick out every telegram or telex containing the word *oil* or the word *Democrat* while voice analysts, scan-guides in hand, listen attentively to every phone call between Washington and London, recording for later dissemination those containing the targeted subjects.

The major advantage of the FISA statute is that NSA is no longer permitted to target or watch-list Americans by name without an FISA warrant, even in international communications — as long as the person happens to be located on U.S. soil. Yet even this welcome reform appears to be undermined by what may be the Agency's most sinister loophole.

"Electronic surveillance," the statute reads, means "the acquisition by an electronic, mechanical, or other surveillance device" of the approved targets. But nowhere does the statute define the meaning of the key word *acquisition*. Rather, it is left to NSA to define — which it does in a top secret document. "Acquisition," according to the document, "means the interception by the National Security Agency through electronic means of a communication to which it is not an intended party and the processing of the contents of that communication into an intelligible form intended for human inspection."

By carefully inserting the words "by the National Security Agency," the Agency has skillfully excluded from the coverage of the FISA statute as well as the surveillance court all interceptions received from the British GCHQ or any other non-NSA source. Thus it is possible for GCHQ to monitor the necessary domestic or foreign circuits of interest and pass them on to NSA through the UKUSA Agreement. Once they were received, NSA could process the communications through its own computers and analysts, targeting and watch-listing

Americans with impunity, since the action would not be covered under the FISA statute or any other law.

That such action is far from improbable can be seen by the way NSA processed its domestic civil disturbance watch lists. According to the still classified Justice Department investigation into illegal NSA surveillance, "MINARET intelligence, except one category of international voice communications involving narcotics, was obtained incidentally in the course of NSA's interception of aural and non-aural (e.g., telex) international communications *and the receipt of GCHQ-acquired telex and ILC [International Licensed Carrier] cable traffic (SHAMROCK)*." [Emphasis supplied.]

Likewise, it is important to recall former Deputy Director Tordella's comment when referring to the CIA's withdrawal of support from NSA's drug monitoring: "It was in their General Counsel's opinion beyond CIA's charter to monitor radio communications on U.S. soil and I was told that if they could move a group of Cubans up to Canada it would be quite all right, but they would not do it in the United States."

Another worrisome aspect of the NSA definition is the inclusion of the words "through electronic means." This may be interpreted as excluding from the FISA statute the receipt of hand-delivered magnetic tapes from the communications companies, as was done in Operation Shamrock. In fact, the Church Committee in its final recommendations, from which much of the FISA statute is drawn, included specific language to prohibit just such transfers: "NSA should not request from any commercial carrier any communication which it could not otherwise obtain pursuant to these recommendations."

No such exclusion, however, was ever included in the final FISA statute. Instead, the statute now calls for what one constitutional law expert has termed "compulsory spy service," requiring "communications common carriers, their officers, employees, and agents . . . to provide information, facilities, or technical assistance to persons authorized by law to intercept wire or oral communications or to conduct electronic surveillance" and also ordering them to protect the secrecy of the operations.

Then there is the last, and possibly most intriguing, part of the definition, which stipulates that NSA has not "acquired" anything until the communication has been processed "into an intelligible form intended for human inspection." NSA is therefore free to intercept all communications, domestic as well as foreign, without ever coming under the law. Only when it selects the "contents" of a particular communication for further "processing" does the FISA take effect.

The same classified document that defines "acquisition" also attempts to resolve another thorny question constantly faced by intercept operators: "If you're intercepting a link," Frank Raven recalled, "let's say from Paris to Stockholm, and you get a message on there — how do you know whether or not the guy is an American citizen? And believe me, the fact that he's got an Anglo name does not make him an American citizen."

The answer was to establish a policy whereby, according to the NSA document,

> a person known to be currently in the United States will be treated as a United States person unless that person is positively identified as an alien who has not been admitted for permanent residence or unless the nature of the person's communications or other indicia in the contents or circumstances of such communications give rise to a reasonable belief that such person is not a United States person.

On the other hand, a person "known to be currently outside the United States, or whose location is not known, will not be treated as a United States person" unless there is positive identification or it can be reasonably determined from the conversation or other factors. Therefore, according to Raven, a person would be presumed to be an American citizen simply because of "the fact that he called from Grand Central Station — you just say 'a possible American citizen.'"

On January 24, 1978, President Jimmy Carter issued an executive order imposing detailed restrictions on the nation's intelligence community. The order was designed to prevent the long list of abuses of the 1960s and 1970s. But four years later President Ronald Reagan scrapped the Carter order and broadened considerably the power of the spy agencies to operate domestically.

First drafted by a working group chaired by CIA (and former NSA) general counsel Daniel B. Silver, a leaked copy of the new order created a storm of protest in March 1981, forcing former deputy director (and former DIRNSA) Admiral Bobby R. Inman to plead ignorance of the plan and publicly disavow the document. Nevertheless, after two more unsuccessful tries, a modified order was finally signed into law on December 4, 1981.

Although the order primarily expanded the activities of the CIA, a number of sections related to the NSA, as well. Under "Conduct of Intelligence Activities," the order formally placed the power to authorize domestic black-bag jobs in the hands of the Attorney General, provided he found "probable cause" to believe that the entry would be directed against a "foreign power or an agent of a foreign power."

The Reagan order also cleared up a long-standing question: whether the NSA has the authority to aid federal and state law enforcement agencies in cryptanalysis not related to signals intelligence. This might be an FBI case involving a coded note passed between two organized crime suspects. To handle such cases, the FBI has long had its own secretive Cryptanalytical and Translation Section, a part of the Technical Evaluation Unit of the FBI Laboratory. For many years the FBI hid the unit in an unmarked, cream-colored building at 215 Pennsylvania Avenue in the southeast section of Washington, a stone's throw from the Capitol.

Hunched over pads of green graph paper, FBI codebreakers spend most of their time attacking "bookie" cryptosystems, in which the betting data — tracks, horses, wagers — are reduced to numbers, and the numbers then enciphered. Hundreds of such systems are broken with little difficulty each year. But every so often in the past a particularly complex system would come up, and the G-men would turn to the Puzzle Palace. The requests would normally be handled very informally; usually a phone call from FBI associate director William C. Sullivan to G Group chief Frank Raven. "The type of message which they brought to us was sometimes quite sophisticated," Raven recalled, "but they did not require major expenditures or even significant expenditures of manpower or equipment . . . We used to give them to our cryptanalysts to take cracks at in their spare time. In short, not on company time take a look at this and see if you can break it, and they would break them over lunch . . . and send them back to the FBI."

The cases sent to G Group ranged from simple bookies to complicated murders. One case involved a massive numbers racket that was centered at the Pentagon. The details of the transactions were enciphered, as were the names of the organizers and players. Once NSA broke the system and the FBI began picking up the individuals, there was a blood bath as the chief numbers runners began taking shots at one another, each believing the other to be the informant.

Not all the cases, however, involved traditional paper-and-pencil ciphers. For months the FBI and postal inspectors were trying to build a conspiracy case against a number of racketeers in various parts of the country, but there was never any communication between them. In fact, there was really only one common denominator — they all mailed their fancy $100 shirts to the same cleaners in Las Vegas.

The FBI, believing the shirts to be a secret code, quietly called in the NSA, and analysts in G Group began setting up charts. Everything was logged — the numbers of shirts, the colors, the sizes, the buttons. One person even searched for a hidden pattern in the odors and religiously sniffed each intercepted shirt, dutifully logging the results (presumably from sweet to foul). In the end, the key was determined to be the number of shirts sent each time — and the FBI rounded up the culprits.

As each case was attacked and, with luck, solved, the chances of NSA's involvement being discovered grew appreciably, and by the early 1970s all cooperation had ceased. At one point the Agency was requested to aid in solving a number of cryptic notes left by a mass murderer but the answer remained no.

Under the Reagan executive order, the NSA can now, apparently, be authorized to lend its full cryptanalytic support — analysts as well as computers — to "any department or agency" in the federal government and, "when lives are endangered," even to local police departments.

But it was not the interception of dirty laundry that caused the Church Committee to issue the warning that "NSA's potential to violate the privacy of American citizens is unmatched by any other intelligence agency." It was, instead, a fear similar to that expressed by David Watters, the telecommunications engineer who formerly worked with the CIA's communications research and development branch:

> Tons of electronic surveillance equipment at this moment are interconnected within our domestic and international common carrier telecommunications systems. Much more is under contract for installation. Perhaps this equipment is humming away in a semi-quiescent state wherein at present "no citizen is targeted"; simply scanned . . . How soon will it be, however, before a punched card will quietly be dropped into the machine, a card having your telephone number, my telephone number, or the number of one of our friends to whom we will be speaking?

In the thirty years since Harry Truman issued NSA's birth certificate, the nation has undergone two parallel revolutions. On the one hand, microwaves and satellites have so transformed telecommunications that the wire has become almost obsolete. Today there are nine domestic satellites* in orbit and many more in use for international

* Three are operated by Western Union, two by RCA American Communications, Incorporated (RCA Americom), three by COMSAT General Corporation (for the use

communications, each with a capacity of thousands of circuits. Each of COMSAT's four domestic COMSTAR satellites alone has eighteen thousand long-distance circuits. Traveling over these invisible pathways are not only millions of telephone conversations, but tens of billions of words and numbers, ranging from simple telegrams and telex messages to complex computer data transfers. Even the mail is now beginning to travel by microwave and satellite.

In 1980 the United States Postal Service inaugurated an international electronic mail system known as INTELPOST (international electronic post), whereby anything from letters to blueprints can be transmitted rapidly to an addressee via satellite and cooperating overseas post offices.* Closer to home, the Postal Service in January 1982 launched an enormous domestic electronic mail service. Known as Electronic Computer-Originated Mail, or ECOM, the system permits the post office to sort and transmit electronic, computer-generated messages by satellite to post offices around the country. Each office can then print the contents and automatically fold, seal, and stamp the messages for delivery by letter carrier.

In 1982 the system is expected to handle twelve million messages, but by 1990 RCA, the major builder of the system, envisions that fully one third of the nation's projected seventy-five billion pieces of letter mail handled by the post office will travel invisibly through the air. So promising is electronic mail that IBM, AT&T, Xerox, and other major technology giants are planning to get in on the act with their own systems.

At the same time, a similar revolution has transformed the nation's intelligence collection system. Where once America's chief source of raw intelligence was the clandestine agent with his or her Minox camera, today that source is the same worldwide blanket of microwave signals and rivers of satellite transmissions that gives us our telephone calls, our remote banking, telegrams and, soon, our mail. Diverted into the Puzzle Palace by the Agency's far-flung network of dish-covered intercept stations, the processed signals yield a rich cargo of economic, political, diplomatic, and military intelligence.

"HUMINT [Human Intelligence] is subject to all of the mental aberrations of the source as well as the interpreter of the source," Lieutenant General Marshall S. Carter once explained. "SIGINT isn't.

---

of the American Telephone & Telegraph Company and GTE Satellite Corporation), and one by Satellite Business Systems (a data communications consortium of COMSAT, IBM, and the Aetna Insurance Company).

* INTELPOST serves fifty foreign cities. Messages are routed to Canada via terrestrial circuits, then by international satellite to other participating countries.

SIGINT has technical aberrations which give it away almost immediately if it does not have bona fides, if it is not legitimate. A good analyst can tell very, very quickly whether this is an attempt at disinformation, at confusion, from SIGINT. You can't do that from HUMINT; you don't have the bona fides — what are his sources? He may be the source, but what are *his* sources?"

Having served as deputy director of the CIA and director of the NSA, Carter was one of the very few people to have been intimately associated with both collection systems, and in his opinion SIGINT won by a wavelength. "Photo interpretation," he explained, "can in some cases be misinterpreted by the reader or intentionally confused by the maker in the first place — camouflage, this sort of thing. SIGINT is the one that is immediate, right now. Photo interpretation, yes, to some extent, but you still have to say 'Is that really a fake, have they confused it?' It is better than HUMINT, it is more rapid than HUMINT [but] SIGINT is right now; its bona fides are *there* the minute you get it."

The major problem with the two revolutions, the tremendous advances in the use of satellite and microwave technology and the enormous growth of SIGINT, is that they have left a void where there should have been a third revolution: the law. Three decades after its creation, the NSA is still without a formal, statutory charter, the first reform called for by the Church Committee. Instead, there is a super hush-hush surveillance court that is virtually impotent; the FISA, which has enough loopholes and exceptions to render it nearly useless; and an executive order that was designed more to protect the intelligence community from the citizens than citizens from the agencies. In addition, because it is an executive order, it can be changed any time at the whim of a President, without so much as a nod toward Congress.

Like an ever-widening sinkhole, NSA's surveillance technology will continue to expand, quietly pulling in more and more communications and gradually eliminating more and more privacy. The task will become increasingly easy throughout the 1980s as voice communications are converted to digital signals, a goal expected to be reached by 1990. When that happens, it will be as easy to run a telephone conversation through a computer, preprogrammed with watch words, as it is now to run through data communications. Of course, by then the ultimate computer may have been developed, one that will be able instantly to transcribe a spoken conversation.

More than fifty years ago, writing a dissenting opinion to a case which held that the Fourth Amendment warrant requirement did not apply to the seizure of conversations by means of wiretapping, Supreme Court Justice Louis D. Brandeis envisioned a day when technology would overtake the law:

> Subtler and more far-reaching means of invading privacy have become available to the government . . . [and] the progress of science in furnishing the government with means of espionage is not likely to stop with wiretapping. Ways may some day be developed by which the Government, without removing papers from secret drawers, can reproduce them in court, and by which it will be enabled to expose to a jury the most intimate occurrences of the home . . . Can it be that the Constitution affords no protection against such invasions of individual security?*

If there are defenses to such technotyranny, it would appear, at least from past experience, that they will not come from Congress. Rather, they will most likely come from academe and industry in the form of secure cryptographic applications to private and commercial telecommunications equipment. The same technology that is used against free speech can be used to protect it, for without protection the future may be grim. Referring to the NSA's SIGINT technology, Senator Frank Church concluded:

> At the same time, that capability at any time could be turned around on the American people and no American would have any privacy left, such [is] the capability to monitor everything: telephone conversations, telegrams, it doesn't matter. There would be no place to hide. If this government ever became a tyranny, if a dictator ever took charge in this country, the technological capacity that the intelligence community has given the government could enable it to impose total tyranny, and there would be no way to fight back, because the most careful effort to combine together in resistance to the government, no matter how privately it was done, is within the reach of the government to know. Such is the capability of this technology . . .
>
> I don't want to see this country ever go across the bridge. I know the capacity that is there to make tyranny total in America, and we must see to it that this agency and all agencies that possess this technology operate within the law and under proper supervision, so that we never cross over that abyss. That is the abyss from which there is no return.

---

* Justice Brandeis answered his own question when he quoted from *Boyd* v. *United States* (116 U.S. 616): "It is not the breaking of his doors, and the rummaging of his drawers that constitutes the essence of the offense; but it is the invasion of his indefensible right of personal security, personal liberty, and private property." (277 U.S. 438, at pages 474–475.)

Appendix

Notes

Acronyms and Abbreviations

Index

APPENDIX

NSA Career Panels and Professions

Cryptanalysis
    Cryptanalyst

Traffic Analysis
    Traffic Analyst

Signals Collection
    Collection Officer

Language
    Linguist

Data Systems
    Computer Systems Analyst

Communications Security
    Communications Security Analyst

Engineering and Physical Science
    Engineer
    Physical Scientist
    Engineering Specialist

Telecommunications
    Telecommunications Officer

Mathematics
    Mathematician
    Cryptologic Mathematician

Signals Analysis
    Signals Analyst
    Signals Conversion Officer
    Telemetry Specialist
    Conversion Specialist
    Electronic Signals Specialist
    Communications Signals Specialist

Special Research
    Special Research Analyst
    Information Science Analyst
Industrial Production
    Industrial Production Officer
Logistics
    Logistician
Education and Training
    Education and Training Officer

Directors of the National Security Agency

Lieutenant General Ralph Julian Canine, USA
November 4, 1952–November 1956

Lieutenant General John Alexander Samford, USAF
November 1956–November 1960

Vice Admiral Laurence Hugh Frost, USN
November 1960–June 30, 1962

Lieutenant General Gordon Aylesworth Blake, USAF
June 30, 1962–June 1, 1965

Lieutenant General Marshall Sylvester Carter, USA
June 1, 1965–August 1, 1969

Vice Admiral Noel Gayler, USN
August 1, 1969–August 24, 1972

Lieutenant General Samuel C. Phillips, USAF
August 24, 1972–August 15, 1973

Lieutenant General Lew Allen, Jr., USAF
August 15, 1973–July 5, 1977

Vice Admiral Bobby Ray Inman, USN
July 5, 1977–March 10, 1981

Lieutenant General Lincoln D. Faurer, USAF
March 10, 1981–

Deputy Directors of the National Security Agency

Rear Admiral Joseph Numa Wenger, USN (Vice Director)
November 4, 1952–Fall of 1953

Brigadier General John B. Ackerman, USAF (Vice Director)
Fall of 1953–June 1956

Lieutenant General John Alexander Samford, USAF (Vice Director)
June 1956–November 1956

Joseph H. Ream
November 1956–October 1957

Dr. Howard Theodore Engstrom
October 1957–August 1958

Dr. Louis William Tordella
August 1958–April 21, 1974

Benson K. Buffham
April 21, 1974–May 1, 1978

Robert E. Drake
May 1, 1978–April 1, 1980

Ann Z. Caracristi
April 1, 1980–

NOTES

ABBREVIATIONS OF SELECTED SOURCES

Draft Report   U.S. House of Representatives, Committee on Government Information and Individual Rights Subcommittee, "Interception of International Telecommunications by the National Security Agency," Draft Report. This report was prepared in the fall of 1977 by Robert S. Fink, professional staff member of the committee, but was never published or released to the public.

Final Report   U.S. Senate, Select Committee on Intelligence, Book I, *Foreign and Military Intelligence*, Book II, *Intelligence Activities and the Rights of Americans*, Book III, *Supplementary Detailed Staff Reports on Intelligence and the Rights of Americans*, Final Report, April 23, 1976.

GPO   Government Printing Office

HMCAH   U.S. House of Representatives, Committee on Appropriations, *Military Construction Appropriations*, Hearings.

NSAN   *National Security Agency Newsletter*

The Friedman Papers, in the George C. Marshall Research Library, have not yet been completely sorted. Some of the citations in the notes that follow will not have the box and item number, but all of the papers cited are in the library and usually can be found in the alphabetical file under the last name of the correspondent.

Chapter 1: Birth

page

1 "the foundation upon which all": Affidavit of Staff Secretary of the National Security Council quoted in *Kruh* v. *General Services Administration*, 412 F. Supp. 965 (1976), at p. 968, note 5.

"This Memorandum remains": Affidavit of the director of the NSA, in ibid.

2 Even a congressional committee: See p. 296.

"one of the deepest secrets": Daniel Schorr, *Clearing the Air* (Boston: Houghton Mifflin, 1977), p. 183.

"not one American in 10,000": Harrison E. Salisbury, "Big Brother Is Alive and Monitoring 400,000 Calls a Day," *Penthouse* (November 1980), pp. 114–115.

"It has been observed that": Yuriy Petrov, "AGRs at Sea, AGRs in the Air . . ." (Moscow) *Literary Gazette* (April 30, 1969), p. A37. This article, translated by the NSA, is found in the Marshall S. Carter Papers, George C. Marshall Research Library, Box 9, Item 2.

"By the budget yardstick": U.S. Senate, Select Committee to Study Governmental Operations with Respect to Intelligence Activities, *Foreign and Military Intelligence,* Final Report, Book I, 94th Cong. 1st Sess., pp. 333–334.

"It was unrealistic"; "while he, as DCI": Victor Marchetti and John D. Marks, *The CIA and the Cult of Intelligence* (New York: Dell, 1974), p. 114.

3 "as Director of the CIA": U.S. Senate, *Foreign and Military Intelligence,* p. 333.

sparked a bitter battle: Lee Lescaze, "Pentagon vs. CIA: Control of Intelligence Community Sparks Major Institutional Battle," *Washington Post* (June 10, 1977), p. A1.

820 employees; twelve hundred to fourteen hundred; "the CIA's first mutiny"; peak of eight thousand; less than four thousand: "The CIA: How Badly Hurt?," *Newsweek* (February 6, 1978), p. 21.

4 still controlled 68,203 people: U.S. National Credit Union Administration, *List of Potential Number of Members of Tower Federal Credit Union for 1978.* This list was developed in response to a Freedom of Information Act request by the author. The Tower Federal Credit Union is located at NSA, and its membership is limited to NSA employees and their families. The list of "potential" members indicates the number of actual employees in the Agency. The number would include the military personnel attached to NSA headquarters and NSA installations but would not include members of the three military cryptologic organizations assigned to military installations or listening posts. In addition to the number of potential members of the credit union for 1978, the list also included the numbers of both actual and potential members from 1956 to 1978.

"No statute establishes the NSA": U.S. Senate, Senate Select Committee to Study Governmental Operations with Respect to Intelligence Activities, *The National Security Agency and Fourth Amendment Rights,* Hearings, 94th Cong., 1st Sess., p. 1.

"possibly the most": Ibid., p. 35.

"That capability": National Broadcasting Company, "Meet the Press" (Washington, D.C.: Merkle Press, 1975), transcript of August 17, 1975, p. 6.

Chapter 2: Prelude

page

5 Herbert Osborne Yardley . . . China: Interviews with Mrs. Herbert O. Yardley, October 20, 1979, and January 23, 1981. See also David Kahn, *The Codebreakers* (New York: Macmillan, 1967), pp. 351–369.

6 "As I asked myself this question": Herbert O. Yardley, *The American Black Chamber* (Indianapolis: Bobbs-Merrill, 1931), p. 20.
"friendly connections": Ibid., p. 21.
"Colonel House must be": Ibid., p. 22.

7 "I always assume": Ibid., p. 30.
"would soon rule": Ibid., p. 32.
Theodore W. Richards: U.S. Army Security Agency, *Historical Background of the Signal Security Agency* (Washington, D.C.: Army Security Agency, 1946), Vol. II, p. 105.

8 "The situation is so uncertain"; "be retained in toto": Ibid., Vol. III, pp. 41–42.
The proposal . . . called for: Ibid., pp. 48–50.

9 "Where you work": Ibid., p. 47.
"My heart stood still": Yardley, p. 269.

10 "the most important"; "It is necessary"; "All it need do": Ibid., pp. 312–313.

12 Western Union; "had put all our cards": U.S. Army Security Agency, *Historical Background,* Vol. III, p. 80.
lawyer named L. F. H. Betts; through W. E. Roosevelt and Robert W. Goelet: Ibid., p. 80.

12–13 *Robert C. Clowry;* British monopoly: "Sub-Chaser's Shot Stops Cable Ship; Crew Are Arrested," *New York Times* (March 6, 1921), p. 1; "Second Sub Chaser on Guard at Miami," Ibid. (March 7, 1921), p. 15; George T. Odell, "The Cable Control Controversy," *The Nation* (February 2, 1921), pp. 169–170.

13 learned that the British were secretly eavesdropping: U.S. Senate, Committee on Interstate Commerce, *Cable-Landing Licenses,* Hearings, 66th Cong., 3rd Sess. (Washington, D.C.: GPO, 1921), pp. 182–199, 312–318.
J. C. Willever; work out a modus operandi: U.S. Army Security Agency, *Historical Background,* Vol. III, pp. 80–81.

14 "mobile tractor" units: For an interesting article on these units, see NSA, "Umbrellas, Loops, and Tractors," *Cryptologic Spectrum* (Summer 1980), pp. 4–14.
special mission to China: Army Security Agency, *Historical Background,* Vol. III, pp. 81–83.

15 "there existed in the office": Ibid., p. 83.
"We learn from a source": Ibid., p. 85.

16 "In 1919 our organization": Army Security Agency, *Historical Background,* Vol. III.

"I have no fears": *The National Experience* (New York: Harcourt, Brace & World, 1968), p. 659.

laid on the Secretary's desk; immediate and violent: Army Security Agency, *Historical Background,* Vol. III, p. 143.

solved coded messages from Argentina, Brazil: Yardley, p. 332.

17 "gentlemen do not": Henry L. Stimson and McGeorge Bundy, *On Active Service in Peace and War* (New York: Harper & Brothers, 1947), p. 188.

"indiscretions which could": Army Security Agency, *Historical Background,* Vol. III, p. 145.

"Ever since the war"; "they may make such a violent": Ibid., p. 166.

"because it proved": Ibid., p. 171.

18 "a prominent publisher"; "would not be for the best": Memorandum, Lieutenant Colonel O. S. Albright, War Department, to Colonel Alfred T. Smith, Assistant Chief of Staff, G-2, March 24, 1931. National Archives, Record Group 457, SRH-038 NSA, pp. 138–140.

"it was possible that": Ibid.

19 "the most sensational": W. A. Roberts quoted in *Book Review Digest,* (March 1931–February 1932).

In two months: Telephone interview with Marie Stuart Klooz, April 12, 1979.

20 *Diplomatic Eavesdropping* and *Embassy Keyholes:* Marie Stuart Klooz, *Japanese Diplomatic Secrets, 1921–22* (unpublished manuscript), title page.

ghost writer put her name: Klooz interview.

secretly notified Nugent Dodds: Petition of the Bobbs-Merrill Company for permission to sell copies of *The American Black Chamber,* June 21, 1933, National Archives, Record Group 60, Department of Justice Central File, 235 334.

"I cannot too strongly urge": Memorandum, Division of Far Eastern Affairs, September 12, 1932, National Archives, Record Group 59, Department of State Decimal File, Item 894.727/20.

requested that Bobbs-Merrill wire him: Letter, Dodds to Bobbs-Merrill, September 13, 1932, National Archives, Record Group 60, Department of Justice Central File, 235 334.

a Western Union telegram: Telegram, Bobbs-Merrill to Dodds, September 13, 1932, National Archives, ibid.

"This demand must be made"; "The Secretary of War": Memorandum, Adjutant General to Commanding General, Fort Hayes, Ohio, September 13, 1932, National Archives, ibid.

21 "I am not interested": Endorsement on above memorandum, Commanding General, Fort Hayes, to Adjutant General, September 17, 1932, National Archives, ibid.

22 "will endeavor"; "relative to the inadvisability": Memorandum, "Major Yardley's Manuscript," September 14, 1932, National Archives, Record Group 457, SRH-038 NSA, p. 183.

vowed to cooperate in any way; "I can readily see": Letter, Brett to Dewey, October 4, 1932, National Archives, Record Group 60, Department of Justice Central File, 235 334.

"anything which the government": Ibid.

"I assume the Department": Letter, Dodds to United States Attorney George Z. Medalie, October 8, 1932. National Archives, ibid.

23 sent the document off: Letter, Dodds to Secretary of War, October 11, 1932, National Archives, ibid.

"Can you advise me": Letter, Medalie to Dodds, October 26, 1932, National Archives, ibid.

"appreciates his courtesy": Letter, Dodds to Dewey, October 28, 1932, National Archives, ibid.

Brett called Dewey; "The important thing": Letter, Medalie to Parrish, February 16, 1933, National Archives, ibid.

"There is a pressing time element": Letter, Medalie (dictated by Dewey) to Parrish, February 17, 1933, National Archives, ibid.

24 Dewey sent a U.S. marshal; Brett arrived first: "Code Expert's MS. on Japan Is Seized," *New York Times* (February 21, 1933), p. 3.

25 not publish any information; inserted accidentally: William F. Friedman, notes following a conversation with Yardley on February 25, 1933, dated February 26, 1933, Friedman Papers, Item 840, George C. Marshall Research Library.

in Dewey's office the next day: Ibid.

26 "We cannot get the truth": *Congressional Record*, LXXVII, May 10, 1933, p. 3129.

27 May 10, 1929: Army Regulation 105–5, December 15, 1926, Change 1.

William F. Friedman: See, generally, Ronald Clark, *The Man Who Broke Purple* (Boston: Little, Brown, 1977). See also Kahn, pp. 369–393.

28 "by various and entirely surreptitious means": William F. Friedman, *Six Lectures on Cryptology* (NSA, April 1963), p. 106.

30 "preparation and revision": Army Security Agency, *Historical Background*, Vol. III, p. 182.

Friedman was authorized: Ibid., p. 202.

knowledge of at least one: Interview with Frank B. Rowlett, January 28, 1981.

John B. Hurt: Rowlett interview.

31 Signal Intelligence School: Army Security Agency, *Historical Background*, Vol. III, pp. 269–283.

Battery Cove: Ibid., p. 294.

During this period: Ibid.

32 By 1938, in addition; between Rome and Tokyo: Ibid., pp. 297–298.

33 "to maintain and operate": Ibid., p. 300.

33–34 "We were just a few"; Shanghai: Kahn, pp. 387–388.

34 with eavesdropping posts in: Ibid., p. 12.

Angooki Taipu A; Angooki Taipu B: Rowlett interview.

a fourth floor; fire broke out: Ibid.

35 "The method of processing": National Security Agency, Committee Appointed to Survey Communications Intelligence Activities of the Government, *Report to the Secretary of State and the Secretary of Defense* (*Brownell Committee Report*), June 13, 1952, p. 8.

36 In December 1941 American COMINT: *History of the Special Branch, MIS, War Department, 1942–1944,* National Archives, Record Group 457, SRH-035, pp. 4–5.
first Sunday in December 1941: U.S. Congress, Joint Committee on the Investigation of the Pearl Harbor Attack, *Pearl Harbor Attack,* Hearings, 79th Cong., 2nd Sess. (Washington, D.C.: GPO, 1946). See also Kahn, Chapter 1.

37 "Will the Ambassador": *Pearl Harbor Attack,* Part 12, p. 248.

38 "Please go out": Ibid., Part 9, pp. 4524–4525.

40 "In 1929 . . . the world": Kahn, p. 360.
McCormack soon discovered that: *History of the Special Branch,* p. 1.

42 breakthrough was at last made; three streamlined sections: Ibid. p. 26.
like transmitters in: Ibid., p. 61–62.

43 more homogeneous organization: Ibid., p. 63.
wrested operational control: George Raynor Thompson and Dixie R. Harris, *United States Army in World War II, The Technical Services, The Signal Corps: The Outcome* (Washington, D.C.: Department of the Army, Chief of Military History, GPO, 1966), pp. 348–350.
half billion dollars; Nimitz rated its value; Handy is reported to have said; In the Pacific: *Brownell Committee Report,* p. 22.
Throughout the war; In the land war; Even before Pearl Harbor: Ibid., pp. 23–26.

44 avoiding any physical compromise: Memorandum, Bissell to Marshall, August 11, 1945, National Archives, Record Group 457.
gentleman's agreement: *Brownell Committee Report,* pp. 9, 12.
"giving the Navy something to do": Ibid., p. 18.

45 presidential memorandum; ANCICC; ANCIB; STANCIB: Ibid., pp. 13–16.
NSCID No. 9: Ibid. pp. 42–48.

46 "The special nature": Department of Justice, "Prosecutive Summary," March 4, 1977, p. 12. For details on this "Prosecutive Summary," see notes for pages 157 and 242.

47 Stone Board: *Brownell Committee Report,* pp. 20–21.
"under the direction"; "to provide for": Ibid., p. 47.

48 Admiral Stone: Navy biography.
considered top secret; But he had to be replaced: Memorandum, Chief of Naval Operations to Secretary of Defense, July 8, 1949, National Archives, Record Group 218, CCS-334 NSA, Section 1.
final recommendation: Memorandum, Chairman, JCS, to Secretary of Defense, August 31, 1949, National Archives, ibid.
AFSA thus became . . . in total secrecy: Memorandum, Secretary of Defense to Secretaries of the Army, Navy, and Air Force, June 29, 1949, National Archives, ibid.
Stone quietly assumed office: Memorandum, Stone to JCS, July 15, 1949, National Archives, ibid.
"the agency of the Joint Chiefs": *Brownell Committee Report,* pp. 49–50.

49 method used for selecting targets: Ibid., pp. 64–74.

"the North Korean Peoples' Army": Ibid., pp. 66–67.

"A list of sensitive": Ibid., p. 67.

50 nine separate lists: Ibid., p. 68.

51 requirements went to AFSA-28: Ibid., pp. 74–89.

"beachheads": Ibid., pp. 88–89.

watch lists: Ibid., p. 98.

52 "the present scale": Memorandum, Chairman, USCIB, to Executive Secretary, National Security Council, July 19, 1950, National Archives, Record Group 218, CCS-334 NSA, Section 4.

number of military personnel; budget of $60.9 million: Memorandum, Army Chief of Staff to Secretary of Defense, July 28, 1950; Memorandum, JCS to AFSA, July 28, 1950; Memorandum, Chairman, AFSAC to JCS, July 24, 1950; Memorandum, Chairman, JCS, to Secretary of Defense, March 5, 1951. All in National Archives, ibid., Section 5.

"In theory the Joint Chiefs": *Brownell Committee Report*, p. 119.

53 CONSIDO plan: Ibid., Exhibit I, pp. 11–13.

British since 1920; "it would drastically": Ibid.

54 "If, as things develop": Ibid., p. 125.

"This memorandum should provide": Ibid., p. 122.

"AFSA is now under": Ibid., p. 128.

Chapter 3: Anatomy

page

56 more than 130: *Road Atlas* (Chicago: Rand McNally, 1979), pp. 106–107.

Stranger Unchallenged: Linda I. Posner, "A Tape Is Born," *NSAN* (October 1979), p. 8.

eighteen thousand pieces of mail: "More Than Meets the Eye," *NSAN* (August 1980), p. 6.

57 thirty thousand calls: "NSA's Telephone Exchange . . . Communications Focal Point," *NSAN* (October 1979), p. 12.

own power station: U.S. House of Representatives, Committee on Appropriations, *Military Construction Appropriations for 1971*, Part 3, 91st Cong., 2nd Sess., p. 814.

city of fifty thousand: Interview with official from Boston Edison Company.

recurring nightmare: Memorandum, General Omar N. Bradley, Chairman, JCS, to Secretary of Defense, March 14, 1950, National Archives, Record Group 218, CCS-334 NSA, Section 3, pp. 1–10.

"the increase in efficiency"; "In the Pacific"; "immediately preceding": Ibid., pp. 3–5.

58 Ten days later: Memorandum, Secretary of Defense Louis Johnson to JCS, March 24, 1950, National Archives, ibid.

appointed an ad hoc site board: Memorandum from Director, AFSA, to members of board, April 21, 1950, National Archives, ibid., pp. 1–4.

Fort Knox: *The Selection of a Site for the Proposed Cryptologic Establishment Outside the Washington Area,* Report by the Chairman, Armed Forces Security Agency Council, to the JCS, February 6, 1951, National Archives, ibid., Section 4.

59 April 10, 1951: Briefing Sheet for the Chairman, JCS, JCS meeting, January 30, 1952, National Archives, ibid., Section 7.

2.05 percent attrition rate: "They Paint Our Picture in Figures," *NSAN* (March 1955), p. 3.

"As the director": Transcript of telephone conversation, December 10, 1952, National Archives, JCS file, Record Group 218, CCS-334 NSA, Section 7.

rescinded his order; possible locations; Fort George G. Meade: Briefing Sheet for the Chairman, JCS, JCS meeting, January 30, 1952, National Archives, ibid.

Omar Bradley sent: Memorandum, Bradley to Secretary of Defense, January 30, 1952, National Archives, ibid.

Project K: *National Security Agency Construction Project,* Report by the Joint Intelligence Committee to the JCS, November 12, 1952, National Archives, ibid.

$19,944,451: David Kahn, *The Codebreakers* (New York: Macmillan, 1967), p. 676.

59–60 squared-off A; main building; supply building: "Construction Bids Invited in May for New NSA Building, Fort Meade," *NSAN* (March 1954), p. 3.

60 $35 million: Kahn, p. 676.

J. W. Bateson; $12 million; 512,000 square feet; 140,000 feet: "Concrete Facts — Annex I," *NSAN* (November 15, 1963), pp. 6–8.

7,560,000 linear feet; 16,000 light fixtures; eleven million gallons: "Annex I Construction 60% Completed," *NSAN* (January 1965), p. 5.

980 feet: *NSAN* (April 1955), p. 5.

The entire complex: Author's observations.

62 Walter Aiken: "Anniversary Celebrants," *NSAN* (November 1977), p. 18.

180 people: "Agency's Appetite Keeps Cafeterias Busy," *NSAN* (May 1965), p. 13.

full-service medical center: "Our Modern Medical Center Offers Complete Facilities for NSAers," *NSAN* (May 1968).

63 Mycenaean documents: "The NSA Library," *NSAN* (February 1958), p. 4.

watch a tape: "Learning Center Acquires FLACS Library," *NSAN* (November 1979), p. 6. The library contains recordings of foreign-language radio and television programs, each with an accompanying transcript. Languages include Cambodian, Egyptian, Arabic, Indonesian, Japanese, Persian, Thai, and Hebrew.

"You will notice": "Simplicity Marks Impressive Dedication," *NSAN* (July 1966).

64 S Building: *HMCAH* for 1966, Part 4, 89th Cong., 1st Sess., p. 407.

printing facility: National Security Agency, *Careers in Printing Technology at the National Security Agency*, prepared by NSA office of Employment (undated).

thirty-five hundred men and women; mess hall: *HMCAH* for 1973, Part 3, 92nd Cong., 1st Sess., pp. 53–55.

Troop Support Building: *HMCAH* for 1969, Part 2, 90th Cong., 2nd Sess., pp. 632–641.

Sensitive Materials Center: *HMCAH* for 1972, Part 3, 92nd Cong., 1st Sess., pp. 428–431.

65 NSA couriers: "Getting the Mail to Its Destination Is Job of Delivery and Courier Branch," *NSAN* (August 1965), p. 12.

Armed Forces Courier Service . . . and diplomatic couriers: "More Than Meets the Eye," *NSAN* (August 1980), p. 6.

SAB 4: *HMCAH* for 1974, Part 4, 93rd Cong., 1st Sess., pp. 456–457.

Half a million cubic feet: "Office of Material Management," *NSAN* (November 1980), p. 5.

"That means": General Accounting Office, Report to the Congress by the Comptroller General of the United States, *Oversight of the Government's Security Classification Program — Some Improvement Still Needed*, LCD–81–13, December 16, 1980 (Washington, D.C.: GPO, 1980), p. 14.

"Is the National Security Agency": Senator Clarence D. Long addressing Brigadier General Thomas B. Wood, USAF, Assistant Director, Installations and Logistics, NSA, *HMCAH* for 1974, 93rd Cong., 1st Sess., p. 461.

turned into pulp: Ibid., pp. 462–463.

66 White Elephant No. 1: Douglas Watson, "NSA Secrets-Swallower Chokes Up," *Washington Post* (June 3, 1975), p. A1.

Disney World; $2 million: *HMCAH* for 1974, 93rd Cong., 1st Sess., p. 466.

"Our research": *Washington Post,* p. A6.

67 "We are": "Action Line," *NSAN* (April 1972), p. 3.

addition to Headquarters-Operations Building: *HMCAH* for 1978, Part 4, 95th Cong., 1st Sess., pp. 446–447, 456.

68 On January 19, 1951: Memorandum, JCS, to Chairman, Armed Forces Security Agency Council, January 19, 1951, National Archives, Record Group 218, CCS-334 NSA, Section 4.

committee met on January 29: Memorandum, Chairman, Armed Forces Security Agency Council to JCS, February 2, 1951, National Archives, ibid.

Canine was a shoo-in: Note by the Secretaries, February 17, 1951, National Archives, ibid.

At fifty-five: Army biography. Canine died on March 8, 1977, at Walter Reed Army Hospital at the age of seventy-three.

"The people who make up": "General Canine and NSA," *NSAN* (November 1956), p. 3.

69 "Lady, I know": "Recalling the Early Days of NSA," *NSAN* (November 1977), p. 10.

John Alexander Samford: Air Force biography; "General Samford," *NSAN* (December 1956), p. 2; "He Knows the Password," *New York Times* (September 7, 1960), p. 14. He died on November 20, 1968, at Andrews Air Force Base Hospital at the age of sixty-three.

Laurence Hugh (Jack) Frost: Navy biography; "Vice Admiral Frost Is New Director," *NSAN* (December 1, 1960), p. 2. He died on May 22, 1977, in Norfolk, Virginia, at the age of seventy-four.

70 Gordon Aylesworth Blake: Air Force biography; "Lieutenant General Gordon A. Blake, USAF, Is Appointed Director, NSA," *NSAN* (August 1962), p. 2; Lieutenant General Gordon A. Blake to Retire on May 31," *NSAN* (May 1965), p. 5.

Travis Trophy: "Air Force Security Service Wins Travis Trophy for Outstanding Contributions," *NSAN* (October 1965), p. 7.

TO BE AWARDED: NSA, *Travis Trophy Award, Eighth Annual Presentation,* September 27, 1972.

71 Reginald H. Parker: Photo, Director's Photo Album, Lieutenant General Marshall S. Carter (Ret.).

25 percent: Interview with Lieutenant General Marshall S. Carter, July 17–18, 1980.

"pornography": Letter, Carter to Arthur Lundahl, Director, National Photographic Interpretation Center (NPIC), CIA, July 12, 1965, George C. Marshall Research Library, Carter Papers.

tangled with Defense Secretary McNamara: Letter, Carter to Eugenia, (his secretary), August 29, 1970, Carter Papers.

72 "I had the word"; "McNamara could never": Carter interview.

"When Admiral Raborn": Letter, Carter to Miss Maxine S. Taylor, April 30, 1965, Carter Papers.

"I was in effect": Carter interview.

73 "sometimes quite awkward"; "In the case": Oral History Interview, Laurence H. Frost (July 7, 1970), John F. Kennedy Presidential Library, Boston, Massachusetts.

under one condition: Carter interview.

" 'peculiar' types": Letter, Carter to a potential recruit, June 17, 1964, Carter Papers.

Baby Doll: Letter, Carter to Sergeant Ralph Smith, Camp Peary, Carter Papers.

74 "Should you ever": Letter, Henry Knoche to Carter, July 28, 1969, Carter Papers.

"Carter's 'skill' ": B. Karpovich, "Pat — the Electronic Ear: NSA Chief's Empire Thrives on No Publicity," *Soviet Russia* (September 22, 1968), p. 3. I am grateful to General Carter for sending me this translated article.

"most of you": "Visit of Vice President Humphrey Highlights Security Week 1967," *NSAN* (October 1967), p. 2.

Dulles; Rowley; Smith; Lay; Coyne: "Commander, Diplomat, Executive Ends Distinguished Military Career," *NSAN* (Special Edition, July 1969), p. 3.

75 "a separately organized agency": Office of the Federal Register, *United States Government Organization Manual, 1977–1978* (Washington, D.C.: GPO, 1977), p. 235.

"You know I was fighting": Carter interview.

battle of the seal: Ibid.

"I want United States": Ibid.

76 "So then": Ibid.

Noel Gayler: "Vice Admiral Noel Gayler, USN, Becomes Agency's New Director," *NSAN* (August 1969), p. 2; Navy biography.

77 "At the end": Department of the Army, Major Commanders' Annual Report to Headquarters of the Army, *Command Presentation United States Army Security Agency* (October 7, 1971), p. 19.

78 ninety-five thousand people: Testimony of Secretary of Defense James Schlesinger, U.S. House of Representatives, Committee on Appropriations, Subcommittee on Department of Defense, *Department of Defense Appropriations for 1975,* Part 1, 93rd Cong., 2nd Sess., p. 598.

"monstrous": Carter interview.

"you couldn't"; "I just took it"; "The damned thing": Ibid.

"declaration of war": Interview with Richard P. Floyd, former Chief, Procurement Support Division, Office of Procurement, NSA, January 19, 1981.

79 "The strategy"; "He wasn't": Ibid.

space and missile program: "General Samuel Phillips Receives Thomas D. White Space Trophy," *NSAN* (September 1972).

Lew Allen, Jr.: "Lieutenant General Lew Allen, Jr., USAF, Named Director, NSA/Chief, CSS, by President," *NSAN* (August 1973), p. 2; Air Force biography.

80 Bobby Ray Inman: "Vice Admiral B. R. Inman Becomes Agency Director," *NSAN* (July 1977), p. 2; "An Interview with Agency's New Director," *NSAN* (September 1977), pp. 4–5; Navy biography.

"They were obviously"; "I stood my first watch": Harvard University, Center for Information Policy Research, Program on Information Resources Policy, *Seminar on Command, Control, Communications, and Intelligence* (Cambridge: Harvard University, 1980), Inman lecture, p. 141.

"I was an analyst": Ibid., p. 142.

81 "I try to do it": Ibid., p. 152.

82 that he was . . . gay; "if the case"; "lower the heat": Interview with Franklin E. Kameny, January 22, 1981.

84 "mend fences": Ibid.

"They had read": Ibid.

"there remain people": Michael Getler, "Homosexual to Keep High-Security Job," *Washington Post* (December 30, 1980), pp. A1, A6.

85 make money; "If ever there was": "The CIA's New Super Spy," *Newsweek* (February 16, 1981), p. 37.

Lincoln D. Faurer: Air Force biography; Department of Defense Telephone Directory (Defense Intelligence Agency section), (Washington, D.C.: GPO, 1977), pp. O–9 to O–10, for division of activities at DIA.

86 "I sure as hell": Carter interview.
Joseph Numa Wenger: *Who's Who in America, 1958–1959,* Vol. 30, p. 2939.
John B. Ackerman: "NSA's New Vice Director: Brigadier General John B. Ackerman," *NSAN* (February 1954), p. 2.
Joseph H. Ream: *Who's Who in America, 1962–1963,* Vol. 32, p. 2563.
Howard Theodore Engstrom: *Who's Who in America, 1960–1961,* Vol. 31, p. 882; "Dr. Engstrom Assumes New Posts," *NSAN* (November 1957), p. 1. He died on March 8, 1962, at the age of fifty-nine.

87 Louis Tordella: Jacques Cattell, ed., *American Men of Science: 1955* (Lancaster, Pennsylvania: The Science Press, 1955), Vol. 1; "Outstanding Cryptologic Leader Ends Career," *NSAN* (May 1974), pp. 2–3.
"world's largest": "Outstanding Cryptologic Leader," p. 3.
"to . . . the director"; he . . . nominated Tordella: Carter interview.

88 When Tordella retired: "Outstanding Cryptologic Leader," pp. 1–3.
Benson K. Buffham: "Benson K. Buffham Named as NSA Deputy Director," *NSAN* (May–June 1974), p. 4.
Robert E. Drake: "Robert E. Drake Named to Post of Deputy Director, NSA," *NSAN* (May 1978), p. 2.
Ann Z. Caracristi: *Who's Who of American Women,* p. 131; "Ann Caracristi Named NSA Deputy Director," *NSAN* (March 1980), p. 4; "Ann Caracristi Receives Federal Women's Award At Washington Banquet," *NSAN* (March 1965), p. 5; "Ann Caracristi Becomes First NSA Woman in Grade 18," *NSAN* (June 1975), p. 4.

89 Oliver R. Kirby: "Oliver Kirby Resigns to Accept Executive Position with Private Industry," *NSAN* (March 1968).
Pine Gap: Desmond Ball, *A Suitable Piece of Real Estate: American Installations in Australia* (Sydney, Australia: Hale & Tremonger, 1980), p. 63.
John E. Morrison: "Retires from Military After 32 Years," *NSAN* (March 1973), p. 6.
Herbert E. Wolff: List of personnel and organizations of NSA, provided to author by Daniel C. Schwartz, general counsel to NSA.
"wheels-up"; machine gun; "ate civilians": Floyd interview.

90 George L. McFadden: Schwartz list.
Henry J. Davis: Ibid.
Robert E. Rich: "Awards and Honors," *NSAN* (March 1980), p. 10.
ADVA; GENS; ACOM: Interviews with Francis A. (Frank) Raven, July 23, 1981, August 11, 1981, and November 4, 1981.
ALLO-34: NSA, *Recommendation for Promotion to GGD-15: Richard P. Floyd,* December 1, 1975, p. 2. Filed in *Floyd* v. *NSA,* Civil Case No. J79–1808, September 27, 1979, Federal District Court, Baltimore, Maryland.
MPRO: Kahn, 719.

91 A Group; Arthur J. Levenson: Raven interview.
Caracristi: "Ann Z. Caracristi Becomes Chief of A Group; Becomes First NSA Woman in Grade 18," *NSAN* (June 1975), p. 4.
B Group; Milton Zaslow: Raven interview.
G Group; PO5; Juanita M. Moody; PO4: Ibid.
W Group: Interview with Raymond T. Tate, former Deputy Director for COMSEC (1973–1978), November 3, 1981.

92 signals analysis; communications signals analysis; electronic signals analysis; telemetry analysis; signals conversion: NSA, *Personnel Management Manual,* pp. 30–32, Chapter 402, Annex B: Career Fields and Effective Dates of Criteria.
"the largest single": Harvard University, *Seminar on Command,* Tate lecture, p. 30.

93 "automatic look-up": NSA, *NSA Technical Journal,* Special Linguistics Issue, p. 3.
"The Soviets today": U.S. House of Representatives, Committee on Appropriations, Subcommittee on the Department of Defense, *Department of Defense Appropriations for 1978,* Part 3, 95th Cong., 1st Sess., p. 639.
"We have ample evidence": Ibid. for 1977, Part 6, 94th Cong., 2nd Sess., p. 50.

94 Robert E. Sears: "Exceptional Civilian Service Awards," *NSAN* (October 1979), p. 10.

95 KY-28: *Department of Defense Appropriations for 1978,* pp. 740–742.
"A fighter pilot": Ibid., p. 741.
"We operated": Carter interview.

96 Ray Tate: *Department of Defense Appropriations for 1977,* p. 49.
barium salts: Interview with Solomon Kullback, former Assistant Director, Research and Development, NSA, January 29, 1981.
REMP; RADE; STED: Statements of defectors Martin and Mitchell, "Text of Statements Read in Moscow by Former U.S. Security Agency Workers," *New York Times* (September 7, 1960), p. 10.
Mathematical Research Techniques Division; Cryptography Equipment Division; Arthur Hausman; Howard Barlow: Kullback interview.

97 "I could talk": Carter interview.
Mitford M. Mathews, Jr.: "Mitford M. Mathews, Jr., Dies Suddenly While on Business Trip in Rochester," *NSAN* (February 1971), p. 2.
Howard E. Rosenblum; James V. Boone: Schwartz list.

98 "I had five and a half acres": Carter interview.
"It's double that today": Interview with NSA official.
NSA . . . computer growth: NSA, *Influence of U.S. Cryptologic Organizations on the Digital Computer Industry,* May 1977, pp. 1–28, plus seven-page appendix. The author of this report was Samuel S. Snyder, a cryptanalyst and computer specialist who served at NSA and its predecessors from 1936 to 1964 and was one of those who supervised the Harvest project.
"policy of anonymity": Ibid., p. 1.

100 "Dammit, I want": Ibid., p. 24.
101 Carillon; Loadstone: Interview with NSA official.
   Built by Cray Research; The supercomputer is: "The CRAY-1 S Series
   of Computers," booklet produced by Cray Research, Inc.; Bradford W.
   Ketchum, "From Start-Up to $60 Million in Nanoseconds," *INC.* (No-
   vember 1980).
102 With a random access: "The CRAY-1 S Series."
   On top of this; Among those included: Interview with NSA official.
103 Eugene S. Ince: "Captain Ince Promoted to Rank of Rear Admiral,"
   NSAN (March 1976), p. 4; Schwartz list.
   "It's all right": Interview with NSA official.
   Milton Zaslow: Schwartz list.
   Kermith H. Speierman: "Kermith H. Speierman Receives Department
   of Defense Distinguished Civilian Service Award" and "A Retrospec-
   tive View of Kermith Speierman," both in *NSAN* (September 1979),
   p. 7.
   door pasted with warning signs and controlled by cipher lock: Author's
   observations.
   CLASSIFIED: Confidential COMINT channels message from UKC 201
   (the British GCHQ SIGINT base at Little Sai Wan in Hong Kong) to
   DIRNSA, November 14, 1966, Carter Papers.
   dish antennas; control facility: *HMCAH* for 1976, Part 2, 94th Cong.;
   1st Sess., pp. 295–297.
104 traced a Soviet bomber: "U.S. Electronic Espionage: A Memoir," *Ramparts* (August 1972), p. 43.
   spot reports; PENREPs: Tad Szulc, "The NSA — America's $10 Billion
   Frankenstein," *Penthouse* (November 1977), pp. 55 ff.
   DIN/DSSCS: Department of the Navy, U.S. Naval Security Group Activ-
   ity Sabana Seca (Puerto Rico), *Annual OPNAV Command History Report*,
   May 3, 1974, Annex A, Communications Facilities, A1, Naval Historical
   Center, Operational Archives.
   Streamliner: Ibid., dated February 27, 1978, Enclosure (1), p. 2, Naval
   Historical Center, Operational Archives.
   Room 406: Author's observations.
105 Charles Raduazo: "Atlanta and Boston Recruitment Offices to Open,"
   NSAN (September 1980), p. 4.
   without ever once; "Some time before": NSA, *Careers for Engineers, Mathematicians, Computer Scientists at the National Security Agency* (undated and
   unpaged). The NSA replaced these pamphlets in 1981.
   PQT: Educational Testing Service, *National Security Agency: 1981 Professional Qualification Test* (Berkeley, California: Educational Testing Service,
   1981).
106 usually about 150; new recruits: Interview with Robert A. Dedad, Chief,
   Office of Employment, NSA, October 31, 1980.
   numerous small offices: Author's observations.
108 Those who pass: See NSA, "NSA Career Service Occupational Struc-

ture," *Handbook of NSA Occupational Specialties.* Occupational Group 13, for example, is Cryptanalysis, which is broken down into three occupational specialties, or COSCs. COSC 1341 is Cryptanalysis Technician, with a grade range of GG-5 to GG-12; COSC 1331, Cryptanalysis Intern, has a range of GG-7 to GG-11; at the highest level is COSC 1311, or Cryptanalyst, with a grade range of GG-11 to GG-18. Before becoming deputy director of NSA, Ann Caracristi was a GG-18 Cryptanalyst.

"Garbled Telegrams"; "Matrices"; "Digit Identification"; "Number Series": NSA, "Description of the CQB Subtests," *NSA Personnel Management Manual,* pp. 30–32, Table 2, p. 11.

twenty-three professions; fourteen . . . career fields: NSA, "Career Fields and Effective Dates of Criteria," *NSA Personnel Management Manual,* pp. 30–32, Annex B, p. 11.

109 seven thousand contracts; $900 million; 8 percent; Rainmaker; Silkworth; Maroon Shield: Briefing Paper for Director, NSA, January 19, 1977.

"Maryland Procurement Office"; contracting: Floyd interview.

110 Richard P. Floyd: NSA, *Recommendation for Promotion to GGD-15: Richard P. Floyd.*

"the people": Floyd interview.

111 "Within two weeks": "Legality of National Security Agency's Purchases Challenged in Suit," *New York Times* (February 5, 1980), p. A20.

111–112 "a number of explosive"; "did not show"; "find no indication"; "exceptional talents"; "full consideration": Morton Mintz, "A Firing and the 'Secret' Workings of NSA," *Washington Post* (August 4, 1977), pp. 1, 2.

112 Silkworth came up for review: R. J. Cox, L411, Maryland Procurement Office, Memorandum for the Record, March 31, 1977.

"that the amount of time": Memorandum from Louis J. Bonanni, Acting Assistant Director, Installations and Logistics, to Richard P. Floyd, Chief, L41, May 3, 1977.

Louis J. Bonanni; Charles E. Shannon: Schwartz list.

113 DDPP; Richard N. Kern: Ibid.

NSA's Pacific command . . . Lester R. Schulz: Letter, Schulz to Carter, July 21, 1969, Carter Papers.

"This means war": U.S. Congress, Joint Committee on the Investigation of the Pearl Harbor Attack, *Pearl Harbor Attack,* Part 10, 79th Cong., 2nd Sess. (February 15, 1946), testimony of Commander Lester Robert Schulz, USN, p. 4662.

Howard M. Estes, Jr., ADPR; DDPR: Schwartz list.

Smith; suggestion . . . post . . . be abolished: Floyd interview.

113–114 Gerard P. Burke; Daniel B. Silver: Schwartz list.

114 "the magnitude"; "I made a survey": Carter interview.

Training School: "School Moves to New Quarters," *NSAN* (July 1954), p. 5.

seven-story tower: "School to Move," *NSAN* (January 1981), p. 8. Before moving to "the Tower," it was housed in the long, two-story FANX II.

CY-600: "CY-600 Course Participants Presented Diplomas at Special NCSch Ceremony," *NSAN* (July 1976), p. 2.

Intensive Study Program: "Intensive Study Program Grads Receive Diplomas," *NSAN* (September 1978), p. 13.

115 Guru: "Lieutenant General Lew Allen, Jr., Becomes Honorary Dundee Society Member," *NSAN* (July 1974), p. 7.

Lambros D. Callimahos: "Lambros D. Callimahos: Salasio and Snuff, Concerts and Cryptology," *NSAN* (October 1965), pp. 10–11.

116 died of cancer: "Lambros D. Callimahos, Flutist and Cryptologist," *Washington Post* (October 30, 1977), p. B6.

honorary membership to . . . Turner: "Dundee Society Holds 11th Reunion; Guru Honors Admiral Stansfield Turner," *NSAN* (July 1977), p. 4.

Frank B. Rowlett: "Frank Rowlett Retires," *NSAN* (Special Edition, January 1966), pp. 1–4.

117 Eugene J. Becker: "Exceptional Civilian Awards," *NSAN* (January 1980), p. 11.

19,000 students; five hundred different courses: Molla Siegel, "That's Academic," *NSAN* (December 1980), p. 7.

Crypto-Linguistic Association; "whose achievements": NSA, *Crypto-Linguistic Association* (NSA, February 1973).

eavesdropper . . . of the year: "First Ardisana Award Winner," *NSAN* (August 1980), p. 4. Brigadier General Bernard (Ben) Ardisana served as Assistant Deputy Director for Operations at NSA from June 1977 until his death in January 1978. The award focuses, according to Director Inman, "on the front end of the system."

Chapter 4: Penetration

118 "YOU ARE": *NSAN* (November 1976), p. 11.

"You don't have": "Security Wise," *NSAN* (March 1955), p. 7.

SNOOPER BOWL: *NSAN* (January 1981), p. 16.

electronic signs: Author's observations.

"security in depth": "Marine Guard Departure Will Bring End to an Era," *NSAN* (October 1977), p. 4.

October 15, 1954: "The Marine Guard: Protector of the Agency's Security," *NSAN* (November 1966), p. 10.

Alert Force: "Marine Guard — NSA's First Line of Defense," *NSAN* (May 1970), p. 4.

color-coded . . . badges: Interview with NSA official.

119 Courier badge; "tabs": Author's observations.

additional badges had to be issued: "Temporary Badges in Use During the Move," *NSAN* (November 1957).

key-punched: Author's observations.

HANDLE VIA COMINT CHANNELS ONLY: This caveat has appeared in the public domain on at least several occasions. See U.S. Senate, Select Committee on Intelligence, *Intelligence Activities, Huston Plan,* Hearings, 94th Cong., 1st Sess., p. 202. Also, U.S. House of Representatives, Select Committee on Intelligence, *U.S. Intelligence Agencies and Activities: Committee Proceedings,* 94th Cong., 1st Sess., p. 1516.

120 UMBRA; Trine; Dinar; Harum; Spoke: David Wise, *The Politics of Lying: Government Deception, Secrecy, and Power* (New York: Vintage Books, 1973), pp. 82–83, 88.

Umbra: See also Duncan Campbell, "Threat of the Electronic Spies," *New Statesman* (February 2, 1979), p. 145.

Trine: Bob Woodward, "Messages of Activists Intercepted," *Washington Post* (October 13, 1975), p. A1.

Gamma; Gupy; Gilt; Gout; Gult; Gant; Gabe; Gyro; Delta; Dace; Dice; Dent: Ibid.

121 HOLYSTONE DESKTOP: James Coates and Jack Fuller, "The Perils of Undersea Espionage," *Boston Globe* (December 17, 1977), p. 1.

profiling . . . McGeorge Bundy: Max Frankel, "The Importance of Being Bundy," *New York Times Magazine* (March 28, 1965), p. 33.

photograph of Bundy; "Hey, Mac"; "We've got to get": Interview with Lieutenant General Marshall S. Carter (Ret.), July 17–18, 1980. Also Wise, pp. 81–82.

122 RESTRICTED DELIVERY, DELIVER TO ADDRESSEE ONLY, POSTMASTER: Letter, NSA to author, November 29, 1978.

Philip F. Berrigan . . . protesters: Jim Landers, "Berrigans Use the Same Tactics, But Doubt Their Effect," *Washington Post* (March 23, 1974), pp. D1–D2.

NSA's clearance process: U.S. House of Representatives, Permanent Select Committee on Intelligence, *Security Clearance Procedures in the Intelligence Agencies,* Staff Report (September 1979), pp. 9, 11–13.

"The polygraph shall": Department of Defense Directive 5210.48, *The Conduct of Polygraph Examinations and the Selection, Training and Supervision of DoD Polygraph Examiners,* Section III-A.

123 access to the front lobby; take a seat; Actual examples: Author's observations.

Public Law 86–36: *The National Security Agency Act of 1959,* 50 U.S.C. 402 note (May 29, 1959), Section 6.

"covert assignments": Meeting between author and Mr. Schwartz, NSA headquarters, January 28, 1980.

"lives or safety"; "might be endangered": Letter, Schwartz to author, March 4, 1980.

124 front parking lot: Author's observations.

military seeking to switch to civilian status: *Security Clearance Procedures,* pp. 11–13.

S. Wesley Reynolds: Interview with S. Wesley Reynolds, April 13, 1979.

125 bugging: Reynolds interview.

Leonard P. Bienvenu: "Leonard P. Bienvenu," *NSAN* (September 15, 1962), pp. 1–2.

126 External Collection Program: U.S. Senate, Select Committee on Intelligence, *Supplementary Detailed Staff Reports on Intelligence and the Rights of Americans,* Final Report, Book III, April 23, 1976, p. 783.
"Nonaffiliates of NSA": Final Report, Book III, pp. 779–780.
Innumerable hours: Ibid.

127 At one point: Ibid.
"a possibly valuable"; "further low-key"; "would discuss": NSA, Memorandum from Carter to Chairman, USIB, April 13, 1966. Lieutenant General Marshall S. Carter Papers, Box 44, Folder 29, George C. Marshall Research Library.
Macmillan agreed to turn over: NSA, Memorandum, Carter to Chairman, USIB, July 13, 1965; Memorandum, Carter to Chairman, USIB, March 28, 1966. Both in Carter Papers, ibid.
"deplored"; "it would not": NSA, "Discussion of the Publication of The Code-Breakers by David Kahn," transcript of meeting in director's office, July 26, 1966, Carter Papers, ibid.

128 "We blew it!": Interview with Lieutenant General Marshall S. Carter, July 17–18, 1980.
refused to put anything in writing; "chose not to sign anything": NSA, "Discussion of the Publication," Carter Papers, ibid.
"This will serve to introduce": NSA, Draft letter to Lee C. Deighton, undated, Carter Papers, ibid.
GCHQ was putting pressure: William F. Friedman, handwritten note that states: "I was told that Geoffrey Evans of GCHQ interceded with Macmillan's in London on behalf of GCHQ and at the request of Brigadier Tiltman." See William F. Friedman Papers, George C. Marshall Research Library.

129 "that when a publisher"; "I pointed out": NSA, "Discussion of the Publication," Carter Papers, ibid.
"they said that": Ibid.
"Another agency outside": Contained in envelope in Friedman Papers, on which is a note written by William F. Friedman stating: "This contains the only paragraphs which were deleted from Kahn's Mss. at the request of GCHQ authorities." See Friedman Papers.

130 buried in the notes: See Kahn, notes for page 730, on page 1097.
Joseph Sidney Petersen, Jr.: "U.S. Security Aide Accused of Taking Secret Documents," *New York Times* (October 10, 1954), pp. 1, 33; "Pipeline via Paris?" *Time* (October 18, 1954), p. 17; U.S., *Department of State Bulletin* (November 1, 1954), p. 654; "To Avoid Embarrassment," *Time* (January 3, 1955), p. 18; "Petersen Gets 7 Years as a Spy for Taking Security Documents," *New York Times* (January 5, 1955), pp. 1, 10; "Petersen at Medical Center," *New York Times* (January 8, 1955), p. 7; "Jail for Petersen," *New York Times* (January 9, 1955), Section IV, p. 2; "The Petersen Case," *Time* (January 31, 1955), p. 4; "Hush-Hush Suspect," *Newsweek* (October 18, 1954), p. 32; "Fate of the Shy Spy," *Newsweek* (January 3, 1955) p. 16; Kahn, pp. 690–691.

131 Petersen's behavior was brought; "Verkuyl!": Interviews with Francis

A. (Frank) Raven, July 23, 1981; August 11, 1981; and November 4, 1981.

a surreptitious entry: Reynolds interview.

American-type staples had been replaced: Raven interview.

132 The problem was brought before: Interview with Frank B. Rowlett, January 28, 1981.

133 "The pith": Kahn, p. 691.

As a precaution: Reynolds interview.

134 Bernon F. Mitchell; William H. Martin: "Flight to Where?" (August 15, 1960), pp. 17–18; "The Defectors" (September 19, 1960), pp. 33–37; "The Risk, The Danger" (September 26, 1960), p. 58, all in *Newsweek*; "Security Risks" (August 15, 1960); "Traitor's Day in Moscow" (September 19, 1960), p. 20, both in *Time*; "They Are All an Abomination," *Nation* (September 17, 1960).

135 Martin and Mitchell at NSA: U.S. House of Representatives, Committee on Un-American Activities, *Security Practices in the National Security Agency*, Report, August 13, 1962.

137 air war with the Soviet Union: "Another Incident — The U.S. Aircraft and the 10-Year Record," *New York Times* (July 17, 1960), p. E5.

138 Samford . . . to suggest: "Text of Statements Read in Moscow by Former U.S. Security Agency Workers," *New York Times* (September 7, 1960), p. 10.

"in order": Ibid.

139 appointment with Congressman Wayne Hays: Ibid.

"but that": Sanche de Gramont, *The Secret War* (New York: Putnam's, 1962), p. 400.

Tom Morgan; two . . . sent from CIA: Jack Raymond, "House Units Map Defector Studies," *New York Times* (September 9, 1960), p. 9.

140 Clarence Schilt: "The Defectors," *Newsweek* (September 19, 1960), p. 37.

141 "Keep your chin up": Ibid.

142 Reynolds; without bothering: Reynolds interview.

1959 Ford: "Security Risks," *Time* (August 15, 1960).

"We hope to explain": Departure statement, "Text of Statements Read."

143 "Officials vainly hoped": "2 Defectors' Note Suppressed by U.S.," *New York Times* (September 11, 1960), p. 22.

"It must be assumed": Jack Raymond, "U.S. Fears Two Security Aides Have Gone Behind Iron Curtain," *New York Times* (August 6, 1960), p. 1.

"could in no way": Ibid.

144 "Information furnished me": Jack Raymond, "Defectors' Data Called Valuable," *New York Times* (August 31, 1960), p. 15.

U-2: Ibid.

145 "This thing was"; "under duress": "Fathers of Defectors Hold Duress Was Used," *New York Times* (September 7, 1960), p. 11.

"self-confessed"; turncoats: Jack Raymond, "President Calls Pair Traitorous," *New York Times* (September 7, 1960), p. 11.

"they ought to be shot": "Truman Agrees to Stump State," *New York Times* (September 10, 1960), p. 44.

Maurice H. Klein: Department of Justice, memorandum from Nathaniel E. Kossack, Fraud Section, to Herbert J. Miller, Jr., Assistant Attorney General, Criminal Division, December 14, 1961, pp. 1–18; *Security Practices in the National Security Agency*, pp. 10–12.

147 "The form 57"; Pentagon . . . investigation: *Security Practices*, pp. 11–12.

Klein was ousted: Laurence M. Stern, "Security Aide Ousted, Prosecution Requested," *Washington Post* (November 21, 1961), p. A2.

Reynolds . . . asked to step down: John G. Norris, "NSA Security Director Is Fired by McNamara," *Washington Post* (November 22, 1961), p. 1.

148 Martin . . . flee to Russia: Theodore Shabad, "Defector from U.S. Resigned to Soviet," *New York Times* (June 24, 1962), p. 1.

In late 1979 the Leningrad computer specialist: Telephone interview with Emery Mitchell, January 14, 1981.

148–149 The inquiry triggered; "We found him"; "he gave valuable": Telephone interview with James Webb, Bureau of Security and Consular Affairs, Department of State, January 14, 1981.

149 Persistent, Mitchell then: Ibid.

'I don't think there": Mitchell interview.

Jack E. Dunlap: Don Oberdorfer, "The Playboy Sergeant Who Spied for Russia," *Saturday Evening Post* (March 7, 1964), pp. 40, 44–45; "G.I. Suicide Sold Secrets to Russia," *New York Times* (October 11, 1963), p. 1; Paul Healy, "Suicide Bares Soviet Spy in Our Code HQ," (New York) *Daily News* (October 11, 1963), pp. 1, 2, 48.

150 "coolness under fire": Oberdorfer, "The Playboy Sergeant," p. 44.

"need to know" policy: Department of Defense, Regulation 5200.1R, *Information Security Program Regulation*, November 7, 1978, p. 1.

151 KH-11 . . . manual: George Lardner, Jr., "13 Copies of Classified Data Missing," *Washington Post* (November 7, 1978), p. 1.

152 "thirty to forty times": David Wise and Thomas B. Ross, *The Invisible Government* (New York: Vintage Books, 1974), p. 209.

153 Victor Norris Hamilton: "Ex-U.S. Employee Defects to Soviet; Accuses Code Unit," *New York Times* (July 23, 1963), p. 4.

"concerns itself"; "The duties of my colleagues": David Kahn, *The Codebreakers* (New York: Macmillan, 1967), p. 728.

Chapter 5: Platforms

page
155 Rumors; Secret Service: "Radio Station at Van Buren," *Houlton Times* (October 30, 1918), p. 1.

wire; Arthur E. Boeder: "Radio Station for Houlton," *Houlton Times* (November 13, 1918), p. 1.

first transatlantic eavesdropping station: Army Security Agency, *Historical Background of the Signal Security Agency,* April 12, 1946, Vol. 3, p. 78, National Archives, Record Group 457, SRH-001.

Kingdom Hall: Author's observations.

156 "to provide a more": Office of the Federal Register, *United States Government Organization Manual, 1977–1978* (Washington, D.C.: GPO, 1977), p. 235.

Central Security Service; "was a half-assed"; "I was in on"; "tower of babel": Former senior NSA official who also held a senior position with the President's Foreign Intelligence Advisory Board.

157 "Since the elimination": U.S. House of Representatives, Committee on Appropriations, Subcommittee on Department of Defense, *Department of Defense Appropriations for 1975,* Hearings, Part 1, 93rd Cong., 2nd Sess., p. 600.

NSCID No. 6: Department of Justice, *Report on Inquiry into CIA-Related Electronic Surveillance Activities* (June 30, 1976), p. 78. This report, classified TOP SECRET UMBRA/HANDLE VIA COMINT CHANNELS ONLY, resulted from an investigation conducted by a Justice Department task force into illegal CIA and NSA eavesdropping activities. This was one of two documents that the Justice Department sought to suppress by issuing a secrecy order against the author. (See note for page 242.)

158 "enemy communications": *Historical Background,* p. 191.

The implementing order did authorize: Ibid., p. 194.

Battery Cove: Ibid., p. 294.

six listening posts: Ibid., pp. 296–297.

Navy . . . intercept stations: David Kahn, *The Codebreakers* (New York: Macmillan, 1967), p. 12.

Aleutians to Australia, India to Africa: United States Army, Office of the Chief of Military History, *The Signal Corps: The Outcome* (Washington, D.C.: GPO, 1966), p. 341.

159 Wakkanai: *HMCAH* for 1961, Part 2, 86th Cong., 2nd Sess., p. 437.

Chitose: *HMCAH* for 1960, 86th Cong., 1st Sess., p. 319.

Sakata: *HMCAH* for 1958, 85th Cong., 1st Sess., p. 442.

Kamiseya; Hanza: *HMCAH* for 1966, 98th Cong., 1st Sess., p. 360.

Sobe: Ibid., p. 359.

Futema: *HMCAH* for 1965, Part 1, 88th Cong., 2nd Sess., p. 462.

Red Cloud Compound: *HMCAH* for 1960, 86th Cong., 1st Sess., p. 327.

Karamursel: Ibid., p. 737.

Main Site: *HMCAH* for 1959, 85th Cong., 2nd Sess., p. 909.

Wiff, Token, Mushroom, and Neptune: US EUCOM ELINT TECHNICAL SUBGROUP (Turkey), Minutes of the 8th Meeting, February 8, 1956, p. 2, National Archives, Record Group 218, CCS 334 NSA Section 17.

159–160 Samsun; Diyarbakir: Ted Greenwood, "Reconnaissance and Arms Control," *Scientific American* (February 1973), p. 22.

160 Sinop: Department of the Navy, *Command History of TUSLOG Detachment 28, Karamursel, Turkey: 1 January–30 September 1977* (OPNAV Report 5750–1) (29 September 1977), pp. 1–3, Naval Historical Center, Operational Archives.

Anadolu Kavak: *HMCAH* for 1960, 86th Cong., 1st Sess., p. 735.

"The 'OPS' Compound": *Command History of TUSLOG*, p. 2.

"supplementary agreement"; "Agreement for Cooperation": Claudia Wright, "America's Sticky Turkish Delight," *New Statesman* (June 20, 1980), pp. 921–922.

"All intelligence": Ibid.

Bremerhaven: *HMCAH* for 1966, Part 1, 89th Cong., 1st Sess., p. 360.

161 IDP; 4120 worldwide: Joint Chiefs of Staff, *NSA Peacetime Requirements for Research and Development Positions*, July 5, 1956, pp. 693–694, National Archives, Record Group 218, CCS 334 NSA, Section 17.

26,233 people; ninety-nine separate units: Department of the Army, *The Secretary of the Army's Program for Command Supervision of Readiness, Command Presentation by USASA*, September 2, 1965, p. 2, Center of Military History.

Edzell: *Introduction to U.S. Naval Security Group Activity Edzell, Scotland: Commanding Officer's Welcome* (August 1, 1976), pp. 1–7, Naval Historical Center, Operational Archives.

Wullenweber . . . antenna: Naval Education and Training Support Command, *Cryptologic Collection Equipments* (Washington, D.C.: GPO, 1977), pp. 26–27, Naval Historical Center, Library.

162 Bullseye: *HMCAH* for 1965, Part 1, 88th Cong., 2nd Sess., p. 463.

163 Vint Hill Farms; Two Rock Ranch: U.S. House of Representatives, Committee on Appropriations, *Military Public Works Appropriations for 1952*, 82nd Cong., 1st Sess., pp. 883–885.

"We had a whole": U.S. Senate, Select Committee on Intelligence, Subcommittee on Intelligence and the Rights of Americans, *Foreign Intelligence Surveillance Act of 1978*, Hearings, 95th Cong., 2nd Sess., pp. 176–177.

rhombic array: *Cryptologic Collection Equipments*, pp. 21–22.

"We built them": Interview with Brigadier General W. Preston Corderman, USA (Ret.), March 8, 1981.

164 "Take for instance": Ibid.

Operations Department: Letter, Commanding Officer, U.S. Naval Security Group Activity, Kamiseya, Japan, to Chief of Naval Operations with enclosure: *Command History for Calendar Year 1969*, March 3, 1970, Naval Historical Center, Operational Archives.

Karamursel; TEXTA; "roll onto": "U.S. Electronic Espionage: A Memoir," *Ramparts* (August 1972), pp. 35–50.

165 "They couldn't get": Ibid., pp. 42–43.

166 Lester R. Schulz: Navy biography.

Robert E. Drake: Letter, Carter to L. G. Shreve, June 12, 1967, Carter Papers, George C. Marshall Research Library.

NSAPAC Representative, Taiwan: Message, Tsai Chien, NRTAI [NSA

Representative, Taiwan] to DIRNSA, July 29, 1969, Carter Papers.

Camp Fuchinobe: Testimony of Dr. Louis W. Tordella, U.S. House of Representatives, Committee on Armed Services, *Military Construction Authorization, Fiscal Year 1965,* Hearings, 88th Cong., 2nd Sess., pp. 8594–8595.

JSPC: *HMCAH* for 1960, 86th Cong., 1st Sess., p. 315. See also *Military Construction Authorization, Fiscal Year 1965,* and testimony of Dr. Louis W. Tordella, U.S. Senate, Committee on Appropriations, *Military Construction Appropriations for 1965,* 88th Cong., 2nd Sess., pp. 681–682.

JOSAF: Testimony of Lieutenant General Marshall S. Carter, U.S. Senate, *Military Construction Appropriations for 1967,* 89th Cong., 2nd Sess., pp. 409–410.

Kunia: Testimony of Theodore L. Newberg, Chief of Installations, NSA, U.S. House of Representatives, Committee on Armed Services, Military Installations and Facilities Subcommittee, *Fiscal Year 1981 Budget for the Military Construction Program,* 96th Cong., 2nd Sess., pp. 54–55.

The establishment: Committee Appointed to Survey Communications Intelligence Activities of the Government (Brownell Committee), *Report to the Secretary of State and Secretary of Defense* (Brownell Report), June 13, 1952, pp. 76–77.

167 Quiet Zone: State of West Virginia, *Radio Astronomy Zoning Act,* House Bill No. 2 (August 9, 1956).

167–168 $60 million; $18 million; Thirty thousand tons: *HMCAH* for 1962, Part 1, 87th Cong., 1st Sess., pp. 242–245. It should be noted that the sanitized hearings contain no references to the intelligence mission of Sugar Grove.

168 "almost beyond"; thirteen components; ninety-two separate formulas; IBM 704: *HMCAH* for 1961, Part 1, 86th Cong., 1st Sess., pp. 568–571.

$135 million; $65 million: *HMCAH* for 1963, Part 1, 87th Cong., 2nd Sess., pp. 319–321.

"from the intelligence": The White House, Jerome B. Wiesner, *Memorandum for the President,* July 2, 1962, John F. Kennedy Presidential Library, Executive File, ND11/FG125.

ideal replacement facility: *HMCAH* for 1964, Part 2, 88th Cong., 1st Sess., pp. 362–365.

169 "to tune in on": Tommy Thompson, "Mountain Navy Station Formally Activated at Sugar Grove, W. Va.," (Harrisonburg, Virginia) *Daily News-Record* (May 12, 1969).

was uncovered in an unclassified file: Author's research on August 27–28, 1980.

immediately summoned back: Letter, D. C. Allard, Head, Operational Archives Branch, Department of the Navy, Naval Historical Center, to author, September 4, 1980.

stamped SECRET: Letter, Eugene F. Yeates, Chief, Office of Policy, NSA, to Dr. D. C. Allard, October 1, 1980.

double set of Wullenwebers: Author's observations.

continued to operate: Author's observations. See also *HMCAH* for 1964, Part 4, 88th Cong., 1st Sess., p. 73.

built in 1957: *HMCAH* for 1964, Part 2, 88th Cong., 1st Sess., pp. 362–365.

relieved the NRL and took over: Letter, Commanding Officer, U.S. Naval Radio Station (R), Sugar Grove, West Virginia, to Administrative Officer, Naval Communication Area Master Station LANT, Norfolk, Virginia, October 6, 1976, enclosure (1) *Summary of Operations.*

Buffham led a group: Letter, Officer in Charge, Naval Security Group Detachment, Sugar Grove, West Virginia, to Director of Naval History, Washington, D.C., April 6, 1979, enclosure (1).

Other groups followed: Ibid.

continued throughout much of 1979; Estes; O'Neil: Letter, Officer in Charge, Naval Security Group Detachment, Sugar Grove, to Director of Naval History, March 31, 1980, enclosure (1).

170 ranged in size; partly from materials; Linn Operations Building: Author's observations; interview with Commander Louis Lashley, USN, Commanding Officer of Sugar Grove, June 18, 1981.

chief of G Group: Letter, Officer in Charge, Naval Security Group Detachment, Sugar Grove, West Virginia, to Director of Naval History, Washington, D.C., April 6, 1979, enclosure (1).

seventy thousand words a minute: COMSAT Corporation, *Andover Earth Station.*

nearly all nongovernmental: *COMSAT Guide to the INTELSAT, MARISAT, and COMSTAR Satellite Systems,* Office of Corporate Affairs, Communications Satellite Corporation, p. 27.

171 "the trick, of course": Telephone interview with James Warren, General Manager of COMSAT's Etam Earth Station, June 12, 1981.

Completed early in 1980: Lashley interview.

150-, 60-, and 30-foot dishes: Author's observations.

Not even; Only by: Ibid.

"Interception of microwave": U.S. House of Representatives, Committee on Government Operations, Government Information and Individual Rights Subcommittee, *Interception of Nonverbal Communications by Federal Intelligence Agencies,* Hearings, 94th Cong., 1st and 2nd Sess. (1976), p. 202.

"the Agency's mission": National Security Agency, *Careers for Engineers, Mathematicians, Computer Scientists at the National Security Agency* (undated), p. 3.

William O. Baker: See Chapter 9, "Competition."

"the actual interception": Interview with Dr. Solomon Kullback, January 29, 1981.

171–172 "unless the receiving"; ideal spot; thirty feet: *Interception of Nonverbal Communications,* p. 202.

172 enormous 261,057-acre: *HMCAH* for 1966, Part 2, 89th Cong., 1st Sess., p. 219.

Yakima Herald: Telephone interview with Jim McNickey, October 28, 1980.

"a real top secret–like place": Telephone interview with postal employee, November 10, 1980.

"sensitive information": Telephone interview with Tom Land, Chief, Yakima Research Station, November 10, 1980.

173 "To intercept a cable": Federal Communications Commission, transcript of proceedings, *Future Licensing of Facilities for Overseas Communication,* docket 18875, Hearings, August 7, 1978, pp. 310–311.

TATs: J. Randolph MacPherson, Regulatory Counsel, Defense Communications Agency, in supplementary filings to docket 18875, p. 3.

174 Green Hill: Author's observations during tour of Green Hill and interviews with station manager and with Jeff Stoll, AT&T Long Lines, May 29, 1981.

Montville; Cheshire: Ibid.

175 4.2.1. *Microwave Radio Signal Acquisition:* The MITRE Corporation, *Selected Examples of Possible Approaches to Electronic Communication Interception Operations* (January 1977), p. 11.

61,800: AT&T Long Lines, Bedminster, New Jersey, press release, January 1, 1981.

176 "There's your smoking": Interview with David L. Watters, January 19, 1981.

"It is understandable": U.S. Senate, Select Committee on Intelligence, Subcommittee on Intelligence and the Rights of Americans, *Foreign Intelligence Surveillance Act of 1978,* pp. 152–153.

"broadband sweeping"; "let there be no": Ibid., p. 155.

177 1961 negotiated; $4500 per year; $48,500: Testimony of Dr. Louis W. Tordella, U.S. Senate, Committee on Appropriations, *Military Construction Appropriations for 1965,* 88th Cong., 2nd Sess., p. 682.

location consists of: Author's observations.

$250,000 and $350,000: Tordella testimony, *HMCAH* for 1967, Part 2, 89th Cong., 2nd Sess., pp. 180–181.

178 "for the conduct": U.S. Senate, *Military Construction Appropriations for 1965,* p. 682.

"we are on Kent Island": *HMCAH* for 1967, p. 181.

"I'm the chief": Telephone interview with Harry (Link) George, November 10, 1981.

"It happens to be": Tordella testimony, U.S. House of Representatives, Committee on Armed Services, *Military Construction Authorization Fiscal Year 1965,* 88th Cong., 2nd Sess., p. 8596.

"I am 201": "Documents on U.S. Plane's Disappearance Over Soviet Union," *New York Times* (February 6, 1959), p. 2.

180 The EC-130: "6 U.S. Fliers Lost in Plane Downed in Soviet Armenia," *New York Times* (September 15, 1958), p. 1.

181 "investigation"; "witnesses": "U.S. Urges Soviet Account for Men on Downed Plane," *New York Times* (September 14, 1958), p. 1.

Robert Murphy met with: *New York Times* (February 6, 1959), pp. 1, 2.

182 Anastas I. Mikoyan: Ibid.

183 went completely public: Ibid.

"fake"; "gross forgery"; "concocted": "Moscow Charges U.S. 'Faked' Tape of Plane Attack," *New York Times* (February 8, 1959), p. 1.

Prodded by: "President Prodded on Missing Airmen," *New York Times* (February 25, 1959), p. 23.

met privately: Edwin L. Dale, Jr., "U.S. Prods Soviet on Missing Fliers," *New York Times* (May 5, 1959), p. 1.

"presumed dead": "U.S. Gives Up Hope for Airmen," *New York Times* (November 21, 1961), p. 27.

"eleven of the seventeen": Osgood Caruthers, "U.S. Fliers Downed in '58 Held in Soviet, Moscow Journal Hints," *New York Times* (January 24, 1961), p. 1.

denounced: "Soviet Magazine Admits Error on 11 U.S. Fliers," *New York Times* (April 5, 1961).

184 "Sighted two": Jack Raymond, "2 MIGs off Korea Attack U.S. Plane," *New York Times* (June 17, 1959), pp. 1, 5.

"This is the first time": Ibid.

most serious incident: U.S. House of Representatives, Committee on Armed Services, Special Subcommittee on the U.S.S. *Pueblo, Inquiry into the U.S.S. Pueblo and EC-121 Plane Incidents* (1969), 91st Cong., 1st Sess., pp. 889–929.

185 airborne radio direction-finding (ARDF): See Headquarters, Department of the Army, Field Manual 30–476, *Radio Direction Finding* (Washington, D.C., April 8, 1977), pp. 4–10.

185–186 Combat Cougar; "The first bombing": "U.S. Electronic Espionage: A Memoir," *Ramparts* (August 1972), pp. 48–49.

186 Abrams Acres: Ibid.

SR-71: For an excellent examination of this aircraft, see Robert R. Ropelewski, "SR-71 Impressive in High-Speed Regime," *Aviation Week & Space Technology* (May 18, 1981), pp. 46–56, and "SR-71 Imposes Burden on Maintenance Units," Ibid., pp. 105–108.

In November 1978: Robert Kaylor, "U.S. Spy Jets Check out MIGs in Cuba," *Boston Globe* (November 18, 1978), p. 2.

One year later: "Blackbirds Over Cuba," *Time* (October 2, 1979), p. 46.

187 U-2: For a detailed look at the U-2, see Major Phillip L. Jarvinen, "Everything You've Always Wanted to Know About a U-2 Navigator — But Didn't Know Where or How to Ask!" *The Navigator* (Spring 1978), pp. 5–9.

Bissell; ARC; NSA joined; COMOR: Final Report, Book I, pp. 84–85.

centralized administrative; Air Force and CIA informally agreed: Ibid., p. 117. Because the NRO is never mentioned by name, it must be inferred.

188 Midas; Vela: Reginald Turnill, *The Observer's Spaceflight Directory* (London: Frederick Warne, 1974), pp. 177–179.

189 two years of battles, EXCOM: Final Report, Book I, pp. 117–118.
     NPIC: Ibid.

190 COMIREX: Ibid., pp. 84–85, note 40.
     Standing in front: Photo, Director's Photo Album, Lieutenant General Marshall S. Carter.
     "If we start": Harvard University, Center for Information Policy Research, Program on Information Resources Policy, *Seminar on Command, Control, Communications and Intelligence* (Cambridge: Harvard University, 1980), Tate lecture, p. 30.

191 NRO's most recent director: Philip Taubman, "Secrecy of U.S. Reconnaissance Office Is Challenged," *New York Times* (March 1, 1981), p. 12.
     Robert J. Hermann: U.S. House of Representatives, Committee on Appropriations, Subcommittee on the Department of Defense, *Department of Defense Appropriations for 1979,* Part 4, 95th Cong., 2nd Sess., p. 396.

192 "his lifetime ambition"; told to clean out his desk; Appointed by President Reagan: Interview with Raymond T. Tate, November 3, 1981.
     Lew Allen, Jr.: "Lieutenant General Lew Allen, Jr., USAF, Named Director, NSA/Chief, CSS, by President," *NSAN* (August 1973), p. 2.

193 DSP: Barry Miller, "U.S. Moves to Upgrade Missile Warning," *Aviation Week & Space Technology* (December 2, 1974), pp. 16–18.
     Byeman: See Robert Lindsey, *The Falcon and the Snowman* (New York: Simon & Schuster, 1979), p. 57; also, David Wise, *The Politics of Lying: Government Deception, Secrecy, and Power* (New York: Vintage Books, 1973), p. 81.
     DSP Code 949: "Data Relay Satellite Sought for Early Warning Network," *Aviation Week & Space Technology* (January 19, 1970), p. 21.
     twelve-foot Schmidt: Miller, "U.S. Moves to Upgrade Missile Warning," pp. 16–18.
     9.9 degrees: "DoD Accelerates Plan to Deploy Early Warning Satellite System," *Aviation Week & Space Technology* (January 12, 1970), p. 18.

193–194 Singapore; South China Sea; Indian subcontinent; Saigon; Jakarta: Desmond Ball, *A Suitable Piece of Real Estate: American Installations in Australia* (Sydney, Australia: Hale & Tremonger, 1980), p. 67.

194 To compensate: "DoD Accelerates Plan to Deploy Early Warning Satellite System."
     Vela-type detectors: Miller, "U.S. Moves to Upgrade Missile Warning," pp. 16–18.
     the Panama Canal: Turnill, p. 179.
     most important; full coverage: Ball, p. 70.
     more than a thousand: Miller, "U.S. Moves to Upgrade Missile Warning," pp. 16–18.
     "It could pick up": Quoted in Ball, p. 70.

195 ferret launches: Philip J. Klass, *Secret Sentries in Space* (New York: Random House, 1971), p. 191.
196 twelve hundred miles away: Klass, p. 190.
piggyback; under a hundred miles; merely an inventory; through a computer; three to five per year: Ibid., p. 193.
too highly directional: Ball, p. 73.
197 "Each satellite carried": Lindsey, p. 57.
March 6, 1973; Horn of Africa; microwave transmissions; second Rhyolite: Philip J. Klass, "U.S. Monitoring Capability Impaired," *Aviation Week & Space Technology* (May 14, 1979), p. 18.
"sucking up": Victor Marchetti quoted in Ball, p. 72.
Two more of the satellites: Klass, "U.S. Monitoring Capability Impaired," p. 18.
"not to interfere with": Article XII of the Treaty on Limitation of Anti-Ballistic Missile Systems.
197–198 Apparently believing; never bothered: Ball, p. 73.
198 changed in mid-1977; spy working at TRW: Robert Lindsey, "Soviet Spies Got Data on Satellites to Be Used for Monitoring Missiles," *New York Times* (April 29, 1979), p. 1.
"tape bucket": Clarence A. Robinson, Jr., "Soviets Push Telemetry Bypass," *Aviation Week & Space Technology* (April 16, 1979), pp. 14–16.
major sticking points: David Nyhan, "Kennedy Sees Mideast Accord," *Boston Globe* (January 12, 1979), p. 29. See also William Beecher, "U.S. Wants a Ban on Coded Space Talk," *Boston Globe* (December 5, 1978), p. 9.
Tracksman 2: Klass, "U.S. Monitoring Capability Impaired," p. 18.
"a 21st-century": Hedrick Smith, "U.S. Aides Say Loss of Post in Iran Impairs Missile-Monitoring Ability," *New York Times* (March 2, 1979), p. 1.
one one-thousandth; Argus: Klass, "U.S. Monitoring Capability Impaired," p. 18.
199 "Carl Duckett": William E. Colby, *Honorable Men* (New York: Simon & Schuster, 1978), p. 37.
vetoing Argus: Klass, "U.S. Monitoring Capability Impaired," p. 18.
$200 million: Smith, "U.S. Aides Say," p. 1.
200 Iranian airmen . . . at Kabkan; "Kabkan is not replaceable": Ibid., pp. 1, 8.
201 "Sending airplanes": "Administration's Verification Claims Hit," *Aviation Week & Space Technology* (April 16, 1979), p. 16.
Big Bird: Ball, pp. 78–79.
twelve-ton, fifty-five-foot; planes . . . near Plesetsk: "The Motto Is: Think Big, Think Dirty," *Time* (February 6, 1978), pp. 12–13.
202 TOP SECRET UMBRA; "Spool Label": James Ott, "Espionage Trial Highlights CIA Problems," *Aviation Week & Space Technology* (November 27, 1978), pp. 21–22.
203 "the Shuttle may not": Benjamin F. Schemmer, "U.S. Needs More Rock-

ets to Launch Vital National Security Satellites," *Armed Forces Journal International* (July 1980), p. 38.

Intelligence Committee cancelled; rocket instead: "Washington Roundup," *Aviation Week & Space Technology* (June 4, 1979), p. 11.

verge of shutting down: Schemmer, "U.S. Needs More Rockets," pp. 38–39.

twelve "vital national security launches"; "would probably make them": Air Force Secretary Mark quoted in ibid.

204   "That technique was": Interview with Lieutenant General Marshall S. Carter, USA (Ret.), July 17–18, 1980.

sometimes exceeding $100 million: Taubman, "Secrecy of U.S. Reconnaissance Office Is Challenged," p. 12.

"No. They were knowledgeable": Carter interview.

"If you knew": Taubman, "Secrecy of U.S. Reconnaissance Office Is Challenged," p. 12.

205   Richard Lee Stallings; negotiations: Ball, pp. 58–60.

In honor of the wife; size of Rhode Island: Alan Villiers, "The Alice," *National Geographic* (February 1966), pp. 230–257.

206   new road; Mereenie water bores; June 1966: Ball, p. 62.

454 people, eighteen . . . buildings; igloolike radomes; "buffer zone"; aircraft are forbidden; "Joint Defense": Ibid., pp. 60–62, 64.

207   visible-light sensor (VLS): Ibid., p. 69.

"Pine Gap is described": "Uncle Sam and His 40,000 Snoopers," (Australian) *National Review* (October 5–11, 1973), p. 1612.

November 1969; Casino: Bell, p. 65.

"Conditions of Entry": Howell Walker, "South Australia, Gateway to the Great Outback," *National Geographic* (April 1970), p. 452.

208   136.46°E and 31.19°S: Ball, p. 65.

concentrates on . . . imagery; ten minutes: Philip J. Klass, "Australian Pressure on U.S. Bases Eases," *Aviation Week & Space Technology* (April 30, 1973), pp. 67–68.

Grand Hotel: "Civilians to Take Over at U.S. Base," *Harrogate Herald* (July 9, 1966).

briefed extensively never to admit: Interview with an NSA official formerly stationed at Menwith Hill.

"Well, we're not happy": "War Office Negotiates for 500 Acres Near Harrogate," *Harrogate Herald* (March 2, 1955), p. 1. See also "Military Want Land in May," *Harrogate Herald* (April 9, 1955).

September 15, 1960; $6.8 million; four-hundred-man: Department of the Army press release: "13th USASA Field Station" (undated).

209   continually denied: Linda Melvern, "Harvest," unpublished article (July 2, 1980), p. 2. I am grateful to Linda Melvern for this article, a portion of which was later incorporated in "America's Big Ear on Europe," *New Statesman* (July 18, 1980), pp. 10–14, by Duncan Campbell and Linda Melvern.

MINISTRY OF DEFENCE: Campbell and Melvern, "America's Big Ear on Europe," cover photo.

"The Army fought"; Principal targets; "It wouldn't be"; back to Fort
Meade: Interviews with Francis A. (Frank) Raven, July 23, 1981, August
11, 1981, and November 4, 1981.
"Intercepted telegrams came through": Melvern, "Harvest", p. 4.

210 ideal for the collection: See Ted Greenwood, "Reconnaissance and Arms
Control," p. 14.
Lockheed Corporation: NSA, (Menwith Hill) *Daily Bulletin.*
choice assignment; three-year tours; live on station; round the clock;
"trick trash"; "day ladies": Interview with an NSA official formerly sta-
tioned at Menwith Hill.
Tower Federal Credit Union: NSA, (Menwith Hill) *Daily Bulletin.*
"All employees": Campbell and Melvern, p. 12.

211 Mission Briefing Conference Room: NSA, (Menwith Hill) *Daily Bulletin.*
"In fact": Interview with NSA official formerly stationed at Menwith
Hill.
Albert Dale Braeuninger; "technician"; relay station: Melvern, "Har-
vest," p. 3.
Buckley; Aerospace Data Facility: Miller, "U.S. Moves to Upgrade Missile
Warning," p. 16.
may control: Ball, p. 68.

211–212 secrecy surrounding Buckley; "witch hunt"; "shanghaied": Bernard
Weinraub, "An Air Force Inquiry on Drugs Criticized," *New York Times*
(March 27, 1978), pp. A1, A15.

212 As the chief of GENS; Under the reorganization: Interviews with Francis
A. (Frank) Raven, July 23, August 11, and November 4, 1981.
Whereas the Soviet Union: *HMCAH* for 1960, 86th Cong., 1st Sess.,
pp. 316–318 for Asmara; Chet Flippo, "Can the CIA Turn Students
into Spies?" *Rolling Stone,* pp. 28, 30, for Sidi Yahia.
In April 1960: Jack Raymond, "Soviet Trawler Called Spy Ship," *New
York Times* (July 14, 1960), p. 8; *Newsweek* (August 22, 1960), p. 29.

213 "hundreds of miles": Raymond, "Soviet Trawler."
In the spring of 1962: *Soviet Spy Ships Monitor U.S. Nuclear Tests,* report,
June 1, 1962, Executive Files, ND21–1, John F. Kennedy Presidential
Library, pp. 1–3.
"What we wanted": Raven interview.
"the *Valdez* was a dream boat"; Following commissioning; Although the
fact: Ibid.
Originally named: Department of the Navy, Military Sealift Command,
"U.S.N.S. VALDEZ (T-AG 169)," information sheet (undated).

214 Picked to be: Department of the Navy, Military Sealift Command,
"U.S.N.S. MULLER (T-AG 171)," information sheet (undated).
As the *Valdez* crawled; Shortly after the NSA began: Raven inter-
view.

215 On July 8, 1961: *Jane's Fighting Ships, 1964–1965* (New York: Franklin
Watts, 1964), p. 395.
In October, one of the two: Trevor Armbrister, *A Matter of Accountability*
(New York: Coward-McCann, 1970), p. 82.

Manned by a crew; On January 5, 1965; In 1966 the SIGINT ship: Department of the Navy, Office of the Chief of Naval Operations, OPNAV Report 5705.4, *U.S.S. Georgetown, Annual Revision of Ship's History, 1964, 1965, 1966, 1967.* Naval Historical Center, Operational Archives.

215–216 As the *Georgetown* concentrated; Two and a half months later: U.S.S. *Jamestown*, (AGTR-3), letter with enclosure, "Submission of Ship's History, 1964," January 1, 1965; U.S.S. *Jamestown*, "Familygram," June 26, 1966, pp. 1–8. Both in Naval Historical Center, Operational Archives.

216 After several shakedown: U.S.S. *Belmont* (AGTR-4), letter with enclosure, "Submission of Annual Historical Report of Ship's Operations," 1965, 1966, 1967, 1968, 1969, Naval Historical Center, Operational Archives; U.S.S. *Belmont*, Cruise Book, 1966, Naval Historical Center, Naval Library.

The *Belmont* remained on station; At exactly 4:43; On February 1, 1967: Ibid.

217 Five weeks before: U.S.S. *Liberty* (AGTR-5), letter with enclosure, "Submission of Command History, 1967," March 11, 1968.

"I do not wish to be": Robert J. Donovan and the staff of the *Los Angeles Times, Israel's Fight for Survival* (New York: New American Library, 1967), p. 71.

"an act of aggression": Ibid., p. 158.

Anticipating the possibility: Raven interview.

But G Group also had to; "Now, frankly"; It took her about: Ibid.

218–219 At 8:20 P.M.; On the morning of June 1: Department of the Navy, Office of the Judge Advocate General, *Court of Inquiry Report on the* U.S.S. *Liberty*, June 18, 1967, Summary of Proceedings and Transcript of Testimony.

At NSA, G Group began; "By God"; The need for Arabic; According to the original: Raven interview.

219 "You can sit": Ibid.

Within hours of her arrival; The problem was; This time the problem: James M. Ennes, Jr., *Assault on the Liberty* (New York: Random House, 1979), pp. 21–22, p. 21 note 1.

220 At 8:49: *Court of Inquiry Report.*

"For God's sake"; "At this point": Raven interview.

But the Navy: Ibid.

Reluctantly, the Navy: *Court of Inquiry Report.*

221 "one of the most": U.S. House of Representatives, Committee on Armed Services, Armed Services Investigating Subcommittee, *Review of Department of Defense Worldwide Communications, Phase I,* Report, 92nd Cong., 1st Sess., May 10, 1971.

Throughout much of the morning: *Court of Inquiry Report.*

One Israeli general: Donovan, p. 124.

222 "any instrument": Dr. Richard K. Smith, "The Violation of the *Liberty,"* *United States Naval Institute Proceedings* (June 1978), pp. 63–70.

At 1:50, Commander McGonagle: All details of the attack from *Court of Inquiry Report.*

223 Now dead in the water: Ennes, pp. 95–96.
224 But as ready aircraft; Crew members of the *America:* Ibid., pp. 76–78.
   Panic immediately broke out: Ibid., pp. 100–101.
226 Also unmistakable were the giant: Smith, p. 65.
   It is even more unlikely: Ennes, p. 154, for location of *El Quseir.*
   "The Israeli government": Ennes, Ibid.
227 "Indeed . . . it is likely": Smith, p. 69.
   Or that the often faulty; cutting TRSSCOMM communications: Ennes, p. 72.
228 "He said that": Central Intelligence Agency, *Comment on Known Identity of U.S.S. Liberty,* Report, July 27, 1967.
229 "[The sources] commented on the sinking": Central Intelligence Agency, *Attack on the U.S.S. Liberty Ordered by Dayan,* Report, November 9, 1967.
230 Among those most troubled: Armbrister, pp. 81–85.
   "These trawlers"; Originally, Fubini's dream: Ibid.
231 "conduct tactical surveillance": U.S. House of Representatives, Committee on Armed Services, Special Subcommittee on the U.S.S. *Pueblo, Inquiry into the U.S.S. Pueblo and EC-121 Plane Incidents,* Hearings, 91st Cong., 1st Sess. (Washington, D.C.: GPO, 1969), pp. 762–765.
   After arriving at Yokosuka: Armbrister, p. 87.
232 In the three years: *Inquiry into the U.S.S. Pueblo,* pp. 734–735.
   According to Trevor Armbrister: Armbrister, pp. 116–117.
233 Throughout the fall: *Inquiry into the U.S.S. Pueblo,* p. 766.
   Of these, the NSA: Armbrister, p. 186.
   "sample electronic environment": *Inquiry into the U.S.S. Pueblo,* p. 767.
   "the size of a Sears": Armbrister, p. 192.
   Yet there was one lingering: Ibid., pp. 196–199.
234 "The following information": Ibid., p. 197.

Chapter 6: Targets

page
236 "I have been informed": National Security Agency, Lieutenant General Lew Allen, Jr., memorandum for the record, May 12, 1975.
   "probably the largest": Final Report, Book III, p. 765.
   Operation Shamrock: Ibid., pp. 765–776.
   end of censorship: See 47 U.S.C. 606.
237 "the necessary"; "very definitely"; "his company": Ibid., pp. 767–768.
238 "Two very evident fears": Ibid., p. 768.
   "all traffic"; "Western Union personnel": Ibid., pp. 772–773.
239 W. H. Barsby: Testimony of William Sidney Sparks, U.S. House of Representatives, Committee on Government Operations, Government Information and Individual Rights Subcommittee, *Interception of Nonverbal Com-*

munications by Federal Intelligence Agencies, Hearings, 94th Cong., 1st and 2nd Sess., (1976), p. 208.

William Sidney Sparks . . . the assignment: Ibid., pp. 207–222.

Signal Center; teletypewriter: George Raynor Thompson and Dixie R. Harris, *United States Army in World War II, The Technical Services, The Signal Corps: The Outcome* (Washington, D.C.: Department of the Army, Chief of Military History, GPO, 1966), p. 584.

"everybody and his brother": *Interception of Nonverbal Communications,* p. 212.

240 "I knew in my own mind": Ibid., p. 219.

Captain Ahern: RCA internal memorandum included in ibid., p. 250.

241 "sergeant"; "corporal": Ibid., p. 24.

not limited to . . . New York: Final Report, Book III, p. 773.

"It can be stated": Ibid., p. 769.

Letter of Appreciation: Ibid., p. 769, note 138.

242 James Forrestal asked . . . to meet: Final Report, Book III, pp. 740, 769–770.

Sosthenes Behn; Harry C. Ingles: Draft Report, note 47.

"because the intelligence": Department of Justice, "Prosecutive Summary" (March 4, 1977), p. 33. This report, labeled TOP SECRET/HANDLE VIA COMINT CHANNELS ONLY, was prepared for Robert L. Keuch, Deputy Assistant Attorney General, Criminal Division, by George W. Calhoun, Chief, Special Litigation. It analyzed the feasibility of bringing criminal charges against members of the intelligence community for questionable and illegal intelligence operations. This was one of two documents that the Justice Department sought to suppress by issuing a secrecy order against the author. (See note for page 157.)

"so long as the present": Ibid., p. 34. See also Final Report, Book III, p. 769.

"while it was always": "Prosecutive Summary," p. 33.

met . . . with Senate Judiciary Committee Chairman: Final Report, Book III, pp. 769–770.

243 "we [do] not desire": Ibid., p. 770.

"plots"; "conspiracies"; "trying to get me"; In the early morning; *Ajax:* A. A. Rogow, *James Forrestal* (New York: Macmillan, 1963), pp. 1–18.

244 May 18, 1949: Department of Justice, *Report on Inquiry into CIA-Related Electronic Surveillance Activities* (June 30, 1976), p. 33. For details on this document, see note for page 54.)

T.C.C.; "OK'd. by the President": "Prosecutive Summary," p. 34.

Joseph Wolanski; Bob Sage; Mr. Feeney: RCA internal memorandum included in *Interception of Nonverbal Communications,* p. 250.

245 converted to magnetic tapes: Final Report, Book III, p. 775.

personal charge of . . . Shamrock: Ibid., pp. 775–776.

met with Thomas Karamessines: *Report on Inquiry into CIA,* p. 18.

246 "concerned about any": Final Report, Book III, p. 775.

"Get out of it": Ibid.

FBI . . . to obtain necessary cable traffic: "Prosecutive Summary," pp. 31–33.

bookkeeper: Ibid., p. 241.

247 "When we got there": Telephone interview with Herbert J. Miller, Jr., January 25, 1980.

watch list of leading racketeers: According to the top secret *Report on Inquiry into CIA*, which the Justice Department had suppressed from publication, "NSA notes that since 1962, the Criminal Division of the Department of Justice has sent hundreds of names of racketeers to NSA requesting information NSA might have, or subsequently obtain, concerning them." *Report on Inquiry into CIA*, p. 87. It is interesting to note that the report gives no indication when, if ever, this activity came to a halt.

248 NSA intercepts on Cuba: Final Report, Book III, pp. 744–745.

"Of the raw traffic": Ibid., p. 745.

249 "I would appreciate": U.S. Senate, Select Committee to Study Governmental Operations with Respect to Intelligence Activities, *The National Security Agency and Fourth Amendment Rights*, Hearings, Vol. 5, 94th Cong., 1st Sess. (1976), pp. 145–146.

"unprecedented . . . It is": Final Report, Book III, p. 746.

civil disturbance unit: Ibid., p. 745.

"the 'big' question": *The National Security Agency and Fourth Amendment Rights*, p. 145.

"concentrating additional": Final Report, Book III, p. 746.

The Secret Service; "the activities": Ibid., pp. 751–752.

250 such well-known figures: Bob Woodward, "Messages of Activists Intercepted," *Washington Post* (October 13, 1975), pp. A1, A14.

multiplier effect; Captured in NSA's net: Final Report, Book III, p. 750.

Focal point in the Agency for the watch lists: Interviews with Francis A. (Frank) Raven, July 23, 1981, August 11, 1981, and November 4, 1981.

250–251 principal point of contact; she would forward: Raven interview.

251 Yale; "An official would"; GENS; G Group; was well aware: Ibid.

"key to the keys": David Kahn, *The Codebreakers* (New York: Macmillan, 1967), p. 23.

Deputy chief of G Group: "Federal Woman's Award Presented to Polly Budenbach at Annual Banquet," *NSAN* (March–April 1969).

A proposal was made; Clark was strongly opposed; probably be unconstitutional; eventually dropped: U.S. House of Representatives, Select Committee on Assassinations, *Investigation of the Assassination of Martin Luther King, Jr.*, Hearings, Vol. 13 (March 1979), 95th Cong., 2nd Sess., pp. 187–189.

received a direct order; directly from the office: Raven interview.

252 though Clifford himself: Interview with Clark M. Clifford, November 3, 1981.

"I tried to object"; "We just wasted": Raven interview.

"asinine"; "When J. Edgar Hoover"; Hoover's belief that; "There's one school of thought": Raven interview.
252–253 "The other school"; Raven would note; most often would not; "scan-guides"; "A scan-guide is": Ibid.
Trine, Gamma Gupy: Woodward, "Messages of Activists Intercepted," p. A14.
253 "Charter for Sensitive SIGINT": *The National Security Agency and Fourth Amendment Rights*, p. 150.
254 "From 1969 on": Final Report, Book III, p. 749.
"I consider keeping": *Report on Inquiry into CIA*, p. 59.
255 White House Task Force on Heroin Suppression; Office of Narcotics Coordinator: Ibid., pp. 14–15.
"flash rolls"; reports; bow out: Ibid., pp. 15–16.
256 "is to remove": Ibid., p. 85.
Grand Central: Final Report, Book III, p. 753.
"primary responsibility": *The National Security Agency and Fourth Amendment Rights*, p. 152.
257 no simple matter; "That requires special"; "Not voice": Raven interview.
Initially, the monitoring; began again in March: Final Report, Book III, p. 753.
Northwest, Virginia; $10 million: Charles Osolin, "Military Snooping: Pentagon Listened in on Americans' Calls," *Atlanta Journal and Constitution* (September 14, 1975), pp. 1A, 20A. See also "Long Distance Wiretaps," *Miami News* (September 17, 1975), p. 12A.
Although only six: Final Report, Book III, p. 753.
transit points; NSA could pick up calls: Ibid., note 68.
In all, NSA monitored: Final Report, Book III, p. 753.
258 IGCP; "subelements": *Report on Inquiry into CIA*, pp. 95–99.
259 "all information on the venereal disease"; "a worthless"; "The first priority": Raven interview.
"We were required to report": Ibid.
"that such effort": *Report on Inquiry into CIA*, pp. 95–99.
"imperative that the illicit"; CCINC; "formulation and coordination"; Krogh: Ibid., pp. 46–48.
260 "During the past year"; Line Item 8: Ibid., pp. 97–98.
NARCOG: Ibid., p. 16.
261 ONNI; "the development and maintenance": Ibid., p. 56.
"We are living": Ibid., p. 58.
"the dark cone": David B. Guralnik, ed., *Webster's New World Dictionary* (New York: Popular Library, 1975), p. 647.
"because of the sensitivity": Interview with Lieutenant General Marshall S. Carter, USA (Ret.), July 17–18, 1980.
Tordella waited a year or so: *The National Security Agency and Fourth Amendment Rights*, pp. 26–27.
"Consumers and NSA": *Report on Inquiry into CIA*, p. 96.
262 "SIGINT Information on Narcotics": Ibid., p. 101.

fears were realized: "U.S. Electronic Espionage: A Memoir," *Ramparts* (August 1972), pp. 35–50.

Perry Fellwock: Tom Topor, "Identify *Ramparts'* Code Man," *New York Post* (July 18, 1972), p. 14.

Tordella had withheld; "NSA had tasked": Final Report, Book III, pp. 754–755.

263 memorandum to the acting chief of Division D: Ibid., p. 755, note 73.

"I was told": Ibid., p. 755, note 76.

"Five or six years before"; One such bust; "NSA could really": Raven interview.

264 "No more such techniques"; "I note that requests": U.S. Senate, Select Committee to Study Governmental Operations with Respect to Intelligence Activities, *Huston Plan*, Hearings, Vol. 2, 94th Cong. 1st Sess. (1976), pp. 275–276.

"If these techniques"; meeting with Hoover: Final Report, Book III, p. 932.

265 "someone got"; "I couldn't go"; "not a topic": Ibid.

"When you see": David Wallechinsky and Irving Wallace, *The People's Almanac* (New York: Doubleday, 1975), p. 254.

266 "present intelligence": *Huston Plan*, p. 204.

"whether — because of": Final Report, Book III, p. 934.

Huston . . . relied on Sullivan: Ibid., p. 936.

267 "The President chewed": Ibid., p. 937, note 45.

"I am convinced"; "hard information": Ibid., p. 937.

meeting: Ibid., pp. 938–945.

268 "operational details"; "objectives": *Huston Plan*, pp. 225–226.

TOP SECRET . . . HANDLE VIA COMINT CHANNELS ONLY; "Bigot List": Ibid., p. 222.

Raymond James Gengler; Leonard J. Nunno: Ibid., p. 220.

representing G Group; representing Juanita: Raven interview.

269 "to define and assess": Final Report, Book III, p. 940.

millions of dollars: Ibid., p. 948.

"that Admiral Gaylor [sic]": *Huston Plan*, p. 235.

270 "— Present interpretation"; "Electronic Surveillances"; "has been": Final Report, Book III, pp. 945–946.

"from COMINT without": *Huston Plan*, p. 172.

"For years and years": Final Report, Book III, p. 942.

"would not oppose": *Huston Plan*, p. 173.

271 "Any comments"; "We got down": Final Report, Book III, p. 942.

272 "Domestic Intelligence Gathering": *Huston Plan*, pp. 189–192.

"Operational Restraints": Ibid., pp. 193–197.

274 "nothing less": Final Report, Book III, p. 965.

"The President has carefully": *Huston Plan*, pp. 199–200.

"went through": Final Report, Book III, p. 956.

275 "sit tight"; "inimical to the best"; "pulled the rug": Ibid., pp. 957–959.

276 "I don't object": *Huston Plan*, p. 251.

"I was, for all": Final Report, Book III, p. 960.

no one challenged Hoover: Ibid., p. 933.

"A key to the entire": Ibid., p. 974.

277 IEC: Ibid., pp. 974–979.

Buffham; Gengler: U.S. Senate, Committee on the Judiciary, Subcommittee on Constitutional Rights, *Military Surveillance*, Hearings, 93rd Cong., 2nd Sess. (1974), pp. 205–207.

"intelligence in the possession": *Huston Plan*, p. 267.

"All those who have been": Final Report, Book III, p. 975.

"NSA Contribution to Domestic": *The National Security Agency and Fourth Amendment Rights*, pp. 156–157.

278 memo to Laird's . . . Mitchell's office: *Report on Inquiry into CIA*, pp. 83–84. The report also quotes from a January 26, 1971, memorandum from Admiral Gayler, stating that the document was read "in presence of Secretary Laird and accepted by Attorney General Kleindienst 1 July 1972." See also Final Report, Book III, pp. 762–763.

Gayler; Helms; Mitchell; Hoover: Final Report, Book III, pp. 977–979.

"most desirous"; "was not at all": Ibid., p. 978.

"that NSA and FBI Director Hoover": *Report on Inquiry into CIA*, p. 107.

279 "an in-depth examination": *Huston Plan*, p. 272.

"were tested"; "institute all possible coverage"; December 26: Ibid., pp. 392–393.

Chapter 7: Fissures

page

280 government document: Office of the Federal Register, *United States Government Organization Manual, 1957–1958* (Washington, D.C.: GPO).

"I should have": Harrison E. Salisbury, "Big Brother Is Alive and Monitoring 400,000 Calls a Day," *Penthouse* (November 1980), pp. 114–115.

281 "policy of anonymity": NSA, *Influence of U.S. Cryptologic Organizations on the Digital Computer Industry*, May 1977, p. 1.

282 "The specific functions": U.S. House of Representatives, Committee on Un-American Activities, *Security Practices in the National Security Agency*, Report, August 13, 1962, p. 4.

"Often the agency enshrouds": David Kahn, *The Codebreakers* (New York: Macmillan, 1967), p. 701.

started publishing: Neil Sheehan, "Vietnam: Pentagon Study Traces 3 Decades of Growing U.S. Involvement," *New York Times* (June 13, 1971), p. 1.

turncoat KGB agent; passed to the Soviet embassy: Seymour M. Hersh, "The President and the Plumbers: A Look at 2 Security Questions," *New York Times* (December 9, 1973), pp. 1, 73.

Although the agent: "Tale of a Double Agent," *Newsweek* (September 14, 1981), p. 25.

283 USM-2; VIPAR: Ernest Volkman, "U.S. Spies Lend an Ear to Soviets,"
    Newsday (July 12, 1977), p. 7.
    "gave us extremely": Laurence Stern, "U.S. Tapped Top Russians' Car
    Phones," *Washington Post* (December 5, 1973), pp. A1, A16.
    conversations had been referred to; more mundane: Hersh, "The Presi-
    dent and the Plumbers," p. 73.
284 Buzhardt; Hess; "Then we can't": Harrison E. Salisbury, *Without Fear
    or Favor* (New York: Times Books, 1980), pp. 296–297.
285 *Times* hired Kahn; *Pueblo;* Judge Murray Gurfein: David Wise, *The Politics
    of Lying: Government Deception, Secrecy, and Power* (New York: Vintage Books,
    1973), pp. 233–235.
286 "The security of the Nation": *United States* v. *New York Times* 328 F.
    Supp. 324.
    "Milton was the most": Interview with Richard P. Floyd, former Chief,
    Procurement Support Division, Office of Procurement, NSA, January
    19, 1981.
    Zaslow . . . and Bancroft; pistol: Salisbury, *Without Fear or Favor,* pp.
    315–318.
287 "the kingpins": Jack Anderson, "CIA Eavesdrops on Kremlin Chiefs,"
    Washington Post (September 16, 1971), p. F7.
288 invited . . . to lunch; In defense: Stern, "U.S. Tapped Top Russians'
    Car Phones," p. A16.
    plumbers: U.S. Senate, Select Committee on Presidential Campaign Ac-
    tivities, *Investigation of Illegal or Improper Campaign Activities in the Presidential
    Election of 1972* [Watergate Investigation], Final Report, 93rd Cong.,
    2nd Sess., Report No. 93–918 (June 1974), pp. 119–124.
288–289 "the President wants"; "Mr. David Young"; "intends to use"; "to
    be able": Department of Justice, *Report on Inquiry into CIA-Related Electronic
    Surveillance Activities* (June 30, 1976), pp. 113–114. (See notes for pages
    157 and 242.)
289 codebreaking and COMINT: Hersh, "The President and the Plumbers,"
    p. 76.
    still at least one: See Stern, "U.S. Tapped Top Russians' Car Phones,"
    p. A16.
    FBI and Secret Service watch lists: See Final Report, Book III, pp. 757–
    758.
290 "to permit procurement": John M. Crewdson, "Documents Show Nixon
    Approved Partly 'Illegal' '70 Security Plan," *New York Times* (June 7,
    1973), pp. 1, 36, 37.
    "espionage techniques": Agis Salpukas, "U.S. Foregoes Trial of Weath-
    ermen," *New Tork Times* (October 16, 1973), p. 1.
    "there were other considerations": "Government Defies Court on
    Weatherman Taps," *New York Times* (June 8, 1973), p. 19.
291 "The Government doesn't believe": William K. Stevens, "FBI Backs
    Data on Weathermen," *New York Times* (June 26, 1973), p. 37.
    "perfunctory": William K. Stevens, "Judge to Review Plea of Radicals,"
    New York Times (July 10, 1973), p. 29.

"sworn statements": Athan Theoharis, *Spying on Americans: Political Surveillance from Hoover to the Huston Plan* (Philadelphia: Temple University Press, 1978), p. 123.

"any disclosure": Final Report, Book III, p. 758.

dropped the project; five years; destroy everything: Final Report, Book III, p. 756.

"of which we had": Ibid., p. 739, note 18.

"the extent of the FBI's": Ibid., pp. 758–759.

292 *United States* v. *United States District Court:* 407 U.S. 297 (1972).

"protect our Government": Final Report, Book III, p. 757.

"concerning organizations"; "We do not believe"; "in excess": Ibid., pp. 759–760.

"the FBI and Secret Service": Ibid., p. 760.

293 "ever-increasing": U.S. Senate, Select Committee to Study Governmental Operations with Respect to Intelligence Activities, *The National Security Agency and Fourth Amendment Rights*, Hearings, Vol. 5, 94th Cong., 1st Sess. (1976), pp. 158–159.

"It has recently come": Ibid., pp. 160–161.

294 "the liberty to exercise": Theoharis, p. 123.

moved to dismiss: Salpukas, "U.S. Forgoes Trial of Weathermen," p. 1.

295 Operation Chaos: Seymour Hersh, "Huge CIA Operation Reported in U.S. Against Antiwar Forces," *New York Times* (December 22, 1974), p. 1.

296 Reagan . . . managed to miss: Linda Charlton, "Reagan Misses 3 Sessions of CIA Spying Inquiry," *New York Times* (February 6, 1975).

"an international": Commission on CIA Activities within the United States, *Report to the President*, June 6, 1975 (Washington, D.C.: GPO, 1975), p. 142.

"the Director and other": Ibid., p. 222.

"It seems incredible": William Greider, "House CIA Probe Subpoenas 1952 Order Creating NSA," *Washington Post* (August 6, 1975), p. A2.

Les Aspin; Colby: William Greider, "Telephone Taps by NSA Confirmed," *Washington Post* (August 7, 1975), pp. A1, A10.

297 Allen; Banner: National Security Agency, *Statement of Lieutenant General Lew Allen, Jr., Director National Security Agency, Before the House Select Committee on Intelligence*, pp. 1–17.

"involves extremely sensitive"; "top national security": Nicholas M. Horrock, "NSA Says It Is Not Eavesdropping," *New York Times* (August 9, 1975), p. 22.

298–299 "panic" trip; "We have a real problem": Interviews with Francis A. (Frank) Raven, July 23, 1981, August 11, 1981, and November 4, 1981.

reluctance to comment; "Philly, talk!"; "Philly, keep your"; "They were *hanging* NSA"; "Now, as I sat there": Ibid.

299 issued an ultimatum; "I wasn't going to"; "Well, you might consider"; "I thought Mondale"; "too defensive": Ibid.

300 last-minute campaign: George Lardner, Jr., "Intelligence Hearings Delayed; Oversight Panel Asked," *Washington Post* (October 9, 1975), p. A2.
reversed itself: Nicholas M. Horrock, "Senate Unit Sets Hearings on NSA," *New York Times* (October 22, 1975), p. 14.
violating the COMINT statute: Allen testimony, *The National Security Agency and Fourth Amendment Rights,* pp. 38–39.
Allen; Buffham; Banner: Ibid., pp. 5–46.
Palestinian terrorists: Nicholas M. Horrock, "NSA Chief Tells of Broad Scope of Surveillance," *New York Times* (October 30, 1975), pp. 1, 27.

301 "You believe": *The National Security Agency and Fourth Amendment Rights,* p. 25.
"Legality?"; Banner, Mondale: Ibid., pp. 45–46.

302 into the record: Ibid., pp. 57–60.
"for matters concerning": Draft Report, Part I, p. 20.
Joe Craig: U.S. House of Representatives, Committee on Government Operations, Government Information, and Individual Rights Subcommittee, *Interception of Nonverbal Communications by Federal Intelligence Agencies,* Hearings, 94th Cong., 1st and 2nd Sess. (1976), pp. 2–3, 145–149, 242, 310.

303 delegation: Draft Report, Part I, p. 3; *Interception of Nonverbal Communications,* pp. 53–54.
"containing the most": *Interception of Nonverbal Communications,* p. 56.

304 "On behalf of the President": Ibid., p. 99.
"I must respectfully": Ibid., p. 67.
middle-level NSA employee . . . West Virginia University: Telephone interview with Joseph J. Tomba, December 5, 1980.
C1 Group; Supervisory Level Course (MG-110): "National Security Agency Awards," *NSAN* (June 1965), p. 11.
Mr. Feeney: See *Interception of Nonverbal Communications,* p. 250.
"General Allen has asked": Ibid., pp. 80–81.

305 "on behalf of the President": Ibid., pp. 125–126.
"extraordinary capability"; "no other": Draft Report, Part II, p. 2.
"obsessive and unfounded": Ibid., Insert B, p. 23.

306 "Let there be no doubt": U.S. Senate, Select Committee on Intelligence, Subcommittee on Intelligence and the Rights of Americans, *Foreign Intelligence Surveillance Act of 1978,* Hearings, 95th Cong., 2nd Sess. (1978), p. 85.
"misleading": Draft Report, Part II, note 88.
"while an American citizen": Ibid., p. 3.
"attitudes ranged": *Report on Inquiry into CIA,* p. i.

307 twenty-three categories; "clearly possess"; "While the high": Ibid., pp. 171–172.
"too much discretionary": Ibid.
"Orders, directives": Department of Justice, "Prosecutive Summary" (March 4, 1977), pp. 12, 38. (See notes for pages 157 and 242).
"Its birth certificate": Ibid., p. 12.

308 "It is not illegal": Ibid., p. 37.

"We may as well": Vera Ruth Filby, "More Beans," *Cryptolog* (February 1978). This is a TOP SECRET/COMINT CHANNELS ONLY NSA in-house newsletter, limited to select operations personnel.

Chapter 8: Partners

page

309 "Dependence is so great": Chapman Pincher, *Inside Story* (New York: Stein & Day, 1979), p. 38.

Little Sai Wan: See Duncan Campbell, "The Spies Who Spend What They Like," *New Statesman* (May 16, 1980), pp. 738–744; Duncan Campbell, "GCHQ: The Cover-Up Continues," *New Statesman* (May 23, 1980), pp. 774–777.

IRSIG: Duncan Campbell, "Threat of the Electronic Spies," *New Statesman* (February 2, 1979), p. 142.

"blood . . . sweat": Churchill addressing Parliament on May 12, 1940, quoted in Robert Leckie, *The Wars of America*, Vol. 2, *San Juan Hill to Tonkin* (New York: Bantam Books, 1969), p. 175.

310 "Wizard War": Winston S. Churchill, *Their Finest Hour* (Boston: Houghton Mifflin, 1949), p. 362.

"Should you approve": Ronald Clark, *The Man Who Broke Purple* (Boston: Little, Brown, 1977), pp. 153–154.

311 Tizard arrived in Washington: Clark, pp. 154–155.

"a full exchange": Ladislas Farago, *The Broken Seal* (New York: Random House, 1967), p. 253.

312 Friedman . . . medical exam: Department of the Army, Walter Reed General Hospital, "Report of Physical Examination," September 20, 1946, Friedman Papers, George C. Marshall Research Library.

"proceed to London": War Department, The Adjutant General's Office, Orders for Lieutenant Colonel William F. Friedman, December 26, 1940, Friedman Papers.

officially cancelled: War Department, The Adjutant General's Office, Revocation of Orders, January 24, 1941, Friedman Papers.

Sinkov, accompanied by: Farago, p. 253.

Marconi-Adcock: Ibid., p. 254.

313 left for England; for the first time: *History of the Special Branch, MIS, War Department, 1942–1944*, National Archives, Record Group 457, SRH-035, pp. 20–24.

Edward W. Travis: *Who Was Who, 1951–1960*, p. 1097.

took charge of the diplomatic branch; "above Peggy Carter's": Interview with Frank B. Rowlett, former Special Assistant to the Director, NSA, on January 26, 1981.

314 PERMIT TO ENTER: Friedman Papers.

May 17; paragraph eight: Letter, Major General Clayton Bissell to Major General Stewart G. Menzies, May 22, 1944, National Archives, Record

Group 457, SRH-034, p. 4. The term BRUSA does not appear in these sanitized documents.

It provided for: *History of the Operations of Special Security Officers Attached to Field Commands, 1943–1945*, National Archives, Record Group 457, SRH-003, p. 2.

October 1943: Letter, Bissell to Menzies.

formal regulations: *Regulations for Maintaining the Security of Special Intelligence in the Pacific and Asiatic Theaters*, May 19, 1944, National Archives, Record Group 457, SRH-034, p. 8.

Dexter; Corral; Rabid: *United States Army Security Regulations for RABID Intelligence*, National Archives, Record Group 457, SRH-044, pp. 8–10.

code words: *Memorandum on the Dissemination of Signal Intelligence Within the British and American Forces*, National Archives, Record Group 457, SRH-044, p. 33.

315 "Security of Ultra Dexter": War Department, The Adjutant General's Office, *Security of Ultra Dexter Intelligence*, National Archives, Record Group 457, SRH-044, pp. 16–17.

Joint Allied Conference: Photo, Friedman Papers, photo file.

dinner . . . menu: Friedman Papers.

UKUSA Agreement: "U.S. Electronic Espionage: A Memoir," *Ramparts* (August 1972), p. 45.

316 "Leaving GCHQ": Letter, Travis to Friedman, March 13, 1952, Friedman Papers, Box 8, Item 24.

Eric Malcolm Jones: *Who's Who for 1980*, p. 1359.

Clive Loehnis: Ibid., p. 1549.

"It is a fascinating": Letter, Jones to Friedman, March 13, 1952, Friedman Papers, Box 4, Item 39.

317 London Communications Security Agency: Letter, Major General W. R. C. Penney, Director, London Communications Security Agency, to Friedman, September 9, 1955, Friedman Papers, Box 6, Item 23.

Prescott C. Currier; executive secretary: Letter, Friedman to Currier, June 26, 1958, Friedman Papers, Box 3, Item 16.

John J. Larkin: Letter, Larkin to Friedman, October 14, 1955, Friedman Papers, Box 5, Item 22.

British Joint Services Mission: Letter, Peter Bayne to Friedman, September 15, 1955, Friedman Papers, Box 1, Item 21.

Freddy Jacob: Letter, Friedman to Major General W. R. C. Penney, Director, London Communications Security Agency "c/o Colonel F. Jacob, SUKLO," November 15, 1955, Friedman Papers, Box 6, Item 33.

318 Under BRUSA, the United States was to have control; "It is toward": Joint Chiefs of Staff, Memorandum for Director, NSA, June 15, 1954, National Archives, Record Group 218, CCS-334 NSA, Section 12.

British had other ideas: Joint Chiefs of Staff, Memorandum for Director, NSA, June 1, 1954, National Archives, ibid.

CCCCs: Joint Chiefs of Staff, *Concept of Operations Involved in the Communications Support of NSA by the Military Services,* February 14, 1956, National Archives, ibid., Section 16.

seven units: Joint Chiefs of Staff, Note by the Secretaries, March 13, 1951, National Archives, ibid., Section 5.

318–319 300 to 674; "it would appear": Message, CINCFE TOKYO to DA WASH DC, November 16, 1950, National Archives, ibid., Section 4.

319 suggested that the British unit go: Joint Chiefs of Staff, Memorandum for the Chairman, Armed Forces Security Agency Council, February 20, 1951, National Archives, ibid., Section 5.

"any time": Message, Department of the Army to CINCFE TOKYO, January 18, 1952, National Archives, ibid., Section 7.

tents: Message, CINCFE TOKYO to DEPTAR WASH DC FOR JCS, April 28, 1951, National Archives, ibid., Section 5.

320 "We had no": Quoted in David Kahn, *The Codebreakers* (New York: Macmillan, 1967), p. 729.

"Here intelligence": Allen W. Dulles, *The Craft of Intelligence* (New York: Signet Books, 1963), p. 157.

"cracked": "Briton Says U.S. Solved Secret Code of Allies," *New York Times* (November 23, 1956).

321 "profitable"; "Needless to say": Letter, Jones to the Friedmans, November 2, 1956, Friedman Papers, Box 4, Item 39.

was airborne toward England: Clark, pp. 238–239.

322 Jones . . . knighthood: Letter, Friedman to Jones, January 8, 1957, Friedman Papers, Box 4, Item 39.

"has been won": Letter, Jones to Friedman, January 20, 1957, ibid.

Boris Caesar Wilhelm Hagelin: Kahn, pp. 425–432.

323 "serious concern"; "the book might": Clark, p. 4.

324 "I have also to report": Letter, Friedman to Engstrom, August 8, 1958, Friedman Papers.

"I am very anxious": Letter, Engstrom to Friedman, September 2, 1958, Friedman Papers.

"writes very rarely": Letter, Hedden to Friedman, April 11, 1955, Friedman Papers.

325 Leonard James Hooper: *Who's Who for 1972,* p. 1544, and *Who's Who for 1980,* p. 1231.

Arthur Wilfred Bonsall: *Who's Who for 1980,* p. 257.

Brian J. M. Tovey background: *Who's Who for 1980,* p. 2562.

picked Cecil C. Corry: Interview with Lieutenant General Marshall S. Carter, USA (Ret.) on July 17–18, 1980.

326 "Corry was very"; "He was not"; "We had a rule"; "We don't let": Ibid.

"I said": Ibid.

327 an effort at fence-mending: Interview with Dr. William O. Baker on July 13, 1981.

"It is always": Letter, Parker to Carter, July 19, 1969, Carter Papers, George C. Marshall Research Library.

"admin. officer": Department of State, *Employees of Diplomatic Missions,* May 1981, p. 37.

"It has long been"; "the interception of correspondence": Kenneth Ellis, *The Secret Office in the Post Office and the Office of Decipherer,* Friedman Papers, Item 952. Attached were the notes, handwritten by William F. Friedman: "Lecture by Kenneth Ellis; delivered during the time that GCHQ was at Eastcote, London, about 1948–50. This copy was photostatted from a copy sent me by the Director of GCHQ, Sir Edward Travis." "These three books were bound for me in 1960 by Brigadier John H. Tiltman while in Washington at NSA. W.F.F."

328 opening and copying; Secret Office; "Private Office": Ibid. See also Kenneth Ellis, *The Post Office in the Eighteenth Century: A Study in Administrative History* (London: Oxford University Press, 1958).

"In every case": *Report of the Committee of Privy Councillors Appointed to Inquire into the Interception of Communications,* Command 283 (London: Her Majesty's Stationery Office, 1962), p. 32.

329 interception of . . . telephone conversations: See *Attorney General* v. *Edison Telephone Company,* 6 Q.B.D. 244 (1880), where it was held that a telephone conversation is a "telegraphic communication" for the purposes of the Telegraph Acts. See also *Report of the Committee of Privy Councillors,* p. 15.

"In July, 1919": U.S. Senate, Committee on Interstate Commerce, *Cable-Landing Licenses,* Hearings, 66th Cong., 3rd Sess. (1921), p. 193.

"They replied"; "No; we cannot": Ibid., pp. 184–186.

serious breach: "Diplomatic Breach Is Laid to British," *New York Times* (December 24, 1920), p. 7.

330 "the originals and transcripts": *An Act to Amend the Official Secrets Act, 1911,* 10 & 11 Geo. 5, Chapter 75, December 23, 1920 (known as the Official Secrets Act, 1920), pp. 3–4.

"one of His Majesty's": British cable-landing license, issued December 30, 1919, to Commercial Cable Company.

"If you do not mind": *Cable-Landing Licenses,* pp. 314–317.

One year earlier: See Army Security Agency, *Historical Background of the Signal Security Agency,* Vol. 3, April 12, 1946, National Archives, Record Group 457, SRH-001, pp. 78–81.

331 In London: Chapman Pincher, "Cable Venting Sensation" (London) *Daily Express* (February 21, 1967), p. 1.

And in New York: See Operation Shamrock in Chapter 6.

"MINARET intelligence": Department of Justice, *Report on Inquiry into CIA-Related Electronic Surveillance Activities* (June 30, 1976), p. 160. (See notes for pages 157 and 242 for details concerning this document.)

332 "The Post Office": Duncan Campbell and Linda Melvern, "America's Big Ear on Europe," *New Statesman* (July 18, 1980), p. 10.

"The heaviest communications": Peter Laurie, *Beneath the City Streets* (London: Granada, 1970), pp. 237–238.

primarily to eavesdrop on Europe and the Soviet Union: Interview with former senior NSA official.

also has a detachment: Interview with an NSA official.

333 third and fourth busiest: *COMSAT Guide to the INTELSAT, MARISAT and COMSTAR Satellite Systems,* Office of Corporate Affairs, Communications Satellite Corporation, Washington, D.C., p. 27.

INTELSAT: Ibid., pp. 1–21.

"I know that I have": Letter, Hooper to Carter, July 27, 1969, Carter Papers.

334 "I think what he's probably": Carter interview.

"had insisted that we": Ibid.

"accumulated substantial evidence"; "recommended no reductions": Victor Marchetti and John D. Marks, *The CIA and the Cult of Intelligence* (New York: Dell, 1974), pp. 112–113.

335 "But equally I hope": Letter, Hooper to Carter, July 27, 1969, Carter Papers.

Communications–Electronic Security Department: *The Diplomatic Service List,* 1969 (London: Her Majesty's Stationery Office, 1969), p. 4. See also *The British Imperial Calendar and Civil Service List,* 1969 (London: Her Majesty's Stationery Office, 1969), p. 181.

"they were a long time": Carter interview.

John O. H. Burrough: *Who's Who for 1980,* p. 370.

"It could be Director"; "In either case": Letter, Burrough to Carter, July 29, 1969, Carter Papers.

became a director of Racal: *Who's Who for 1980,* p. 370.

336 "I have often felt"; "As you can understand": Letter, Hooper to Carter, July 27, 1969, Carter Papers.

Hooper letter: Carter Papers.

"Between us": Letter, Hooper to Carter, July 27, 1969, Carter Papers.

Chapter 9: Competition

page
338 "Dear sir": Letter, Earnest to Chief Signal Officer, January 28, 1937, Friedman Papers, Item 192.

"It is": Letter, J. W. Hough to Robert D. Lansing, Secretary of State, November 26, 1918, National Archives, Record Group 59, Box 1093, 119.25/382.

"nut file": Interview with Solomon Kullback, January 29, 1981.

339 NSASAB: Begun in 1953 (*NSAN* [January 1967], p. 4), the board was formally chartered under NSA Regulation 11–3, dated January 31, 1967, which provides that the board be composed of two government members and eight public members having industrial, nonprofit institution, and academic backgrounds in science and technology (Linda E. Sullivan, Anthony T. Kruzas, eds., *Encyclopedia of Government Advisory Organizations* [Detroit: Gale Research Co.], p. 273).

SIGINT . . . Panel; Electromagnetic . . . Panel: Federal Advisory Committees, *Fifth Annual Report of the President,* covering the calendar year 1976, p. 57.

early members of the board: Photo, Friedman Papers, photo file.

Chairman . . . Howard P. Robertson: Letter, Robertson to Friedman, May 14, 1957, Friedman Papers.

adviser to President Kennedy: Obituary, *Washington Post* (August 28, 1961).

not putting enough time; lack of guidance: Letter, Friedman to Professor Robert F. Rinehart, January 19, 1961, Friedman Papers.

appointed Robert F. Rinehart: Letter, Solomon Kullback, Executive Secretary, NSASAB, to Friedman, December 16, 1960, Friedman Papers.

"lack of previous": Letter, Rinehart to members of NSASAB, January 16, 1961, Friedman Papers.

Board members: Photos, NSASAB 1965 and 1969, Director's Photo Album, Lieutenant General Marshall S. Carter, USA (Ret.).

340 Willis H. Ware: "RAND Corporation Executive," *NSAN* (January 1967), p. 4.

Howard T. Engstrom: "First Exceptional Service Award Presented to Dr. Howard T. Engstrom," *NSAN* (March 15, 1960), p. 1.

Joseph H. Ream; CBS biography: Telephone conversation with librarian, CBS headquarters, New York City.

340–341 They concluded; Such a goal: Interview with Dr. William O. Baker, July 13, 1981.

341 Project Lightning: NSA, *Influence of U.S. Cryptologic Organizations on the Digital Computer Industry,* May 1977, p. 24.

dedicate the latest building: Princeton University program, Friedman Papers, Box 5, Item 23.

John von Neumann Hall: Author's observations.

Project Focus: Baker interview.

342 IDA: Paul Dickson, *Think Tanks* (New York: Atheneum, 1971), p. 146.

$1.9 million: David Kahn, *The Codebreakers* (New York: Macmillan, 1967), p. 677.

"completely independent": David Bird, "Faculty Consultants Support Studies for Defense," *New York Times* (May 3, 1968), p. 52.

J. Barkley Rosser: *American Men and Women of Science,* 12th edition, p. 5374.

Richard A. Leibler: *American Men and Women of Science,* 14th edition, p. 2920.

"our lonely isolation": "For reasons": Letter, Leibler to Friedman, September 18, 1969, Friedman Papers.

A. Adrian Albert: *American Men and Women of Science,* 12th edition, p. 52; see also Kahn, *The Codebreakers,* p. 410.

"It would not": Kahn, *The Codebreakers,* p. 410, p. 1046 note.

343 Leibler; chief of the Office of Research: *NSAN* (January 1980), p. 11.

Lee P. Neuwirth: *American Men and Women of Science,* 12th edition, pp. 4550–4551.

"the most secret": Dickson, p. 147.

demonstration: "A Target of Campus Protesters Is a 'Think Tank',"
New York Times (May 3, 1968), p. 53.

issue was finally resolved: Ibid.

boxy, three-story: Author's observations.

By February 1970: Institute for Defense Analysis, *Annual Report*, 1970,
p. 11; one-year contracts, p. 21.

344 Cleared and indoctrinated: Letter, Friedman to Professor E. G. Begle,
Department of Mathematics, Yale University, May 25, 1958, Friedman
Papers.

would arrive; be paid directly: Memorandum, Professor J. D. Swift, University of California at Los Angeles, to SCAMP Participants, February
24, 1959, Friedman Papers.

competition within private industry: *Influence of U.S. Cryptologic Organizations on the Digital Computer Industry*, p. 27.

"NSA": Ibid., p. 28.

computer crime: See National Criminal Justice Informational and Statistics Service, Law Enforcement Assistance Administration, U.S. Department of Justice, *Criminal Justice Resource Manual, Computer Crime* (Washington, D.C.: GPO, 1979).

345 code-named Lucifer: Paul Kinnucan, "Data Encryption Gurus: Tuchman
and Meyer," *Cryptologia* (October 1978), pp. 371–381.

charged since 1965: *Automatic Data Processing and Equipment Act*, Public
Law 89–306 (Brooks Act).

"the tiniest": David Kahn, "Cryptology Goes Public," *Foreign Affairs* (Fall
1979), p. 151.

346 "IBM was involved": Gina Bari Kolata, "Computer Encryption and the
National Security Agency Connection," *Science* (July 29, 1977), p. 440.

"It goes on all the time": Interviews with Francis (Frank) Raven, July
23, 1981, August 11, 1981, and November 4, 1981.

347 IBM agreed: U.S. Senate, Select Committee on Intelligence, *Unclassified
Summary: Involvement of NSA in the Development of the Data Encryption Standard*
(1978), p. 4.

"deep analysis": Kinnucan, "Data Encryption Gurus," p. 376.

"free of any": *Unclassified Summary*, p. 4.

"The codebreaking": Kahn, "Cryptology Goes Public," p. 151.

347–348 two computer experts; How long it takes: Kolata, "Computer Encryption and the National Security Agency Connection," p. 439.

348 cost: Ibid.

Dennis Branstad: Ibid.

Arthur Levenson; group chief: Photo, Director's Photo Album, Carter.

349 $200 million: Kinnucan, "Data Encryption Gurus," p. 378.

"Most data": Robert Morris, N. J. A. Sloane, and A. D. Wyner, "Assessment of the National Bureau of Standards Proposed Federal Data Encryption Standard," *Cryptologia* (July 1977), p. 286.

"NSA convinced": *Unclassified Summary*, p. 4.

American Banking Association: Kahn, "Cryptology Goes Public," p. 152.

Bell Telephone Company: Kolata, "Computer Encryption and the National Security Agency Connection," p. 439.

Code Compilation Company: Kahn, *The Codebreakers,* p. 359.

350 "the most revolutionary": Kahn, "Cryptology Goes Public," p. 153.

351 Cecil Corry . . . Fred Weingarten: U.S. House of Representatives, Committee on Government Operations, Government Information, and Individual Rights Subcommittee, *The Government's Classification of Private Ideas,* 96th Cong., 2nd Sess., House Report 96–1540 (1980), pp 77–80.

"had sole": Ibid., p. 77.

351–352 "coordinate"; "secret reviews"; "First — NSA": Ibid., p. 78.

352 "We are grateful": Ibid., p. 79.

353 destined to be as ignored: Harvard University, Center for Information Policy Research, Program on Information Resources Policy, *Seminar on Command, Control, Communications, and Intelligence* (Cambridge: Harvard University, 1980), Inman lecture, p. 144.

Joseph A. Meyer: Deborah Shapley and Gina Bari Kolata, "Cryptology: Scientists Puzzle Over Threat to Open Research, Publication," *Science* (September 30, 1977), pp. 1345–1349.

"unless clearances": Ibid.

"unclassified information": International Traffic in Arms Regulations (ITAR), 22 *Code of Federal Regulations,* pp. 121–128 (1980).

354 Inman asked the committee: Harvard University, *Seminar on Command,* p. 144.

issued two reports: *Unclassified Summary.*

back of a garage: Sylvia Sanders, "Data Privacy: What Washington Doesn't Want You to Know," *Reason* (January 1981), p. 25.

technical "Kelly girl": Deborah Shapley, "NSA Slaps Secrecy Order on Inventor's Communications Patent," *Science* (September 8, 1978), p. 891.

SECRECY ORDER: See Sanders, "Data Privacy," p. 27, for copy of the order.

Invention Secrecy Act: Public Law 82–593 (approved July 19, 1952), 35 U.S.C. pp. 181–188. For history of act, see *The Government's Classification,* pp. 33–62.

"be detrimental": Ibid., p. 12.

355 "in effect": Ibid., p. 13.

September 1978: The enactment in 1976 of the *National Emergencies Act* (Public Law 94–412, 50 U.S.C. 1621, 1976), to be effective two years later, terminated existing declared emergencies.

"in any way": Sanders, "Data Privacy," pp. 25, 27.

SUPER SECRECY; BLUE SLIP: *The Government's Classification,* p. 40.

Secret Group: Ibid., p. 17.

supported by Air Force and Navy but not Army: Shapley, "NSA Slaps Secrecy Order," p. 893.

final decision: Harvard University, *Seminar on Command,* p. 144.

"John Doe"; three hundred secrecy orders: *The Government's Classification,* p. 3.

356 seed for Phasorphone: Sanders, "Data Privacy," p. 25.

356–357 secrecy order . . . Davida: Shapley, "NSA Slaps Secrecy Order,"
        pp. 891–894.
357 "minimal due process": Deborah Shapley, "DoD Vacillates on Wisconsin
        Cryptography Work," *Science* (July 14, 1978), p. 141.
        "appears part": Kahn, "Cryptology Goes Public," p. 155.
        "very well-meaning": Harvard University, *Seminar on Command*, p. 144.
        "attempt to hold": *The Government's Classification*, p. 24.
        "There I was": Ibid.
        "bum rap": Deborah Shapley, "Intelligence Agency Chief Seeks 'Dia-
        logue' with Academics," *Science* (October 27, 1978), p. 407.
        "immediate damage"; "sources and methods": Vice Admiral B. R. In-
        man, USN, "The NSA Perspective on Telecommunications Protection
        in the Nongovernmental Sector," *Cryptologic Spectrum* (a top secret/COM-
        INT channels NSA in-house publication), (Winter 1979), p. 1.
358 manipulate the NSA: Shapley, "Intelligence Agency Chief Seeks 'Dia-
        logue,' " p. 409.
        Inman told *Science:* Ibid., pp. 407–410.
        "A public address": Vice Admiral B. R. Inman, USN, "The NSA Perspec-
        tive," *Signal* (March 1979), pp. 6–13.
359 "While some": Ibid., p. 13.
360 "central core": American Council on Education, *Report of the Cryptography
        Study Group* (February 7, 1981), p. 9.
        "Two years": Ibid., "The Case Against Restraints on Non-Governmental
        Research in Cryptography: A Minority Report by George I. Davida,"
        pp. 1–6.
361 Atkinson suggested; "sensitive areas"; $2 to $3 million: *The Government's
        Classification*, p. 81.
        "most attractive": Ibid., p. 82.
        "authorized observer"; "Chief, Office of Research, Department of De-
        fense": Ibid., p. 95, note 90.
        "NSA would take over": Comment recorded by staff member of Govern-
        ment Information and Individual Rights Subcommittee who was present
        at meeting. Ibid., p. 96, note 92.
361–362 On Thursday; "interagency matter"; "In the present climate": Gina
        Bari Kolata, "Cryptography: A New Clash Between Academic Freedom
        and National Security," *Science* (August 29, 1980), pp. 995–996.
362 "It's a very frightening collusion": Ibid.
        "not that of"; *The Government's Classification*, pp. 85–86.

                            Chapter 10: Abyss

page
364 "The PLO sends a man"; "There was a big": Interviews with Francis
        A. (Frank) Raven, July 23, 1981, August 11, 1981, and November 4,
        1981.
364–365 Thus, according to Raven; Malcolm X; "Tricky Dicky": Ibid.

365 "secondary testing": Ibid.

150,000 per month; twenty-four million international telegrams; fifty million telex: Letter from R. Michael Senkowski, Legal Assistant to the Chairman, Federal Communications Commission, quoted in prepared statement of David L. Watters in U.S. Senate, Select Committee on Intelligence, Subcommittee on Intelligence and the Rights of Americans, *Foreign Intelligence Surveillance Act of 1978*, Hearings, 95th Cong., 2nd Sess., p. 171.

In the past: Raven interview.

366 "You get a guy": Ibid.

In fact, in one: Ibid.

"on a first class spot!": Ibid.

In 1977 she was: Charles R. Babcock and Scott Armstrong, "Ethics Unit to Summon Four Officials," *Washington Post* (June 9, 1977), pp. A1, A11. See also Jack Anderson and Les Whitten, "U.S. Intercepted Seoul's Messages," *Washington Post* (October 7, 1977), p. D29.

367 "If the Russian": Raven interview.

Foreign Intelligence Surveillance Act: S.3197.

369 "foreign powers"; "directed and controlled": Foreign Intelligence Surveillance Act of 1978, Public Law 95–511 (1978).

"national security, defense": Ibid.

370 It sits in secret; "On its face": Helene E. Schwartz, "Oversight of Minimization Compliance Under the Foreign Intelligence Surveillance Act: How the Watchdogs Are Doing Their Jobs," *Rutgers Law Journal* (Spring 1981), Vol. 12, No. 3, p. 436.

has even tried to keep: Larry Tell, "The Cloak-and-Dagger Court," *National Law Journal* (August 10, 1981), p. 63.

518 applications: Ibid. p. 62.

"nonresidential premises under": *In the Matter of the Application of the United States for an Order Authorizing the Physical Search of Nonresidential Premises and Personal Property* (Washington, D.C.: U.S.F.I.S.C.), filed June 11, 1981.

371 Presiding Judge Hart, in the court's: Ibid.

"I would point out": Testimony of Admiral Stansfield Turner, in U.S. Senate, Select Committee on Intelligence, Subcommittee on Intelligence and the Rights of Americans, *Foreign Intelligence Surveillance Act of 1978*, p. 49.

"some of the most": U.S. House of Representatives, Permanent Select Committee on Intelligence, *Report on the Foreign Intelligence Surveillance Act of 1978*, Report 95–1283, Part 1, 95th Cong., 2nd Sess., p. 68.

372 "Acquisition," according to the document: "Standard NSA Minimization Procedures," included in Schwartz, pp. 501–507. (This sanitized document was released to Ms. Schwartz pursuant to a Freedom of Information Act request.)

373 "MINARET intelligence": Department of Justice, *Report on Inquiry into CIA-Related Electronic Surveillance Activities* (June 30, 1976), p. 160.

"It was in their": Final Report, Book III, p. 755.

"NSA should not request": Final Report, Book II, p. 310.

"compulsory spy service": Prepared statement of Professor Christopher H. Pyle in U.S. Senate, Select Committee on Intelligence, Subcommittee on Intelligence and the Rights of Americans, *Foreign Intelligence Surveillance Act of 1978*, p. 106.

374 "If you're intercepting a link": Raven interview.

"a person known": Schwartz, p. 504.

"the fact that": Raven interview.

On January 24: Executive Order No. 12036.

First drafted by: See Robert Pear, "Intelligence Groups Seek Power to Gain Data on U.S. Citizens," *New York Times* (March 10, 1981), p. A1; Hedrick Smith, "President Opposes Domestic CIA Role," *New York Times* (March 17, 1981), p. A1; George Lardner, Jr., "CIA Official Advises Against Domestic Role," *Boston Globe* (March 14, 1981), p. 3.

"Conduct of Intelligence Activities": Judith Miller, "Reagan Widens Intelligence Role; Gives CIA Domestic Spy Power," *New York Times* (December 5, 1981), pp. 1, 18–19.

375 Cryptanalytical and Translation: U.S. Department of Justice, Federal Bureau of Investigation, *Handbook of Forensic Science* (Washington, D.C.: GPO, 1979), pp. 88–89.

215 Pennsylvania Avenue: David Kahn, *The Codebreakers* (New York: Macmillan, 1967), pp. 819–820.

"The type of message": Raven interview.

One case involved: Ibid.

Not all the cases: Ibid.

376 "any department"; "when lives": Executive Order No. 12333, quoted in Miller, p. 19.

"NSA's potential to violate": Final Report, Book II, p. 201.

"Tons of electronic": Prepared statement of David L. Watters in U.S. Senate, Select Committee on Intelligence, Subcommittee on Intelligence and the Rights of Americans, *Foreign Intelligence Surveillance Act of 1978*, p. 158.

377 Closer to home; In 1982: Ronald Rosenberg, "Electronic Mail Is Just a Post Office Away," *Boston Globe* (December 20, 1981), pp. A21–A22.

"HUMINT": Interview with Lieutenant General Marshall S. Carter, July 17–18, 1981.

379 "Subtler and more": *Olmstead* v. *United States,* 277 U.S. 438, at pp. 473–474 (1928).

"At the same time": National Broadcasting Company, "Meet the Press" (Washington, D.C.: Merkle Press, 1975), transcript of August 17, 1975, p. 6.

ACRONYMS
AND
ABBREVIATIONS

A-2: Air Force Intelligence
ACOM: Asian Communist; one of the four major operational divisions of NSA's Production Organization; now known as B Group
ADLA: Assistant Director for Legal and Legislative Affairs
ADPL: Assistant Director for Policy and Liaison
ADPR: Assistant Director for Plans and Resources
ADT: Assistant Director for Training
ADVA: Advanced Soviet; one of the four major operational divisions of NSA's Production Organization; combined with GENS into A Group
AEC: Atomic Energy Commission
AFESC: Air Force Electronic Security Command
AFSA: Armed Forces Security Agency
AFSAC: Armed Forces Security Agency Council
AFSAC/IRC: Armed Forces Security Agency Council Intelligence Requirements Committee
ALLO: All Others; one of the four major operational divisions of NSA's Production Organization; now known as G Group
ALP: Advanced Language Program
ANCIB: Army-Navy Communications Intelligence Board
ANCICC: Army-Navy Communications Intelligence Coordinating Committee
ARC: Ad Hoc Requirements Committee
ARDF: Airborne Radio Direction-Finding
ARFCOS: Armed Forces Courier Service
ASA: Army Security Agency
ASPAB: Armed Services Patent Advisory Board
AT&T: American Telephone and Telegraph Company
AUTODIN: Automatic Digital Network
BI: Background Investigation
BNDD: Bureau of Narcotics and Dangerous Drugs
BRUSA: British–United States Agreement
C³I: Communications, Command, Control and Intelligence
CBNRC: Communications Branch, National Research Council
CBS: Columbia Broadcasting System

CCCC: Centralized COMINT Communications Center

CCINC: Cabinet Committee on International Narcotics Control

CCP: Consolidated Cryptologic Program (CCP)

CCPC: Critical Collection Problems Committee of the United States Intelligence Board

CDAA: Circularly Disposed Antenna Array

CIA: Central Intelligence Agency

CINCPAC: Commander-in-Chief, Pacific

COMINT: Communications Intelligence; the interception and processing of foreign communications passed by radio, wire, or other electromagnetic means, and by the processing of foreign encrypted communications, however transmitted. Interception comprises search, intercept, operator identification, signal analysis, traffic analysis, cryptanalysis, decryption, study of plain text, the fusion of these processes, and the reporting of results. Excluded from this definition are the interception and processing of unencrypted written communications, press and propaganda broadcasts. (From National Security Council Intelligence Directive [NSCID] No. 6)

COMIREX: Committee on Imagery Requirements and Exploitation

COMOR: Committee on Overhead Reconnaissance

COMSAT: Communications Satellite Corporation

COMSEC: Communications Security; the protection resulting from any measure taken to deny unauthorized persons information derived from the national security–related telecommunications of the United States, or from any measure taken to ensure the authenticity of such telecommunications (From Senate Bill S.2525, *National Intelligence Reorganization and Reform Act of 1978*)

CONSIDO: Consolidated Special Information Dissemination Office

COS: Chief of Station

CRITIC: Critical Intelligence message

CRITICOM: Critical Intelligence Communications network

CSS: Central Security Service

DCI: Director of Central Intelligence

DDA: Deputy Director for Administration

DDF: Deputy Director for Field Management and Evaluation

D/DIRNSA: Deputy Director of NSA

DDO: Deputy Director for Operations (Office of Signals Intelligence Operations)

DDPP: Deputy Director for Plans and Policy

DDPR: Deputy Director for Programs and Resources

DEFSMAC: Defense Special Missile and Astronautics Center

DES: Data Encryption Standard

DIA: Defense Intelligence Agency

DIN/DSSCS: Digital Network–Defense Special Security Communications System

DIRNSA: Director of NSA

DIS: Defense Investigative Service

DONCS: Director of Operations Narcotics Control Reports
DSP: Defense Support Program
DSU: Direct Support Unit
ECOM: Electronic Computer-Originated Mail
ELINT: Electronics Intelligence; the collection (observation and recording) and the processing for subsequent intelligence purposes of information derived from foreign, noncommunications, electromagnetic radiations emanating from other than atomic detonation or radioactive sources (From NSCID No. 6)
ENIAC: Electronic Numerical Integrator Computer
EPQ: Embarrassing Personal Question
ERA: Engineering Research Associates
EXCOM: Executive Committee
FANX: Friendship (Airport) Annex
FBI: Federal Bureau of Investigation
FCC: Federal Communications Commission
FISA: Foreign Intelligence Surveillance Act
G-2: Army Intelligence
GAO: Government Accounting Office
GCCS: Government Code and Cypher School
GCHQ: Government Communications Headquarters
GENS: General Soviet; one of the four major operational divisions of NSA's Production Organization; combined with ADVA into A Group
GG-: Government Grade; because the NSA is exempted from the normal Civil Service regulations, the employee ranking of GG-1 to GG-18 is used instead of the Civil Service GS-1 to GS-18
HFDF: High Frequency Direction Finding
HUAC: House Un-American Activities Committee
HUMINT: Human Intelligence
IBM: International Business Machines Corporation
ICBM: Intercontinental Ballistic Missile
ICI: Interagency Committee on Intelligence
IDA-CRD: Institute for Defense Analysis-Communications Research Division
IDP: Intercept Deployment Plan
IEC: Intelligence Evaluation Committee
IEEE: Institute of Electrical and Electronic Engineers
IG Staff: Possibly, Intelligence Guidelines Staff
IGCP: Possibly, Intelligence Guidelines for COMINT Priorities
ILC: International Licensed Carriers
INSCOM: U.S. Army Intelligence and Security Command
INTELPOST: International Electronic Post
INTELSAT: International Telecommunications Satellite
IPB: Intercept Priorities Board
ITAR: International Traffic in Arms Regulations
ITT: International Telephone and Telegraph Corporation
JCS: Joint Chiefs of Staff

JOSAF: Joint Operations Support Activity Frankfurt
JRC: Joint Reconnaissance Center
JSPC: Joint Sobe Processing Center
KGB: Komitet Gosudarstvennoy Bezopasnosti (Committee for State Security) (USSR)
LASP: Low-Altitude Surveillance Platform
LOB: Raymond E. Linn Operations Building
LPMEDLEY: CIA cryptonym for an operation in support of the NSA
M5: NSA Office of Security
MI-8: Military Intelligence, Section 8 (Codes and Ciphers)
MID: Military Intelligence Division
MIT: Massachusetts Institute of Technology
MPRO: Machine Processing section of NSA's Production Organization
MSTS: Military Sea Transportation Service
NARCOG: Narcotics Coordination Group
NASA: National Aeronautics and Space Administration
NATO: North Atlantic Treaty Organization
NBS: National Bureau of Standards
NCS: National Cryptographic School
NOG: NSA Pacific Operations Group
NORAD: North American Air Defense Command
NPIC: National Photographic Interpretation Center
NRL: Naval Research Laboratory
NRO: National Reconnaissance Office
NSAPAC: National Security Agency, Pacific
NSASAB: National Security Agency Scientific Advisory Board
NSCID: National Security Council Intelligence Directive
NSES: National Security Electronic Surveillance
NSG: Naval Security Group
NVA: North Vietnamese Army
ONC: Office of Narcotics Coordinator
ONI: Office of Naval Intelligence
ONNI: Office of National Narcotics Intelligence
OP-20-G: Section G (Communications Security) of the 20th Division (Office of Naval Communications) of the Office of Chief of Naval Operations (OP)
OSS: Office of Strategic Services
PFIAB: President's Foreign Intelligence Advisory Board
PLO: Palestine Liberation Organization
PO4: Fourth staff office within PROD/DDO: Office of Operational Policy and Plans
PO5: Fifth staff office within the NSA Production Organization (now Office of SIGINT Operations); Consumer Staff Liaison Office
PQT: Professional Qualification Test
PROD: Office of Production
R and D: Office of Research and Development
R and E: Office of Research and Engineering

RADE: Research and Development Division within NSA's Office of Research and Development (now Office of Research and Engineering)

RADINT: Radar Intelligence

RCA: Radio Corporation of America

RCV: Receive Only Station

REMP: Research, Engineering, Mathematics, and Physics Division within NSA's Office of Research and Development (now Office of Research and Engineering)

ROK: Republic of Korea

SAB: Support Activities Building

SALT: Strategic Arms Limitation Treaty

SAMSO: U.S. Air Force Space and Missile Systems Organization

SBI: Special Background Investigation

SCA: Service Cryptologic Agency

SCAMP: Summer Campus, Advanced Mathematics Program

SDS: Students for a Democratic Society

SIGINT: Signals Intelligence; comprises communications intelligence (COMINT), electronics intelligence (ELINT), foreign instrumentation signals intelligence (technical and intelligence information derived from the collection and processing of foreign telemetry, beaconry, and associated signals), and information derived from the collection and processing of nonimagery infrared and coherent light signals (From Senate Bill S.2525, *National Intelligence Reorganization and Reform Act of 1978*)

SIGLEX: Special Interest Group on Lexicography

SIGTRAN: Special Interest Group on Translation

SIGVOICE: Special Interest Group on Voice

SIPG: Special Intercept Priorities Group

SIS: Signal Intelligence Service

SLBM: Submarine Launched Ballistic Missile

SPINTCOM: Special Intelligence Communications

SSA: Signal Security Agency

STANCIB: State-Army-Navy Communications Intelligence Board

STED: Standard Technical Equipment Development Division within NSA's Office of Research and Development (now Office of Research and Engineering)

SUKLO: Senior United Kingdom Liaison Officer

SUSLO: Senior United States Liaison Officer

T/A: Traffic Analysis

TAT: Transatlantic Telephone Cable

TELINT: Telemetry Intelligence

TEXTA: Technical Extracts of Traffic

TRESSCOMM: Technical Research Ship Special Communications

UAR: United Arab Republic (now Egypt)

UBG: Underground Building

UKUSA: United Kingdom–United States Agreement

USAFSS: United States Air Force Security Service

USCIB: United States Communications Intelligence Board
USCIB/IC: United States Communications Intelligence Board Intelligence
  Committee
USFISC: United States Foreign Intelligence Surveillance Court
VHF: Very High Frequency

INDEX